Seamus Heaney, Virgil and the Good of Poetry

For Annabel Stevenson Mills

Seamus Heaney, Virgil and the Good of Poetry

Rachel Falconer

Edinburgh University Press is one of the leading university presses in the UK. We publish academic books and journals in our selected subject areas across the humanities and social sciences, combining cutting-edge scholarship with high editorial and production values to produce academic works of lasting importance. For more information visit our website: edinburghuniversitypress.com

© Rachel Falconer, 2022

Grateful acknowledgement is made to the sources listed in the List of Plates for permission to reproduce material previously published elsewhere. Every effort has been made to trace the copyright holders, but if any have been inadvertently overlooked, the publisher will be pleased to make the necessary arrangements at the first opportunity.

Edinburgh University Press Ltd
The Tun – Holyrood Road
12(2f) Jackson's Entry
Edinburgh EH8 8PJ

Typeset in 10/12pt Goudy Old Style
by Cheshire Typesetting Ltd, Cuddington, Cheshire, and
printed and bound by CPI Group (UK) Ltd,
Croydon, CR0 4YY

A CIP record for this book is available from the British Library

ISBN 978 1 4744 5439 1 (hardback)
ISBN 978 1 4744 5441 4 (webready PDF)
ISBN 978 1 4744 5442 1 (epub)

The right of Rachel Falconer to be identified as the author of this work has been asserted in accordance with the Copyright, Designs and Patents Act 1988, and the Copyright and Related Rights Regulations 2003 (SI No. 2498).

Contents

List of Plates	vii
Acknowledgements	viii
Abbreviations	xi
Introduction	1
1 The Golden Bough and the Absent Tree	13
I. A Local Virgil	14
II. 'The Golden Bough'	21
2 Threshold Crossings in *Seeing Things*	40
I. 'In the end is my beginning': Virgil and Dante	41
II. The Golden Bough, Again	50
III. Charon's Boat	54
IV. The Father's Ghost	59
3 Orpheus in a Major Key	67
I. *The Midnight Verdict*	70
II. *The Redress of Poetry*	74
III. 'Orpheus and Eurydice'	77
IV. 'The Death of Orpheus'	82
4 Pastoral, *Pietas* and Stealth	91
I. 'Bann Valley Eclogue'	96
II. '*Eclogues IX*'	107
III. 'Glanmore Eclogue'	113
IV. 'Electric Light'	116
V. 'The Staying Power of Pastoral'	118
5 'Terra tremens': *District and Circle*	124
I. *Katabasis* in Our Time	126

II. 'Anything Can Happen'	131
III. 'District and Circle'	136
IV. 'The Tollund Man in Springtime'	146
6 'In river country': *The Riverbank Field*	150
I. The River Lethe	153
II. 'The Riverbank Field'	156
III. 'Route 110'	160
7 Raids, Settlement and Sounding Line	177
I. Virgil on Air	179
II. 'Freed Speech' and Settlement	182
III. The Wanderings of Palinurus	187
IV. Ted Hughes, Keats and the Sea	192
V. Palinurus 'Enlarged'	197
8 Cadence and Lapse in *Human Chain*	204
I. Three Virgilian Lapses	206
II. The Phantom, *Verus*	209
III. 'The second life of art'	217
IV. 'Wind-drink' and Windfall	223
9 A Double Music: *Aeneid Book VI*	229
I. Introducing *Book VI*	230
II. Between Two Rhythms	234
III. He Do the *Aeneid* in Different Voices	239
IV. *Katabasis* as Poetic Redress	247
Coda: 'Mossbawn via Mantua'	259
Appendix: 'Palinurus': *Aeneid Book VI*, lines 349–83	264
Bibliography	267
Index	288

Plates

Plate 1 Joseph Mallord William Turner (1775–1851), 'The Golden Bough', exhibited 1834. Oil paint on canvas, support: 1041 × 1638 mm; frame: 1455 × 2046 × 110 mm. Tate Britain, London.

Plate 2 Gustave Caillebotte (1848–94), 'Banks of a Canal, near Naples', c. 1872. Oil on canvas, 39.7 × 59.7 cm. National Gallery of Ireland. Photo © National Gallery of Ireland.

Plate 3 Paul Cézanne (1839–1906), 'Aeneas Meeting Dido at Carthage', 1873–6. Graphite on cream laid paper, 22.9 × 30.5 cm. The Henry and Rose Pearlman Foundation on long-term loan to the Princeton University Art Museum / photo Bruce M. White.

Plate 4 Martin Gale (b. 1949), 'Crows', c. 2006, reproduced in Seamus Heaney, *The Riverbank Field*, Dublin: The Gallery Press, 2007. © Martin Gale.

Acknowledgements

Firstly, I would like to thank the Heaney Estate and Faber for their permission to quote from Seamus Heaney's work, and Catherine Heaney for her gracious support and meticulous reading of this study. I am grateful to the University of Lausanne for granting me a year's research leave, with special thanks to Dean Dave Lüthi and the Décanat of the Faculty of Arts.

For permission to quote archival material relating to Seamus Heaney, I would like to thank the Heaney Estate, the Manuscripts Library and the National Library of Ireland, RTÉ Archives, BBC Archives, the Sound Recording Department (Rare Books and Music) of the British Library, the Woodward Poetry Room of Harvard University, and the Stuart A. Rose Manuscript Archives and Rare Book Library of Emory University. Thanks are also due to Stephanie Bredbenner and the Beineke Library at Yale University, to Anne Chesher and the Magdalen College Library, Oxford University, and to the Accademia Pascoliana di San Mauro.

My very warm thanks to Sarah Ruden, gifted poet and translator of Virgil, for her generous permission to quote from a 2008 typescript draft of Seamus Heaney's *Aeneid Book VI*, and personal correspondence concerning the composition of his translation (2008–9). Special thanks, also, to Peter Fallon, poet, translator and editor of The Gallery Press, Dublin, for permission to quote from Heaney's *The Last Walk* (2013) and *The Riverbank Field* (2007); to David Constantine, co-editor with Helen Constantine, of *Poetry in Translation*, for permission to quote from Heaney's 'Three Freed Speeches'; to Herbert Leibowitz, former editor of *Parnassus*, for permission to reproduce Heaney's translation, 'Palinurus', as an Appendix to this study; to the poet Gerald Dawe, for permission to quote from his interview, 'The Riverbank Field: An Interview with Seamus Heaney'; to the artist Martin Gale and The Gallery Press, for kind permission to reprint a copy of his painting, 'Crows'; to the artist Jan Hendrix, for permission to quote from his collaborative works with Heaney, and for sending me a copy of their magnificent volume, *Yagul: Three Books with Seamus Heaney* (2002); to the learned John Elderfield, of the Princeton University Art Museum, and to the Henry and Rose Pearlman Foundation for permission to reprint Cézanne's sketch, 'Aeneas Meeting Dido at Carthage'. All these people have kindly shared their memories of Seamus Heaney and reflections on his writing, greatly enriching my understanding of the poet, the man and his work.

Thanks are also due to Stephen Weir, Picture Library Executive at the National Museums Northern Ireland, for permission to reproduce Edward McGuire's portrait of Heaney, the National Bardo Museum of Tunis for permission to reproduce the mosaic of Virgil, and Louise Morgan of the National Gallery of Ireland, for permission to reproduce Caillebotte's 'Banks of a Canal, near Naples'. Material from Chapters 5, 6 and 9 has previously appeared in *Comparative Literature* (2017); *Essays and Studies* (2021); *A Companion to Poetic Genres*, edited by Erik Martiny (Blackwell, 2011); *A Quest for Remembrance: The Underworld in Classical and Modern Literature*, edited by Madeleine Scherer and myself (Routledge, 2019); and *Seamus Heaney and the Classics*, edited by Stephen Harrison et al. (Oxford University Press, 2019).

As a professor of English literature with a distant BA in Classics, I am particularly indebted to Nicholas Horsfall's authoritative two-volume edition of Virgil's *Aeneid VI*, as well as the scholarship of learned friends, particularly Damien Nelis, Professor of Latin at the University of Geneva. For their helpful comments on chapter drafts, I am indebted to Annabel Mills, Gerald Dawe, Graham Falconer, Stuart Gillespie, Stephen Heiny, Margaret Kean, Philip Lindholm, Marie McMullin, Bernard O'Donoghue, Michael Parker, Neil Roberts, Nicholas Roe, Marco Sonzogni and Graham Topping. For informative exchanges on Seamus Heaney, Virgil and/or poetry in general, I am most grateful to Simon Armitage, Matthew Bevis, Susanna Braund, Franco Buffoni, Lindsay Clarke, Lucy Collins, Neil Corcoran, Robert Crawford, Patrick Crotty, Eamon Duffy, Edith Hall, Paul Hamilton, Adam Hanna, Philip Hardie, Robert Pogue Harrison, Stephen Harrison, Hugh Haughton, Martine Hennard Dutheil de la Rochère, Rui Carvalho Homem, Kathleen Jamie, Sebastian Knowles, Herbert Leibowitz, Michèle Lowrie, Fiachra MacGorain, Tom Mackenzie, Stephen Regan, Richard Russell, Ann Saddlemyer, Kirsten Stirling, Malcolm Sutherland, Simon Swift, Helen Vendler and Olivier Thévenaz. At Yale University, Ralph Hexter and Gordon Williams furthered my encounters with Virgil in Latin. Later, my D.Phil. supervisors at Oxford, John Carey and Anthony Nuttall, deepened my appreciation of Virgil's presence in the English literary tradition.

At the University of Lausanne and other Swiss universities, I have had the good fortune to work with gifted, polylingual students, many of whom have studied Heaney's poetry with me. For their special insights and enthusiasms, I would especially like to thank Leila Benallal, Ezra Bennisty, Lily Dessau, Patrick Jones, Alexandre Jordan, Philip Lindholm, Lila Mabiala, Sam MacDuff, Oran McKenzie, Marie McMullin, Sarah-Jane Moloney, Céline Naito, Rachel Nisbet, Amy Player and Francesca Scala.

I am indebted to my dear father, Graham Falconer, for giving me the upstairs of Quince Cottage in which to write this book, for surviving Covid together, for his stimulating conversation and music, and for patiently enduring my cooking. Living in Iffley, I have been surrounded by the presence of absent loved ones: my mother, Elisabeth Ann Falconer; grandparents, Gaby and Herbert Davis; godparents, Noony Knowles and Helen Gardner; and grandmother to us all, Nell Gray. For present friendship, I am grateful to my hedge-school master of the cello, Johanna

Messner; to fellow musicians Jessica, Anthony and Graham, who kept our garden quartet going in spite of Covid, Brexit and English weather; and to my fellow eco-warriors and friends in Iffley. Most of all, I am grateful for the love and support of my family, Graham, Julia, Bob and Corinne Falconer, Tom, Jenny, Sara and Madi Schneidermann, my late uncle Jeremy, and Janey, Sebastian, Jay and Tim Knowles. Finally, this book is dedicated to Annabel Mills, my best friend and first reader from the age of three.

Abbreviations

  Ae   P. Vergilius Maro (Virgil), *Aeneid* (c. 19 BC)
   G   Virgil, *Georgics* (c. 29 BC)
   E   Virgil, *Eclogues* (c. 38 BC)

   A   Seamus Heaney, *Aeneid Book VI* (2016)
 BBC 'Greek and Latin Voices: Virgil' (2/4), *The Essay*, BBC Radio 3 (2008)
  DC *District and Circle* (2006)
  DD *Door into the Dark* (1969)
  DN *Death of a Naturalist* (1966)
  EL *Electric Light* (2001)
  FK *Finders Keepers: Selected Prose, 1971–2001* (2002)
  FW *Field Work* (1979)
  GB 'The Golden Bough' (1989)
  GT *The Government of the Tongue: Selected Prose, 1978–87* (1988)
  HC *Human Chain* (2010)
  HL *The Haw Lantern* (1987)
  LP Seamus Heaney Literary Papers, National Library of Ireland, Dublin
  MV *The Midnight Verdict* (1993)
   N   *North* (1975)
  OG *Opened Ground: Poems 1966–1996* (1998)
   P   *Preoccupations: Selected Prose, 1968–1978* (1980)
  Pa 'Palinurus' (2008)
  RF *The Riverbank Field* (2007)
  RP *The Redress of Poetry* (1995)
 RTÉ Gerald Dawe interview with Heaney, *The Poetry Programme*, RTÉ (2008)
  SI *Station Island* (1984)
  SL *The Spirit Level* (1996)
  SS Dennis O'Driscoll, *Stepping Stones: Interviews with Seamus Heaney* ([2008] 2009)

ST *Seeing Things* (1991)
WO *Wintering Out* (1972)

LiS H. G. Liddell and R. Scott, *Greek–English Lexicon*, 9th edn (Oxford: Clarendon, 1996)
LS   Charlton T. Lewis and Charles Short, *A Latin Dictionary* (Oxford: Clarendon, 1879)
OED *The Oxford English Dictionary* (Oxford: Oxford University Press, 2019)

A NOTE ON THE LATIN

Quotations of Virgil are taken from R. A. B. Mynors, *P. Vergili Maronis Opera* (Oxford Classical Texts, 1969). The 'u' for the semi-vowel '/w/' is used in the OCT edition and is retained here. Note, however, that in Heaney's Church Latin pronunciation, this 'u' is pronounced 'v'. In 'The Riverbank Field', Heaney refers to the 1978 Loeb edition, *Eclogues, Georgics, Aeneid 1–6*, translated by H. R. Fairclough, where the semi-vowel is printed as 'v'. The name 'Publius Vergilius Maro' is anglicised to 'Virgil' (rather than 'Vergil') in Heaney's writing and is the spelling used here.

Introduction

Heaney's Virgil is a poet of tragic pathos and melancholy, who gives voice to the *lacrimae rerum*, the weight of the world's suffering. And yet he is also the farmer–poet from Mantua, who delights in the earth's renewal, and possibilities of civic renewal from one generation to the next. For Heaney, Virgil's Aeneas offers a model of the poet's *pietas*, the feelings of affection and obligation that bind him to a particular community and place. At the same time, the hero's venture into the underworld provides a mythic analogue for the poet's ability to outstrip the given, to credit the marvellous and ultimately to offer poetic redress to actual, historical conditions. All of Virgil's major works, the *Eclogues*, *Georgics* and *Aeneid*, contribute to shaping Heaney's later verse, while the very trajectory of Virgil's life, from farmer's son to famous poet, offers Heaney a companionable biography with which he could closely identify. This study aims to shed light on all these aspects of Heaney's dialogue with Virgil, which leads continually to one of the central preoccupations of his poetry and poetics: namely, what is the good of poetry and the arts in the life of an individual, and in society as a whole?

Most of Heaney's readers will already know that Virgil is a major figure in Heaney's literary pantheon. In translation or adaptation, his poetry features prominently in three of Heaney's volumes, *Seeing Things*, *Human Chain* and his posthumously published translation, *Aeneid Book VI*. But Heaney's dialogue with Virgil runs much deeper than is generally acknowledged.[1] He had begun reading Virgil from a very young age, which is one reason for the particular intimacy, warmth and affection that mark his engagement with Virgil in his later poetry and prose. In the last two decades of his writing life, Virgil reappears to him as a 'familiar compound ghost', summoned directly from his own childhood and adolescent memories, as well as mediated through his later reading of Dante and T. S. Eliot.[2]

---

1. Occasionally, one finds Virgil's influence being dismissed altogether: 'canonical classical figures such as Homer, Virgil, Ovid and Dante have of course provided important stimulus to writers in Ireland as elsewhere, but of these four Virgil tends to be the least prominent in Heaney's poetry' (Moi, 2007), 179.
2. Eliot, 'Little Gidding', II.42 (2015), Vol. I, p. 204.

As a school boy at St Columb's College in the 1950s, Heaney had studied parts of the *Aeneid* in Latin, as well as its entirety in J. W. Mackail's prose translation.[3] Latin was familiar to him from the Catholic Mass, and the language came easily to him at school, which led on to his feeling at ease with Virgil's hexameters.[4] At Queen's University, Belfast, Heaney became fascinated by the history of language, 'etymology, roots, where words came from, the whole mix-up between Irish and English and Latin.'[5] Amongst the Belfast Group in the 1960s, according to Heaney, a number of poets were 'ploughing up the common ground of the old school classics, Longley with his Homer, me with my Virgil, all of us with our Greek tragedies in translation.' (SS 167)

From the mid-1960s, Heaney's poetry demonstrates a strong interest in Greek and Latin literature. Amongst the typewritten 'groupsheets' of the Belfast Group is a translation by Heaney of Horace's ode, 'To a Wine Jar'.[6] And there are allusions to Virgil's poetry in *Death of a Naturalist* (1966), *Wintering Out* (1972), *Field Work* (1979) and *Station Island* (1984).[7] The sequence of 'Glanmore Sonnets' in *Field Work* is particularly indebted to the *Eclogues* and *Georgics*, while in the same volume, 'Triptych' invokes Aeneas' encounter with the Cumaean Sibyl in *Aeneid VI*. Of this familiarity with the classics, Heaney commented, 'I don't think of my cultural baggage as "learned". I just happen to belong to the last generation that learned Latin, that read Virgil, that knew about the descent into the underworld.' (SS 295)

All the same, Heaney's early poetry manifests a particular fascination with underground journeys and descents into the underworld of memory, as evidenced in the title of his second collection, *Door into the Dark* (1969). '[I]nclined to / the appetites of gravity' (N 37), with a 'hankering for the underground side of things' (P 21), Heaney demonstrates an affinity with Virgil's descent hero long before he engages in explicit dialogue with *Aeneid VI*. In his first published volume, *Death of a Naturalist*, the opening poem, 'Digging', famously descends into the past to retrieve a memory of Heaney's father and grandfather digging potato drills (DN 1). And in its final poem, 'Personal Helicon', he declares that he rhymes 'to set the darkness echoing'

---

3. Heaney's schoolboy marginalia in his copy of Mackail's *Aeneid* already demonstrate a marked sympathy for Turnus and the Latin tribes; for a full consideration of the marginal markings, see Hall (2019), 223–43. He studied Book IX for A-levels with his Latin master, Father Michael McGlinchey, and at sixteen or seventeen he purchased an edition of Book VI at Smithfield Market, Belfast (*RTÉ*).
4. 'I got off to a good start in Latin . . . because of the early schooling . . . at Anahorish School . . . I always was a little bit ahead of myself in the Latin area, which probably explains why I was more at ease with Virgil' (*RTÉ*). See also, Heaney, 'Postscript', *The Golden Bough* (1992), 31.
5. Heaney in conversation with Mike Murphy, in Ní Anluain and Kiberd, eds (2000), 84.
6. The unpublished translation is dated 1965; see Ní Ríordáin (2003), 174 and S. J. Harrison (2019), 244–7.
7. In *DN*, 'At a Potato Digging' alludes to *Georgics*; in *WO*, 'Anahorish', 'Toome', 'Broagh' and 'Gifts of Rain' allude to *Eclogues* and *Georgics*; in *FW*, 'The Toome Road' and 'An Afterwards' borrow from *Georgics*; and in *SI*, 'The Underground' and 'Sandstone Keepsake' refer to *Aeneid VI*. See Travaglia (2017) for a helpful enumeration of Virgilian allusions in Heaney's English poetry.

(*DN* 44).[8] In subsequent volumes, notably *Wintering Out* and *North*, Heaney meditates on bodies exhumed from peat bogs, and converses with the ghosts of men and women killed in the Troubles. Structurally and thematically, these invocations of the dead bear close resemblance to the classical forms of *nekyia* and *katabasis*.[9]

All of the above signals that Virgil is already a notable influence on the poetry of the first half of Heaney's career. The present study, however, focuses on Heaney's dialogue with Virgil from the mid-1980s, when the Roman poet becomes a major presence in Heaney's writing. Tellingly, the second of two volumes of *New Selected Poems* published by Faber, covering the period 1988 to 2013, opens with Heaney's translation of the golden bough episode from *Aeneid VI*.[10] Virgil's mysterious bough operates like a talismanic charm in Heaney's later poetry, and in itself comes to symbolise the transformative powers of poetry. Other motifs and episodes from *Aeneid VI*, such as Aeneas' crossing of the Styx in Charon's boat, the exchange with the drowned helmsman, Palinurus, and the hero's attempt to embrace his father's ghost, acquire totemic significance in Heaney's later writing, where they are commingled with scenes from his own life and times.

The mid-1980s is also, not coincidentally, the period in which Heaney announces a decisive turn in his poetry and poetics. In his Nobel Prize address, 'Crediting Poetry', Heaney describes his 'changed orientation' in this way:

> for years I was bowed to the desk like some monk bowed over his prie-dieu, some dutiful contemplative pivoting his understanding in an attempt to bear his portion of the weight of the world, knowing himself incapable of heroic virtue or redemptive effect, but constrained by his obedience to his rule to repeat the effort and the posture. . . . Then finally and happily, and not in obedience to the dolorous circumstances of my native place but in spite of them, I straightened up. I began a few years ago to try and make space in my reckoning and imagining for the marvellous as well as for the murderous.[11]

---

8. In '"Apt Admonishment"' (2008), Heaney retrospectively associates this poem with Hesiod, the founder of georgic poetry in the Western literary tradition. At the beginning of *Works and Days*, Hesiod relates how the muses called him from the 'field-dwelling shepherds on Helicon' for a life in poetry (20). His biography, as recounted by Heaney, falls into the same pattern as Virgil's: farmer-turned-poet, inspired by the gift of a plucked branch of laurel (33), which anticipates the golden bough, and the laurel tree foretelling Virgil's birth.
9. The *nekyia*, or conversation with the dead, originally comprised a separate literary tradition from *katabasis*, the descent and return of a living being into the underworld. Raymond Clark also distinguishes *katabasis* from visionary *ecstasis*, where only the soul undertakes a journey while the body remains earthbound, and from religious fertility rites, in which a god descends rather than a mortal human being (1979, 32–44).
10. Heaney, *New Selected Poems 1988–2013* (2013), 1. Heaney edited the first volume of *New Selected Poems 1966–1987* himself, while the second volume was compiled from selections he had made for *Opened Ground*, together with his selections for an edition of poems in Italian translation, compiled by Marco Sonzogni (see 'Publisher's Note').
11. OG 458. Cf. also 'The Placeless Heaven' (1985), 371; 'A soul on the washing line' (1991).

In Heaney's poetry, we see space being cleared for the marvellous in *The Haw Lantern* (1987) and *Seeing Things* (1991), the two volumes published after the deaths of his mother and father. In 'Fosterling', Heaney describes a shift from '*Heaviness of being. And poetry / Sluggish in the doldrum of what happens*' to poetry that can 'credit marvels. . . . Time to be dazzled and the heart to lighten.' (*ST* 50) This new phase in Heaney's writing has been understood by some scholars as a conscious return to and re-embrace of the poet's Catholic upbringing. Indeed, for John Dennison, Heaney's later writing is problematically dependent on the redemptive logic of Christian doctrine.[12] Heaney finds himself in a 'fiduciary predicament', according to Dennison, when he claims a curative role for poetry that is essentially imported from the 'collapsed eschatology' of his former Catholic faith (220).

Over the same period, however, Heaney's interest in classical literature deepens and develops, leading other scholars to claim that the Irish poet's turn to 'crediting marvels.'' announces precisely a new distance from his Catholic origins. Florence Impens suggests that Heaney's turn to the classics is precipitated by a loss of religious faith in the mid-1980s. She observes a shift in Heaney's literary influences from Catholic Dante in *Station Island*, to Virgil and Dante as paired and equal authorities in *Seeing Things*, to Virgil presiding alone in *Human Chain*, with a further secularisation of Heaney's language in the *Aeneid Book VI* translation.[13] Helen Vendler similarly suggests that Virgil's *Aeneid VI* offered Heaney 'a compelling poetic account of pre-Christian myth that would counter the Christian narratives of his Catholic upbringing.'[14] But as Vendler herself points out, Heaney's early poetry also draws amply on pre-Christian, Celtic and Scandinavian myth. His resistance to Christian redemptive narratives is, if anything, more strongly marked in early volumes such as *Wintering Out* and *North*. And meanwhile, Dante remains an important presence in Heaney's later work, as evidenced in the *terza rima* form of many of his poems in *Human Chain*.[15] Finally, his engagement with the classics seems to me to have complicated and enriched, rather than dislodged, the primary, Catholic contours of Heaney's imagination.

Heaney's translations are major works in themselves and deserve to be studied with as close attention as any of his original English poems; Heaney the translator is no less Heaney the poet. One reason for the persuasiveness of his translations is that they are texts in which readers can hear the poet exploring his own preoccupations, exposing his doubts, clarifying his values and furthering his art. The scholarly conversation about Heaney's relation to the classics is currently growing apace, and my reading should be seen as part of this broadening field of research. Bernard O'Donoghue's pioneering work on Heaney's use of the classics in his English poems is particularly valuable for the way it connects the classical references to the

---

12. Dennison (2015), 190–223 *et passim*.
13. Impens, *Classical Presences* (2018), 59; and '"Help me please"' (2017), 256.
14. Vendler, 'Introduction', in Heaney, *Stone from Delphi* (2012), 10.
15. In Heaney's 'Mossbawn via Mantua' (2012), Dante is named as an entire 'zone' of influence, outweighing any other single writer named in the essay (based on a lecture delivered in Vienna in 2009). See Coda.

broader questions that animate Heaney's entire corpus. In his most recent study, O'Donoghue asks, 'why did Heaney turn so much to Virgil? What "imaginative need" did he meet for him?'[16] This sense of an 'imaginative need' being answered is precisely what makes Heaney's translations so compelling for the contemporary reader. His classical translations, and English poetry relating to the classics, are the focus of a ground-breaking collection of essays, *Seamus Heaney and the Classics*, edited by Stephen Harrison, Fiona Macintosh, Claire Kenward and Helen Eastman (2019). For the first time, we can appreciate the range and depth of Heaney's engagement with Greek and Latin authors, from Hesiod, Aeschylus and Sophocles to Horace and Virgil. In the field of Irish Studies, Florence Impens offers a useful, contextual survey of the classics in the poetry of Heaney, Michael Longley, Derek Mahon, Eavan Boland and other contemporary Irish poets (2018). Meanwhile, Heaney also features in Philip Hardie's magnificent cultural history of Virgil's *Aeneid* (2014), as well as in Susanna Braund and Zara Martirosova Torlone's volume of collected essays on Virgil in translation (2018).

Too often, however, Heaney's translations are still treated in academic discussions as works apart from his main body of writing. In modern literary criticism, much of the richness of Heaney's intertextual dialogue with the classics is lost, since the translations are considered only as an aid to interpreting the original English poems. And in studies of Heaney's poetics, the classical translations have received even less critical attention. In several major studies of Heaney's prose writing, which are otherwise well researched, judiciously argued and illuminating, Heaney's writing about the classics is largely ignored.[17] And yet, Heaney's engagement with classical literature contributes greatly to his overall understanding of the 'do-goodery of poetry and of the arts in general'.[18] At the other end of the scale, detailed close reading of individual translations, while highly valuable, can reveal only a small slice of the multi-layered conversation that Heaney is conducting, between himself and the originary text, and between himself and other modern writers. Heaney's reading of Virgil, as we shall see, is intricately implicated in his dialogues with Dante, Wordsworth, Keats, Kavanagh, Yeats, Eliot, Mandelstam, Czesław Miłosz, Elizabeth Bishop and Ted Hughes. The presences of these other writers enrich his translations, and draw the reader into a conversation that stretches from Ireland across the globe, and from prehistoric times to our own age.

Most pertinent of all is the way the translations form part of Heaney's dialogue with himself, demonstrating time and again his notion that poetry can 'extend people's chances of getting into dialogue with themselves.'[19] Virgil is Heaney's inner interlocutor in at least seven of the later volumes of poetry: *Seeing Things, The Midnight Verdict, Electric Light, District and Circle, The Riverbank Field, Human Chain* and, of course, *Aeneid Book VI*. Heaney mused on the shape of Virgil's life and the enduring impact of his writing in two national radio broadcasts, as well as numerous

---

16. O'Donoghue (2009) and (2019), alluding to Heaney, 'Envies and Identifications' (1985), 5.
17. See Cavanagh (2009), Dennison (2015), Lavan (2020).
18. Heaney, 'The Whole Thing' (2002).
19. Heaney, 'Further Language' (1997), 13.

lectures, interviews and essays, most notably 'Envies and Identifications' (1985), *The Redress of Poetry* (1995), 'Secular and Millennial Miłosz' (1999, rpt. *FK* 2002), *Sounding Lines* (1999), 'On Elegies, Eclogues, Translations, Transfusions (2001), 'Towers, Trees, Terrors' (2001), '*Eclogues in Extremis*' (2003), 'Glory be to the world' (2004), 'Suffering and Decision' (2007) and 'Mossbawn via Mantua' (2012). When this rich array of writing is considered as a whole, it becomes abundantly clear that Heaney values Virgil's poetry not only for its talismanic motifs and images, and its orchestration of diction, syntax, pace and hexameter pulse, but also for the way it bridges cultures between ancient Greece and Rome, and again between Rome and medieval Christendom. In Virgil's poetry, from *Eclogues IX* to *Georgics IV* and *Aeneid VI*, Heaney finds examples of the good of poetry, in its capacity for remembering and forwarding the past, and conversely, in its capacity to break from the past, let fly and strike its own, fresh note.

With respect to Heaney's translations of the classics, it is useful to distinguish the different kinds of engagement Heaney conducts with Greek and Latin literature. The Greek translations are predominantly written for public performance on stage, while much of the Latin material is voiced with the subjective interiority of modern lyric. For the Field Day Theatre Company in Northern Ireland, Heaney produced *The Cure at Troy*, a version of Sophocles' *Philoctetes* (1990). His 'Mycenae Lookout', a sequence of five searing, sometimes brutal monologues, is voiced by the figure of the watchman from Aeschylus' *Agamemnon* (*SL* 29–37). In 2004, Heaney published translation extracts from Sophocles' *Oedipus at Colonus* and *Ajax*, and in the same year produced a version of Sophocles' *Antigone*, entitled *The Burial at Thebes*, again for the Field Day Theatre Company.[20] Apart from the Greek tragedians, Heaney was increasingly drawn to Hesiod's *Works and Days*, the model for Virgil's *Georgics* and one of the earliest songs of earth in the Western literary tradition.[21] Inspired by Theocritus' *Idylls* and a trip to Greece, he composed the 'Sonnets from Hellas' and eventually published this sequence together with his Virgilian eclogues (*EL* 38–43). In *Stepping Stones*, Heaney comments that 'with the Greeks, you're hand to hand with the world' whereas 'much of the Roman stuff was texted to them' (*SS* 294). Heaney's Theocritean sequence is more direct and bluntly pessimistic than his Virgilian eclogues, which, while consciously 'texted' and literary, are also confiding, tender and intimate. Vendler suggests that Heaney's works borrowing from the Greeks 'are in great part savage, cruel, bloody, and elemental' while his poems alluding to classical Latin 'can be elegiac, tender, dignified – and even self-mocking'.[22] That general distinction should be qualified, for Heaney draws on Virgil's portrait of the horrifically mutilated warrior Deiphobus in *Aeneid VI*, and many other depictions of military conflict, especially the Roman civil wars, as we shall see. Similarly, it is a tender scene

---

20. 'Testimony: The Ajax Incident' (adapted from Sophocles' *Ajax*, Tecmessa, 285–323/4), first published in *Times Literary Supplement* (26 November 2004), then in *A Shiver* (2005). 'What Passed at Colonus' (based on Sophocles' *Oedipus at Colonus*, 1586–1666), published in *The New York Review of Books* (7 October 2004), 14.
21. See Rowena Fowler, 'Heaney and Hesiod', in Harrison et al., eds (2019), 38–49.
22. Vendler, *Stone from Delphi* (2012), 25.

from Sophocles' *Oedipus at Colonus* that Heaney chooses for his own epitaph, and quotes from, in his memorial address for his mentor at Harvard, Robert Fitzgerald.[23] Broadly speaking, however, I would agree that while Heaney confronts the abattoir of history with Aeschylus and Sophocles, he elegises the loss of his first world with Virgil. The family farm with its Lethean riverbank field, and the ghostly presences of lost loved ones, are layered with Virgilian associations in Heaney's later poetry. And yet, whether the dialogue is with Sophocles or Virgil, Heaney's 'pity survives undamaged', as Vendler rightly argues: 'he hopes still for a viable ethical synthesis of the best in Christian and classical systems.'[24] Heaney's dialogue with Virgil develops in concert with a new openness to Catholic mysticism in the latter part of his career.

Moreover, while Heaney's Greek-inspired poetry is powerfully visceral and sometimes quite savage, it is largely based on translations and adaptations of the originary texts. The Latin material, although 'texted' from the Greeks, is written in a language which Heaney could read with ease and intimate familiarity. In 'Alphabets', the opening poem of *The Haw Lantern*, he recalls how 'Declensions sang on air like *hosannah*', and if at first Latin seemed 'Marbled and minatory' to the primary schoolboy, later he would be able to see 'the figure of the universe / And "not just single things"' because of the different worlds opened up to his imagination by learning Latin, Irish and other languages (*HL* 1, 3). His translations of Horace's *Odes* I, 34 and Ovid's *Metamorphoses* X and XI engage closely with the phrasing, sounds and rhythms of the Latin texts.[25] In translating Virgil, Ovid and Horace, Heaney is pursuing a double-helixed quest for artistic freedom and for social justice.

As Heaney wrote, 'When poets turn to great masters of the past, they turn to an image of their own creation'.[26] Heaney's love of Virgil is very far from Milton's sense of the Roman poet as *summus artifex decori* ('the master craftsman of style'), known to an elite circle of learned men, the 'fit audience though few' to whom *Paradise Lost* is addressed.[27] Heaney's 'hedge-schoolmaster' is a demotic presence with whom Heaney engages as friend, alter ego and co-conspirator for poetry.[28] As a Northern

---

23. 'Seamus Heaney: Out of the Marvellous', *RTÉ* (2009); Heaney, 'An Evening for Robert Fitzgerald' (6 May 1993), audiofile courtesy of Woodward Poetry Room, Harvard University.
24. Vendler, *Stone from Delphi* (2012), 25. On Virgil's debt to Greek tragedy, see Philip Hardie (1997) and Fiachra MacGóráin (2018).
25. Heaney's translation of Horace's 'Ode to a Wine Jar' was finally published in 1994; see S. J. Harrison, 'Heaney as Translator: Horace and Virgil', in Harrison et al., eds (2019), 244–8. His translations of Ovid's *Metamorphoses* and Horace's *Odes* I, 34 are discussed in Chapters 3 and 5, respectively. Heaney also published a translation of Ovid's 'Actaeon' in *The Guardian* (6 July 2012). As discussed in Chapter 7, versions and extracts of Virgil's *Aeneid Book VI* were published in various journals, in 2008, 2009 and 2012. See Marco Sonzogni's forthcoming edition of *Given Notes: The Complete Translations of Seamus Heaney* (Faber). With thanks to the editor for allowing me to read the manuscript in advance.
26. Heaney, 'Envies' (1985), 5.
27. Donald Mackenzie translates the Latin phrase as 'unsurpassed in the creation of what was appropriate', Milton, *Defensio pro Populo Anglicano* [1651], in *Complete Prose* 4.1:445; 'fit audience', *PL*.VII.31.
28. 'Bann Valley Eclogue', *Times Literary Supplement* (1999), 32, l. 4. On 'hedge-schoolmaster', see page 99.

Irish poet raised in rural County Derry, Heaney identifies with Virgil as a 'child of the countryside, starting at eye level with the ripening grain and the grazing beasts' (FK 411), and as a 'scholarship boy' who gravitated towards the city to find himself at the heart of violent political conflict (RTÉ). As author of the *Aeneid*, Virgil gives 'plangent and abundant expression' to the *lacrimae rerum*: in Heaney's translation, 'tears at the heart of things'.[29] Like Miłosz in the twentieth century, Virgil as author of the *Aeneid* is 'a man at work in the mineshafts of language whom others regarded as a guide to the corridors of power' (FK 413). As author of the *Eclogues*, Virgil is the consummate artist who can combine 'the realism of Breughel [sic]' with 'the exquisite landscapes of *Les Tres Riches Heures du Duc de Berry*'.[30] At home 'in the fields at the back of the house', Virgil can shift easily into the 'heightened, cadenced voice of poetic tradition.' (ibid.) And as author of the *Georgics*, Virgil is the poet of the earth who, like the mythical Antaeus and Heaney himself, derives staying power from his 'love of the land, the physical ground that is the people's home ground'.[31]

But standing for, and standing up for, the home ground requires more than pastoral or georgic songs of earth, if the home ground in question is Northern Ireland or Virgil's *Italia*. Both *patriae* are contested places, riven by civil war and at turning points of their political histories.[32] As a child of Ulster's Nationalist, Catholic community, Heaney could find no ally in Virgil the poet of Augustan *imperium*. But he could identify with Virgil the inner *émigré*, ousted from his home farm by Augustan resettlement schemes, a man compelled to see and sing both sides of the conflict. Thus, for Heaney, there is 'something implacable' in the very sheen and polish of Virgil's pastoral poems; their 'almost vindictive artistry' should be understood as Virgil's comeback 'against the actual conditions of the times.' (SS 389) Repeatedly, Heaney draws our attention to Virgil's ability to bestride two worlds, to speak in two languages and two poetic traditions at once. The ground he stands for, and stands over, is doubled, both foreign and familiar. Similarly, Heaney stands over the ground of a conflicted community, and his poetry draws on the resources of conflicting languages, including Anglo-Saxon, Irish, Old Norse, Latin and English.

Aeneas' underworld journey also provides Heaney with a mythic structure for poetic reverie or dream-work, for reaching into the past and projecting into the future.[33] The underworld is not only the place you descend to in search of wisdom or the lost beloved, as is true of *katabatic* narratives dating back to *The Epic of Gilgamesh*

---

29. FK 411, quoting Virgil, '*sunt lacrimae rerum et mentem mortalia tangunt*' (Ae.I.462). Heaney's translation is taken from BBC (2008). Wordsworth renders this, 'Tears for the frail estate of human kind / Are shed; and mortal changes touch the mind' (*Translations of Chaucer and Virgil* (1998), I.633–4).
30. Heaney,'"Glory be to the world"' (2004) and cf. BBC (2008).
31. Heaney, 'Glory' (2004).
32. Seamus Deane has explored the different senses in which 'ground' is contested in Irish writing, the word variously connoting 'land' and the question of legal and political rights, 'soil' as a matter of 'material–metaphysical possession', and 'earth' as 'vegetative and material' (Deane, 'The Production of Cultural Space' (1994), 129, 131. See also his *Strange Country* (1999)).
33. Cf. Heaney, 'we go to poetry, we go to literature in general, to be forwarded within ourselves', from 'Joy or Night', in FK 328.

(c. 2000 BCE). In Heaney's later writing, the discovery of the golden bough, the crossing of the Styx, and even more, the return via the River Lethe become tropes for the afterlife that is poetry itself. Ultimately, such poetry encourages us to reflect on the mortal condition, not by explicating a system of absolute judgement in the after-realm, but by providing broader frames of reference for individual judgement *en route*, and bringing us closer together in the appreciation of shared cultural memories.

In order to illuminate several facets of Heaney's intertextual dialogues with Virgil, we shall look more closely at Heaney's translations of the Latin texts, as well as the versions, adaptations and direct and indirect allusions to Virgil in his English poetry, and the prose writing, lectures and interviews in which Heaney makes explicit or implicit reference to the Roman poet. Succeeding chapters will examine a particular volume and/or collection of texts, and can be read in isolation, or as one stage in Heaney's evolving dialogue with Virgil. Chapter 1 explores how Virgil's golden bough functions as a catalyst for Heaney's thinking about poetic divination, and the contrasting virtues (properties, powers) of epic and lyric poetry. Focusing on the longer translation of the golden bough episode, published in 1989, this chapter explores Heaney's interest in the bough's fusion of φύσις and τέχνη (nature and artifice), and its combined masculine and feminine sources of authority in Virgil's underworld narrative. Additionally, this chapter traces how Heaney weaves the legend of Virgil's birth, heralded by the magical appearance of a laurel tree, together with his own personal memories of a chestnut tree planted in the year of his birth. In Chapter 2, I explore the implications of the truncated extract of this translation, positioned as the threshold crossing into Heaney's pivotal collection, *Seeing Things*. The seven poems originally published together in 1989, under the title of 'Crossings', feature the Virgilian images of threshold crossing that will become central to the dynamics of the 1991 volume as a whole. Not only the golden bough, but the Stygian crossing and Aeneas' attempted embrace of his father prove to be mythic analogues for the poet's self-interrogation and release, remembered and reimagined as checkpoint crossings on the border between Northern Ireland's divided Catholic and Protestant communities.

Chapter 3 explores Heaney's engagement with the Orpheus myth, as evidenced in his translation of Ovid's *Metamorphoses* X and XI, and the allusions to Orpheus in his 1995 essay collection, *The Redress of Poetry*. This chapter argues that Heaney's Ovid translation is influenced by Virgil's treatment of the myth in *Georgics IV*, and more importantly, that Orpheus becomes Heaney's classical analogue for the modern artist living under historical conditions of extreme duress. In Heaney's treatment of the myth, Orpheus first responds to the death of his wife by attempting to create art that can transcend mortal limit; hence his song takes him over the threshold of Hades and at first succeeds in retrieving Eurydice, as recounted in *Metamorphoses* X. But this attempt fails and Orpheus is driven into fresh extremity when his wife dies a second time. His art attains its greatest maturity at the moment he confronts the enraged mob in the Thracian mountains; there, as narrated in *Metamorphoses* XI, Orphic song acknowledges its human limitations and is transmuted beyond itself into pantheistic music. This song of immanence, rather than religious transcendence, is celebrated in Heaney's translation of *Metamorphoses XI*, the end of which, in my view, is particularly sympathetic to Orpheus' antagonists.

At the turn of the millennium, Heaney's treatment of the Orpheus myth leads him on to a sustained engagement with classical pastoral poetry, and Virgil's *Eclogues* in particular. In Chapter 4, I consider the Virgilian slant of Heaney's 2001 collection, *Electric Light*, focusing on his translation, adaptation and transfusion of Virgil's eclogues in the context of the 1998 Good Friday Agreement, and his substantial body of prose writing on classical and modern pastoral, composed in the aftermath of 9/11. For Heaney, pastoral delights in its own self-sufficient artistry but it also speaks within and against particular, adverse historical conditions, and it speaks *for* men and women made vulnerable by civil war and sectarian division. Heaney also personally identifies with Virgil's experience of civil war, and in this period adopts the Roman poet as his 'hedge-schoolmaster', a revered yet local and familiar literary exemplar.

This pastoral voice extends into Heaney's next collection, *District and Circle*, leading some reviewers to characterise his poetry as nostalgic and out of place in a post-9/11, global-capitalist world.[34] Chapter 5 argues, on the contrary, that Heaney's 2006 volume constitutes a far-reaching meditation on the current state of our fragile, mortal earth. His title poem, modelled on Aeneas' *katabasis*, along with his translation of Horace's *Odes I*, 34, form the heart of this collection. Both poems register the sense of shock, fear and apprehension felt by many in the wake of terrorist bomb attacks on New York City and London at the beginning of the new millennium. Filtering his response through Horace and Virgil provides Heaney with a measure of artistic and ethical distance from the immediate events, and a means of stepping outside the escalating cycle of violence. Once again, the poetry aspires not to transcend history but to understand it more comprehensively and to find ways of mentally surviving tragedy and loss.

Heaney's own life takes a seismic turn in late 2006, when he suffers a stroke and is briefly hospitalised. As will be explored in Chapter 6, he turns for refreshment and recovery to Virgil's Book VI, and in 2007 publishes an autobiographical sequence of poems loosely modelled on Aeneas' journey, under the title *The Riverbank Field*. While Heaney's dialogue with Virgil in *Electric Light* and *District and Circle* is driven by an ethical imperative to engage with contemporary events, in *The Riverbank Field* the dialogue is channelled in the direction of what, for Heaney, are the primary impulses of lyric poetry, the pleasures of rhythmic cadence and the spontaneous generation of poetic form.

In terms of his dialogue with Virgil, 2008 might be described as Heaney's *annus mirabilis*. In this year, he drafted his translation of Virgil's *Aeneid VI* in its entirety for the first time, produced a radio essay on Virgil for BBC 3, gave an interview about Virgil and *The Riverbank Field* on RTÉ, and published a free translation of Virgil's Palinurus episode, along with other extracts from the forthcoming translation. It was a year for major reflection on his art and the arts of poetry in general, as evidenced by his magisterial book of interviews with Dennis O'Driscoll, *Stepping Stones*, first

---

34. Bedient (2007), Schneider (2006).

published in the same year. Chapter 7 examines this range of Virgilian material, much of which has not been considered by Heaney scholars before. The BBC radio interview gives us insight into Heaney's reading of Virgil's ideological slant in the *Aeneid*, which he interprets as more complex than a straightforward celebration of the Augustan *pax romana*. Translation extracts from *Aeneid VI*, published as 'Three Freed Speeches', give further indication of Heaney's anti-imperialist approach to the epic as a whole. Even more importantly, Virgil emerges as a bridge-builder between local cultures, forwarding ancient Greek poetry into what would become a heterogeneous European culture. Heaney's self-standing translation of the Palinurus episode is a little-known work of major significance, which I take here as a sounding line into his late poetry and poetics. Composed shortly after a memorial address on Ted Hughes, Heaney's translation has absorbed the Anglo-Saxon rhythms of Hughes's poetry, as well as Hughes's view that a poem must be 'a statement from the powers in control of our life, the ultimate suffering and decision in us.'[35] In Heaney's strikingly original translation, Virgil's Palinurus episode unfolds as a three-act drama in which a Hughesian or Keatsian intelligence is schooled into a soul through suffering and acceptance of a difficult fate. Ultimately, Palinurus comes to stand for the poetry that speaks from Keats's 'human shore', offering steadfast renewal rather than transcendent bliss.[36]

Heaney's final volume of original English poems, *Human Chain*, incorporates as its centrepiece the two Virgilian poems ('The Riverbank Field' and 'Route 110') that had been published earlier as *The Riverbank Field*. In Chapter 8, I explore the tracery of Virgilian language that animates the entire volume, particularly Virgil's description of souls lapsing across the River Styx, ghosts slipping from a son's embrace, and spirits gathering beside the River Lethe in preparation for their release back into the material world. Heaney draws on these Latin resonances to meditate on the fleetness of time, the cadences of mortal being and the cadences of artistic creation, from the first 'visitation' of inspiration to the second life of art as it enters cultural memory.

My final chapter considers Heaney's translation of *Aeneid Book VI* as the last act in his decades-long dialogue with Virgil. In this seminal translation, we find Heaney celebrating Virgil's love of *patria*, and taking on Virgil's role as the mediator between different languages and artistic traditions. Heaney bridges the temporal distance between Virgil's times and our own by mediating between two poetic rhythms and two tonal registers, creating a continuous dialogue at the heart of his translation. This powerful blend of intimate and public voicing constitutes Heaney's most successful amalgamation of what he had earlier described as lyric and epic impulses in his own poetry, the former connoting artistic spontaneity and self-sufficiency, and the latter, *pietas* or obligation and attachment to community and the past. The translation also demonstrates Heaney's exceptional skill as poet and translator to bridge different worlds and cultural values, just as Virgil had done in his own times. Through Virgil's Latin, Heaney conducts his poetic quest which, at heart, consists of a search for inner resilience and renewed hope, for peace and the healing of

---

35. Heaney, 'Suffering and Decision' (2013), 230.
36. Keats, 'Bright Star', ll. 5–6 (2003), 247.

fractured communities. What Virgil's poetry brings home to Heaney is something akin to the insight he says Wordsworth gains from the leech gatherer he meets on the lonely moor: the conviction 'that human beings, given the right conditions, have an immense and heartbreaking capacity for dignified endurance; and furthermore to witness such endurance helps the rest of us endure.'[37]

---

37. Heaney, "'Apt Admonishment'" (2008), 27.

1. The Golden Bough and the Absent Tree

When asked if Virgil's underworld journey had been a seminal influence on his work, Heaney responded, 'the motifs of Book VI have been in my head for years – the golden bough, Charon's barge, the quest to meet the shade of the father.' (SS 389) Of those three motifs, Virgil's description of the golden bough is the first that Heaney translated and published as a self-standing fragment of epic-turned-lyric. Many readers will know that Heaney's translation of the golden bough episode appears at the beginning of *Seeing Things*, providing a threshold crossing into that volume's exploration of the underworld of the poet's memory.[1] But fewer may be aware that a longer version (corresponding to lines 98–211 of *Aeneid VI*, rather than *Seeing Things*' lines 98–148) had already appeared in the journal *Translation* two years earlier, in 1989.[2] Why should this matter, and why does the longer version merit our attention, alongside the extract now firmly established as one of the canonical poems of Heaney's poetic corpus?

What this earlier version does, in my view, is underline the presence of Virgil, and the significance of his golden bough motif, at a crucial turning point in Heaney's career as a poet and writer. His immersion in Virgil's underworld book is usually associated with the death of his father, Patrick Heaney, in 1986. But the longer, self-standing translation, with its inclusion of the burial rites for Misenus and the hero's discovery of the bough, point to associations with Heaney's mother as well. Virgil's golden bough episode, in fact, provides a threshold crossing into two,

---

1. In this study, 'the poet' generally refers to the image of the artist depicted in the text itself (the 'I' in the poem, the speaker, voice), not the autobiographical author. On the problems of using terms such as persona, speaker, voice or voicing when referring to lyric subjectivity and address, see Culler (2015), 186–200. For the biographical author, I try to use Heaney's name but I have not adhered rigorously to a particular terminology. I hope the reader's discretion will guide them through any grey areas.
2. Seamus Heaney, 'The Golden Bough', from Aeneid Book VI, ll. 98–211, *Translation* (1989), 197–201. Lines 98–148 were republished, in this version though with minor revisions, in: *Seeing Things* (1991); *Poetry Review* (Spring 1991), paired with 'Man and Boy'; and Vendler, ed., *Stone from Delphi* (2012).

pivotal, collections, *The Haw Lantern* (1987) and *Seeing Things* (1991), written after the death of the poet's mother and father, respectively.[3] Another key link between the golden bough and the uncanny space opened up by his mother's absence is Heaney's essay, 'The Placeless Heaven: Another Look at Kavanagh', based on a lecture delivered in 1985. The same year, 1985, saw the publication of 'Envies and Identifications', which, while in many ways an anomalous and atypical essay, sheds additional light on Heaney's preoccupations at this time of radical transition in his own poetry. These various texts suggest that Heaney's turn to Virgil in the mid-1980s forms part of a multi-layered conversation about the good of poetry in times of personal, as well as collective, historical crisis and change. The longer Virgilian extract, published in 1989, reveals a more enabling dialogue with the Roman poet than is immediately apparent in the fifty lines reprinted in *Seeing Things*.

I. A LOCAL VIRGIL

Heaney identifies with the filial instincts that drive *pius* Aeneas to seek his father's ghost in the underworld. But his engagement with the golden bough episode is literary, cultural and political, as well as personal. Aeneas' journey in search of his father, Anchises, seems to validate a patrilinear history stretching from Rome's legendary past to imperial future. But in Heaney's translation it is clear that the paternal line is being affirmed in resistance to a mainstream, colonialist legacy. In 'The Golden Bough' extract, this manifests itself as a resistance to the iambic pentameter line traditionally used for translations of classical epic into English. In shaping his epic line, Heaney is negotiating not only with Virgil's dactylic hexameter, but also with epic tendencies in Yeats and Eliot, which he largely admired, and in Tennyson, which appealed to him less. At the same time, Heaney turns to Virgil in pursuit of the demands of lyric poetry, and in this direction his dialogue with Virgil is laced with crosstalk from Patrick Kavanagh, Osip Mandelstam and Czesław Miłosz. To some extent, these poetic dialogues divide along lines which Heaney, in his early, Jungian, essays, contrasted as 'masculine' and 'feminine' poetic functions. The motif of the golden bough, in particular, had long been a symbol in Heaney's work for poetry that combined 'masculine' with 'feminine' poetic functions, or to put it in other terms, epic *pietas* and will to form and structure, with lyric freedom and spontaneity.

In Virgil's *Aeneid VI*, the golden bough is already a potent, complex and ambivalent symbol. Virgil describes the bough as a hybrid growth, composed of both leaf and metal: that is, of φύσις (*LiS* AI, II, original, natural form) and τέχνη (AI, art, skill). Its secret whereabouts are known to the Cumaean Sibyl, and she derives her prophetic authority from the sun-god, Apollo. Heaney's translation emphasises the masculine source of authority, in his description of the Sibyl undergoing one of her Apollonian seizures:

---

3. Heaney's mother died of a stroke in 1984, and his father of colon cancer in October 1986 (McCrum, 'Seamus Heaney: A Life of Rhyme' (2009)).

> ea frena furenti
> concutit et stimulos sub pectore uertit Apollo. (*Ae*.VI.100–1)[4]

> Apollo turned and twisted
> His spurs at her breast, gave her her head, then reined in her spasms. (*GB*.4–5)

Virgil's '*frena*' (reins) turns the seer into a mare being subdued by the male god, and Heaney elaborates the metaphor, giving three stages to the animal-taming. By the time she comes to speak of the golden bough, however, the Sibyl's 'mad mouthings' ('*rabida ora*') have ceased.[5] She addresses Aeneas rationally and sympathetically, as one human being to another. And what she tells Aeneas is that the bough belongs to Proserpina (Persephone), whom she respectfully refers to as '*Iunoni infernae*' ('infernal Juno'): that is, queen of the underworld (*Ae*.VI.138). Aeneas is to pluck the bough from its hidden grove and plant it in the underworld as an offering to the goddess, which he eventually does (*Ae*.VI.636). The Sibyl derives her authority from both male and female divinities.

Aeneas' descent journey is loosely modelled on the *nekyia* in Homer's *Odyssey* XI, in which Odysseus encounters his mother's ghost. Aeneas' mother is immortal so his *katabasis* is motivated, instead, by a yearning to see his father's shade (*Ae*.VI.108).[6] In this respect, the Roman poet's *katabasis* might be seen as reoriented to a patri-linear history. At the same time, though, Aeneas' descent is made possible by the intervention of two female authority figures: the Sibyl and Aeneas' mother, Venus, who together guide the hero to the golden bough, an image not found in Homer's epic. Heaney's translation underlines the doubleness of the bough's composition, and its double-gendered authority, being both the property of Persephone and the instrument by which Aeneas finds his father's ghost.

We know from 'Route 110, I' and his interview with Gerald Dawe in 2008 that Heaney purchased his first copy of *Aeneid VI* at a second-hand bookshop in Smithfield Market, Belfast, around the age of sixteen or seventeen.[7] The edition he most likely bought was the Modern School Classics *Aeneid VI*, in standard use for A-levels in Northern Ireland in the late 1950s.[8] The editors of this volume underline the originality of Virgil's golden bough episode,[9] and they compare its

---

4. The Latin text is taken from *Vergili Opera*, ed. R. A. B. Mynors (Oxford: Clarendon, [1969] 1980).
5. *Ae*.VI.102; *GB*.6. Numbers refer to line numbers in *Vergili Opera* and 'The Golden Bough' respectively.
6. Raymond Clark defines *katabasis* as 'a Journey of the Dead made by a living person in the flesh who returns to our world to tell the tale' (1979, 34). Generically, its aim is the recovery of wisdom lost or concealed in the past.
7. HC 48; RTÉ (2008).
8. Vergil, *Aeneid Book VI*, eds H. E. Gould and J. E. Whiteley (London: Macmillan, 1946, rpt. 1960). Damien Nelis, who studied Latin with the same teacher as Heaney, confirms the Gould and Whiteley Schools edition was used at St Columb's College (email to author).
9. 'There is no other reference in Greek or Roman literature to the Golden Bough' and 'it must be identified with the mistletoe.' (Gould and Whiteley (1946), xxii, xxiii) Scholars have since uncovered many possible classical antecedents and parallels, amongst which the most

magical properties to that of mistletoe, which is used 'in modern folklore as a divining rod to unlock the secrets of the earth' and 'as a key to gain admission to the lower world' (xxiii).[10] This description of the golden bough resurfaces in one of Heaney's earliest published poems, 'The Diviner', which Heaney then uses as a basis for discussion of 'masculine' and 'poetic' functions in his *Preoccupations* essay, 'Feeling into Words'.[11]

In 'The Diviner', Heaney attributes quasi-magical powers to the skilled craftsman who could detect the presence of water using a V-shaped hazel stick. Bystanders would have a try but only the skilled diviner could work the bough's magic (hazel wood being associated with the supernatural in Celtic folklore, it makes a native equivalent to the golden bough[12]):

He handed them the rod without a word.
It lay dead in their grasp till, nonchalantly,
He gripped expectant wrists. The hazel stirred. (*DN* 23)

Heaney invests the diviner's rod with powers granting access to a hidden resource, as he will do with many familiar objects in subsequent poems, whether a garden spade, fountain pen, walking stick, tinker's clock, or bunch of rushes or oat stalks. In each case, the cherished object will guarantee the poet's right of way through a forbidden realm, as the golden bough safeguards Aeneas in his passage through Hades.[13]

In the lines quoted above, 'The Diviner' ends with a sexual innuendo which genders the diviner's technique as decidedly masculine. But in most of the essays collected in *Preoccupations*, Heaney rather associates divination with what he calls the 'feminine' function in poetic creativity. In 'Feeling into Words', for example, the diviner in the poem above is cited as a figure for 'the poet in his function of making contact with what lies hidden' (*P* 48). The poem rhymes 'stirred' with 'word' to indicate how the 'divining, vatic, oracular function' sets in motion 'that first stirring of the mind round a word or an image or a memory' (*P* 49, 48).[14] The divining function is spontaneous, intuitive, 'feminine' and receptive to external forces. In various early

---

interesting for Heaney's poetry is the golden staff, or *caduceus*, carried by Hermes in Homer's *Odyssey* V.87. Heaney associates his father with Hermes, 'god of travellers and marketplaces' (*SS* 293). For a review of classical precedents for Virgil's bough, see Horsfall (2013), pp. 152–7.

10. Divining or dowsing has a long history in geology, psychology and literature, for which, see Barrett and Besterman (1926).
11. 'The Diviner', first published by the Poetry Book Society (Christmas 1965), then in *Eleven Poems* (1965) and *DN* (1966). 'Feeling into Words' (1974) is collected in *P* (1980), 41–60.
12. Cf. 'A Hazel Stick for Catherine Ann' (*SI* 42–3).
13. A golden bough or some local equivalent appears in the following poems: 'Digging' (*DN* 1); The Harvest Bow (*FW* 55); 'A Hazel Stick for Catherine Ann' (*SI* 42–3); 'The Haw Lantern' (*HL* 8); 'Clearances, 8' (*HL* 34); 'The Ash Plant' (*ST* 19); '1.1.87' (*ST* 20); 'Fosterling' (*ST* 50); 'Settings, xiii' (*ST* 69); 'Settings, xv' (*ST* 71); 'Crossings, xxvii' (*ST* 85); 'The Rain Stick' (*SL* 1); 'The Stick' (1998); 'Tollund Man in Springtime' (*DC* 57); 'The Conway Stewart' (*HC* 9); 'Route 110, v' (*HC* 52); 'Route 110, xii' (*HC* 59); 'On the Gift of a Fountain Pen' (2013).
14. Heaney may have the golden bough in mind when he describes how poetic divination 'ensures that the first gleam attains its proper effulgence.' (*P* 48)

essays, Heaney relates poetic divination to Wordsworth's wise passiveness, Keats's negative capability and Eliot's auditory imagination (P 68, 81, 84). The opposing function, exemplified in Yeats's and Hopkins's poetry, is the 'masculine' will to impose structure and form on poetic material (P 75, 88).

In a key interview with Seamus Deane (1977), Heaney discusses these contrasting functions in terms of an epic instinct for structure and form, 'the search for myths and sagas, the need for a structure and a sustaining landscape', which in this discussion he associates with Yeats, as opposed to the 'lyric' instinct for spontaneity and freedom, the 'need to be liberated and distanced from it, the need to be open, unpredictably susceptible, lyrically opportunistic', here associated with Patrick Kavanagh. Seamus Deane then asks Heaney whether he is seeking a 'resolution between Kavanagh and Yeats' in search of 'a poetry that would be neither a matter of the day-to-day spontaneities alone, nor of a schematic mythologizing alone, but a matter of making the day-to-day become a form embedded in the day to day from which it arises?'[15] To this, Heaney responds, 'That is exactly it.'

At the same time, Heaney appreciates how Yeats's search for myths and sagas was being conducted in a spirit of counter-cultural resistance to the scientific, secular discourses that were ascendant at the time. As he comments in 'The Sense of Place',

> when the spirit of the age was becoming increasingly scientific and secular, when Sir James Frazer's *Golden Bough* was seeking to banish the mystery from the old faiths and standardize and anatomize the old places, Yeats and his friends embarked upon a deliberately counter-cultural movement to reinstate the fairies, to make the world more magical than materialistic, and to elude the social and political interpretations of society in favour of a legendary and literary vision of race.[16]

As this passage shows, Heaney is familiar with Sir James Frazer's monumental study, *The Golden Bough*, which launches its sprawling comparison of ancient myths and primitive religions by enquiring,

> who does not know Turner's picture of the Golden Bough? The scene, suffused with the golden glow of the imagination in which the divine mind of Turner steeped and transfigured even the fairest landscape, is a dream-like vision of the little wood-lake of Nemi – 'Diana's mirror', as it was called by the ancients.[17]

In the Turner painting to which Frazer alludes, the Sibyl holds the golden bough aloft and gestures toward a gleaming lake behind her – in fact, Lake Avernus rather

---

15. Heaney and Deane, 'Unhappy and At Home' (1977), 66.
16. P 135. Later, Heaney more accommodatingly embraces the 'pulse of an old energy beating in terms as far apart as Dante's *Selva oscura* and Fraser's [sic] *Golden Bough*' (Heaney, 'Ramifications', in *Yagul* (2002), 229).
17. Frazer, *The Golden Bough* (1922), 4th edn, 1.

than Nemi (see Plate 1).[18] Turner's scene has no exact equivalence in Virgil, but it does very strikingly place the golden bough in the female diviner's upraised hand.

Frazer's study went through many subsequent editions, and in 1959, the contested Turner reference was dropped, to be replaced by a two-page, prefatory citation of all the passages in *Aeneid VI* that mention the bough.[19] An opening chapter relates how the bough was protected by a priest of Diana, known as the King of the Wood, who held his priesthood until the bough was plucked by another candidate. The pretender then had to kill the incumbent King before taking his place (3–6). While modern scholars doubt the connection between Virgil's bough and the mystery cult of Diana at Lake Nemi, the King of the Wood might well have reminded Heaney of the myth of the Fisher King and Eliot's *The Waste Land*.[20] But apart from positing this connection with the mystery cult at Nemi, Frazer makes no further mention of Virgil's bough. In Heaney's view, his study serves to expose and demystify 'the old places', which Yeats's mythological poetry aims to preserve as sacred.

In the mid-1980s, it is Eliot whom Heaney characterises as the exemplary mythicising or 'epic' poet, while Osip Mandelstam becomes the champion of spontaneous, demotic and democratising lyric. In his 1985 essay, 'Envies and Identifications', Heaney contrasts the two poets' approach to Dante.[21] While Eliot elevates Dante to an 'expresser of a universal myth' and a 'seer and repository of tradition', Mandelstam restores Dante's language to its local habitation (*FK* 175). For Eliot, Dante's Italian can speak for 'the whole mind of Europe' because of its 'roots in classical and ecclesiastical Latin' (170–1).[22] In the famous opening lines of the *Commedia* the words '*nostra vita*', '*selva oscura*' and '*diritta via*' conjure the 'ghosts of first declension Latin nouns' (171). Because of the authority of Latin in the medieval, Catholic world, Virgil comes to Dante as 'a figure of completely exemplary force'. Indeed, 'Virgil comes to Dante, in fact, as Dante comes to Eliot, a master, a guide and authority, offering release from the toils and snares of the self, from the *diserta*, the waste land.' (172) Thus, if we follow Eliot, Dante is transformed into the 'dreamer of a world obedient to the spiritual authority of an uncorrupt Papacy and under the sway of a just emperor, where, without bitterness or compromise, Christ and Caesar would be

18. J. M. W. Turner, 'The Golden Bough' (1834), oil on canvas, Tate Britain.
19. Frazer, *The New Golden Bough* (1959), xxix–xxx, *Aeneid* 6, trans. C. P. Cranch.
20. The Fisher King legend is related in Jessie Weston's *From Ritual to Romance*, from which Eliot claims to have derived the structure of *The Waste Land*. Frazer's association of the golden bough with the worship of Diana was first suggested by Servius in the fourth century but is no longer generally credited by Virgil scholars. See Julia Dyson, *King of the Wood* (2001), and Horsfall, p. 152.
21. 'Envies and Identifications' appeared in *The Irish Review* (1985), then was collected in *FK*, 168–79. This essay is somewhat anomalous for Heaney, who is usually much more admiring of Eliot, if sometimes guardedly so (see Cavanagh 2009, 145–65). Heaney 'pirated' some of these pages praising Mandelstam's lyric Dante, restating them in 'The Government of the Tongue' (*GT* x, 94–6). Mandelstam is again praised for his lyric 'obedience to poetic impulse' in *GT* xix–xx. See O'Donoghue (1994), 137–52.
22. For Matthew Arnold and Eliot's promotion of 'the idea of a "mind of Europe"' as an antidote to what they would have called provincialism', see Heaney, 'Between North and South' (1995), 102; and Dennison (2015).

hand in glove.' (170) The 'familiar compound ghost' in Eliot's 'Little Gidding' is an amalgam of Aeneas, Dante's Virgil, and Christ, an 'alien judging figure who walks among them, the thoroughly human presence who casts a shadow and displaces water when he steps in Charon's boat.' (173)[23]

In refreshing contrast to this sternly judging figure of monologic, 'latinate-classical-canonical' authority, Heaney offers us Mandelstam's Dante, 'the most eager, the most inspiring, the most delightfully approachable recreation we could hope for' (174–5). This 'essentially lyric' Dante babbles and stutters and cavorts in the local vernacular and, like Shakespeare, delights in the local-associative and the free, spontaneous play of language (176). As Michael Cavanagh points out, Heaney's own translations of Dante are nothing like Mandelstam's; nor, indeed, are his translations of Virgil. But in 'The Golden Bough' extract, Heaney works to prise Virgil free from the weight of Eliotic *gravitas*, so that he no longer speaks with the 'universal' voice of a composite, 'latinate-classical-canonical' authority. Instead what we hear, as I hope to show, is something like the 'axle-roll of a rut-locked cart' that Heaney admires in Patrick Kavanagh.[24]

In the mid-1980s, however, Heaney is also after the shimmer and luminosity of Kavanagh's later poetry, the poetry of place transfigured by absence and loss. It is this later poetry, plucked out of its local habitation, that Heaney comes to associate with Virgil's golden bough and the poet's entry into the underworld of memory. In 'The Placeless Heaven', Heaney offers an extended analogy between the early and late poetry of Kavanagh, and the change of direction in his own aesthetics in the mid-1980s.[25] This was the period when Heaney lost both his parents but also when he took up his professorship at Harvard, then coming under the mentorship of Robert Fitzgerald, the distinguished translator of Homer and Virgil. Fitzgerald was working on his translation of the *Aeneid* when Heaney arrived, and indeed, they spent an afternoon discussing how to translate the *Aeneid*'s famous opening, '*arma uirumque cano*'.[26] The dialogue over Virgil touches on Heaney's reading of Kavanagh's late style because the transformation he describes in his predecessor is that of a lyric poet being transformed through the prism of classical epic. For Heaney, Kavanagh's early poetry has the receptive and reactive quality of a poet diviner, where the poet 'is pervious to this world's spirit more than it is pervious to his', so that 'the experienced physical reality of Monaghan life imposes itself upon the poet's consciousness'.[27] In the poetry of Kavanagh's later period, embodied first in his poem 'Epic', 'the world is more pervious to his vision than he is pervious to the world. When he writes about places now, they are luminous spaces in his mind.' (ibid.)

The shift from Wordsworthian receptivity to Yeatsian control is unmistakable, as is the gendering of Heaney's poetic categories. Thus, Kavanagh's late poetry

---

23. Eliot, 'Little Gidding', II.42, (2015), Vol. I, p. 204.
24. Kavanagh, 'Spraying the Potatoes', qtd in Heaney, 'The Placeless Heaven: Another Look at Patrick Kavanagh' (1987), 376, based on a keynote address delivered in November 1985.
25. Heaney, 'The Placeless Heaven', 371–80.
26. Literally, 'I sing of arms and the man'. Heaney, *Sounding Lines* (1999), 16.
27. Heaney, 'The Placeless Heaven', 372.

does arise from the spontaneous overflow of powerful feelings, but the overflow is not a reactive response to some stimulus in the world out there. Instead, it is a spurt of abundance from a source within and it spills over to irrigate [a] world beyond the self. (379)

But if late Kavanagh moves closer to Yeats, he is also more than ever the 'local-associative', lyric poet of small farm life. Only now there is 'a change of focus from outer to inner reality' (377); the poetry of place has become a poetry of memory. For example, in Kavanagh's 'In Memory of My Mother', there is still an exacting specificity in the 'catalogue of actual memories of the woman as she was and is bound to a true-life Monaghan by its image of cattle and fair-days.' And yet, at the same time, 'all these solidly based phenomena are transformed by a shimmer of inner reality. The poem says two things at once: mother is historically gone, mother is a visionary presence forever' (377).

In this commentary on Kavanagh's elegy, Heaney could have been describing 'Clearances', the sequence of poems written in memory of his own mother. And indeed, the essay on Kavanagh very strikingly begins where the 'Clearances' sequence ends, with the story of a chestnut tree planted in 1939, the year of Heaney's birth and the year that Patrick Kavanagh arrived in Dublin. Heaney relates that, in time, 'I came to identify my own life with the life of the chestnut tree', along with the affection of the 'green-fingered aunt' who planted it (371). When the Heaney family moved from Mossbawn to a different farm, the chestnut tree was felled by the new owners (ibid.). In 'Clearances 8', Heaney's auditory imagination conjures the tree's fall:

> I heard the hatchet's differentiated
> Accurate cut, the crack, the sigh
> And collapse of what luxuriated
> Through the shocked tips and wreckage of it all. (HL 34)

In the previous poem, Heaney has been reflecting on his mother's absence, which he describes as a 'bright nowhere' that 'had been emptied / Into us to keep' (HL 33). Like the felled tree, the mother has been transfigured into a visionary presence.

In 'The Placeless Heaven', Kavanagh's early poetry is associated with this 'childhood tree in its home ground; it is supplied with a strong physical presence and is . . . symbolic of affections rooted in a community life' (372). Like the affectionate aunt and mother, Kavanagh is the exemplar who first confirms Heaney in his identity as a poet: he 'gave you permission to dwell without cultural anxiety among the usual landmarks of your life.' (375) Correspondingly, the absent tree comes to symbolise Kavanagh's later poetry and Heaney's own altered appreciation of Kavanagh's work:

> I began to think of the space where the tree had been or would have been. In my mind's eye I saw it as a kind of luminous emptiness, a warp and waver of light . . . I began to identify with that space just as years before I had identified with the young tree. // Except that this time it was not so much a matter

of attaching oneself to a living symbol of being rooted in the home ground; it was more a matter of preparing to be unrooted, to be spirited away into some transparent yet indigenous afterlife. (371)

In terms of his own material circumstances, Heaney had good reason to identify with the 'unrooted' quality of Kavanagh's late verse. From 1982, Heaney had begun to teach part-time at Harvard, succeeding Fitzgerald as Boylston Professor of Rhetoric and Oratory in 1984, which meant that, like Persephone wintering in Hades, he would spend four months of every year away from home in Dublin.[28]

But there are also textual grounds for associating the luminous emptiness of Heaney's absent chestnut tree, and Kavanagh's late style, with Heaney's turn to the golden bough episode in *Aeneid VI*. We should first recall the famous legend of Virgil's birth, which, like Heaney's, is closely associated with the seeding and growth of a miraculous tree. As Suetonius relates it, Virgil's mother, while pregnant with her son, dreamed she gave birth to a laurel branch which, when it touched the earth, sprang up into a mature tree 'stuffed with diverse fruit and flowers'.[29] The next day, she gave birth to Virgil in a ditch adjacent to the magic laurel tree. In associating his own, and Kavanagh's, late poetry with the absent chestnut tree, Heaney is grafting a personal myth on to this legend of Virgil's birth. As a symbol of poetic inspiration, moreover, the chestnut tree happily encompasses both Kavanagh's late visionary poetry and the 'daring and extravagant imagination' of Yeats's late style, which for Heaney is illustrated in 'Among School Children', especially its concluding apostrophe, 'O chestnut tree, great rooted blossomer, / Are you the leaf, the blossom or the bole?'[30]

II. 'THE GOLDEN BOUGH'

In translating the episode of the golden bough, Heaney is interweaving his own autobiographical myth with his predecessors' transition from the poetry of materially rooted place to that of visionary memory. In *Aeneid VI*, the golden bough episode forms 'a perfect little narrative in itself', as Heaney says; it is artfully structured as a triptych, with the first and last sections (lines 98–155 and 183–211) concerning how Aeneas is to find and pluck the magic branch.[31] In the middle section (lines 156–82), Aeneas discovers that his crewman Misenus has died in mysterious circumstances. Hard as it is to credit the marvellous tale ('*si credere dignum est*', l. 173), when Misenus blasted his trumpet out to sea, the sea-god Triton had responded in a jealous rage, and 'seized him and drowned him in a foaming surge among rocks'.[32]

---

28. From Boylston Professor of Rhetoric, he became Emerson Poet in Residence, resigning his Harvard post in 2007. See SS xxxvi, and Ní Anluain and Kiberd, eds (2000), 88.
29. Ziolkowski and Putnam (2008), 190.
30. Heaney, Introduction, xxii, in *W. B. Yeats: Poems Selected by Seamus Heaney* (2000), a revised version of his Introduction to Yeats in *The Field Day Anthology of Irish Writing* (1991), Vol. 11. Yeats, 'Among School Children', ll. 61–2 (1992), 261.
31. Heaney, *Sounding Lines*, 16.
32. Heaney, GB.89; '*inter saxa uirum spumosa immerserat unda*' (Ae.VI.174).

Due funeral rites must now be conducted for Misenus before Aeneas can embark on his underworld journey. Aeneas therefore instructs his men to ascend into the ancient forest, and fell huge trees for the funeral pyre:

> itur in antiquam siluam, stabula alta ferarum;
> procumbunt piceae, sonat icta securibus ilex
> fraxineaeque trabes cuneis et fissile robur
> scinditur, aduoluunt ingentis montibus ornos. (Ae.VI.179–82)

> They head into virgin forest, up among the wild beasts,
> Making the holm-oaks echo the crack of their axes,
> Pitching down spruce trees, splitting up beams of ash wood
> And grained oak, with their wedges, rolling immense rowan trees
> To the foot of the slopes. (GB.94–8)

Virgil's '*antiquam siluam*' and '*stabula alta*' are archaic, emotionally evocative terms, which introduce an impressive catalogue of trees. As he names each species, Virgil presses through the stages of felling, from the first axe-blow to dragging the trees down to the funeral pyre.

As in Heaney's description of the chestnut tree's fall, what impacts on the imagination most is the thunderous sound of the trees' fall. In '*prōcŭmbŭnt*' and '*ādŭōlŭŭnt īngēntīs*', for example, Virgil uses heavy *molossi*, or three long syllables in a row. The sonorous felling of ancient trees, in response to the news of Misenus' death, then leads directly to the discovery of the golden bough. Tragedy, absence and loss are therefore countered in the final scene of the episode, the 'moment of discovery and triumph when Aeneas finds the bough and the bough comes away in his hand and he has been given the right of way'.[33] Taking into account Heaney's translation of the entire golden bough episode, rather than the partial extract republished in *Seeing Things*, we can appreciate its symbolic significance for Heaney, with its associations with Kavanagh, and the two matriarchal figures governing Heaney's childhood.

At the same time, though, we should not downplay the golden bough's strong, paternal associations. As he said on many occasions, filial pieties led Heaney to identify with Aeneas' desire to seek out his father's ghost in Hades. Moreover, Robert Fitzgerald, who had become a 'father figure in my life at Harvard', died in January 1985, and as Heaney recalls to Robert Hass, it was the occasion of a memorial reading in Fitzgerald's honour that turned his thoughts to translating Virgil:

> I'd been translating the opening sections of the *Inferno*, and was interested in the whole theme of descent. And I had been thinking of the finding of the golden bough and of being given the branch as symbolic of being given the right to speak.[34]

---

33. Heaney, *Sounding Lines* (1999), 16.
34. Ibid.

Heaney's memorial address begins with an explicitly Virgilian homage to Fitzgerald: 'I am as bewildered as I am honoured to be standing here, Aeneas to his Anchises, as it were, except that it was he who had to carry me on his founding shoulders.'[35] Then came his own father's death in the following year. When an invitation came to contribute to a guest issue of *Translation*, Heaney recalls thinking, 'I'll go and get permission to go down to the underground to see him.'[36] The invitation to contribute to *Translation* came from the nephew of Jack Sweeney, Curator of the Woodberry Poetry Room at Harvard, a man for whom, Heaney said, 'I had developed feelings that were to some extent filial and *pius*.'[37] Jack Sweeney had died in the same year. All these fresh absences compelled Heaney to undertake the Virgil translation in memory of these absent, paternal figures.

When Aeneas plucks the golden bough and is given the right of way into Hades, Heaney tells Hass, 'It's like finding a voice, the beginning and end at once.'[38] At that stage in his own life, Heaney had already had eleven volumes of poetry and prose published by Faber; he was Boylston Professor of Rhetoric at Harvard, and in 1989 he was to be appointed Professor of Poetry at Oxford. He was not, then, in any immediate need of permission to write, and clearly he had already found a poetic voice. But Virgil's golden bough taps into an inner resource that fuels a new phase of writing. As Gaston Bachelard writes, 'it is not until late in life that we really revere an image, when we discover that its roots plunge well beyond the history that is fixed in our memories.'[39] Heaney continued to work on his golden bough translation, and was still doing so in 1989, when he retreated to Glanmore Cottage to escape the publicity of his election as Oxford Professor of Poetry.[40] In one form or other, Heaney continued to publish and read aloud versions of the golden bough motif from the 1980s to the end of his life.[41] As his collaborator, the Dutch artist Jan Hendrix remarked,

---

35. Heaney, 'Robert Fitzgerald: Memorial Address' (1985). Courtesy of the Stuart A. Rose Manuscript, Archives, and Rare Book Library, Emory University.
36. Heaney, *Sounding Lines*, 16.
37. Heaney, *The Golden Bough* (1992), 32. The 1989 issue of *Translation*, as well as Heaney's extract in it, are dedicated 'in memory of Jack and Máire Sweeney'.
38. Heaney, Sounding Lines, 16.
39. Gaston Bachelard, *The Poetics of Space* [1958], Beacon Books edn (1969), 33.
40. A notebook entry about intense publicity coverage of the Oxford Poetry election, dated 5 June 1989, ends with: 'Had to get down here to do the Virgil.' LP I.xi.7. 1989–90.
41. All the published versions of Heaney's 'Golden Bough' known to me are as follows: 'The Golden Bough from *Aeneid* Book VI, lines 98–211', *Translation* (1989); 'Man and Boy' (Parts I, II) and 'The Golden Bough from *Aeneid* Book VI, lines 98–177' in *Poetry Review* (Spring 1991), 72–4 ['177' is an error; it is in fact l. 148], based on 1989 text, with minor revisions; 'The Golden Bough' (*Aeneid* Book VI, ll. 98–148), in *Seeing Things* (London: Faber, 1991), 1–3, based on 1989 text, with minor revisions; with Jan Hendrix (screenprints), *The Golden Bough*, ll. 98–211, English above Latin text (Mexico City: Los Tropicos, and Bannholt, Netherlands: In de Bonnefant, May 1992), text from Faber 1991 edition; audio version, The Essay, 'Greek and Latin Voices: Virgil 2/4', Radio 3, an earlier version of the Faber 2016 edition, with some variations; 'The Golden Bough' (*Aeneid* Book VI, ll. 98–148), in *The Stone from Delphi: Poems with Classical References*, selected with an introduction by Helen Vendler (San Francisco: The Arion Press, 2012), 1–3, text from *Seeing Things* (Faber, 1991). And posthumously, the

Aeneid VI was 'like a talisman that he always carried with him all the time, to tinker with and work on and change'.[42] The golden bough episode, in particular, proved to be as constantly renewable a resource as the magical bough itself.

In the extract published in *Translation* (1989), Heaney stakes his ground at a deliberate distance from the sound of English iambic pentameter, although this is the verse form into which classical epic is usually translated. Notable pre-twentieth century translations had been composed in rhyme. In the seventeenth century, Sir John Harington had published a translation of the sixth book alone, of which Heaney was aware, though the strong Protestant bias of the work (most evident in Harington's introduction) cannot have appealed to Heaney. A long-time translator of Ariosto, Harington unusually rendered his *Aeneid VI* in Italian *ottava rima*.[43] Dryden's enduring translation of the *Aeneid* is composed in Augustan heroic couplets (rhyming iambic pentameters).[44] Alexander Pope called it 'the most noble and spirited translation that I know in any language', and Heaney's mentor, Robert Fitzgerald, agrees: 'We cannot call ourselves acquainted with English poetry in his age and in the next unless we have read his translation.'[45] And Wordsworth, though he disliked Dryden's translations of Virgil, felt that he could not escape using the same meter in his own version of *Aeneid I–III*.[46] Robert Fitzgerald remarks that, surprisingly, there is no classic, pre-modern translation of the *Aeneid* into English blank verse, although, he suggests, one might have expected one from Marlowe, Shakespeare, Milton, Keats or Tennyson.[47] But amongst modern translators, unrhymed iambic pentameter (blank verse) has become the standard meter for classical epic translation. And Fitzgerald himself produced a critically acclaimed blank verse translation of the *Aeneid*, published just a year after Heaney had succeeded him at Harvard.[48]

golden bough episode, corresponding to lines 98–211 of Virgil, taken from the forthcoming Faber edition of *Aeneid Book VI*, published in *The Guardian*, 27 February 2016; *Aeneid Book VI* (London: Faber, 2016), including the golden bough episode on pages 5–13, text substantially altered from the version in *Seeing Things*; Heaney and Jan Hendrix (screenprints), *Aeneid Book VI* (Bannholt, Netherlands: In de Bonnefant Press, 2016), including the golden bough episode, same as Faber 2016 edition.

42. Jan Hendrix, Arts Section, *The Irish Times* (24 January 2017). Heaney and Hendrix produced four Virgilian volumes together: *The Golden Bough* (1992), *The Light of the Leaves* (1999), *Yagul* (2002) and, posthumously, *Aeneid Book VI* (2016). With grateful thanks to the artist Jan Hendrix, and Mr Hans van Eijk of Bonnefant Press.
43. The rhyme scheme of *ottava rima* is ABABABCC. See *The Sixth Book of Virgil's* Aeneid *Translated and Commented on by Sir John Harington* [1604], ed. Cauchi (1991). Heaney refers to Harington's *Aeneid VI* in RTÉ.
44. Stuart Gillespie notes that Dryden's *Aeneid* 'has been almost continually in print since 1697', and cites Jasper Griffin's review of Fitzgerald's Virgil, *Times Literary Supplement* (24 February 1984): 'Dryden, he wrote, "remains the lion in the path of any translator of Virgil"' (email to author).
45. Fitzgerald (1963), quoting Pope, 22.
46. On Wordsworth's translation, see Falconer, 'Wordsworth's Soundings in the *Aeneid*' (2020).
47. Fitzgerald (1963), 17–18. Keats's youthful translation of the *Aeneid* is sadly lost.
48. Gordon Williams writes of Fitzgerald's translation, 'it is a work of high scholarship and real poetic genius, a truly adequate equivalent for our times to Virgil's epic.' ('Review', 1984)

Despite the 'founding shoulders' of his predecessor, though, Heaney does not follow Fitzgerald's lead in rendering Virgil into English iambic pentameters. In a lecture delivered to Harvard students, in the autumn of 1985, Heaney criticises the 'twilit Elysian melancholy' of Tennyson's 'In Memoriam', suggesting that its iambic rhythm conveys a false sense of consolation.[49] The basic metrical unit of Tennyson's epic elegy is iambic tetrameter, as in this quatrain, quoted in Heaney's lecture:

Be near me when I fade away,
To point the term of human strife,
And on the low dark verge of life
The twilight of eternal day.[50]

Here the regular iambics ('the twílight óf etérnal dáy') toll like a 'hymn tune', according to Heaney.[51] If Tennyson admired Virgil as creator of the 'stateliest measure / Ever moulded by the lips of man',[52] Heaney clearly felt that Virgil's 'lambent hexameters' should be translated into something other than this very English sound.[53] His own ear had indeed been trained in this tradition and 'baked from the beginning into the iambic pace'.[54] But, for some years, he had felt that 'the melodious grace of the English iambic line was some kind of affront, that needed to be wrecked.'[55] If, by the early 1990s, Heaney had 'made his peace with the tyranny of the iamb', in Bernard O'Donoghue's phrase, still, as regards Virgil translation, he seems to have remained resistant to the iambic melody.[56]

---

49. Heaney, 'English 186' Lecture, delivered 27 February 1985. Audiofile courtesy of Woodberry Poetry Room, Harvard University.
50. Tennyson, 'In Memoriam', Vol. II, p. 367.
51. Heaney, 'English 186' Lecture. I adopt traditional metrical markings because of the way they bridge classical quantitative prosody and English accentual–syllabic prosody. Thus, I use [¯] to mark a long syllable in Latin, and [´] for a stress or metrical beat in English; and [˘] marks a short syllable in Latin, or unstressed syllable in English. It should be noted, though, that the way the lines might actually be pronounced, either aloud or in the mind's ear, is far more fluid than this conventional marking allows. Hanson and Kiparsky (1996) propose a more flexible system, with [w] for a weak syllable, and [s] for a strong syllable, marked below the line, with variant stresses marked above. While attractive as an approach to modern, part-metered verse, their system distances English poetry from its roots in classical meter and so is not much help in the present study.
52. Tennyson, 'To Virgil', Vol. III, p. 102. The rhythm in this poem is trochaic (˜), however, not iambic: |'Státelĭest | meắsŭre /| Évĕr | moúldĕd | bý thĕ | líps ŏf | mán'.
53. Heaney, 'Postscript', in *The Golden Bough* (1992), 31.
54. 'An Interview with Seamus Heaney by James Randall', *Ploughshares* (1979).
55. Interview with Frank Kinahan, quoted in Neil Corcoran, *Student's Guide to Seamus Heaney*, 107, and Cavanagh, *Professing Poetry*, 85. The politics of Northern Irish poets using iambic pentameter is explored in full in Jason David Hall's *Seamus Heaney's Rhythmic Contract*, especially Chapter 2. Hall also discusses there the contrary, un-iambic rhythms of the English poet Gerard Manley Hopkins, who greatly influenced Heaney, 31.
56. O'Donoghue (1994), 9.

His 'Golden Bough' translation is composed in a long line of between ten and eighteen syllables per line, rather than the ten syllables of blank verse; and its predominant meter is dactylic. Around a third of the 129 lines of the translation have the six stresses equivalent to the long syllable of the classical hexameter line; the rest vary from five stresses to seven.[57] To my knowledge, the closest precedent for Heaney's long line is the Anglo-Irish poet C. Day Lewis's war-time translation of the *Aeneid*, although Heaney's use of dactyls is much more pronounced. In this line, for example, Heaney produces the six stresses of classical epic:

índeūbĭ uénēreād faucés graŭeŏléntĭs Áuérni, (*Ae*.VI.201)
Thén whĕn thĕy cáme tŏ thĕ górge ŏf thíckly fúmĭng Ávérnus, (*GB*.118)[58]

Heaney's 'thíckly fúmĭng Ávérnús' falls in the same place in the line as it does in the Latin, and follows the Latin rule of a dactyl followed by spondee in the fifth and sixth feet. In the whole line, three of Heaney's six feet are dactylic, which again emphasises the strong Latin rhythm to the line.

Published in 1952, Day Lewis's *Aeneid* is noted for its use of the idioms of modern warfare, whereas Heaney mostly avoids explicit reference to the Troubles, the thirty-year conflict over the constitutional status of Northern Ireland.[59] In this respect, his 'Golden Bough' translation contrasts markedly with his approach to Dante's 'Ugolino' in the 1970s (*FW* 60), where he quite explicitly compares the Count's starvation to the Northern Irish hunger strikers.[60] In the mid-1980s, Heaney's political allegiances are being deflected and channelled through artistic forms. Aeneas becomes Heaney's figure for the lyric poet in search of inner ratification for his writing.

Heaney's self-standing extract, 'The Golden Bough' (1989), captures this approach to Aeneas as a figure for the questing artist. The first section of the translation (lines 1–68) concerns Aeneas' encounter with the Sibyl, and in their exchange, Heaney mingles the everyday with the mythic, and colloquial with elevated lan-

57. More precisely, the 129 lines vary from ten to eighteen syllables in length, of which roughly three-quarters comprise lines of fourteen syllables, plus or minus one. Around a third of the 129 lines of his translation begin or end with a falling rhythm, whether dactylic or trochaic. And around a third have the six stresses of a hexameter line.
58. Classical poetry is scanned in patterns of long and short syllables, noted as [ō, ŏ], whereas English meter is accentual–syllabic, varying between stressed and non-stressed syllables, noted here as [é, ĕ].
59. 'It is the speaking voice that I have throughout attempted to follow' (C. Day Lewis, *Virgil: The Aeneid*, [1952] 2009), 8. Along with World War II terms such as 'evacuation', 'shock-troops', 'field commanders' and 'manning the trenches', Day Lewis draws liberally from the language of the Bible and Shakespeare. The 'Troubles' date back to the twelfth century, but in modern history refer to the conflict between Unionists, or loyalists, who wanted Northern Ireland to remain part of the United Kingdom, and Nationalists, or Republicans, who wanted to become part of the Republic of Ireland.
60. 'Then hunger killed when grief had only wounded.' (*FW* 62) There are, however, connections between the two translations. For example, Ugolino's heart 'foresuffers', as does Aeneas' (*FW* 61).

guage. A brief comparison with Dryden's heroic couplets and Day Lewis's long line version should illustrate the distinctiveness of Heaney's sound:

Talibus ex adyto dictis Cumaea Sibylla
horrendas canit ambages antroque remugit,
obscuris uera inuoluens; (Ae.VI.98–100)

Thus, from the dark Recess, the Sibyl spoke,
And the resisting Air the Thunder broke;
The Cave rebellow'd; and the Temple shook.
Th' ambiguous God, who rul'd her lab'ring Breast,
In these mysterious Words his Mind exprest:[61]

Thus from her sanctum spoke the Cumaean Sibyl, pronouncing
Riddles that awed them; her voice came booming out of the cavern,
Wrapping truth in enigma: she was possessed. (Day Lewis, p. 158)

So from the back of her shrine the Sibyl of Cumae
Chanted scaresome equivocal words and made the cave echo
With sayings where clear truths and mysteries
Were inextricably twined. (GB.1–4)

Dryden's lines have an electric energy. His 'rebellowed' catches the animal sound of '*remugit*', and 'ambiguous god' is cleverly derived from the sound of '*ambages*' (which, with '*horrendas*', can just mean 'roundabout expressions'). But Apollo's presence predominates in his translation, whereas in the Latin the Sibyl is the subject of '*canit*' and '*remugit*'; even when possessed, she has agency as the oracle of the divine. In terms of sound, the midline caesurae and end-rhymes strongly shape the Latin into Augustan heroic verse.

For a modern reader, Day Lewis's long lines allow for a natural variation in rhythm, along with a rich patterning of sound (notably, the 's' alliterations in the first line). But Heaney's translation marries a colloquial register with a shaping dactylic rhythm that manages to sound both classical and Hiberno-English. As in his *Beowulf* translation (also undertaken in the mid-1980s), Heaney begins with the word 'so', the 'Hiberno-English Scullion-speak . . . that obliterates all previous discourse and narrative, and at the same time functions as an exclamation calling for immediate attention.'[62] The first two lines are dactylic, varying with trochees: 'Só frŏm thĕ báck ŏf hĕr shríne' and 'Chántĕd scárĕsŏme ĕquívŏcăl wórds'. The first line even ends with a dactyl and spondee ('Síbyl ŏf Cúmaé'), as would a classical epic hexameter line. But the rhythmic effect is subtle and understated, in part because of the run of monosyllables beginning line one and ending line two.

Heaney's Sibyl is both a mythic prophetess and a flesh-and-blood, maternal guide to Aeneas, so her 'sayings' contain both 'clear truths' and 'mysteries'. A translation

---

61. Dryden, *The Works of Virgil, The Sixth Book*, ll. 147–51 (Vol. 5, p. 531).
62. Heaney, 'Introduction', *Beowulf* (1999), p. xxvii.

less sympathetic to the Sibyl might have rendered '*obscuris uera inuoluens*' as 'mixing lies with truth'. For Virgil's '*horrendas canit ambages*', Heaney hooks together the familiar, Hibernian 'scaresome' with the more formal, Latinate 'equivocal',[63] while 'Chanted' retains *cano*'s associations with enchantmewnt and lyric song. Meanwhile, 'the back of her shrine' is plainer and less elevated than either Dryden's 'dark recess' or Day Lewis's 'sanctum'. Heaney's Sibyl herself combines formal, Latinate diction with an earthier Anglo-Saxon register. She describes the underworld river, '*Cocytusque sinu labens circumuenit atro*' as 'Cocytus winds through the dark, licking its banks' (*Ae*.VI.132, GB.39), where Heaney reproduces Virgil's alliterative *k*'s, but with short, Anglo-Saxon words. 'Licking' for '*labens*' (literally, gliding down) introduces a colloquial hint of the scary monster in the great river's flow.[64] The Sibyl tells Aeneas that if he wishes 'to inspect / The murk of Tartarus' ('*nigra uidere / Tartara*'), he must first find the golden bough (*Ae*.VI.134–5, GB.42). Her alliterative 'inspect the murk' again combines Latinate with Anglo-Saxon language. So if she has poise and *gravitas*, it is certainly something other than Tennyson's English stateliness.

It is also worth stressing what Heaney has left out of the Sibyl's exchange with Aeneas. He begins his extract after Aeneas and the Sibyl have concluded their public business, in which Aeneas pleads for, and receives, her oracular prophecy about the Trojans' future in Italy. But it turns out he is not here interested in her predictions of grim wars, '*bella, horrida bella*', in his future (*Ae*.VI.86).[65] Aeneas now speaks of his personal need to enter the underworld, and these are his first words in Heaney's extract:

> incipit Aeneas heros: 'non ulla laborum,
> o uirgo, noua mi facies inopinaue surgit;
> omnia praecepi atque animo mecum ante peregi.
> unum oro: quando hic inferni ianua regis
> dicitur et tenebrosa palus Acheronte refuso,
> ire ad conspectum cari genitoris et ora
> contingat; doceas iter et sacra ostia pandas.' (*Ae*.VI.103–9)

> Heroic Aeneas began: 'No ordeal, O Priestess,
> That you can imagine would ever surprise me
> For I have already foreseen and foresuffered them all.
> But one thing I pray for especially: since they say it is here
> That the King of the Underworld's gateway is to be found,

---

63. Cf. 'The fire dragon / was scaresomely burnt' in Heaney's *Beowulf*, l. 3041. Cf. Heaney's use of the adjective in colloquial speech: 'I do remember a scaresome fight at the end of Broagh Road, just a couple of hundred yards from our house in Mossbawn.... It was the unprepared nature of the fight and the fury of it that was so scaresome.' (*SS* 241)
64. '*labens*' becomes a very important Virgilian motif in *Human Chain*, for which, see Chapter 8. In 2016, Heaney alters this to 'a ring of dark waters, the river Cocytus, furls / And flows round it' (A.181–2), which is even more beautiful, with the Anglo-Saxon alliteration of paired verbs.
65. In 2009, however, Heaney publishes a self-standing translation of this more political section of the Sibyl's speech. See Chapter 7.

Among these shadowy marshes where Acheron comes flooding through,
I pray for one look, one face-to-face meeting with my dear father.
Please teach me the way and open the holy doors wide.' (GB.7–14)

In line 7, Heaney's initial placement of the word 'heroic' underlines Aeneas' epic stature. The hero addresses the Sibyl formally, 'O Priestess', and later he will add, 'kind lady, . . . you who have power to do everything' (GB.21–2). She, in turn, will hail him as 'Blood relation of gods' (GB.31). In line 9, Heaney has Aeneas echo Eliot's Tiresias in 'The Fire Sermon' of *The Waste Land*.[66] This, in effect, establishes a vocational rapport between Aeneas and the Sibyl, since he is claiming a measure of her prophetic powers. Virgil probably means, in the more Roman, Stoic sense, that Aeneas has mentally steeled himself for bad news (Ae.VI.105). And in this passage, Day Lewis comes closer to the Latin, in making Aeneas sound like a veteran soldier; here he says,

> Maiden, there's nothing
> New or unexpected to me in such trials you prophesy.
> All of them I have forecast, worked out in my mind already. (p. 158)

By contrast, Heaney's Aeneas is an initiate, seeking access to underworld mysteries via 'the King of the Underworld's gateway'. Thus, he begs the priestess to 'teach me the way and open the holy doors wide'. The capitalisation, and the Biblical language, preserve the mystery cult associations of Virgil's '*sacra ostia*'. Like Yeats, Heaney responds to the mythic attraction of sacred, 'hidden places' (GB.49).

At the same time, what drives his Aeneas to enter Hades is love and personal loss. At *Ae*.VI.108, the iteration of '*conspectum*' (the sight of) in '*ora*' (face) gives an intensity to Aeneas' plea to see his father in the afterlife. Heaney heightens the lyric subjectivity by turning Virgil's '*contingat*' ('let it be granted') into a first-person verb, 'I pray'. The homonymic '*oro*' (I beg) is also echoed in '*ora*' (face), which Heaney catches with the affective repetition, 'one look, one face-to-face meeting' (GB.13). The Sibyl responds to the son's desperate wish:

'. . . si tantus amor menti, si tanta cupido est
bis Stygios innare lacus . . .
et insano iuuat indulgere labori' (*Ae*.VI.133–5)

'if love torments you so much and you so much need
To sail the Stygian lake twice . . .
. . . if you will go beyond the limit' (GB.40–2)

Virgil's '*cupido*' ('desire') and '*insano*' are strong words, not unrelated to the '*demens*' that drives Misenus to a fatal contest with the gods (*Ae*.VI.172). But rather than implicating a charge of dangerous hubris to the hero, the Sibyl in Heaney's

---

66. 'And I Tiresias have foresuffered all', *The Waste Land*, l. 243 (2015), Vol. I, p. 64.

translation seems to acknowledge the need for risk-taking in aesthetic terms, as an artist's response to loss: 'if you will go beyond the limit'. Among the legendary descent heroes to whom Aeneas next compares himself is Orpheus, the ultimate lyric risk-taker. Heaney underlines the Orphic allusion with the addition of a musical pun; Aeneas asks, '*quid memorem?*' ('why should I mention?', *Ae*.VI.123), which Heaney gives as, 'But why harp on them?' (GB.28).[67] Orpheus will become a major preoccupation of Heaney's in the early 1990s, as we will see in Chapter 3. For the moment, Virgil's Aeneas is at once a legendary hero, a figure for the poet, and an everyman who has suffered the kind of loss we will all know. As Heaney writes in the 'Postscript' to the Heaney–Hendrix *Golden Bough*, Aeneas is for him 'the grateful son' who 'seeks to enter the land of the dead in order to see again the face of his lost and cherished parent.'[68]

The Sibyl provides the key to the success of Aeneas' quest. She explains clearly and distinctly what the dangers are and why he must find the bough. In one of the *Aeneid*'s most often quoted passages, she tells the hero,

> facilis descensus Auerno:
> noctes atque dies patet atri ianua Ditis;
> sed reuocare gradum superasque euadere ad auras,
> hoc opus, hic labor est. (*Ae*.VI.126–9)

>   the way down to Avernus is easy.
> Day and night black Pluto's door stands open.
> But to retrace your steps and get back to upper air,
> This is the real task and the real undertaking. (GB.32–5)

The black, open door as a metaphor for death recurs frequently in Heaney's late poetry, and generally it bears the memory of Virgil's line (127, above), along with one of his favourite passages of Sophocles (see p. 62). Virgil's line is slow and weighty, opening with a Lucretian formula, with a first-foot, self-contained spondee, '| nōctēs | ātquĕ dĭ | ēs', an unelided '*atque*' and elaborate alliteration (c-t-s-d-t).[69] Heaney matches the slow rhythm of the Latin with a heavily stressed line, full-stopped at the end: 'Dáy ănd níght bláck Plútŏ's doór stánds ópĕn.'[70] But apart from these weighty trochees and spondees, Heaney maintains his predominantly dactylic rhythm. And he sticks to a very homely register in translating the Sibyl's most famous lines (126, 128–9), favouring monosyllabic plain speech over marbled *gravitas*: 'the way down is easy', 'get back to' and 'real' twice (matching the parallelism of *hoc, hic*).

The Sibyl's advice regarding the golden bough is also practical and direct. She explains its hybrid composition, metal and living wood, its magical, regenerative properties and protective powers, stemming from the authority of Persephone. Most of all, it is hidden, and can be plucked only by a chosen initiate:

67. The pun is removed in the version published in *Seeing Things*.
68. Heaney, *The Golden Bough* (1992), 32.
69. See Horsfall, Vol. 2, pp. 148–9.
70. Or, with heavier stress: Dáy ánd níght bláck Plúto's doór stánds ópen.'

                        latet arbore opaca
aureus et foliis et lento uimine ramus,
Iunoni infernae dictus sacer; hunc tegit omnis
lucus et obscuris claudunt conuallibus umbrae.
sed non ante datur telluris operta subire
auricomos quam quis decerpserit arbore fetus.
hoc sibi pulchra suum ferri Proserpina munus
instituit. primo auulso non deficit alter
aureus, et simili frondescit uirga metallo.
ergo alte uestiga oculis et rite repertum
carpe manu; (Ae.VI.136–46)

Virgil disrupts normal Latin word order to start the sentence with the key verb: '*latet*' (there lurks, or hides), and follows with the '*arbore opaca*' (dark tree) that conceals the bough. The next line uses enveloping syntax to withhold it from view a moment longer: '*aureus et foliis et lento uimine*' (literally, 'of gold, both in leaves and in pliant stem'). And finally, '*ramus*' (branch) appears at the end of the line. In line 144, '*aureus*' and '*metallo*' are deftly juxtaposed, at the beginning and end of the line.

Heaney's School Classics edition notes the debate over whether '*aureus*' here means 'gold-coloured' or 'made of gold'.[71] Heaney opts decidedly for the latter, where φύσις and τέχνη are blended:

Hidden in the thick of a tree is a bough made of gold
And its leaves and pliable twigs are made of it too.
It is sacred to Underworld Juno, who is its patron,
And is all roofed in by a grove, where deep shadows mass
Along far wooded valleys. No one is ever permitted
To go down to earth's hidden places unless he has first
Plucked this golden-fledged growth out of its tree
And handed it to fair Proserpina, to whom it belongs
By decree, her own special gift. And when it is plucked
A second one always grows in its place, golden again,
And the foliage growing on it has the same metal sheen.
Therefore look up and search deep and when you have found it
Take hold of it boldly and duly. (GB.44–56)

In general, the translation is less compact than the Latin (two lines longer, and more syllables per line), and wordier than is usual for Heaney's English poetry. But the additional syllables allow him to maintain a hexameter-like pattern of tri-syllabic feet, varying the dactyls with anapests. And key lines begin with a strong, even

---

71. 'There are two views. Some authorities think the Bough is actually of gold.... On the other hand, many believe that it is the branch of a real tree or plant.' (Gould and Whiteley, eds, xxiii) Cf. Horsfall, p. 157: '"Golden" in the sense not so much of "gold-coloured" (though that, necessarily, it is) but rather "made of gold".'

anti-iambic, opening beat. Thus, 'Hídděn ĭn', 'Plúcked thĭs góldĕn', 'Thérefóre' and 'Táke hóld'. Where the enveloping syntax performs concealment in the Latin, Heaney uses sprung rhythm to emphasise the obscuring landscape: 'áll roófed ín', 'deép shádŏws máss' and 'fár woódĕd válleys', while 'Hidden' is picked up again in another, double-stressed phrase, 'eárth's hídden pláces' (l. 49). Virgil's *'auricomos'* ('golden-haired') becomes a 'gólden-flédged grówth' (again, double-stressed).

Why 'fledged'? As we will see below, Dryden draws on *'auricomos'* to personify the bough as a human seductress. But for Heaney, the bough is a metaphor for poetry, or art more generally, which fledges into a life separate from its creator. Underworld Juno, or Persephone, becomes a 'patron' of art (a free translation of *sacer*, or 'sacred to'). And the bough, or poem, is 'her own special gift' (*munus*). One of the important characteristics of poetry achieved by vatic divination is that it is gifted from sources of power below, above or deep within the artist, rather than imposed by the artist's conscious will. Thus, Heaney invariably presents the bough as a thing gifted to Aeneas: 'he has been given the right of way'; he is 'given the branch as symbolic of being given the right to speak'.[72] And the Sibyl's instructions, delivered here in three crisp, un-iambic imperatives, are exactly those appropriate to the poet as diviner: 'loók úp ănd seárch deép', 'Táke hóld . . . bóldly ănd dúly'. 'Duly' underlines the respectful character of *pius Aeneas*, the 'grateful son', which Aeneas goes on to exemplify in conducting due burial rites for Misenus, in the middle section of the golden bough episode.

As argued above, Heaney associates the tree-felling for Misenus with his own memories of the felled chestnut tree on his former homestead. While the tree's collapse is linked with his mother's death, in 'Clearances' 7 and 8, Heaney presents Misenus himself as an anti-type to *pius Aeneas* and the opposite of a poet diviner. Misenus is 'a man unsurpassed at inflaming the spirits of fighters / With his bronze trumpet, and rousing up Mars when he played' (GB.78–9). As a type of artist, he aligns his art with military causes, as Heaney himself had refused to do. And this is perhaps why Heaney drops Virgil's *'cantu'*, with its positive connotations of lyric song (Ae.VI.165). After his leader, Hector, dies in the fall of Troy, this 'staunchest of heroes' switches his allegiance to Aeneas, 'Refusing to follow any inferior cause.' (GB.83–4) Once again, Misenus' susceptibility to take up military causes contrasts starkly with the actions of 'Aeneas the Good' (GB.91) himself, who, at least in the golden bough episode, is motivated by personal attachment, grief and reverence for the gods.

In this second section of the episode (GB.69–98), Misenus' fall is that of an artist who projects his ego into art, rather than waiting for the fledged thing to be gifted to him:

sed tum, forte caua dum personat aequora concha,
demens, et cantu uocat in certamina diuos, (Ae.VI.171–2)

---

72. Heaney, *Sounding Lines*, 16. On the importance of the gift to Heaney's late poetics, see Hart (2016).

But a mad moment came, when impulse drove him to blow
Resonant notes from a conch shell over the waves
And to challenge the gods themselves to a musical contest. (GB.85–6)

Once again, Heaney's translation excludes '*forte*' and '*cantu*' ('by chance', 'in song'), both words positively connotated with divination in his poetics. Instead, he attaches the chancy element to '*demens*' ('madman'), resulting in 'a mad moment came', suggesting a failure of artistic judgement with fatal consequences. Triton overwhelms the unsanctioned music in a storm of noise: '*inter saxa uirum spumosa immerserat unda*' (Ae.VI.174; 'And seized him and drowned him in a foaming surge among rocks', l. 89). As Milton writes of Orpheus, this is what happens when the Muse fails to 'defend / her son'; when the poetry is not rightly inspired, 'the savage clamor drown[s] / Both harp and voice'.[73]

After the negative example of Misenus, Aeneas discovers the bough by following the Sibyl's advice and exercising his own skills of divination. In Heaney's symbolism, this is a model for the poet being 'given the right to speak' because he pursues his art in the right way. Aeneas invokes his divine mother's aid, and when two doves appear, he credits their authority and follows where they lead:

uix ea fatus erat, geminae cum forte columbae
ipsa sub ora uiri caelo uenere uolantes,
et uiridi sedere solo. (Ae.VI.190–2)

        And immediately then
A pair of doves happened to fly down out of the sky
Under the man's very eyes, and settled on the green grass; (GB.106–8)

This 'chance' descent of the doves ('*forte*') comes in answer to Aeneas' prayer, which also occurs by chance, as Virgil somewhat oddly asserts ('*sic forte precatur*', Ae.VI.186; 'he happened to pray', GB.102). In the Latin, '*uiri*' ('the man') chimes with '*uiridi*' ('green'), but this allows Heaney to portray Aeneas as an everyman figure, or archetype of the artist, at this moment of supreme good fortune. Not only does poetry arrive as a gift, in Heaney's self-deprecating poetics, but it comes to the artist who happens to be lucky.[74]

The poet diviner has additionally to seize upon his or her good fortune. Thus, Aeneas responds decisively to the apparition of the birds: '*este duces o, . . . cursumque per auras / derigite*' (Ae.VI.194–5). Heaney gives three imperatives for Virgil's two, thus underlining Aeneas' rapid transition from doubt, over the '*caecos euentus*' ('blind outcome'), to certainty. He follows Venus' doves through the wood to the edge of Lake Avernus, and there immediately sees the two-fold tree ('*gemina arbore*') of the golden bough,

---

73. Milton, PL.VII.34–8; and cf. 'Lycidas', ll. 58–63.
74. Cf. 'The Sounds of Rain': '*You are steeped in luck,* / I hear them say, *Steeped, steeped, steeped in luck.*' (ST 49)

> discolor unde auri per ramos aura refulsit.
> quale solet siluis brumali frigore uiscum
> fronde uirere noua, quod non sua seminat arbos,
> et croceo fetu teretis circumdare truncos,
> talis erat species auri frondentis opaca
> ilice, sic leni crepitabat brattea uento.
> corripit Aeneas extemplo auidusque refringit
> cunctantem, et uatis portat sub tecta Sibyllae. (Ae.VI.204–11)
>
> the twofold tree, where the contrasting waft of gold shone through the branches, as mistletoe is used, in the woods, in the chill of winter, to turn green with new growth, mistletoe that its own tree does not engender, and to gird the smooth trunks with its yellow growth. Such was the appearance of the leafy gold upon the dark ilex, and so the gold leaf rustled upon the dark holm-oak. Aeneas seized it forthwith and eagerly snapped it off. (trans. Horsfall, p. 15)

Virgil's writing is exceptionally resonant here, especially in the echo of '*aura*' ('emination') in '*auri*' ('of gold'). In the last line, too, he adds sound to the visual image of the bough, the metal leaves rustling ('*crepitabat brattea*') against wood. The scene then concludes very swiftly, the energy of Aeneas' grasp ('*corripit extemplo auidus*') matched against the bough resisting him ('*cunctantem*'). The hard enjambment of '*refringit / cunctantem*' throws weight on the participle, notoriously underlining the bough's failure to respond as predicted. It does not come '*uolens facilisque*' ('easy and willing'), as the Sibyl had said would happen if, indeed, Aeneas had been summoned by the fates (Ae.VI.146–7).

Classical scholars of the 'Harvard' or 'pessimist' school interpret these lines as a sign of Virgil's latent critique of Augustan politics: for if Aeneas' seizure of the bough is unsanctioned by the gods, then perhaps the vision he is granted of Rome's future glory is false, along with the legitimacy of Augustus' imperial rule in Virgil's present.[75] Others have suggested that Virgil uses the reluctant bough to signal his own distance from the religious views of the afterlife Aeneas will shortly encounter.[76] But for Heaney, no critique or reserve on Virgil's part is implied here: on the contrary, Aeneas' eager gesture shows him marrying instinct with will, lyric divination with epic purpose. This is not to suggest that Heaney's reading of the *Aeneid* is apolitical;

---

75. For 'Harvard school' or 'pessimist' readings of the *Aeneid*, see, for example, R. F. Thomas, *Virgil and the Augustan Reception* (Cambridge University Press, 2001); R. O. A. M. Lyne, *Further Voices in Vergil's* Aeneid (Clarendon Press, 1987, rpt. 2004); and Craig Kallendorf, *The Other Virgil: Pessimistic Readings of the* Aeneid *in Early Modern Culture* (Oxford University Press, 2007). For an overview of different possible interpretations, see Horsfall, pp. 158–9.
76. Agnes Michels and David West argue that Virgil derives the image of the golden bough from Plato (or, more precisely, from a Greek anthology praising Plato's epigrams as an ever-golden bough). For West, the ambivalence of this passage, and the Ivory Gate, indicate that Virgil, like Plato in the Myth of Er, is distancing himself from Anchises' Orphic–Pythagorean doctrine of reincarnation. See Michels (1945) and West (1987).

but the political gesture here consists of claiming an (Irish, Catholic) affinity with Virgil's Latinity, which dislodges the Roman poet from his place in the mainstream of English heroic verse.

A comparison with Dryden's translation of this passage should help to illustrate the distinctiveness of Heaney's approach, and the way it 'unroots' Virgil from the English epic tradition. Here are Dryden's lively heroic couplets:

> Perch'd on the double Tree, that bears the golden Bough.
> Thro' the green Leafs the glitt'ring Shadows glow;
> As on the sacred Oak, the wintry Mistleto:
> Where the proud Mother views her precious Brood,
> And happier Branches, which she never sow'd.
> Such was the glitt'ring; such the ruddy Rind,
> And dancing Leaves, that wanton'd in the Wind.
> He seiz'd the shining Bough with griping hold,
> And rent away, with ease, the ling'ring Gold;[77]

The 'proud mother' nesting in the mistletoe is Dryden's invention, as is the suggestion of sexual wantonness in the golden bough. Elaborating on Virgil's earlier description of the '*auricomos*' ('golden-haired') branch, Dryden turns this into a seduction scene with echoes of the fall of Eve portrayed in Milton's *Paradise Lost* (*PL*; published thirty years before Dryden's *Aeneid* and much admired by the younger poet[78]). With its 'ruddy rind', 'glitt'ring' branches and leaves that 'wanton'd', the golden bough manages to combine the attractions of Milton's 'ruddy and gold' fruit (*PL*.IX.578), glistering snake (*PL*.IX.643) and wanton-ringleted Eve (*PL*.IV.306), herself turned temptress of Adam. Aeneas seizes the bough with violent strength, but unlike Adam's fall, this turns out to be a divinely sanctioned rapture. Dryden exonerates Aeneas by adding that the bough comes away 'with ease', although any sense of '*uolens facilisque*' is precisely what is missing from the Latin. That the bough lingers can be attributed to its own, Eve-like, waywardness.

Heaney exploits Virgil's ambivalence in this passage as well, though for different reasons. His golden bough is at once a homely and a marvellous thing. Though glowing with a gold aura, it is also a convincingly real, botanical plant. He begins with a naturalistic interpretation of '*gemina arbore*' (twin, or two-fold, tree), and he continues to focus on the plant's vivid, hardy growth, its yellow berries bright against a dark trunk of oak:

> a tree that grew like two trees
> For a glow came from it, and a gold aura tarnished its branches,
> Like mistletoe shining with cold in the mid-winter woods,
> Gripping its tree but not grafted to it, always in leaf,

---

77. Dryden, *The Works of Virgil, The Sixth Book*, ll. 296–304 (Vol. 5, p. 535).
78. With Milton's wry permission to 'tag his verses', Dryden had produced a rhymed, musical opera version of *Paradise Lost* (*The State of Innocence*, 1677).

Its yellowy berries in sprays all curled round the bole –
The leaf-sprouting gold looked like that in the gloom of the oak
While its bright foil chimed in the breeze. There and then,
Aeneas took hold of it and although it resisted
He greedily tore it away and carried it back
To the Sibyl's retreat. (GB.120–9)

Evidently relishing the sheen of gold, combined with green shoots, Heaney also aims here to free Virgil from the traditionally elevated style of English heroic verse.[79] This bough seems vigorously alive and actually planted in home soil, partly by virtue of the fact that Heaney deploys an almost exclusively earthy, Germanic linguistic register, as, for example: 'glow' (*glowan*, Old English), 'gold' (Germanic, Old Frisian *gold*), 'gripping' (*gripfen*, Middle High German), 'grafted' (*grif*, Dutch), 'leaf' (*laf*, Old Frisian), 'yellowy' (Germanic, cf. Old Saxon *gelo*), 'sprays' (cf. *sprag*, Swedish dialect), 'curled' (*krollen*, German), 'bole' (*bol-r*, Old Norse), 'sprouting' (*spruta*, Old Frisian), 'bright' (*berht*, Old Saxon; *beraht*, Old High German) and so on. Indeed, the only Romance words that stand out in this passage are 'aura' (*aura*, Latin, meaning 'breath' or 'breeze') and 'foil' (brilliantly appropriate in its connection to *foil*, Old French, from *folium*, Latin for 'leaf'). The description recalls early Kavanagh, I would say, in the colloquialism of 'yellowy', the Germanic compound 'leaf-sprouting', the plainness of 'looked like that', and the directness of Heaney's monosyllables, as in 'the gloom of the oak'. Heaney, moreover, adheres to Ezra Pound's principle that 'the natural object is always the adequate symbol', in contrast to Dryden, who royalises the oak and sexually personifies the bough.[80] The music of this passage comes from the mid-line double and triple stresses ('góld áura', 'leáf-sproúting', 'bríght foil chímed', with that lovely assonance) and the complex alliterative patterns: 'glow' / 'gold'; 'grew' / 'gripping' / 'grafted'; 'sprays' / 'sprouting'; and 'bright' / 'breeze'.

Beyond its material rootedness in northern soil, though, this passage also has the 'angelic strangeness' of Kavanagh's late poetry. Aeneas immediately recognises the bough because the Sibyl has described it to him in advance, and for the same reason the reader experiences that feeling of recognition at first sight. This gives it an aura of the uncanny, being both familiar and a weirdly impossible thing (a metal yet growing plant). Its own luminosity is also mysterious in the way it emanates from an inner source (a 'glow came from it'), yet also provides a carapace of brightness ('gold aura tarnished its branches'). As a natural symbol of art, its gold aura combines inner, vatic power with willed, poetic form, to invoke Heaney's earlier terms. Moreover, as Heaney writes of late Kavanagh, the bough's function in the *Aeneid* is

---

79. Cf. 'The force that through the green fuse drives the flower', a line of Dylan Thomas's that Heaney quotes admiringly in *RP* 132, and his praise of the constancy and gleam of gold in *Beowulf*, xvii.
80. Heaney, 'On Home Ground' (2012–13), 22. Heaney quotes from Ezra Pound's 1912 letter: 'it is in the laconic speech of the Imagistes [. . .] Objective—no slither; direct—no excessive use of adjectives, no metaphors that won't permit examination. It's straight talk' (Pound, *Selected Letters*, 1971, 11).

not to remain 'rooted in the home ground' but 'to be unrooted, to be spirited away into some transparent yet indigenous afterlife'. Indeed, it is not clear from Virgil whether the bough 'belongs' in the forest grove above Cumae, where Aeneas breaks it off from its tree, or in the underworld, where he plants the severed branch on a sacred threshold for Persephone. In the forest grove, the branch will be immediately replaced by another, grown in its place, and it exists there, so it would seem, in order to be transplanted from a physical location to a spirit world, or from an actual place to the realm of memory.

From this perspective, when Aeneas seizes hold of the bough, although he is laying hands on the magical object (materialising the marvellous, as it were), he is also initiating a process of *de*-materialisation. He is opening the doors to the underworld. Unlike Heaney's earlier figure of the diviner, Aeneas, as a type of the artist, has to combine both poetic techniques: passive divination and active mastery of form. The Sibyl has encouraged him: '*carpe manu; namque ipse uolens facilisque sequetur, / si te fata uocant*' (*Ae*.VI.146–7); 'Take hold of it boldly and duly. If fate has called you / The bough will come easily, and of its own accord.' (*GB*.56–7) In the heat of the moment, however, the hero's grasp of the bough is more bold than due: 'Aeneas took hold of it and although it resisted / He greedily tore it away'. Heaney shifts the bough's resistance ('*cunctantem*') to the end of the line, but he preserves the tug and pull of the branch over the line end pause. And his translation of '*auidus*' as 'greedily' preserves the implication of a possible transgression (Day Lewis, for example, writes, 'eagerly').

When he comes back to this passage, twenty years later, he will retain the same ambivalent translation. This 'greedy tearing' is the more striking when we remember that, in prose, Heaney invariably remembers the bough as being *given* to Aeneas, symbolising the giftedness of poetry and the poet's entitlement to speech. In the translation itself, however, Heaney acknowledges, and indeed fully exercises, the poet's wilful shaping of poetic material. Creative work, he comments elsewhere, is a matter of '*impulse discovering direction, about potential discovering structure, about chance becoming intention.*'[81] So, in *Seeing Things*, when Heaney lifts the latch on Glanmore Cottage and tells himself, 'raise your right hand / Make impulse one with wilfulness, and enter', he is in a sense re-enacting Aeneas' encounter with the golden bough (*ST* 87). It requires wilfulness, or a feeling for epic structure and design, as well as impulse, or lyric freedom and spontaneity, to enter his house of poetry.

This applies, too, to the lyric poet who sets himself to break off, and translate, extracts of ancient epic poetry. There has to be both an imposition of will and a willingness to lose oneself in foreign ground. In conversation with Robert Hass, Heaney describes translations as either 'Raids' or 'Settlements', like the two kinds

---

81. 'Varieties of Irishness' (1989), 10 (ital. in original). In *RP*, Heaney describes 'what typically happens in lyric poetry of the purest sort. Suddenly the thing chanced upon comes forth as the thing predestined: the unforeseen appears as the inevitable.' (*RP* 108) 'Design', as opposed to 'predestination' or 'inevitability', requires a more explicit exercise of poetic will, which Heaney associates with Yeats, and the feeling for epic, I would suggest.

of Viking invasion.[82] If this distinction holds true, then in his 1989 translation of 'The Golden Bough', Heaney is like Aeneas, '*auidus*', driven by love and grief, to make a first, opportunistic raid on Virgil's underworld.[83] The longer settlement was to come later. However greedily he lays hold of it, Aeneas' seizure of the bough is legitimate, in Heaney's eyes, because he does not seek to possess it. He seeks rather to be dispossessed, allowed into the spirit world, where he will duly lay the branch on Persephone's threshold. By extension, when Heaney lays claim to Virgil's underworld journey as a mythic analogue to his own experience, his aim is not to contribute to Virgil's canonisation as the founding poet of Western literature; nor is it to see himself among the English poets, as Keats wished for. He ventures into Virgil's underworld so that he can find his way home through memory and imagination.

*

In the late 1990s, Heaney bequeathed a walking stick, once owned by Charles Parnell and given to him by Conor Cruise O'Brien, to the poet Nuala Ní Dhomhnaill. Along with the stick, he composed a poem for her, in which he suggests that the golden bough is a gift not to be possessed, but to be borrowed and passed on. He pictures her as inner *émigré* like himself, wandering far from home,

> Astray like Aeneas
>
> Conducting himself
> By the light of the leaves.
> I'd see it rehearsed
>
> Back into the thickets
> And thick of the languages,
> Into that *selva*
>
> *Selvaggia et forte*
> We cull and come through
> As poets, if we're lucky.[84]

The poem hybridises Ní Dhomhnaill with Heaney, and Dante with Aeneas, and Aeneas with the hero of the medieval Irish saga, *Buile Suibhne*, in Heaney's translation, *Sweeney Astray* (1983). The mad Irish King, half-man, half-bird, living in

---

82. Heaney, *Sounding Lines*, 1. With thanks to Marco Sonzogni, whose chapter '"Out of the Marvellous" as I Have Known It: Translating Heaney's Poetry' (2018) explores Heaney's translation metaphor.
83. Heaney, *Sounding Lines*, 16.
84. Heaney, 'The Stick', in English and Skelley, eds, *Ideas Matter* (1998), 53. Also rpt. in Heaney and Hendrix, *The Light of the Leaves* (1999). Heaney quotes from 'The Stick' at the end of his 2002 essay, 'Ramifications: A Note on Jan Hendrix', in Heaney and Hendrix, *Yagul* (2002), 231.

exile, had already become an alter ego for Heaney in *Station Island*.[85] Here, Heaney merges Latin, Italian and Irish *personae* to create a compound figure of the lyric poet embarked on an epic *katabasis*. Each poet hopes to be among the fortunate, guided and protected by the golden bough. But ultimately, the quest ends in a release of the poem back into the underworld of cultural memory.

---

85. *Sweeney Redivivus*, in *SI* (1984), 97–121. Heaney describes Sweeney as 'a figure of the artist, displaced, guilty, assuaging himself by his utterance', in *Sweeney Astray* (1983), vi.

2. Threshold Crossings in *Seeing Things*

Heaney's pivotal volume *Seeing Things* (1991) announces a lighter mode, a lifting of weight in the line, a change of element from earth to water and air, and a shift from 'poetry / Sluggish in the doldrums of what happens' to poetry that can 'credit marvels' (*ST* 50). Published shortly after the death of his parents and his fiftieth birthday in 1989, *Seeing Things* registers a significant change of orientation in Heaney's life and writing. There is a conscious distancing from contemporary political events and a new emphasis on the transformative power of the imagination. 'Skylight', for example, dramatises the volume's shift of spatial coordinates as the 'perfect, trunk-lid fit' of Heaney's attic study in Glanmore Cottage is transformed by the installation of a skylight: 'extravagant / Sky entered and held surprise wide open' (*ST* 37).

Two translation extracts, placed as bookends to the volume, indicate that Virgil and Dante are integral to this transitional phase in Heaney's writing. Both extracts concern the attempt of a living human being to cross the threshold into the underworld. In the prefatory extract from *Aeneid VI*, the Cumaean Sibyl advises Aeneas how to find the golden bough and descend into Hades.[1] And in the concluding extract from *Inferno III*, Charon ferries the souls of the dead across the Styx in his barge, but he refuses to give passage to Dante and his guide, Virgil.[2] In contrast to Heaney's translation of the entire golden bough episode, published two years earlier, both translation extracts in *Seeing Things* break off at points of narrative uncertainty, with the protagonist not yet safely across the threshold into the underworld. In these extracts and in the Virgil and Dante allusions that recur throughout the volume, the poet finds himself on the border between two different orders of reality.

The Virgilian images and motifs in this volume provide Heaney with an imaginative language and landscape for questioning himself as an artist, for balancing his

---

1. 'The Golden Bough (*Aeneid*, Book VI, lines 98–148)', *ST* 1–3.
2. 'The Crossing (*Inferno*, Canto III, lines 82–129)', *ST* 111–13. Dante's depiction of the ferryman and his barge in *Inferno III* itself reworks Virgil's *Aeneid* VI.384–416. Heaney's translation of Dante in *ST* is also extracted from a longer translation of the opening cantos of *Inferno*, published in Halpern, ed., *Dante's Inferno* (1993), 3–15.

artistic needs and impulses against conflicting social obligations and loyalties to particular communities. The models of Virgilian *katabasis* and Christian *via negativa* offer Heaney a means of strategically distancing himself from the actual, material hells of sectarian conflict in Northern Ireland. In turning to the classics, Heaney gives himself licence to remember the past and return to the home ground with a new sense of detachment and imaginative freedom.

1. 'IN THE END IS MY BEGINNING': VIRGIL AND DANTE

The two translation extracts, at the beginning and end of *Seeing Things*, position Aeneas and the pilgrim Dante, respectively, on the threshold of their transformative journeys into the underworld. The 1989 translation of 'The Golden Bough' had gone further, depicting Aeneas plucking the magical bough and 'finding a voice, the beginning and end at once' of the supernatural journey.[3] The shorter extract in *Seeing Things* is exactly fifty lines long, surely marking the milestone of Heaney's fiftieth birthday in April 1989. But there is, too, a new note of uncertainty in the truncated extract, since Aeneas has not yet obtained permission to enter the underworld. Here the translation ends with the Sibyl warning Aeneas,

> 'If fate has called you,
> The bough will come easily, and of its own accord.
> Otherwise, no matter how much strength you muster, you never will
> Manage to quell it or cut it down with the toughest of blades.' (*ST* 3)

Her speech ends on a strongly negative note, the alliterating verbs 'quell' and 'cut' even suggesting Aeneas could meet a hydra-headed adversary in the golden bough.[4]

The concluding extract from Dante's *Inferno* breaks off at a similarly negative threshold moment. Dante has the faring poets encounter the boatman Charon on the banks of the Acheron. His scene is closely modelled on Virgil's but, partway through, he veers away from the classical text and has the surly boatman refuse the poets entry on to his barge. Dante's guide, Virgil, reassures him, saying (in Heaney's translation):

> 'No good spirits ever pass this way
> And therefore, if Charon objects to you,
> You should understand well what his words imply.' (*ST* 113)

The ferryman's rejection implies that Dante cannot board the barge because he is not among the damned souls who are destined for Hell. As readers of *Inferno* will know, the two poets do manage to get across the infernal river without Charon's

---

3. Sounding Lines, 16.
4. Virgil's pair of alliterating verbs has an elegant economy: '*uincere* nec duro poteris *conuellere* ferro.' (Ae.VI.148, my ital.) By contrast, Heaney's line is prosy and abrasive, with its monosyllabic run of 'k's and 't's.

help. Moreover, further down in Hell they will meet another Virgilian ferryman, named Phlegyas, and he will be persuaded to row them across the Styx. But Heaney chooses to end *Seeing Things* with the passage in which Dante and Virgil are still facing an *impasse* on the threshold of the underworld.

Enclosed within this frame of two threshold crossings, Heaney's volume is divided into two parts, with Part II comprised of a forty-eight-poem sequence of skimming, aerial poems entitled *Squarings*.[5] Seven of the poems from this long, experimental sequence were originally published in *The New Yorker* in 1989, under the title 'Crossings'.[6] This smaller clutch of threshold-related poems already contain the key elements of the intertextual dialogue with Virgil and Dante which will be elaborated in the forty-eight-poem sequence, and in *Seeing Things* as a whole. All but one are set in Northern Ireland or the Republic of Ireland. The one set abroad takes place on a bus ride from San Francisco airport to Berkeley.[7] There are glimpses of the classical underworld in the third, fifth and sixth poems, while all depict threshold crossings of some kind. In the seventh poem, Dante and Virgil emerge as enabling literary exemplars, steering Heaney through a painful memory of crossing a Loyalist military checkpoint in Northern Ireland.

Virgilian motifs appear in several of the seven poems, particularly the three motifs mentioned in *Stepping Stones* as long-time favourites: the golden bough, Charon's barge and the encounter with the ghostly Anchises (SS 389). The first poem in 'Crossings' recalls a distinctly Irish, rural scene, in which men and women step through girdles of straw rope on St Brigid's Day.[8] Undergoing this ritual proves to be a kind of transitional passage out of the actual into the marvellous: 'The open they came into by these moves / Stood opener, hoops came off the world' (ll. 7–8). There are traces of the golden bough in the magical properties of St Brigid's hoops of rope, which 'fray and flare' in the sun, unexpectedly like 'an unhindered goldfinch over plowland' (ll. 11–12). The flight of the goldfinch mirrors the way the poem suddenly takes off from the ordinary communal rites to hint at supernatural transformation. The golden hoops are also instruments of divine female power, being made in honour of St Brigid, just as Virgil's golden bough is associated with the powers of the underworld queen, Persephone, the Cumaean Sibyl and Aeneas' mother, Venus.

In the third poem, 'Running Water' (*Squarings*, xxxii), Heaney remembers crossing water, where 'Stepping stones were stations of the soul' (l. 3). The memory is bound up with the Ulster-Scots word 'kesh', meaning a causey or bridge. Again, this local scene merges into a Virgilian one, where Anchises' ghost is met in Elysium: 'I cannot mention keshes or the ford // Without my father's shade appearing to me' (ll. 8–9). The turf-cutters' strewn clothes remind him of 'souls cast off' as they gather

---

5. *Squarings* was published as a self-standing volume by Hieroglyph Press (Dublin, 1991), and by Arion Press (San Francisco, 2003); both are now rare and extremely costly, the former especially so.
6. The seven 'Crossings' poems, published in *The New Yorker* (1989), 35, were revised and republished as part of the *Squarings* sequence: Part III 'Crossings', Poems xxx–xxxvi (ST 88–94).
7. Heaney was a visiting lecturer at the University of California, Berkeley, in 1970–1 and 1976 (SS xxv–vi).
8. Later published as *Squarings*, xxx (ST 88); these lines are revised in ST.

at the riverside, readying for their crossing into (or perhaps out of) the underworld. In the fourth poem (*Squarings*, xxxiii), the poet returns to a bleak memory of the day his father died. He recalls his father's plans for a house, 'a paradigm of rigour and correction / . . . a shrine to limit' (ll. 8–9). But in the last line, the sketched house shrugs off its burden of rigour and correction, and escapes (like the vanishing goldfinch) into an unexpected simile, 'like a printed X-ray for the X-rayed body' (l. 12). In the fifth poem of 'Crossings' (*Squarings*, xxxiv), the face of a young American soldier reminds the poet of one of the 'newly dead come back' (l. 9). Freshly arrived from the land of the dead, the young soldier is tragically bound for the material Hell of the war in Vietnam. The threshold crossings thus become progressively darker until we arrive at the last poem, in which the poet recalls a memory of border crossing in Northern Ireland.

In the opening tercet of this seventh poem (*Squarings*, xxxvi), Heaney immediately encloses the memory within a composite, Biblical and classical frame of reference:

And yes, my friend, we too walked through a valley.
Once. In darkness. With all the street lamps off.
When scaresome night made *valley* of that town.[9]

The halting rhythm and italic font underline the allusions to two famous *viae negativae*: the valley of darkness in Psalm 23: 4, and the *selva oscura* in the opening lines of Dante's *Inferno*. The heavy stops of the opening lines mime the tentative steps of one lost in the dark. Dante is then invoked by name in the second tercet, where the night-time arrival at the checkpoint elicits this analogy:

Scene from Dante, made more memorable
By one of his head-clearing similes –
Fireflies, say, since the policemen's torches

Clustered and flicked and tempted us to trust
The unpredictable, attractive light.

Dante alludes to fireflies in a wood when describing the tongues of flame belonging to Ulysses and other 'false counsellors' in *Inferno XXVI*, where both tenor and vehicle of the simile (eloquent tongues, flickering lights) are misleading to the faring poets.[10] The simile is 'head-clearing', then, not for the participants, but for the reader, who is given a clear, bright point of comparison for Ulysses' dangerous eloquence.

But in Heaney's poem, the analogy continues to flicker ambiguously because the Dantean parallel he has in mind is actually the approach to the Styx in *Inferno III*,

---

9. In *Squarings*, xxxvi, l. 3 is revised to 'As danger gathered and the march dispersed' (*ST* 94).
10. Philip Lindholm suggests an allusion to Wordsworth's 'Scorn not the Sonnet': 'The Sonnet glittered a gay myrtle leaf / Amid the cypress with which Dante crowned / His visionary brow: a glow-worm lamp, / It cheered mild Spenser, called from Faery-land / To struggle through dark ways' (*Last Poems 1821–1850* (1999), 82).

where Dante and his fictional Virgil encounter souls waiting to board Charon's barge. Thus, he continues:

We were like herded shades who had to cross
And did cross, in a panic, to the car
Parked as we'd left it, that gave when we got in
Like Charon's boat under the faring poets.[11]

This extended simile again slides off in an unexpected direction because Heaney likens their treatment by the border guard to that of the weightless souls whom Charon crowds roughly on to his barge, whereas the way the car sinks under their weight ('gave when we got in') shows that they are living bodies climbing aboard. So Heaney's two travellers have slipped from being damned souls to being poets exempt from punishment (the pilgrim Dante, a living man, would cause the barge to sink; the journey through Hell will help to save his soul, while Dante's Virgil resides in Limbo, without infernal torment).

There is a final slide, in the last line, from the scene as portrayed by Dante to the scene from Virgil on which Dante's is modelled. Dante's Charon refuses to allow the wayfaring pilgrim into the boat for the encouraging reason that he is not destined for Hell. Heaney reminds us of this refusal in his translation extract at the end of *Seeing Things* (ST 111–13). But the allusion in the final line swerves from Dante's scene to Virgil's, where two mortal figures – Aeneas and the Sibyl – do climb into Charon's boat, causing it to sink low in the water. Meanwhile, at the checkpoint in Northern Ireland, a situation that had become dangerous and threatening is suddenly resolved, and the poet and his companion escape unharmed. In the dynamics of the poem, the two men are arraigned at a physical border, which is also a psychological trial, and they escape via the dark valley of the Psalms and Dante's *selva oscura*, finally crossing into Virgil's underworld by means of Charon's barge. The simile is both stealthy and 'head-clearing' in the way it creates a distance between Heaney's present self and the memory of the scaresome night-time encounter with armed guards in Northern Ireland.

Although unnamed in the seventh 'Crossings' poem, Virgil is the guide who ushers the faring poets into the car cum barge that will transport them to safety. This mythicised crossing can be read as a response to an actual border crossing described in 'From the Frontier of Writing', a poem published in *The Haw Lantern*. The earlier poem dwells on remembered details of the actual experience: 'that space / when the car stops in the road' and the troops inspect its interior, 'and everything is pure interrogation / until a rifle motions and you move' (HL 6, ll. 1–2, 7–8). Each time the interrogation at the border leaves him 'a little emptier, a little spent . . . subjugated yes, and obedient.' (ll. 10, 12) But at the frontier of writing, this memory of the actual border crossing is transformed in the poem, becoming the place where 'suddenly you're through, arraigned yet freed' (l. 19). In the final 'Crossings' poem,

---

11. 'Crossings', *The New Yorker*, 35; unrevised in ST 94.

both the arraignment and the release happen on the plane of literary allusion, where the border has been mythicised as an entryway into another world. As Heaney puts it in 'Fosterling', the poet has escaped 'the doldrums of what happens' by means of an imaginative release into Dante and Virgil's underworlds (*ST* 50).

This 'Frontier' poem originally bore the title, 'The Place of Writing', a title Heaney eventually used for a volume of essays based on a lecture series delivered at Emory University.[12] In the three essays, Heaney meditates on the examples of writers who create imaginative sanctuaries to help negotiate their way through difficult and dangerous circumstances. Introducing the volume, Ronald Suchard suggests these 'places of writing' are points of mediation between 'the free creative imagination and the constraints of religious, political, and domestic obligation'.[13] In *Seeing Things*, the threshold crossing is repeated in many different forms, and on different levels, frequently with a Virgilian or Dantean parallel in view. So one has a sense that the freedom gained from crossing the border must be continually re-earned, with a fresh arraignment and release being conducted in each succeeding poem. Just so, the two translation extracts from Virgil and Dante offer the poet a glimpse of release while more immediately placing obstacles in his path. It is as if the threshold of the marvellous can be broached only by means of a double-negative optics: a not not-seeing of things.[14] A comparable ambiguity hangs over Virgil's famous exit from Hades by means of the twin Gates of Sleep, where one gate is for '*ueris . . . umbris*', true shades, and the other for '*falsa . . . insomnia*' or false dreams.[15]

The sense of release from the burden of the actual which Heaney describes in 'Fosterling' is, then, a more complicated moment of transition than it might seem at first glance. The turn to 'crediting marvels' happens in a period of Heaney's life marked by the loss of both parents, and as Heaney puts it in *Stepping Stones*, the 'loss of faiths, of all kinds,' including 'religious faith' (*SS* 287). It has been suggested that Heaney turns from Dante to Virgil in this transitional period because he is breaking from the religious faith he had once shared with Dante.[16] By his own account, however, Heaney's 'secularisation' happened much earlier, while he was an undergraduate at Queen's University.[17] In the 1980s, he was translating and publishing extracts from Dante as well as Virgil.[18] And Virgil, a deeply religious

---

12. Draft title, 'The place of writing' (*LP* I.x). Heaney, *The Place of Writing* (1989), based on three lectures delivered in 1988, for the inaugural Richard Ellmann Lectures in Modern Literature at Emory University, in Atlanta, Georgia.
13. Ronald Suchard, 'Introduction', in Heaney, *The Place of Writing* (1989), 7.
14. See also Vendler, for whom the title suggests 're-inspecting the phenomenal world in the aftermath of death' and 'quasi-visionary insight, or numinous *frisson*, "seeing things" with "Wordsworthian imagination"' (1998, 138).
15. *Ae*.VI.894, 896. See Chapter 9, Section IV.
16. Vendler (2012), 10; Impens (2017), 256, and (2018), 59.
17. Interview with Dawe, *RTÉ*.
18. Extracts from his translation of 'Cantos I, II, III' of Dante's *Inferno* were published under various individual titles: 'The Dark Wood' (a translation of Canto I, in Welch, 1988), 'The Lost People' (a translation of 'Canto II.22–52', in Connor, 1991) and 'The Crossing' (a translation of Canto III, ll. 82–129, in *Agenda*, 1989, a Seamus Heaney 50th Birthday Issue).

poet himself, was widely regarded as the poet who bridged classical antiquity and medieval Christendom.[19] The 'loss of faith' Heaney describes undergoing in the 1980s seems to be a sense of being cut off from his 'first world', his upbringing in rural County Derry. In that first world, it is true, Catholicism was a given, 'so pervasive that it hardly counted as an influence at all; it was a reality like oxygen'; but then so, too, was Latin, the language of Virgil as well as the Catholic Mass.[20] When Heaney describes his father's death as 'the final "unroofing" of the world', he seems to be referring to this first world, the loss of which affected him 'in ways that were hidden from me then and now.' (SS 322)

Moreover, Heaney immediately qualifies his recollection of experiencing a 'loss of faiths, of all kinds' by adding that there was also 'a countervailing impulse at work, a refusal to discredit "the real thing"' (SS 287). When asked whether Yeats had led him to crediting marvels in 'Fosterling', Heaney replied that Patrick Kavanagh's 'fundamentally Catholic mysticism' was the more immediate influence (SS 317–18). In *Seeing Things*, both impulses are at work: the loss of the first world, as well as the countervailing impulse of crediting the Catholic imagination. As Karl Miller writes,

> a Catholicism of the imagination is voiced in the book, in contrast with his position in the Sixties, when he would have been 'diffident' in answering questions about the teachings and ceremonies associated with the 'first visionary world' of this cradle Catholic.[21]

Heaney's forty-eight *Squarings* poems test out a full spectrum of perspectives on the question of faith, from the secular to the deeply religious.[22] In *Squarings*, i, for example, Heaney shifts from the Catholic doctrine that 'the particular judgement' determines the fate of a soul in the afterlife to the rationalist position of an 'old truth dawning: there is no next-time-round.' (ST 55) But a feeling for the spirit world lingers in such phrases as 'knowledge-freshening wind', where 'wind' recalls *anima*, breath of life or soul, and 'soul-free cloud-life' suggests a drift of clouds either 'free *of* soul' or 'free *as* the soul'. *Seeing Things* thus hovers between both possibilities: the daylight clarity of a postlapsarian world without gods or ghosts, and the gleam of lost or spirit worlds conjured by memory and imagination. At the level of metaphor and mythic analogy, these spirit worlds continue to exist in Heaney's poetic imagination.

As I suggested in Chapter 1, Heaney turns to Virgil's underworld when absence and loss activate his memories of his 'first world' from a newly distanced perspective. His translation of the golden bough episode brings the sound of Kavanagh's late poetry into Virgil's hexameters, which is one sign of Heaney's imaginative

---

19. See T. S. Eliot, 'Virgil and the Christian World', in *On Poetry and Poets* (1957); Heaney, FK 168–79.
20. Heaney interview, Haffenden, ed., *Viewpoints* (1981), 100.
21. Karl Miller, *Tretower to Clyro* (2011), Chapter 6 (no pag.). See also the excellent discussion of Heaney's sacramentalism, in Gail McConnell (2014), esp. 52–121.
22. While composing the *Squarings* poems, Heaney was closely reading the Catholic writer Jacques Maritain's *Creative Intuition in Art and Poetry*. See Heaney's 'Sixth Sense' (2002); and Russell (2016), 154.

refiguration of the Catholic world of his childhood. The withdrawal of the old world simultaneously triggers the desire to cross the threshold into memory, and the work of poetry is to credit the absent spirit world as present and real. A similar claim is made by the French poet Yves Bonnefoy:

> Poetry is the memory of those instants of presence, of plenitude experienced during the years of childhood, followed by the apprehension of non-being underlying those instants which become translated as doubt, and then by that hesitation that constitutes life; but it's also a reaffirmation, it is our *willing* that there should be meaning at the moment meaning falls away. This takes work, certainly. A long exercise of transgression within the image. . . . It is the task of a lifetime. A difficult task. . . .[23]

This description of poetry's *opus* and *labor* sounds Virgilian in itself. But it is particularly striking in Heaney's later poetry that the work of transgression proceeds by invocation and transformation of Virgil's underworld motifs.

As he remarks in *Stepping Stones*, the images and motifs from *Aeneid VI* are ones that Heaney has 'internalized and lived with long and dreamily.' (SS 440) Revisiting *Aeneid VI* in the wake of his parents' death, with the freedom of a sabbatical year from Harvard in 1988–9 and the chance to retreat to Glanmore Cottage, his 'house of poetry', proved to be a decisive encounter with a familiar but newly significant exemplar. While geographically and temporally far removed from his experience of personal loss, Virgil's poetry is also inextricably a part of the first world of Heaney's childhood.

For a Northern Irish poet, moreover, there would be present from the beginning a latent cultural tension in coming to terms with Virgil's lambent hexameters. Quoting Proinsias MacCana in 'Varieties of Irishness' (1989), Heaney recalls that the Latin language, together with Roman, international culture, was introduced by Catholic settlers in the sixth century to an Irish society that was largely '"mythopoeic . . . innocent of secular chronology"'; Latin brought to Ireland '"a view of time and history - of secular and sacred, of artistic and religious, categories - that was radically at variance with native Irish society."'[24] This cultural colonisation, Heaney adds, 'has obviously been repeated in traumatic ways since – and in none more traumatic than in the shift from Irish to the English language.' (15) Virgil's Latin is, then, both an intimate feature of Heaney's rural, Catholic first world of childhood innocence, and a sign of the cultural complexities already palpable in the mixed linguistic inheritance of that first world.

An address delivered in London, and then published as 'Anglo-Irish Occasions' (1988), gives a sense of the immediate socio-political context within and in resistance to which Heaney began to absorb, dream over and reimagine Virgilian motifs in his own poetry. The address begins with a polite acknowledgement of the warm

---

23. Yves Bonnefoy, 'The Place of Grasses', in *The Arrière-pays*, 191. Cited by Neil Corcoran, 'Melt of the Real Thing' (2015).
24. MacCana, in R. Kearney (1984), quoted by Heaney, 'Varieties of Irishness' (1989), 15.

reception of his poetry, but then proceeds to criticise the British media in very strong terms for biased and hypocritical reportage of a series of violent clashes in Northern Ireland, in March 1988. Rosie Lavan summarises the events as follows:

> the killing in Gibraltar of three members of the IRA by undercover members of the SAS; the attack on Milltown cemetery by a loyalist gunman during the funerals of those IRA members; and the reprisal killing of two British corporals at the funerals of those who died at Milltown.[25]

Heaney insists that 'the act of writing is, after all, an act of detachment and differentiation', but that nevertheless '"every serious artist knows he cannot enjoy public celebration without making subtle public commitments."'[26] Speaking then as an Irish poet with a public responsibility to defend his community and nation, he goes on to accuse the British government and media of betraying the Anglo-Irish Agreement of 1985, which had sought to establish an 'eye-level equilibrium' between Irish and British Governments (ibid.). Within this context, his turn to Virgil can be understood as a means of both detaching himself artistically from the worsening political situation, and reaffirming the shared tribal, historical and literary memories of his community and nation.

Heaney returns to Virgil in the mid-1980s from a point both geographically and intellectually distanced from his earlier poetic encounters. He discusses translating the *Aeneid* with Robert Fitzgerald at Harvard and, in his essay 'Envies and Identifications', he quarrels with T. S. Eliot's notion of a single, universal voice of European poetry transmitted through Dante and Virgil to the present day. But Eliot's lines about 'the use of memory' clearly struck a chord with him; they appear at the end of two mid-1980s essays, 'Varieties of Irishness' and 'Place, Pastness, Poems' (1986).[27] In the latter, Heaney contrasts different kinds of memory - tribal, historical and literary - in the work of a number of his favourite poets.[28] For all poets, 'pastness is to a greater or lesser degree enabling', and the literary imagination 'unites the most ancient and most civilized mentalities' (38, 39). Yet the 'use of memory' is different in poets with a sense of tribal belonging to place, as opposed to those who draw on a literary inheritance of tropes and images. With Pablo Neruda and Thomas Hardy, 'we are at the tribe's centre of feeling and belonging, where the spirits of the ancestors are pressing actively in upon the consciousness of the living.' (43)

On the spectrum between tribal and literary memory, Gerard Manley Hopkins, though 'anxious and scholastically self-justifying', proves to be closer to Hardy than the literary Keats, in that his 'poetry does not spacewalk in the ether of literary associations but is grounded in the insular landscape which, in the month of May, blooms and greens in a way that is still Marian, sacramental, medieval English

---

25. Lavan (2020), 140.
26. Heaney, quoting Lowell, 'Anglo-Irish Occasions' (1988), para. 5.
27. 'this is the use of memory: / For liberation – not less of love but expanding . . .' (Eliot, 'Little Gidding', III.7 (2015), Vol. I, p. 206).
28. Heaney, 'Place, Pastness, Poems: A Triptych' (1986), 30–47.

Catholic.' (45) Heaney writes with particular admiration for the poetry of Hardy and Hopkins: that is, for poetry which finds 'a point of entry into a common emotional ground' of tribal memory and belonging (31). Far removed from this kind of memory work is Ezra Pound's retrieval of the past, which is eclectic, historical and literary; with Pound and the symbolists, 'the literary past, the tradition – became a category of our thinking at precisely that moment when, politically and culturally, the centre could not hold' (47).

For Heaney at this stage, the challenge seems to be to find a way of bringing together these different senses of the past, in particular the tribal sense of belonging to place with the modern, free-ranging literary imagination. As he puts it,

> the actual poetic task is to find a way of melding the intuitive and affection-steeped word-world of personal memory with the form-hungry and projecting imagination, to find an idiom at once affective and objectified, as individual as handwriting and as given as the conventions of writing itself. (41)

This fusion cannot be achieved only through immersion in memories of the first world, but must also invoke a broader sense of embeddedness in a literary tradition, since 'literary tradition is what links the periphery to the centre – wherever that imaginary point may be – and to other peripheries.' (47) As he acknowledges in 'Envies and Identifications', Virgil and Dante are key figures in any account of Western European literature. But what Heaney seeks is a way of bringing the 'affection-steeped word-world of personal memory' into contact with the broader European cultural heritage. Virgil emerges as an essential exemplar because he belongs so thoroughly to both worlds, that of Heaney's personal memory and that of European literary culture.

Virgilian motifs recur throughout *Seeing Things* as part of Heaney's reaffirmation of the plenitude of the past, to borrow Bonnefoy's phrase. But they do more than will forth the lost first world; they also connect that emotional centre to the broader circumference of European or Western culture. And in doing so, they offer a sense of detachment from the tribe, or at least an alleviation of the burden of tribal memory. At the same time, because Virgil is rooted in Heaney's first world, the Roman poet never loses his particularity at the margins, never gets assimilated to a single, hegemonic voice of mainstream European culture, as (according to Heaney) happens to Virgil and Dante in Eliot's writing. In *Squarings*, Heaney's 'form-hungry imagination' takes the shape of Dantean *terza rima*, each of the forty-eight poems being comprised of four tercets (two lines short of a sonnet). In the volume as a whole, though, his affection for his first world seems largely mediated through Virgilian motifs and images.

Heaney mixes together Virgilian and Dantean material with his own personal memories to produce the fusion of lyric and epic that he found and admired in Kavanagh's late poetry. One sign of this merging of lyric and epic modes is Heaney's distillation of the narrative arc of the *katabatic* journey into singular, recurrent moments of threshold encounter in *Seeing Things*. For Russian philosopher Mikhail Bakhtin, the threshold is associated with 'the breaking point of a life, the moment of crisis, the decision that changes a life (or the indecisiveness that fails to change a life)' and so the chronotope, or represented time-space, of the threshold is 'metaphorical and symbolic' and 'highly charged with emotion and value'.[29] The chronotopic images of the threshold in Seeing Things seem to me to bear this symbolic value of a breaking point and radical change in life requiring also a change in poetic form and in the poet's relation to his poetic exemplars. In his title essay, 'The Government of the Tongue', Heaney characterises poetry as 'more a threshold than a path, one constantly approached and constantly departed from, at which reader and writer undergo in their different ways the experience of being at the same time summoned and released.' (GT 108)

Heaney's imagination of this poetic arraignment draws on personal memory, as in the memory of border crossing discussed above, but these intimate memories are blended with three emotionally charged points along Aeneas's *katabatic* journey: discovering the bough, boarding Charon's barge, and meeting his father's shade beside the last riverbank. These become lyric, threshold encounters in poems such as 'Seeing Things, III', 'Man and Boy' and *Squarings*, xxxii and xxxiii, where Heaney encounters the shade of his own father, Patrick Heaney. The risky boat crossing is recurrently imagined, most memorably in 'Seeing Things, I' and *Squarings*, viii, ix and xxxvi. And Hibernicised golden boughs are sought and found in 'The Ash Plant', 'Fosterling' and *Squarings*, xiv–xv. I would like now to observe more closely in a number of these poems how Heaney reimagines the bough, the boat and the ghost, respectively, as motifs that help him to renegotiate his relation to the home ground and to the wider European literary tradition.

II. THE GOLDEN BOUGH, AGAIN

Heaney composed 'The Ash Plant' soon after his father's death and before he undertook his 'Englishing of "The Golden Bough"'.[30] In form, it recalls neither Virgil nor Dante, being in near-rhyming quatrains (ABBA). But in the last two quatrains, a cherished familiar object, such as would stir Neruda's ancestral memory, is bestowed with the mythical aura of Virgil's golden bough, so that without losing its domestic intimacy, this paternal memory gains an ampler resonance and durability. The poem attributes this transformative power to the golden bough itself which, unusually, is placed in the ghostly father's hands. At the beginning of the poem, Heaney locates his father at an existential crossroads:

29. Bakhtin, 'Forms of Time and of the Chronotope' (1938), in *The Dialogic Imagination* (1981), 248. The 'chronotope' in Bakhtin's coinage signifies the representation of 'time space' in a text; more generally, it is a term which highlights 'the intrinsic connectedness of temporal and spatial relationships' (86).
30. 'the most potent factor in the choice of these lines [*Aeneid* VI.98–211] was my own father's death in 1986. I had in the meantime written a poem where his cattle-dealer's stick, the seasoned ash plant which he habitually carried, became "a silver bough". The next, obvious step had to be the Englishing of "The Golden Bough".' (Heaney and Hendrix, 'Postscript', *The Golden Bough*, 32)

> He'll never rise again but he is ready.
> Entered like a mirror by the morning,
> He stares out the big window, wondering, (ST 19, ll. 1–3)

The third-person stance is partly focalised through the father's eyes, so that we both see the light falling on the figure in bed, and experience his light-headedness from within (l. 13). Looking out from the upstairs window like a forgotten and forgetful sentry (l. 9), he seems to preside over an exterior domain that has itself become dream-like:

> First milk-lorries, first smoke, cattle, trees,
> In damp opulence above damp hedges – (ll. 6–7)

As in the 'Clearances' sequence, this poem conveys the sense of a first world absenting itself in the wake of a parent's death.

But here the touch of a familiar object offers resistance to the sensation of dematerialisation. The father reaches out a hand for the cattle-dealer's stick which he habitually carried:

> Gropes desperately and finds the phantom limb
> Of an ash plant in his grasp, which steadies him.
> Now he has found his touch he can stand his ground
>
> Or wield the stick like a silver bough and come
> Walking again among us: the quoted judge.
> *I could have cut a better man out of the hedge!*
> God might have said the same, remembering Adam. (ll. 14–20)

With 'Or' in the final stanza, the poem lifts away from the father's perspective, offering first the analogy of Virgil's bough (silvered as the head of the stick) and then a more layered Biblical allusion, which draws upon Genesis and the Apostles' Creed,[31] and perhaps the image of Moses' staff or Aaron's rod. Thus, while Virgil's bough offers protection to a living man travelling through the land of the dead, this composite silver bough also apparently wields the power of Christian resurrection, judgement and redemption.

Only 'apparently', though, because the entire stanza beginning with 'or' has lifted off from the 'ground' (l. 16) of verifiable reality and entered an arena of speculation. But what the poem does recover with certainty is the father's native, idiomatic speech, heard as if being spoken at that moment: '*I could have cut a better man out of the hedge!*' (l. 19) To this the poem offers its own rueful response, 'God might have said the same, remembering Adam.' Although the tone is clear enough, it is not

---

31. 'The third day he rose again from the dead. He ascended into heaven, and sitteth on the right hand of God the Father almighty. From thence he shall come to judge the quick and the dead', or in Latin, '*inde uenturus est iudicare uiuos et mortuos*'.

clear to me whether Heaney means that God remembers having done a better job with Adam, or that God is thinking a hedge-cut Adam might have turned out to be a better man than the Biblical one made of clay. A familial or local reader would perhaps not have to hesitate. Still, we can see how the allusion to Virgil's bough bridges the local and the wider readerships: it lends a supernatural aura and authority to his father's cattle-dealer's stick, and it claims a local habitation for the classical image of the bough. In the three-line poem following this one, the poet inherits the stick from his father, and he thereby comes into symbolic possession of this hybridised authority himself ('1.1.87', ST 20).

Together with 'The Haw Lantern', the title poem of Heaney's previous volume, 'The Ash Plant', associates the image of Virgil's bough with the notion of being held up for judgement.[32] The truncated translation extract at the start of *Seeing Things* throws the same weight of emphasis on the trial and judgement of the hero: 'If fate has called you / The bough will come easily, … / Otherwise, … you never will / Manage to quell it or cut it down' (*ST* 3). But the mid-volume poem 'Fosterling', by contrast, puts a distinctly bough-like object to the opposite purpose of liberating its subjects from judgement and moral obligation. In this way, the golden bough comes to preside over both lyric and epic modes: that is, both the 'lyric' impulse towards freedom, and the 'epic' sense of obligation to a wider community.

While the sonnet 'Fosterling' functions as a pivot between Parts I and II of *Seeing Things*, it also forms a bridge between early and late poetry in Heaney's corpus as a whole. In the opening octet, Heaney remembers the 'music of what happens' from his earlier 'Song' (*FW* 53). And he anticipates one of his very last poems, 'Banks of a Canal' (2014), written in response to the painting of a canal in Naples by the French painter Caillebotte. All three poems bear a close affinity with Patrick Kavanagh's Canal Bank sonnets.[33] Both 'Fosterling' and 'Banks of a Canal' celebrate the presence of the luminous in the everyday, which Heaney associates with Kavanagh's late style. It is easy to walk past Caillebotte's small, quiet painting, where it hangs unassumingly between larger works at the National Gallery in Ireland (Plate 2). But once caught, your eye is drawn deep into the painting by the placid, luminous curve of the water and the worn, brown towpath as they converge toward the sky.

The transition from a 'lowlands of the mind' to a marvellous lightness of being occurs part-way through the sestet in 'Fosterling':

Me waiting until I was nearly fifty
To credit marvels. Like the tree-clock of tin cans
The tinkers made. So long for air to brighten,
Time to be dazzled and the heart to lighten. (*ST* 50, ll. 11–14)

---

32. The haw lantern, held aloft and glowing before him, like the golden bough, reminds Heaney of Diogenes the Cynic, 'seeking one just man; / so you end up scrutinized from behind the haw / he holds up at eye-level on its twig, / and you flinch before its bonded pith and stone' (*HL* 8).
33. Heaney, 'Another Look at Kavanagh' (1985).

Just as Aeneas does not actually get to the bough in the prefatory extract of *Seeing Things*, so no transformation actually takes place in this sestet, which conspicuously lacks a main verb. But the way the passage swings from gerunds ('me waiting') to infinitives ('to credit, to brighten') helps convey the impression of an imminent, radical change of being. In between the first infinitive and the cluster at the end, Heaney inserts a sentence fragment describing a 'tree-clock of tin cans'. If we take 'like' to mean 'such as', then the tree-clock is an instance of the 'marvels' the older poet is now prepared to take seriously. But how is it marvellous, apart from dazzling the eye with refracted light? In *Stepping Stones*, Heaney offers a fuller explanation of its provenance and symbolic import (SS 317f.). In Wicklow, a local legend tells of a community who had made a pact with the devil, agreeing that, at a certain hour, he could come and collect their souls and bring them down into Hell. But an ingenious band of tinkers fashioned 'a fantastic tin clock' with arms set to the wrong time. When the devil arrived, he believed he had missed the appointed hour and so let them be. Heaney goes on to comment that the 'image of that strange flashing tin-flanged tree' stayed with him, leading to the idea of 'crediting marvels' in 'Fosterling', although its exact import remained mysterious: 'Not a very clear image, not even to me.' (SS 317)

This mysterious tree-clock is associated with Virgil's golden bough in several respects. First, in *Stepping Stones*, Heaney compares its glittering light to D. H. Lawrence's Bavarian gentians, which 'lead the spirit down to the halls of Dis'; the tinker's tree-clock, by contrast, 'pointed an Orphic hand up towards the light', which is what the golden bough does for Aeneas in the underworld (SS 317). In 'Route 110', Heaney similarly dismisses Lawrence's *katabatic* flower ('So reach me not a gentian') in favour of a foil-decorated oat-stalk, which serves him as a golden bough ('it as good as lit me home', HC 52). Whereas Lawrence's gentians merely lead down into Hades, the golden bough leads the bearer down with a promise of reascent so its gleaming light is ultimately *anabatic*, upward-bearing and homeward bound. As already noted, 'Fosterling' also functions as a threshold poem in *Seeing Things*, bringing Part I to a close, and opening the gateway to the *Squarings* sequence of Part II. In view of the possible numerological link to Heaney's fiftieth birthday in the fifty-line Virgil extract and the placement of 'Fosterling' on page 50, it is also worth pointing out that the golden bough and the tree-clock are both associated with an appointed hour for a supernatural intervention.

And most importantly, both magic talismans offer the bearer protection from life-threatening danger. But whereas Virgil's golden bough offers divine aid to a destined hero, the Wicklow tree-clock is invented by local craftsmen for the rescue of an entire community from a seemingly inescapable, infernal pact. This Northern Irish take on the classical bough transforms an epic motif into a lyric one, where the bearer escapes a preordained fate. And conversely, this symbol of individual, lyric release gains a social, epic dimension, for the tree-clock can magically free an entire community from ensnarement with the devil.

III. CHARON'S BOAT

In *Seeing Things*, the poet's element is water, more responsive and malleable than his earlier earth-bound volumes, but also more treacherous and alien. The poem, or poetry in general, is the craft that sustains the artist's imagination, moving fluently and buoyantly over the surface of the actual. Thus, for example, in 'The Biretta', Heaney imagines a Catholic priest's cap turned upside-down and transformed into a boat like Dante's:

> the one that wafts into
> The first lines of the *Purgatorio*
> As poetry lifts its eyes and clears its throat.
>
> Or maybe that small boat out of the bronze age
> Where the oars are needles and the worked gold frail
> As the intact half of a hatched-out shell,
> Refined beyond the dross into sheer image (*ST* 27)

Both these boats are marvellously light and aerial, the former especially in the way it overgoes Charon's infernal barge, met earlier in *Inferno III*, and the latter because of its tiny size and rare gold substance.[34] In *Stepping Stones*, Heaney offers his own transformation of the priest's biretta into a 'boat of imagination' as a symbol for 'poetry's impulse to outstrip the given' (*SS* 327). The dreamwork of lightening the weight of 'the given' is clearly an unalloyed good in this instance, as is the lightening of various bulky objects that appear in *Seeing Things*, such as a heavy old settle bed and a grounded boat (*ST* 28, 63).

Heaney's most complex transgression of the image of the boat-as-poetry occurs when he engages in dialogue with Virgil's portrayal of Aeneas, as the living hero climbs into Charon's barge and crosses into the land of the dead (*Ae*.VI.296–330, 384–416). The classical barge is Hibernicised in the first section of the title poem, 'Seeing Things', where Heaney describes a boat trip from Inishbofin, an island off the Galway coast. The poem centres on a group of passengers boarding a small motorboat on a calm Sunday morning:

> One by one we were being handed down
> Into a boat that dipped and shilly-shallied
> Scaresomely every time. We sat tight
> On short cross-benches, in nervous twos and threes,
> Obedient, newly close, nobody speaking
> Except the boatmen, as the gunwhales sank
> And seemed they might ship water any minute. (*ST* 16, 3–9)

---

34. The tiny Bronze Age ship is from the Broighter Hoard, on display in the National Museum of Ireland (cf. *SS* 327).

The individual handing-down of passengers, the nervous crowding along the benches and the fearful dip of the boat into the water are all details that feature in Virgil's description of the boat crossing into Hades:

> inde alias animas, quae per iuga longa sedebant,
> deturbat laxatque foros; simul accipit alueo
> ingentem Aenean. gemuit sub pondere cumba
> sutilis et multam accepit rimosa paludem. (*Ae*.VI.411–14)

In *Aeneid Book VI* (2016), Heaney will translate the above passage thus:

> Other souls ensconced on the long thwarts
> He hurries off up gangways, then at once
> Hands mighty Aeneas down into the vessel.
> Under that weight the boat's plied timbers groan
> And thick marsh water oozes through the leaks, (A.550–4)

Just as Aeneas dares to undertake this journey because he wants to see his dead father's face, so the memory of this Irish boat trip will bring Heaney face to face with his 'undrowned father' in the third section of 'Seeing Things'.

As in the 'Crossings' poem (*Squarings*, xxxvi), however, Heaney seems readier to identify with Virgil's herded shades than with the heroic Aeneas. At the end of this section, the 'I' splits into two, and an exalted, angelic self looks down on the self among the passengers below, knowing them to be doomed, like the souls huddled in Charon's boat:

> It was as if I looked from another boat
> Sailing through air, far up, and could see
> How riskily we fared into the morning,
> And loved in vain our bare, bowed, numbered heads. (ll. 19–22)

This floating, aerial self looks like the mirror opposite of Virgil's '*ingentem Aenean*', whose huge bulk sinks the boat low in the water. And, although exempt from the immediate danger of drowning, the aerial self is made more anxious by his privileged vantage point because he cannot save the 'bowed, numbered heads' below, including his own mortal, material self. If this boat is to stand for poetry, it has somehow to accommodate the collective, mortal condition, and not only bear the solitary, faring poet on a journey into the marvellous.

In *Stepping Stones*, Heaney remarks that he was uncomfortably conscious of 'a disjunction between the unscathed life I was living in Harvard and Dublin and the conditions being experienced on the ground in Northern Ireland' (SS 323). And as noted above, he had voiced deep concern over those worsening conditions in his 1988 address, 'Anglo-Irish Occasions'. In *Seeing Things*, even as he defends the artist's detachment from 'the doldrums of what happens', he expresses anxiety over that very detachment. The figure of the chosen Aeneas, borne safely over the Styx, comes to express some of Heaney's ambivalence about the poet in search of artistic freedom. In 'A Royal Prospect', for example, the poet and his wife are identified with a royal couple approaching Hampton Court by boat: the 'royal favourites'

> alone are borne downstream unscathed,
> Between mud banks where the wounded rave all night
> At flameless blasts and echoless gunfire – (ST 40)

And in 'A Retrospect', a seventeenth-century deputy of the English King travels through Ireland, provoking stares from the locals '"as Virgil's ghosts / Wondered to see Aeneas alive in Hell."' (ST 43)[35] Both allusions acknowledge the ambiguity of Aeneas' presence in the underworld; however sympathetically he addresses the underworld ghosts, they cannot meet on equal terms since he will emerge unscathed from Hades and they will not.[36]

In 'A Basket of Chestnuts', Heaney recalls a favourite portrait of himself, painted by Edward McGuire in 1974 (reproduced on the cover of this study).[37] The poet is seated behind a small table in the recess of a gable window, and the gleam on his boots, Heaney suggests, is transposed from the bowl of chestnuts the artist chose not to paint (SS 328). If the gleam introduces the suggestion of a threshold crossing into the marvellous, the painting itself depicts Heaney in a cramped, inhibited position. Wedged in the narrow space, the poet looks uncomfortably *ingens*, like Aeneas weighing down Charon's rickety boat. The poet's legs are awkwardly splayed, his shoulders slumped and his eyes alert and wary. Heaney describes his expression in the painting as 'slightly at bay, penned in, staring out' and 'constantly watchful' (SS 328). He admired the portrait's 'gathered up, pent-up, head-on quality', which, for him, portrays the poet as 'a keep of tensions.' (SS 329) In the window behind him, oversized birds appear amongst dark foliage, like Virgilian souls newly transported into the underworld. The painting is closely cropped around the sitting figure, which gives the illusion that he is somehow receding into the dark foliage behind, as if he were indeed an Aeneas being ferried into the land of the dead. If the painting and its companion poem do depict a threshold crossing into the supernatural, the moment of transformation is fraught with inner conflict and danger.

In 'Seeing Things, I', Heaney seems undecided which position to identify with: the divinely protected wayfarer Aeneas or the ordinary doomed soul in Charon's boat. The split into two consciousnesses at the end of the section suggests an unwillingness to choose between the two. In 'Elegy', an earlier poem written in memory of

---

35. The name 'Hell' is another instance of Heaney freely overlayering Virgil's classical underworld with Dante's Catholic one.
36. At least, until the classical epic conception of the underworld is challenged by Anchises' Pythagorean explanation of the doctrine of metempsychosis in the final scene by the River Lethe. See Chapters 6 and 9.
37. ST 24–5. Edward McGuire (1932–86), 'Portrait of Seamus Heaney b.1939' (1974), BELUM. U2107, reproduced on my book cover with kind permission of the National Museums NI Collection, Ulster Museum. Heaney commented of McGuire, who died in 1986, 'when it came to seeing things, he was very good indeed' (SS 329).

Robert Lowell, Heaney expresses similar fears about being on water, and contrasts his own hydrophobia with Lowell's confident mastery of a boat at sea. Command of the boat becomes a metaphor for the poet's wilful command of language. Lowell the 'helmsman, netsman, *retiarius*' is also the 'master elegist / and welder of English', who rode on 'the swaying tiller / of yourself' and 'bullied out / heart-hammering blank sonnets' (FW 25–6). Heaney thus presents his friend as an epic warrior at sail in a modern, industrial vessel:

> Not the proud sail of your great verse . . .
> No. You were our night ferry
> thudding in a big sea,
>
> the whole craft ringing
> with an armourer's music
> the course set wilfully across
> the ungovernable and dangerous. (FW 26, ll. 39–44)

Although Heaney obviously admires this willed and welded verse, he presents his own craft and character in diametrically opposite terms. At the end of the poem, he pictures himself standing safely on land, at the gate of his cottage at Glanmore.

In this affectionate comparison between his own ungoverned poetry and Lowell's 'deliberate, peremptory' art (FW 25, l. 22), Heaney could be casting himself as a lyric Horace to Lowell's epic Virgil. In *Odes I*, 3, an ode composed after his friend had set sail for Greece, Horace prays for Virgil's safety and worries over the audacity of the human race, daring to venture wildly into sea and sky. The ode playfully associates Virgil's poetry with the epic *nauis* bearing him over dangerous seas, while Horace's own *carmen* will be linked with a nimbler, lyric boat in *Odes I*, 32.[38] Like Horace's craft, the Inishbofin ferry has the 'buoyancy and swim' Heaney associates with lyric. And yet, within the poem, the ferry's 'guarantee' of physical safety (and, metaphorically, of being able to write lyric) brings no release from fear and doubt:

> I panicked at the shiftiness and heft
> Of the craft itself. What guaranteed us –
> That quick response and buoyancy and swim –
> Kept me in agony. (ST 16)

The very shiftiness of the craft is what causes him to panic, so that some bridging of perspectives, that of the material self in the boat and the free, artistic imagination in the sky, seems necessary to escape the agony of this lightness of being. A mediation between these two perspectives is achieved in *Squarings*, viii, 'The annals say' (ST 62).

---

38. With thanks to Olivier Thevenaz, for his thoughts on *Odes I*, 3. Horace is drawing on Virgil's own association between epic verse and Aeneas' ships, at the beginning and end of *Aeneid VI*. On Horace's *proempticon*, see Basto (1982).

This is the eighth poem in the 'Lightenings' sequence, Part I of *Squarings*, and one of many poems linking the two parts of the volume in an intricate, intratextual dialogue. The most widely known and quoted of the *Squarings* poems, 'The annals say' recounts a medieval legend in which the monks of Clonmacnoise are said to have witnessed a miracle ship appearing in thin air, above the altar in their oratory. When its anchor catches on the altar, a crewman shins down the rope and struggles to unhook it. The abbot realises that, for the otherworldly crewman, their natural air is an alien, watery element, and he urges the monks to help him,

> . . . So
> They did, and the freed ship sailed, and the man climbed back
> Out of the marvellous as he had known it. (ST 62, ll. 10–12)

Elsewhere, Heaney explains that the little crewman who descends from the dreamship is a figure for the poet, and the poet in the reader, who 'will drown in actual historical conditions' unless helped by the monks; and the monks in turn experience 'an immense enlargement when the dreamship appears there'.[39]

The episode as a whole becomes, for Heaney, 'an allegory about the two dimensions or the two poles or the two calls to poetry, to art of all sorts. To bear witness to what's on the floor of history and at the same time to portray what's in the heaven of the imagination'.[40] Or, as he explains on another occasion, it is 'about the necessity of being in two places at the one time, on the ground with the fatherly earthiness, but also keeping your mind open and being able to go up . . . and live in the world of fantasy . . . For your wholeness you need to inhabit both worlds.'[41] In the poem itself, it is the mediation or threshold crossing between these two dimensions of poetry that is of primary importance: the crewman shinning down the rope and the abbot unhooking the caught anchor. The action may seem far removed from Aeneas and the weightless souls boarding Charon's barge, but in *Stepping Stones* Heaney gives the poem a more classical gloss, describing the crewman as a 'successful Orpheus' in a *katabatic* narrative (SS 322). The crewman descends in order to save his shipmates, and he succeeds because he is helped by underworld forces; the same might be said of the abbot when the scene is viewed from upside-down, for he rescues his community by opening their minds to the marvellous.

As will be explored in the following chapter, Aeneas' *katabasis* is modelled in many ways on that of Orpheus, which Virgil relates at the end of *Georgics IV*. Here, the abbot and the crewman are Orphic types in that they are able to 'hear' beyond the 'herd', to borrow a favourite pun of Heaney's, yet they are also firmly rooted in their respective communities.[42] Practical and supernatural wisdom converge in the legend as Heaney relates it: 'the magic casement opens for a moment only and the marvellous occurs in a sequence that sounds entirely like a matter of fact.' (SS 322)

---

39. Heaney, interview with Christopher Lydon, quoted in Russell (2016), 268.
40. Ibid.
41. Heaney, in conversation with Mike Murphy, in Ní Anluain and Kiberd, eds (2000), 90.
42. See Chapter 3, note 48.

The dreamship of Clonmacnoise manages to negotiate between our actual, mortal condition and a free, imaginary response to it. In the context of *Seeing Things*, it offers a redress to the Virgilian motif of Aeneas boarding Charon's boat, where the hero's safety is guaranteed by the evacuation of the gathered souls of the dead. In this Hibernicised version of the classical motif, two Aeneases, or poets, guarantee the safety of gathered souls in the other's marvellous world. And their imaginary, mutual understanding opens up the possibility of a better future for the doomed souls in their own, material worlds.

IV. THE FATHER'S GHOST

Of the three Virgilian motifs mentioned in *Stepping Stones*, Aeneas' meeting with his father's ghost is perhaps the one Heaney identifies with most closely and personally. He describes the thought of meeting his own father in the underworld as 'the most potent factor' in his decision to translate the golden bough episode, the work that initiated his intense engagement with Virgil's works, lasting from mid-career to the end of his life.[43] The scene of the father and son meeting on the banks of an otherworldly river (*Ae*.VI.679–702) forms the emotional climax of Heaney's book-length translation. As we will see in Chapter 9, the translation of this passage in the 2016 volume is remarkably intimate and familial in tone. In his original English poems, Heaney freely adapts the father–son meeting in Hades to the shape of his own memories. His identification with Aeneas over the loss of his father is perhaps the most obvious proof that, in turning to classical literature, Heaney was far from abandoning his Catholic, Northern Irish identity.

Loss of the first world is also a central theme of the *Aeneid*, and Heaney identifies specifically with Aeneas' nostalgia for his fallen city and lost homeland. While the motifs of the golden bough and Charon's boat are deployed in *Seeing Things* to celebrate the transformative power of the imagination, the motif of meeting the father's ghost rather brings out the theme of personal loss, and more generally, the sense of a unbreachable divide between present and past. Aeneas tries and fails three times to embrace the bodiless shade of his father, and this motif, known as the *ter conatus* (literally, 'tried three times'), connotes the unrecoverability of the past in Virgil's *Aeneid*. Coming upon his father's ghost in Elysium, Aeneas reaches out:

> ter conatus ibi collo dare bracchia circum;
> ter frustra comprensa manus effugit imago,
> par leuibus uentis uolucrique simillima somno. (*Ae*.VI.700–2)

> Three times he tried to reach arms round that neck.
> Three times the form, reached for in vain, escaped
> Like a breeze between his hands, a dream on wings. (A.942–4)

---

43. Heaney, 'Postscript', in Heaney and Hendrix, *The Golden Bough* (1992), 32; see also *Sounding Lines*, 16.

The desire that motivates Aeneas' entire *katabatic* journey is to see his father face to face, and this meeting in a sense represents the culmination of his quest. But the *ter conatus* reveals his deeper, impossible desire to restore the past and bring his father back to life.

Not only does the gesture convey the son's longing for his dead father; it also signifies the traumatic repetition and return of his sense of loss, since these three lines are repeated word for word from *Aeneid II*, where, in the midst of the fall of Troy, Aeneas has tried and failed to rescue his wife, Creusa (Ae.II.792–4). Having brought his father and son out of the burning city, Aeneas discovers his wife has fallen behind. Returning to look for her, he finds her ghost instead. Looking strangely larger than life ('*nota maior imago*'), she urges Aeneas to accept the loss of Troy, and herself, and his entire first world, and to embrace his future instead, where another city, another wife and a new world await him (Ae.II.773, 776–89). Intra- and intertextually, Virgil himself seems trapped in a recursive spiral of remembered grief, since he is repeating himself, both within the *Aeneid* and in his larger corpus, where the loss of Creusa recalls the loss of Eurydice, told in *Georgics IV*, and other empty embraces in the *Aeneid*, while intertextually he is repeating and rehearsing earlier ghostly encounters found in his Greek model, Homer.[44]

Aeneas must go on, he can't go on, he goes on.[45] But as he goes, he brings the spectre of the past with him. This idea is beautifully expressed in a sketch of a scene from *Aeneid VI* by Paul Cézanne, an artist Heaney much admired. I do not know if Heaney knew of this sketch, or even if he was aware of Cézanne's particular fascination with Virgil.[46] But in Cézanne's drawing 'Aeneas meeting Dido at Carthage' (Plate 3), one finds the same blend of melancholy and hope that imbues many of the encounters described in *Seeing Things*. In the picture, Aeneas is stepping away from the sea, where his anchored ship is still waiting, and he is moving towards a figure of the marvellous: Dido as the African queen, reclining semi-naked on a throne backed by enormous peacock feathers. But at his heels, the ghost of his former wife, Creusa, still follows. Her dark, shrouded figure, '*nota maior imago*', dominates the picture. With right arm raised over her head, she is a monument of the sorrow Aeneas carries within him, and perhaps also a proleptic image of the tragic figure Dido will herself become, when Aeneas flees Carthage at the end of *Aeneid IV*. The outline of Creusa's bent right knee almost touches Aeneas' sword but does not quite make contact. Aeneas and Dido are likewise nearly but not quite touching; each extends an arm towards the other but two attendants fill and block the space between them. So Aeneas is suspended between past and future, with both women just beyond his sensory reach.

44. The principal *ter conatus* scenes are in Homer, *Iliad* xxiii.99–101 (Achilles–Patroclus); *Odyssey* XI.206–9 (Odysseus–Anticleia); Virgil, G.IV.498–502 (Orpheus–Eurydice); Ae.I.407–9 (Aeneas–Venus), I.715–17 (Aeneas–Ascanius), II.792–4 (Aeneas–Creusa), VI.469–73 (Aeneas–Dido), and VI.700–2 (Aeneas–Anchises).
45. 'you must go on, I can't go on, I'll go on.' (Beckett (1953), 134)
46. For Cézanne on Virgil, see Danchev (2012), especially 352–3; and Tuma (Spring 2002), 56–85. Cézanne wrote to Zola that he had translated Virgil's *Eclogues* (30 December 1859, in Danchev, ed., 2013). With grateful thanks to John Elderfield.

In *Seeing Things*, the son's attempted embrace of his father's ghost constitutes a critical threshold moment in which poetry strives to recover a lost, material reality:

> what the reach
> Of sense despairs of as it fails to reach it,
> Especially the thwarted sense of touch. (ST 24)

While many poems in the collection allude to Heaney's recently deceased father, two poems, in particular, evoke and transform Virgil's *ter conatus* motif: 'Man and Boy' and 'Seeing Things, III'. In 'Man and Boy', Heaney remembers the 'slow, bright river evenings' of his childhood, spent fishing with his father (ST 14, l. 5). The second part of the poem develops into a more abstract, symbolic mode, beginning with a death-like mower, who 'leans forever on his scythe' in the centre of a field ploughed in perfect, concentric circles (l. 16). 'Man and Boy' was first published together with 'The Golden Bough' translation in *Poetry Review* (1991), which would have invited readers to look for Virgilian parallels in the autobiographical poem.

In the poem itself, there is only one obvious allusion to Aeneas and it comes as a surprising twist in the final line. But the *ter conatus* also helps to structure the whole poem: there are triple repetitions in each of the poem's two parts, and performatively, 'Man and Boy' attempts to recover and preserve a memory of the father's touch. In Part I, Heaney condenses the beatitudes of St Matthew's Gospel from eight to three, as he sings his father's praises:[47]

> Blessed be the down-to-earth! Blessed be highs!
> Blessed be the detachment of dumb love
> In that broad-backed, low-set man (ST 14, ll. 8–10)

And in Part II, he links the memory of losing his father with a second-hand account of his own father hearing of *his* father's death, so that three Heaneys are bound up in the one experience of loss:

> My father is a barefoot boy with news,
> Running at eye-level with weeds and stooks
> On the afternoon of his own father's death. (ST 15, ll. 23–5)

The use of the present tense here (in contrast to the past tense for Part I) suggests the poem has slipped into a dream-time that wavers between daydream and nightmare; the deceased father is brought back to life as a barefoot boy, but only to face the moment he learns of his father's death. As the boy runs across the fields, 'The open, black half of the half-door waits' (l. 26), where the half-door connotes both death and originary birthplace (Mossbawn having the characteristic split stable-door of a

---

47. Matthew 5: 3–12, 'Blessed are the poor in spirit, for theirs is the Kingdom of Heaven.'

simple, one-storey farmhouse). The deathly door recalls Sibyl's warning to Aeneas, *'noctes atque dies patet atri ianua Ditis'* (Ae.VI.127).[48]

In one of Heaney's favourite passages from Sophocles' *Oedipus at Colonus*, the dark door is welcoming, rather than menacing: the King's friends suggest that, when Oedipus was ready to die, 'the underworld / Opened in love the unlit door of earth.'[49] But here, death's door seems ready to engulf fathers and sons in one undifferentiated temporality, where past has collapsed into present. Freud gave the name 'repetition compulsion' to the form of remembering the past in which 'the patient does not remember anything of what he has forgotten and repressed, but acts it out. He reproduces it not as a memory but as an action.'[50] In a later paper, he distinguished mourning from melancholia, arguing that the latter behaves like an open wound which can never heal because the past is never experienced *as* past.[51] In the circling movement of 'Man and Boy', Heaney re-enacts the iterative gesture of Aeneas as he tries to embrace his father's ghost.

More broadly speaking, Heaney's turn to Virgil in this poem can be understood as a way of reaching out to the literary tradition at a point in his own life when, politically, intellectually and emotionally, he senses a loss of connection to his first world, the *omphalos* of Mossbawn and his local district. 'Man and Boy' attempts a marvellous rescue of this lost world by bridging personal memories of his own father together with a literary memory of Aeneas' archetypal father, Anchises. Just as the salmon leaps backwards 'through its own unheard concentric soundwaves' (l. 15), so Heaney pursues a connection between cultural centre and periphery, moving backward in time and outward from Moyola's riverbank to the edge of the Mediterranean Sea.

This connection is bridged in the last five lines of the poem, where there is an identification with the father as a running, barefoot boy:

I feel much heat and hurry in the air.
I feel his legs and quick heels far away

And strange as my own – when he will piggyback me
At a great height, light-headed and thin-boned,
Like a witless elder rescued from the fire. (*ST* 15, ll. 27–31)

The last line refers to Aeneas' escape from Troy bearing his elderly father on his shoulders, a now iconic image of filial piety in European art and literature

---

48. 'Day and night black Pluto's door stands open.' (*GB*.33)
49. Sophocles, *Oedipus at Colonus* 1661–2, trans. Robert Fitzgerald (Chicago, 2013). A colleague of Fitzgerald's read out these lines at a memorial service held for him at Harvard University. At the end of the service, Heaney, who regarded Fitzgerald as a father figure, quoted the same passage, saying 'Robert is under the clay roof, behind the unlit door of earth but I hope there is a little skylight through which all this is coming through to him.' ('An Evening for Robert Fitzgerald', 6 May 1993, quotations from 5" and 52" respectively).
50. Freud, 'Remembering, Repeating and Working Through' [1914], 150.
51. Freud, 'Mourning and Melancholia' [1917], 163.

(*Ae*.II.707–24). What is dizzying about Heaney's simile is how it telescopes time and inverts the perspectives of father and child. In Virgil's scene, Aeneas also leads his son Ascanius by the hand. But here, the roles are all compressed together: Heaney's father is at first a running child, then a father bearing *his* son, then the aged father, himself borne aloft on his adult son's shoulders. This transformation stems from an act of imaginative sympathy between son and father: 'I feel much heat and hurry . . . I feel his legs and quick heels . . .'. Conjuring living sensation into his father's legs, he is then able to reverse the *ter conatus*, and recover the earlier image of Aeneas successfully rescuing his father from death. At the same time, the lost father bears and rescues the son, as the remembered piggyback ride is projected forward with the future tense of 'will' (l. 29). The childhood linguistic register of 'piggyback' dovetails into the sophisticated, literary allusion of the 'witless elder rescued from the fire', and thus casts a bridge between the poet's child and adult worlds (l. 31).

And yet this act of poetic rescue and recovery seems tenuous at best. The very moment when the poet reaches to feel what his father feels, the image of the child begins to recede in time and space, appearing 'far away // And strange'. Not only does his father appear remote, but so too does the poet's childhood self, whose light-headedness is so surprisingly compared to that of an old man. The child is father of the man, as Wordsworth says, but Heaney pushes this further in showing how ghosthood is immanent in the child. If, in the last line, Heaney transgresses the Virgilian image in order to rescue his father from the past, what is lost in the allusion to 'a witless elder' is precisely the linguistic plenitude of the father's idiomatic speech and the folkloric wisdom captured in the poem's opening lines. So the poetic rescue is partial, and it paradoxically deepens the severance between present and past.

In 'Seeing Things, III', Heaney's remembrance of his father begins with this doubled sense of poetry performing a rescue and/or witnessing the repetition of loss. Although there is no direct allusion to Virgil, the poem is even more visibly structured as a *ter conatus* episode, with three attempts made by the son to embrace his father's ghost. Unlike 'Man and Boy', the poem is framed from the start as a fairy tale, a *mirabile dictu* not to be read as literally true. It begins thus: 'Once upon a time my undrowned father / Walked into our yard.' (*ST* 18, ll. 1–2) The first line frames the memory as a Shakespearean romance, where the drowned father's death can be reversed by Prospero's magic. Within the romance frame, though, the poem then relates a miraculous survival that did actually happen: the poet's father was pitched into the river while spraying his crops and nearly drowned, along with his horse and crop-sprayer. Relating the story as a miracle has a double-edged effect: it inclines one to believe in romance endings since this one proved true; and it reminds us of the impossibility of fairy-tale truths, since this story is recalled in the context of the father's recent death. Maintaining this precarious balance between credulity and incredulity, the poem rehearses the story twice more, like Aeneas unable to escape the desire to give substance to his father's ghost.

The second attempt adopts the point of view of the childhood self, reluctantly separated from his father:

> He had gone to spray
> Potatoes in a field on the riverbank
> And wouldn't bring me with him. (ll. 2–4)

This time, viewed from the child's perspective, the father returns radically altered from his experience:

> scatter-eyed
> And daunted, strange without his hat,
> His step unguided, his ghosthood immanent (ll. 11–13)

One meaning of that last, obscure phrase is that the father's ghostly appearance anticipates his future death. Another, as Bernard O'Donoghue suggests, is that 'his post-mortal nature is present while he is still in his living form.'[52] In any case, while the father is miraculously saved, he seems to have been enghosted by the near-death experience. The adult self then returns to imagine the accident as if he had personally witnessed it:

> the whole rig went over into a deep
> Whirlpool, hoofs, chains, shafts, cartwheels, barrel
> And tackle, all tumbling off the world,
> And the hat already merrily swept along
> The quieter reaches. (ST 18, ll. 17–21)

The accumulated jumble of nouns, heavily accented in line 18, is then lightly swept away as if by a magical flood. The idea of 'tumbling off the world', together with the echo of the nursery rhyme in 'merrily', suggest a fairy-tale catastrophe, where any harm to the good can be overturned.[53] But the jaunty tone is offset by the image of the hat floating downstream and its resemblance to a soul's crossing over water into the afterlife (cf. *Squarings*, xliv). This scene of shipwreck seems to encompass two temporalities, the childhood story and the time of the adult self's recent loss.

The third telling of the miraculous return then attempts to redress both these experiences of loss. The narration is at once a plain statement of fact and a luminous account of a visionary resurrection:

> That afternoon,
> I saw him face to face, he came to me
> With his damp footprints out of the river,
> And there was nothing between us there
> That might not still be happily ever after. (ll. 21–5)

---

52. O'Donoghue, '"Chosen Ancestors"' (2018), 16. In O'Donoghue's reading, the father returns in the poem as a revenant from the land of the living: 'The appearance of the living father is startling in the same way as living bodies were among the dead shades.' (16–17)
53. J. R. R. Tolkien's *eucatastrophe* (Tolkien, 1964). The nursery rhyme lyrics are: 'Row, row, row your boat, gently down the stream, merrily, merrily, merrily, merrily, life is but a dream.'

Along with the romance reversal of tragedy, there are obvious Christian overtones to the dead father's resurrection here. But there is also a more specific attempt to redress the filial longing of Aeneas: '*ire ad conspectum cari genitoris et ora / contingat*' (*Ae*.VI.108, 'I pray for one look, one face-to-face meeting with my dear father.' (*GB* 13)) Going beyond Aeneas, Heaney conjures a flesh-and-blood father who can imprint the riverbank with his corporeal weight. The double negative of 'nothing between us . . . That might not be', together with the fairy-tale ending 'happily ever after', invite us to credit the marvellous against the odds.

At the same time, the fairy-tale ending can be read as delusional, 'seeing things' in the negative sense. As Bernard O'Donoghue notes, what is absent from the fairy-tale formula is the word 'lived'.[54] The temporal marker, 'That afternoon', pushes the resurrection scene into the distant past. The chiastic repetition of pronouns, 'I saw him . . . he came to me', holds the two figures in close relation but slightly apart, like Cézanne's drawing of Aeneas and Creusa's ghost. And the phrase 'nothing between us' recalls the melancholy of Aeneas' embrace of empty air. Thus Heaney's treatment of the *ter conatus* motif in 'Man and Boy' and 'Seeing Things, III' is highly ambivalent in tone, mixing the possibility of miraculous transformation with a lingering elegiac tone. In both poems, the lyric qualities of lightness and mobility that he celebrates elsewhere in *Seeing Things* are also associated with the lightness of senescence and ghosthood. As in Virgil's *ter conatus* scene, the father can be 'undrowned' through the poet's imagination and memory, but only within the provisional threshold time-space of the poem.

As a final example, in *Squarings*, xxvii, the cattle-dealer father is transfigured into Hermes, Greek god of thresholds and crossroads:

Everything flows. Even a solid man,
A pillar to himself and to his trade,
. . .
Can sprout wings at the ankle and grow fleet
As the god of fair days, stone posts, roads and cross-roads, (*ST* 85, ll. 1–2, 4–5)

Here, the very act of associating his father with the Greek god brings lightness and mobility to the remembrance: the stone pillar sprouts wings. But this transfiguration of tribal to literary memory does not lose touch with the home ground either. At play here are Irish mythical and literary associations: mad, half-bird King Sweeney, and Yeats's 'Cuchulain Comforted', where the legendary hero, bound to a tree, is approached by bird-like shrouds.[55] The time-space of the threshold is one of transformation, but in both directions, away from and back to home. In his guise as Hermes, the apotheosised father-figure becomes Heaney's guide on his travels. The advice the father gives to his sister is also meant for the poet: '"Look for a man with an ashplant on the boat, . . . / And you'll be safe."' (l. 7) That this man is equipped like Aeneas – but also Joyce's Dedalus – with boat and bough contributes to the

---

54. O'Donoghue, '"Chosen Ancestors"', 17.
55. Yeats, 'Cuchulain Comforted' (1992), 379.

sense that Heaney is returning home, even as the poem looks abroad and backwards in time. As he writes in 'Markings', 'All these things entered you / As if they were both the door and what came through it.' (*ST* 9)

*

The poet's father is continually recalled in *Seeing Things* as a figure of solidity and weight, embodying the plenitude of Heaney's first world. As this figure is forwarded from the past, it undergoes complex transformations, from weight to lightness, and historical specificity to myth. Lightness signifies lyric freedom, but also the rootless condition of the inner *émigré*, forcibly exiled from his first world. In Cézanne's drawing, Aeneas' ship floats uncannily close to shore and hardly imprints the surface of the sea. To the viewer, it recalls Aeneas' flight from Troy and many years wandering at sea. It signifies both his luck in escaping the burning city and the burden of the past that goes with him. It also foreshadows his swift escape from Carthage, which will destroy Dido, and the city itself in later wars with Rome. In his dialogue with Virgil in *Seeing Things*, Heaney explores all these implications of lightness, both the positive and the negative. Seeking parallels with Virgil is a vital part of the dreamwork, the self-extraction and the escape from the burden of communal bonds and the history of sectarian conflict. But meeting Virgil in the underworld also proves to be his surest route to rediscovering and conjuring forth the lost home ground.

3. Orpheus in a Major Key

After *Seeing Things*, Heaney's next in-depth engagement with Latin literature is a translation of the Orpheus myth as recounted by Ovid in *Metamorphoses* X and XI.[1] Composed in the early 1990s, Heaney's Ovid translations extend and develop the dialogue with Virgil, in that they represent the archetypal poet Orpheus *in extremis*, testing the powers of his art against threats of violence and death. In *Metamorphoses* X, Orpheus descends into the underworld to rescue his dead wife, Eurydice, and in *Metamorphoses* XI, he is overcome by a crowd of maenads who, infuriated by his rejection of heterosexual love, rip him to pieces and throw his severed limbs into the River Hebrus. For Heaney, the *katabasis* in *Metamorphoses* X constitutes the poet's lesser trial, since he uses the enchanting power of his song to charm the underworld shades into believing that death can be denied or transcended. The violent confrontation in *Metamorphoses* XI, although it results in the poet's death, nevertheless elicits the major art, in Heaney's view, since here Orpheus must face up to and accept the mortal condition, but his suffering is transmuted into a song that comprehends the wholeness of life-in-death and death-in-life.[2]

These translations are closely related to Heaney's earlier meditations on Aeneas, as he seeks to go beyond human limit in search of his lost first world. Rather than fixing on Aeneas' threshold crossing into Hades and isolated, transitional encounters, Heaney now follows Orpheus down into the underworld and beyond, to the legendary poet's encounter with his own death. In translating Ovid's *Metamorphoses*, Heaney knew that Ovid was himself responding to and rewriting Virgil's account of the Orpheus myth in *Georgics* IV.[3] Where Ovid deliberately undercuts and satirises Virgil's high tragic style, Heaney's translation reintroduces a fuller note of pathos,

---

1. P. Ovidius Naso, *Metamorphoses*, ed. R. J. Tarrant (2004); unless otherwise noted, translations are from *Ovid, Metamorphoses Books 9–15*, trans. Frank J. Miller, rev. G. P. Goold (1984).
2. For further criticism on Heaney's Ovid translations, see O'Brien (2004), Coughlan (2007), Wheatley (2018). For other 'Ulster Ovids', see Kerrigan (1992).
3. On Virgil's *Georgics*, see Volk, *Oxford Readings in Classical Studies: Vergil's Georgics* (2008), 1–13, for a review of criticism.

thus bringing the Orpheus myth closer in line with the *Aeneid*'s sense of the *lacrimae rerum*, the tragedy of loss. In *The Redress of Poetry*, Heaney refers to the death of Orpheus as related by both Virgil and Ovid (*RP* 58). And he paraphrases various passages from Charles Segal's *Orpheus: The Myth of the Poet* (1989), in which Virgil and Ovid's versions are compared in detail.[4]

The Orphic voice is also associated with Virgil in a slightly later essay, where Heaney describes Czesław Miłosz as 'somewhere between the Orphic and the Tiresian' and then proceeds with an extended comparison between the lives of the Polish poet and Virgil (*FK* 410). For Heaney, 'there is something Virgilian about the curve of Miłosz's whole destiny', and the late work of both poets gives 'plangent and abundant expression to their sense of "lacrimae rerum"' (*FK* 411).[5] In both cases, 'the felicity of the art was in itself a heartbreaking reminder of the desolation of the times' (*FK* 412). While elsewhere Heaney admires Virgil's ability to bridge rural and urban worlds, as well as different cultures and historical eras, in this essay he portrays the Roman poet as an Orpheus ensnared by historical forces inimical to his art.

Both Virgil and Miłosz lived through periods of violent political conflict, and in this sense their biographies find answerable form in the mythic archetype of Orpheus, when set upon by wild maenads. In the Miłosz essay, Heaney recalls Hermann Broch's dark prose-poem about Virgil's death, which offers the portrait of

> a man hallucinating at the centre of the world of *real-politik*, a man in thrall to memory even as he was turned to for prophecy, a man at work in the mine-shafts of language whom others regarded as a guide to the corridors of power, (*FK* 413)

This intensely tragic image of Virgil informs Heaney's reading of the Orpheus myth in the early 1990s, and is closely associated with his reading of Miłosz and other modern European poets caught up in war, as well as his general reflections on 'history' as a 'No' to life.[6] A less tragic view of Virgil emerges in Heaney's later essays, but the sense of a disjunction between the poet and his times remains a constant theme. As he will later claim, Virgil had 'a temperament made for Arcadia but forced to take stock of Actium.'[7]

One obvious point of attraction about the *katabasis* of Orpheus over that of Aeneas is that it concerns a poet rather than a political leader whose destiny is to lay the foundation of a future empire. But Heaney also emphasises what they share in common: both the Trojan prince and the legendary seer are impelled by love

---

4. Segal (1989, 73–94) compares Virgil and Ovid's Orpheus. Heaney directly paraphrases Segal's reading of Rilke's Orpheus myth (*RP* 143–4).
5. On Heaney and Miłosz, see Parker, '"Past master"' (2013), and Kay (2018).
6. For close analyses of Heaney's tragic view of 'history', see Dennison (2015) and Lavan (2020). Heaney discusses Orpheus, in relation to modern European writers, and history as 'No' in 'Between North and South' (1995).
7. Heaney, 'Towers' (2007), 153.

to enter the underworld, and both struggle to balance private instinct and social responsibility. In any case, for Virgil scholars the parallels between the descent of Orpheus in *Georgics IV* and that of Aeneas in *Aeneid VI* are already multiple and well attested. In Virgil's predecessor Ennius' *Annales*, Aeneas' Trojan wife, Creusa, is called *Eurydica*.[8] Cumae, where Aeneas enters the underworld, is known to have been one of the centres of Orphism and Bacchic mystery cults in the Roman world, which has encouraged some scholars to believe that *Aeneid VI* was modelled on a now lost *katabasis* of Orpheus.[9] Whether or not this earlier descent text was a source, Virgil himself echoes his own account of the Orpheus myth in the *Aeneid*; Orpheus' attempted embrace of Eurydice (G.IV.499–501) is played out again in the *ter conatus* scenes of *Aeneid II* and *VI*.

Ovid's relation of the Orpheus myth in *Metamorphoses* (*Meta.*) compounds these parallels with the *Aeneid*. All three of Heaney's favourite motifs from *Aeneid VI*, for example, are taken up and transformed in *Metamorphoses X* and *XI*: the *ter conatus*, Charon's barge (which is denied to Orpheus, *Meta.X.73*), and Orpheus' lyre as the precursor to Aeneas' golden bough. It is his enchanting lyre that wins the poet access to the underworld but then fails to save him when subjected to human violence in the material world (*Meta.XI.18*). In interview with Richard Kearney in 1992, Heaney finds 'a steadiness and a durability' and a 'mystical sense of value' in 'the word, Orpheus'.[10] By the time Henri Cole interviewed Heaney for *The Paris Review* in 1994, the myth of Orpheus had become part of Heaney's mental furniture, a narrative to live with dreamily alongside the motifs of *Aeneid VI*. Amongst the furnishings of Heaney's study, Cole takes note of: 'A stone from Delphi. A view of Tintern Abbey. Orpheus on a vase. And on a plate. And on a medal.'[11] Heaney's Orpheus is a compound ghost, drawing some of his features from *Georgics IV* and the *Aeneid*, alongside the principal source of Ovid's *Metamorphoses*.

The importance of this mythical figure to Heaney is further exemplified in the series of lectures he delivered as Professor of Poetry at Oxford, from 1989 to 1993. His 1995 volume, *The Redress of Poetry*, offers an edited and rearranged selection of these Oxford lectures.[12] As published, the lecture series proceeds from consideration of lighter to more substantial examples of poetic redress in writers such as Marlowe, Merriman, Clare, Wilde, MacDiarmid, Dylan Thomas, W. B. Yeats, Elizabeth Bishop and Louis MacNeice. The Introduction to *The Redress* alludes to Virgil's *lac-*

---

8. See Grillo, 'Leaving Troy and Creusa' (2010), and 'Eurydice' in Hornblower and Spawforth, eds, *Oxford Classical Dictionary*, 575.
9. Norden (1903, 5). This view is more recently upheld by Bremmer (2014), who finds similar descriptions of the tortured souls in Tartarus (*Ae.VI.548–636*) in Orphic papyri (see, further, Horsfall's review of the criticism, in his note on *Ae.6.548–636*). G.IV, however, does not seem to be based on the same source (for example, there is no reference to Tarturus in the Georgic epyllion). On Orpheus and Orphism, see Tom Mackenzie, '*Georgica* and *Orphica*: The *Georgics* in the Context of Orphic Poetry and Religion', in Nicholas Freer and Bobby Xinyue, eds, *Reflections and New Perspectives on Virgil's Georgics*.
10. Heaney, interview with Kearney, 1992, published as 'Between North and South' (1995), 104.
11. Henri Cole interview with Seamus Heaney, 'The Art of Poetry No. 75' (1997), 119.
12. For detailed analysis of *RP*, see Dennison (2015), esp. 157–87, and Lavan (2020), 127–39.

rimae rerum and Rilke's 'Sonnets to Orpheus' (xvii), and in the volume as a whole, the allusions to Orpheus are also arranged in an ascending scale from minor to major feats of poetic redress.

In the opening essay, 'The Redress of Poetry', Heaney begins by defending poetry in a 'court of appeal' against prosecutors such as Plato, who demanded to know how poetry is '"of present use"' within the *polis* (*RP* 1). In interview with Kearney, Heaney admits the justice of Plato's charge, whenever poets aim merely to enchant and entrance, like the young Orpheus, rather than 'taking on the role of the artist [as] oppositional'.[13] The 'fully empowered artist', on the other hand,

> goes beyond entrancement into what Yeats called 'the desolation of reality'. And there you have Orpheus, not as the puller of the harp string that puts everybody to sleep, but Orpheus confronting the fact of death and love, going into the underworld, always defiant but always failing to overcome death, always failing to absolutely make the perfection cohere.[14]

If we take *The Midnight Verdict* and *The Redress of Poetry* together, then, Heaney's treatment of the Orpheus myth in the early 1990s can be understood as part of a broader project to articulate his poetics of 'redress'. In its major, oppositional role, poetry attempts to harness beauty and truth in resistance to what Eliot described as 'the immense panorama of violence and futility which is contemporary history'.[15]

I. *THE MIDNIGHT VERDICT*

More immediately, Heaney's engagement with the Orpheus myth was prompted by the invitation to contribute to a collected volume of translations of the *Metamorphoses*, published as *After Ovid* (1994). Having deployed the Orpheus and Eurydice myth in an earlier, original poem, 'The Underground', Heaney offered the editors of *After Ovid* a translation of the first eighty-five lines of *Metamorphoses* X, concerning the pair of lovers, and he subsequently sent them a second extract,

---

13. Heaney, 'Between North and South' (1995), 107. Similarly, in a lecture delivered at the Melbourne Writers' Festival, Heaney argues, 'Orpheus in one aspect is the ecstatic poet who moves not only human beings but creatures but the world [sic] by rhythmical sound. He chants. When he plays the world becomes entranced. It's like playing an Irish jig – people start to beat their feet and begin to move ... And Plato said "Not too good"' (Heaney, 'God Moves in Mysterious Metres' (1994), MSS 960 Box 46: 4, Stuart A. Rose Manuscript, Archives, and Rare Book Library. With thanks to Michael Parker.
14. 'Between North and South', 108.
15. Eliot, 'Ulysses, Order, and Myth' ([1923], 1975), p. 177. See also Dennison (2015), 33. While I disagree with some of his conclusions, Dennison very convincingly traces the influence of Eliot on Heaney's pessimistic view of history. His comment that Heaney's 'effortful yea-saying' in 'Joy or Night' (*RP* 146–63) is 'not so much "Orphic" as it is Sisyphean' (171), however, fails to register the complex dynamics of the Orpheus myth in Heaney's work or elsewhere.

'The Death of Orpheus', comprising the first eighty-four lines of Book XI.[16] In the meantime, he published the Ovid extracts in his own volume, *The Midnight Verdict*, together with two translation extracts from the eighteenth-century Irish poem *Cúirt an Mheán-Oíche* (*The Midnight Court*) by Brian Merriman.[17]

Merriman's poem is a spoof on the traditional genre of the *aisling*, in which a male poet dreams of a beautiful, afflicted woman, a figure for Ireland, lamenting her state of thraldom (SS xix, RP 48). In *Cúirt an Mheán-Oíche*, a pseudo-autobiographical poet named 'merry' and 'Brian' (MV 33) has a nightmare that he has been arraigned by a court of fairy women, who charge him, and all young Irishmen, with sexual neglect. The fairy queen, Aoibheall, finds him guilty and condemns him to a general whipping by the women's court. In 'Orpheus in Ireland', Heaney praises the poem's 'libertarian and adversarial stance' against the sexually repressive moral codes of Merriman's society, as well as its 'overall drive to celebrate the creaturely over the ethereal in human beings, male or female'.[18] In response to recent feminist critique, he then offers a defence of Merriman's poem despite 'the phallocentrism of its surface discourse', a point we will return to below (RP 61).

In his 'Translator's Note' to *The Midnight Verdict*, Heaney describes the Latin and Irish translations as 'all part of a single impulse' (MV 11). By his own account, 'Orpheus and Eurydice' was completed in July 1993, and the Merriman translation undertaken in the same summer. It was while putting 'bits of the Irish into couplets' that he came to think of the Irish poem in relation to the death of Orpheus; in particular, 'The end of *The Midnight Court* took on a new resonance when read within the acoustic of the classical myth' (ibid.). Thematically, the trial of Merriman reverses that of Orpheus, with the Irish poet escaping violent punishment only by a last-minute exit from the dream-vision (comparable to Aeneas' ascent via the Gates of Sleep). Formally, Heaney's choice of loosely rhymed, Augustan heroic couplets for both the Ovid and the Merriman translations underlines his strategy of coupling opposing genres, moods and values in *The Midnight Verdict* as a whole.[19] While his translations of Virgil always incorporate, to some degree, the dactylic hexameter meter of classical epic, Heaney may have felt licensed to adopt the Augustan form with Ovid because of Ovid's own use of couplets in his earlier verse (in

---

16. SS 313. 'The Underground' was first published separately in *Thames Poetry* (February 1981), *Sequoia* (Autumn 1983) and *Poetry Ireland Review* (Winter 1983). It was then collected in *Station Island* (1984), where it heads the volume and anticipates the poet's own *katabasis*, much in the way the translation of Virgil's 'golden bough' prefaces the *katabatic* content of *Seeing Things*.
17. MV (1993). This Gallery Press edition has no line numbers, so citations will be noted by page number.
18. RP 38–62 (53, 56). Delivered in October 1993, published 3/10 in RP.
19. Cf. the heroic couplets used in George Sandys's *Ovid's Metamorphosis Englished* (1632), and Samuel Garth, ed., *Ovid's Metamorphoses in Fifteen Books Translated by the Most Eminent Hands* (London: Shakespear's-Head, 1717), where Book X is translated by William Congreve and Book XI by Samuel Croxall. Arthur Golding's 1567 *Metamorphosis*, still considered a masterpiece, is composed in heptameter rhyming couplets.

Metamorphoses itself, however, Ovid adopts dactylic hexameter, after the *Aeneid*).[20] In any case, Heaney's use of the couplet allows him to accentuate the connections and contrasts between Merriman's bawdy satire and the classical tragedy of Orpheus. And as we shall see, the form of the couplet is also deployed to contain and structure the complex tensions at the end of Heaney's Ovid translation, contributing to his notion that poetry offers psychological 'redress' at the level of patterned sound.

Delving further, one finds a paradoxical combination of contrasting moods already present in each of the originary texts. Merriman's *Cúirt an Mheán-Oíche* hybridises traditional *aisling* and Augustan satire, while Ovid injects legalistic discourse and down-to-earth pragmatism into the extreme pathos and high tragedy of Virgil's narrative.[21] In a marginal note on a typescript draft of his Ovid translation, Heaney has penned along the bottom and up the side of the page: 'On the whole, wonderful. Also, on the whole, Ovid's style is paradoxical. I.e., the next line overrules what the previous line states. Almost the rhythm principal [. . .] before rhyme.'[22] As a whole, *The Midnight Verdict* multiplies and amplifies this sense of paradox, one utterance being continually challenged by another, both within each translation, and in the juxtaposition of the Latin and Irish material. All these tensions contribute to the complexity of the debate Heaney is conducting about what poetry can do, and what it should do, when placed under historical conditions of extreme duress.

The Midnight Verdict has itself undergone trial and verdict in a critical controversy that has unfortunately obscured the broader implications of Heaney's reading of Orpheus. In *Stepping Stones*, Heaney recalls coming under fire for the publication of an androcentric anthology of Irish writers, published by the Field Day Company (of which Heaney was one of the board of directors), and he compares himself to the composite Merriman–Orpheus of *The Midnight Verdict*: 'the merry man in me couldn't help seeing the beleaguered Orpheus as a General Editor figure, being attacked' (*SS* 313). In interview with Henri Cole, moreover, he characterises his critics as maenads or fairies in Merriman's dream-trial: 'It became a whipping boy, or a boy-whipping. A real hosting of the *she*.'[23] In 'Orpheus in Ireland', however, Heaney suggests that *Cúirt an Mheán-Oíche* can be read against 'the phallocentrism of its surface discourse' to reveal a more profound 'male anxiety about suppressed female power, both sexual and political' (*RP* 61). One of his professed aims in the Merriman translation is to bring out 'the under-music of the women's voices' in a way that previous translations had failed to do (*RP* 56). Heaney also uses the translation to place his own early poetry on trial: in particular, his celebrated 'Bog' poem, 'Punishment', in which the skeleton of a female sacrificial victim is held up for close scrutiny by an anxious male gaze.[24] As David Wheatley rightly comments, 'it is left to the reader to decide whether the stance of self-accusation excuses or compounds the offence'.[25]

---

20. On Ovid's meter, see D. E. Hill, Introduction, Ovid, *Metamorphoses* (1999), 2–3.
21. See further, O'Brien (2004), 277–90.
22. Heaney, *LP* III.ii, underlining in original; [. . .] is illegible.
23. Heaney, 'Interview with Henri Cole', 135. N.B. 'she' is an Irish word for 'fairy'.
24. For a critique of 'Punishment', see Edna Longley (1986) and Coughlan (1997).
25. Wheatley (2018), 229.

In *Seeing Things*, as we saw in Chapter 2, Heaney draws on the Virgilian motif of Aeneas boarding Charon's barge to explore some of his own anxieties concerning a poet's responsibility towards his community. With the Orpheus myth, he deliberately places on trial his much-cherished notion of the poet as a creature of free, self-generated, lyric impulse. What the trial in Thrace reveals is another, more demanding form of verse-making, which admits to the reality of violence and death, and seeks a comprehension beyond it. In the process, the binary opposition between male poet and lethal, female antagonists in the originary myth is exposed, challenged and finally 'transfigured, in another pattern'.[26]

A key to understanding Heaney's reading of Orpheus is the idea of the mythical poet facing two different kinds of trial, first in Hades and then in the mountains of Thrace. The idea of a modulation of keys is further supported by the existence of two classical versions of the Orpheus myth, one tragic and the other comedic. In *The Midnight Verdict*, by splicing together Merriman's comic tale with Ovid's tragic version of the Orpheus myth, Heaney attempts to deliver a double-sided experience of the poet's trial as both tragic and comedic at the same time. In 'Orpheus in Ireland', Heaney suggests that in placing Merriman side by side with Orpheus, 'what transposed the parallel from a minor to a major key' was finding a connection between the trial scene and the *death* of Orpheus (*RP* 58). The Merriman trial is in 'a major key' in the sense of playing out a comedic version of Orpheus' trial, where the mythic poet escapes trial at the hands of the maenads (which does not happen in any extant classical version). Understood in the sense of progression, though, Orpheus' death is the major, more serious trial, after the lesser (minor) trial of his art in Hades. The later episode, related in *Metamorphoses XI*, is 'far more grievous and ... sombre' than the poet's attempted rescue of Eurydice, and it is this latter trial that raises the more urgent questions about the value of poetry, both for Merriman's poet and for Heaney himself (*SS* 313).

Heaney seems to have gleaned both senses of 'minor' and 'major' art from his reading of Charles Segal's study of the Orpheus myth.[27] Segal begins by pointing out that, from antiquity, the myth of Orpheus and Eurydice has existed in two different versions. In the comedic version (that of Euripides' *Alcestis*, for example, and later, the medieval romance *Sir Orfeo*), Orpheus successfully recovers Eurydice from the underworld, while in the better-known, tragic version, he loses her by looking back, and later suffers a violent death himself. Virgil and Ovid, while choosing the tragic version, integrate aspects of the comedic one in different ways, as Segal explains. Virgil embeds the tragic story of Orpheus and Eurydice within a comedic frame narrative: he has Aristaeus the beekeeper placed on trial by the naiads of Eurydice's retinue, since it was in fleeing from Aristaeus' sexual advances that Eurydice stepped on a poisonous snake and died. Aristaeus eventually wins forgiveness from the naiads and the shade of Orpheus, and he emerges from the trial unscathed. Virgil's *Georgics IV* is thus one probable model for *The Midnight Verdict*'s

---

26. Eliot, 'Little Gidding', III.16 (2015), Vol. I, p. 206.
27. Segal (1989) cited in *RP* and Heaney's Melbourne lecture, 'God Moves' (MSS 960 Box 46: 4, Stuart Rose Archives).

composite, tragi-comedic narrative structure. Ovid introduces no framing, comedic narrative but he also interweaves comedic strains into the tragedy of Orpheus itself: his Orpheus finds solace in other love, and in the end is reunited with Eurydice in the underworld.

As Segal goes on to argue, these tragic and comedic versions of the myth have given rise to two contrasting schools of poetics, 'the immanentist and the transcendent' (7). 'Transcendent' poetics place greater emphasis on Orpheus' first descent into Hades, for his initial success (whether or not he later fails) demonstrates the power of song, or art in general, to transcend mortal limit. Heaney thus describes Orpheus' trial in Hades as demonstrating the 'ability of art – poetry, music, language – to triumph over death' (*RP* 144). By contrast, 'immanentist' poetics focus on the death of Orpheus and the posthumous survival of his song, as illustrated in Rainer Maria Rilke's 1923 *Duino Elegies* and *Sonnets to Orpheus*. In a letter quoted by Heaney, Rilke writes of the *Duino Elegies* that '"death is a *side of life* that is turned away from us . . . the true figure of life extends through both domains . . . *there is neither a here nor a beyond, but a great unity*"' (*RP* 140). As Segal further explains, the Orpheus myth 'oscillates between the power of form to master intense passion and the power of intense passion to engulf form' (8). While Orpheus' intense passion leads him to transcend mortal limit in Hades, his posthumous song illustrates the power of form to contain and master passion. It is this latter song that Rilke celebrates in the *Duino Elegies*. For Heaney too, the passionate, transcendent song which wins Orpheus entrance into Hades represents a minor poetics, when contrasted with the immanentist Orphic song that comprehends the 'great unity' of life as it extends through both domains, over- and underworlds.

II. *THE REDRESS OF POETRY*

Heaney's allusions to Orpheus in *The Redress of Poetry* are consistent with the Rilkean idea that poetry's major labour involves the confrontation with death and transmutation of suffering into forms of endurance in the mortal, material world. In 'Dylan the Durable?', Heaney associates Dylan Thomas's early poetry with the lesser, 'transcendent' poetics of *Metamorphoses* X, while his later, most 'durable' work evinces the major, 'immanentist' qualities of Orpheus' posthumous song in *Metamorphoses* XI.[28] Like that of Orpheus, Thomas's early verse had an 'immediate spellbinding power', charming and captivating its first audiences with its sheer physicality and 'sonic boom' (125, 127). But this 'genius for lyricizing' led to avoidance of the 'suffered world', in Eavan Boland's phrase (135, 134). So Thomas's lush and verdant poems, such as 'Fern Hill' and 'Poem in October', fall short of great poetry, in Heaney's view, because, 'like the backward look of Orpheus', they 'avert their eyes from the prospect of necessity.' (144) In these aurally rich, enchanting early poems, Heaney suggests, Thomas fails to confront the fact of mortality:

---

28. *RP* 124–45; Delivered 21 November 1991; published 7/10 in *RP*.

> It is as if Orpheus, grown older, had reneged on his larger task, that of testing the power of his lyre against the gods of the underworld and wresting life back out of death, and had gone back instead to his younger, happier if less world-saving task of casting musical spells upon the whole of nature. (*RP* 143)

Although it resembles the earlier trial in Hades, the 'larger task' here is that of wresting '"the true figure of life"' out of the evidence of death: that is, discovering life as it '"extends through both domains"'.[29]

In 'Do Not Go Gentle into That Good Night', according to Heaney, Dylan Thomas performs the major, immanentist art, in a poem that 'keeps its gaze firmly fixed on the upward path and works against the gradient of relapse.' (144) As Heaney reminds us, this poem was composed when Thomas's father was dying of cancer and Thomas was confronting 'the return journey out of mortality into ghosthood.' (138) The poem's passion is closer to that of Aeneas than Orpheus, as it recalls 'the father's remoteness – and the remoteness of all fathers', as well as, 'in an almost sobbing counterpoint, the protest of the poet's child-self against the separation' (137). This grievous matter is contained in the tightly controlled form of a villanelle so that, in Heaney's words, the 'backtracks and double-takes, turns and returns' of the rhyme scheme and rhythm become 'a vivid figure for the union of opposites, for the father in the son, the son in the father, for life in death and death in life.' (139) Moreover, the 'mixture of salutation and farewell' in Dylan's 'good night' mirrors the Janus-facing ambivalence of the '*uale*' (hail, farewell) that Eurydice utters as she descends back into the underworld (*RP* 138; *Meta*.X.62).

In 'Joy or Night', Heaney admires the way that W. B. Yeats was 'always passionately beating on the wall of the physical world in order to provoke an answer from the other side', despite not believing in a personal God.[30] And he controversially disparages Philip Larkin because, despite the 'high poetic achievement' of 'Aubade', the poem 'does not hold the lyre up in the face of the gods of the underworld; it does not make the Orphic effort to haul life back up the slope against all the odds.' (158) In terms of the parallel with the classical myth, this 'haulage' work refers not to Orpheus' attempt to rescue his own lost love, but to poetry's *labor* of celebrating the life principle in the face of violence and death. Admittedly, Heaney is not always clear about this distinction; here and in the passage quoted above, he seems to elide the two episodes (*Metamorphoses* X and *XI*) into one model of 'major', oppositional art, contrasting with the 'minor' art of enchanting an audience of trees, animals and

---

29. *RP* 140. And in the Melbourne lecture, 'says Segal, we can think of Orpheus as the figure of the poet who makes art encounter the fact of death and that the poetry which is working its way is going on the upward gradient of the beam of music. It's entranced but it's also working. . . . We want it to have some relationship to the endured life as well as to being called along by the envisaged life. So Orpheus in that aspect is the poet doing the labour of the upward slope . . . [quoting Miłosz, the poet is] stretched between the contemplation of a motionless point and the command to participate actively in history.' ('God Moves', MSS 960 Box 46: 4, Stuart Rose Archives).
30. *RP* 146–63 (149). Delivered 21 November 1990; published 8/10 in *RP*.

stones.[31] But generally, he follows Segal's lead in suggesting Orpheus faces 'the devastation of reality' only in the latter episode. This would mean pronouncing an even greater *Yes* to 'the enormous *No* which reality pronounces constantly in the face of human life', as Heaney writes, paraphrasing John Barth (153, 163). Barth's notion of the 'enormous *Yes* at the centre of Mozart's music' finds its equivalent in Yeats's poem 'Man and the Echo', which, for Heaney, 'has weight and significance because it overpowers and contains a *No*.'[32] In his 1994 interview with Henri Cole, he elaborates on what 'Mozartian poetry' might sound like, offering Marlowe's 'Hero and Leander' as an example: 'underneath all that banner-flying beauty and merriment, there was terrific veteran knowledge. Real awareness of hurt and vindictiveness and violence.'[33] Drawing on W. H. Auden's symbolisation of Ariel and Prospero, he suggests that Marlowe's poem 'has a Prospero awareness of all the penalties but it still retains an Ariel ability to keep itself sweet and lively.'[34]

In *The Redress of Poetry*, the 'Ariel' qualities of sweetness, swank and liveliness are generally associated with the minor poetics of Orphic transcendence. Thus, in the collection's opening essay, 'Extending the Alphabet', Marlowe's poem is praised for its 'casual technical virtuosity' and 'happy inner freedom' (*RP* 36). Likewise, in the fifth essay, Oscar Wilde is celebrated for his 'over-the-topness' and 'exhilarated high-wire word-play.' (*RP* 97) Like Orpheus on his way down to rescue Eurydice, in Wilde's writing, 'the lighter his touch, the more devastating his effect. When he walked on air, he was on solid ground.' (ibid.) But Wilde's death-defying art cannot survive a Prospero-awareness of the suffered world; in 'The Ballad of Reading Gaol', his genius for transcendence fails him and 'the master of the light touch came to submit to the heaviness of being' (*RP* 102). In a similar way, 'Orpheus's fatal backward look must . . . represent "the failure of art before the ultimate reality of death"' (*RP* 144, quoting Segal). It is only when Orpheus has faced mortality as an inescapable reality that his song can comprehend death as '"*a side of life* that is turned away from us"' (*RP* 140, xviii, quoting Rilke). In this respect, Heaney's gloss on his notion of 'poetry as redress' in *Stepping Stones* is particularly useful: 'I don't mean as compensation or as consolation, more as comprehension, a comprehension which has to be its own reward' (*SS* 431). Compensation and consolation are what Orpheus seeks in his first descent to Hades, whereas 'comprehension' is the music conveyed by his posthumous song, as shown in Heaney's Virgil-inflected translation of *Metamorphoses XI*.

In *The Redress of Poetry*, it is arguably Elizabeth Bishop who comes closest to Heaney's understanding of Orpheus' major art, in the sense of art which 'compre-

---

31. There is a similar conflation of the two Orphic episodes in 'Between North and South', 107–8.
32. Yeats (1992), 392; Heaney, *RP* 163.
33. Heaney, 'Interview with Henri Cole', 102.
34. Heaney, 'Interview with Henri Cole', 102. In 'The Sea and the Mirror' (1965), Auden discusses Shakespeare's Ariel as a symbol for poetry's instinct for beauty or, more generally, the artistic imagination, while Prospero represents its instinct for truth, or its disillusioned acceptance of reality. He refers to the Ariel–Prospero dichotomy in his essay 'Robert Frost', which Heaney also alludes to in *RP* (*The Dyer's Hand* (1987: 239–50)). For Heaney on Auden, see Dennison (2015), 39–40.

hends' the 'suffered world', rather than offering 'compensation or consolation' for loss. In 'Counting to a Hundred', Heaney begins by relating a harrowing incident from Bishop's early childhood, when she heard a piercing scream from her mother just before her mother was committed permanently to a mental asylum.[35] From this originary traumatic experience, Bishop develops her artistic ability 'to be able to ingest loss and to transmute it.' (RP 165) Her short story 'In the Village' converts this scream into the 'clang' of a blacksmith's anvil; thus, the suffering is comprehended and contained in an artistic form that is a 'capable match for disaster.' (167) In her early poem, 'The Monument', Bishop constructs a poem like boxes piled upon boxes: 'it seems to be standing over something which it also stands *for*. Once again, a withdrawn pressure, an inscrutable purpose or missing element is what the resulting structure exists to express or shelter.'[36] As an Orpheus singing in a 'major key', Bishop is not attempting to transcend her loss, but rather giving it shelter in the containing form of her verse.[37] Heaney's ultimate example of Bishop's major Orphic art is her poem 'One Art', composed in the strict form of a villanelle and addressed to the Orphic theme of the loss of a beloved. The containing form of the villanelle again, as in Thomas's case, allows the poet not to transcend but to 'survive the devastation' (184). Thus, Heaney sees the end-rhyme of the final couplet, and the homonym of 'right' latent in 'write', as poetry's forms of redress to loss:

the art of losing's not too hard to master
though it may look like (*Write* it!) like disaster. (RP 185)

Emotional 'disaster' is matched by formal 'mastery' here, and the parenthetical '*write it*' is a way of setting 'the balance *right*.' (185) So, if the lyric impulse begins in the articulation of enchanting, pleasurable sound (as in Dylan Thomas's early poetry) and the bold articulation of inner freedom and going beyond the limit (Marlowe and Wilde), it attains its full maturity in poetry that contains and shelters the sense of loss in a balanced configuration of sound. This 'major' Orphic voicing advances to 'that even more profoundly verifying point' where poetry not only helps us to enjoy life 'but helps us also to endure it.'[38]

III. 'ORPHEUS AND EURYDICE'

In his translation extract from Ovid's *Metamorphoses* X, Heaney maintains an ambivalent tone, varying between Virgil's pathos and Ovid's pragmatism and

---

35. RP 164–85 (165). Delivered December 1992; published 9/10 in RP.
36. RP 171. Cf. Segal, 'Rilke sometimes phrases this paradoxical essence of Orpheus in terms of a tension between "monument" and "metamorphosis"' (1989), 127.
37. Cf. Robert Harrison, *Dominion* (2003), 37–54, and on Orpheus, 150–1.
38. RP 185. Heaney's line about art helping us to endure life paraphrases Dr Johnson, who is also quoted by Auden, as an example of Prospero's art, in his essay on Robert Frost (*Dyer's Hand*, 239).

brisker narrative pace. For Heaney, the lovers' fatal romance is an example of poetry labouring in a minor key, charming its audience and naïvely attempting to transcend mortal limit. The first suggestion of this approach is given in the opening lines, where Orpheus' summons of the marriage god is made to sound like Prospero calling for Ariel in the first scene of *The Tempest*. The poet's name is the first word of the translation, which immediately gives him a commanding presence. And then Hymen rushes to do his bidding with the directness and energy of Shakespeare's island spirit:

> Inde per immensum croceo uelatus amictu
> aethera digreditur Ciconumque Hymenaeus ad oras
> tendit et Orphea nequiquam uoce uocatur. (*Meta*.X.1–3)

> Orpheus called for Hymen and Hymen came
> Robed in saffron like a saffron flame
> Leaping across tremendous airy zones
> To reach the land of the Ciconians. (MV, p. 15)

In the third line, Heaney's 'tremendous' is generated from the sound of '*immensum*' (X.1), but 'Leaping' and 'airy' (for '*tendit*' and '*aethera*') are equally inspired by Prospero and Ariel's opening exchange.[39] Orpheus calls for Hymen, and Hymen is immediately present, robed in saffron that is like saffron fire; these verbal repetitions suggest the power of Orpheus to shape reality according to his will.

Shortly afterwards, Eurydice steps on a poisonous snake and dies, and Orpheus seems unravelled by her death. But his music remains as potent as ever. At the equivalent point in *Georgics IV*, Virgil hears Orpheus singing his most enchanting, plangent song:

> ipse caua solans aegrum testudine amorem
> te, dulcis coniunx, te solo in litore secum,
> te ueniente die, te decedente canebat. (G.IV.464–6)

> He solacing his bitter love with his hollow lyre [literally, 'shell'], sang of you, sweet wife, of you to himself on the solitary shore, you with the coming, you with the falling of day. (my trans.)

Virgil heightens the emotional affect by addressing Eurydice on behalf of Orpheus. His invocation has a sympathetic, Orphic sonority, with the triple repetition of the vocative '*te*', the syntactic symmetry, and the chiming internal rhymes of '*ueni<u>ente</u> die . . . dec<u>ed</u>ente*'. And by describing the song rather than reporting its content directly, Virgil invites the reader to imagine a music even more sublime, which surpasses the limits of verbal representation.

---

39. Prospero: 'Approach, my Ariel. Come!' Ariel: '. . . I come / To answer thy best pleasure; be't to fly, / To swim, to dive into the fire, to ride / On the curled clouds. To thy strong bidding task' (*The Tempest* I.i.188–92).

Ovid imitates Virgil's affective syntax later, in connection with the death of Orpheus himself (*Meta*.XI.44–5). But here he undercuts the Virgilian pathos and more briskly relates,

Quam satis ad superas postquam Rhodopeius auras
defleuit uates, ne non temptaret et umbras, (*Meta*.X.11–12)

When the Rhodopeian seer had wept over her enough in the upper world, he did not hesitate to try the shadows as well (my trans.)

In Segal's reading, '*quam satis*' ('when [he had wept] enough') is intended to be humorous, showing how Ovid 'deliberately dissolves the "high ethos" of Virgil into lower terms' (58, 54). Later, when Ovid has Orpheus say '*uicit Amor*' ('in the end Love won'),[40] he is quoting Virgil's famous line, '*omnia uincit Amor et nos cedamus Amori*' ('Love conquers all, and we all yield to Love').[41] But Ovid's Orpheus immediately brings this divine '*amor*' down to earth by associating it with Hades' rape of Persephone (*Meta*.X.28).

Heaney, in turn, restores the Virgilian pathos of this passage, reserving his biting satirical tone for the Merriman translation. Going further, he identifies with the mourning Orpheus, invoking a parallel with the mad Irish King Sweeney:[42]

Orpheus mourned her in the world above,
Raving and astray, until his love
Compelled him down among the very shades. (MV 15)

Even in this sympathetic portrait, though, there is a touch of mockery (and self-mockery) in the description of Orpheus as 'raving and astray'. This elegiac love is far from what Rilke would call 'angelic' consciousness.[43] Instead, Heaney's translation grants Orpheus a lyric power comparable to Thomas's early poetry, aurally enchanting but not yet fully answerable to the 'suffered world' beyond his own private grief. Thus, 'among the shadow people', Orpheus 'plucked the lyre-gut for its melodies / And sang in harmony'.[44] In *After Ovid*, Heaney emends this line to 'tuned the lyre-gut to its own sweetness', which underlines his notion of the spontaneous autonomy of lyric and also its potential solecism.[45]

40. *Meta*.X.26, MV 16.
41. Virgil, *E*.10.69.
42. Heaney's translation of the Irish saga, *Buile Suibhne*, is entitled *Sweeney Astray* (1983).
43. "'there is neither a here nor a beyond, but a great unity, in which those creatures that surpass us, the "angels", are at home.'" (Heaney, quoting Rilke, *RP* 140)
44. Heaney, MV 15–16, translating: '*umbrarum dominum, pulsisque ad carmina neruis*' (*Meta*.X.16).
45. *After Ovid* (1994), 222. Cf. his description of Mandelstam as 'a woodcutter singing at his work in the dark wood of the larynx' (*FK* 179). From the version published in *The Midnight Verdict* to that published in *After Ovid*, Heaney introduced about half a dozen emendations. These all occur in 'Orpheus and Eurydice': 'Raving' (MV 15) > 'Lamenting' (*After Ovid*, 222); 'Ghosts of the dead' (MV 15) > 'Ghosts of the buried' (AO 222); 'plucked the lyre-gut for its melodies' (MV 15) > 'tuned the lyre-gut to its own sweetness' (AO 222); 'Scaresome voids and

Having crossed into Hades, Orpheus pleads for Eurydice's life in the presence of the King and assembled spirits of the underworld. Ovid so exaggerates the impact of his singing that, as Segal puts it, it 'verges on the ridiculous' (61). Its exaggerated impact is also comically at odds with the words Orpheus actually delivers. Ovid introduces his speech with '*ait*', meaning 'said' rather than 'sang' (Meta.X.17). He then proceeds to argue his case with the canniness of a seasoned rhetorician. At times, he sounds elaborately laboured (X.20–2), at times direct and sincere (X.24–5), and at times explicitly litigious (X.37). But Ovid's Orpheus is never the singing nightingale to whom Virgil famously compares the grieving poet (G.IV.511f.).

In Heaney's translation, the impact of Orpheus' song is that of an enchanting lyricist singing in a minor key (minor, in both senses). Once again, the situation invokes parallels with *The Tempest* and the effect of Ariel's music on the shipwrecked crew:

> nec Tantalus undam
> captauit refugam, stupuitque Ixionis orbis,
> ... inque tuo sedisti, Sisyphe, saxo. (Meta.X.41–2, 44)

> Tantalus
> Was so bewitched he let the next wave fill
> And fall without reaching. Ixion's wheel
> Stood spellbound ...
> And Sisyphus, you dozed upon your rock
> Which stood dazed also. (MV 17)

But as in Ovid's text, Heaney's Orpheus is less than enchanting in his actual words. He sounds legalistic, and what's more, he invokes Heaney's own notion of 'crediting poetry' in an unconvincing way. He concludes his song, or speech, by arguing:

> pro munere poscimus usum.
> quod si fata negant ueniam pro coniuge, certum est
> nolle redire mihi; leto gaudete duorum.' (Meta.X.37–9)

> I desire on sufferance
> And want my wife. But if the fates pronounce
> Against this privilege, then you can take
> Credit for two deaths. I shall not go back.' (MV 17)

The formal, stilted expression, 'desire on sufferance', conveys something of the legalese in Ovid's phrase, '*pro munere poscimus usum*' (literally, 'we request the use, or loan [of our wife], as a gift'). And by placing 'I' at the start of two sentences, Heaney adds a touch of egotism to his final words. For Ovid's ironic '*gaudete*' ('you may

> mist-veiled silences' (MV 16) > 'Dark hazy voids and scaresome silences' (AO 223); 'Olenos ... Lethea' (MV 18) > 'Olenus ... Lethaea' (AO 224). To my knowledge, 'The Death of Orpheus' is the same in both editions.

rejoice'), Heaney substitutes the notion of taking 'credit' for death, which seems like a self-mocking twist on Heaney's claim to credit poetry for its truth to life (OG 449). In the Merriman trial, the Irish poet will stand accused on the same terms: 'Where is the credit you've earned with us?' (MV 32). Orpheus' defiant-sounding 'I shall not go back' also rings hollow because we know that, very shortly, he will be forced to do just that. In this first trial of his art, then, Heaney's Orpheus fails to deliver poetic redress in its most potent, persuasive form.

After the second death of Eurydice, Virgil sustains the extreme pitch of the poet's grief right through to his own death. To lose Eurydice is to lose himself, as Milton's Adam would have said. Anticipating Aeneas' *ter conatus*, Virgil's Orpheus grasps after her dissolving shade, but she is already a ghost, cold and afloat on Charon's barge (G.IV.500–6). He mourns her loss for seven months at the riverside, before retreating to the 'Hyperborean glacial peaks', where eventually the poet is discovered by the violent band of maenads (517). By contrast, Ovid, in his strongest revisionary gesture, reduces the extremity of Orpheus' response. First, he compares Orpheus' initial shock to that of a man turned to stone by the sight of Cerberus. The comparison to an unnamed bystander is comic, verging on grotesque:

> Non aliter stupuit gemina nece coniugis Orpheus,
> quam tria qui Stygii, medio portante catenas,
> colla canis uidit; (Meta.X.64–6)

Then, Ovid shortens his seven months of mourning to seven days of fasting and three months of celibacy, after which Orpheus turns to sex with young boys (rather than 'the only bride . . . a boy', as Heaney chastely renders Meta.X.84–5).

In translating the passage above, however, Heaney expands on Ovid's verb '*stupuit*', to reinject the scene of loss with Virgil's emotional intensity:

> The second death stunned Orpheus. He stood
> Disconsolate, beyond himself, dumbfounded
> Like the man who turned to stone because he'd seen
> Hercules lead Cerberus on a chain, (MV 18)

The second line, not in Ovid, recalls the world-shattering loss experienced by Virgil's Orpheus. It is this version of absolute, transformative loss that Virgil replays in the *Aeneid*, first in reference to Aeneas' loss of his wife, Creusa. Failing to look back, Aeneas loses his wife in the midst of escaping from Troy. When he goes back to find her, he meets her ghost instead. At the sight of her, as he relates, '*Obstipui, steteruntque comae et uox faucibus haesit.*' ('I was stunned, my hair stood on end and the voice stuck in my throat.' Ae.II.774, my trans.) Orpheus is 'beyond himself, dumbfounded' because he sees for the first time that his art cannot transcend death. A similar chill of mortality overcomes Milton's Adam when he learns that Eve has eaten the forbidden fruit; he, 'amazed, / Astonied stood and blank, while horror chill / Ran through his veins and all his joints relaxed' (PL.IX.889–91). In *The Midnight Verdict*, this tragic premonition of Orpheus' mortality hangs in the air, while Heaney digresses into comic mode with his translation of Merriman's *Cúirt an Mheán-Oíche* (MV 21–34).

IV. 'THE DEATH OF ORPHEUS'

The suspension of the classical tragedy is entirely in keeping with the 'snake pit' structure of Ovid's *Metamorphoses*, in which many mythic tales are interwoven.[46] In *Metamorphoses* X, Orpheus, having lost Eurydice, proceeds to narrate a long series of love stories which fill the next 650 lines of the book. In the opening of Book XI, we hear that he has been enchanting beasts and trees with these stories, while wandering in the mountains of Thrace (XI.1–3). For Heaney, this is 'minor' art compared to Orpheus' major work of civilising and harmonising human society.[47] When the underworld shades take pity on Orpheus because 'song had made them human' (a phrase Heaney adds to the Latin), we have a foreshadowing of his major art (MV 17). When set upon by the Ciconian women (*'matres'* in Virgil, *'nurus'* or daughters-in-law in Ovid), Orpheus fails to harmonise the hostile crowd because his harp and voice are drowned out by their noise (G.IV.520; Meta.XI.3). The drowning of poetic sound anticipates the actual drowning of severed head and harp in the River Hebrus.

The maenads' violence is sexually motivated in both Virgil and Ovid's accounts, and Heaney's pairing of the myth with the Irish material underlines this theme. Heaney rather jarringly translates the maenads' accusatory epithet for Orpheus, *'nostri contemptor'* ('the man who scorns us'), as 'Orpheus the misogynist' (Meta.XI.7; MV 39). Both Virgil and Ovid portray Orpheus as a love poet undone by *furor* or passion for Eurydice, so the term 'misogynist' obviously does not apply. In Heaney's translation, the phrase is perhaps intended to forge a stronger connection to the trial of Merriman, who does stand accused on precisely that charge. After these opening lines, however, the gender conflict between male poet and female detractors is reconfigured as a binary opposition between solitary artist and crowd violence. The maenads come to represent the entropic force of history as 'No', as an 'immense panorama of violence and futility'.

This polar opposition is played out in *Metamorphoses XI* as a clash between patterned, rhythmic sound and discorded cacophony. In earlier treatments of the myth, Orpheus' enemies are similarly portrayed as cacophonous noisemakers, their disruption of musical harmony being far more threatening than their gender, which is often overlooked. When Milton portrays the death of Orpheus in 'Lycidas', he imagines the poet being destroyed by 'the rout that made the hideous roar' (60). And later, having himself survived political defeat and arrest after civil war, he invokes his muse to drive off:

---

46. Hofmann and Lasdun (1994), xii.
47. Orpheus' song is a civilising force, in Bacon's *De Sapientia Veterum* and Milton's prose tracts (see Falconer (1996), 23–4).

>   the barbarous dissonance
> Of Bacchus and his revellers, the race
> Of that wild rout that tore the Thracian bard
> In Rhodopè, where woods and rocks had ears
> To rapture, till the savage clamour drowned
> Both harp and voice; (*PL*.VII.32–7)

Here in *Paradise Lost*, the pun on 'rapture' contrasts the charm of song with the entropic force of 'savage clamour'. Heaney's rendition of the death of Orpheus sees the opposition in similar terms, with the poet's voice going unheard because of an overwhelming herd-noise, here a 'squealing' that represents the entropic force of political conflict (MV 40).[48]

Ovid's description of the lynching scene, moreover, introduces an element of theatrical performance, where Virgil had aimed for concentrated pathos. Thus, Ovid compares the beleaguered poet to an owl being bombarded by birds of prey, and then to a deer being torn apart by hounds in a Roman theatre (*Meta*.XI.23–7). The first simile ironically revises Virgil's comparison of Orpheus to a nightingale, while the second places the artist on trial in a public arena. The death inflicted on the 'stag that stands / in the amphitheatre early' is an orchestrated act of state-sanctioned violence (*Meta*.XI.26; MV 40). An episode set in the remote mountains of Thrace now suddenly looks like a scene taking place in Rome, which gives an added political dimension to the death of Ovid's Orpheus.

There is a similar shift into a major key in Heaney's translation of the death scene. The diction is restrained and almost monosyllabic, with distinct Biblical overtones:[49]

>   ad uatis fata recurrunt
> tendentemque manus atque in illo tempore primum
> inrita dicentem nec quidquam uoce mouentem
> sacrilegae perimunt, (*Meta*.XI.38–41)

>   then turned to rend the bard,
> Committing sacrilege when they ignored
> His hands stretched out to plead and the extreme
> Pitch of his song that now for the first time
> Failed to enchant. (MV 40)

---

48. 'One of the puns that interests me is to be found in the word 'herd / heard' . . . this goes to the very core of . . . the function of poetry in the public world. What you hear in the sanctum of yourself, that which strikes you as true, convinces you, steadies you, to provide that kind of heard melody is the function of poetry.' (Heaney, in conversation with Mike Murphy, in Ní Anluain and Kiberd, eds (2000), 92).
49. See Wheatley (2018) on the political dimensions of the language of sacrifice used in modern Irish depictions of Orpheus, including Heaney's.

The poet's suppliant gesture and 'extreme / Pitch of song' contrast with the confident, rhetorical performance of the poet in the earlier, minor episode in Hades. Heaney holds off the '*inrita*' until the end of the sentence, building the suspense before allowing the power of song to fail. Orpheus is here fulfilling Heaney's archetype of the poet *in extremis*, 'when the spirit is called extravagantly beyond the course that the usual life plots for it, when outcry or rhapsody is wrung from it' (RP 16).

While, in the examples considered in *The Redress of Poetry*, such moments of spiritual crisis produce a poet's greatest work, here Orpheus dies with his last outcry going unheard. But the death of the singer immediately activates the immanent potential of posthumous Orphic song. As 'the breath / Of life streamed out of him' it enters into the gathered host of mourners (MV 40). Ovid's birds and other animals, rocks, woods and rivers all take up his lament for Eurydice, with the triple vocative borrowed from Virgil: '*Te maestae uolucres, Orpheu, te turba ferarum, / te rigidi silices, . . . / fleuerent*' ('for you the mourning birds, Orpheus, for you the crowd of beasts, for you the flint rocks wept', *Meta*.XI.44–6, my trans.). Heaney's translation misses out the vocative address, so that a newly animated nature mourns Orpheus without calling him back: 'For Orpheus then the birds in cheeping flocks / The animals in packs, the flint-veined rocks / And woods that had listened . . . / Wept and kept weeping.' (MV 41) This translation effectively shifts the work of mourning from transcendence to immanence, since these creatures are not trying to overcome death but completing the natural cycle of life.

In both classical accounts of the myth, while the dismembered limbs of Orpheus remain scattered on the shore, the poet's head and lyre are swept down the River Hebrus and out to sea. Virgil abandons any semblance of realism in relating this most far-fetched detail of the legend. He has the decapitated head continue to call for Eurydice, and the riverbanks echo back the name in sympathy:

> Eurydicen uox ipsa et frigida lingua,
> a miseram Eurydicen! anima fugiente uocabat:
> Eurydicen toto referebant flumine ripae. (G.IV.525–7)

'Eurydice', his voice and cold tongue kept calling, with departing breath,
'O poor Eurydice!' 'Eurydice' the banks of the stream echoed all the way down. (my trans.)

Virgil's Proteus then breaks off his narration of the story and plunges back into the sea, leaving Aristaeus with the task of appeasing Orpheus' ghost and lifting the curse on his dying bees.

Ovid takes these Virgilian lines in the opposite direction, giving the head something inaudible ('*nescioquid*') to murmur as it is swept downstream:

> caput, Hebre, lyramque
> excipis, et (mirum!) medio dum labitur amne,
> flebile nescioquid queritur lyra, flebile lingua
> murmurat exanimis, respondent flebile ripae.' (*Meta*.XI.50–3)

His head and lyre you received, O Hebrus, and (by a miracle!) while they floated in mid-stream, the lyre wept something or other mournful, the lifeless tongue murmured mournfully, the banks mournfully replied.' (my trans.)

This triple repetition of '*flebile*' (mournfully) again recalls Virgil's repetition of '*Eurydicen*', even as it renders the name inaudible. But the lyre and 'lifeless tongue' of Orpheus still have a voice and they can still enchant the riverbank into sympathetic, human-like response.

In Heaney's translation, however, it is not the severed head that sings, but the water as it ripples between the open mouth and the riverbank. Again the 'miracle' is not that of transcendence but of human music finding an answerable song in the natural environment:

> But his head and lyre
> Were saved by a miracle: the Hebrus River
> Rose for them, ran with them, bore them out midstream
> Where the lyre trembled and the dead mouth swam
> Lapping the ripples that lipped the muddy shore
> And a fluent humming sadness filled the air. (MV 41)

In the third line above, Heaney's Hebrus River is notably more animated and active than Ovid's. And it is the river's own water that 'lips' the 'fluent humming sadness' in the air, a phrase Heaney adds to the Latin. Both the phrase itself and the pantheism of the entire passage recall the 'still, sad music of humanity' that Wordsworth hears on the banks of the River Wye in 'Tintern Abbey'.[50] Moreover, while the 'l' sounds of 'lapping', 'ripple', 'lipped' and 'fluent' may have been inspired by Ovid's '*flebile*', the word 'fluent' itself more specifically alludes to the '*confluere*' of bees, as they hum into life at the end of *Georgics IV*: '*iamque arbore summa / confluere et lentis uuam demittere ramis.*' ('the cloud of bees flow together and cluster under a bough of hanging grapes', G.IV.557–8) This suggests that Orpheus lives on in the regeneration of the natural world.[51]

The memory of Orphic song gives nature a language with which to express its sentient, sympathetic grief. With the complex interweaving of aural music ('-stream', 'trembled', 'swam'; 'lyre', 'lapping', 'air'), moreover, Heaney's translation enacts a formal reparation at the level of poetic sound. In his book-length translation of *Aeneid VI* (2016), Heaney will recall this passage when he describes the River Lethe 'Lapping those peaceful haunts' in the Elysian Fields, and the gathered shades

---

50. Wordsworth, 'Lines Written a Few Miles above Tintern Abbey', l. 92 (1992, 118). Sheats (1973, 220) and Averill (1980, 154), point out that Wordsworth's thinking about the 'one mind' is influenced by Anchises' speech (*Ae*.VI.724–8).
51. Bees have longstanding symbolic associations with poetry, and the specifically Yeatsian symbolism is discussed in Chapter 6. The original dust jacket of Heaney's *Spirit Level* (1996) features a beehive on its cover ('Detail of Bees from MS Ashmole 1511, fol. 75v', courtesy of the Bodleian Library, Oxford).

'Humming with life, like bees in meadows' (A.948–51). There he suggests that the natural cycle continually revives the finite, human song, making possible the ongoing conversation between the living and the dead.

This sad Orphic hum is also heard in the poem Miłosz sent from his deathbed to his friend Leon Wieseltier, 'Orpheus and Eurydice', written in memory of his late wife.[52] The poem ends with Orpheus losing consciousness to the sound of bees:

> It happened as he expected. He turned his head
> And behind him on the path was no one.
> Sun. And sky. And in the sky white clouds.
> Only now everything cried to him: Eurydice!
> How will I live without you, my consoling one!
> But there was a fragrant scent of herbs, the low humming of bees,
> And he fell asleep with his cheek on the sun-warmed earth.[53]

The 'low humming of bees' is an instance of the 'untranscendent music' Heaney celebrates in his elegy for Miłosz, 'Out of This World' (*DC* 51).

While Virgil reserves the comedic ending for his frame narrative of the beekeeper Aristaeus, Ovid incorporates the upward, comedic movement within the story of Orpheus and Eurydice itself. He produces a surprise happy ending for Orpheus in the underworld, as well as vengeance on his living enemies. In what Segal calls a tour-de-force (69), Ovid imagines the shade of Orpheus reuniting with his Eurydice after all:

> inuenit Eurydicen cupidisque amplectitur ulnis.
> hic modo coniunctis spatiantur passibus ambo,
> nunc praecedentem sequitur, nunc praeuius anteit
> Eurydicenque suam iam tuto respicit Orpheus. (*Meta*.XI.63–6)

> And when he found her, wound her in his arms
> And moved with her, and she with him, two forms
> Of the one love, restored and mutual –
> For Orpheus now walks free, is free to fall
> Out of step, into step, follow, go in front
> And look behind him to his heart's content. (*MV* 41–2)

With this emphasis on interlocking limbs and freely looking behind and ahead, Ovid answers back to the tragedy of Virgil's tale. Heaney responds with a free translation of Ovid, adding the internal assonance of 'found' and 'wound', and the idiomatic phrase, 'to his heart's content'. But his major addition to the Latin is the runover line, 'two forms / Of the one love, restored and mutual'. Here, he refers to Plato's idea, articulated by Aristophanes in the *Symposium*, that love attempts to reunite

---

52. The poem is quoted in Wieseltier's 'Czesław Miłosz' (2004).
53. Miłosz, 'Orpheus and Eurydice' (2011), 263.

the two halves of what was once a single, four-limbed body, prior to its severance by a jealous Zeus.⁵⁴ This Platonic union of Orpheus and Eurydice offers us a 'true figure of life', as it extends through the 'here' and 'beyond' (*RP* 140, quoting Rilke). Orpheus has overcome Hades' law, separating the living and the dead, and he also seems to have overcome the Christian division of the damned and the saved as well. Or, at least, in Orpheus' 'free to fall', there is a riposte implied to Milton's God, who protests, 'I made him just and right, / Sufficient to have stood, though free to fall' (*PL*.III.99–100). Formally speaking, the coupling of end-rhyme, the pairing of pronouns, parallel syntax and free use of alliteration all contribute to the aural sense of poetry 'complet(ing) the circle of one's being' in this passage (*RP* 9).

And yet, while Ovid pictures Orpheus reunited with Eurydice, it is a silent interlocking of limbs; the poet no longer sings in the underworld. The second life of art unfolds in mortal time, as Ovid returns us to the overworld for the last act of the Orpheus story. As Ovid relates, the angry mob is punished by Bacchus, who turns the women into trees. Ovid's depiction of the arboreal metamorphosis is a final piece of flamboyant theatre, demonstrating that everything living is subject to constant change. While it begins with the idea of vengeance, the crime ('*scelus*') against the seer of Bacchus' sacred rites ('*sacrorum uate suorum*') not going unavenged ('*non inpune*'), the sympathy of Ovid's epic narrator shifts midway to the women being punished (*Meta*.XI.67–8). Paradoxically, while they were less than human in their violent rage, they become most human when they are being transformed into trees:

> utque suum laqueis, quos callidus abdidit auceps,
> crus ubi commisit uolucris sensitque teneri,
> plangitur ac trepidans adstringit uincula motu,
> sic, ut quaeque solo defixa cohaeserat harum,
> exsternata fugam frustra temptabat; at illam
> lenta tenet radix exsultantemque coercet.
> dumque ubi sint digiti, dum pes ubi quaerit et ungues,
> aspicit in teretes lignum succedere suras
> et conata femur maerenti plangere dextra
> robora percussit; pectus quoque robora fiunt,
> robora sunt umeri, porrectaque bracchia ueros
> esse putes ramos - et non fallare putando. (*Meta*.XI.73–84)

> And, as a caught bird struggles to get free
> From a cunningly set snare, but still can only
> Tighten the mesh around its feet still tighter
> The more it strains its wings and frets and flutters,
> So each of the landlogged women heaved and hauled
> In vain, in agony, as the roots took hold
> And bark began to thicken the smooth skin.
> It gripped them and crept up above their knees.

---

54. Plato, *Symposium*, 189e–193e (ed. Lamb, 1991).

> They struggled like a storm in storm-tossed trees.
> Then, as each finger twigged and toe dug in,
> Arms turned to oak boughs, thighs to oak, oak leaves
> Matted their breasts and camouflaged their moves
> So that you couldn't tell if the whole strange growth
> Were a wood or women in distress or both. (MV 42)

Ovid compares each struggling figure to a trapped bird, thus linking their suffering to that of Orpheus when he is compared to an owl (*Meta*.XI.25) and a nightingale (G.IV.511). His close-up focus elicits sympathy for each Bacchante, and pity for the terror ('*exsternata*') she sees and feels ('*adspicit*', '*percussit*') as her limbs harden into oak ('*robora*' being repeated three times). In the last line, though, Ovid withdraws from both sympathy and judgement as he turns to address the reader directly: 'you would think her jointed arms were real branches, and in thinking so, you'd not be mistaken' (my trans.). The progression from '*putes*' ('you would think') to '*non fallare putando*' ('you'd not be mistaken') finalises the metamorphosis and confirms the change as irrevocable.

Arthur Golding's classic *Metamorphosis* (1567) adeptly conveys Ovid's sense of finality, with a final couplet of strong end-rhymes, underlined with the triple repetition of 'tree' (for '*robora*'):

> Shee felt them tree: her brest was tree: her shoulders eeke were tree.
> Her armes long boughes yee myght have thought, and not deceyved bee.[55]

Heaney's final couplet, by contrast, is far less definitive. The 'you' (whether the reader or narrator) is doubtful about what he is seeing, and the metamorphosis from 'women in distress' to 'wood' is not conclusively finalised. If this is a containment of the women's power, it is notably more ambiguous than Ovid's text or subsequent translations.[56] Compare, for example, Heaney's 'whole strange growth' to the pleasant Arcadian grove depicted in Samuel Garth's canonical, eighteenth-century *Metamorphoses*, where the translator, Samuel Croxall, glides smoothly from suffering to delight:

> A rugged bark their softer neck invades,
> Their branching arms shoot up delightful shades;
> At once they seem, and are, a real grove,
> With mossy trunks below, and verdant leaves above.[57]

---

55. The.XV.Bookes of P.Ouidius Naso, entytuled Metamorphosis, trans. Arthur Golding (1567).
56. For an alternative, highly critical, interpretation, see Coughlan (2007), 34 et passim.
57. *Ovid's Metamorphoses in Fifteen Books* (1717), ed. Garth. Cf. Andrew Marvell, 'The Gods, that mortal Beauty chase, / Still in a Tree did end their race: / Apollo hunted Daphne so, / Only that She might Laurel grow.' ('The Garden', ll. 27–30).

By contrast, Heaney sustains Ovid's shift of sympathy towards the women, right through to the final couplet. Their punishment is made to sound like an inversion of Orpheus' release, so that they become, in a sense, two aspects to the one circle of life: he 'when he found her [Eurydice], wound her in his arms / And moved with her' while 'in a web of roots, he [Bacchus] wound / And bound the offending women to the ground.' (MV 41, 42) If, at the beginning of *Metamorphoses* X, Heaney's Orpheus resembles Auden's Ariel as a symbol of the free, lyric imagination, then these 'landlogged women' resemble that same Ariel spirit, now constrained by Prospero's veteran knowledge of pain and conflict. 'The more it strains its wings and frets and flutters,' the more history binds each of these figures to the ground (MV 42). But the inconclusiveness of Heaney's metamorphosis suggests the struggle is ongoing, and the women's 'camouflaged ... moves' allow for the possibility of a stealthy comeback.

While Orpheus is, for Heaney, the classical archetype of the poet fallen victim to political violence, the durable Orphic song is the sympathising impulse of art, which seeks to comprehend the whole picture, the perpetrator's and the victim's, the light and the dark. His phrase 'strange growth' has the paradoxical double-sidedness of '*hospes*' (meaning both friend and stranger). And this wood of women in distress recall Virgil's Polydorus, transformed into a tree and discovered by Aeneas, in Orpheus' home ground of Thrace. When Aeneas tries to tear off a branch (a precursor to the golden bough), the tree cries out, '*parce pias scelerare manus. non me tibi Troia / externum tulit aut cruor hic de stipite manat.*' ('cease to wound me with your pious hands. Troy bore me, so I am not a stranger to you, nor does my blood flow from wood.' Ae.III.42–3) Upon hearing the tree speak, Aeneas decides to leave the place at once, after conducting burial rites for his murdered kinsman.[58] Similarly, there is little of alien otherness, '*externum*', in the 'strange growth' of Heaney's last two lines. The form of the couplet itself is pressed to encompass the perspectives of both sides of the conflict. Rhyming 'growth' with 'both' allows us to read this ending as 'both' a conclusion for Orpheus and a beginning for future Ariels, seeking their liberation in turn.

*

When Heaney puts poetry on trial in *The Redress of Poetry*, he imagines a 'court of appeal' that will answer back to Plato and other sceptics who would banish it from a free commonwealth (*RP* 1). As his translation of the *Metamorphoses* shows, one of the strengths of Orphic poetry is its ability to sympathise and shift ground to the perspective of the other. The development of such imaginative arts bodes well, as he claims in his final essay in *The Redress*, 'for the evolution of a political order, one tolerant of difference and capable of metamorphoses within all the multivalent

---

58. Dante draws on the image of Virgil's Polydorus in his description of the wood of suicides, where a thornbush bleeds when the pilgrim snaps off a twig from its branch: '*Perché mi scerpi? / non hai tu spirto di pietade alcuno?* ('Why do you tear me? Have you no spirit of pity?' *Inf*.XIII.35–7, trans. Singleton).

possibilities of Irishness, Britishness, Europeanness, planetariness, creatureliness, whatever.' (*RP* 200) Forming an important bridge between his *Aeneid* translations and his Virgilian eclogues, Heaney's Orphic song laments for loss while also affirming the circle of life, a 'No' contained within a greater 'Yes'.

4. Pastoral, *Pietas* and Stealth

In the mid-1990s, Heaney began experimenting with pastoral, composing a series of Arcadian sonnets and three Virgilian eclogues which would eventually be collected in his millennial volume, *Electric Light* (2001). His dialogue with the *Eclogues* is further developed in a number of essays, lectures and interviews which argue for the staying power of pastoral poetry in general. Reading Alpers's magisterial study, *What is Pastoral?* (1997), encouraged Heaney to view these country poems as part of a wide-ranging literary tradition encompassing many different subgenres, from comedy to elegy, and naïve to dark, postlapsarian pastoral.[1] Heaney's Virgilian eclogues, composed just after the Good Friday Agreement of 1998, explore the possibilities of peace within a culture already acclimatised to violence.[2] His lectures and essays are written within the context of a darker political climate, with increased military conflict following the terrorist attacks of 9/11.[3] Pastoral comes to represent the ultimate test case for poetry as it attempts to reconcile art's two conflicting impulses or demands: the impulse towards the free play of imagination (Ariel's 'covenant with beauty') and the ethical imperative to oppose the 'brutality of the historical onslaught' (Prospero's 'covenant with truth').[4]

---

1. Heaney, 'Eclogues *in Extremis*: On the Staying Power of Pastoral' (2003), 5, citing Alpers (1997). On modern forms of 'post'-pastoral, see Gifford, 'Evolving Pastoral', in *Pastoral*, 2nd edn (2019).
2. On Heaney's Virgilian eclogues, see also Burris (1991), Tyler (2005), Moi (2007), Homem (2009), O'Donoghue, 'Heaney's Classics and the Bucolic', (2009), Potts (2011), Twiddy (2012). On 'Eclogue IX', see also Heiny (2018), O'Hogan (2018), 403–4, Putnam (2010), Washizuka (2011). On 'Bann Valley Eclogue', see Bloomer (2005), S. J. Harrison (2008).
3. Heaney, 'Lux Perpetua' (2001), 'Time and Again: Poetry and the Millennium' (2001), 'On Elegies, Eclogues, Translations, Transfusions' (2001), 'Towers, Trees, Terrors, a Rêverie in Urbino' (delivered 2001), 'The Whole Thing: On the Good of Poetry' (2002), 'Staying Power' (Harvard lecture, 2002), 'Eclogues *in Extremis*' (2003). In 2002, Heaney also delivered three Tanner Lectures on Human Values at Cambridge University, one of which was on Virgil's *Eclogues*, but the lectures are unpublished to date.
4. Heaney, 'Sounding Auden' (GT 107, 110).

In an early version of 'Bann Valley Eclogue', published in 1999, Heaney praises Virgil for 'holding your own / In your own way. *Pietas* and stealth.'[5] To my knowledge, this is the first time Heaney attributes the celebrated *pietas* of Aeneas to Virgil himself. And it signals his much closer identification with Virgil's life history (or what little is known of it) during this period of intense preoccupation with pastoral verse.[6] Published in the late 30s BCE, Virgil's *Eclogues* were composed during a turbulent period in Roman history. Having defeated the tyrannicides (murderers of Julius Caesar) at the Battle of Actium in 42 BCE, Octavian Augustus rewarded his soldiers with confiscated land, which led to a further escalation of violence and an attempt at containment with the Treaty of Brundisium in 40 BCE. Legend has it that Virgil's father's farm near Mantua was among the estates confiscated, although the decision was later revoked. Modern scholars now approach the *Eclogues* as autonomous works of fiction rather than veiled autobiography.[7] But within their literary, Theocritean frame, the ten eclogues do address the subject of the recent land confiscations, and *Eclogues* I and IX are voiced by pairs of herdsmen whose lives have been radically altered as a result of the Augustan resettlement scheme. And for Heaney, it is an important aspect of their covenant with truth that Virgil's *Eclogues* have their basis in the poet's lived experience, 'in his own deadly Roman times'.[8] Heaney's 2001 address to the Royal Academy focuses on *Eclogues* I and IX in particular, linking both poems to the legend of Virgil's father's eviction. He considers whether Tityrus' praise of Augustus in *Eclogues* I might even be regarded as 'propaganda on Virgil's part' insofar as it is 'paying tribute to the emperor Octavian and thanking him for having restored his father's estates.'[9] But the eclogue also allows the unfortunate shepherd Meliboeus to complain of having been arbitrarily evicted. Thus, Heaney concludes, *Eclogues* I 'passes . . . the honesty test' because it 'still keeps harsh reality in mind' (ibid.).

In an early review, Heaney had distinguished two separate poetic traditions, 'rural' as opposed to 'pastoral' verse, and his strong preference was for the former.[10] By the time he came to engage closely with Virgil's *Eclogues*, however, he saw the two traditions as closely intertwined. Indeed, it has been argued that classical 'bucolics' were originally a mixed mode, combining fantasy and realism; only later was pastoral associated with an idealised state of innocence.[11] While Theocritus rarely

---

5. Heaney, 'Bann Valley Eclogue', *Times Literary Supplement* (1999), 32.
6. In 'Towers, Trees, Terrors' (2001), Heaney reiterates that, of his favourite trio of Roman poets (Virgil, Livy, Horace), Virgil 'is the most like his dutiful hero, the *pius Aeneas*.' (154)
7. For an overview of scholarship on Virgil's *Eclogues*, see Volk (2008). On the life of Virgil, see Peter Levi (1997) and Ziolkowski and Putnam (2008).
8. 'Eclogues *in Extremis*', 2.
9. 'Eclogues *in Extremis*', 4.
10. Heaney, 'In the Country of Convention', in *Preoccupations* (1980), 173–80, reviewing Barrell and Bull (1975).
11. Volk (2008), 8. Conversely, many critics of the English literary tradition view pastoral as 'wedded to outmoded models of harmony and balance' (Garrard (2011), 65). On the Greek term 'bucolics', see Suetonius's *Life of Virgil*: 'there are three kinds of herdsmen that have standing in things pastoral. The least of these are called aipoloi [goatherds] . . . Somewhat

names real people or events in his *Idylls*, Virgil often brings characteristics of the Mantuan countryside into his literary Arcadia, and amongst his stock-named shepherds we also find allusions to actual poets of his day.[12] The *Eclogues'* very mixture of elaborate artistry and plain, country realism is, in fact, what Heaney comes to admire most about them: 'it's as if the ideal landscapes of *Les Très Riches Heures du Duc de Berry* were encroached upon by a couple of hard-wrought, hard-bitten countrymen from the more realistic and relentless world of Peter Brueghel.'[13]

Paul Alpers argues that 'we will have a far truer idea of pastoral if we take its representative anecdote to be herdsmen and their lives, rather than landscape or idealized nature.' (22) The reason for this, Alpers suggests, is that 'in their simplicity and vulnerability, shepherds fittingly represent those whose lives are determined by the actions of powerful men or by events and circumstances over which they have no control.' (24) Heaney concurs entirely with Alpers's view of pastoral when he argues that the *Eclogues* are about 'the troubles that farmers must face in contemporary Italy. Eviction, expropriation, refugee status overnight.'[14] While seeming to praise Augustus in *Eclogues I*, Virgil is also laying bare the 'power of Rome and the brutal might of the legions', which proves to be 'as arbitrary as it is irresistible. . . . One man is struck by misfortune, the next, for no reason, is immune.'[15] Alpers further observes that pastoral poems very often take place on a country lane or road, as a sign of the vulnerable, itinerant status of the herdsmen singing the songs.[16] Invoking Bakhtin, we could identify the country road as the dominant chronotope of pastoral, where it functions as the time and 'space for exchanging conversation and song.'[17]

The *Eclogues* are intricately crafted, with phrases and images recurring in symmetrical patterns across the series of ten poems. The same shepherds appear in different poems and in different relationships, while in each poem the paired songs complement each other in length and structure. As Wendell Clausen notes, the 'Book of *Eclogues*' was conceived as a unified whole, even though individual poems had been composed for separate occasions.[18] While he values their truth to harsh reality, Heaney also admires the *Eclogues* for their sheer, self-delighting artistry. They are, he writes, 'a kind of Crystal Palace, beautifully structured and strong

more esteemed are melonomoi poimenes [sheepgrazing herdsmen] . . . The greatest and best-esteemed are the boukoloi [oxen-drivers]' (Ziolokowski and Putnam, eds (2008), 19).
12. Clausen (1994), xix. Varius and Cinna are contemporary Roman poets, named in *Eclogue IX*. On Virgil's dialogue with Theocritus, see Clausen (1982, 1994).
13. BBC (2008). Heaney makes the same comparison in his admiring review of Peter Fallon's translation of Virgil's *Georgics* ('"Glory be to the World"', 2004).
14. '*Eclogues in Extremis*', 2.
15. '*Eclogues in Extremis*', 2–3.
16. Alpers (1997), 5.
17. Bakhtin (1981, 86) defines 'chronotope' as the representation of 'time-space' in literature, and chronotopic images as those highlighting 'the intrinsic connectedness of temporal and spatial relationships'. For Alpers, pastoral is 'fictionally and metaphorically a space for exchanging conversation and song' (1997, 5).
18. Clausen (1982), 209. See also R. G. M. Nisbet, 'The Style of Virgil's *Eclogues*', in Volk (2008), 48–63.

because of inner relationships and symmetries'.[19] Reading David Ferry's 1999 translation, Heaney is reminded of the 'beauty of these poems and their strangeness'.[20] In their intricate weave, concentrated clarity and resilient wholeness, Virgil's *Eclogues* are in some sense a showcase for the virtue or haleness of poetry in general. Thus, Heaney argues, poetry 'has virtue, in the first sense of possessing a quality of moral excellence and in the sense also of possessing inherent strength by reason of its sheer made-upness, its *integritas, consonantia* and *claritas.*'[21]

Much as he admires their crystalline structure and symmetry, however, Heaney does not attempt anything like Ferry's complete translation of the whole 'Book of *Eclogues*'.[22] His three eclogues are not interlinked by any structural *integritas*. Indeed, they are markedly dissimilar. 'Bann Valley Eclogue' is an intertextual response to Virgil's *Eclogues IV*; the translation of *Eclogues IX* attempts a 'faithful rendering' of the originary Latin; and 'Glanmore Eclogue' is a semi-autobiographical 'transfusion' of *Eclogues I*, newly embedded in a contemporary Irish context.[23] 'Bann Valley' features in the opening section of *Electric Light*, while 'Virgil: Eclogues IX' and 'Glanmore Eclogue' are paired in reverse order of composition, half-way through Part I (*EL* 11, 31, 35).[24] While the Latin translation seems the most 'foreignising', the most distanced from Heaney's immediate historical circumstances, of the three eclogues it is the one he comes to identify with most closely. Some years later, he describes the translation as 'a poet's *apologia pro vita mea* over the previous thirty years.'[25] Its subject is no less than 'the frail but vitally necessary work of poetry in a time of violence' (ibid.). On the evidence of these three compositions, what Heaney values most about Virgil's *Eclogues* is not so much their sophisticated, cross-hatched *integritas*, as the '*pietas* and stealth' of their pastoral voice. In these ten slight poems, traditionally the lowest step on the Virgilian *cursus honorum*, Heaney hears the voice of a 'young poet coming back with an almost vindictive artistry against the actual conditions of the times'.[26] He turns to Virgil's *Eclogues* in the late

---

19. 'Eclogues *in Extremis*', 6.
20. Heaney, 'On Elegies' (2001), 25, alluding to a new translation that triggered his own engagement with the *Eclogues*. David Ferry's translation is quoted in 'Eclogues *in Extremis*'. Ferry's introduction cites Clausen's commentary, and praises the 'Book of *Eclogues*' as an intricate, harmonious whole (1999, x).
21. SS 467, quoting Augustine; plus 'Eclogues *in Extremis*', 7; and again, 'its sheer and clear made-upness' in 'Articulations' (2008), 19. For the 'haleness' of poetry, see Heaney, 'The Whole Thing' (2002).
22. His last volume, *The Last Walk* (2013), does translate an entire cycle of Italian songs, Pascoli's *Myricae*. See Falconer, 'Heaney, Pascoli and the Ends of Poetry' (2019).
23. Heaney, 'Mossbawn via Mantua' (2012), describes his translation of *E IX* as 'a faithful rendering', 21. Dryden, in *Preface to the Fables* (1700), uses the term 'transfusion' for the process by which 'another writer transfuses himself or his gifts or his voice into yours' (quoted by Heaney, 'On Elegies' (2001), 27).
24. In 'On Elegies', Heaney identifies the composition order: 'BV', 'GE' then 'Virgil: Eclogues IX' (2001, 25).
25. Heaney, 'Mossbawn via Mantua' (2012), 22.
26. Heaney, SS 389. Traditionally, the three tiers of the Virgilian *cursus honorum* are (1) pastoral, (2) georgic and (3) epic. On *Eclogues* as the first tier, see Volk (2008), 3.

1990s, then, to articulate his own forms of comeback against actual conditions, and to mount his own *apologia* for a poet's life.

Heaney's relation to more modern literary exemplars, from Dante, Wordsworth and Hopkins to Yeats, Eliot, Lowell and others, has received considerable scholarly attention, while the exemplarity of Virgil and other classical authors has been largely overlooked.[27] Neil Corcoran argues that, for Heaney, '"exemplary" . . . compounds a moral and an aesthetic judgement: it implies the poet's life as well as his work . . . is in some sense accountable, available to scrutiny, proposed as pattern and imitation.'[28] With this definition in mind, it seems beyond question that, in the late 1990s, Heaney turns to Virgil as a major literary exemplar whose life, as well as work, could fortify his own poetic labours. Virgil's Latinity, in addition to his combination of country origins and literary sophistication ('very much the learned poets' poet'), made him particularly hospitable to the Catholic, Northern Irish, grammar school-educated Heaney.[29]

After receiving the Nobel Prize for Literature in 1995, Heaney was very soon exposed to the full glare of international celebrity. Finding ways to meet his new, global responsibilities, Heaney also sought cover for his independent, creative life.[30] For Heaney, Virgil's '*pietas* and stealth' suggests ways of 'holding your own' under pressure of difficult circumstances. In the *Eclogues*, Virgil's *pietas* manifests itself in an undisguised affection for the Mantuan countryside and sense of attachment to its rural community. His 'stealth', on the other hand, lies in the careful orchestration of opposing points of view, so that no single singer could be identified with Virgil himself. As Alpers observes, the ninth eclogue has provoked an 'almost comical division of critical opinion' on the question of Virgil's own stance, whether pro- or anti-Octavian, whether hopeful or pessimistic about the unstable political situation.[31] Virgil's obliquity evidently impressed Heaney for it produced an answerable style in his own pastoral poems. The 'staying power' of pastoral is asserted more confidently and overtly in Heaney's lectures and essays, to which we will turn below.[32] But we should begin by considering the three eclogues in turn, since each in its own way offers a stealthy form of resistance to actual, historical conditions.

---

27. For example, Cavanagh (2009) and Dennison (2015), both excellent studies of Heaney's poetics, but they make little or no mention of Virgil.
28. N. Corcoran (1987), 118.
29. 'Eclogues *in Extremis*', 3.
30. Heaney, 'On Elegies' (2001), 29.
31. Alpers (1979), 136; qtd by Heiny (2018), 54. Heiny explores the mixture of optimism and pessimism in *Eclogues IX* and Heaney's translation (2018), esp. 62, 58. Virgil's 'stealth' is also perhaps intended to recall the 'hazel stealth' of ST 69.
32. O'Donoghue, 'Heaney's Classics and the Bucolic', (2009), also observes that the poems seem less confident than the essays 'that poetry can help – that it can offer "redress"' (106). Heiny (2018) responds that 'Eclogues *in Extremis*' offers an optimistic response to balance the pessimism of the *Eclogues IX* translation (58, 62).

1. 'BANN VALLEY ECLOGUE'

Heaney's 'Bann Valley Eclogue' was first published on the eve of the new millennium, with part of the poem aired on BBC Radio's 'Thought for the Day' and the full text published in the December 1999 edition of the *Times Literary Supplement*.[33] The poem consists of a dialogue between 'Virgil' and an unnamed but semi-autobiographical Poet. Quoting lines from Virgil's prophetic *Eclogues IV*, the two speakers speculate about the possibility of a coming Golden Age. Heaney's poem is therefore consciously addressed to a broad, public audience, on the occasion of an epochal moment in the world's history. In interview, he mentions a number of other factors contributing to the composition of his Virgilian eclogue: the unexpected birth of a great-niece, his own sixtieth birthday in April 1999, a total solar eclipse in August of the same year (the death of Julius Caesar was marked by a solar eclipse), and a recent visit to Greece (in fact, he was in Arcadia when he heard he had won the Nobel Prize).[34] But he does not mention the most significant and obvious parallel between Virgil's *Eclogues IV* and his own 'Bann Valley Eclogue': that they were both written in the aftermath of a peace agreement promising to bring an end to sectarian military conflict.

Virgil's fourth eclogue famously conjures the vision of a *pacatum orbem*, a 'world brought to peace' by the birth of a miraculous child. His readers would have recognised the fictional child as the infant boy hoped for and expected from the marriage of Antony and Octavia, sister of Octavian Augustus.[35] Their marriage sealed the Pact of Brundisium in 40 BCE, which was to have ended the war between Octavian and Antony, following the murder of Julius Caesar. *Eclogues IV*, addressed to the Consul Pollio, is thought to have been composed as an epithalamium in celebration of this political marriage.[36] Unlike the other eclogues, this one is voiced by a solitary speaker, who declares that the Golden Age foretold by the Cumaean Sibyl has finally dawned. The Sicilian muses of Theocritus, invoked in the first line, are to expand their pastoral repertoire to include matter drawn from Hesiod, Aratus and the Jewish sibylline oracles.

Heaney's 'Bann Valley Eclogue' in turn celebrates the birth of an Irish child, whose arrival may augur a new era of peace.[37] In an essay published more than a decade after the poem's publication, Heaney describes 'Bann Valley' as 'a millennium poem set in post-ceasefire Ireland'.[38] He cites this poem, together with his translation of *Eclogues IX*, as a response to a contemporary historical crisis, and his

---

33. Heaney, 'Bann Valley Eclogue', *Times Literary Supplement* (8 October 1999), 32. For MS of BBC Radio 4 'Thought for the Day' (aired September 1999), see *LP* I.xv.10.
34. Heaney, 'On Elegies' (2001), 25. Heaney refers to 'a niece' in the essay, but more particularly, it was a great-niece (with thanks to Catherine Heaney).
35. Clausen (1994), 121.
36. For the political background and literary antecedents, see Clausen (1994), 119f.
37. The baby whose birth is celebrated in the eclogue is grand-daughter to Heaney's brother, Colm (with thanks to Catherine Heaney).
38. Heaney, 'Mossbawn via Mantua' (2012), 21.

own way of 'approaching terror via Holyhead'.[39] The Good Friday Agreement, consisting of a multi-party accord between most of Northern Ireland's political parties, and an international agreement between the British and Irish governments over the governance of Northern Ireland, the relationship between Northern Ireland and the Republic of Ireland, and between the Republic and the UK, was signed in Belfast on 10 April 1998. While it was composed in the wake of this historical ceasefire, 'Bann Valley Eclogue' makes no explicit mention of the Agreement. Instead, Heaney approaches the subject via a pastoral exchange with 'Virgil', in which the two poets remember the confiscation of Virgil's family estate by veteran soldiers returning home from war. In the course of their dialogue, 'Virgil' expresses a cautious optimism about the newly brokered peace in the Poet's world and hopes for a better future for the new-born infant.

In the opening lines of *Eclogues IV*, Virgil's pastoral singer is initially diffident about launching into a prophecy of world peace. He invokes the Muses' help to sing of 'slightly grander things' than 'bushes and lowly tamarisks' ('*paulo maiora canamus*' instead of '*arbusta . . . humilesque myricae*', E.IV.1–2). But soon he is commanding a more elevated style, as in the climactic passage where he welcomes the miraculous child of destiny:

Adgredere o magnos (aderit iam tempus) honores,
cara deum subolēs, māgnūm Iouis īncrēmēntum! (*E*.IV.48–9)[40]

Assume, I pray, great dignities (the time will soon be here),
dear offspring of the gods, great increase of Jupiter (trans. Clausen, 62)

The end-stopped rhythm in these lines is a mark of elevated style, as are the patterned distributions of noun and adjective pairs, and use of slow *molossi*, or three long syllables (marked in line 49 above).[41] Throughout *Eclogues IV*, this grander style is interwoven with a homelier pastoral discourse, which the herdsmen use, for example, in describing their '*capellae*' ('little goats', l. 21).

Virgil imagines Hesiod's mythical Golden Age, which was set in the distant past, being miraculously realised in his own historical era. First, the boy must grow up to see ancient conflicts being replayed on every side, but as an adult he will witness a world brought to peace. By the time Virgil had finished the *Eclogues*, however, the fragile peace had collapsed (and in the event, a girl was born, not a boy). The poem underwent some revision before being included in the *Eclogues*, and if originally the father celebrated for his heroic deeds was meant to be Antony, in the surviving version of the poem his identity is uncertain. Overall, the revised poem's political stance is deliberately opaque. At the end of the poem (whether or not as a result of revision) Virgil's description of the future Golden Age sounds deliberately far-

---

39. Heaney, 'Mossbawn via Mantua', 22, adapting Joyce's 'the shortest way to Tara [seat of the High Kings of Celtic Ireland] is via Holyhead [in Anglesey, Wales]', in *A Portrait of the Artist as a Young Man*: that is, to understand Ireland, you have first to leave it.
40. Quotations of Virgil's *Eclogues* are from *Vergili Opera*, ed. Mynors (1980).
41. See Nisbet (2008); Segal (1965).

fetched: the fields will bear every kind of crop at once and sheep will grow multi-coloured wool (ll. 39–44).[42]

In the closing section of *Eclogues IV*, Virgil shifts abruptly from prophetic to pastoral mode, further distancing himself from this extravagant vision of world peace. In the end, he appeals for authority, not from Jupiter or the Fates as one might expect (ll. 47, 49), but from Arcadia, the country of imagination:

> Pan etiam, Arcadia mecum si iudice certet,
> Pan etiam Arcadia dicat se iudice uictum. (E.IV.58–9)

> Even Pan if he were to compete with me with Arcadia as judge, even Pan with Arcadia as judge would say he is defeated.[43]

An intimate family scene follows, in which the imagined baby is entreated to smile at his mother ('*Incipe, parue puer, risu cognoscere matrem*', l. 60). If *Eclogues IV* adopts a prophetic style, perhaps to please a great politician, it closes on a much more domestic note.[44]

For hundreds of years, *Eclogues IV* was interpreted as an inspired prophecy of the birth of Christ, and the Golden Age understood as the beginning of the Christian era. In 'Virgil and the Christian World', Eliot dismisses the interpretation but retains the traditional view that Virgil was *anima naturaliter Christiana*, 'uniquely near to Christianity'.[45] In 'Bann Valley Eclogue', Heaney restores the poem's original Roman context, while also steering its Christian associations towards a more culturally specific connection with Northern Irish Roman Catholicism. The extensive dialogue between the Poet and 'Virgil' is reduced in the later version of the poem printed in *Electric Light*, with three of the middle stanzas excised (*EL* 11–12). But in both versions, 'Virgil' appears to the contemporary Poet, not as a prophet of Christendom or Roman Empire, but as an enabling friend, mentor and literary exemplar.

In *Relating Narratives* (2000), Adriana Cavarero argues that a person's true biography can be told only by an intimate other, a member of the family or lifelong friend who can narrate the person's origins in a way that is unavailable to that person alone. One's life is always therefore a relational narrative rather than a story one can individually possess. Such a relational exchange is enacted in the longer, 1999 version of 'Bann Valley Eclogue', where one poet recalls the other poet's history,

---

42. In her review of *Electric Light*, Edna Longley objects that 'all' has too much work to do in it, but Heaney may be imitating Virgil's recurrent use of '*omnia*' in this passage (Longley, 'Too Much Confectionery?', *Metre* (2002), 15).
43. Translation by Wendell Clausen (Clausen, 1994), 62.
44. 'I used to compare small things with great ones' (*E.I.23*). Heaney's 'Secular and Sacred Miłosz' (1999) concludes by quoting Miłosz's paraphrase of this line, '"What once was great, now appeared small."' (*FK* 416)
45. 'Virgil and the Christian World' in Hayward, ed., *T. S. Eliot: Selected Prose* (1953), 98, extracted from Eliot, *On Poetry and Poets* (1957), 121–31 (Heaney read Hayward's edition at Queen's University, see *FK* 33).

and reflects on the possible shape of the other's future. This structure of antiphonal exchange would have been familiar to Heaney, not only from the other nine Virgilian eclogues, but also from the Roman Catholic liturgy he had grown up with as a child.[46]

In the opening stanza of 'Bann Valley', the Poet expresses a wish to make a grand, theatrical entrance, in the manner that Virgil had done in *Eclogues IV*. The implicit comparison leads him to invoke Virgil's presence, although he still falls short of the Roman poet's grander style. And he sounds less confident in his prognosis for peace:

> Poet: Bann Valley Muses, give us a song worth singing,
> Something that rises like the curtain in
> Those words *And it came to pass* or *In the beginning.*
> Help me to please my hedge-schoolmaster Virgil
> And the child that's due. Maybe, heavens, sing
> Better times for her and her generation. (ll. 1–6)[47]

The dactylic rhythm, particularly in the opening feet ('Bánn Vălley', 'gíve ŭs ă', 'Sómethĭng thăt', 'Hélp mĕ tŏ', 'hér gĕnĕration'), gives an immediate feeling of Latinity to this opening stanza. But the hexameter rhythm is relaxed and flexible, many lines resolving into hendecasyllables, a meter Heaney might have found in the war-time eclogues of Miklós Radnóti and Louis MacNeice.[48]

In a typescript version of this stanza, prepared for the BBC radio broadcast, the Poet invokes the Muses simply to 'help me to write a northern pastoral'.[49] That phrase is struck out in pen and amended to 'to please my hedge-schoolmaster Virgil', a far more culturally specific invocation. Following the proscription of educational practices of Catholics and Presbyterians in Ireland, in 1695, popular schools had begun to be organised, often outdoors, near hedges and rivers, in barns and chapels, and in private homes, coming to be known as 'hedge schools'. By the end of the long eighteenth century, around 9,000 of such schools are thought to have been running, the ban on Catholic education being lifted in 1793.[50] Heaney associates this kind of school more broadly with a country resistance to the Anglophone cultural mainstream, and with

---

46. The Catholic liturgy reflects Christ's historical practice of sending the twelve disciples out to preach in pairs (Mark 6: 7–13), a practice that was continued after Christ's death (Acts 13: 1–3).
47. 'Bann Valley Eclogue', *Times Literary Supplement* (1999), 32; and *EL* 11 (the opening stanza is the same in both versions).
48. See also Twiddy (2012), 129. In *Camp Notebook* (2000), Radnóti adheres very strictly to eleven syllables (see Szirtes, 'Introduction', 9). The MacNeice eclogues vary between five and six beats per line (*The Collected Poems*, 1966, 33f.). Day Lewis's translation of the *Eclogues* (1983) similarly varies between five and six beats per long line. These examples differ from David Ferry's translation, which adheres to iambic pentameter throughout.
49. Ink correction on typescript, *LP* I.xv.10.
50. Lyons (2016), who cites this poem by Pádraic Colum (1882–1972): 'My eyelids red and heavy are / With bending o'er the smould'ring peat / I know the Aeneid now by heart / My Virgil read in cold and heat.'

a vernacular language 'still fresh from the folk-speech and hedge-school of the shires' (*FK* 172). Introducing his translation of *Buile Suibhne*, Heaney describes Sweeney as a 'figure of the artist' who embodies the 'green spirit of the hedges' in the countryside of south County Antrim and north County Down (*Sweeney Astray*, vi, vii). In 'Bann Valley', then, the Poet hails Virgil as a parochial authority figure, a master familiar from a marginalised, rural Catholic education system.

The 'hedge-schoolmaster' then promptly responds, in the next stanza, with a string of words to be rehomed in the Bann Valley:

> Virgil: Here are my words you'll have to find a place for:
> *Carmen, ordo, nascitur, saeculum, gens*
> *Ferrea, aurea, aetas, scelus, Lucina.*
> Their gist in your tongue and province should be clear
> Even at this stage. Poetry, order, the times,
> The nation, wrong and renewal, iron and gold. (1999, ll. 7–12)

The Latin words in lines 8–9, condensed to one line in *Electric Light*, are all drawn from the opening paragraph of *Eclogues IV*, in which the poet announces that the Sibyl's prophecy of a Golden Age has come true:

> Vltima Cumaei uenit iam *carminis* aetas;
> magnus ab integro *saeclorum nascitur ordo*.
> iam redit et Virgo, redeunt Saturnia regna,
> iam noua progenies caelo demittitur alto.
> tu modo nascenti puero, quo *ferrea* primum
> desinet ac toto surget *gens aurea* mundo,
> casta faue *Lucina*: (E.IV.4–10, my ital.)
>
> Now is come the last age of Cumaean song; the great line of the centuries begins anew. Now the Virgin [*Diké*, Justice] returns, the reign of Saturn returns; now a new generation descends from heaven on high. Only do you, pure Lucina, smile on the birth of the child, under whom the iron brood shall at last cease and a golden race spring up throughout the world. (trans. Fairclough)

Virgil's passage imports from Hesiod's *Works and Days* the story of the generations of mankind, passing from an ideal golden race to silver, bronze and finally iron, which is used to denote the degraded race of the present. It was Virgil's innovation to prophesy a return to the Golden Age, in the aftermath of the Pact of Brundisium. Heaney's 'Virgil' lifts the key words out of the prophecy in such a way as to alter the idea of historical progression to the motion of a pendulum swing: '*Ferrea, aurea, aetas, scelus*', that is, 'iron, gold, the age, crime'. We are closer here to the 'widening gyre' of Yeats's 'The Second Coming'.[51] Where Virgil declares optimistically that

---

51. Yeats, 'The Second Coming', where 'twenty centuries of stony sleep / Were vexed to nightmare by a rocking cradle' (1992, 235).

'the order of centuries is born', the 'Virgil' in Heaney's poem translates '*nascitur*' ('is born') as a floating noun, 'renewal', which falls short of claiming that the Golden Age has indeed come to pass, or that it definitely will.

Moreover, 'Virgil' pairs 'renewal' with 'wrong', a translation of *scelus*, which is culled from a subsequent passage in *Eclogues IV*, where the consul Pollio is seen presiding over the new peace:

> te duce, si qua manent *sceleris* uestigia nostri,
> inrita perpetua soluent formidine terras. (*E*.IV.13–14, my ital.)

> under your sway [Pollio] any lingering traces of our guilt shall become void and release the earth from dread. (trans. Fairclough)

Virgil applies the strong term '*scelus*' (also used for the murder of Orpheus, in *Georgics IV*) for the wars between Antony and Octavian because Romans regarded civil war as evil and polluting, in contrast to wars against other nations. The '*sceleris uestigia nostri*' ('traces of our crime') would also have reminded Roman readers of Romulus' legendary murder of his brother, Remus, an original *scelus* on which the Roman state was founded.[52]

Heaney's 'Virgil' tells the Poet that the 'gist' of his Latin words should be clear, and he obligingly translates them, 'Poetry, order, the times, / The nation, wrong and renewal, iron and gold' (ll. 11–12). But, stripped of any semantic structure, their import is far from clear. He seems to have been provoked into speech by the Poet's hesitant attempt at prophecy in the opening stanza: 'Maybe, heavens, sing / Better times' (ll. 5–6). In place of 'maybe', he offers these fragments of 'marble Latin', out of which to assemble a prophecy.[53] In the 1999 version, 'wrong and renewal, iron and gold' are left as unresolved polarities. In 2001, after 'wrong and renewal', 'Virgil' goes further, to predict 'an infant birth / And a flooding away of all the old miasma' (the Greek word *miasma* similarly denotes a polluting crime such as that of Oedipus[54]). The image of a cleansing flood may have been suggested by Day Lewis's free translation of Virgil's '*sceleris uestigia nostri*' as 'All stains of our past wickedness being cleansed away'.[55] Incorporating the Judeo-Christian image of a cleansing flood, both Heaney and Day Lewis are nodding toward the longstanding Christian interpretation of *Eclogues IV* as prophesying the birth of Christ.

But in Heaney's eclogue, the Poet studiously ignores the prophetic strain and instead chooses to find a place for just one of Virgil's words: '*Lucina*'. In *Eclogues*

---

52. See Putnam (2010), 13.
53. Martin Bloomer finds the 'drum roll of fragments' harsh and forbidding, an instance of 'marble Latin' being foisted on an unwilling schoolchild (2005, 214). But the Poet is a prompt, willing and able student of Latin, much as Heaney remembers himself to have been (SS 295–6).
54. Sophocles uses '*miasma*' in *Oedipus at Colonnus* (l. 1374) and *Antigone* (l. 172), in reference to a polluting act, committed intentionally or not. For Aristotle, '*to miaron*' (the repugnant or disgusting) is a topic unfit for tragedy as it 'arouses neither fellow-feeling nor pity nor fear.' (*Poetics* 13.35 (1453a))
55. *Virgil: The Eclogues, The Georgics*, trans. C. Day Lewis [1940], 18.

IV, Virgil invokes several of the major deities of Greek myth (Saturn, Apollo, the Parcae/Fates and Jupiter/Zeus), along with a single Roman deity, this being Lucina, goddess of childbirth. In 'Bann Valley', the Poet chooses the one goddess linked by locality to Virgil and then associates this name with an Irish, Roman Catholic one. Taking on the role of pupil in Virgil's hedge-school, he correctly parses the Latin, then builds a kind of prophetic utterance out of her name:

> Poet: *Lucina*. Rhyming with Sheena. Vocative. First
> Declension. Feminine gender. The Roman
> St Anne. Who is *casta Lucina*, chaste
> Star of the birth-bed. And secular star,
> Meaning star of the *saeculum*, brightness gathering
> Head great month by month now, waiting to fall. (1999, ll. 13–18)

'Sheena' is, more particularly, the name of Heaney's eldest sister. 'Lucina' also rhymes best with 'sheena' when pronounced with the soft 'c' of Church Latin, hence reinforcing a kinship with the Catholic St Anne. The Roman Lucina is associated with moonlight, and here the Poet imagines her brightness gathering into a full moon, 'waiting to fall'. The phrase anticipates the birth of the child, but it also suggests (along with the lapse of faith implied in 'secular') a possible fall into 'the old miasma', the *scelus* of civil war. The Poet's vision of a 'brightness gathering', in other words, still falls short of predicting a historical realisation of the mythical Golden Age.

Over the next two stanzas, in the 1999 version, the Poet then relates Virgil's biography, alluding to his country origins, the threat to the family farm from the land resettlement schemes, and his move to Rome where he could recite his poems to the most powerful man in the land, Octavian himself. For Cavarero, this would be an instance of relational biography, where a person's life assumes a coherent shape in the discourse of, and as a gift from, an intimate other. Within their exchange, the Poet's recollection of the life of 'Virgil' is prompted by *pietas* for a beloved schoolmaster. But there is also stealth involved because, by focusing on the political tensions in Virgil's era, Heaney is deflecting the reader's attention away from his own immediate circumstances. Instead of invoking a contemporary politician (John Hume, for example), in the way Virgil addresses Pollio, the Poet reminds 'Virgil' of how 'ex-servicemen' flooded into Mantua, Virgil's homeplace.[56]

Moreover, while the hedge-schoolmaster's life is recounted sympathetically, it is also recalled in such a way as to make the life of 'Virgil' rhyme with Heaney's own:

> You were raised on the land they drove your father off.
> You had his country accent and little to learn
> Of the facts of life when you read your first poems out

---

56. John Hume, the Northern Irish politician regarded by many as the main architect of the Good Friday Agreement, died on the day this paragraph was being written, 3 August 2020. He had been a contemporary of Heaney's at St Columb's College, in Derry.

To Octavian, feeling the length of the line
As if you were dressing husks off a hank of tow
Or measuring wheal for thatch. Holding your own

In your own way. *Pietas* and stealth. If ex-servicemen
Were cocks of the walk at home, hexameters
Would rule the roost in Rome. You would understand us
Latter-day scholarship boys and girls, on the cusp
Between elocution and *duchas* . . . (1999, ll. 19–29)

The historical Virgil was reputed to have a country accent, just as Heaney's is distinctively from County Derry. But Heaney also recalls the country labour of 'Virgil' using distinctly Northern European, rather than Latinate, vocabulary ('dressing husks of a hank of tow', 'measuring wheal for thatch'[57]). 'Virgil', measuring his poetic line by a length of wheal, imitates the young poet Heaney, measuring his pen by the action of his father's spade in his signature poem, 'Digging' (*DN* 1).

'You would understand us', the Poet tells 'Virgil'. His speech creates a two-way flow of sympathy, honouring 'Virgil' by remembering his biography, and giving coherence to his own life by seeing it patterned in another's. It takes this mirroring of the life of 'Virgil' for the Poet to recognise the difficulty of bridging 'elocution and *duchas*', the latter meaning 'heritage, birthright' (*SS* xix). Heaney had experienced militia behaving like 'cocks of the walk at home'. As he tells Dennis O'Driscoll, 'there was an affront to *dúchas* in being questioned about my name and address by these uninformed cubs in uniform at the end of my own loaning,' 'loaning' being another Hiberno-English word for a small country lane (*SS* 212, xix). Here, by the Poet's account, 'Virgil' sidesteps the sense of affront, to practise *elocutio* ('a speaking out', *LS* 1) in Rome, all the while stealthily strengthening his attachment to home.

'Virgil' responds, in turn, by reflecting on the Poet's life history (the texts are almost identical in the two versions, from here until the final stanza). In his speech, it is the notion of an originary stain that links their experience. Thus 'Virgil' makes the Poet's life rhyme with a Roman's: 'Earth mark, birth mark, mould like the bloodied mould / On Romulus's ditchback' (1999, ll. 32–3). Alluding to the murder of Remus, 'Virgil' implies that fratricidal civil war has been written into Ireland's history from its earliest days. This history is indelibly inscribed on later generations. Now fortified by their antiphonal exchange, 'Virgil' directs his prophecy of a Golden Age into the Poet's territory, predicting an end to the old divisions:

> When the waters break
> Bann's stream will overflow, the old markings
> Will avail no more to keep east bank from west.
> The valley will be washed like the new baby. (1999, ll. 33–6)[58]

57. A 'tow', from Middle English *towe*, is 'a fibre of flax, hemp, or jute prepared for spinning' (*OED*, n.1), while 'wheal', from Old English *hwele*, means 'a ridge' (*OED*, n.2).
58. In *EL* 11, Heaney adds 'But' before 'when', marking a stronger transition from history to prophecy.

Foreseeing the commingling of west and east banks, 'Virgil' shows how closely he can speak to the Poet's home ground, since the Bann River traditionally divided Catholic communities on its Western side from Protestants on the eastern side.[59] But the local prophecy also has a global resonance: 'Virgil' implies peace between Palestine and Israel, the conflict over the West Bank resolved, and peace between Eastern and Western Europe. In the 1999 version, it is clear that 'Virgil' projects his Roman prophecy into the modern world in response to the Poet's sympathetic narration of his own life history. He derives hope, in other words, from his exchange with the later Poet. As a result, Heaney's 'Virgil' ends up sounding more optimistic about the prospect for peace than the Virgil of *Eclogues IV* does.

The Poet, however, remains to be convinced by the growing optimism of 'Virgil'. He finds the idea of '*Pacatum orbem*', a world brought to peace, 'too much nearly' (the delayed adverb indicating the Hibernian inflection of his speech, l. 37). The word '*orbem*' instead triggers his recent memory of witnessing a solar eclipse, as Heaney had himself:

> Poet: And then, last month, mid-morning, the wind dropped.
> An Avernus chill, birdless and dark, prepared.
> A firstness steadied, a lastness, a born awareness
> As name dawned into knowledge: I saw the orb. (ll. 39–42)

The 2001 version changes 'mid-morning' to 'noon-eclipse', clarifying the reference to the darkened orb of the eclipsed sun. Instead of a world at peace, he sees a dark, fallen world, 'dawned into knowledge'. In 2001, line 40 becomes 'A millennial chill, birdless and dark', but as the name of the underworld lake, 'Avernus', literally means 'birdless' (*a-vernus*), he retains this foreboding sense of underworldly, mortal knowledge. Agreeing with Alpers, Heaney understands pastoral to be a knowing genre, projecting a vision of innocence against a backdrop of known experience (sentimental rather than naïve, in Schiller's terms).[60] But here, the Poet takes the eclipse as a vision of the opposite, the known world (Earth) blocking out the Sun's brightness and the recovery of innocence.

In *Electric Light*, this idea is reinforced in a dark pastoral poem entitled 'Known World', in which Heaney recalls a visit to a festival in Macedonia, in 1978 (SS xxvi). The poem is dated 'May 1998', therefore after the genocidal war which led to the break-up of Yugoslavia in the early 1990s (*EL* 23). Given that hindsight, there is tragic irony in the jaunty '*Nema problema!*' of the Macedonian taxi-driver, in the first and last lines of the poem. In the 'known world' of this postlapsarian pastoral, shepherds have become refugees, and the meeting-place of the road now signifies their homelessness and exile:

> And now the refugees
> Come loaded on tractor mudguards and farm carts,

---

59. See Russell (2016), 175.
60. 'Eclogues *in Extremis*', 8.

On trailers, ruck-shifters, box-barrows, prams,
On sticks, on crutches, on each other's shoulders, (*EL* 20)

May 1998 is also one month after the signing of the Good Friday Agreement, suggesting that the peace treaty has not cancelled out Heaney's memory of long years of conflict at home.[61]

In 'Bann Valley', however, 'Virgil' deliberately refuses this worldly knowledge: 'Eclipses won't be for this child' (l. 43). Instead, responding to the Poet's melancholy awareness of the *lacrimae rerum*, he narrows his prophecy to the domestic sphere:

> The cool she'll know
> Will be the pram over her vestal head.
> Big dog daisies will get fanked up in the spokes. (ll. 43–5)

This diminution of scale mirrors the last section of *Eclogues IV*, which closes with a direct address to the expected child: '*Incipe, parue puer, risu cognoscere matrem*' ('Begin, baby boy, to recognise your mother with a smile', E.IV.60). In Heaney's poem, 'Virgil' adopts the Irish child's linguistic register, predicting 'dog daisies' 'fanked up' in the pram's wheels. That 'Virgil' speaks in this northern idiom suggests how fully his imagination has entered the world of his addressee. Once there, the 'chug and slug going on in the milking parlour' triggers the memory of clashing weaponry (l. 47). The prophecy of 'Virgil' then turns to Yeatsian prayer in his last, anxious line: 'Let her never hear close gun fire or explosions.' (l. 48)[62]

If the Poet cannot quite believe in the vision of a *pacatum orbem*, he is nevertheless responsive to the tender evocation of 'Virgil' of the child in her pram. This image activates a memory from his own past, when as a child he was sent by his mother to gather trefoil from the railway line. The fragility of the plant recalls the '*munuscula*' offered to the child in *Eclogues IV*:

> At tibi prima, puer, nullo munuscula cultu
> errantis hederas passim cum baccare tellus
> mixtaque ridenti colocasia fundet acantho. (*E*.IV.18–20)

But for you, child, the earth untilled will pour forth its first little gifts, wandering ivy with foxglove everywhere, and the Egyptian bean blended with the laughing briar. (trans. Fairclough, modified)

In the Poet's memory, the little plant is unmistakeably Irish, and its ground-level fecundity suggests the natural world's ability to rejuvenate after war:

---

61. Nor did the Good Friday Agreement bring an end to the violence altogether. On 15 August 1998, a car bomb in Omagh, Co. Tyrone, killed twenty-nine people. The attack was said to be orchestrated by a splinter group of the IRA opposing the Agreement ('Omagh Bombing: Key Events', *The Irish Times*, 12 August 2018).
62. For the echo of Yeats's 'A Prayer for My Daughter' (1992, 236), see Twiddy (2012), 130.

>   the little trefoil, untouchable almost, the shamrock
> And its twining, binding, creepery, tough, thin roots
> All over the place . . .
> Dew-scales shook off the leaves. Tear-ducts asperging. (ll. 51–4)

The last line also admits the possibility of a social and cultural rejuvenation. 'Tear-ducts asperging' conjoins Virgil's *lacrimae rerum* with the ritual beginning of the Catholic Mass, *asperges me, Domine* ('thou shalt sprinkle me, Lord'). In place of the flooding Bann River, the Poet creates out of memory a much smaller-scale (but to him, credible) act of purgation.

The Poet then returns to the present and to the 'Child on the way'. He is emboldened to imagine the world again, though suspended in the present tense:

> Poet: Planet earth like a teething ring suspended
>   Hangs by its world-chain. (ll. 58–9)

This image borrows from the most stately, elevated line in *Eclogues IV*, where Virgil dares to make hope and history rhyme:

> aspice conuexo nutantem pondere mundum,
> terrasque tractusque maris caelumque profundum; (E.IV.50–1)
>
> See how the world bows with its massive dome – earth and expanse of sea and heaven's depth! (trans. Fairclough)

Heaney foregoes the enveloping syntax and end-line rhyme, but his simile daringly diminishes the orb to the size of the new baby's teething ring.[63] The possibility of rejuvenation, suggested in the remembered image of the trefoil, now hangs in the balance. Against the innocence of the teething ring, the 'world-chain' suggests the drag of postlapsarian knowledge. A few pages later, in 'Known World', the 'world-chain' will be linked to the Styx and the material Hell of warfare:

> I see its coil again like a syrup of Styx,
> An old gold world-chain the world keeps falling from
> Into the cloud-boil of a camera lens. (*EL* 20)

In 'Bann Valley', the Poet follows 'Virgil' and retreats from the global to the domestic scene, where the child's birth is soon expected:

>   Your pram waits in the corner.
> Cows are let out. They're sluicing the milk-house floor. (ll. 59–60)

---

63. By contrast, Milton retains Virgil's stateliness in his own beautiful version of this line, in the Nativity Ode: 'And the well-balanced world on hinges hung' (*Complete Shorter Poems*, 1997, 109).

Even this innocent-seeming image has a dark subtext when conjoined with 'The Augean Stables' (the fourth of the 'Sonnets from Hellas'). There, the poet's travels through Arcadia are interrupted by news from Northern Ireland of a sectarian murder in his home town.[64] He thinks of the blood being hosed away after the murder, 'And imagined / hose-water smashing hard back off the asphalt' (*EL* 41). But at the end of 'Bann Valley', the milk-house floor is also connected to the image of the pregnant mother, on 'her sunset walk among big round bales' (l. 57). So 'Planet earth' remains in delicate suspension, between 'teething' innocence and 'world-chain' knowledge. What keeps the vision of innocence alive in the poem is the Poet's retreat into memory, where he recovers the image of trefoil and 'tear-ducts asperging'. It is the act of memory that asperges, the memory being triggered by a sympathetic exchange with his 'hedge-schoolmaster Virgil'.

11. '*ECLOGUES IX*'

In his 2001 interview with Rui Homem, Heaney mentions rather casually that after writing 'Glanmore Eclogue', he went on to produce a translation of *Eclogues IX* 'to give a bit more context'.[65] Ten years later, though, he refers to this translation as 'a poet's *apologia pro vita mea*', composed 'in the aftermath' of the Good Friday Agreement.[66] In *Electric Light*, the translation is prominently placed, just before 'Glanmore Eclogue' and midway through Part I of the volume. The context of Virgil's poem allows Heaney the opportunity to reflect stealthily on the Belfast Agreement. Still more importantly, though, the dialogic exchange between the herdsmen provides an example of fellowship in the reception, practice and handing on of poetry, an idea that is central to Heaney's own practice.

Lycidas and Moeris, the two herdsmen in *Eclogues IX*, have survived the civil war but are now living at the mercy of new landowners. The older shepherd, Moeris, has lost ownership of his goats and is going to town to sell them on behalf of a new owner. If the fear of war and political injustice are central themes in *Eclogues I*, the question in this eclogue is whether the herdsmen's poetry will survive the peace: whether they can recall their former songs, and whether their new lives will allow them space and leisure to sing.

Through Moeris and Lycidas, Virgil offers two opposing views on the recent change of power in Rome and its implications for the lives of ordinary farmers and herdsmen, as well as for Rome's leading poets.[67] Virgil's ninth eclogue is notably

---

64. The sixty-one-year old Seán Brown was abducted and shot by loyalist militia, as he was locking up the Wolfe Tone Gaelic Athletic Association premises in Heaney's home town of Bellaghy, Co. Derry ('Killing led to claims of collusion', *The Irish Times*, 9 January 2004). For O'Donoghue, this allusion to the murder is an example of the way Heaney's pastoral is always set up to be shot down ('Heaney's Classics and the Bucolic', 2009, 117).
65. 'On Elegies' (2001), 26.
66. 'Mossbawn via Mantua' (2012), 21–2.
67. See Alpers (1979), 136; Heiny (2018), 54.

darker and more pessimistic than its Greek model, Theocritus' *Idylls VII*.[68] On the other hand, the relation between the herdsmen is warmer and more sympathetic than in *Eclogues I*, where the fortunate shepherd ignores the plight of the unlucky one. Here, the two herdsmen face the same predicament, having suffered the same losses. They are clearly old friends, as Moeris repeatedly speaks of 'us' and refers to himself as '*tuus hic Moeris*' ('your Moeris here', l. 16). He expects a sympathetic ear from Lycidas when he complains, '*aduena nostri / . . . ut possessor agelli*' ('that a stranger should come to our little farm', E.IX.2–3). And Lycidas, who knows several of Moeris' songs by heart, soon induces the older man to take part. In the Homem interview, Heaney admits to 'a little secret, personal link' with Lycidas, the younger and less experienced singer who begins by saying, 'well, "I'm not sure: I have done nothing yet"'; as an undergraduate, he had felt the same, publishing his first poems under the pseudonym *Incertus*.[69] But Virgil himself maintains a stealthy anonymity behind the stock-pastoral names in *Eclogues IX*.

The reason for secrecy, from Heaney's perspective, is that these herdsmen are surviving 'in a desolate and no longer nourishing landscape of fact', rather than an Arcadian 'land of heart's desire', as he puts it in 'Eclogues *in Extremis*'.[70] The beech trees they pass by are old and 'scraggy-headed' ('*fracta cacumina*', E.IX.9; *EL* 31). Lycidas has heard a story that their most highly skilled singer, Menalcas, has rescued them from trouble: '*omnia carminibus uestrum seruasse Menalcan*' ('How your song-man's singing saved the place', E.IX.10; *EL* 31). If that had been true, then Menalcas would have had the powers of Orpheus on his first descent to Hades, able to reverse history with his music. Moeris, however, has just seen Menalcas fail:

> carmina tantum
> nostra ualent, Lycida, tela inter Martia quantum
> Chaonias dicunt aquila ueniente columbas. (*E*.IX.11–13)

> songs and tunes
> Can no more hold out against brute force than doves
> When eagles swoop. (*EL* 31)

The bird metaphors, along with the rendering of '*tela Martia*' as 'brute force', link this passage to Heaney's earlier translation of the *sparagmos* of Orpheus.[71] Here, Menalcas and Moeris have escaped death, but only just. And Lycidas, shocked by the news, imagines a loss comparable to Orpheus' death:

> Heu, cadit in quemqam tantum scelus? heu, tua nobis
> paene simul tecum solacia rapta, Menalca! (*E*.IX.17–18)

---

68. See Segal (1965), 252f.
69. Heaney, 'On Elegies' (2001), 25–6.
70. Heaney, 'Eclogues *in Extremis*', 6. 'Landscape of fact' is Hugh's phrase in Brian Friel's *Translations* (1981), 43.
71. *MV* 40, translating Ovid, *Meta*.XI.38–41. See Chapter 3.

Shocking times. Our very music, our one consolation,
Confiscated, all but. And Menalcas himself
Nearly one of the missing. (*EL* 32)

The crime ('*scelus*') is a fall ('*cadit*') of the worse kind, the seizure ('*rapta*') amounting to a theft of identity, and belief in the transcendent power of art. Both herdsmen believe that Menalcas is still alive (E.IX.55, 67), but he is somewhere off-stage and silent. Their act of *pietas* is to keep the pastoral song going in his absence.

In the postlapsarian world of *Eclogues IX*, the pastoral road traversed by the two herdsmen is marked at either end by a sense of mortal limit. Behind them is the memory of their song-man's failure; ahead lies the tomb of Bianor. Between these mortal *termini*, Moeris and Lycidas exchange fragments of half-remembered pastoral song. Lycidas feels he is 'a squawking goose among sweet-throated swans' ('*argutos inter strepere anser olores*', E.IX.36; *EL* 33). And Moeris complains, 'I'm forgetting song after song / And my voice is going' ('*nunc oblita mihi tot carmina, uox quoque Moerim / iam fugit ipsa*', E.IX.53–4; *EL* 34). Lycidas proposes that they sit in the shade and sing, '*hic, ubi densas / agricolae stringunt frondes*' ('here, where the farmers are stripping off thick leaves'), where the sense is that the leaves will be used to feed their animals (E.IX.60–1). In Heaney's version, this becomes 'Here where they've trimmed and faced / The old green hedge,' a reminder of the provisional secret character of the rural Catholic hedge-schools (*EL* 34). Hence, the two herdsmen's conversation has the character of a passing, road-side exchange.

As in 'Bann Valley', Heaney here deploys a mixed prosody that consciously hybridises traditional English iambic pentameter with the falling rhythms and longer line of Virgil's dactylic hexameter. The hexameter effect is more muted than in 'Bann Valley', with around half the translation's eighty-three lines beginning with a stressed first syllable. But Heaney still uses the falling rhythm for dramatic emphasis, as in the opening question, 'Whére ăre yoŭ góing?', and again, in Lycidas's response to Moeris's misfortune, 'Shŏckĭng tímes. Our véry músĭc, oŭr óne cŏnsŏlátĭŏn' (l. 20). Dactyls also formalise Moeris's remembered snatch of song, 'Whát's ĭn thĕ séa ănd thĕ wáves?' (l. 49), and strengthen Lycidas's claim that 'Sĭngĭng shórtĕns thĕ róad, sŏ wĕ'll wálk' (l. 80).

In terms of diction and register, as well, Heaney crosses Hibernicisms with Latinity to produce a sense of doubled localism, rather than a composite, classical–canonical voice.[72] As Cillian O'Hogan has ably shown, Heaney's two herdsmen use specifically Hibernian turns of phrase throughout the poem.[73] The speech of the older herdsman, Moeris, is particularly idiomatic. He regrets having to take his own goats to market, to sell for his new landlord: '*hos illi (quod nec uertat bene) mittimus haedos*' is rendered as 'we send off these kid-goats (may it not turn out well!)' (E.IX.6). Heaney's version Hibernicises in at least three details: 'And these kid-goats in the creel / Bad cess to him – these kids are his. All's changed.' (*EL* 31) 'Bad cess' is an Irish expression for 'bad luck', while 'creel' is a kind of basket commonly

---

72. Cf. *FK* 174, and Chapter 1.
73. O'Hogan (2018), 403–6.

used in parts of Scotland and Ireland.⁷⁴ And 'All's changed' recalls Yeats's famous refrain in his poem 'Easter, 1916': 'All changed, changed utterly: / A terrible beauty is born.'⁷⁵ Elsewhere, he transforms a Roman expression into a northern one when, for '*lupi Moerim uidere priores*' (E.IX.54), he writes, 'maybe the wolves have blinked it [my voice]', 'blinked' being a Scots–Irish word for 'jinx' or 'bewitch' (*EL* 34). Lycidas also uses colloquial word order, when regretting their music has been 'Confiscated, all but', and an idiomatic register in a line of song: 'watch / The boyo with the horns doesn't go for you.' (*EL* 32) In Heaney's translation, there is no doubting that these herdsmen come from the Irish countryside.

At the same time, though, they are inextricably rooted in the otherness of their Roman district, language and context. Moeris describes his near-escape from ruin using the expression, common from Roman augury, that it is good luck to see a bird on the left: '*quod nisi me . . . / ante sinistra caua monuisset ab ilice cornix*' (E.IX.14–15).⁷⁶ Heaney makes no attempt to naturalise the expression, and in fact carries over the Latin alliterative pattern ('c̲aua, ili̲c̲e, c̲ornix') thus: 'If I hadn't heard the c̲row c̲aw on my left / In our hollow oak̲' (*EL* 31).

He also retains the Roman names of people and places whose significance is unlikely to be familiar to most of his readers, as in this song-fragment recalled by Moeris:

'Vare, tuum nomen, superet modo Mantua nobis,
Mantua uae miserae nimium uicina Cremonae,
cantantes sublime ferent ad sidera cycni.' (E.IX.27–9)

Heaney negotiates the specificity of the reference by having Moeris partly paraphrase the song before launching into quotation. But the reference is still likely to be obscure:

And then there was that one . . .
Addressed to Varus, about a choir of swans
Chanting his name to the stars, 'should Mantua
Survive, Mantua too close to sad Cremona.' (*EL* 32)

Mantua is Virgil's birthplace, and there were swans on the River Mincius as it flowed past the town, while Cremona was the nearby administrative centre, where the land redistribution took place under the supervision of the Roman official, Varus.⁷⁷ A modern commentary would equally be needed to decode an invocation commonly found in Augustan poetry and familiar to Roman readers: '*Sic tua Cyrneas fugiant examina taxos,/ . . . incipe*' (E.IX.30, 32).⁷⁸ Heaney's translation preserves the

---

74. *OED: cess*, n.5, *OED: creel*, n.1.
75. Yeats, 'Easter 1916', ll.15–16 (1992), 228.
76. Clausen (1994), 273.
77. Clausen (1994), 275.
78. Clausen (1994), 276.

oddness of the proverb: 'sing it now / So that your bees may swerve off past the yew trees' (*EL* 32). What this mixture of insistently rural Derry and Roman language does is demonstrate pastoral's attachment to place and, at the same time, its continual displacement and deportation across time and space.

The pastoral singer serves poetry by planting two feet astride different cultures, creating a channel or bridge so that the poetry can flow from one to the other. Such a singer functions like the bridge described in 'Ten Glosses': 'Its feet on both sides but in neither camp, / It stands its ground, a span of pure attention, / A holding action' (*EL* 54). This bridging attention is evidenced in all four fragments of song exchanged between Moeris and Lycidas. In *Eclogues IX*, each shepherd sings one fragment of song closely derived from Theocritus, and one fragment drawn from their own, Roman context. Lycidas' Theocritean fragment (E.IX.23–5) is contrasted with Moeris' Roman choir of swans chanting about Mantua (E.IX.27–9). And conversely, Moeris' Theocritean love song (E.IX.39–43) is followed by Lycidas' Roman song celebrating a new star in the heavens, the apotheosised Caesar (E.IX.46–50).[79]

In translating these songs within pastoral songs, Heaney registers their layered origins and extends the dialogic process of transmission. He does this by translating one song 'faithfully', retaining its Roman otherness, while the other he freely transfuses with northern vocabulary, rhythmic and rhyming patterns, and literary allusion. Virgil's Moeris is the better, more experienced singer of the two, and in his translation Heaney gives Moeris' song the bolder, more imaginative, Ariel flight. The Latin text, on the other hand, closely imitates Theocritus' *Idylls XI*:

'huc ades, O Galatea; quis est nam ludus in undis?
hic uer purpureum, uarios hic flumina circum
fundit humus flores, hic candida populus antro
imminet et lentae texunt umbracula uites.
huc ades; insani feriant sine litora fluctus.' (E.IX.39–43)

Fairclough's more literal, prose translation of the above reads:

'Come here, Galatea! What pleasure lives in waves? Here is rosy spring; here, by the streams, Earth scatters her flowers of a thousand hues; here the white poplar bends over the cave, and the clinging vines weave shady bowers. Come to me; leave the wild waves to lash the shore.'

Heaney's translation makes much more of the contrast between sea and land. Virgil's alliterative pattern, *flumina*, *fundit*, *flores*, *fluctus*, is transformed into Anglo-Saxon pairs of rhyming verbs. And the '*insani fluctus*' (wild, or mad, waves) are given a postcolonial resonance:

'What's in the sea and the waves that keeps you spellbound?
Here earth breaks out in wildflowers, she rills and rolls

---

79. Segal (1965), 247; Clausen (1994), 280.

The streams in waterweed, here poplars bend
Where the bank is undermined and vines in thickets
Are meshing shade with light. Come here to me.
Let the mad white horses paw and pound the shore.' (EL 33)

Heaney abandons Virgil's chiastic repetitions (*huc, hic, hic, huc*) but doubles '*undis*' into 'sea and waves', giving him a dactylic rhythm in the opening line, 'Whát's ĭn thĕ séa and the wáves', and a run of rhyming 'w's across three lines. He doubles '*fundit*' to produce the Anglo-Saxon rhyming pair, 'rills and rolls', contrasted with the waves that 'paw and pound'. For '*antro*' he ingeniously suggests 'undermined', which initiates the triple assonance of 'mined', 'vines' and 'light', to which delight is added the hush of 'meshing shade'. As Michael Putnam observes, 'mad white horses' (for Virgil's '*insani fluctus*') alludes to the white-capped waves in Kipling's poem, 'White Horses'.[80] Since Kipling's whitecaps are metaphors for the British navy, Heaney has Moeris pleading with Galatea to put aside her admiration for British imperial power and return to her native ground.

In *Eclogues IX*, Lycidas responds to Moeris' Theocritean song with a song by Moeris himself. With this compliment to his friend, he also turns the focus of the eclogue back to the immediate Roman context, reminding Virgil's audience of the appearance of a comet during Julius Caesar's games in July 44 BCE:[81]

'Daphni, quid antiquos signorum suspicis ortus?
ecce Dionaei processit Caesaris astrum,
astrum quo segetes gauderent frugibus et quo
duceret apricis in collibus uua colorem.' (E.IX.46–9)

'Daphnis, Daphnis, why
Do you concentrate your gaze on the old stars?
Look for the star of Caesar, rising now,
Star of corn in the fields and hay in haggards,
Of clustered grapes gone purple in the heat
On hillsides facing south.' (EL 33)

Like the hills in the last line, this song fragment consciously 'faces south' to Virgil's Roman context and Latin text. Thus, Heaney exactly mirrors Virgil's placement of *Daphni, Ecce* and *astrum* at the head of the line ('Daphnis . . . Look . . . Star'). And apart from the light alliteration, there is little attention drawn to the English words, the sense of '*mirum*' being focused on the apotheocised Caesar, now rising in the sky.

This exchange of song concludes in an atmosphere of muted melancholy. Lycidas proposes to rest by the hedge or walk on, but at any rate, to continue singing as the evening breezes fall. Virgil's '*ceciderunt aurae*' (l. 58) can be interpreted in various ways. Fairclough opts for a deathly chill: 'lo! every breath of the murmuring breeze

---

80. Putnam (2010), 11.
81. Clausen (1994), 283.

is dead.' (p. 89) But Heaney's Lycidas feels something much more benign in the fall of the evening air: 'now this hush has fallen / Everywhere – look – on the plain, and every breeze / Has calmed and quietened.' (*EL* 34) Twilight is the time for more song: '*hic, Moeri, canamus*', 'here, Moeris, let us sing' (E.IX.61). And his final lines repeat the emphasis on *poesis*, the active making of song: '*cantantes . . . eamus; / cantantes ut eamus*', 'so we'll walk and sing, / Walk then, Moeris, and sing.' (E.IX.64–5)

For Moeris, however, it is time for pressing on with the journey in silence. The eclogue concludes with his brusque reply:

Desine plura, puer, et quod nunc instat agamus;
carmina tum melius, cum uenerit ipse, canemus. (E.IX.66–7)

That's enough of that, young fellow. We've a job to do.
When the real singer comes, we'll sing in earnest. (*EL* 34)

He might just be saying they have sung enough for that day, but coming at the end of the poem, the lines also convey the impression of a more general finality, as if Moeris' sense of '*mortalia tangunt*' has silenced the younger poet's delight in song. That said, Moeris' reply still takes up Lycidas' '*canamus*' (let us sing) and repeats it twice in his reply: '*carmina*' (songs), '*canemus*' ('we will sing'). Of Moeris' final '*canemus*', Michael Putnam comments that this 'astonishing word [is used] one more time in the corpus of major classical Latin literature as the final word in the last ode of Horace', where its meaning 'suggests hope'.[82] This farewell transmission perfectly illustrates how pastoral song is forwarded in an exchange of discourse with an intimate other. In the context of Heaney's transmission of Virgilian pastoral, the translation 'we'll sing in earnest' leaves their dialogue precisely poised between elegy and hope, in a mixed gesture of *pietas* and stealth. There is a promise of continuity in the very act of deferring the pastoral song to another time and place.

III. 'GLANMORE ECLOGUE'

Fellowship between poets, and the relationship between a poet and his community, are the central themes of Heaney's 'Glanmore Eclogue', which was initially composed for a collection of essays devoted to the Irish playwright John Millington Synge.[83] Heaney had, in 1988–9, purchased Glanmore Cottage, which stood on the Synge estate in County Wicklow. His eclogue commemorates Synge in the guise of an absent shepherd named Meliboeus, who is reputed to have known all the old Wicklow songs. In Heaney's poem, an unnamed but, again, quasi-autobiographical Poet exchanges verses with a farmer named Myles (*EL* 36). 'Myles' is probably a pseudonym for Flann O'Brien (Myles na Gopaleen), though it has also been

---

82. Putnam (2010), 7.
83. 'Glanmore Eclogue' was originally published in Grene, ed., *Interpreting Synge* (2000), 17–19. This earlier version contains more extensive allusions to Synge, and to Ann Saddlemyer, Heaney's 'Lady Augusta'. This chapter quotes from the later version, in *EL* 35–7.

suggested that it stands for Milesius, mythical founder of the Gaelic Irish race.[84] The Poet lets his own mask slip when he tells Myles, 'Meliboeus would have called me "Mr Honey"', near-rhyming with 'Heaney' (*EL* 36). The appellation also graciously nods to Synge, 'mister honey' being a name addressed to Christy Mahon, the main character in Synge's most famous play, *The Playboy of the Western World*.[85] But Heaney again disguises the immediate context of the poem, and stages a dialogue based on Virgil's *Eclogues I*, where an unlucky farmer, also called Meliboeus, trades stories with a fortunate shepherd, named Tityrus.

While Virgil's Tityrus has gained land (and possibly manumission) from Octavian's resettlement scheme, Meliboeus has been arbitrarily evicted from his farm. In Heaney's poem, Myles is the unlucky farmer, who is finding times hard as wealthier incomers buy up the old smallholdings. And Myles regards the Poet as the 'lucky man' of Virgil's poem: 'No stock to feed, no milking times, no tillage / Nor blisters on your hands' (*EL* 36). Myles also addresses the Poet as 'Augusta's tenant', which places their dialogue in the 1970s, when Heaney was renting Glanmore Cottage from Ann Saddlemyer, the well-known Canadian Synge scholar.[86] The nickname 'Augusta' was modelled on Yeats's name for his patroness, Lady Gregory (*SS* 208). Heaney's arrival at Glanmore Cottage, in the summer of 1972, is regularly construed in his autobiographical reflections as a moment of artistic self-affirmation. In a sense, the house does for him what the pastoral mode does for its composer or audience:

> It's a silence bunker, a listening post, a holding, in every sense of the word. It holds meanings and things, and even adds meaning. In my life, Glanmore Cottage stands for what Wallace Stevens said poetry stands for, the imagination pressing back against the pressures of reality. (*SS* 325)

In 'Glanmore Eclogue', Heaney's 'house of poetry' also stands for, and shelters behind, the image of Virgil's rural homestead: thus, the poem 'turn[s] a rented smallholding in Co. Wicklow at the end of the 20th century into the equivalent of a farm in the Mantuan countryside, confiscated and resettled on the eve of the first.'[87]

But if Virgil provides cover, he also offers a testing ground, a space for inner dialogue and self-questioning. Heaney's Poet is associated with the fortunate Tityrus of *Eclogues I*, perhaps, because of the lucky swerve Heaney's own life has taken, 'the accident of my life (being called to Stockholm)'.[88] If this is so, then the challenge he sets himself (or the Poet) in 'Glanmore Eclogue' is to hear and respond to the undermusic of the dispossessed farmer, in a way that Tityrus had failed to. With the Virgilian analogy in mind, moreover, one is likely to hear in the name 'Mr Honey'

---

84. Twiddy (2012), 132.
85. Michael: 'that was a hanging crime, mister honey.' (J. M. Synge, *The Playboy of the Western World*, Act I, p. 73, in *Collected Works*, Vol. 4)
86. He bought the cottage in 1988 (*SS* xxv, xxviii).
87. Heaney, 'Lux Perpetua' (2001).
88. Heaney, 'On Elegies', 29.

an allusion to the canny beekeeper, Aristaeus, in *Georgics IV*. Virgil's Aristaeus is an ambivalent figure, a lucky survivor of the tragedy of Orpheus. He is called upon to make an account of himself and appease the offended deities before his bees can thrive. When the Poet calls himself 'Mr Honey', then, it may be to call himself to account in the midst of his good fortune.

Unlike 'Bann Valley', 'Glanmore Eclogue' is composed in a prosy register and loose rhythm, with between nine and thirteen syllables, and mostly five beats per line. In the last section, the Poet delivers a country ballad, distinguishable from the pastoral dialogue by its shorter-lined quatrains and regular tetrameter beat. Myles and the Poet begin by comparing memories of Meliboeus, or Synge; both the works and the life of the absent singer are presented as exemplary of the pastoral mode. If, according to Paul Alpers, pastoral's true subject is 'those whose lives are determined by . . . circumstances over which they have no control' (24), then the Irish Meliboeus has found his way to the heart of the matter. As Myles recalls,

> All the tramps he met tramping the roads
> And all he picked up, listening in a loft
> To servant girls colloquing in the kitchen. (*EL* 35)

The Poet agrees, and again mentions the singer's fondness for the country road as a sign of his instinctive sympathy for the vulnerable and dispossessed:

> Was never happier when he was on the road
> With people on their uppers. Loneliness
> Was his passport through the world. Midge-angels
> On the face of water (*EL* 36)

The Poet then remembers Meliboeus with a line taken from Synge's play *In the Shadow of the Glen*; he was a 'stranger on a wild night, *out in the rain falling.*' (*EL* 36)[89] This is another instance of Cavarero's relational narrative, since Heaney is effectively gifting this memory of Synge's line to Synge himself. In the process, Heaney's fictionalised Synge (Meliboeus) is made to sound very similar to one of Heaney's own alter egos, the migrant King Sweeney.

When Myles asks for one of the old songs, in 'words that the rest of us / Can understand', the Poet offers him a summer ballad as a gift 'for the glen and you' (*EL* 36–7). Heaney might have got the idea of an inset song from C. Day Lewis's translation of *Eclogues V*, which incorporates set pieces with indications of the popular tunes to which they should be sung.[90] But Day Lewis's songs are ornately metered pieces, in eighteenth-century style, which contrast with the colloquial exchange of conversation between the shepherds. Heaney's inset song works in the other

---

89. Nora: 'Good evening kindly, stranger, it's a wild night, God help you, to be out in the rain falling.' (Synge, 'In the Shadow of the Glen', in *Collected Works*, Vol. III, 33)
90. For example, 'tune: 'The Lark in the Clear Air' (*Virgil: The Eclogues*, trans. Day Lewis [1940], 22).

direction, introducing a simple folksong at the request of the down-to-earth farmer. While the first quatrain of the song recalls the well-known Middle English lyric 'Sumer is icumen in', the last echoes the Northern Irish folksong 'The Blackbird of Belfast Lough'. Heaney had translated the song in *Preoccupations* ('The small bird / let a chirp / from its beak', P 181). In one of his last public appearances, he quotes the little poem by heart, in a spontaneous response to a real blackbird that had been singing all through his reading.[91] Within the context of 'Glanmore Eclogue', the Poet, too, appears to be improvising when he produces this lyric from memory:

> A little nippy chirpy fellow
> Hits the highest note there is;
> The lark sings out his clear tidings.
> Summer, shimmer, perfect days. (*EL* 37)

With the absence of a verb in the last line, the Poet's ballad conveys a sense of full summer stillness, a glimpse of a truly naïve Arcadia, imaginary but specifically located in a northern glen, with its 'heather, whins and bog-banks'. In *Preoccupations*, Heaney had praised the 'brightness' and 'steel-pen exactness' of 'The Blackbird of Belfast Lough' and claimed that, in such early Irish nature poems, we are 'nearer the first world' (*P* 181, 185). Here the Poet recites this naïve ballad within the frame of a 'sentimental', postlapsarian exchange, as a gift to a farmer whose livelihood he knows is under threat. Since there is no closing frame to the pastoral dialogue, the ballad is left to resonate open-endedly, in the hope of being well received.

IV. 'ELECTRIC LIGHT'

Heaney's Virgilian eclogues are collected in *Electric Light* (2001), a millennial volume divided into two parts. Part I includes the eclogues and 'Sonnets from Hellas', and other poems more or less explicitly written in the pastoral mode. The Theocritean 'Sonnets from Hellas' are loosely based on Heaney's 1995 trip to the actual Arcadia in Greece.[92] These are collected with other travel poems based on visits to the Asturias, Belgrade, Montana and the Aran Islands. Thus across the range of poems in Part I, the poet appears as a kind of Virgilian Meliboeus, a traveller recording chance encounters on a country road. With Part II devoted to elegies for friends, family and fellow artists, the whole volume could 'carry a Virgilian epigraph', as Heaney remarked; 'it is full of mortalia ... *Sunt lacrimae rerum et mentem mortalia tangunt*.'[93]

---

91. The reading was at the *Marché de la Poésie* festival in Paris, 13 June 2013, <https://www.youtube.com/watch?v=NuUhPovZuB8> (last accessed 14 December 2020).
92. Earlier versions appeared as 'Sonnets from the Peloponnese' (*Cara*, September/October 1998, and *Persephone*, Harvard, 1999), 'The Augean Stables' (*The New Yorker*, 20 March 2000), 'Sonnets from Hellas' (*The Guardian*, 7 April 2001).
93. Heaney, 'Lux Perpetua' (2001), quoting Ae.I.462, here glossing '*mortalia*' as 'people and things

In contrast to *Seeing Things*, where the dominant element is water, here light is a recurrent leitmotif, though the real-world Arcadian light is distinctly postlapsarian. In 'At Toomebridge', water comes pouring over the weir as if it had 'fallen shining to the continuous / Present of the Bann.' (*EL* 3) Radiant as it is, the sheet of water emits a fallen light. The shining waterfall recalls the '*lux perpetua*' of the Catholic Mass for the dead.[94] An occluded, fallen light is associated with the Virgilian *lacrimae rerum* in the volume's titular and final poem, 'Electric Light', where Heaney recalls a memory of his maternal grandmother.[95] The poem begins with a close-up view of his grandmother's smashed thumbnail, a 'puckered pearl, // Rucked quartz, a littered Cumae.' (ll. 3–4) Heaney then recalls a frightening night in his childhood, when he was left to stay with her alone: the 'scaresome cavern waters' of her sibilant speech were an 'eddy of sibylline English.'[96] In the remembrance, the grandmother has become a Cumaean Sibyl, initiating the child into the mysteries of poetic language. But she seems a more alienating figure than the Sibyl who leads Aeneas into Hades in the golden bough episode. There she was young, and in Heaney's symbolism, a poetic diviner such as Aeneas would become himself. In 'Electric Light', the hero and his guide have grown apart in age, the initiate being much younger and the Sibyl very much older, like the frail creature helplessly suspended at the start of Eliot's 'The Waste Land'.[97] Her sibylline speech does not fortify the child. On the contrary, the archaism of her repeated question, 'What ails you, child?', fills him with fear; he 'wept and wept / Under the clothes, under the waste of light' (ll. 10–12).

At the same time, this memory of his grandmother's house comes back to him later as a source of wonder and connection to modernity and futurity, as indeed the Sibyl's prophecy potentially is in *Eclogues IV*. It is in his grandmother's house that the boy first encounters electricity and is allowed to work the light switch and the radio controls, roaming 'at will the stations of the world.' (l. 36) So this aged, modern Sibyl is still a poetic diviner and the child is still an initiate, learning to tune in to the frequencies of other people's lives. In the middle section of the poem, the poet is an adult emerging from the London Underground into an Eliot-like

---

we must pass away from or that have had to pass away from us'. Elsewhere, Virgil's *lacrimae* are associated with Wilfred Owen's 'the eternal reciprocity of tears' (*SS* 119); Robert Frost's 'leaving poetry free to go its way in tears' (see Potts, (2011), 48); and Miłosz's 'tears, tears' in 'From the Rising of the Sun' (*FK* 415).

94. '*et lux perpetua luceat eis*', 'And let perpetual light shine upon them' (Heaney, 'Lux Perpetua', 2001). Cf. his comment on 'Toome' in *SS* 135: 'I was more conscious of the strong bright lumen and numen of the Bann River, the big lift of light over Lough Neagh'.
95. *EL* 80–1. Heaney identifies his grandmother in *SS* 27.
96. *EL* 80, ll. 14, 16. Cf. 'So from the back of her shrine the Sibyl of Cumae. / Chanted scaresome equivocal words and made the cave echo' (*GB*.1–2). See Chapter 1.
97. '"Nam Sibyllam quidem Cumis ego ipse oculis meis vidi / in ampulla pendere, et cum illi pueri dicerent: Σίβυλλα τί θέλεις; / respondebat illa: ἀπο θανεῖν θέλω."' (T. S. Eliot, epigraph, 'The Waste Land', quoting Petronius' *Satyricon*, 'I saw with my own eyes the Sibyl at Cumae hanging in a cage, and when the boys said to her: "Sibyl, what do you want?" she answered: "I want to die."' (2015), 53).

waste land: 'From tube-mouth into sunlight, / Moyola-breath by Thames's "straunge stronde".' (ll. 29–30) One of the memories that sustains him in later life is the fearful hardness of the smashed nail of his grandmother, now buried in Derry: 'it must still keep / Among beads and vertebrae in the Derry ground.' (ll. 44–5) However small and frail this 'glit-glittery' fragment of memory is, it exemplifies the hardness and durability of that now distant, rural community (l. 44). Throughout *Electric Light*, Virgil's presence is invoked in this way, to preside over the careful transport of such fragments of memory.

V. 'THE STAYING POWER OF PASTORAL'

It was soon after composing these Virgilian poems that Heaney developed his theory of pastoral poetry and its cultural staying power. Most of his essays, lectures and interviews on pastoral were also delivered shortly after 11 September 2001, and reflect the mood of apprehension and fear that affected many in the wake of that cataclysmic event. Virgil's life and works continue to feature prominently in these lectures and essays, including the address to the Royal Academy, 'Eclogues in Extremis', in which Heaney articulates his most formal *apologia* for the mode of pastoral.[98]

He begins this major address by presenting his compatriot Michael Longley as a modern Orpheus, 'a love poet' closely related to 'the shepherds and goatherds of classical eclogue' (2). As Heaney explains, Longley's poem 'The Beech Tree' alludes to the four-line *sphragis* (seal, or signature) with which Virgil concludes his *Georgics*. In these lines, Virgil relates how he persisted in singing of local matters, the peaceful tending of fields, trees and animals, while Octavian and his army thundered away ('*fuminat*') in the East (G.IV.559–63).[99] In the last line, he reminds his readers of his beginnings in pastoral: '*Tityre, te patulae cecini sub tegmine fagi*' ('Tityrus, [I] sang / Of how you lay in ease in the beech tree's shade').[100] Recalling these lines, Longley himself reinforces the link between georgic and pastoral, between country labour and an Arcadian ideal of social harmony.[101] His long, twelve-beat line and single, ramifying, unbroken sentence offer a naïve pastoral ideal of wholeness in deliberate resistance to the modern, public consciousness that in Northern Ireland had been conditioned 'by the old sectarian and ideological divisions' (2).

The subtitle of Heaney's address is 'the staying power of pastoral', where 'staying' has two senses: 'resisting or standing up to power' and 'tholing it', or enduring suffering and keeping going.[102] Robert Frost's dictum that 'a poem is a momentary stay

98. 'Eclogues *in Extremis*' (2003), delivered 6 June 2002.
99. On Virgil's *sphragis* and its political ambivalence, see *Virgil: Georgics*, ed. R. F. Thomas, (2001), 241.
100. G.IV.566. Trans. Ferry, *The Georgics of Virgil* (2006).
101. Heaney, 'Eclogues *in Extremis*', 2. Longley's poem ends, 'And improvises a last line for the georgics / About snoozing under this beech tree's canopy.' (M. Longley, *The Weather in Japan* (London, 2000), 62)
102. On 'tholing', see Heaney, 'Further Language' (1997), 11. See also, S. Kearney, 'The Staying

against confusion', often quoted by Heaney, contributes to this sense of pastoral's double staying power.[103] While Frost contributes greatly to Heaney's appreciation of pastoral, it is arguably the Eastern European and Russian poets whose writing encouraged him to view classical pastoral as a poetic form capable of resisting or enduring extreme political violence in modern times.[104] As he told Richard Kearney in 1992, 'what you find in poets like Miłosz, Sorescu or Holub is an invocation of classical mythology . . . in a totally contemporary, angry way.'[105] The classics proved to be a 'quickening' and 'vivifying' resource for such writers as they faced the atrocities of twentieth-century world wars, occupation and genocide.[106]

In 'Eclogues *in Extremis*', Heaney's examples of modern pastoral range from the serenity of Longley's 'The Beech' to poems composed in much darker circumstances: Miłosz's 'The World', Louis MacNeice's 'An Eclogue for Christmas', written before the outbreak of world war in 1933, and bleakest of all, Radnóti's 'Eighth Eclogue'.[107] The Hungarian poet Miklós Radnóti composed his eclogues while in a labour camp, and on a forced march which drove him to exhaustion and death. A notebook containing his eclogues was rescued from the poet's body, exhumed from a mass grave after the war.[108] Radnóti's 'Eighth Eclogue' records his experience of walking on that grim, interminable road: '"this time still grinds me down like a stone in a swift-surging stream"' (ibid.). The classical form of the poem (its Ariel 'beauty'), Heaney argues, allows the poet's rage to sound forth in such a way that leaves the reader vivified and nourished rather than wholly overwhelmed by the poem's 'terrible realism'.[109]

If the appalling circumstances of Radnóti's death bring him closest to the fate of the mythical Orpheus, Czesław Miłosz is the modern poet whom Heaney most frequently likens to Virgil. And while he once described the 'curve of Miłosz's whole destiny' as Virgilian (*FK* 411), it is generally Virgil's *Eclogues* he has in mind when comparing their work. In the Academy lecture he argues that 'the integrity, consonance and radiance that I've claimed for Virgil's *Eclogues* can also be claimed for

---

Power of Poetry: Interview with Seamus Heaney' (2007), 14; and Heaney's lecture 'Staying Power' and post-lecture remarks (Harvard, 22 October 2002). Audiofile, courtesy of Woodberry Poetry Room, Harvard University.

103. Frost, 'The Figure a Poem Makes' (Preface to *Collected Poems*, 1939). Frost's claim that poetry provides 'a momentary stay against confusion' is quoted by Heaney on numerous occasions (such as *P* 193; *RP* xiv–xv, 198; 'Above the Brim' (1997), 66; 'The Whole Thing' (2001), 10). Quoting Frost's 'Directive' (which ends, 'Drink and be whole again beyond confusion'), Heaney comments that the poem 'provides a draught of the clear water of transformed understanding and fills the reader with a momentary sense of freedom and wholeness' (*RP* xv).
104. For Frost's influence on Heaney, see Buxton (2004) and Potts (2011).
105. 'Between North and South' (1995), 104–5.
106. Ibid.
107. Heaney also admired Joseph Brodsky, who quotes Virgil in 'Eclogue 4: Winter'. See Putnam (2010), 12.
108. M. Radnóti, *Camp Notebook* (2000), quoted in Heaney, 'Eclogues *in Extremis*', 12. On Radnóti as a twentieth-century Virgil, see Takács (2013).
109. Heaney, 'Eclogues *in Extremis*', 12, alluding to Shakespeare's 'Sonnet 65', 'How with this rage shall beauty hold a plea?'

another sequence ['The World'] . . . by the poet whom I regard as the greatest one alive among us today.'[110] Miłosz's 'The World' resembles *The Eclogues* in that it celebrates the rural idyll of a family farm, which for Miłosz was a small woodland estate in Lithuania.[111] This *locus amoenus* is now definitively lost; the poem was composed in Nazi-occupied Warsaw, in 1943. 'The World' is subtitled 'A naïve poem', which, as Heaney points out, nods ironically to Schiller's distinction between 'naïve' and 'sentimental' pastoral. It is 'sentimental' or postlapsarian in the way it deliberately conjures a remembered, childhood idyll as a defence against 'one of the most atrocious moments of World War II', when 'concentration-camps were opening like hell-mouths all over Europe'.[112] For Heaney, what is important is 'not so much the consoling innocence of the memories themselves as the artistic intransigence with which the innocence is presented. There is something bullet-proof about Miłosz's crystal palace.' (ibid.) The poet aims for 'a pure calligraphic line' in 'The World' because if you had attempted to describe what the world was actually like at that time, says Heaney, quoting Miłosz, '"you'd have had to scream, to speak"' (ibid.). Miłosz's deliberately 'naïve' poem and Radnóti's searing, war-time eclogues are both instances of what Heaney describes as 'pastoral used to devastating effect'.[113]

But while he compares Miłosz to Virgil on several occasions, on closer scrutiny his classical pastoral exemplar does not much resemble the intransigent, mentally bullet-proof artist being lauded in his Academy address. Heaney elevates Miłosz to heroic status in part because of the horrific wars he had lived through; he refers to the Polish poet, for example, as 'the Master . . . an imagined site of authority, an imagined completeness'.[114] This is quite distinct from the familiar tone he uses to invoke 'my hedge-schoolmaster Virgil'. His admiration for both poets is beyond question, but Heaney's image of Virgil is homely rather than heroic. In terms of the Orpheus myth discussed in the last chapter, if Miłosz is the Orphic–Tiresian prophet, Virgil combines the virtues of Orpheus with Aristaeus, the canny 'Mr Honey' who survives the crisis and preserves his hives. And to both these characters, Virgil now brings the *pietas* of Aeneas. When incorporated into the chronotope of pastoral, Aeneas' princely *pietas* becomes tangibly familiar and even domestic, as here: 'for the sake of the future I believe we must carry our possessions, we must do Aeneas's job and, you know, get Daddy on our back, and get the household materials together and carry them along.'[115] This is to see Aeneas, after the fall of Troy, in the condition of a migrant herdsman, travelling the open road and vulnerable to powerful forces beyond his control. And conversely, Virgil's herdsmen are recognised as preserving the cultural history of a displaced people in their exchange of pastoral song.

110. 'Eclogues *in Extremis*', 7. In *FK* 411, Heaney again describes 'The World' as 'a kind of twentieth century equivalent of Virgil's *Eclogues*.' Parker quotes Heaney (12 August 1997) describing Miłosz as 'my hero amongst the living' ('"Past master"', 2013), 844.
111. 'Eclogues *in Extremis*', 7. On Miłosz's 'The World', see Parker (2017).
112. 'Eclogues *in Extremis*', 7. Cf. 'On Elegies', which also likens 'The World' to Virgil's *Eclogues*.
113. 'On Elegies', 26.
114. 'On Elegies', 30.
115. 'On Elegies', 29.

Heaney's notion of the staying power of pastoral is most fully developed in 'Eclogues in Extremis', and for that reason has been widely discussed by his academic readers. In terms of his dialogue with Virgilian pastoral, however, another, little-known essay is equally, if not more, illuminating. Since this essay is not easily accessible, I take the liberty of quoting from it somewhat liberally below. 'Towers, Trees, Terrors, a Rêverie in Urbino' is based on a lecture delivered in 2001, at the University of Urbino, where Heaney received an honorary degree.[116] The occasion demanded a celebratory note, and yet the terrorist attacks in New York City had occurred only a month earlier. The title of the lecture alludes to the twin towers of the World Trade Center, while the address itself gathers a triumvirate of Italian poets, Dante, Virgil and Horace, to ward off the recent images of destruction from the United States. If ever there were a time to offer the *Eclogues'* crystalline *integritas* as a mental shield against violent conflict, this would surely have been it. But Heaney remits the apotropaeic function of poetry to Dante, while he summons Virgil as a gentle companion met along the roadside, found travelling in company with shepherds and cattle-drovers (152).

Before paying homage to Italy's poets, Heaney establishes the Irish connection with W. B. Yeats, who was inspired by the sight of a tower in Urbino to purchase Thoor Ballylee in Galway. This place of writing leads Heaney to speak of Dante, and his translation of 'Ugolino', thus moving from a tower of poetry to a tower in *inferno*. From Ugolino's tower Heaney shifts his attention to the Twin Towers in New York, and the Horatian ode he translated in response to these new 'terrors'.[117] Heaney's next move is to step away from these global conflicts, and return to pastoral's country road:

> But to be honest, I am more at home among trees than among towers. More familiar with the farmer in the doorway of his barn than the sage in the door of his tower. More fitted by temperament for conversation with cattle drovers on a country road than for passionate argument with the damned in the deep circles of hell. I am more equipped, in other words, for Virgilian pastoral than for Dantesque epic.
>
> When Virgil appears to me, it is not as someone who is heaven-sent by a Beatrice but rather as somebody encountered by chance on the road to the village.[118]

This neighbourly portrait of Virgil is quite striking when one recalls that, a decade earlier, Heaney had been focused on the divinely sanctioned *katabasis* of Virgil's epic hero, Aeneas. But as suggested above, Heaney finds parallels between Aeneas'

---

116. 'Towers, Trees, Terrors, a Rêverie in Urbino', in *In forma di parole: Seamus Heaney poeta dotto, a cura di Gabriella Morisco* 23:2 (2007), 145–56 (based on a lecture delivered in Urbino, 23 November 2001).
117. See Chapter 5 for Heaney's response, via Horace and Virgil, to 9/11 and 7/7 (the 2005 London bombings).
118. 'Towers, Trees, Terrors', 152.

migrant wanderings and the herdsmen's precarious conditions of life. More fundamentally, his interest has shifted to the poet Virgil himself, and the country origins they share in common:

> He had his beech-trees ... I grew up under beech trees ... Virgil had his River Mincius, I have my River Moyola. Virgil moved from his father's farm in the North to a poet's retreat outside Naples in the South, I made [a] similar move from Ulster to Wicklow and Dublin. Virgil lived through civil war in the aftermath of Julius Caesar's assassination. I have experienced not only the civic violence of Ulster, but thanks to the age of technology, I have witnessed civil wars and ethnic conflicts all over the globe, blanket bombing and terrorist attacks. (152–3)

Whether or not this biography of Virgil is historically verifiable, Heaney is drawing on its broad outlines to structure and fortify his own life history. His displacement from Derry to Wicklow and Dublin is, in a sense, alleviated and offset by being mirrored in the displacement of Virgil from Mantua to Rome.

In the following passage, Heaney's postlapsarian awareness intensifies, but he continues to derive 'staying power' from the parallelism of Virgil's history and his own:

> Virgil saw the roads of Italy full of dispossessed labourers and erstwhile estate owners, people like Virgil's own father driven out of their holdings by Caesar's veterans, forced to yield up their homes and their land at sword-point; I have seen the streets of Belfast burn and then fill with neighbours, driven out by other neighbours, but I have also lived to see refugees return to the roads of Europe and Asia and Africa, to the ports, to the border posts, even to the local traffic lights where they plead to be allowed to sell you a flower or to wash your wind-screen. (153)

The pastoral roads have multiplied and extended from 'Hibernia and Italia' to all over Europe, but this trans-European perspective remains at street level, in sympathy with the displaced refugee.[119] Heaney's eye then pursues the tide of displaced humanity until it turns, and the refugees flow back into Europe and across the world, working and reclaiming the same streets.

Heaney's concluding remarks are undisguised in their affection for Virgil as a man, a poet and an exemplar. In contrast to the intransigent artist holed up in his solitary tower, with which he began his essay, Virgil inspires in him a sense of fellowship so strong that it manages to bridge the distance of 2,000 years:

> I bring up Virgil simply because I love to think of him, the genius of his language who is also so local in his origins, an artist at once naturally endowed

---

119. Cf. the realism of the first 'Sonnet from Hellas': 'And then it was the goatherd / With his goats in the forecourt of the filling station / Subsisting beyond eclogue and translation.' (EL 38)

and totally educated, *poeta natus* and *poeta doctus*, a poet with a gift for pastoral song who nevertheless had the imaginative power to make pastoral song accomodate [sic] the brutalities and injustices of his time; a temperament made for Arcadia but forced to take stock of Actium. (153)

As we saw in Heaney's Virgilian eclogues, the Arcadian temperament is never very far from an awareness of actual, historical circumstances. The word 'local', appearing in both quotations above, answers back to Eliot's portrayal of Virgil as a universalised figure, a 'familiar compound ghost' of 'latinate–classical–canonical' authority (*FK* 174). While Virgil's poetry forms the bridge between antiquity and modern European literature for both poets, Heaney's Virgil differs from T.S. Eliot's in this important respect: he is the poetic exemplar for a pluralistic Europe, where individual languages remain distinctly rooted in their own, local grounds.

*

It was Eliot who wrote, in an essay that Heaney had read as an undergraduate at Queen's, that Virgil's writing lacked Dante's *amor*, that he was 'more tepid' than other Latin poets, and that 'we feel ourselves, with Virgil, to be moving in a kind of emotional twilight.'[120] By contrast, Heaney's essays on pastoral, along with his Virgilian eclogues, portray Virgil as an exceptionally empathetic writer, attuned to the needs and hardships of ordinary country people. Later, he remarks on this same quality of empathy in Basho and Japanese poetry with its heightened sense of *mono no aware* (literally, 'the pathos of things'). It is the 'closeness to common experience' and 'sensitivity to *lacrimae rerum*, to the grievous aspects of human experience', that make such poetry 'a permanent and ever more valuable resource.'[121] As an example of *mono no aware*, Heaney quotes a stanza from Eliot's 'Preludes' that might almost have been spoken by his own hedge-schoolmaster Virgil:

> I am moved by fancies that are curled
> Around these images, and cling:
> The notion of some infinitely gentle
> Infinitely suffering thing.[122]

---

120. Eliot, 'Virgil and the Christian World' (1951), in Hayward, ed., *Selected Prose*, 98–9.
121. Heaney, 'Afterword: Petals on a Bough' (2007), 218.
122. Eliot, 'Preludes', ll. 10–13 (2015), Vol. I, p. 16. Quoted by Heaney, 'Afterword: Petals on a Bough', 216.

5. 'Terra tremens': *District and Circle*

In his address to the Royal College of Surgeons in Ireland in 2001, Heaney spoke about the sense of apprehension and fear experienced by many in the wake of the bombings of the World Trade Center in New York City. There was, he said, a 'feeling that a crack had run through the foundations of the world, that the roof was blown off, that the border between the imaginable and the possible had been eradicated.'[1] This millennial awareness of a fractured, destabilised world runs throughout Heaney's next collection of poems, *District and Circle* (2006). In terms of his dialogue with Virgil, while *Electric Light* incorporates Aeneas' epic wandering into a pastoral framework, his next collection moves the other way and casts the pastoral chronotope on to the vertical axis of an epic *katabasis*, a freshly imagined descent into the underworld and return.

Heaney is therefore revisiting earlier preoccupations with Aeneas' underworld quest, the golden bough, and the threshold crossing into the marvellous. But several years' immersion in classical and modern European pastoral has also shifted his perspective on Virgil's *katabatic* narrative. In *District and Circle*, the descent journey is about coming to terms with the damaged world, and reimagining the modern city through the lens of pastoral. Some reviewers objected to this pastoral dimension, taking it as a sign of escapist nostalgia: 'the world has changed, but Heaney's art has not', and 'as a 21st-century poet of the pastoral, he verges perilously toward a nostalgia out of place in a post-9/11, global–capitalist world'.[2] But this is to miss both the actively oppositional dynamics of pastoral in *Electric Light*, and the new relation of pastoral to urban poetics that Heaney is exploring in *District and Circle*. Once again, this new direction is stimulated by Heaney's ongoing dialogue with Roman writers, in this case with Virgil, Horace and Livy.

---

1. Heaney, 'The Whole Thing' (2001), 11. Lecture delivered as the Annual Distinguished Lecture, Department of International Health and Tropical Medicine, The Royal College of Surgeons in Ireland, 5 November 2001.
2. Bedient (2007), Schneider (2006).

Heaney reread Horace's *Odes I*, 34 in the days after September 11, 2001, when he was feeling 'called upon to do something that would be an answer', a rising 'to the challenge of the historical moment'.[3] Horace's ode describes the poet's shock and awe on hearing Jupiter, the god of thunder, drive his chariot across a clear sky. In the aftermath of 9/11, the poem struck Heaney as possessing 'an uncanny strength and sooth-saying force' with 'an eerie contemporary applicability.'[4] For Heaney in 2001, the ode is 'about *terra tremens*, the opposite of *terra firma*. About the tremor that runs down to earth's foundations when thunder is heard and about the tremor of fear that shakes the very being of the individual who hears it.'[5]

A similar tremor of fear is captured in the five-sonnet sequence 'District and Circle', which Heaney expanded from two existing sonnets, in the weeks after the bombing of the London Underground on 7 July 2005. The semi-autobiographical poem reflects back on the summer of 1962, when a young Heaney commuted to work at the London Passport Office on the Tube (SS 410). In the expanded sequence, the young man's dreamy descent into the Underground takes on echoes of Aeneas's descent into Hades, and the appearance of his father's ghost triggers a crucial turning point in his journey (*DC* 17–19). This expanded version becomes the title poem in Heaney's 2006 collection, *District and Circle*, a volume that meditates on the current state of our fragile, mortal earth, our '*terra tremens*'.

The roof has blown off the known world not only because of international terrorism, but also because of global-scale, human-induced climate change. A sense of threat to the natural environment surfaces in poems such as 'Höfn', 'Moyulla', 'The Birch Grove', 'On the Spot' and 'The Tollund Man in Springtime'. These poems reflect the growing public awareness that the earth's ecosystem is being fundamentally altered by human activity.[6] In 'The Tollund Man in Springtime', Heaney's Iron Age archetype rises out of his museum display case to enter a polluted urban landscape. He gathers his ancient powers of endurance to face the new reality of the Anthropocene (*DC* 55–7).[7]

Speaking in Urbino, a month after the 9/11 attacks, Heaney took the occasion to reflect on the city's name and its etymological origin in *urbs* (Latin for 'city').[8] Reading the Roman historian Livy at school, Heaney remembers how 'the noun *urbs*, feminine and radiant, gleamed constantly at the centre of the historian's narrative.' (148) While Livy's narrative was 'mostly concerned with matters military and masculine,' occasionally he would refer to Rome 'simply as the *urbs*, and for a moment the city turned from being the site of government and imperium to being a mixture of *alma mater* and muse.' (148–9) In *District and Circle*, while many poems register the shock of the 'military and masculine' city under attack, Heaney is also

---

3. 'The Whole Thing', 17.
4. 'The Whole Thing', 18. Cf. *Anything Can Happen* (2004), 15; and 'Reality and Justice' (2002/3), 51.
5. 'The Whole Thing', 17–18.
6. See, for example, McKibben (1989); Latour (2004), 25–31.
7. Heaney, SS 410; 'One Poet in Search of a Title' (2006).
8. Heaney, 'Towers, Trees, Terrors' ([2001] 2007), 146. See also Chapter 4.

pursuing the gleam of Livy's 'feminine and radiant' *urbs*: that is, a centre of culture and education, offering protection to strangers rather than attracting the world's envy and resentment.[9]

As collected in *District and Circle*, Heaney's millennial poems fall into the roughly tripartite shape of a *katabatic* journey, beginning with the disruption of ordinary reality by a cataclysmic event, then a descent into the mythic underworld that is triggered by the shock of disruption, and finally, a return to the altered, material world. The narrative arc is traversed in several individual poems but it also provides an overarching structure to the collection: the Horatian ode, 'Anything Can Happen', marks the opening phase (dis-orientation, orientation towards Hades); 'District and Circle' enacts the poet's Virgilian descent; and 'The Tollund Man in Springtime' effects a regenerative return from the underworld. Before turning to these poems in detail, we should consider some of the broader ramifications of Heaney's return to underworld motifs and the archetype of the descent journey.

1. *KATABASIS* IN OUR TIME

In his lecture to the Royal College of Surgeons, Heaney observed how 'religious language sprang naturally to the lips of leaders' in the aftermath of 9/11, as 'talk of good and evil fulfilled a need and gave an order to the threatening chaos'.[10] The righteous militarism of US and UK governments in the early 2000s brought back, for Heaney, the 'high rhetoric' of World War I: 'high rhetoric in high places,' with their 'high certainty about God on our side, high flags and high patriotism' (ibid., 12). In the war poems of Wilfred Owen, by contrast, Heaney finds such patriotic certainties being challenged and exposed as comforting falsehoods (13). Owen borrows from the Judeo-Christian iconography of Hell to convey its actual materialisation in the trenches of World War I. And, having invoked the idea of Hell, Owen then 'proceeded to elaborate it to the fullest of his emotional and technical ability, using the richest deposits of the civilization he was in the trenches to defend.'[11]

One of the most ancient of these 'deposits' is the narrative of a descent into the underworld and return. From *The Epic of Gilgamesh* and Homer's *Odyssey XI* down to the literature and film of our own time, the *katabatic* journey has offered writers and artists a way of structuring, giving shape, coherence and possibilities of resistance to the experience of extreme suffering and loss.[12] For Heaney, Wilfred Owen's

---

9. Cf. Heaney's comments, in an early notebook, on the early settlements of medieval Catholic Britain: 'those worlds centred round a divine purpose, and an *urbs* at once of earth and heaven, pegged together concentrically by the cross' (*LP* I.vi.2, 'Notebook, 1966–75').
10. 'The Whole Thing', 11.
11. 'The Whole Thing', 13. For the materialisation of Hell in modern history, see Steiner (1971), 47.
12. Raymond Clark defines *katabasis* as 'a Journey of the Dead made by a living person in the flesh who returns to our world to tell the tale' (1979), 34. See also Falconer (2007), Martiny (2009) and Thurston (2009).

poem 'Strange Meeting' belongs in this *katabatic* tradition, where the aim is not only to give an account of a real, material hell but also to 'ma[k]e a homeopathic gesture towards healing' (14). In 'Strange Meeting', which Heaney quotes in full, the poet meets a dead soldier in a 'profound dull tunnel', a space he recognises immediately: 'I knew that sullen hall, / By his dead smile I knew we stood in Hell.' (15) In an echo of Virgil's *lacrimae rerum*, Owen's poem attempts to deliver 'the truth untold, / The pity of war, the pity war distilled.'[13] More than simply witnessing the actualisation of Hell in history, Owen actively reshapes the Judeo-Christian iconography he has inherited. There, writes Heaney, 'in the hell upon earth that the twentieth century soldier-poet inhabits and reinterprets', instead of a confrontation with the Satanic other of the Judeo-Christian tradition, 'sympathy is given, blame is removed and enmity is replaced by friendship.'[14] Owen's 'Strange Meeting' administers its curative poison through the voice of the dead soldier who tells the poet, 'I am the enemy you killed, my friend.'

There is a similar resistance to demonising the other in Heaney's *The Burial at Thebes*, a version of Sophocles' *Antigone* that he produced for the Abbey Theatre in Dublin, in 2004. In an afterword to the volume, Heaney likens the Bush administration to Sophocles' Creon, who pushed the citizens of Thebes into an either/or choice over Antigone's defiance of the law: 'Either you are a patriot, a loyal citizen, and regard Antigone as an enemy of the state because she does honour to her traitor brother, or else you yourselves are traitorous because you stand up for a woman who has broken the law and defied my authority.'[15] After 9/11, President Bush likewise demanded of Americans, 'Are you in favour of state security or are you not? If you don't support the eradication of this tyrant in Iraq and the threat he poses to the free world, you are on the wrong side of the "war on terror".' (ibid.) In Heaney's view, Sophocles achieves an even, dramatic balance between Antigone's world-view and Creon's, allowing the audience space to reflect rather than immediately take sides. As in Owen's 'Strange Meeting', Sophocles' tragedy creates a space for reflection and an imaginative shift to the point of view of the 'stranger'.

The terrorist attacks on New York City in 2001 seemed to many like another eruption of Hell in the material world.[16] But if this religious iconography is still deeply embedded in our cultural consciousness, so too are the wisdom-seeking dynamics of *katabatic* narrative.[17] That is, the descent to the underworld is, or can be, a *via negativa* whose aim is a fuller comprehension of injustice, suffering and loss, rather than a demonisation of the enemy as evil incarnate. Heaney's familiarity with sectarian conflict in Northern Ireland, from the killings in Derry on Bloody

---

13. Owen, 'Strange Meeting' (1977), 35, quoted in 'The Whole Thing', 14–15. As noted above (p. 118, note 93), for Heaney, Virgil's *lacrimae rerum* conjures close associations with modern poets such as Wilfred Owen ('the eternal reciprocity of tears'), Robert Frost and Czesław Miłosz, who all draw on Virgilian pastoral to 'devastating effect'.
14. 'The Whole Thing', 14.
15. Heaney, 'A Note on The Burial at Thebes', in *The Burial at Thebes*, 75–9 (76).
16. See Falconer, 'Hell in Our Time' (2010), 217–36.
17. As Clark writes, the *telos* of ancient *katabatic* narratives is the recovery of wisdom lost or concealed in the past (1979, 34).

Sunday, 30 January 1972, to the car bombing in Omagh, County Tyrone, in August 1998, made him acutely aware that polarised opposition would lead to an escalation of violence. Thus, in the attack on the Twin Towers he already foresaw the brutal military retaliations that would follow:

> the irruption of death into the Manhattan morning produced not only world-darkening grief for the multitudes of victims' families and friends, but it also had the effect of darkening the future with the prospect of deadly retaliations. Stealth bombers pummeling the fastnesses of Afghanistan, shock and awe loosed from the night skies over Iraq, they all seem part of the deadly fallout from the thunder cart in Horace's clear blue afternoon.[18]

Horace's ode speaks to him in the aftermath of 9/11 because it witnesses this eruption of deadly violence without being drawn into a polarised response. The US government did succumb to the mimetic desire for retaliation and unleashed its own version of *inferno* on the city of Baghdad.[19] As a consequence, millions of people suffered in the vortex of destruction that followed the attack on thousands of people in New York City. The former US soldier Roy Scranton remembers how his company 'convoyed all day, all night, past Army checkpoints and burned out tanks, till in the blue dawn Baghdad rose from the desert like a vision of hell'.[20] Inevitably, images inherited from Homer, Virgil and Dante shape his perception of this materialised vision of hell: 'flames licked the bruised sky from the tops of refinery towers, cyclopean monuments bulged and leaned against the horizon, broken overpasses swooped and fell over ruined suburbs, bombed factories, and narrow, ancient streets.' (ibid.) Infernal monsters and flaming towers are imbedded in the Western cultural imagination of Hell. But *katabatic* narratives attempt to trace a meaningful journey through this violent chaos, giving the infernal experience shape and perspective where possible.[21]

In *District and Circle*, Heaney adopts the vantage point of a road-side witness; meditating on global destruction, his gaze is most often at street level, in sympathy with the civilian casualties of war. Three pieces of 'Found Prose' describe road-side encounters, and in one, 'The Lagans Road', Heaney's primary school has the provisional appearance of a refugee shelter: 'a couple of low-set Nissen huts raising their corrugated backs above the hedges.' (*DC* 36). *District and Circle* is dedicated to his pastoral muse, Ann Saddlemyer; and in the last poem of the volume, 'The Blackbird of Glanmore', Heaney is on a gravel walk, recalling the fatal road accident of his

---

18. Heaney, *Anything Can Happen* (2004), 18.
19. In *Violence and the Sacred*, René Girard argues that violence typically escalates mimetically until a sacred scapegoat can be found to arrest the cycle (1977).
20. Scranton (2015), 13.
21. Susan Neiman (2002) argues that on the subject of evil, there are broadly two schools of philosophy: one which holds that evil must be meaningful (Leibniz, Kant, Marx), and the other that it must be meaningless (Hume, the Marquis de Sade, Schopenhauer). Arguably, *katabatic* literature shares its generic world-view with the former of these schools.

four-year-old brother; by the end of the poem, he is imagining himself gone and the gravel path empty. Like the pilgrim Dante, or the herdsman on the country road, the speaker in many of these poems is displaced from centres of power and detached from the escalating cycle of violence.

In an essay on translating Horace's ode, Heaney describes how two American friends, on holiday in Florence at the time of the 9/11 attacks, turned to Renaissance art to work through their shock and grief.[22] Heaney explains that they were drawn to art because of its 'capacity to distinguish itself from us and our needs and at the same time to make ourselves and our needs distinct and contemplatable'.[23] Both the art itself, and their geographical distance from home, afforded these New Yorkers the time and space to absorb their shock and come to terms with the altered reality. In this way, as Heaney later reflects, art can create 'a pause in the action, a freeze-frame moment of concentration' (SS 382–3). In Heaney's translation of Horace, sympathy and detachment are distributed in equal measure, as we shall see below. The translation has attracted some critical censure, both for its detachment and for its hint of sympathy for the perpetrators of the 9/11 attack. But Heaney draws on Horace precisely to detach himself from taking sides.

The title of his 2006 collection, *District and Circle*, is a further indication of Heaney's aim to embrace global concerns as well as reaffirm ties to his own childhood 'district' in County Derry. Mirroring the circular and linear trajectory of the two London Tube lines, Heaney's *katabatic* journey both circles back in time and projects forward into the millennial present. In terms of poetic form, the cultural 'deposit' being forwarded and transformed in *District and Circle* is the sonnet, in both Shakespearean and Petrarch varieties. The echo of Shakespeare in 'A Shiver' is underlined with the near-rhyming couplet at the end. But elsewhere, as in 'District and Circle', Heaney uses the Petrarchan sonnet, with its ninth line *volta*, to map the trajectory of a mythic descent and return.

The first ten poems of the collection, six of which had been published earlier in a pamphlet entitled *A Shiver* (2005), make up the opening movement of the volume's tripartite, *katabatic* shape. Most of the poems in this first section are set in Heaney's childhood around the family farm at Mossbawn (DC 1–12). Although based on the daily life of a rural community, they are still 'coloured by a darkened understanding' of war and therefore 'capable of bearing the brunt of present realities'.[24] Thus, in 'Anahorish 1944', Heaney recalls the arrival of American troops in tanks and jeeps, headed for the war in Normandy (DC 7). And before the soldiers arrive, the community is already ringing with the prescient noise of turnip-snedders, sledgehammers and blacksmiths' anvils (DC 3, 25, 26, 51). As Heaney explains, 'The blow struck on the local anvil and the strike against the twin towers are the tuning forks for poems that appear in the early pages of . . . *District and Circle*.'[25]

---

22. Heaney, 'Reality and Justice' (2002/3).
23. Ibid., 50.
24. LP I.xvii.10 ('PBS Bulletin', 28 February 2006).
25. Heaney, 'One Poet in Search of a Title'.

Originally, Heaney had 'Midnight Anvil' in mind as the title poem of the volume, as 'its suggestions of hammering force and ominous dark matched the mood of the new age of anxiety.'[26]

The title poem of the earlier pamphlet likewise centres on a hammer blow landing with shattering force. In 'A Shiver', Heaney recalls being taught to use a sledgehammer as a young child:

> The way you had to stand to swing the sledge,
> Your two knees locked, your lower back shock-fast
> As shields in a *testudo* (DC 5)

The 'you' being addressed here is not only the poet's childhood self but any human being who has delivered a deadly stroke, from the Roman army implied in '*testudo*' (a military 'tortoise' formation) to contemporary terrorists, soldiers and heads of state. Heaney compares the 'gathered force' of the hammer blow to 'a long-nursed rage / About to be let fly'. In his essay on Horace, he faces this kind of rage with Shakespeare's question in Sonnet 65: 'How with this rage shall beauty hold a plea / Whose action is no stronger than a flower?'[27] While Horace's ode gives no human agency to the violent blow, in 'A Shiver' Heaney directly accosts the 'you' with responsibility:

>   does it do you good
> To have known it in your bones, directable
> Withholdable at will.
> A first blow that could make air of a wall,
> A last one so unanswerably landed
> The staked earth quailed and shivered in the handle? (DC 5)

The question 'does it do you good?', while primarily directed at the author of the hammer blow, also challenges the artist to 'hold a plea' against the rage, however ineffectual such resistance might seem. As Czesław Miłosz asked himself, in a phrase Heaney often quoted, 'what is poetry which does not save / Nations or people?'[28] As collected in *District and Circle*, 'A Shiver' and the other anxious, accusatory poems set in Heaney's rural childhood thus constitute a kind of dark pastoral limbo, which is shattered by the arrival of Horace's sky-god, Jupiter (DC 13).

---

26. Heaney, SS 410; 'One Poet in Search of a Title', borrowing from Auden's *The Age of Anxiety: A Baroque Eclogue* (1947).
27. Heaney, *Anything Can Happen*, 13.
28. Miłosz, 'Dedication', in *Collected Poems* (1988).

11. 'ANYTHING CAN HAPPEN'

Heaney's translation of Horace's *Odes I, 34* is positioned in *District and Circle* to initiate a *katabatic* movement that is furthered in the title poem and 'The Tollund Man in Springtime'. But it also holds its own plea against the rage of military conflict, having already been published in a wide variety of contexts, as a self-standing poem. It was first published with the title 'Horace and the Thunder' in *The Irish Times*, 17 November 2001. In the same month, Heaney read the poem in public on two formal occasions, in Urbino and Dublin; and it subsequently appeared (in slightly differing versions) in the *Times Literary Supplement*, as well as a multilingual volume produced in support of Art for Amnesty, and a range of other journals in Ireland and abroad, before being collected in *District and Circle*.[29] The translation itself makes no explicit reference to the bombing of the World Trade Center, but in at least two lectures and two publications the poem appears alongside an essay explicitly stating that it was written in response to 9/11. The Amnesty volume includes Heaney's translation of Horace, together with twenty-three translations of Heaney's poem, strikingly paired in the 'languages of conflict', so that English and Irish, German and Russian, and Hebrew and Arabic translations appear side by side on facing pages.[30] The stealthy detachment of Heaney's poem, alongside the strategic publication and pointedly explicit prose commentary, are two complementary aspects of Heaney's ethically driven, artistic response to the international outbreak of violence at the start of the millennium.

When Heaney first reread Horace's ode, just after 9/11, he was immediately struck by its 'uncanny soothsaying force'.[31] The tone of Heaney's translation heightens the sense of Horace as a familiar acquaintance, and he starts up a conversation without preamble or ceremony:

> Anything can happen. You know how Jupiter
> Will mostly wait for clouds to gather head
> Before he hurls the lightning? Well, just now
> He galloped his thunder cart . . . (*DC* 13)

---

29. Heaney's translation of Horace is published in at least ten places: (1) Quoted in 'The Whole Thing' (lecture delivered 5 November 2001, Dublin); (2) 'Horace and the Thunder', *The Irish Times* (17 November 2001: Weekend 10); (3) Quoted in 'Towers, Trees, Terrors' (lecture delivered 23 November 2001, Urbino); (4) 'Horace and the Thunder' (New York: Pressed Wafer, 2002, ltd edn); (5) 'Horace and Thunder' [sic], *Times Literary Supplement* (18 January 2002), 40; (6) 'Horace and the Thunder' published together with 'Reality and Justice: On Translating Horace, Odes I, 34', in *Translation Ireland* (Spring 2002), 8–11; (7) 'Horace and the Thunder, After Horace, Odes, I, 34' published together with 'Reality and Justice: On Translating Horace, Odes I, 34', *Irish Pages* I:2 (Autumn, Winter, 2002/3), 50–3; (8) 'Anything Can Happen, *after Horace, Odes, I, 34*', *Anything Can Happen: A Poem and Essay by Seamus Heaney with Translations in Support of Art for Amnesty* (Dublin: Townhouse, 2004), 11; (9) 'Horace and the Thunder', *A Shiver* (Thame: Clutag Press, 2005); (10) 'Anything Can Happen', *District and Circle* (London: Faber, 2006), 13.
30. *Anything Can Happen* (2004).
31. *Anything Can Happen*, 15. Cf. 'Reality and Justice', 51.

This translation corresponds loosely to Horace's second stanza:

> . . . namque Diespiter
> igni corusco nubile diuidens
> plerumque, per purum tonantis
> egit equos uolucremque currum, (*Odes I*, 34, ll. 5–8)

In his essay on Horace's ode, Heaney reprints an unnamed prose translation as the basis for a comparison with his own translation in verse:[32]

> For the father of the sky, who mostly cleaves the clouds with a gleaming flash, has driven through the undimmed firmament his thundering steeds and flying car.

Heaney's opening stanza is more colloquial than Horace's, with a relaxed, second-person address ('you know . . . well, just now') and a Kavanaghesque 'cart' for Horace's formal '*currus*'. From this informal beginning, Heaney's poem then shifts into a more elevated style for the middle two stanzas, describing Jupiter's thunderclap and Fortune's eagle-like swoop. The fourth stanza concludes in terse, end-stopped sentences, with no first- or second-person address, or indeed any mention of human presence at all. It is this newly alien, infernal reality that necessitates the poet's journey into the underworld.

While he preserves the four-quatrain structure of the Latin ode, Heaney drops Horace's first stanza and adds a fourth of his own invention.[33] In Horace's poem, the urbane poet is jolted out of his free-wheeling attitude to the gods by a sharp reminder of their infinite powers. The Latin first stanza describes the poet's return to proper religious observance. Heaney's decision to cut this first stanza distances the ode from its religious context. Whatever moral we draw from Heaney's poem, it cannot be the terroristic one that the gods exact vengeance on non-believers. God, or Jupiter, is also conspicuously absent from Heaney's rendering of '*ualet ima summis / mutare . . . deus*' ('the god has power to change the highest things to/for the lowest'[34]) as 'anything can happen'. In the poem's final version, this theologically neutral phrase appears twice, in the first and eighth lines, and is also adopted as the title of the Art for Amnesty volume containing the twenty-three translations of Heaney's poem. The familiar expression thus comes to denote a collective artistic decision to voice both sides of these longstanding, military conflicts, with god and divine right belonging to neither side.

32. Heaney provides Horace's Latin text followed by a prose translation in *Anything Can Happen*, 17. The source of the translation is not mentioned but it appears to be a modified version of James Lonsdale and Samuel Lee's *The Works of Horace Rendered into English Prose*, 8th edn (London: Macmillan, 1874).
33. An earlier draft includes his translation of the first stanza: 'Never much of a one for religion, / I've gone with the flow, strayed seriously / Off course, steered by my own lights always, / But now I'm forced to re-set sail and head // Back into port.' (*LP* I.xvii.2)
34. The prose translation is Heaney's, from 'Reality and Justice', 52.

In his second stanza, corresponding to Horace's third, Heaney introduces three slight changes of emphasis which draw the poem into the orbit of 9/11 and its aftermath. Both poets declare that Jupiter's thunder shakes the earth and the underworld (Heaney suppresses the more obscure reference to Taenarus but retains Styx as synecdoche for Hades). Horace says it even shakes '*Atlanteus . . . finis*' (l. 11), a compressed phrase suggesting the Pillars of Hercules, at the Western end of the Mediterranean and eastern limit of the Atlantic.[35] In Heaney's version, this becomes 'the Atlantic shore itself', where New York's World Trade Center stood. Secondly, Heaney changes the verb '*concutitur*' ('is rocked') from passive, simple present to active, historical past ('shook'), so that the event of Jupiter's thunderous arrival comes to stand for a specific, world-altering catastrophe: 'his thunder cart . . . shook the earth . . . Styx . . . the Atlantic shore itself' (ll. 4–7). Although he then switches back to Horace's simple present tense, to suggest that this can happen any time, a modern reader now has a particular disaster in mind. And this is reinforced in the final 2006 text, where Heaney changes 'things' to 'towers' in his eighth line. All earlier versions of the poem had read 'Anything can happen, the tallest things / Be overturned' (a free rendering of '*valet ima summis / mutare . . . deus*'). But reading the poem in the aftermath of 9/11, few would miss the allusion to New York City's Twin Towers in Heaney's 'tallest towers . . . overturned'.

In his Urbino lecture, Heaney meditates on the 'world-darkening' impact of the assault on the Twin Towers, and he offers by way of resistance the counter-image of two ruined, medieval towers, one located in the Apennines, near Urbino, and the other in the West of Ireland. W. B. Yeats had discovered the first while walking towards Urbino (as Heaney cites) '"amid a visionary, fantastic, impossible scenery"', and this vision inspired him to purchase the second, Thoor Ballylee, in County Galway.[36] From his stay at Ballylee, Yeats produced two major collections, *The Tower* and *The Winding Stair*, and thus, Heaney maintains, 'the image of a tower on the road to Urbino helped the greatest Irish poet of our age to attain the fullest expression of his powers' (148). For Heaney and 'all subsequent Irish poets', the road to Urbino would therefore always 'be a pilgrim's road' (ibid.). In Heaney's translation of Horace, the 'tallest towers' belong to the 'military and masculine *urbs*', rather than any visionary, 'feminine and radiant' city. But what restores 'a certain balance to a world unbalanced by political violence' is the very urbanity of Horace's voice: 'his resilient intelligence, his ability to move unpredictably within a poem yet maintain its integrity, the combination of formal mastery and sheer human credibility, the mixture of light touch and clued-in worldly wisdom' (156, 154).

The third stanza (Horace's fourth) contains the correspondences that Heaney found uncanny in their close fit between the original Latin and the 2001 context. Here is Horace's fourth and final stanza, and the prose translation, followed by Heaney's version:

---

35. S. J. Harrison (2019), 251.
36. Yeats quoted by Heaney, 'Towers, Trees, Terrors', 147.

> ... Valet ima summis //
> mutare et insignem attenuat deus,
> obscura promens; hinc apicem rapax
> Fortuna cum stridore acuto
> sustulit, hic posuisse gaudet. (*Odes I*, 34, ll. 12–16)

> To change the highest for the lowest, the god has power; he makes mean the man of high estate, bringing what is hidden into light: Fortune, like a predator, flaps up and bears away the crest from one, then sets it down with relish on another. (p. 17)

> Anything can happen, the tallest towers //
> Be overturned, those in high places daunted,
> Those overlooked regarded. Stropped-beak Fortune
> Swoops, making the air gasp, tearing the crest off one,
> Setting it down bleeding on the next. (*DC* 13)

Heaney finds an 'eerie correspondence' between Horace's image of the highest brought low and the 'dreamy, deadly images of the Twin Towers'.[37] And there is 'an equally unnerving fit' between the 'conventional wisdom of the Latin "*obscura promens*" (bringing the disregarded to notice)' and the '*realpolitik* of the terrorist assault'. For Heaney, the Latin phrase conveys how the assault brought to 'new prominence the plight of the Palestinians and much else in and about the Arab world.' (ibid., 53) In his 2001 version, published in *The Irish Times*, Heaney translates '*obscura promens*' as 'those overlooked esteemed', though later this line is slightly toned down, from being 'esteemed' to being 'regarded'. Even in the latter version, few voices in the Western media took such an even-handed stance on the attacks, especially as early as 2001.

Horace's *rapax Fortuna* draws on the Roman legend that an eagle crowned the head of the future King Tarquin the Elder.[38] For Heaney, '*rapax Fortuna* ... becomes an image for the impulse to attack or to retaliate,' referring in this case to the violent attack of the terrorists, as well as the recriminations by the US government that were to follow (ibid., 53). The shift from the simple past tense of 'It shook the earth' to the present of 'Anything can happen' and 'Fortune swoops' contributes to the sense that a single act of violence has set in motion a recurring cycle of attack and retaliation. Heaney's poem thus studiously avoids attributing human agency to the violence, and while this has disturbed some readers, it could be considered as one of the poem's strengths. By keeping his gaze steadily on the victims of violence, he withholds any oxygen of publicity from the perpetrators, who in this poem have lost their human faces entirely. Along with the Roman eagle, Heaney's phrase 'Stropped-beak Fortune' alludes to his friend, Ted Hughes's, poem, 'Crow's Song

---

37. Heaney, 'Reality and Justice', 52; as in 'The Whole Thing', 19.
38. See S. J. Harrison (2019), 251.

of Himself', in which 'Crow stropped his beak and started in on the two thieves'.[39] In Hughes's series of Crow poems, the bird inhabits a degraded, polluted world, what Heaney sums up as 'the Crow-cursed universe', devoid of grace (*FK* 409). So although Heaney withholds blame from either side, the violent blow itself is given the face of a predatory bird, associated with godlessness and empire.[40]

Horace's poem ends with the raptor Fortune's stoop, but Heaney adds another quatrain, dense with classical allusion. And here, not only is human agency excluded, but the consequences of the violence are registered on a vast, geological scale, rather than a human one:

> Ground gives. The heaven's weight
> Lifts up off Atlas like a kettle-lid.
> Capstones shift, nothing resettles right.
> Telluric ash and fire-spores boil away. (*DC* 13)

The one reference to the man-made environment is the 'kettle-lid', a decidedly human-scale, quotidian object that seems out of place in the volcanic movement of the rest of the quatrain. The lifting of Atlas's burden (the sky, in classical mythology) may also trigger a positive counter-image for Biblically schooled readers. When Heaney explains how 'the shaken earth called up an image of the lifted roof' (53), he calls attention to the same motif in the New Testament story of a roof being lifted off, at Capernaum, so that a paralysed man could be lowered inside, to be healed by Jesus.[41]

But the allusions to Virgil in the last three lines are more ominous. Atlas being relieved of his burden of sky is an image that recurs five times in the *Aeneid*, as Stephen Harrison notes.[42] In *Aeneid IV*, Mercury alights on thunder-crowned Mount Atlas on his way to commanding Aeneas to leave Carthage (*Ae*.IV.247f.). And in *Aeneid VI*, Anchises mentions Mount Atlas as the outer limit of Augustus Caesar's expanding empire (*Ae*.VI.792–7). In both cases, the allusion to Atlas is associated with Rome's aggressive imperial ambitions, which in Heaney's poem take on an additional association with the US government's 'high rhetoric' in the wake of the 9/11 attacks. If the ash and smouldering fire-spores recall the 'dreamy, deadly images' of the crumbled Twin Towers, there is already a counter-movement implied in the mention of ground giving and 'telluric ash' boiling. The rare adjective 'telluric' means 'of the earth', from the Latin *tellus*, and if the ground gives, the portals of the underworld could well be opening already. Heaney's neologism 'fire-spores' seems very closely related to Virgil's '*semina flammae*' ('seeds of flame').[43] In Book VI, just before Aeneas undertakes his descent, his ships land at Cumae and the Trojan

---

39. With thanks to Neil Roberts for this reference.
40. Cf. Hughes's tyrannical bird of prey in 'Hawk Roosting': 'I kill where I please because it is all mine. /. . . My manners are tearing off heads – / The allotment of death' (2005, 69).
41. Matthew 9: 1–8, Mark 2: 1–12 and Luke 5: 17–26. Cf. Heaney, 'Miracle' (*HC* 17).
42. S. J. Harrison (2019), 252.
43. S. J. Harrison agrees with this conjecture (2019, 252).

youths leap ashore to seek the '*semina flammae*' hidden in the flinty rock (Ae.IV.6). 'Ground gives' before Aeneas when he follows the Sibyl into her cave and down to the shores of the Styx.

Thus, Heaney invokes Horace's 'resilient intelligence' to achieve a certain distance and detachment from the experience of a contemporary political atrocity. By structuring and formalising sound, introducing complex layers of allusion and correspondences in Graeco-Roman myth, Heaney arrests our judgement while inviting sympathy for the street-level witness, on both sides of the conflict. As a self-standing poem, Heaney's translation of Horace offers different forms of redress to the *lacrimae rerum*. In the context of the 2006 volume as a whole, though, 'Anything Can Happen' initiates a poetic descent to recover a sense of identity in the heart of the modern metropolis itself.

III. 'DISTRICT AND CIRCLE'

District and Circle explores a wide variety of traditions relating to the underworld, from classical Hades to Arthurian Avalon, the Pacific Northwest Indians' land of the dead and the dark matter of contemporary physics. But the ethical imperative driving Heaney's exploration of different cultural underworlds is most clearly discernible in the title poem, 'District and Circle' (*DC* 17–19). In this five-sonnet sequence, the poet's recollection of a habitual commute on the London Underground takes on the dimensions of a Virgilian *katabasis*. A busker with whom he exchanges glances at the entrance of the station becomes a sibylline gatekeeper, while the approaching train rumbles and growls like a three-headed Cerberus (ll. 4–8, 19–20). The poet steps on to the train amid a crowd of commuters, from whom he feels separate and estranged, like Aeneas amongst the dead souls when he steps on to Charon's barge (ll. 31–5, 42–50). Then, as the train ferries him under the streets of London, he catches a glimpse of his father's face in his own reflection, as if, like Aeneas, he were greeting his dead father in the underworld (l. 58). The sonnet sequence thus jolts backward in time as the poet descends into the underground.

The first and final stanzas of 'District and Circle' originally comprised a diptych of two sonnets about the Tollund Man.[44] One of the 'Bog People', preserved in peat for 2,000 years and exhumed in 1950, the Tollund Man had become a poetic archetype for Heaney in *Wintering Out*.[45] Heaney's diptych portrayed the Tollund Man travelling between Earls Court and St James's Park, and was already entitled 'District and Circle', after the Tube lines that serve those stations (SS 410). Formally, each sonnet in the diptych had a distinct *volta*, or turn, between the

---

44. Heaney, SS 410; 'One Poet in Search of a Title'; 'The Tollund Man', in WO (1972), 36–7.
45. 'The Tollund Man', in WO (1972), 36–7, inspired by P. V. Glob's archeological study of *The Bog People* (1969); see Heaney, SS 350. The original head and a replica body of the Tollund Man are on display at the Silkeborg Museum, Denmark. There is extensive criticism on Heaney's *Bog Poems*; for a recent, excellent discussion, see Hickey, 'The Haunted Bog and the Poetry of Seamus Heaney' (2018).

eighth and ninth lines, as is characteristic of the Petrarchan sonnet. With this two-stanza poem, Heaney had, then, already forged a connection between the mid-poem *volta* of a Petrarchan sonnet and the doubling-back movement of a *katabatic* descent and return.[46] The Tollund Man rises from the underworld to confront 'a world of surveillance cameras and closed-circuit TV, of greenhouse gases and acid rain'.[47] Although the diptych was not yet autobiographically voiced, Heaney was already exploring the sense of a disconnect from his Northern Irish identity when, in the summer of 1962, he worked for the Passport Office in London. The title of the diptych signified Heaney's 'inclination to favour a chosen region and keep coming back to it', and eventually he adopted it as the working title of the collection in progress (ibid.). This account of the poem's genesis reveals the close link between the autobiographical, five-sonnet 'District and Circle' and 'The Tollund Man in Springtime', which introduces the final section of the 2006 volume.

The London Underground was bombed on 7 July 2005, as part of four coordinated suicide attacks which killed fifty-two people and injured more than 700 others. Heaney's poetic response to this terrorist atrocity was once again both highly specific and deliberately veiled, as had been his decision to translate Horace's ode. In the months following 7/7, he expanded 'District and Circle' into a five-sonnet sequence. Incorporating the original diptych was, he said, a way of 'keep[ing] faith with the London lines', while the added sections allowed for a 'deeper dwelling with the motif' of the descent journey.[48] In an introduction of the poem written for the Poetry Book Society, Heaney identified the context of the July bombings but then changed his mind, and faxed another version of the introduction with the contextual reference removed.[49] Rather than making the poem sound 'occasional / topical', he explained, he wanted readers to notice 'the oddness / oldness of the memories'.[50] This remark shows Heaney's stealth and wariness in engaging with contemporary politics, but it also indicates his familiarity with *katabasis* as a quest for uncanny knowledge, for a discovery of the known in the unfamiliar and vice versa.

The three additional sonnets were 'not particularly to do with the atrocity', Heaney later wrote, with a similar caginess; rather, they were composed with the awareness that a poem about the underground would now 'have to bear additional scrutiny' (SS 410). In the longer version, the first-person voice has shifted from the Tollund Man to a younger version of Heaney himself:

> The figure who speaks in the five sonnets that make up 'District and Circle' is at a remove from the people among whom he finds himself. This is partly because I'm remembering the other, younger person I was when I first journeyed on a

---

46. See Meg Tyler on Heaney's use of the sonnet in *DC*, in '"The Whole of Me A-Patter"' (O'Brien, 2016), 135f.
47. 'One Poet in Search of a Title' (2006). On the poem's negotiation of urban and natural environments, see, further, Carruth (2011).
48. 'One Poet in Search of a Title'.
49. LP I.xvii.4 (letter to Chris Holifield, 28 February 2006).
50. Ibid.

London tube train; somebody who was much less at home, more anxious and 'out of it' than I would come to be later on. But the feeling of unease is also there because the figure is haunted by all kinds of new awarenesses: awareness of the potential danger of a journey nowadays on a London tube train and awareness of the mythical dimensions of all such journeys underground, into the earth, into the dark. (SS 410)

The first-person voice in the poem is, then, both autobiographical and detached, at one remove from his environment. An earlier draft records his encounter with London stereotyping of the Irish; his supervisor at the Passport Office, for example, habitually rebuked him for lateness: '"Slow coach on the Green Line, were you, Paddy? / Out with the navvies last Night?"'[51] So the young Northern Irish poet was struggling with the migrant's double sense of being at a remove: feeling guilty for having left, but also not accepted into the new city. At the same time, the revised poem is more inclusive in the feelings of apprehension and dread it invokes. In its final version, the first-person voice in the poem is also potentially any reader's, who might feel a similar unease when journeying across London on the Tube after the 7/7 bombings.

If the poem conveys this mixture of private and collective unease, it also offers redress in the form of the poet's, and potentially the reader's, transformation of consciousness in the course of his journey underground. Like the motif of Charon's barge itself, Heaney's poetic strategy hearkens back to his procedure in *Seeing Things* (1991), where the burden of historical reality is alleviated by a shift into visionary, dream-like perception. 'District and Circle' immediately conveys the oneiric quality of the repeated, daily commute underground; an early draft of the poem contains the line 'As if I had entered not a train but knowledge.'[52] But here, the poet's train ride also summons echoes of the displaced herdsman on the country road, along with Aeneas venturing down into Hades and preparing to face the terrors of the underworld (SS 410).

In 'Anything Can Happen', there is one main tense shift from habitual action to a singular event. By contrast, in 'District and Circle', the tense sequencing is extremely complex and elastic, underlining the oneiric atmosphere of the poem. Such a disordering of time is again a characteristic, generic feature of *katabatic* narratives.[53] In the first sonnet, the poet's enigmatic exchange of nods with a sibylline busker seems to be a habitual, even ritual, practice: note the 'would' in 'I'd trigger and untrigger a hot coin'. In the second, third and fourth stanzas of 'District and Circle', the verb tenses shift into the simple past: 'I missed the light' (l. 22), 'I re-entered the safety of numbers' (l. 30), 'I reached to grab' (l. 43). And here the dream-time crystalises into the narrative of a single, singular journey, whose mythic goal is the recovery of loss, or discovery of secret, otherworldly wisdom. At the same time, though, a series of participial verbs continue to imply repeated action:

51. *LP* I.xvii.2.
52. *LP* I.xvii.2.
53. See Falconer (2007), 42–62.

'newcomers / jostling and purling ... then succumbing' (ll. 33, 35), and the poet 'waiting', 'Stepping', 'Listening', 'craning' (ll. 39, 42, 49, 59). The whole journey, then, seems suspended between eternal recurrence and the 'now-or-never whelm' of a cataclysmic event (l. 40).

When the poet asks himself 'had I betrayed or not, myself or him?', this seems like a question posed once, if enigmatically. But it turns out to be a habitual self-accusation:

always new to me, always familiar,
This unrepentant, now repentant turn
As I stood waiting (37–9)

This guilty thought being described as a 'turn', along with the 'turned' (doubled and reversed) adjective 'unrepentant/repentant', alerts us to the disturbances that occur at the sonnet's *volta* here, and in every sonnet in the sequence. In the third sonnet, the key question, 'Had I betrayed or not', comes slightly too soon, curtailing the second quatrain and hastening the sestet, so that the sonnet falls one short of fourteen lines. In the first sonnet, lines eight and nine are short lines, which again disturbs the *volta* from octet to sestet. And in the final sonnet, the disturbance comes early, with short lines disrupting the transition between quatrains in the octet. Then the poem ends abruptly, with a final line of three syllables, a compound adjective thrown free of the sestet, both grammatically and visually on the page. All of these rhythmic stutters in the sonnet form contribute to the impression of a disordered, dream-like temporality, now cyclical and regular, now accelerated and discontinuous.

Most *katabatic* journeys depict some version of a threshold crossing, a ground-zero trial and a reascent to light.[54] While the image of threshold crossing is repeatedly replayed in *Seeing Things*, and there associated with loyalist checkpoints in Northern Ireland, here the motif is developed further, revealing stronger tensions between the poet and the souls crowding the shore, and a stronger narrative drive to get over the threshold, into the underground journey itself. The poet at first stands aloof from the jostling crowd at the platform, 'Street-loud, then succumbing to herd-quiet' (l. 35). In contrast to 'Seeing Things, I', there is no 'we', no self-identification with the 'human chain' (l. 32) at this point in the poet's descent. He is absorbed in his own thoughts, and an ellipsis in line 35 (indicating the missing line of the octet) separates him from the other commuters. He asks himself, 'Had I betrayed or not, myself or him?'

At a border control in County Derry, a betrayal might involve denying your ties to a particular Catholic or Protestant community. Here the sense of betrayal seems both more personal and more detached. The identity of the 'him', at first obscure, is made clear in the final sonnet, where he sees his father in the glass reflection of the train window. So, one way of construing his inward questioning is to suggest he has 'repentant' feelings of *pietas* towards his father, as well as worries about having

54. See Falconer (2007), 42–50, 68–70.

betrayed his own Northern Irish Catholic identity in an 'unrepentant' pursuit of poetic vocation. Whether his pious obligations to his father and to himself are one and the same, or in conflict, is unclear from the syntactic structure of the question. But either way, he keeps himself separate from the London crowd as he stands waiting for the train (l. 39). For a section of the poem composed months after the July bombings in London, this is notably distanced from the strong feelings of identification and outrage that were then circulating in the British media. As in the Horace translation, Heaney's response to political violence is carefully distanced.

The poet's threshold crossing on to the Tube train conflates two scenes from *Aeneid VI*: Aeneas's seizure of the golden bough and his boarding of Charon's barge. Here the order is reversed, so that the poet steps in with the crowd, 'caught up in the now-or-never whelm / Of one and all', like the souls thronging on to Charon's barge. On a literal level, this depicts the poet thrown together with fellow commuters, recollected from the summer of 1962; but metaphorically, the parallel with *Aeneid VI* suggests he is also stepping in with the shades of the dead, specifically the fifty-two people killed in 2005. Once on the train, he reaches for the carriage strap, in a gesture that resembles Aeneas' clutch for the bough, even as the train takes on the function of Charon's barge:

> Stepping on to it across the gap,
> On to the carriage metal, I reached to grab
> The stubby black roof-wort and take my stand
> From planted ball of heel to heel of hand
> As sweet traction and heavy down-slump stayed me.
> I was on my way, well girded, yet on edge,
> Spot-rooted, buoyed, aloof, (*DC* 18)

The poet's stance, 'well girded, yet on edge … buoyed, aloof', recalls the many Virgilian boat scenes in *Seeing Things*, while his 'heavy down-slump' specifically recalls Aeneas' unusual weight in the barge: '*gemuit sub pondere cumba*' ('Under that weight the boat's plied timbers groan').[55]

The echo of Aeneas' threshold crossing into Hades here adds a socio-political dimension to the poet's oneiric reverie. In its earlier, two-sonnet version, when the Tollund Man boarded the Tube train, the crossing had been more straightforwardly a gesture of lyric release, of Ariel flight. Thus, an early version of the above passage reads:

> Stepping on to it … I felt
> Not … down-drag but an up
> And airy lift … my foot
> Like Sweeney's safely landed on a bough.[56]

---

55. *Ae.*VI.413; Heaney, *A.*553.
56. *LP* I.xvii.2.

When the figure of the bird-king gets crossed with Virgil's Aeneas, the poem is burdened with a heftier cultural weight. Sweeney, himself divided between the exercise of the 'free creative imagination and the constraints of religious, political, and domestic obligation', now crosses the Styx with a Prospero-awareness of recent tragedy.[57]

The poet grabbing for the overhead strap handle, in the poem's expanded version, mirrors Aeneas' exercise of will and purpose as he reaches out for the golden bough: '*corripit Aeneas extemplo auidusque refringit*' (Ae.VI.210, 'There and then, / Aeneas took hold of it'; Heaney, GB, ll. 126–7). While, physically, the gesture merely steadies the poet in the moving train, metaphorically the poet's Northern Irish identity is being stayed and affirmed in this transformative, threshold crossing. This metaphorical significance is suggested by the sudden thickening of language with consonant clusters, spondaic accents and Anglo-Saxon root words, notably in the phrase, 'stúbby bláck roóf-wórt'. A *wort* is an archaic word (from the Old English *wyrt*), meaning a plant used in stews or medicine (OED 1.a), but when used in compound nouns it refers to the second element in the names of plants (for example, 'figwort', 'woundwort'). *Roof* also has an Old English origin, from *hrof*, meaning 'ceiling' or 'roof' (OED 1.a), One of its etymological meanings is also 'coffin lid', an apt term for a growth hanging from the ceiling of the underworld, although that may be pressing Heaney's etymological subtext too far. In any case, the image of a strap handle as an organic ceiling growth links to the vocabulary of farming that Heaney deploys in the fourth sonnet: he is 'Spot-rooted' by 'sweet traction', with 'planted ball of heel' and (in Sonnet 5) 'lofted arm a-swivel like a flail' (l. 57). Like Virgil's golden bough, this 'roof-wort' combines natural and technological, and symbolically speaking, urban and pastoral poetics. If discovering the bough is 'like finding a voice', grasping the strap handle releases a flood of words that reconnects the poet to his farmer father and his rural origins in County Derry.[58]

In the last two sonnets, this personal affirmation broadens out to a more collective redress, offering a visionary connection to the 'feminine and radiant' *urbs* of Livy's prose, and the city of Carthage where Aeneas falls in love with Dido. In a way, this alternative, radiant *urbs* persists as a mirror image of the 'military and masculine' cities of Rome and London. When 'country' language infiltrates the enclosed space of the train, there is a bridging of urban and rural worlds. And the modern, high-speed city comes to seem closer, less 'blindsided' (l. 55) to its ancient origins. In the fifth and final sonnet of the sequence, the train hurtles its passengers, including the poet, into the underground network of tunnels. 'So deeper into it', the poet tells himself, and by 'it', he means both the District and Circle lines and the memories of his home district in rural County Derry. In stance, he is like Aeneas holding the golden bough before him: 'My lofted arm a-swivel like a flail' (l. 57). A 'flail' is not only an ancient military weapon but a rod used to flatten crops, so like the golden bough, it combines links to nature and technology. And as with Aeneas, the aim of his journey turns out to be a longed-for meeting with his father's shade.

---

57. *Sweeney Astray* (1983), vi.
58. Sounding Lines, 16.

This he glimpses in his own face, reflected in the train window: 'My father's glazed face in my own waning / And craning . . .' (ll. 58–9). There is, conspicuously, no main verb in this entire last sonnet, so these floating participial verbs contribute to the impression that the poet is here adrift in a dream-time cut off from the narrative present.

And in themselves, the paired verbs 'waning and craning' capture the two-way trafficking movement of this poem. 'Waning' implies ageing (hence, starting to look like his father), but 'craning' suggests a straining to see ahead, and into the future, like the small boy at the window in 'Seeing Things'. More broadly, this glimpse of his father holds the poet still, in a temporal limbo, while at the same time he is being 'hurtled forward' by the train, its 'jolt and one-off treble' and 'long centrifugal / Haulage of speed' become a figure for linear, chronological time itself. Being able to stand still, with 'planted ball of heel', while travelling forward at speed suggests learning to balance opposing allegiances between rural Northern Irish past and urban British present. All the formal and thematic pairings in the poem, from the exchange of nods with the busker and the pairing of verbs throughout (ll. 10, 16, 20, 31 and so on), to the end-line near-rhymes and the sestet's fold-back on the octet, contribute to this notion of finding a balance between opposing tensions, rather than giving way to a single direction of travel. Yet again, what distinguishes this glimpse of the 'father's glazed face' from the recognition scene in 'Seeing Things' ('I saw him face to face, he came to me') is that it is not trapped in the recursively repetitive time of romance, but is being hurtled forward in the train and, by implication, in the movement of historical time (*ST* 18).

Heaney would have found similar formal and thematic symmetries in Virgil's description of the infernal barge carrying Aeneas across the Styx, the passage that had so preoccupied him in *Seeing Things* (*Ae*.VI.411–16). In the Charon episode, Virgil pairs verbs, such as *deturbat*, *laxat* (hurls out, clears) and *accipit*, *accepit* (takes on, took in); nouns, as in *uatemque uirumque* (both prophet and man) and *limo*, *ulua* (mud, swamp-grass); and adjectives, such as *informi*, *glauca* (shapeless, gleaming). The light *alias animas* (souls of the dead) are balanced grammatically against *ingentem Aeneam* (huge Aeneas). And the boat's sinking under the weight is balanced against its sure, forward passage *tandem trans fluuium*, across the river. This balance of tensions in the boat point to Aeneas' need to find a spirit level between a longing for the past (his lost home city of Troy) and his future destiny to found Rome.

The poet's glimpse of his father's face, in 'District and Circle', establishes a link with the past that is not only personal and patrilinear, but also socially conscious and decidedly feminine, for while the primary parallel is with Aeneas when he finds Anchises' shade in Elysium, there is also a secondary echo of Aeneas' tragic encounter with Dido in the Fields of Mourning. Aeneas recognises Dido despite the uncertain light, and her 'wavering form' is compared to a rising moon:

> . . . Phoenissa recens a uulnere Dido
> errabat silua in magna; quam Troius heros
> ut primum iuxta stetit adgnouitque per umbras

obscuram, qualem primo qui surgere mense
aut uidet aut uidisse putat per nubila lunam, (Ae.VI.450–4)[59]

This is Heaney's translation of the passage, in *Aeneid VI* (2016):

> . . . still nursing her raw wound,
> Dido of Carthage strayed in the great forest.
> As soon as the Trojan came close and made out
> Her dimly wavering form among the shadows,
> He was like one who sees or imagines he has seen
> A new moon rising up among the clouds
> On the first day of the month; (A.VI.604–10)

Heaney translates *'Phoenissa'* as 'of Carthage' to underline the historic rivalry between Carthage and Rome, in which Aeneas and Dido's affair is already implicated from the beginning of the *Aeneid*. The last line of Virgil's description, *'aut uidet aut uidisse putat per nubila lunam'*, has been much imitated in English poetry (in one of Milton's most famous underworld similes, for example, a

> belated peasant sees,
> Or dreams he sees, while overhead the moon
> Sits arbitress (*PL*.I.783–5)

Heaney quotes Virgil's line in the eighth poem of 'Route 110', when comparing the ending of a relationship to Aeneas' betrayal of Dido: '*As one when the month is young sees a new moon.*' (*HC* 55, ital. in original) The classical allusion there is commingled with feelings of guilt and regret, with recollections of a social context of religious repression and impending political violence. Here, when Heaney compares his father's face to a crescent moon, glimpsed in the underworld, the metaphor comes laced with echoes of Aeneas' encounter with Dido. It will be carried forward later in the volume, when the Tollund Man remembers 'moony water' from his former life.

Here, the parallel is underlined when, a few lines later, the poet describes himself as 'the only relict / Of all that I belonged to' (ll. 65–6). The primary meaning of 'relict' is 'widow' (*OED* I.a). Virgil's 'Widow Dido' is a character already at home in English tragedy, from Marlowe's 1593 play, *Dido Queen of Carthage*, to Purcell's 1680 opera, *Dido and Aeneas*. Heaney was also fond of Shakespeare's haunting description of the Queen in *The Merchant of Venice* (c. 1599):

> In such a night
> Stood Dido with a willow in her hand

---

59. 'with wound still fresh, Phoenician Dido was wandering in the great forest, and soon as the Trojan hero stood near and knew her, a dim form amid the shadows – even as, in the early month, one sees or fancies he has seen the moon rise amid the clouds' (trans. Fairclough, p. 565).

Upon the wild sea banks and waft her love
To come again to Carthage.⁶⁰

The word 'relict' also has a specifically Irish connection, as it appears frequently on gravestones, describing widows of soldiers killed in battle. Hence Steven Mathews credibly suggests that Heaney is aligning himself with the survivors of massacre, and perhaps we could add the survivors of the London bombings.⁶¹ When the poet describes himself as a 'relict', he is, then, taking on the burden of a communal sense of belonging, one that notably hybridises feminine and masculine ancestries (Dido, Irish war widows and Aeneas' father, Anchises). Widow Dido herself has a complicated afterlife in Latin and English literature, becoming, on the one hand, a symbol of the abandoned Queen whose city will be defeated by Rome, and on the other, a symbol of the faithless widow, whose reputation is mended only when she returns to her husband Sychaeus' ghost in Hades.⁶² But Heaney's allusions to Dido tend to fall in the former group, as a figure betrayed rather than betraying.

So why should Heaney call up this image of Dido and the underworld moon, when seeing his father's face in his own? This takes us back to the question the poet asks at the start of the descent: 'Had I betrayed or not, myself or him?' The question is already complex enough for a rural, Northern Irish poet feeling out of touch with his roots amongst Londoners in the 1960s. But for the poet reflecting on this experience in 2005, after the terrorist attacks on London, there is an additional tension which further complicates his poetic identification with Virgil's hero, Aeneas. As Brian Friel's play, *Translations*, illustrates, there is a strong tradition in Irish literature of identifying Virgil's Rome with London, and Carthage with the Irish cultures silenced by British colonisation.⁶³ Weaving Anchises and Dido together into an image of the lost past would thus seem to be a way of not choosing sides between Virgil's warring cities or, by extension, London and its present-day antagonists. Virgil's feeling for the *lacrimae rerum*, tears of things, is still present but it is being abstracted from a particular partisan stance. Heaney is building an invisible bridge between two warring cities.

In 'Towers, Trees, Terrors', Heaney praises 'that lovely, elegiac cadence' at the beginning of the *Aeneid*, 'which introduces and swiftly dispenses with the history and destiny of Carthage: *Urbs antiqua fuit* . . .' (149). He continues, 'the word *urbs* is sounded very sweetly and very lovingly, but this time sadly because Virgil is telling us that all of its mystery and beauty and essential *urbanitas* is now to pass from Carthage to the new city of Rome' (ibid.). This praise of Virgil as a poet of the city is rare in Heaney's writing. The pity of war, and feeling for the land, are Virgilian preoccupations he identifies with and deeply admires, but *urbanitas* is a

---

60. Shakespeare, *The Merchant of Venice*, V.i.9–12. Heaney quotes this passage in 'The Real Names' (*EL* 48) and SS 400.
61. Mathews (2007), 93.
62. On Dido's ambivalent reputation for faithfulness and infidelity in classical literature, see Joyce Green MacDonald (2010), 73.
63. Friel (1981), 68.

quality he associates with the 'sceptical, susceptible spirit' of Horace.[64] But in the lecture delivered in Urbino shortly after 9/11, Heaney discovers in the opening lines of the *Aeneid* a powerful evocation of the beauty and mystery of the ancient *urbs*. What makes this evocation of the city characteristically Virgilian, for Heaney, is the melancholy awareness of its impermanence. The adverbs 'sweetly', 'lovingly' and 'sadly' also suggest that, for Heaney, Carthage represents the lost, 'feminine and radiant' *urbs* that he finds gleaming off the pages of Livy. In Virgil's epic, the lost *urbs* gets forwarded in time, as Virgil weaves Aeneas' memories of fallen Troy and Dido's Carthage into the history of Rome and its future destiny. In 'District and Circle', the poet's dreamily free association of his roots and his reading play on this shared history to link London, Belfast and his own abandoned rural district into one and the same human chain.

Descent journeys typically end with the hero's return from the underworld, so we might expect to find an upward movement in the final sestet of 'District and Circle'. Heaney subverts this generic expectation by portraying himself continuing the journey underground:

And so by night and day to be transported
Through galleried earth with them, the only relict
Of all that I belonged to, hurtled forward,
Reflecting in a window mirror-backed
By blasted weeping rock-walls.
                    Flicker-lit. (*DC* 18)

The first line above retains the sound of Virgil's '*tandem trans fluuium*' (*Ae*.VI.415), where the description of Aeneas' passage across the Styx also, dreamily, lacks a main verb. If the reflection of his father's face recalls Dido in the lines above, here the poet applies the widow sobriquet to himself, 'the only relict / Of all that I belonged to', so he is, on several levels, taking up the burden of his political and cultural history. Later, in his translation of *Aeneid VI* (2016), Heaney will describe Aeneas and his followers as 'the last ... relicts' of 'Troy's name and fame' (ll. 95, 93), a phrase suggesting that Aeneas is a kind of war widow himself, in that he survives the massacre at Troy and suffers many years of migratory exile. Heaney identifies with this condition of exile, as is reflected in his choice of 'Relict' as a working title for the poem in one of its early drafts.[65]

Relicts are also religious or sacred objects (*OED* 2a, 3), and in this final sestet, Heaney seems to be imagining himself as just such an object, passively 'hurtled forward' in time. In the penultimate lines, the words 'blasted' and 'weeping', though referring literally to the tunnel walls, also resonate with the memory of bomb blasts and weeping survivors, so that the final adjective, 'Flicker-lit', describes the poet-as-relict, 'hurtled forward' by the force of that explosion. But even while describing that experience of fragmentation, the sestet offers resistance to it, in the sense

---

64. Heaney, 'Towers, Trees, Terrors', 154.
65. *LP* I.xvii.2, p. 4.

that 'reflecting' and 'mirror-backed' oppose the rush of 'forward' movement. And also, though a solitary 'only relict', the poet is also blasted forward 'with them', the London commuters of his earlier memory, as well as the 'herded shades' of the victims of 7/7. This is only the second use of a collective pronoun in the entire poem (he mentions 'we' descending the escalators in line 18), and here it underlines the poet's stance of solidarity, if not identification, with the London travellers.

The poet's own identity remains ambiguous, his apartness implied by the isolation of 'Flicker-lit' in the final line, his memoriousness by the internal rhyme of 'flicker-lit' with 'Reflecting' and 'relict'. And of course, 'Flicker-lit' itself combines the opposites of darkness and light, or lightness in the dark, like the golden bough gleaming in its hidden grove.[66] Thus if the poet identifies with Aeneas, on a heroically self-willed journey of descent, he also sides with those who suffer fates not of their choosing, and over which they have no control. Indeed, the fragmentation and distillation of an epic narrative (the *katabasis* of *Aeneid* VI) into a five-sonnet lyric sequence seems designed expressly to allow these other relicts of the past to be forwarded in time.

IV. 'THE TOLLUND MAN IN SPRINGTIME'

There is no return from the underworld in 'District and Circle', but the *katabasis* there is complemented by the *anabatic* or upward movement of 'The Tollund Man in Springtime' (*DC* 55–7). Formally, within the 2006 collection, this sequence of six regular sonnets firms up and fills out the five ragged sonnets of the title poem. Thematically, the Tollund Man reascends from the underearth, or rather, from the museum case in which his exhumed body has been on display. Like the earlier sonnet sequence, this one is voiced in the first person. Here the 'I' is neither autobiographical nor a dramatised *persona*, but in Heaney's words, 'a transfusion', a 'soul guide' and 'a kind of guardian other, risen out of the Jutland bog.'[67]

Though less overtly than in 'District and Circle', the Tollund Man's ascension also mirrors and doubles Aeneas' journey through Hades. Questions of faith and betrayal play over in his mind, activating echoes of Dido at the start of the poem: 'Faith placed in me, me faithless as a stone . . . I'd hear soft wind / And remember moony water in a rut.' (ll. 39, 41–2). He also wields a homely golden bough to ensure his safe passage through the alien world of the urban environment:

Through every check and scan I carried with me
A bunch of Tollund rushes – roots and all –
Bagged in their own bog-damp. (*DC* 57)

---

66. Compare the face of the protagonist, illuminated by a rotating police siren light, at the end of the *banlieue* film *La Haine* ('Hate', 1995), dir. Mathieu Kassovitz.
67. 'One Poet in Search of a Title'.

While, in 'District and Circle', the poet feels unease and danger in the London Tube, for the Tollund Man, the modern city is toxic due to environmental pollution:

> I smelled the air, exhaust fumes, silage reek,
> Heard from my heather bed the thickened traffic
> Swarm at the roundabout five fields away
> And transatlantic flights stacked in the blue. (DC 56)

In this poem, as in *District and Circle* as a whole, the entire earth has suffered a mortal blow, from the Atlantic shore to underearth and heaven's lid. There is a sense of pervasive environmental damage that extends well beyond the specific arenas of political conflict depicted in the Horatian ode and the volume's title poem. In 'Höfn', Heaney catches a glimpse from a plane window of polar ice caps melting and glaciers on the move, where the awakening of this 'undead grey-gristed earth-pelt, aeon-scruff' foreshadows the end of human culture and 'every warm, mouthwatering word of mouth.' (DC 53) And in 'Moyulla', he returns to his personal Helicon, the River Moyola which flows near the grounds of the family farm at Mossbawn (DC 58–9). The 'clear vowels' of the river's name have 'suffered muddying' (the 'o' darkening to 'u' in 'Moyulla'[68]) because the river itself is '[m]ilk-fevered' and 'froth[ing] at the mouth / of the discharge pipe' (ibid.). In the twenty-first century, the Earth has, to invoke Milton, 'felt the wound' of human presence, and 'sighing through all her works, g[ives] signs of woe'.[69]

The Tollund Man leaves the safe preserve of his museum case to enter this muddied and 'milk-fevered' world. He steps directly out of the Iron Age into the Anthropocene, 'the world of surveillance cameras and closed-circuit TV, of greenhouse gases and acid rain.'[70] In *Stepping Stones*, Heaney describes him as somebody who has gathered his 'staying powers' and returned to 'the living world by an act of will that is equally an act of imagination.' (SS 411) His staying powers derive from contact with the earth, like Anteaus, and more specifically, from his former life as a herdsman or cattle-drover:

> Cattle out in rain, their knowledgeable
> Solid standing and readiness to wait,
> These I learned from. (DC 57)

And Heaney, in turn, claims to have imbibed from this soul-guide inspiration for the volume's environmental poems 'about glacier melt and river flow, crab apples and fiddlehead ferns, birch groves and alder trees.'[71]

---

68. 'I wanted the darkening of the vowel from 'ola' to 'ulla' to suggest the darkening of the ecological climate, the pollution of the river over time' (SS 406).
69. After the fall of Eve, 'Earth felt the wound, and nature from her seat / Sighing through all her works gave signs of woe, / That all was lost.' (PL.IX.782–4)
70. 'One Poet in Search of a Title'.
71. 'One Poet in Search of a Title'.

The Tollund Man has staying powers, in this alienating, urban environment, in part because he has not come from a world of pristine, Arcadian innocence. On the contrary, in his past life and death, he was already a victim of religious and political violence, his perfectly preserved corpse showing signs of having been killed in an ancient fertility ritual. Thus, in Heaney's poem, he says his spirit was 'strengthened when they chose to put me down / For their own good' (*DC* 55). Sounding much like Heaney, he steels himself to this brave new world by recalling a line from Miłosz, '"The soul exceeds its circumstances"', and he agrees, 'Yes, / History not to be granted the last word' (*DC* 56).

Like Aristaeus' dying bees, which recover once the underworld gods have been appeased, the Tollund Man is a 'principle of regeneration' that is released by an act of human imagination and will (*SS* 411). He awakens with 'newfound contrariness', with the stealth of an urban pastoralist (*DC* 57). Although the bough-like rushes have disintegrated by the time he is ready to make his ascent, he breathes in their dust and pollen (death and new life), which afford him protection as he enters his urban existence:

> Dust in my palm
> And in my nostrils dust, . . .
> / . . . As a man would, cutting turf,
> I straightened, spat on my hands, felt benefit
> And spirited myself into the street. (*DC* 57)

Like the 'relict' thrown forward by the bomb blast in 'District and Circle', the Tollund Man is thrown forward in time, and his *anabasis* completes the descent journey initiated in the earlier sonnet sequence. He comes back from the dead not to transcend the actual, historical world, but to live in it as he finds it. There is an ongoing sense of his living in exile:

> in those queues
> Of wired, far-faced smilers, I stood off
> Bulrush, head in air, far from its lough (*DC* 57)

But it is the presence of this alien, dark, pastoral figure, with bulrush head, phantom limbs and snakeskin-lidded eyes (56), that guarantees the city a measure of natural regeneration at its heart. '[N]either god nor ghost' (55), he is the ancient double of the *urbs*, not on the margins but in the midst of us, lost but waiting to be found.

*

In the volume as a whole, then, Heaney draws on Virgil's narrative of the underworld journey as a means of articulating his desire as an artist to keep faith with the past, with memories of his father and the local, rural community of County Derry. At the same time, he takes a stand in the present, alongside those who lost their lives in the bomb attacks of 2001 and 2005. Filtering his response through Horace and Virgil provides him with a measure of distance and detachment from the events, and a means of stepping outside the escalating cycle of violence. Invoking the memorious tradition of classical *katabasis*, alongside his own imaginative descent and return with the Tollund Man, allows Heaney to bestride rural and urban worlds in ancient and contemporary history, in order to sustain his double identity as a Northern Irish poet, and as an international poet laureate with social responsibilities on the world stage.

6. 'In river country':
The Riverbank Field

> 'And if ever tears are to be wiped away,
> It will be in river country'
> ('Clonmany to Ahascragh', *EL* 76)

A year after *District and Circle* was published by Faber in London, Heaney produced a slim volume entitled *The Riverbank Field*, with The Gallery Press in Dublin. Though separated by only a year, the two volumes could not be more different in scope and tone. Virgil is present as hedge-schoolmaster and guide in both volumes, but whereas Heaney explores global concerns in *District and Circle*, he shifts gear to the local and deeply personal in *The Riverbank Field*. The slim Dublin volume contains a prefatory poem called 'The Riverbank Field', and a sequence of twelve short poems called 'Route 110'. The title poem rehearses thoughts about translating a passage from the end of *Aeneid VI*, while the sequence of linked poems recalls scenes from Heaney's early life, in parallel with a range of different episodes from *Aeneid VI*. In the volume as a whole, we get a strong sense of Heaney's longstanding affection for Virgil as a poet he first encountered in adolescence, a presence thus intermingled with his memories of growing up in rural County Derry.

Heaney's change of focus from the global to the local can be understood in part as a response to a very unexpected turn in his own life. Since receiving the Nobel Prize in 1995, he had been leading a high-pressured existence, with a punishing schedule of public performances around the world. The Virgilian poems in *Electric Light* and *District and Circle* evince his awareness of this wider public context, and his determination to meet the challenge of his new, international role. In late August 2006, however, Heaney suffered a stroke and was briefly paralysed down one side. He was hospitalised for six weeks before making a full recovery, and in response to this brush with mortality he cut back drastically on his schedule of public appearances.[1] He resigned as Poet in Residence at Harvard University and cancelled almost all of his

---

1. H. McDonald (2009); Heaney, 'A Life of Rhyme' [Interview with Robert McCrum] (2009); *SS* 461–3.

lecture engagements for the following year. It was another major consecration of his time and attention to writing poetry, comparable to his move to Glanmore Cottage in County Wicklow, in 1972 (SS 150). While recovering from the stroke, Heaney was also expecting the birth of his first grandchild, and this combination of circumstances, he said, happily produced a 'little surgette' of inspiration.[2] By November, he had completed his sequence of twelve Virgilian poems, in time to present to his son Christopher at the birth of Anna Rose.[3]

While it is easy to understand why a globally renowned poet, when suffering a serious health setback, would choose to take a year off to recuperate away from the public eye, the question remains: why turn to Virgil in this retreat from the global stage? Colin Burrow has suggested that, in his later work, Heaney presents *Aeneid VI* as 'more like a family drama than a political one', implying that the later 'domesticated' responses to Virgil are less provocative and interesting.[4] But Heaney's return to Mossbawn via Mantua is, in a sense, entirely in accord with the central preoccupation of his poetry and poetics, which is to ask: what good is poetry, what are its virtues or curative powers?[5] The radical diminution of scale that occurs in *The Riverbank Field* is already implicit in the Virgilian eclogues of *Electric Light*, and in 'The Blackbird of Glanmore', the tender elegy that closes *District and Circle*. Most of all, *The Riverbank Field* builds on his discovery of a principle of regeneration in the *katabases* of Aeneas and the Tollund Man, in *District and Circle*. But whereas his previous two volumes had been driven by an ethical imperative to respond to national and global crises, in *The Riverbank Field* Heaney follows what he would call his primary lyric impulses, the pleasures of rhythmic cadence and the spontaneous generation of poetic form. The idea that poetry generates newness – new energy, new artistic form, new ways of thinking – lies at the heart of his series of Virgilian vignettes in 'Route 110'.

Heaney later described his procedure in 'Route 110' as 'a matter . . . of a relatively simple "mythic method" being employed over twelve sections'.[6] His 'mythic method' alludes to T. S. Eliot's description of Joyce's use of Greek myth in *Ulysses*:

> in manipulating a continuous parallel between contemporaneity and antiquity, Mr. Joyce is pursuing a method which others must pursue after him . . . It is simply a way of controlling, of ordering, of giving a shape and a significance to the immense panorama of futility and anarchy which is contemporary history. . . . Instead of narrative method, we may now use the mythical method.[7]

---

2. Interview with Mark Lawson (2009).
3. Heaney's son Christopher told Deirdre Falvey, 'When Anna Rose was born he did send to myself and Jenny the last section of *Route 110*, which is about her birth. He said he finished that the night she was born': that is, in November 2006 ('Seamus Heaney, Our Dad the Poet', *The Irish Times*, 30 June 2018). On 'Route 110', see also Heiny (2013), Hickey (2019), Impens (2018), K. Murphy (2016), Parker, '"Back in the heartland"' (2013) and Putnam (2012).
4. Burrow (2016) is commenting on the later work, in a review of Heaney's *Aeneid Book VI*.
5. Cf. Heaney, 'Mossbawn via Mantua: Ireland in/and Europe' (2012).
6. Heaney, 'Translator's Note' (A.viii).
7. Eliot, 'Ulysses, Order and Myth', in *Selected Prose of T. S. Eliot* (1975), 177–8. On the descent myth in modernism, see Pike (1997).

Heaney's twelve poems, each twelve lines long, correspond to the twelve books of Virgil's *Aeneid*. But his continuous parallels are drawn between 1950s Derry and the sixth book of the *Aeneid*, where the otherworldly setting softens the brunt of history's 'futility and anarchy'. Heaney also reduces and fragments the narrative arc of *Aeneid VI*, so that Aeneas' journey through the underworld is transformed into a swift series of independent lyric episodes.

Each of the twelve poems is comprised of four tercets, combining Dantean flow with the compressed, dramatic structure of the Petrarchan or Shakespearean sonnet, like the forty-eight poems of *Squarings* (ST 51–108). Heaney admired the 'deliberately chosen and executed *terza rima*' in Yeats's late poem, 'Cuchulain Comforted', where the poet prepares 'to meet his unmaker and confront him with made things'.[8] But the free-flowing movement of 'Route 110' owes still more to Mandelstam's idea of Dante's form creation 'as the apotheosis of free, natural, biological process, as a hive of bees, a process of crystallization, a hurry of pigeon flights, a focus for all the impulsive, instinctive, non-utilitarian elements in the creative life' (FK 178). In 'Route 110', there is a similar principle of generation at work, in spirit close to the '"infantile . . . phonetics"' that Mandelstam heard in Dante's vernacular Italian, with '"its beautiful child-like quality, its closeness to infant babbling"' (FK 176). 'Route 110' similarly culminates in the birth of a child, an event that is symbolically bound up with a return of language to its *in-fans-*y, or pre-speech babbling.

Despite the elegiac content of many of the 'Route 110' poems, the tone of the entire sequence is remarkably tranquil and light-hearted, especially when encountered in the original 2007 volume (it reappears in 2010, in slightly revised form, as the centrepiece of *Human Chain*). As published by The Gallery Press, *The Riverbank Field* is a beautiful book, casebound in plain, olive green, linen covers, and illustrated with paintings and sketches by the Dublin artist, Martin Gale. The two paintings, reproduced in colour plates, depict the River Liffey flowing through fields close to the artist's home in County Kildare (see Plate 4).[9] As bookends to *The Riverbank Field*, they provide a visual analogue for the twilit walk Heaney describes in the title poem, as well as the riverbank scene in the eleventh poem of 'Route 110'. While nodding to Joyce's River Liffey in *Ulysses* (later personified as Anna Livia Plurabelle in *Finnegans Wake*), Gale's tranquil river scene also commingles Heaney's River Moyola with Virgil's River Lethe. The boat on the bank invites the viewer to cross the river, while the crows on the farther shore recall Virgil's bird-like souls flocking to the river's edge. The quiet evening scene depicted by Gale thus seems both materially real, and suggestive of a supernatural otherworld.

---

8. Heaney, SS 465; Yeats (1992), 379.
9. Email from Martin Gale to author, 13 November 2018. The paintings were specially commissioned for the volume, around December 2006.

I. THE RIVER LETHE

Turning the page from Gale's river painting, the reader comes upon the prefatory poem, 'The Riverbank Field', in which Heaney conjoins his own memories of the Moyola river with Virgil's description of the River Lethe, at the end of *Aeneid VI*. While we have previously seen Heaney's fascination with the threshold crossing *into* Hades by means of Charon's barge, this is the first volume to highlight the *return* crossing, via the oblivion-inducing waters of the Lethe. The prominence of this motif suggests that, for Heaney, Virgil is not only the poet of elegiac memory who mourns the *lacrimae rerum*; he is also the exemplary guide who, like the ghost of Joyce in *Station Island*, encourages Heaney to 'let go, let fly, forget' (*SI* 93). Virgil's river of oblivion will feature again in the last two sections of 'Route 110', suggesting that Heaney's mythic method in 'Route 110' involves deliberately forgetting or disburdening oneself of the memory of sectarian conflict and violence.

His interpretation of the Lethean crossing is, in itself, a deliberately forgetful or hazy reading of the originary Virgilian episode. At the end of *Aeneid VI*, Aeneas realises his quest and discovers his father's ghost in Elysium. Having tried and failed to embrace the insubstantial shade, he then turns to see thousands of shades flocking to a riverbank and wonders what it means. Anchises explains that these are souls gathering to drink from the River Lethe, to forget their former selves and return to the material world. Aeneas is baffled by their desire to return to the world, where he has witnessed so much war, violence and loss, and asks his father, '*quae lucis miseris tam dira cupido?*' (*Ae*.VI.721, 'what terrible desire possesses the wretches?'[10]). Anchises explains, borrowing from Lucretius, Plato, and Pythagorean and Orphic doctrine, that the souls have undergone many years of suffering before reaching this stage, and all their past stains and crimes have been burned away by purgatorial fire (*Ae*.VI.736–47).[11] Each soul suffers its own torment, and then, after a thousand years have passed, is sent to drink from the Lethe and return to the world:

> '*has omnis, ubi mille rotam uoluere per annos,*
> *Lethaeum ad fluuium deus euocat agmine magno,*
> *scilicet immemores supera ut conuexa reuisant*
> *rursus, et incipiant in corpora uelle reuerti.*' (*Ae*.VI.748–51)

> 'All these others, when they have turned the wheel for a thousand years, the god summons to the river Lethe in a great column, to the end that they revisit the vault of the sky with no recollections.' (trans. Horsfall, p. 51)

For Virgil, then, drinking from the Lethe is part of the purgatorial process which the souls are summoned to endure. Since memory was such an important part of Roman culture, becoming '*im-memores*' would have been regarded as a particularly

---

10. Trans. Horsfall (2013), p. 51.
11. Major influences on Virgil's metempsychosis passage include Pythagoras, the Orphic mysteries, Plato, Cicero's *Somnium Scipionis*, Lucretius and Ennius. For a review of scholarship on this famous passage, see Horsfall (2013), pp. 484–6, 499–508.

horrifying punishment.[12] According to Virgil's lines, only a few blessed souls are exempt from this punitive cycle, souls like Anchises who are permitted to dwell in Elysium forever. The entire passage, so out of keeping with traditional representations of the afterlife in classical epic, has attracted much scholarly debate. Even the order of the lines is uncertain, some finding it unlikely that souls would be sent back *after* they had reached Elysium.[13] But most scholars agree that Virgil had a practical reason for introducing the doctrine of reincarnation at the end of Aeneas' underworld journey: it allows Anchises to show Aeneas the souls of future Roman leaders and generals, waiting to assume their destined lives.[14]

For Heaney, however, the Lethean crossing offers the possibility of extracting oneself mentally from the trauma of military conflict. Two years before publishing *The Riverbank Field*, while on a visit to Portugal, he had come across the legend of a Roman legion crossing an actual River Lethe on their campaign to colonise Lusitania (as they named Portugal).[15] The story is recorded in Strabo's *Geographica*, where the River Lethe is identified as the Limaeas (the Lima River), or Belion (possibly a corruption of the Latin, *oblivio*) in Lusitania.[16] According to Strabo, the Roman soldiers refused to follow their general across the Lethe as they feared losing their memories. But the general reassured them by summoning each legionary across the river by individual name, thus proving that his memory had survived the crossing. Heaney alludes to the legend in a poem entitled 'To the Poets of St Andrews', which purports to be a translation of a Renaissance Latin poem by Arthur Johnston:[17]

> As when in Lusitania once the legions
> Stood under halted standards by Lima River

---

12. Cf. Virgil's direct apostrophe to Orpheus, '*immemor heu!*' ('o forgetful one!'), as he fails in his quest and turns to look back at Eurydice (G.IV.491). Alain Gowing writes, 'Romans attached a heightened importance to memory, which manifests itself in almost every aspect of their existence, from celebrations of the dead to oratory to law, suffusing and animating their art, their buildings, and their literature' (2005, 1). The state punishment of *damnatio memoriae* entailed removing all images, monuments, inscriptions or other memorials of the condemned person (see Tola, 'Memories of Rome's Underworld', in Scherer and Falconer, eds (2020), 87–107.
13. On the classical afterlife, see Alice Bennett (2019). In 'The Riverbank Field', Heaney follows the line order of the Mynors Oxford Classical Texts (OCT) and 1978 Loeb edition (not the 1986 edition, revised by Goold, who proposes a different line order at Ae.VI.743–7). Heaney also follows the OCT and Fairclough editions at a textual crux in line VI.383.
14. 'That doctrine . . . is what makes it possible for V. to reveal to us the pageant of great, unborn Romans.' (Horsfall (2013), p. 486)
15. With thanks to Marco Sonzogni for this information, and for drawing my attention to Heaney's poem, 'To the Poets of St Andrews'. The visit to Portugal is mentioned in a fax to Liam O'Flynn, 7 June 2004 (*LP* I.xvii.4).
16. *The Geography of Strabo* III.3.4, trans. H. L. Jones, Vol. 2, p. 69.
17. No such original Latin poem exists. The fiction is a nod to the poet and scholar Robert Crawford, who had published translations of the Scottish poet and physician Arthur Johnston (1587–1641). Heaney's poem is published in Crawford's anthology, *The Book of St Andrews* (2007). With thanks to Robert Crawford, email to author, 26 June 2020.

> And refused to wade across the water north
> To make war on the clans because the clans
> Had spread a rumour that Lethe flowed to Ocean[18]

In Heaney's poem, the Lusitanian tribes try to trick the Romans into abandoning their campaign, playing on their superstitious fear of the Lethe's powers. But the Roman leader dispels the rumour by crossing the river and retaining his memory, in accordance with Strabo's account:

>   one veteran commander
> (To show this was no bourne of forgetfulness)
> Splashed into the shallows and kept going
> Under the campaign gear, his spear-shaft firm
> And his grasp on memory when he'd got across[19]

In the last section of the poem, Heaney likens himself to the veteran commander, as he crosses into Scotland over the Forth river. But rather than a soldier's weapon, he bears a poet's walking stick ('instead of spear-shaft grasp my crummock'). Even in making the comparison, his sympathies seem more inclined to the Lusitanian clans than the veteran commander. As well as complimenting his Scottish host, Robert Crawford, Heaney's attribution of the poem's authorship to Arthur Johnston gives the power of language back to the clans, thus undoing the legacy of the Roman conquest inscribed in the legend. Moreover, while the legend still centres on the Roman fear of Lethean oblivion, Heaney's poem plays with two new possibilities that he would not have found in Virgil: one, that memory could be retained in crossing the Lethe, and two, that forgetfulness might be deployed strategically, by those attempting to escape military conflict.

When he turns to Virgil's Lethe in 2006, Heaney gives a strongly positive valency to the idea of drinking forgetfulness from the mythical river. In an interview with the Irish poet Gerald Dawe, broadcast on RTÉ shortly after the publication of *The Riverbank Field*, Heaney describes the Virgilian setting of his title poem:

> when Aeneas gets down to the very end to the river of Lethe when he meets his father, it is in a beautiful riverbank situation on the *broagh* of the river . . . there are thousands of people moving around, and the father tells him, these people are – after a thousand years, they'll go over that river, they'll go through the River Lethe. They'll forget they were in the underworld, and they'll be reborn, up, under the dome of the sky again . . . So, there's that kind of transition: youth and age, age and youth . . . generations passing, generations arriving.[20]

---

18. Heaney, 'To The Poets of St Andrews' (ll. 1–5), in *The Book of St Andrews* (2007), 11.
19. Ibid., ll. 7–11.
20. Heaney, interview with Gerald Dawe, Irish poet and Fellow Emeritus, Trinity College, *The Poetry Programme* (RTÉ). Audiofile, courtesy of RTÉ and Gerald Dawe. The broadcast was recorded around 28 April, according to Dawe, and broadcast 4 October 2008. Email to author.

The 'riverbank situation', as Heaney describes it, is both the scene of the son's reunion with his father and a place strongly associated with a Hibernian landscape. *Broagh* derives from the Gaelic *bruach*, meaning 'riverbank', a word that strangers are said to find 'difficult to manage' (WO 17). In this tranquil description of generations crossing the Lethe, there seems to be little trace of Virgil's notion of purgatorial suffering. The scene by the riverbank now offers Heaney a metaphor for the resurgence of natural life, which had been embodied in the Tollund Man in his previous collection. As a psychological metaphor, furthermore, the Lethean crossing offers the possibility of escaping the traumatic memory of war. In this sense, 'they'll forget they were in the underworld' offers a welcome release to those who lived in the 'age of ghosts' in pre-Troubles Ireland (HC 53, l. 1).

II. 'THE RIVERBANK FIELD'

The title poem of *The Riverbank Field* is positioned immediately before 'Route 110', and functions as a threshold-crossing into the twelve-part *katabatic* journey. Paratextually, it creates a bridge between the poet's present-day reality, in the midst of translating Virgil, and the underworld of his memory, where we find him entering a bookshop in 1950s Belfast, in Poem I of 'Route 110'. 'The Riverbank Field' also conducts its own mini-*katabasis*, in the sense that Heaney begins by quoting the classic Loeb translation of Virgil, then descends into an encounter with the Latin text, and finally translates the lines as if speaking directly from Virgil's underworld. Arrestingly, this threshold poem initiates the descent journey from the 'beautiful riverbank situation' at the end of Book VI, where the souls are gathering by the River Lethe and preparing to re-enter the material world. Descending into Hades via Lethe alters the traditional dynamics of *katabatic* narrative in at least two fundamental ways. From the perspective of the descent hero, the journey becomes less threatening and dangerous, since the way out is already known from the beginning. And for the poet, descending via Lethe suggests that forgetfulness, as well as memory, will shape his narration of the journey and ultimately the *telos* or aim of his artistic quest. Thus, in 'Route 110' we will find that Heaney recounts his adolescent experience in disjointed flashbacks, as if his memory has been altered, but not erased by drinking the mysterious river water.

'The Riverbank Field' prepares us for this light-footed journey into the past. The tone of the opening tercet is relaxed and informal, the poet beginning in mid-conversation:

Ask me to translate what Loeb gives as
'In a retired vale . . . a sequestered grove'
And I'll confound the Lethe in Moyola [21]

---

21. Since *RF* (2007) is unpaginated, citations are taken from *HC* (2010), unless otherwise noted. Significant differences between the two editions will be given in the notes.

Plate 3 Paul Cézanne (1839-1906), 'Aeneas Meeting Dido at Carthage', 1873-76. Graphite on cream laid paper, 22.9 × 30.5 cm. The Henry and Rose Pearlman Foundation on long-term loan to the Princeton University Art Museum / photo Bruce M. White.

Plate 4 Martin Gale (b. 1949), 'Crows', c. 2006, reproduced in Seamus Heaney, The Riverbank Field, Dublin: The Gallery Press, 2007. © Martin Gale.

Plate 3 Paul Cézanne (1839-1906), 'Aeneas Meeting Dido at Carthage', 1873-76. Graphite on cream laid paper, 22.9 × 30.5 cm. The Henry and Rose Pearlman Foundation on long-term loan to the Princeton University Art Museum / photo Bruce M. White.

Plate 4 Martin Gale (b. 1949), 'Crows', c. 2006, reproduced in Seamus Heaney, The Riverbank Field, Dublin: The Gallery Press, 2007. © Martin Gale.

The third line announces the 'mythic method' that Heaney will deploy in 'Route 110'. In its etymological sense, 'confound' (from Latin *confundere*, 'flow together') here connotes the conjoining of two rivers, the one remembered and real, the other literary and mythical. The Moyola river flowed past Heaney's childhood homestead at Mossbawn, where one of the planting fields running down to the river was known as 'the riverbank field' (SS 18). In this neutral sense, then, the commingling of rivers indicates the parallels Heaney will find between Virgil's underworld and his memories of County Derry. But additionally, the adversarial sense of 'confound' (meaning 'defeat utterly', 'discomfit' or 'overcome', *OED* 1) indicates his readiness to refashion Virgil's lines to his own artistic needs. This proves to be true of Heaney's Lethe, in particular, which temporarily forgets its ancient, punishing aspect in *The Riverbank Field*.[22]

In the second tercet, Heaney reclaims Virgil from Fairclough's Loeb translation, which, with elevated words like 'vale' and 'grove', reserves Elysium for a cultural elite.[23] Here 'grove' is rehoused in the local landscape where the poet remembers strolling, from 'Back Park down from Grove Hill / Across Long Rigs' (ll. 4–5). Likewise, the 'riverbank' is Hibernicised in 'Upper Broagh' (l. 8), with its 'difficult to manage' name. The '*domos placidas*' are made to sound local and familiar, with the demonstrative adjective preceding the translation: '"those peaceful homes"' (l. 7). In the RTÉ interview, when Heaney reads the poem aloud, he pronounces '*placidas*' with the soft 'c' of Church Latin, an auditory reminder of the way Virgil's Elysium is being relocated in County Derry.

Then, in the middle section of the poem, something unexpected happens which jolts the poet on to a new course. Until this point, he has seemed confident of his Joycean method, 'manipulating a continuous parallel' between Virgil's Elysium and his memory of home. With minimal adjustments, one landscape could be superimposed on the other: 'Moths then on evening water' and 'Midge veils instead of lily beds, but *stet* / To all the rest' (ll. 8–11). But at the river's edge, the poet seems to lose control of the poem as his remembered world suddenly becomes more otherworldly than real. There grows 'grass so fully fledged // And unimprinted' that it seems already to combine age and innocence, like the oxymoronic 'full-grown lambs' in Keats's 'o'er-brimm'd' autumn.[24] Then a double negative, with four sharp plosives, nicks the fabric of the real, revealing the presence of supernatural beings:

---

22. In HC, 'The Riverbank Field' follows 'Canopy', a poem which describes the transformation of Harvard Yard by an installation of fairy lights (HC 44–5). Heaney declares the artist has transformed a Dantean forest of suicides (*Inferno* XIII) into a lover's lane. In a draft version of 'Canopy', Heaney writes, '"Thus I confound Hell in Elysium."' (*LP* I.xviii.1), quoting Marlowe's defiant Dr Faustus, 'This word Damnation, terrifies not me, / For I confound hell in Elizium' (*Doctor Faustus* I.iii.286–9, *The Complete Works* (1981), Vol. II, 170. Faustus probably means he is indifferent to Hell and Heaven, not that he disbelieves in their existence.
23. The word 'grove' belongs to 'translations from the classics', suggesting 'a sunlit treeline, a tonsured hillock approached by white-robed priests' (*P* 36). The Irish equivalent of 'groves' would be *dirraghs*.
24. Keats, 'To Autumn', ll. 30, 11 (2003), 361, 360.

>   it <u>c</u>an'<u>t</u> no<u>t</u> <u>c</u>onjure thoughts
> Of passing spirit-troops, *animae, quibus altera fato*
> *Corpora debentur*, 'spirits', that is, //
> 'To whom second bodies are owed by fate'. (HC 46, ll. 13–16)

The Latin words drift into the English mid-sentence, as if surfacing dreamily from the underworld. Heaney preserves Virgil's rhythm and word-order placement, so that line 14 ends on a dactyl-spondee (*āltĕră fātō*), and line 15 resumes with a dactyl (*cōrpŏră*) line, exactly as occurs in *Aeneid VI*, lines 713–14.[25]

While line 16 above is still Fairclough's translation, the poet now begins to translate the Latin passage '"In my own words"' (l. 18). The quotation marks suggest that he is remembering the familiar prompt of a teacher, and that he is translating now 'as enjoined to often' in his schooldays (l. 17). In a sense, his translation is being addressed to this former schoolmaster, whether that implies Heaney's actual Latin master, Father Michael McGlinchey, or his exemplary hedge-schoolmaster, Virgil himself.[26] Either way, in this final section of the poem, he seems to forget the mythic method and instead enters wholly into Virgil's imaginary world. He translates the passage in which Anchises explains how the underworld shades are gathering by the river to return to life:

> 'has omnis, ubi mille rotam uoluere per annos,
> Lethaeum ad fluuium deus euocat agmine magno,
> scilicet immemores supera ut conuexa reuisant
> rursus, et incipiant in corpora uelle reuerti.' (*Ae*.VI.748–51)

> 'All these presences
> once they have done their turn of a thousand years
> are summoned here to drink the river water
>
> so that memories of life on this side are shed
> and soul repines to dwell in flesh and blood
> under the dome of heaven.' (*RF* no pag.)

These last two tercets are offered in Heaney's 'own words', rather than filtered through Loeb, as he is 'enjoined to' by a silent teacher. But at the same time, as the quotation marks indicate, these lines are spoken by a character in Virgil's narrative: Anchises is addressing his son, Aeneas. So they are Virgil's words, and Anchises', and the poet seems to be hearing them, rather than uttering them himself. Descending into Virgil's otherworld, then, he has been dispossessed of sole authorship of the poem. At the same time, these lines still are distinctly Heaney's, in that they give a newly positive spin to Virgil's account of Pythagorean metempsychosis. Heaney notably skips over Anchises' description of the torments the shades will have to

---

25. The first typescript draft of 'The Riverbank Field' has 'says Loeb' in place of 'that is', underlining that this is still Fairclough's translation being quoted (*LP* I.xviii.1).
26. On McGlinchey, see A.vii–viii.

endure (the poem's by-line, '*after* Aeneid VI, 704–15, 748–51', indicates the ellipsis). He also softens the stretch of time in purgatory ('once they have done their turn'), and he gives Hades a touch of the Celtic faery world (with a contiguous relation to 'life on this side'). And, finally, he invests the Lethean crossing with implications of a Biblical resurrection ('soul repines to dwell . . . under the dome of heaven').

Evidently, Heaney thought this translation almost *too* forgetful of the originary text, for he later revised it, and in *Human Chain* the same passage reads:

'All these presences
Once they have rolled time's wheel a thousand years
Are summoned here to drink the river water

So that memories of this underworld are shed
And soul is longing to dwell in flesh and blood
Under the dome of the sky.' (HC 46–7, ll. 19–24)

Line 20 offers a more literal version of Virgil's '*mille rotam uoluere per annos*' (*Ae*.VI.748).[27] And the Biblical language is more muted, with 'repines' changed to 'longing', and 'heaven' altered to 'sky'.[28] But in both versions, Heaney omits to mention the *deus* who commands the shades to approach the river, which invites us to suppose they are glad to be summoned to 'dwell in flesh and blood'. And again, in both versions, 'memories . . . are shed': that added verb turns memory loss into a welcome disburdening of the past, with an added connotation of Christian resurrection (symbolised by a snake shedding its skin).[29]

A final touch of forgetfulness in Heaney's translation is his omission of the name Lethe (*Ae*.VI.749) in the penultimate tercet. In a typescript draft of 'The Riverbank Field', he tries out various possibilities: 'Lethe's water', 'Lethe's River' and 'from Lethe River'.[30] But in the end, he settles simply for 'river water', which confounds both rivers together, the Lethe and Moyola. Or perhaps, at this transitional moment, both names are shed as the river fulfils its promise of baptism and rebirth. A similar

---

27. Fairclough translates 'Time's wheel' as well. For a further discussion of this passage, see Chapter 9, p. 253.
28. To me, this alteration does not substantiate the larger claim that Heaney is shifting from a Catholic to a classical world-view (Impens 2017, 2018). In *RTÉ*, Heaney paraphrases the *RF* passage 'they'll be reborn . . . under the dome of the sky'; in other words, he is equally comfortable with 'heaven' and 'sky' in 2007/8. Heaney's December 2008 draft of A.1014–15 reads: 'To dwell under heaven's dome and start again / To wish for the old life of flesh and blood.' Both terms appear in A (2016): *Ae*.VI.751 becomes 'beneath sky's dome' (A.1014), yet later we find 'the whole offspring of Iulus, destined one day / To issue forth beneath the dome of heaven.' (A.1067–8; *Ae*.VI.789–90)
29. In A (2016), Heaney renders this as 'memories are effaced' (A.1013), restoring the notion of purgatorial punishment in the Latin.
30. Draft 1 has 'river water' crossed out and overwritten with 'Lethe river'; Draft 2 hesitates between 'Lethe's water', 'Lethe's River' and 'from Lethe River' (*LP* I.xviii.1). In the book-length translation (2016), he renders Virgil's '*Lethaeum fluvium*' more exactly as 'Lethe river' (A.1012).

translation beyond nomination occurs at the end of Heaney's poem 'St Kevin and the Blackbird', where the saint loses himself in prayer and forgets his aching limbs, 'For he has forgotten self, forgotten bird / And on the riverbank forgotten the river's name' (SL 21). In 'The Riverbank Field', what we are left with is a sensation of lightness and a welcome return to the material world. As Heaney remarks to Dawe, myths of the underworld 'are not hell or heaven or not punishment or not reward . . . they are a kind of continuation.' (*RTÉ*)

III. 'ROUTE 110'

From the threshold of 'The Riverbank Field', Heaney descends into his sequence of twelve flashbacks, each paired with an episode from Virgil's underworld book. At first simply titled 'Book Six', Heaney's sequence was soon baptised with a local name, 'Route 110', after the old bus route running out of Smithfield Market in Belfast up to Magherafelt, Cookstown.[31] In his interview with Dawe, Heaney compares the sequence to James Joyce's 'day in Dublin with *Ulysses* or *The Odyssey* in the background': 'Route 110', he suggests, is a kind of *Ulysses* 'reduced to . . . County Derry dimensions' (*RTÉ*). While Joyce stretches twenty-four hours in Dublin into an Odyssean sea journey, Heaney instead ratchets up the speed of narration, so that our primary impression of the underworld journey is one of swift, unencumbered flight. The 'I' of Poem IV is depicted as a 'creature of cold blasts and flap-winged rain', like Heaney's alter ego, the bird-king Sweeney (*HC* 51, l. 6). And in the Dawe interview, he describes the composition process in terms of an Ariel flight. Thus, the twelve poems are 'more drawings than oil work', 'very swift little things . . . little steals', that 'just had to be caught on the wing', a matter of 'swift annotation' executed 'swiftly and boldly' (*RTÉ*). The time frame is elastic and non-linear: while most of the episodes are set in the mid- to late 1950s, Poem IV shoots forward to a 1967 holiday in Tuscany, and Poem VIII to a relationship in the early 1960s, while Poem IX depicts scenes from 1970s Belfast, and Poem XII refers to two scenes of childbirth, in 1966 and 2006 (the poem's present). These disjunctions contribute to the sense of a spontaneous, self-generated form, rather than a mythical structure architecturally imposed on the material from without. The flashbacks generate further poetic flights by twinning with episodes from *Aeneid VI*.

These independent lyric flights are linked by verbal patterning, rather than by a strictly linear narrative. There are resonant repetitions within individual lines, such as 'booths and the jambs of booths' (Poem II) and 'rooks / Around a rookery' (Poem III). And there are repetitions of images and phrases which hook one poem to the next, in a loose, free-associative sequence: old suits resemble souls in Poem II, and souls flock like rooks in Poem III; a pigeon-grey suit flaps like a soul-bird in Poem IV, and pigeons deliver Heaney to a local golden/foil bough in Poem V. Creating these little verbal links involves the reader in the poet's memory work so that we encoun-

---

31. Heaney, *RTÉ*. Heaney sent a print-out of 'The Riverbank Field' and the sequence then entitled 'Book Six' to Patrick Crotty on 31 December 2006. With thanks to Patrick Crotty.

ter the underworld as an accreting network of memories and metaphors, rather than a fixed system of rewards and punishments.

In the *RTÉ* interview, Heaney describes the separate, autobiographical incidents as 'little flashes, they're little flashbacks, they're little cutaways', while the arc of Aeneas' journey is 'matched a little bit by little incidents on the journey from Smithfield up to Castledawson, Bellaghy.' The repeated adjective 'little' highlights the familiar and intimate mood Heaney manages to capture in his compact sequence, which distils 900 lines of epic hexameter into twelve lyric flits and perchings.[32] In this descent into Virgil's underworld, he discovers the spontaneous, auto-generating voice of lyric that Mandelstam had heard in Dante (*FK* 175, 178). And Dante remains a generative force in Heaney's sequence as well. This is most evident in the Dantean form of loose, unrhymed *terza rima*. But also, as in the *Commedia*, Heaney's descent journey can be read on two levels, with the 'poet-Heaney' descending in search of artistic rejuvenation, while the adolescent 'pilgrim-Heaney' is initiated into the adult life of the community, sharing its rituals of grief and celebration.[33]

Heaney also affirms his ties with Romantic poetry and, in particular, with Wordsworth's autobiographical poem, 'The Prelude'. The River Moyola, flowing past Mossbawn, is Heaney's River Derwent, where Wordsworth located the sources of his creativity. In 'The Prelude', Wordsworth proceeds in a series of episodic, autobiographical flashbacks, or as he called them, 'spots of time, / That with distinct pre-eminence retain / A renovating virtue,' from which 'our minds / Are nourished and invisibly repaired'.[34] Heaney's local district in County Derry similarly becomes a time-space of 'renovating virtue', whose 'greenness' runs through all the region's subsequent experience of sectarian conflict. As he wrote in an uncollected *Squarings* poem, 'green went deep / As the unconscious in *Bann Valley*,' where 'we glossed ourselves with earth tones and with leaf shades.'[35] 'Gloss' derives from the ancient Greek γλῶσσα, meaning 'tongue' or 'language' (*OED*, *gloze*, n. 1). The earth tones of the Bann Valley, reflected in the endpapers of The Gallery Press edition of *The Riverbank Field*, are a primary language for Heaney's poetry, just as the Lake District is for Wordsworth.[36]

In Poem I of 'Route 110', Heaney recalls his former self purchasing his first copy of *Aeneid VI* from a Sibyl-like shopkeeper, in a second-hand bookshop in Smithfield Market, Belfast.[37] For the boy, the *katabatic* journey will trace a route from city to

---

32. Heaney's 'little' also contrasts with the Yeatsian use of 'great', 'intoned like a mantra' in correspondence about the thoor at Ballylee; the medieval tower has 'great beams', 'great chairs', 'great elmwood beds', 'great ground floor' and so on (quoted in Heaney, *The Place of Writing* (1989), 22–3). Heaney criticises Yeats's 'great fur coat of attitude' in *FK* 110.
33. Putnam finds the same analogy with Dante-poet and Dante-pilgrim (2012), 82ff. Impens (2018) argues, contrastingly, that Heaney turns away from Dante's influence after *ST*.
34. Wordsworth, *The Fourteen-Book Prelude*, Book XII.208–15 (1985, 238–9).
35. Heaney, 'Seven Years' (*LP* I.xi.4).
36. On the language of the unconscious, cf. Lacan, 'The Insistence of the Letter in the Unconscious, or Reason Since Freud', in *Écrits* (1977).
37. The bookshop is based on a real place, Henry Hall's, where, as an adolescent, Heaney did in fact purchase a copy of Virgil (*RTÉ*).

countryside, and from market to river, culminating in Poem XI, where he will stand on the banks of the Moyola, fishing alongside his father. The scene in the bookshop corresponds roughly to lines 42–155 of *Aeneid VI*, and the 'old dame' (*RTÉ*) who fetches him a copy of the *Aeneid* is a burlesque, domesticated Sibyl, 'Smelling of dry rot and disinfectant' (l. 4). Poem I has a jaunty tone, bristling with 't's and 'k's, and tripping along in irregular four-beat lines. But there are touches of oracular menace as well: the subject of the opening phrase, 'she', is suspensefully withheld until the fifth line. Less crude than Yeats's 'raving slut / Who keeps the till', Heaney's *cailleach* still commands a mysterious power.[38] As she slides the book through the cubicle mouth, the rhythm of the final tercet shifts to dactylic, so that, playing against the tercets, we get this more classical hexameter beat:

'Dústbrĕath bĕ | stírred ĭn thĕ | cúbĭclĕ | móuth Ĭ ĭn- | háled ăs shĕ |
slíd my | púrchăse | Íntŏ ă | décklĕ-ĕdged | brówn păpĕr | bág'

The dactyls are a rhythmic reminder of the moment when Virgil's Sibyl is breathed into by Apollo, as she stands in her cave mouth at Cumae.[39] A kind of poetic birth takes place here too, the *Aeneid* being delivered, as it were, from the 'slack marsupial vent' of the old dame's shop-coat.

With his 'bagged Virgil' in hand, the adolescent poet steps into the milling chaos of Smithfield Market, Belfast, in Poem II (*HC* 49). Here, he pushes past racks of ancient suits resembling souls gathered at the edge of the River Styx. Smithfield Market, while recalling Virgil's scene beside the Styx (*Ae*.VI.305–16), is also Heaney's version of Yeats's 'foul rag and bone shop of the heart', that 'mound of refuse or the sweepings of a street, / Old kettles, old bottles, and a broken can, / Old iron, old bones, old rags', whence poetry derives its primary images.[40] The Belfast market is similarly glutted with the rags and bones of local life: 'displays / Of canvas schoolbags, maps, prints, plaster plaques, / Feather dusters, artificial flowers' (ll. 8–9). In recollecting these images, poet-Heaney is restoring to life an institution that no longer exists. Smithfield Market was bombed in 1974, and thus, in the poet's present, is 'silent now as birdless Lake Avernus' ('*a-vernus*' meaning, literally, 'without birds', and 'Avernus' being traditionally known as one of the entrances to Hades).[41] Meanwhile, the boy shoulders his way through the market's bric-a-brac, heading for Gresham Street bus station. The old suits are crushed together on their

---

38. Yeats, 'The Circus Animals' Desertion', ll. 37–8 (1992, 394). A *cailleach* is a 'witch-like old woman or crone' (*SS* xix), or 'a hag, a very old woman' (Dolan, *A Dictionary of Hiberno-English* (1999), 48). In an earlier version of Poem XII, the friend who comes in from the garden is accompanied by a feline Sibyl, a '*cailleach* of the dew', who sees the poet through to the end of his journey. The entire scene of Poem XII, with the cat-Sibyl, was originally written as a section of 'Loughanure' (*LP* I.xviii.1; *HC* 61).
39. Putnam also notices the echo of Joyce's Leopold Bloom at the bookseller's ('Onions of his breath came across the counter out of his ruined mouth' ('Wandering Rocks', *Ulysses* Part 10; Putnam (2012, 107)).
40. Yeats, 'The Circus Animals' Desertion', ll. 40, 36–7 (1992, 394).
41. *HC* 49, l. 4; Heaney, *RTÉ*; Parker, '"Back in the heartland"' (2013).

hangers like souls 'close-packed on Charon's barge' (l. 12), a compressed image that combines Virgil with Yeats, while also referring to the fact that the previous owners of these suits lay buried in the cemeteries above the market (*RTÉ*).⁴²

Poem III goes on to compare the crowds at the bus station to a flock of rooks, recalling Virgil's famous description of the souls crossing the Styx:

> quam multa in siluis autumni frigore primo
> lapsa cadunt folia, aut ad terram gurgite ab alto
> quam multae glomerantur aues, ubi frigidus annus
> trans pontum fugat et terris immittit apricis. (*Ae*.VI.309–12)
>
> as many as the leaves in the woods that slip and fall with the first chill of autumn or as many as the birds that mass toward land from the high seas, when the cold season chases them over the sea and consigns them to warm lands. (trans. Horsfall, p. 23)

Virgil's double simile begins elegiacally, with leaves falling in the dying year and winter driving the migrating birds southward. But it ends with a surprisingly optimistic twist, as the glimpse of '*terris . . . apricis*', warm lands, suggests that Hades may not be an entirely dark and gloomy place. There turns out to be a moon in Virgil's underworld and the Elysian Fields are bathed in sunlight. Heaney's Poem III registers this lightening of mood in his description of the Belfast bus driver at work. The driver winds 'a little handle' (a reduced version of Charon's great oar) to indicate the bus route number, and suddenly 'everything // Came to life.' (*HC* 50) The waiting passengers are then hustled on board by the bus conductor, who 'ruled the roost' at the station. They are thus like the shades being herded on to Charon's boat, in a potentially transformative crossing. Virgil's simile, with its lapsing of birds, leaves, seasons and souls, is a complex image encompassing the poet's melancholy awareness of mortality and his optimistic faith in nature's powers of renewal. As we will see in Chapter 8, Heaney will take up this image of lapsing, both out of and into life, in a number of major poems in *Human Chain*. Here, in 'Route 110', he alludes to the *lapsus* motif lightly and fleetingly, passing over its more sombre implications. The swirling, noisy, rook-like crowds in Poem III then dissolve and reassemble into the features of the poet himself, in the opening lines of Poem IV.

In the fourth poem of 'Route 110', time has jumped forward around ten years to discover the poet, first at home and then on holiday in Tuscany, visiting a mountain chapel with friends.⁴³ Despite the time gap between Poems III and IV, he resembles one of the rooks flocking to the Route 110 bus. In the first half of the poem, he wears a wintry 'coal-black . . . railway guard's long coat', which flaps in the rain like bird wings (*HC* 51, ll. 1–2, 6). Not only a lost and displaced

---

42. 'An aged man is but a paltry thing, / A tattered coat upon a stick, unless / Soul clap its hands and sing' (Yeats, 'Sailing to Byzantium', ll. 9–11 (1992, 239)). See Auge, 'Surviving Death' in O'Brien (2016), 29–48.
43. Parker, '"Back in the heartland"' (2013) notes the trip to Tuscany was in 1967, on the occasion of a family wedding.

soul, though, the fiercely garbed poet also causes alarm and fear with his nighttime, 'doorstep arrivals', as Aeneas does when he steps on to Charon's barge (cf. Ae.VI.412).[44] Once again, Heaney's sympathies waver between the massed, herded souls and the venturing hero, when he draws parallels between the Styx-crossing episode and his own memories of border-crossing. Thus, his transformation in the second half of the poem resembles both Virgil's soul-birds as they reach their winter territories, and Aeneas as he receives the blessing and guidance of Venus' doves. He exchanges his heavy black coat for a bargain suit from the market, 'Of finest weave, loose-fitting, summery, grey' (l. 9). Arriving in Tuscany, he visits a chapel, where, presumably because of his Catholic upbringing, he finds himself 'the only one at home'.[45]

Like the word 'forlorn' for Keats, the thought of 'home' (the last word of Poems IV and V) transports 'pilgrim-Heaney' back to his adolescence in 1950s Derry.[46] The grey suit carries forward the image of Venus' doves, who bring Aeneas to the grove of the golden bough (Ae.VI.203–11). Heaney directs us explicitly to the Virgilian parallel in the opening line of Poem V: 'Venus' doves? Why not McNicholls' pigeons' (HC 52, l. 1). In contrast to Virgil's sacred and mysterious grove, though, the McNicholls' kitchen is the epitome of Derry homeliness. Venus is 'old Mrs Nick, as she was to us', and the golden bough, a bunch of oat stalks decorated in tin foil. In a typescript draft of Poem V, Heaney has 'stalk' (in the singular) crossed out, and 'golden bough' penned in the right-hand margin.[47] But the register of the marvellous, associated strongly with the golden bough elsewhere, is deliberately downplayed here. So too are the ominous associations of the smoky blue flowers which 'appear to conduct one into the Halls of Dis' in D. H. Lawrence's 'Bavarian gentians' (SS 317). Here, Heaney declares, 'reach me not a gentian', thus refusing the flower's association with death. Instead, he celebrates the thrift and cheerful economy of the household, epitomised in this decoration of oat stalks with tin foil. Like Roman *lares* and *penates*, the stalks are used to dignify the local hearth and, in Derry idiom, give 'the wee altar a bit of shine' (l. 10).[48] The foil-topped stalks provide a miniature instance of Hopkins's 'grandeur of God', which 'will flame out, like shining from shook foil'.[49] Within the context of pilgrim-Heaney's *katabatic* journey, the oat stalks guarantee the bearer safety against supernatural powers, like the tin tree-clock in *Seeing Things*. When he is handed one of them by old Mrs Nick, the young boy finds the glittery foil 'as good as lit me home' (l. 12).

44. In RF, line 5 reads: 'For the dismay caused by my late night doorsteppings,'; in HC, this is revised to: 'For the dismay I caused by doorstep night arrivals'. The revision regulates the meter to ia⁵, with an initial anapaestic foot and a hypermetric final syllable.
45. RF l. 12, revised in HC to 'the one there most at home'.
46. 'Forlorn! the very word is like a bell / To toll me back from thee to my sole self!' (Keats, 'Ode to a Nightingale', ll. 71–2 (2003, 281).
47. Heaney, LP I.xviii.1.
48. LS define *lares* as 'the tutelary deities of a house' (II), and *penates* as 'the old Latin guardian deities of the household' (I) or the 'dwelling, home, hearth', from *penus*, the innermost part of the house (II).
49. Hopkins, 'God's Grandeur', ll. 1–2 (1990), 139.

As 'poet-Heaney' descends into darker regions of memory, in Poems VI to IX, home is remembered chiefly for its losses. The transition of 'pilgrim-Heaney' into adulthood occurs in 'the age of ghosts' (*HC* 53). Heaney's treatment of these darker memories is still handled with a notably light touch; each mental impasse is sidestepped with an ellipsis, allowing the 'pilgrim' to pass on to the next flashback. In Poem VI, the young poet attends the funeral wake of a drowned neighbour, Michael Mulholland, and he waits with the grieving family while the boy's corpse is retrieved from the Bristol Channel. This funeral scene extends over two poems, the only incident to receive such full treatment in 'Route 110'. Funerals are important in Irish Catholic culture and feature prominently in the 'Hades' section of Joyce's *Ulysses*.[50] Placed midway through 'Route 110', the Mulholland funeral functions as an important rite of passage for the boy seeking entrance into the adult life of the community. The Catholic wake is 'the first / I attended as a full participant' (*HC* 53, ll. 4–5). Heaney parallels this incident with the drowning of Aeneas' helmsman, Palinurus (*Ae*.VI.337–87), an episode which he translates in full and publishes separately (the translation is discussed in Chapter 7).

In *Aeneid VI*, the death of Palinurus remains at least partially unresolved. He is thrown from the ship in mysterious circumstances and survives for three days at sea. On the fourth day, the helmsman is washed ashore in Italy, only to be murdered by local tribes, who cast his body back into the sea (*Ae*.VI.359). Aeneas meets his shade wandering beside the Styx, forbidden to cross into Hades because his body remains at sea, unburied.[51] At the Mulholland boy's funeral, the family have to wait three days before the body is recovered. The family rises from the wake, 'strangers to themselves and us', having lost their 'Sonbrother swimmer.' That compound noun recalls the Heaney family's own loss of Christopher, the 'little stillness dancer / Haunter-son, lost brother' elegised in 'The Blackbird of Glanmore' (*DC* 85). The parallel with Palinurus suggests that this is a loss never to be consoled or compensated for, but Heaney now pursued a lighter theme: his acceptance into the adult community at the wake.

As the funeral rites continue into Poem VII, the Virgilian echoes extend from the unburied Palinurus to Misenus, whose burial is a necessary prelude to Aeneas' descent into the underworld. In *Aeneid VI*, both deaths have a symbolically sacrificial function. As we saw in Chapter 1, the funeral for Misenus prepares the way for Aeneas to find the golden bough (*Ae*.VI.212–35). Since Misenus' death is, to an extent, induced by his own hubris, Virgil treats it as a lesser tragedy than that of Palinurus, whom Aeneas meets further on, by the banks of the Styx. The tragic mood also lightens in Heaney's Poem VII, where 'the corpse house' transforms into a 'house of hospitalities' (*HC* 54, l. 1). The smoke from Misenus' pyre is radically

---

50. For Heaney's thoughts on funerals, see (for example) *SS* 474–5. On the parallel with Joyce, see Putnam (2010).
51. It remains a puzzle to classical scholars that Virgil gives a different account of the death of Palinurus at the end of *Aeneid V*. There it is specifically predicted that he will 'lie ... on an unknown strand' ('*in ignota ... iacebis harena*' (*Ae*.V.871, trans. Fairclough)). See Horsfall (2013), p. 274f.

reduced to the cigarette smoke of the adult visitors, amongst whom the adolescent Heaney is now included (l. 8). In Poem VII, the drowned boy's body is received into its coffin and the community's funeral rites are fulfilled (l. 12). After this rite of passage into adulthood, the young Heaney is then instructed how to find his way home across their fields (ll. 10–12). This assistance from the mother of the family provides another parallel with Aeneas, who is guided by the Sibyl and his divine mother, Venus.

The absolution of trespass, in the last line of Poem VII, creates an associative link with the trespass, or breach of romantic trust, touched on in Poem VIII. Time has again slipped forward a number of years, as Heaney compares the breakup of a relationship he had at university to the tragic separation of Dido and Aeneas (SS 405). Here, the Virgilian analogy is given explicitly, with the first line translating the moment Aeneas first glimpses Dido's shade in the Fields of Mourning: 'As one when the month is young sees a new moon' (HC 55, l. 1; 'aut uidet aut uidisse putat per nubila lunam', Ae.VI.454). Compressing this underworld encounter with Aeneas' flight from Carthage in *Aeneid IV*, Heaney pictures his younger self making a fast getaway in his car. The young man glances back in the rear-view mirror to see his girlfriend watching him leave, 'her hurt still new' (l. 3). This phrase is lifted from Virgil's description of Dido's shade, '*recens a uulnere*' (Ae.VI.450). Like the scarred and disfigured Deiphobus, Dido still bears her suicide wound in the afterlife, thus suggesting a traumatic conflict still unresolved at the time of Aeneas' descent. Virgil's mention of her *uulnus* recalls earlier scenes, when passion for Aeneas first 'wounds' her, and later, when she stabs herself in despair at his desertion.[52] When Aeneas discovers her in Hades, still '*recens a uulnere*', the unhealed wound has become symbolic of the political rift between Carthage and Rome, which would lead in future to more than a hundred years of war and many thousands of deaths.

In Heaney's Poem VIII, the 'hurt still new' is deliberately diminished to a private passion, which seems at first devoid of political ramifications. Recalling Aeneas' guilty, night-time flight from Carthage (Ae.VI.584ff.), the young poet escapes from his lover in a hurry of short, stressed verbs: 'I unlock, / Switch on, rev up, pull out and drive away' (l. 5). Our sympathies are clearly directed to the jilted lover and against the young poet, but the affair is still treated skimmingly, without any sense of tragic depth. In the second half of the poem, though, Heaney suggests that the entire relationship, with its 'holdings on / And holdings back', reflected the socially repressive atmosphere and mounting tensions of Belfast in the 1960s (l. 12). The poet's receding brake lights are likened to 'red lamps swung by RUC patrols / In the small hours on pre-Troubles roads' (ll. 8–9).[53] This allusion adds a major, political dimension to the breakdown of their private affair. While the young people have been struggling with the repressive *mores* of their Catholic community (the 'nay-saying age of piety'[54]), the country is drifting into deadly sectarian conflict. The reference

---

52. Ae.IV.67, 683, 689.
53. The Royal Ulster Constabulary, the Loyalist police force in Northern Ireland, 1922–2001, frequently involved in clashes with the Republican Irish Republican Army (IRA).
54. Revised in the later edition to 'age of impurity' (HC 55, l. 12).

to Dido and Aeneas now points ominously to the onset of violence between Loyalist and Republican forces.

In the opening lines of Poem IX, we find ourselves in the midst of this violent conflict. While the funeral scene in Poems VI–VII had underlined the need for due commemoration of the dead, here the poet brusquely dismisses these communal rites as inadequate: 'And what in the end was there left to bury / Of Mr Lavery, blown up in his own pub'? (*HC* 56, ll. 1–2). A young man's body can be recovered from the sea and laid to rest, but how is one to mourn the victim of a bomb explosion? Heaney's poem refers to the deaths of two Belfast men: John Lavery, killed by an IRA bomb in 1971, and Louis O'Neill, killed by what was probably a Protestant Loyalist bomb in 1972.[55] In terms of the traditional structure of a *katabatic* narrative, Poem IX constitutes the nadir of the descent in 'Route 110'. Its Virgilian analogue is Aeneas' meeting with the shade of the Trojan Prince Deiphobus, who was killed and mutilated by his enemies during the sack of Troy (*Ae*.VI.494–547). This is the horrific nadir of Aeneas' journey as well, since he knew of his friend's death but not how he had been killed: '*te, amice, nequiui / conspicere et patria decedens ponere terra.*' ('you, my friend, I could not lay eyes on, nor place you in your native earth, before leaving', *Ae*.VI.507–8). The encounter follows immediately after the tragic meeting with Dido, so in this case, Heaney preserves both the order of events and the deepening of tragedy into horror in Virgil's narrative.[56] While Virgil honours a fallen military leader, however, Heaney's poem commemorates two ordinary people, members of the local community. He stresses this point in his interview with Dawe: the people mentioned in Poem IX '*weren't* active. They weren't soldiers, they weren't in the British army. They weren't in the provos. They weren't in the violence. They were victims of it.' (*RTÉ*) The shameful dismemberment of their bodies, which makes impossible any ritual return of the human to the *humus*, or earth, brings the poet to the crux of his dilemma in 'Route 110'. How are such civilian victims to be remembered? How are their maimed ghosts to be appeased?

In *Aeneid VI*, Virgil dwells on the memory of the offence, as it is inscribed on the body of Deiphobus and retained even on his bodiless shade. Deiphobus urges Aeneas to remember the crime of the Greeks who tricked and murdered him, and to bear his revulsion and horror into the future. His message to Aeneas is exactly the opposite of Anchises', who exhorts the future Roman race to remember to spare the conquered, a passage Heaney admired enough to translate and publish separately.[57]

---

55. John Lavery was a sixty-year-old Catholic, killed by an IRA bomb in his pub on Lisburn Road, South Belfast, on 21 December 1971. The Heaneys lived 20 metres away, at 16 Ashley Place. Louis O'Neill was a close family friend who ignored an IRA curfew and was killed in February 1972, probably by a Protestant Loyalist bomb (*RTÉ*, and Parker, '"Back in the heartland"', 2013).
56. Aristotle's term for this kind of horror is μιαρός (polluted, abominable, repulsive to the moral sense, *LiS* II, III); he considered it to be beyond representation as tragedy (*Poetics*.13.36 (1995, 68). See also, Dennison on Matthew Arnold's distinction between the painful and the tragic (2015, 168).
57. A.VI.847–54, one of three speeches translated by Heaney, and published in *Modern Poetry in Translation* (2009). See Chapter 7.

In Poem IX, Heaney contrasts the forgotten, 'unglorified' deaths of civilian victims to the soldiers who are ritually remembered, buried in 'war graves with full honours' and 'Fired over on anniversaries' (*HC* 56, ll. 10–11). These official commemorations, where guns are fired 'By units drilled and spruce and unreconciled' (l. 12), prolong the memory of the offence and fuel the desire for revenge. The final word of Poem IX, 'unreconciled', leaves us with the sense of an unhealed wound (*'recens a uulnere'*) on both Loyalist and Republican sides of the conflict.

'Unreconciled' also recalls the famously ambivalent ending of the *Aeneid*, where Aeneas refuses Turnus' plea for mercy and kills his enemy in a passionate rage. In the final line of the epic, the ghost of Turnus flees indignantly to the underworld: *'fugit indignata sub umbras'* (Ae.XII.919). Though a stock term for fallen soldiers, '*indignata*' (offended, indignant, resentful) is especially powerful here because it casts doubt on Aeneas' famous *pietas*. Turnus is precisely one of the '*subiectis*', the vanquished enemies, whom Anchises had exhorted future Romans to spare. By placing 'unreconciled' as the last word in Poem IX, Heaney recalls the disquieting ending of the *Aeneid*, and its foreshadowing of many years of military conflict to follow.

At the same time, Poem IX remembers the two civilian deaths in a different spirit, one that requires a degree of forgetfulness along with active remembrance. As Michael Putnam observes, this is the only poem in 'Route 110' without an 'I'. It is therefore more carefully and consciously public-facing than the rest of the sequence. But it also avoids any officially commemorative language, just as it focuses on civilian deaths rather than fallen military heroes.[58] The appellation 'Mr Lavery' is respectful but also familiar rather than heroising. The parallel with Deiphobus supplies a graphic analogy to the disfigurement both civilians suffered in the bomb explosions. But after the opening question about burial, the poem moves backward in time to the publican's selfless action just before his death:

> As he bore the primed device and bears it still //
> Mid-morning towards the sun-admitting door
> Of Ashley House (ll. 3–5)

It is actually the image of Mr Lavery, still alive and moving towards a sunlit door, that the poem etches into the reader's memory. The repetition and change of tense, 'bore . . . bear', and the double sense of 'still' ('until now' and 'unmoving') insist on this image being thrown forward into the present, rather than the shameful violence done to the publican's body.

There are other, deliberate, ellipses in Heaney's recollection of the two Troubles victims as well. He declines to mention which sectarian party was responsible for their deaths. This contrasts with his earlier poem, 'Casualty', in which he lets it be known that O'Neill had broken 'our tribe's complicity' and ignored an IRA curfew, imposed after Bloody Sunday, thus putting his own life at risk (*FW* 16). In *The Riverbank Field*, this is toned down to an oblique suggestion that O'Neill was

---

58. Putnam (2012), 106, note 36.

'Bomb-blasted after hours' (*RF* l. 6). In sympathy with O'Neill, Heaney alludes to the Loyalist massacre by name: 'the Wednesday / The thirteen Bloody Sunday dead were buried' (l. 7). In the re-edited version in *Human Chain*, the particular circumstances have been all but supressed: O'Neill simply finds himself 'in the wrong place' (rather than time, *HC* 56, l. 6), and without mention of Bloody Sunday Heaney alludes to the 'Thirteen who'd been shot in Derry' (l. 7). The name 'Derry' indicates an enduring, Republican tribal complicity, since the Loyalist name for the city is 'Londonderry'. But otherwise, the poet seems to resist taking sides, remembering instead the bravery of ordinary people and committing the rest to the waters of Lethe.

In the last three poems of 'Route 110', the poet brings his journey full circle to the Elysian Fields and the river of oblivion. Poem X, with its twilit green meadows, comes as a relief after the memory of sectarian conflict in the previous poem. This follows the general arc of Virgil's narrative, which also shifts from tragedy and horror to the sunlit serenity of Elysium. Heaney floods the first two tercets of Poem X with the curative vision of Virgil's '*sedes beatas*'. Rather than offering an analogy, his opening lines directly paraphrase Virgil's description of the underworld games, where the shades wrestle, sing and race their chariots (*Ae*.VI.637–78). The rhythm of Heaney's opening line is slow and measured: 'Virgil's happy shades in pure blanched raiment / Contend' (*HC* 57, ll. 1–2). The trochaic rhythm of the first line spills over into the second, so that at first we read 'contend' with a stress on the first syllable. The elevated Latinate word, thus slowed and lengthened, highlights the shift from military conflict to competitive games. Heaney's Orpheus cuts a homely figure next to Virgil's priestly musician but they are both instruments of social harmony:

nec non Threicius longa cum ueste sacerdos
obloquitur numeris septem discrimina uocum, (*Ae*.VI.645–6)

There, too, in his long robe, the Thracian priest performs in harmony with their tune the intervals of the seven notes [of the scale] (trans. Horsfall, modified)

       Orpheus
Weaves among them, sweeping strings, aswerve//
To the pulse of his own playing and to avoid
The wrestlers, dancers, runners on the grass. (*HC* 57, ll. 2–5)

Picking up on Virgil's '*obloquitur*' ('speaks across'), Heaney imagines Orpheus 'weav[ing]' and 'aswerve' in the crowd. His unencumbered movement might figure for the fluent rhythm of 'Route 110' as a whole as it weaves swiftly through remembered griefs, refusing the temptation to fixate on unhealed and unhealable wounds.

The action then shifts back to happier memories of Heaney's adolescence, and games in his own neighbourhood. The Elysian Fields are 'Not unlike a sports day in Bellaghy', the double negative suggesting this time a passing and casual correspondence with Virgil (*HC* 57, l. 6). Slim Whitman will stand for Orpheus, parked cars for chariots, and 'grown men stripped for action' for wrestlers (l. 10). But Heaney also contrasts the two scenes so that Virgil's dream-like Elysian Fields materialise in full colour, shape and substance in Bellaghy. Heaney's fields are full of flying, sparking objects and rugged sportsmen. And in the last line, unlike Virgil's shadow wrestlers, Heaney's sportsmen 'Leav[e] stud-scrapes on the pitch and on each other' (l. 12). These imprints of physical contact seem already promissory of the new material life to be given to the shades once they cross over the River Lethe.

In Poem XI, the poet recalls evenings spent fishing in 'the riverbank field' (*HC* 58, l. 8). This refers us back to the title poem, except that, here, the names of the Rivers Moyola and Lethe are unspecified, just as the characters in the poem are unnamed. Elsewhere, Heaney glosses the 'we' in the poem as himself and his father, and he locates the time as the summer before he left home to attend St Columb's College as a boarding student.[59] But in the poem, the 'beautiful riverbank situation' is dreamily adrift between the poet's remembered adolescence and Virgil's mythic otherworld. In contrast to the previous poem, the analogy with *Aeneid VI* surfaces only gradually and belatedly. The poet begins with an intimate address to his father, though unnamed, inviting him to recall 'Those evenings when we'd just wait and watch / And fish.' (ll. 1–2) There is an uncanny previousness and familiarity to the scene, not only because it revisits the scene of the title poem, but also because it harkens back to Heaney's earlier poem, 'The Harvest Bow'.[60] The setting of the earlier poem is very similar:

> an evening of long grass and midges, . . .
> Me with the fishing rod, already homesick
> For the big lift of these evenings, (*FW* 55)

In 'The Harvest Bow', the boy is looking ahead to separation, while in Poem XI, he looks back to his homesickness, having already lost his father.

Although one of the figures on the bank is already a ghost, Poem XI reimagines the scene so that they are both still at the riverside together. In this revisionary memory, the father and son experience a glimpse of the marvellous together. As they wait and watch, they see or think they see an otter's head,

> or was it only //
> A surface-ruck and gleam we took for
> An otter's head? No doubting, all the same,
> The gleam, a turnover warp in the black //
> Quick water. (*HC* 58, ll. 3–7)

---

59. 'We used to go fishing, and we were together on the riverbank, and it was a very tender poem to the, to the father.' (Heaney, 'Interview with Mark Lawson' (2008), 20:42).
60. 'In my own head, this poem is a kind of sequel to a poem called 'The Harvest Bow', way back. I used to go with my father in the evenings to fish along the Moyola River and it was the time when we were closest together, really.' (*RTÉ*)

The gleam of the animal's head is the first of the poem's several dispersals of material reality into air. 'No doubting' is followed by 'Or doubting the solid ground' (l. 7), where the syntactically ambiguous 'Or' either reiterates the solidity of the ground or casts it into doubt. The ground dematerialises in the next line, being 'twilit and a-hover / With midge-drifts' (ll. 8–9).

At the same time, the creature's gleaming head has become a 'turnover warp', suggesting some fold-over or transformation of consciousness.[61] According to medieval legend, recalled by Heaney in 'Station Island', an otter had mysteriously retrieved St Ronan's Book of Psalms from the water.[62] Heaney had also admired Elizabeth Bishop's poem 'At the Fishhouses', where a 'rhythmic heave' in the line mirrors the way a seal's head breaks the surface of the water, under the poet's gaze.[63] Of another Bishop poem called 'The Fish', Heaney suggests that 'the fish is recognized as a harbinger of that dearest freshness that lives deep down in things,' recalling one of his favourite of Gerard Manley Hopkins's lines.[64] The 'gleam' in Poem XI, then, may intimate the existence of a marvellous spirit world, or in a late Romantic sense, a 'dearest freshness' at the originary source of one's being. The 'turnover warp' produces a 'surface heave' in the poem's rhythm as well: a stanza break cuts between the two adjectives 'black' and 'quick', with their three sharp plosives ('bla<u>ck</u> // <u>Q</u>uick water'). This division highlights the paradoxical attributes of the Lethe, being at once a river in the land of the dead ('black') and a river of rebirth ('quick', alive). The stuttering rhythm and cutting sound also recall the '<u>c</u>an't not <u>c</u>onjure' of the title poem, which had ushered in the Latin alterity of '*animae quibus altera fato / Corpora*'. In Poem XI, the hovering insects now recall those same Virgilian 'shades and shadows' (l. 10).

In the last lines of Poem XI, the boy and his father appear to join the shades waiting to cross over into new life. In doing so, they are departing from the Virgilian analogue since Anchises does not have to leave Elysium, being one of the *beati*, and Aeneas exits via the Gates of Sleep. Only in Heaney's poem do the father and son join the waiting shades on the bank:

> As if among shadows stirring on the brink
> We had commingled and were standing watching,
> Needy and ever needier for translation. (RF 10–12)

---

61. Parker, '"Back in the heartland"' (2013), explores the links with Ted Hughes's poems about otters, which Heaney knew well, and with Heaney's otter poem in FW 43 (a love poem to his wife, Marie).
62. See Heaney, SI 87. Cf. Paul Muldoon's elegy for Heaney, 'Cuthbert and the Otters', in *One Thousand Things Worth Knowing* (2016).
63. 'here it is, a rhythmic heave which suggests that something other is about to happen – . . . the seal . . . arrives partly like a messenger from another world' (Heaney, GT 105). In an uncollected poem, 'The City', discussed by Peter McDonald (2019, 175), the glimpsed, mystical animal *is* a seal, as in Bishop's poem.
64. RP 174, quoting 'There lives the dearest freshness deep down things' (Hopkins, 'God's Grandeur', l. 10 (1990, 139).

In *Human Chain*, this passage is revised to:

> as if we had commingled', //
> Among shades and shadows stirring on the brink,
> And stood there waiting, watching,
> Needy and ever needier for translation. (HC 58, ll. 9–12)

In *The Riverbank Field*, the confluence of bodies and shades happens in the last tercet, which begins with 'As if', a clear signal of an Ariel shift into the realm of the imaginary. The changes introduced in the *Human Chain* version strengthen the implication that the human pair have joined the Virgilian shades: the 'as if' comes earlier, unseparated from the body of the poem; 'shadows' become 'shades and shadows', a stronger link to the Virgilian *animae*; and in the later edition, they are 'waiting and watching', part of the transformation about to occur rather than merely observers.

Heaney's last line leaves open for speculation exactly what kind of 'translation' the father and son are '[n]eedy and ever needier for'. In interview, Heaney says that he was 'punning on needing the example of the classical myth, and also wanting to be translated into some kind of eternal peace.' (*RTÉ*) He also remarks that his father had been mostly silent during those evenings fishing, 'so it was as if you were waiting for the translation' (ibid).

If we think about the dialogue with Virgil that occurs in 'The Riverbank Field', we can see that, for Heaney, translation is not only a means of forwarding the deep past into the present; it is also a way of *being forwarded* by the classical myth into something beyond your already known artistic, emotional or intellectual territory. Moreover, while the desire for translation to 'some kind of eternal peace' could be glossed purely as a Christian longing for heaven, in my view the Virgilian context insists, as well, on a more material transformation. The souls waiting by the River Lethe are longing to return to the world in *altera corpora*. So Heaney's two figures may be desiring the return to a *pacatum orbem*, the historical, material world brought to peace. Finally, the 'need for translation' may refer to the poet's desire for a fundamental transformation of speech. In 'The Harvest Bow', the son seeks for a way to translate his father's silence, 'Gleaning the unsaid off the palpable' (*FW* 55). And in some ways, Poem XI continues that earlier filial effort of putting silence into words. But here, there also seems to be a need for something more, for words being called up from silence. Or to put it another way, Heaney may be expressing the need for a rebaptism of poetic language.

The birth of Anna Rose, celebrated in Poem XII, brings the sequence back to the present tense of narration. The poet's descent journey into the past comes to a close as he welcomes the arrival of 'one / Whose long wait on the shaded bank has ended' (*HC* 59, ll. 7–8). But as this allusion to Lethe suggests, he has not stepped out of the parallel with the classical myth altogether. The new-born's arrival heralds an 'age of births' (l. 1) to succeed 'the age of ghosts' alluded to in Poem VI. In broadest terms, this proclamation furthers the hope for a world beyond sectarian conflict, which Heaney had associated with an infant's birth in 'Bann Valley Eclogue' (*EL* 12). In terms of the Virgilian analogy, the 'one' who has crossed the Lethe refers not only to Anna Rose, but also to the adolescent 'pilgrim' and the adult poet reascending from the underworld. Thus, the 'I' in 'So now, . . . / I arrive, with my bunch of stalks and silvered heads' (ll. 7, 9) merges the boy, carrying his gift of foil-covered stalks, together with the 'silvered head' of the poet, now grandfather to the new-born child.

If the poet has crossed the River Lethe, according to his continuous parallel with Virgil, he still retains his layered, associative memory. Like the Roman general in 'To the Poets of St Andrews', the first thing he does upon reaching the farther shore is assure himself his memory is still intact. The first two tercets of Poem XII flash back to the birth of his own first child, some forty years earlier: 'As when once / At dawn' (ll. 1–2). Originally composed as part of 'Loughanure', these lines recall how the painter Colin Middleton had arrived with a bunch of flowers to celebrate that earlier infant birth.[65] So if the final poem of 'Route 110' celebrates newness of life, it also insists on the continuity of generations, however translated and transformed by Lethean oblivion. Throughout the poem, temporal markers of past and present are closely interlinked, and images of arrival and departure are threaded together: 'And now . . . once' (l. 1), 'The last to leave came' (l. 3) and 'ended, / I arrive' (ll. 8–9).

And, of course, Heaney is still remembering Virgil's Lethean scene and commingling classical myth with his own lived experience. But it is worth underlining with what strategic forgetfulness he remembers the end of *Aeneid VI* in this final poem. The silvered heads gathering around the infant are a homely, ironic substitution for the parade of Roman leaders and generals that Aeneas watches processing by the riverbank (*Ae*.VI.756–886). And Heaney's bunch of oat stalks and 'fresh-plucked flowers' celebrate the granddaughter's birth, in place of the handful of lilies Anchises calls for to mourn the premature death of Marcellus, Augustus' nephew and heir ('*manibus date lilia plenis*', 'offer lilies with full hands', *Ae*.VI.883). Whereas, traditionally, *katabatic* narratives culminate in the poet's assumption of prophetic authority, Heaney's 'Route 110' concludes with the opposite gesture: a mature poet divests himself of authority and *gravitas* to begin again with infant speech.

The final tercet's short lines contribute to this last poem's light and buoyant mood. Heaney declares the shining foil-tipped stalks are

Like tapers that won't dim
As her earthlight breaks and we gather round
Talking baby talk. (*HC* 59, ll. 10–12)

The phrase 'earthlight breaks' condenses two common expressions, the 'break of day' and 'daylight', and marks the temporal shift from twilight to dawn at the end of 'Route 110'. 'Earthlight' is also the astronomical term for 'sunlight reflected by the earth, especially as illuminating part of the moon's surface not lit by sunlight' (*OED*). Otherwise known as 'earthshine' or 'ashen light', it is a particularly apt word to describe the presencing of a Virgilian shade into corporeal form. 'Earthlight' is both ghostly, being the light visible from the dark side of the moon, and material,

---

65. Draft of 'Loughanure' (*LP* I.xviii.1); Middleton is also identified as the guest in *RTÉ*.

being light reflected off the earth, rather than raining down from heaven. As a light produced by the earth itself, it constitutes a redress to the ominous solar eclipse that preceded the child's birth in 'Bann Valley Eclogue'. The cluster of plosives in the final two lines ('bre<u>a</u>ks . . . t<u>a</u>lking baby tal<u>k</u>') again signals a break and swerve into a new image and mood. While the flashback was narrated in a heightened, formal style ('As when once'), the last line suddenly dips into a tender, colloquial register. Heaney's 'baby talk' recalls the 'infant babbling' that Mandelstam heard in Dante's Italian phonetics (FK 176). The audaciously short final line makes way for silence and new beginnings.

The brevity and fluency of 'The Riverbank Field' and 'Route 110' are consistent with Heaney's overall artistic purpose in *The Riverbank Field*, to remember the past lightly and with strategic forgetfulness. If '*the end of art is peace*', one of poetry's labours is to assist at the complex and delicate translation of memory from one generation to the next.[66] The socio-political aspect of this work is suggested by one of Heaney's revisions to 'The Riverbank Field'. In 2007, the title poem contains the following contrast:

> . . . Moths then on evening water
> it would have to be, not butterflies in sunlight, (ll. 8–9)

'Butterflies', not in Virgil's text, might have been suggested by a passage in Keats's *Endymion* (1818), where, on the edge of the underworld, the eponymous hero sees

> A golden butterfly; upon whose wings
> There must be surely character'd strange things . . .
> Lightly this little herald flew aloft,
> Follow'd by glad Endymion's clasped hands . . .
> It seem'd he flew, the way so easy was;
> And like a new-born spirit did he pass
> Through the green evening quiet in the sun (*Endymion* II.60–71)

The Ariel lift of this passage has much in common with Heaney's lightness of touch in 'Route 110'. But in the *Human Chain* version of 'The Riverbank Field', he exchanges Keatsian butterflies for Virgil's bees, so that his passage now reads:

> . . . Moths then on evening water
> it would have to be, not bees in sunlight, (ll. 8–9)

Virgil does indeed compare the souls on the Lethean riverbank to swarms of bees (*Ae*.VI.707). By restoring them in this revised version, Heaney's negative comparison commingles Virgil's bees with the Moyola's moths rather than cancelling them out: the aural repetition, 'to <u>be</u>, not <u>bees</u>', is a form of *recusatio* that insists on their

---

66. '*The end of art is peace*' is from Heaney's 'The Harvest Bow' (FW 56), quoting Yeats, 'Delight in art whose end is peace', in 'To a Wealthy Man . . .', l. 27 (1992), 159.

lingering presence. In a similar way, the 'low humming of bees' at Orpheus' death guarantees the persistence of life and the continuity of song, in Miłosz's last poem, 'Orpheus and Eurydice'.[67] In Heaney's poem, the presence of moths-not-bees connotes the spontaneous generation of poetic form in the sequence to come. He takes his inspiration, I would suggest, from Mandelstam's comparison of Dante's form-creation to bees constructing a hive: 'Their cooperation expands and grows more complicated as they participate in the process of forming the combs, by means of which space virtually emerges out of itself.' (FK 176)

*

In Heaney's poetry and poetics, Mandelstam's bees are closely related those in Yeats's poem, 'Meditations in Time of Civil War'. In his Nobel Lecture, 'Crediting Poetry' (1995), Heaney had cited this poem as an example of poetry that manages to be true to reality while also being equal to it, in the sense of offering redress, or an alternative vision of how reality might be (OG 464ff.). In 'Meditations' itself, Yeats draws on the image of honey-bees to help him 'build in the empty house' of a society divided and depleted by war. Over many stanzas, Yeats repeatedly invokes the bees to build in an empty starling's nest:

> The bees build in the crevices
> Of loosening masonry, and there
> The mother birds bring grubs and flies.
> My wall is loosening; honey-bees,
> Come build in the empty house of the stare. . . .
>
> We had fed the heart on fantasies,
> The heart's grown brutal from the fare;
> More substance in our enmities
> Than in our love; O honey-bees,
> Come build in the empty house of the stare.[68]

Heaney argues that this poem

> satisfies the contradictory needs which consciousness experiences at times of extreme crisis, the need on the one hand for a truth telling that will be hard and retributive, and on the other hand, the need not to harden the mind to a point where it denies its own yearnings for sweetness and trust. (OG 464)

Mandelstam might also have pointed out how the stanzaic cells of Yeats's poem take shape from the incantatory repetition of his refrain: 'o honey-bees, come build!' Heaney's sequence of 'little flashbacks' into the past might be read, in the

---

67. On Miłosz's Orpheus, see Chapter 3, p. 86.
68. Yeats, 'Meditations in Time of Civil War, VI', ll. 1–5, 15–20 (1992), 250–1; Heaney, OG 463–4.

same spirit, as a form of social rebuilding conducted in miniature. Entering the underworld via Lethe, he journeys lightly, fluently and forgetfully through the past, forging a continuation between generations, but also allowing space for the lyric swerve, the sudden break with the past, the chance to begin afresh.

7. Raids, Settlement and Sounding Line

From the publication of *The Riverbank Field* onwards, Virgil remains at the forefront of Heaney's thinking about the good of poetry and at the heart of his compositional process. He values Book VI of the *Aeneid* for its pathos, 'the twilit fetch of its language' and its 'mythopoeic visions' (A, 51). Still more, he hears an inner quarrel being conducted in Virgil's verse which stimulates the dialogue he is conducting within his own writing.[1] Heaney remains conflicted about two sets of 'virtues', or aesthetic and ethical values, which are often associated in his writing with two kinds of poetry, lyric and epic.[2] When he celebrates the 'lyric' impulse, it is often connoted with the values of inner freedom, spontaneity, Ariel flight, Lethean forgetting and letting go. And by contrast, 'epic' is more often associated with the virtues of steadfastness and endurance, of memory and deep connection to a community and place.[3] He finds both these sets of values in Virgil, or more precisely, Virgil's poetry stimulates his own thinking in both directions. Again, broadly speaking, we can see a pendulum swing between two poles of value in Heaney's late work, from the 'lyric' impulse predominating in *The Riverbank Field* to an 'epic' preoccupation with community, place and the past, in the translation extracts and radio essay he published in 2008–9. There is a further swing from lyric in *Human Chain* to epic in *Aeneid Book VI*. But in these two late, great works, the two sets of opposing virtues, or values, are woven together into a complex, close-knit whole.

1. For Heaney, poetry can 'extend people's chances of getting into dialogue with themselves' ('Further Language', 1997, 13).
2. 'Virtue' has both moral and aesthetic implications in Heaney's usage (SS 467 and 'The Whole Thing' (2001). Cf. Wordsworth's 'renovating virtue' in *The Fourteen-Book Prelude*, Book XII.208–15 (1985), 238–9.
3. While Heaney is consistent in his use of the term 'lyric' for poetry's spontaneous impulses and so on, the term 'epic', for the opposing virtues of social responsibility, poetic *labor* and *pietas*, steadfastness and endurance, occurs more frequently in the earlier essays, discussed in Chapter 1. Virgil's Aeneas is famously the exemplary hero of *pietas*, but in Heaney's writing, he can also be the hero of spontaneous, Ariel flight (positively connoted in the golden bough episode, and more negatively in his flight from Dido).

What is particularly striking about the poetry Heaney produced between late 2006 and 2010 is the close link between original composition and Latin translation. In his 'Translator's Note' prefacing *Aeneid Book VI*, Heaney remarks that composing 'Route 110' gave him 'the impulse to go ahead with a rendering of the complete book.'[4] In itself, that note is a good indication of how a quick 'raid' into another poet's territory often led to a more considered 'settlement' in Heaney's writing process. But it does not fully convey the shuttling movement between original English composition and Latin translation that transpired over this intensely productive, three-year period. In 2008, Heaney published extracts of Latin translation paired with original English poems: thus, 'Album' was first published with 'Palinurus' (a translation of *Aeneid* VI.349–83), and 'Loughanure' was first published alongside 'The Fields of Light' (a translation of *Aeneid* VI.638–78). This suggests that many of the poems collected in *Human Chain* were composed in parallel, and in dialogue, with Heaney's translation of *Aeneid VI*. In the previous chapter, I proposed that 'The Riverbank Field' and 'Route 110' offer us a lyric version of Virgil's underworld book, one in which the governing motif is the forgetful crossing of the River Lethe into new life. Heaney's extracts of Latin translation, published in advance of *Human Chain*, offer a counter-balancing movement towards remembrance of the past, and responsibility to a communal identity. In terms of dominant chronotopic motifs, we are once again on the shores of the River Styx, descending into darkness, rather than emerging into light.

In this chapter, I would like to consider Heaney's radio essay on Virgil, together with the five translation extracts that Heaney published in 2008–9. All five extracts are generated from the longer project of translating Virgil's Book VI entire, a first draft of which Heaney had finished by December 2008. As noted above, two of the extracts, 'Palinurus' and 'The Fields of Light', were published alongside original English poems. The three remaining extracts were published in 2009, as a self-standing triptych entitled 'Three Freed Speeches'. Heaney's translation of the Palinurus episode is the only one of the five extracts to be written in loose *terza rima*: that is, rhythmically midway between 'Route 110' and *Aeneid Book VI*. It is also the only one whose phrasing and diction differ very substantially from those of Heaney's 2008 draft of Book VI. Collectively, the five extracts and radio essay emphasise poetry's role in preserving and transmitting cultural memory. Heaney's hedge-schoolmaster comes to the fore in his more *pius* aspect, as he stands over the cherished home ground, commemorates the dead and forwards cultural values from the ancient past into modern times. We see these preoccupations emerge most clearly in Heaney's 'Palinurus' translation, which deserves to be recognised as one of his major, late poems (the text is given in full in the Appendix to this volume). Before considering this translation in detail, I would like to discuss Heaney's radio essay, the other extracts and the composition of the book-length

---

4. Heaney, A vii. Michael Parker ('"Back in the heartland"', 2013) initially suggested that Heaney's *Aeneid VI* was drafted in 2005 and that 'Route 110' came afterwards, in response to the experience of translating the book. He now agrees this must have been based on a misreading of their correspondence (email to author).

draft, which, amongst other things, shed useful light on his reading of the politics of the *Aeneid*.

1. VIRGIL ON AIR

While working on his 2008 draft of *Aeneid Book VI*, Heaney recorded two radio programmes on Virgil, very different in emphasis and tone. Promoting the recent publication of *The Riverbank Field*, Heaney was interviewed in Dublin by the Irish poet Gerald Dawe, on RTÉ's *Poetry Programme*.[5] As discussed in the previous chapter, this interview brings out Heaney's personal connections with Virgil's poetry: how Latin was embedded in his adolescence, how he identified with Virgil as the 'scholarship boy who makes good', and how he shared with Virgil the experience of sectarian conflict. Indeed, he says, 'all of us [Northern Irish poets] had that sense of coming from a peaceful domain and then entering the domain of violence' (*RTÉ*). In the Dublin interview, Heaney's main focus is on the lightness and speed of composing 'Route 110', his sense of easy familiarity with certain scenes from Book VI, and his particular fondness for the scene on the banks of the River Lethe. Speaking to a fellow Irish poet, Heaney's tone is relaxed and familiar, his accent and idiomatic register both strongly Hibernian. As I suggested, this interview dwells on Virgil in his vitalising, spontaneous and strategically forgetful lyric aspect.

The radio broadcast I would like to consider in this chapter is an essay that Heaney wrote for a series on 'Greek and Latin Voices' that featured on BBC Radio 3's programme, *The Essay*.[6] Heaney's tone in the BBC broadcast is more decorous and literary, and his language is less idiomatic and Hibernian than in the Dublin interview. While he includes extracts from his own translation in progress, his primary focus is on Virgil's own life and work. As well as introducing Virgil to a general audience, the essay argues for the good of poetry in its relation to individual and collective memory. He begins with a pitch for poetry and its 'ongoing place within the consciousness' (*BBC*). Just a few lines remembered over a lifetime can have a transformative effect on any individual reader: 'At every encounter, something revives, or focuses, or steadies, or shines, or perhaps grieves.' (*BBC*) All these things happen at once, he says, 'when I repeat some of the best-known lines of the *Aeneid*... *Urbs antiqua fuit. Facilis descensus averno. Sunt lacrimae rerum.* There was an ancient city. It is easy to descend into Avernus. There are tears at the heart of things.'[7] While both broadcasts invoke Virgil as a familiar presence, in the RTÉ interview Heaney's Virgil is embedded in his own personal history, whereas in the

---

5. Heaney (*RTÉ*). Gerald Dawe has the date '28 April 2008' inscribed in the copy of *The Riverbank Field* which Heaney gave him, probably on the day of their interview. The date could be later, though, as normally the recording would be made a few weeks before transmission. With thanks to Gerald Dawe and Breeda Bennan of RTÉ Archives.
6. The second of a four-part series, 'Greek and Latin Voices'. Recorded on 16 June, broadcast on 15 July 2008, for *The Essay* (cited as *BBC*).
7. Heaney's Latin 'v's are pronounced hard, the 'c's soft, as typical of 'Church' Latin pronunciation.

BBC essay, Heaney offers his attachment to Virgil as proof of a common cultural inheritance. These fragments of remembered Latin verse are 'like a treasure deeply lodged in the European word-hoard' and are available for retrieval by any reader. When exhumed from the common word-hoard, Virgil's 'characters and images . . . retain their aura and attraction' for each and every reader (*BBC*).

But Heaney's essay also reshapes 'the European word-hoard', giving it a strongly northern anchorage. He was introduced to Virgil, he tells his listeners, through the instruction of his Latin schoolmaster at St Columb's, Father Michael McGlinchey. This very personal portrait of his teacher is here deployed to project an image of a reflective, irenic Virgil rather different to the Augustan poet, as enshrined in the English literary tradition. With a glancing reference to Dryden's canonical translations, and the Irish playwright George Bernard Shaw's *Arms and the Man*, Heaney proceeds to describe Father McGlinchey as a man of gentle, melancholic disposition, constitutionally averse to war. A 'tender, inward man', McGlinchey 'dearly wished that our prescribed book had not been the one concerned with the first stages of the war in Italy', *Aeneid IX* being the set text for their A-level exams. This gentle teacher bears a strong resemblance to the Virgil portrayed in 'Bann Valley Eclogue' and elsewhere in Heaney's writing on pastoral.[8] The schoolmaster is also afflicted with longing for a lost past that mirrors the exilic longing of Virgil's hero, Aeneas. It is this very 'note of longing in that involuntary refrain' and 'wistfulness in the tone of the man's voice' that, Heaney says, would 'eventually lead me to the cave of the Sibyl and the golden bough agleam, like yellow mistletoe in the winter woods.' (*BBC*) In this account, Virgil, Aeneas, McGlinchey and now Heaney himself are drawn by grief and loss to enter into the realm of the marvellous. Heaney casts his teacher's affection for Book VI, as well as his own spell-bound descent into the text, as a kind of spirit-led divination. Their common attraction to Virgil's underworld is instinctual, Wordsworthian and 'feminine', in Heaney's earlier gendering of these qualities.[9] In his portrayal of McGlinchey, then, Heaney is indirectly painting a portrait of Virgil as a northern, constitutionally sensitive and irenic poet, the very opposite of the canonical, Augustan Virgil, known for his celebration of Roman *imperium*.

The implication that Virgil was a 'tender, inward man', much like McGlinchey, is then reinforced by the two passages Heaney chooses to convey the overall mood and tone of the *Aeneid*. In the first passage, the only one Heaney remembers from studying *Aeneid IX* at school, Virgil compares the death of the young soldier Euryalus to a flower cut down by a plough. Nodding to a later paternal mentor, Heaney quotes Robert Fitzgerald's translation of Virgil's elegiac simile:

blood streamed on his handsome length and his neck
collapsing let his head fall on his shoulder,
as a bright flower cut by a passing plough
will droop and wither slowly, or a poppy

8. And *FK* 411; see further, Chapter 4.
9. See Chapter 1.

bow its head upon its tired stalk when overborne
by a passing shower of rain.[10]

This image of a beautiful boy dying like a cut flower illustrates the pathos lodged in Heaney's remembered fragment of Virgil, 'Sunt lacrimae rerum'.[11] It is echoed in Giovanni Pascoli's 'L'aquilone', an elegy for a young child's death which Heaney translated and published in 2009: 'We die with our childhood clasped close to our breast / Like a flower in bloom that closes and reforms / Its petals into itself.' ('*si muore / la sua stringendo fanciullezza al petto, / come i candidi suoi pètali un fiore // ancora in boccia!*')[12] In 'A Kite for Aibhín', the final poem of *Human Chain*, Heaney offers a lyric response to both Virgil and Pascoli, transforming Pascoli's elegy into a thank-offering for an infant birth (HC 85). But in the 2008 radio essay, the tragedy of the boy's death is remembered without any consolatory uplift.

Heaney goes on to quote a second famous simile, this time from Book VI, where Virgil describes the souls of the dead flocking to the banks of the River Styx. Here, he quotes from the working draft of his own book-length translation:

> Continuous as the streaming leaves nipped off
> By first frost in the autumn woods, or flocks of birds
> Blown inland from stormy seas, when the year
> Turns cold and drives them to migrate
> To countries in the sun. (*BBC*)[13]

In Poem III of 'Route 110', Heaney invokes this simile to convey the idea of souls coming to life as he remembers the crowds that used to flock to their allotted buses in Belfast Bus Station (*RF, HC* 50). But again, in the radio essay, Heaney stresses the elegiac tone of Virgil's original simile. He offers the two passages together as an illustration of Virgil's

> sympathy and intimacy with the world of nature, of frost and flowers and flocks of birds, his closeness to the life of the land, what it feels like to be a plough-man opening furrows under a shower of rain, and his raw inwardness, with the *lacrimae rerum*, the brutality of war, the reality of cruelty and bloodshed. (*BBC*)

In *Human Chain*, the image of souls as falling leaves (Virgil's '*lapsa cadunt folia*') becomes a leitmotif running throughout the collection, connoting both mortal

10. Ae.IX.433–7; trans. Fitzgerald (1983), 275.
11. Heaney passes over the simile's homoeroticism, which is focalised through the eyes of Nisus, the older soldier who mourns Euryalus and is shortly killed himself. Edith Hall notes that, in his school edition of Virgil's *Aeneid*, the young Heaney marked with a triple line Virgil's apostrophe to the two fallen soldiers, writing in the margins 'foretells their immortality' (Hall (2019), 230).
12. Heaney, '"The Kite" by Giovanni Pascoli', in Mulligan, ed., *Augury* (2009).
13. Heaney, translating Ae.VI.309–12. This version contains one early variant in line 411, 'stormy seas', which by December 2008 has been emended to 'the stormy ocean'.

cadence and nature's cyclical renewal.[14] But in the essay, Heaney stresses the contrast between the poet's inner melancholy and the serenity of the natural image in this simile.

In the radio essay, Heaney goes on to argue that the 'settled, canonical serenity' of Virgil's lines should not obscure the fact that 'under its untroubled surface, a quarrel is being conducted, a quarrel with himself – the quarrel which W.B. Yeats thought of as the real and true source of poetry.' (*BBC*) Concerning the politics of the *Aeneid*, Heaney concedes that the poem 'celebrates, very deliberately, the origins and triumph of Roman power', but nevertheless, 'there is a latent tension between the poetic personality . . . and the official propagandist'. The 'melody and melancholy' of the *Aeneid* stem from Virgil's poetic personality, which witnesses but cannot reconcile itself to 'the savage brunt of Roman history'. While the lyricist in Virgil 'rejoice[s] in those flights and deflections which poetic imagination can devise', his poetry also faces up to the epic task of recording and speaking truth to Roman power.

In the final part of his radio essay, Heaney celebrates Virgil as a poet of memory, who bridges the entire span of European literature from the ancient past to contemporary times. He reminds us that Virgil's poetry offered Romans a memory of their history and a shared mythic origin. By modelling the *Eclogues*, *Georgics* and *Aeneid* on the works of Theocritus, Hesiod and Homer, Virgil 'carried the heritage of ancient Greek poetry forward into the civilisation of Rome and in doing so, preserved it for the Europe that was to come' (*BBC*). Even Virgil's epitaph on his tomb at Naples plants itself in the collective memory: '*cecini pascua, rura, duces* . . . I sang of sheep-hills, farmlands, generals'. In this concentrated line, Virgil captures the 'three aspects of his art, the natural world, the business of agriculture, the conduct of wars' that he would pass on to modern European culture (ibid.). Virgil is, then, a master of the arts of memory, forwarding the Greek and Roman culture we have collectively inherited, but also forwarding his own, conflicted inner consciousness to speak to us as individual readers.

II. 'FREED SPEECH' AND SETTLEMENT

Reflecting on the art of translation with Robert Hass in 1999, Heaney suggested he practised two types of translation, 'raids' and 'settlements'.[15] Translating Dante's 'Ugolino' was a 'raid' that freely altered the rhythm and style of the originary text: 'The Italian swims. But mine is sluggish. I liked it like that. . . . Dante's movement is Chianti-pour, but . . . mine is like poured concrete.'[16] By contrast, the *Beowulf*

---

14. See Chapter 8.
15. *Sounding Lines* (1999), 1. He also described the 'raid' as the 'Lowell method', imposing the poet's roughened up, thicker sound on the originary text.
16. *Sounding Lines* (1999), 4, referring to 'Ugolino', *FW* 60–3. Heaney admires Dorothy Sayers's *terza rima* version of Dante for its swift flow: 'she's just sketching it out. . . . Its swiftness makes it very readable.' (ibid.)

translation adopted the 'settlement approach', where 'you enter an oeuvre, colonize it, take it over - but you stay with it, and you change it and it changes you' (ibid., 1). With a 'settlement', there is 'a different covenant with a work', even 'a kind of conjugal relation' (ibid., 4, 2).

When he comes to 'settle' with *Aeneid VI* almost a decade later, Heaney enters that 'conjugal relation' with an accumulated weight of memories, obligations and gratitude. Translating the whole of Book VI was a notion he had been contemplating for some time (*RTÉ, SS* 440). In his 'Translator's Note', he reiterates his sense of obligation to Father McGlinchey, the translation being 'the result of a lifelong desire to honour the memory of my Latin teacher at St Columb's College' (*A* vii). Having undertaken the project by April or May 2008, he wrote to Sarah Ruden in late July that he had already 'reached the point where Anchises starts his voice-over prophecy / history of Rome.'[17] He 'quailed' over this passage, his least favourite part of the *Aeneid*, but by the end of November he had completed the first draft and sent it out to certain expert readers.[18]

Diverted into preparations for the extensive public celebrations of his seventieth birthday, it was several months before he responded to his readers' comments, but in May 2009, he found the time to 'withdraw and recuperate' with his Virgil translation, at Glanmore Cottage.[19] In his letters to Sarah Ruden, he still sounds hesitant about publication, 'not sure how or if the thing can be published.'[20] He was well aware that new, authoritative translations of the *Aeneid* had been published very recently. In the 2008 issue of *Parnassus* which included Heaney's 'Palinurus', Robert Fagles's 2006 translation of the *Aeneid* was favourably reviewed by Willard Spiegelman, who also wrote at length about his own apprenticeship reading Virgil at school.[21] Spiegelman's 'Virgilian Memoir' is close in spirit to Heaney, in its praise of a much-loved schoolteacher, and appreciation for Virgil's combination of local patriotism and literary savvy, of intimacy and public voice.[22] Still more recently, Sarah Ruden's translation of the *Aeneid* had been published by Yale University Press in 2008. And Heaney, who had formerly taught Ruden at Harvard, was warm in his praise: 'Your translation is a marvel, newness bestowed on the poem and its oldness

17. Heaney, letter to Sarah Ruden, 26 July 2008.
18. Heaney, letter to Ruden, 26 July 2008. Poet and translator Sarah Ruden was one of the expert readers to whom Heaney sent his draft of *Aeneid Book VI* in late November 2008. He received her feedback in late December (letter to Ruden, 24 January 2009). With grateful thanks to Sarah for sharing this correspondence and Heaney's 2008 draft of *Aeneid Book VI*, and to Catherine Heaney for allowing me to quote from the draft where it sheds light on Heaney's interpretation of Virgil or helps to establish a chronology of composition.
19. Heaney, letter to Ruden, 9 May 2009. Seventieth birthday celebrations included: recording all of his published poems for a fifteen-CD box set; an hour-long Irish TV documentary; and a ceremonial unveiling of a bronze sculpture of a turf-cutting man at his home in Co. Derry. Heaney was also working on his translation of Henryson, *The Testament of Cresseid & Seven Fables* (Faber, 2009).
20. Letter to Ruden, 9 May 2009. A similar hesitation is expressed in July 2008.
21. Willard Spiegelman, 'Unforced Marches: A Virgilian Memoir', *Parnassus* 30:1–2 (2008), 81–106.
22. Spiegelman (2008), 104.

respected. . . . The law is laid down, the decisive note struck, the line-for-line *disciplina* mastered immediately.'[23]

His own translation he describes in self-deprecating terms as 'an old-style dutiful sixth formerish bit of construing.'[24] It was 'hard to justify' yet another translation of the *Aeneid*, Heaney writes, but 'one reason I kept going, however, was an old irrational *pietas*.' His *pietas* is directed again towards the memory of 'the gentle Father McGlinchey who . . . was forever sighing, "Och boys, I wish it was Book VI"'. Again, it was his teacher's melancholy yearning that predisposed Heaney to 'wooded Avernus', and led him eventually to produce this 'late classics homework, in a way, for McGlinchey in Elysium'.[25] In his interview with Dawe, too, Heaney mentions writing out of a sense of obligation to his ghosts: 'As you get older yourself, your head is a kind of Elysium . . ., they live with you, and you live in a sense *for* them' (*RTÉ*, Heaney's emphasis). After his swift flight through the underworld in 'Route 110', Heaney returns to Virgil's Latin with a renewed sense of attachment and obligation. The translation work is *pius* in the sense that it is undertaken *for* his ghosts.

Writing about, or for, one's own Elysian ghosts is a connecting theme in the five extracts Heaney published in advance of the book-length translation. In 2008, the UK journal *Archipelago* published 'The Fields of Light', Heaney's rendition of Virgil's 'Groves of the Fortunate Ones' in Elysium.[26] The extract is published alongside 'Loughanure', in which Heaney celebrates the life of the painter Colin Middleton, while also meditating more broadly on our culturally inherited ideas of the afterlife. A classical elegy, Heaney elsewhere suggests, is a poem in which 'the dead person is resurrected in a benign landscape.'[27] By pairing his elegy for Middleton with Virgil's depiction of the '*sedes beatas*', Heaney offers this irreverent, Rabelaisian artist a kind of apotheosis or translation into the afterlife of poetry.

The following year, in an issue of *Modern Poetry in Translation* entitled *Freed Speech*, Heaney published 'Three Freed Speeches from Aeneid VI'.[28] There is a political slant to the entire volume, with the 'freed speech' of poetry in translation intended as a protest against the military conflicts then being waged in Afghanistan and Iraq, Israel and Palestine, the Democratic Republic of Congo, Pakistan, Sudan and elsewhere.[29] David and Helen Constantine write in their Editorial to the volume that 'speech is freed – given utterance – in the writing of the poem' and that, by being translated, the poem 'is *enlarged*: and not just in that word's modern sense

---

23. Letter to Ruden, 26 July 2008. Heaney's remark about her '*disciplina*' responds to Ruden's principle of translating Virgil line for line, often demanding great compression and economy in the English translation.
24. Ibid.
25. Ibid.
26. Heaney, 'The Fields of Light' [trans. Aeneid VI: 638–78] and 'Loughanure', *Archipelago* II (Spring 2008), 9–14 (9). Later collected in *The Stone from Delphi* (2012), ed. Vendler (2012). The translation extract corresponds to A.867–915 (same text but with minor revisions).
27. Heaney, *Out of the Marvellous* (RTÉ film, 2009).
28. Heaney, 'Three Freed Speeches from Aeneid VI' [trans. Aeneid VI: 42–76; 77–97; 847–54], in David and Helen Constantine (eds), *Modern Poetry in Translation* (2009), 58–61.
29. Conversation with David Constantine, 2 April 2019.

– increased, extended – but in the archaic sense too, set free, given its liberty.'[30] The volume contains translated poetry from around the world, in many cases, from regions steeped in military conflict at the time.

All three of Heaney's 'freed speeches' concern the threat of warfare and how it is to be withstood, the themes that had preoccupied him in *District and Circle*. The first two extracts are taken from Aeneas' exchange with the Sibyl, this time not the lines relating to the golden bough, but rather the Sibyl's prediction of 'wars, bloody wars' in Italy. The third extract, from the end of *Aeneid VI*, is taken from Anchises' prophetic vision of those same wars, and his plea to future Romans to be sparing and merciful in the use of force. These three translation extracts are virtually unchanged in the book-length translation published in 2016. But in the context of the *Modern Poetry in Translation* volume, they demonstrate the kind of 'enlargement' poetry can offer in response to political and military rhetoric. In the first extract, Aeneas prays to Apollo to relinquish his divine anger against Troy, 'To spare us, the last of its relicts'.[31] Then he turns to the Sibyl and pleads for help in finding

> home ground for my people
> In Latium, refuge for our wandering gods
> And all Troy ever held sacred.[32]

His exilic desire for a haven will be echoed very shortly in Palinurus' plea to him for a final resting place, which increases the pathos of their exchange.

The Sibyl's reply to Aeneas is grimly pessimistic. In Heaney's second extract, she famously predicts 'wars, / Atrocious wars, and the Tibur surging with blood'.[33] But she also urges Aeneas to have courage:

> follow your fate
> To the limit. A road will open to safety
> From the last place you would expect: a city of Greeks.[34]

By breaking off her prophecy at this point, the Sibyl emphasises the line of friendship that will unexpectedly be extended between warring nations. She also implies that Aeneas arriving in Italy will be adopting the part of a Greek himself:

> again the cause of such pain
> And disaster for Trojans will be as before: a bride
> Culled in a host country, an outlander groom.[35]

30. David and Helen Constantine, eds, *Modern Poetry in Translation* (2009), 1. Ital. in original.
31. Heaney, 'Three Freed Speeches' (2009, 59), '1. Aeneas (lines 42–76)', l. 31; trans. Ae.VI.63. The extract corresponds to A.65–112, where six lines are revised.
32. '1. Aeneas', ll. 34–6; trans. Ae.VI.65–8.
33. '2. The Sibyl (lines 77–97)', ll. 13–14; trans. Ae.VI.86–7. The extract corresponds to A.113–39. The first part is slightly revised, but lines 125–39 are identical in 2009 and 2016.
34. '2. The Sibyl', ll. 25–7; trans. Ae.VI.96–7.
35. '2. The Sibyl', ll. 21–3; trans. Ae.VI.93–4. See also Chapter 9, pp. 247–8.

This is to suggest that Aeneas' pursuit of marriage to Lavinia will repeat Paris' theft of Helen of Troy. Heaney's choice of phrasing, 'an outlander groom' robbing a 'host country', underlines the ambivalence of Aeneas' role, as his exilic wandering leads him to the colonisation and conquest of Italy.

Heaney's third extract is taken from Anchises' address to the souls waiting on the riverbank of Lethe, who would in future become his Roman descendants. The speech is famous for its characterisation of Roman *imperium*:

'tu regere imperio populos, Romane, memento
(hae tibi erunt artes), pacisque imponere morem,
parcere subiectis et debellare superbos.' (Ae.VI.851–3)

'Do you remember, Roman, to rule imperially over the nations (these shall be your skills), to set the force of habit upon peace, to spare those who submit and crush in war the haughty.' (Horsfall, p. 59)

Instructing Romans to remember who they are, Virgil has Anchises employ the rhetorical arts of memorisation in the structure and phrasing of his speech. He places '*memento*' at the end of the line, and three infinitives in a symmetrical pattern (*imponere, parcere, debellare*), to drive home the point that Romans will be remembered for their peace-keeping skills, in contrast to the Greeks who will be remembered for their arts. Virgil's translators often slant this celebration of the *pax Romana* with patriotic sentiment toward their own nations. For example, Dryden glorifies *Britannia* alongside *Roma* in his symmetrically succinct and memorable rendition of lines 852–3: 'Disposing Peace, and War, thy own Majestic Way. / To tame the Proud, the fetter'd Slave to free'.[36]

Heaney's translation is also sonically orchestrated but it deliberately resists stirring the heartstrings with patriotic zeal.[37] He shifts '*memento*' from the end to the beginning of the line, and introduces the notion of 'gifts' that should be correctly used:

'But you, Roman,
Remember: to you will fall the exercise of power
Over the nations, and these will be your gifts –
To impose peace and justify your sway,
Spare those you conquer, crush those who overbear.'[38]

The last line is made memorable by the internal rhyme, 'spare' and '-bear', the midline alliteration of '<u>c</u>onque<u>r</u>, <u>cr</u>ush', and the parallel syntax maintained with an

---

36. Dryden, The Works of Virgil, The Sixth Book, ll. 1175–6, p. 566.
37. Burrow (2016) suggests Heaney was weary by the time he reached this passage, but as this extract shows, it was actually a section he worked up for translation in advance of the book-length publication. In my view, the flatness shows a deliberate resistance to emotive patriotic rhetoric.
38. Heaney, 'Three Freed Speeches': '3. Anchises (lines 847–54)', ll. 6–10; trans. Ae.VI.851–3. Unchanged in 2016: A.1156–9.

adroit shift from active to passive voice: 'those you ... those who'. In the *Aeneid*, this speech has a tragic irony for many readers, since Aeneas will notoriously fail to spare the '*subiectis*' when he kills the suppliant Turnus at the end of the epic. In Heaney's extract, which presents this speech in the context of a volume aimed to give voice to the victims of war, Anchises is celebrating the *pax Romana* as an ideal to which all world leaders should aspire. Heaney's version further challenges those leaders to 'justify' their right to power by acting in the interests of the nations they have colonised. The downbeat tone of the speech, though memorable, makes Anchises an advocate for peace in modern times.[39]

III. THE WANDERINGS OF PALINURUS

Heaney's translation 'Palinurus' was published in the American journal *Parnassus*, together with an early version of 'Album', a set of five snapshots of Heaney's parents, remembered through the prism of Virgil's *ter conatus* scene.[40] The extract relates how Aeneas meets the ghost of his helmsman, Palinurus, on the banks of the Styx, and learns how he came to drown and why he is barred from crossing the river into Hades. The episode is not mentioned in *Stepping Stones*, where Heaney cites other Virgilian motifs he lived with 'long and dreamily' (SS 440). Indeed, Palinurus seems to have become important to him in the months following his stroke, being the only episode to extend over two sections of 'Route 110' (Poems VI–VII).[41] And it is again one of only two episodes given particular mention in his 'Translator's Note' to *Aeneid Book VI* (viii). While, in 'Route 110', the helmsman's story is sketched in lightly and swiftly, in the translation extract Heaney presents him as a fully tragic figure, one of the underworld ghosts whom Aeneas proves powerless to save.

In Books V and VI of Virgil's *Aeneid*, Palinurus is a tragic foil for Aeneas, who survives the dangerous sea crossing and safely lands his ships on the coast of Cumae. At the end of Book V, we learn that the god of sleep closed Palinurus' eyes at the tiller. And, when he resisted the drowsiness, the god drugged him with Lethean dew until Palinurus fell unconscious into a calm sea (V.854). Unlike Misenus, who challenges the sea gods with his trumpeter's blast of a conch shell, Palinurus is innocent of any act of hubris (Ae.VI.171–2). But in Book VI, when Aeneas meets his ghost, Palinurus is allowed to give his own account of his death, and he corrects the

---

39. Virgil 'celebrates, very deliberately, the origins and triumph of Roman power' (*BBC*). In 'Suffering and Decision', Heaney writes that Virgil 'would eventually link his epic ... to the Augustan project of world renewal through the *Pax Romana*' (224). With little enthusiasm, he describes Virgil's 'devotedness to Rome and its heritage' as 'Roman piety and propaganda' (224, 225).
40. Heaney, 'Palinurus' [trans. *Aeneid* VI: 349–83] and 'Now the oil-fired burner comes to life' (untitled version of 'Album'), *Parnassus* (2008), 75–80. 'Album', revised and with title, was also published in *Poetry Ireland Review* (2009). With thanks to Herbert Leibowitz, then editor of *Parnassus*, for providing me with a copy of the text and an eloquent commentary on it. On 'Album' in *HC*, see Chapter 8.
41. *HC* 53–4.

account given in Book V, insisting that a powerful storm had washed him overboard: he did not fall asleep and no god wished him dead.[42]

> '... nec me deus aequore mersit.
> namque gubernaclum multa ui forte reuulsum,
> cui datus haerebam custos cursusque regebam,
> praecipitans traxi mecum. maria aspera iuro
> non ullum pro me tantum cepisse timorem,
> quam tua ne spoliata armis, excussa magistro,
> deficeret tantis nauis surgentibus undis.' (Ae.VI.348–54)

'nor did a god plunge me into the sea, for it was the tiller, torn from me by chance with great violence, to which I was assigned, and stuck to, as my watch, as I guided the course, that I tore away with me as I plunged. I swear by the cruel sea that I experienced no fear so great on my own account as that dread lest your ship, deprived of her gear, and torn from her steersman, should go down amid such swelling waves.' (trans. Horsfall, p. 25)

Throughout the storm, Palinurus says, his concern had been for the ship and its company. The way '*tua*' ('your') is pushed forward of its noun '*nauis*' ('ship') underlines the helmsman's loyal devotion to Aeneas and the ship, over his own safety. By this account, Palinurus is a model of Trojan *pietas*, like his captain, Aeneas.

Palinurus' account of the storm, followed by his glimpse of the Italian coast, also mirrors the Trojan fleet's arrival in Italian waters, recounted in *Aeneid* III.[43] The close parallel between the two episodes, sea storm followed by unlucky landfall, throws into sharp relief the contrasting fates of Aeneas and Palinurus, the leader eventually destined to found a new homeland and the helmsman destined for eternal exile. There is also a stark contrast in the way their stories are received by their addressees in the narrative. Aeneas describes his first glimpse of *Italia* to Queen Dido, who pities his exilic longing and welcomes him into her kingdom. Palinurus recounts the story of his death to his own captain, yet receives from him no word of sympathy.

Heaney's translation is divided into three parts, opening with a gripping, first-person monologue, in which the ghost of Palinurus recounts how he was swept overboard in a storm and murdered by local tribes as he struggled to reach the shore. In the second part, the helmsman turns to Aeneas and begs to be taken across the Styx, and in the third, he receives a sharp rebuke from the Sibyl for his unlawful request, followed by a more comforting prediction. The tripartite division emphasises the dramatic shape of the episode, just as Heaney's 1989 translation had done for 'The

---

42. See R. D. Williams (1972), 480, who lists the inconsistencies between Ae.V.827f. and Ae.VI.337f.: the sea was calm in V but stormy in VI; there are inconsistencies in the time and course of travel – three nights and sighting of Italy on fourth day (VI.356f.), which cannot be squared with Aeneas' journey from 'Lucanian waters' to Cumae, and Aeneas' arrival in the underworld to find Palinurus already there. See also Horsfall (2013), pp. 273–89.
43. The scene in *Aeneid* III itself recalls Odysseus' first glimpse of Phaeacia in Homer's *Odyssey* V.

Golden Bough'. His extract begins with a line that succinctly expresses Palinurus' *pietas*, as well as his mental qualities of endurance and steadfastness. The opening line conveys the sense of the Latin *religare* (to closely bind, from which we derive 'religion'): '"Bound to hold course and hold fast / to the wheel, I refused to let go"'. Yet the line is largely Heaney's invention, as becomes clear if we compare his 2008 draft of the book-length translation with the extract published as a self-standing episode in *Parnassus*:

The steering oar I held and was in charge of	5.11
Snapped in a sudden gale and as I fell	5.10
I dragged it down with me. But I swear by ocean	5.12
My fear then for myself was as nothing	4.11
To the fear I had for your ship.	3.8
Stripped of her tackle, her steersman overboard,	5.11
Would she not wallow and founder	3.8
In those mountainous seas?[44]	
Bound to hold course and hold fast	5.7
to the wheel, I refused to let go	3.8
when gale-force dislodged it - and went down	5.9
when the helm went down.	2.5
But by tempest	2.4
and tide I swear my fear for myself	4.9
was less than my fear for the ship: what hope	4.10
had she then, her tiller torn off	3.8
and her steersman gone overboard, at the mercy	5.12
of mountainous seas? (Pa. 1–10)	

The book-length draft is more accurate in conveying the details of Virgil's text. For example, in Virgil's time, the tiller ('*gubernaclum*') would have been a 'steering oar', not a wheel; 'tackle' is accurate for '*armis*' in this nautical context; and swearing 'by ocean' (capitalised in 2016) is closer to '*maria aspera*' than 'tempest and tide'. In the book-length version, Palinurus' ghost sounds more formal, making use of a conditional indirect discourse ('would she not wallow') that suggests a degree of distance from his traumatic experience.

In the *Parnassus* extract, by contrast, the shorter lines, verbal repetitions and hard enjambments all convey a sense of urgency and heightened emotional pitch. The rhythm of the extract is far more energetically irregular, and the number of beats and syllables in each line (noted in the margin above) correspond neither to iambic pentameter nor to classical hexameter. The run of spondees in the first tercet ('hóld coúrse ... hóld fást ... lét gó ... gále-fórce ... wént dówn') have an incantatory

---

44. A (December 2008 draft), with thanks to Sarah Ruden. Only one minor revision, lines 465–6, from December 2008 to A.463–70 (2016).

force. They are perhaps meant to suggest, onomatopoeically, the movement of waves peaking in a stormy sea. At any rate, the rhythm is stormily disordered, and the fourth line breaks off in an ellipsis just where Palinurus remembers going overboard.

Apart from the ragged tercets of the *Parnassus* extract, what is most striking about these opening lines is the heavy use of paired alliteration and repetition: 'hold course and hold fast', 'by tempest and tide', 'tiller torn', 'mercy of mountainous' and so on. Virgil's passage contains some striking alliteration: for example, the '*u*' in '*u̱exit me u̱iolentus aqua; u̱ix lumine quarto / prospexi*' (VI.356, the wind 'carried me wildly over the water, only just, on the fourth day, I glimpsed . . .'). But Heaney's alliterations are distinctively grouped in pairs. One of them, Palinurus' oath, 'by tempest and tide', recalls the dramatic opening scene of shipwreck in Shakespeare's *The Tempest*. Heaney admired the reckless pace of the play's opening scene ('hurry, hurry, hurry; speed, speed, speed'), and here imports it into Palinurus' narration.[45] The allusion to *The Tempest* suggests further correspondences in this episode between Ferdinand's grief over his drowned father and Palinurus' death and posthumous appeal to Aeneas.[46]

Along with these Shakespearean echoes, the strong alliterative rhythm of the extract gives Palinurus' speech a distinctly archaic, Anglo-Saxon sonority. Modern editions of Old English poetry are printed in units of two half-lines (known as the *a-verse* and *b-verse*). Each unit or 'verse' had two beats or 'lifts', with varying numbers of 'dips', or unstressed syllables.[47] Typically, the first 'lift' of the *b*-verse alliterates with one or both of the 'lifts' in the *a*-verse. The two half-lines, or 'verses', are thus bound aurally over a notional caesura. In Michael Alexander's translation of *Beowulf*, this Anglo-Saxon aural pattern is reproduced in such lines as 'High over head they hoisted and fixed' and 'that leapt into the world, this leader of armies'.[48] And Heaney's *Beowulf* has these patterns too: 'He was four times a father, this fighter prince'.[49] In Heaney's Latin extract, Palinurus' speech draws so extensively on this verse tradition that parts of it might easily be lineated like an Old English poem, thus:

Boúnd to hold coúrse	and hold fást to the wheél,
I refúsed to let gó	when gále-force dislódged it –
and wént dówn	when the hélm went dówn.
But by témpest and tíde	I sweár my feár
for mysélf was léss	than my feár for the shíp:
what hópe had she thén,	her tíller torn óff

45. 'On Elegies' (2001), 26.
46. On the mixture of Dantean tercets and the alliterative line, it is also worth bearing in mind the example of Eliot's 'Little Gidding', Heaney's favourite section of *Four Quartets*. Marjorie Perloff notes 'the shift from alliterative line to iambic tercets as in the "ghost" passage (movement 2) of *Little Gidding*, with its allusion to Dantean terza rima' (Perloff (2019), 72).
47. See Jones (2006), 245.
48. Qtd in Jones, 246.
49. Heaney, *Beowulf* (1999), 4.

and her steérsman gone	overboárd, at the mércy
of moúntainous seás?	A soúth wínd
húrled me and búrled me	through horízonless surge

The helmsman's speech falls naturally into two-beat half-lines, with alliteration or verbal repetition binding the units together. In the second and last lines above, two *b-verses* alliterate with an *a-verse* lift. Each half-line has two beats divided by a notional caesura. And other rhyming patterns bind the half-line units together. The last line is a particularly rich example, with the triple assonance of 'hurled', 'burled' and 'surge' strengthening the triple alliteration. These repetitions give Palinurus' speech an Anglo-Saxon sonority and forcefulness.

The traces of this ancient meter are particularly marked in Palinurus' struggle to reach the coast of Italy. His effortful approach to the shore is implicitly contrasted with that of Aeneas, who has just beached safely at Cumae, in the beginning of *Aeneid VI*. With a clash of word accent and ictus (metrical beat) in the first line below, Virgil underlines Palinurus' physical exertion:

pāulātim‿ádnābām tērræ; iām tūtă těnēbam,
ni gens crudelis madida cum ueste grauatum
prensantemque uncis manibus capita aspera montis
ferro inuasisset praedamque ignara putasset. (*Ae*.VI.358–61)

indeed I was holding on and would have been safe, had not a savage, well-armed people attacked me, weighed down as I was with a sodden garment and grasping with hooked hands at the sharp peak of the crag. (trans. Horsfall, p. 25, modified)

Virgil has alliterating 't's in line 358, and the dramatic imagery of hooked hands on a sharp crag in line 360. Heaney's translation thickens the alliteration with a run of 'g's and 'r's, but these are additionally linked into the alliterative pairs of Old English verse. The tercet below falls naturally into the two-beat 'lifts' of Anglo-Saxon verse, as is evident if one adds the midline break between half-line units:[50]

Líttle by *líttle*	I was máking heádway,
slúgging and strúggling	to lánd in my wáterlogged clóthes
gétting a gríp	on rázor-backed rídges, (*Pa* 16–18)

This strongly Anglo-Saxon rhythm and diction, combined with the *terza rima* stanza form of the extract, is distinctly different to the book-length translation. This raises the question, what is Heaney's special interest in Palinurus, and why does the translation extract take this particular poetic form? Looking closer at the context of its composition, it appears that Heaney's approach to the Palinurus episode is directly

---

50. Cf. Paul Muldoon's translation of 'Caedmon's Hymn', which is lineated in half-lines *and* tercets. See Muldoon, *Moy Sand and Gravel* (2002), 23 (qtd in Jones, 182).

informed by ideas he had been recently exploring in relation to John Keats, and his own close friend and mentor, Ted Hughes.

IV. TED HUGHES, KEATS AND THE SEA

The connection with Ted Hughes is suggested by two memorial addresses, one delivered at Dartington Hall in 2007 and the other at Westminster Abbey in 2011. In both addresses, Heaney meditates on the tragic circumstances of his friend's life, and at the same time pays tribute to Hughes's mastery of Anglo-Saxon verse forms. In the first of these speeches, Heaney associates Hughes's idea of 'suffering and decision' with Keats's celebrated notion of the 'vale of soul-making'.[51] The idea of suffering as a transformative experience is a central theme in the work of both English poets. In Heaney's translation extract, the three-part drama of Palinurus' narration of his drowning, plea for assistance and resignation to his difficult fate follows the trajectory of a Keatsian instruction of the soul. Palinurus' decision to embrace his fate provides Heaney with a classical *exemplum* of Hughes's views on the relation of suffering and *poesis*, as well as a Virgilian analogue for the defining tragedies of Hughes's own life.

With this broader context in mind, the 'Palinurus' extract might be read as a 'sounding line' into Heaney's late poetry and poetics.[52] 'Sounding' in the nautical sense means 'ascertaining the depth of water', and in the plural noun form, 'soundings' refer to places 'at sea where it is possible to reach the bottom with the ordinary deep-sea lead' (*OED*, 'sound' 1a; 'soundings'). 'To take a sounding', in the figurative sense, means 'to try to find out quietly how matters stand' (*OED*, 'sounding', 1b). And 'sounding' can also imply the sense of 'to make sound or whole' (*OED*, 3). In all these senses, Heaney translates Virgil's Palinurus episode as a way of sounding out his ideas about poetry's relation to suffering.[53] Sounding out the case of a contemporary poet by way of a classical analogue gives the subject temporal depth while also affording protection and concealment to the poet concerned. Ted Hughes was one of the Elysian ghosts for whom Heaney was writing when he composed 'Route 110' ('I was still with him in a way, and he was with me' (*RTÉ*)). And he seems to have been a ghostly presence overseeing Heaney's translation of the Palinurus episode as well.

Heaney had been commissioned by the poet's widow, Carol Hughes, to deliver the Ted Hughes Memorial Lecture at Dartington Hall in 2007.[54] This was the one public engagement he chose not to cancel after his stroke in August 2006, and he

---

51. Heaney, 'Suffering and Decision' (delivered at Dartington Hall, 2007), in Gifford et al., eds, *Ted Hughes: From Cambridge to Collected* (2013).
52. Cf. the title of Heaney's interview with Robert Hass, *Sounding Lines: The Art of Translating Poetry* (1999).
53. Cf. Averill, *Wordsworth and the Poetry of Human Suffering* (1980); Wordsworth's *lacrimae rerum*, however (like Heaney's), extend to the natural world, not just the human.
54. Heaney had spoken at Ted Hughes's funeral on 3 November 1998. See Henry Hart (2012).

duly delivered the address the following July (SS xxxi). At his Westminster Abbey Memorial Address for Hughes, in 2011, Heaney celebrated the way Hughes's poetry had absorbed the sound of Anglo-Saxon verse.[55] Quoting from his own translation of Beowulf's funeral, Heaney reminded his listeners of some of the best-known lines of Hughes's verse: 'I imagine this midnight moment's forest' (from 'The Thought-Fox') and 'Here is the fern's frond, unfurling a gesture' ('Fern')[56]. In these, Heaney pointed out, we hear the characteristic 'four beats and three alliterations of the native Anglo-Saxon line.' Equally, Heaney stresses the deep influence of Shakespeare on Hughes's poetry, and praises 'the seriousness and tenacity and supernatural perspective that distinguished his life-long dedication to Shakespeare.'[57] If Palinurus' suffering is, in some respects, an analogy for Hughes's, this would help to explain why Heaney gives an Anglo-Saxon inflection to Palinurus' speech, and why the extract begins with the dramatic, *Tempest*-like storm scene.

In his account of Hughes's life, Heaney also stresses his Virgilian *pietas* and capacity for enduring intense emotional and physical suffering. Heaney begins his Dartington Memorial lecture by relating two anonymous poets' biographies. The first initially reads like a life of Seamus Heaney:

> Once upon a time there was a poet, born in the north of his native country, a boy completely at home on the land and in the landscape . . . Educated first in local schools, he proved himself a gifted son and was chosen for further education . . . [His] early work . . . could not have been written without his memories of that first life in the unfashionable, non-literary world of his childhood . . . His reading voice was bewitching, and all who knew him remarked how his accent and bearing still retained strong traces of his north-country origins. (221)

The poet in question, however, turns out to be Virgil. Virgil's mature poetry, writes Heaney, 'had a tragic visionary quality, darkened by a sense of his own country's history of war (which he had known about from his father's experience)' (ibid.). The second biography is a condensed life of Dante: 'he became the victim of a great hue and cry' and was exiled from his native city; and he was forever changed by a visionary encounter with a woman who, after her 'untimely death', became 'the dark matter of the poet's life' (222).

Having related these two exemplary poets' biographies, Heaney then suggests they both may be read as alternative versions of the life of Ted Hughes (223). Virgil's absorption of his father's suffering during years of civil war, and Dante's

---

55. Heaney, 'Address for unveiling of Ted Hughes MEMORIAL', Westminster Abbey (6 December 2011), no pag. With thanks to Neil Roberts for sharing his signed transcript of Heaney's address. Heaney quotes from his own translation of *Beowulf* (1999), ll. 3156–62.
56. Hughes (2005), 153, 21.
57. He had earlier written, too, that in Hughes's language we find the 'persistence of the stark outline and vitality of Anglo-Saxon that paid into the Middle English alliterative tradition and then went underground to sustain . . . the ebullience of Shakespeare and the Elizabethans.' (P 151)

tragic loss of Beatrice, are paralleled with the two defining tragedies of Hughes's life: his silent, war veteran father and the suicide of Sylvia Plath. Heaney's Westminster Abbey address summarises the two tragedies in this way:

> First he would absorb the tragedy of the First World War at his own fireside, dwelling with a father who had fought and survived and remembered but did not speak. Then in his young manhood fate dealt another blow with the bewildering death of his first wife, Sylvia Plath.[58]

Both tragedies constitute spiritual shipwrecks in the life of the poet, which the poetry has decisively to contain and perhaps transmute through the medium of poetry.

In 'Suffering and Decision', Heaney's reason for invoking the parallels with Virgil and Dante is to suggest the seriousness of Hughes's devotion to 'his poetic calling, the spiritual dimensions within which he conceived of it and the responsibility which he felt to it and for it.' (224) Virgil's '*pietas*' or 'devotedness to Rome and its heritage' led him, in the aftermath of the civil wars in Italy, to aspire to the 'work of healing' in his poetry, whether by celebrating rural labour as a reparation of the land in his *Georgics*, or by endorsing the Augustan promise of 'world renewal' in the *Aeneid* (ibid.). Similarly, Ted Hughes 'from beginning to end . . . had a devotedness to Albion, a care for the land and the language' (224–5).[59] His poetry retains 'back-echoes of the sacred' deriving from the proximity of ancient poetry to divination and prophecy, and 'the power to heal – "heal" in its first sense meaning "to make whole".' (ibid.)

The title of Heaney's published lecture, 'Suffering and Decision', derives from Hughes's statement that '"no poem can be a poem that is not a statement from the powers in control of our life, the ultimate suffering and decision in us."' (230) Heaney argues that Hughes's 'best writing had sprung from an unrealized capacity for suffering and decision within himself' and that 'his divining spirit seeks out creatures and plants and people who have the capacity to bear their predicament, to keep going, hold the line and suffer in silence' (ibid.). He recalls the salmon in Hughes's poem 'Rain-Charm for the Duchy', which hang suspended motionlessly in the river, 'the patient, thirsting ones'; their 'patience' relates closely 'to its root in the Latin word *patiens*, meaning suffering' (226).[60] 'Suffering' transmutes to endurance in the poems Hughes composed out of, and in anticipation of, the tragedies of his own life: poetry 'holds him . . . steady in his wounds'.[61] Like Palinurus (and unlike Aeneas), Hughes was not rescued from this condition by supernatural intervention. Even the

---

58. Heaney, 'Address' (2011).
59. A further indication of Heaney's association of Virgil and Hughes: 'On a New Work', a poem about Ted Hughes, was chosen as the first poem in a collaborative volume entitled *The Light of the Leaves* (1999). This is one of three volumes Heaney produced in collaboration with the Dutch artist Jan Hendrix, all thematically linked to Virgil's underworld book (the other two volumes are *The Golden Bough* and *Aeneid Book VI*. See Heaney and Hendrix, *Yagul* (2002).
60. Hughes (2005), 805.
61. Hughes (2005), 679, qtd by Heaney, 'Suffering and Decision', 227.

name 'Palinurus' could be associatively linked to Hughes. The Latin for 'thistle' is *'paliurus'*, and in his Dartington lecture, Heaney compares Hughes's resilience to the thistles celebrated in one of Hughes's own poems: 'Stiff with weapons, fighting back over the same ground'.[62] Another possible link is suggested by the Latin word *'palinous'*, meaning 'a fair wind'. For some classical scholars, the helmsman Palinurus gives his name to the headland on the Italian coast, because it is a cape where fair and foul winds clash.[63] In his double biography of Dante and Hughes, Heaney relates that 'a great hue and cry descends' on both poets midway through their lives; metaphorically speaking, then, perhaps the weather-beaten promontory of Palinurus reminded Heaney of this 'great hue' descending on the ill-fated poets.[64]

In his Westminster address, Heaney compares Hughes's notion of 'suffering and decision' to Keats's concept of suffering as 'a schooling, in the course of which an intelligence is transformed into a soul.'[65] He quotes Keats's famous letter to George and Georgiana Keats, in April 1819: 'Do you not see how necessary a World of Pains and troubles is to school an Intelligence and make it a soul?'[66] For Keats, it is 'by the medium of the world' that individual intelligences are fashioned into souls. By enduring suffering, an intelligence comes to 'possess a bliss peculiar to each ones individual existence'. This strikes the young poet Keats as 'a grander system of salvation than the chrystain [sic] religion.' (ibid.) According to Herbert Warren, Keats derived his notion of the 'vale of soul-making' from his reading of *Aeneid VI*, particularly the passage in which Anchises' ghost explains to his son Aeneas the doctrine of the *Anima Mundi*, a passage that had also influenced Wordsworth in 'Tintern Abbey'.[67]

Even more than Heaney, Keats was attracted to the *Aeneid* from a young age, and translated the entire epic while a schoolboy at Clarke's Academy in Enfield.[68] In Book II of his epic romance, *Endymion*, the eponymous hero undertakes a Virgilian *katabasis* and descends to the ocean floor in pursuit of his beloved Selene, or Cynthia, goddess of the moon.[69] Keats began composing *Endymion* in April 1817, shortly after he had staged his own sea-crossing, close to the thirteenth anniversary of his father's death. On the late afternoon of 15 April, he sailed from Southampton to

---

62. Heaney, 'Suffering and Decision', 235; Hughes (2005), 147.
63. Horsfall (2013), p. 273.
64. Simon Armitage's version of the Palinurus episode highlights the recent plight of refugees crossing the Mediterranean, thousands of whom have drowned in their attempt to reach safe haven in Italy. See his 'On the Existing State of Things', in *Sandettie Light Vessel Automatic* (2019), 84–5, 187–8.
65. Heaney, 'Address for unveiling of Ted Hughes MEMORIAL', no pag.; referring to Keats, *Letters*, Vol. II (1958), 101–3. In 'Suffering and Decision', Heaney links Hughes's schooling in suffering with passages from Wordsworth and Yeats (233, 235–6).
66. Keats, 'To the George Keatses', 21 April 1819 (*Letters*, Vol. II, 102).
67. Herbert Warren, 'Keats as a Classical Scholar', *The Nineteenth Century* 93 (January 1923), 64, qtd in D'Avanzo (1967), 62. On Anchises and 'Tintern Abbey', see Averill (1980), 154.
68. Charles and Mary Clarke, *Recollections of Writers*, 124. With thanks to Nicholas Roe for this reference.
69. On Keats's *Endymion* and *Aeneid VI*, see D'Avanzo (1967).

the Isle of Wight, a journey that may have helped inspire his sonnet 'On the Sea'.[70] In a letter to his friend Reynolds, he confided that a line from Shakespeare, 'Do you not hear the Sea?', haunted him intensely during the journey.[71] As Nicholas Roe points out, the remembered phrase actually splices together a line from the opening of *The Tempest* ('Do you not hear him?') and one from *King Lear*, where Edgar asks his father, 'Hark! do you hear the sea?'[72] Keats's sonnet seems suspended between tragedy and romance, just as it hovers between two visions of the sea, one as a destructive force, the other as the source of new life. Both are implicit in the sonnet's opening lines:

> It keeps eternal Whisperings around
> Desolate shores, and with its mighty swell
> Gluts ten thousand Caverns.[73]

In the closing line, Keats echoes the sea-nymphs' hourly knell for Ferdinand's still-drowned father in *The Tempest*.[74] When the poet 'start[s]' from his Shakespearean dream, it will not be to find his father magically rescued from the sea. But the sound of the sea, and no less the sound of Shakespeare's lines, continue to resonate as sources of creative renewal. According to Roe, this association between poetry, the sea and Shakespeare lasted for the duration of the poet's life, and it endures into his cultural afterlife in the line he composed for his own epitaph, 'here lies one whose name was writ in water'.[75] Keats's preoccupation with his father during the composition of *Endymion* suggests that, on one level, the poem is re-enacting Aeneas' descent to find his father's ghost. His sonnet 'On the Sea', however, suggests a closer parallel with Palinurus, the sea-wanderer whose quest for a haven is never entirely fulfilled.

A letter from Keats to George and Georgiana Keats, in October 1818, again touches on the image of a soul by the Styx, steadfast in his wandering. The letter also movingly illustrates how Keats's intellect undergoes its 'soul-making', schooled by the experience of suffering. His brother Tom is mortally ill, and Keats abjures thoughts of married life and domestic happiness; instead, he delights in the power of imagination, through which he feels

> that I do not live in this world alone but in a thousand worlds - No sooner am I alone than shapes of epic greatness are stationed around me . . . Or I throw my

---

70. Keats (2003), 59. See Roe (2013), 161–94. I am also indebted to Roe's keynote lecture, 'Keats and the Sea', delivered at the Wordsworth Summer Conference, August 2019.
71. Keats, Letter to J. H. Reynolds, 17 April 1817, in *Letters*, Vol. I (1958), 132, qtd in Roe, 163.
72. Shakespeare, *The Tempest* I.i.12; Roe, 163.
73. Keats, 'On the Sea' (2003), 59, and *Letters*, Vol. I, 132.
74. Shakespeare, *The Tempest* I.ii.402; Roe, 164.
75. A major theme in Roe's biography; see Roe, 19, 162–94, 238–9, 256–8. 'Among the many things he has requested of me to-night, this is the principal one, – that on his grave-stone shall be this, – HERE LIES ONE WHOSE NAME WAS WRIT ON WATER.' (Joseph Severn, letter to Brown, in Rollins (1965), no. 166, 2:91)

whole being into Troilus, and repeating those lines, 'I wander like a lost Soul upon the stygian Banks staying for waftage'.[76]

The 'Soul ... staying for waftage' is again a recollection of *Aeneid VI*, filtered through Shakespeare. The soul on the bank is Palinurus, whose 'staying' means 'waiting' but also 'enduring'; he endures, in this case, as a simile remembered by Keats from Shakespeare.

From a Keatsian perspective, Palinurus is an intelligence being schooled into a soul by the forces of the sea, which are both destructive and ministering. Like the drowned father in Shakespeare's *Tempest*, he suffers the sea-change into ghosthood. But as a ghost in *Aeneid VI*, he narrates his own history and is absorbed into the ocean of poetry that is constantly being remembered and renewed. His steadfastness is that of the poet in Keats's late sonnet, 'Bright Star', who is inspired by the constant movement of the sea: 'The moving waters at their priestlike task / Of pure ablution round earth's human shores.'[77]

V. PALINURUS 'ENLARGED'

The misfortunes of Palinurus contain echoes, in Heaney's translation, of personal tragedies suffered by Ted Hughes and, before him, by Virgil and Dante. But in their retelling, these tragic histories also become narratives of cultural renewal. The sea in which Palinurus drowns figures not only as a destructive force, but also in a late Keatsian sense, as a source of rejuvenation for the human world. At the end of the storm scene, Palinurus recalls how the Lucanian locals set upon him as he struggled to reach the shore:

> gens crudelis madida cum ueste grauatum
> prensantemque uncis manibus capita aspera montis
> ferro inuasisset praedamque ignara putasset. (*Ae*.VI.359–61)

> savage locals came at me
> mad for the kill, and that much the madder //
> at the thought of me as rich pickings. (*Pa* 20–2)

Virgil's locals attack Palinurus in the hopes of booty ('*praedam*'), not knowing ('*ignara*') that he carries nothing of value. Whether their attack kills him or not Virgil does not say. Heaney's translation, by missing out '*ignara*', suggests that the locals are indeed aiming to kill. The proximity of '*gens crudelis*' to '*madida*' (from *madidus*, meaning 'wet', referring here to Palinurus' water-logged clothes) produces

---

76. Keats slightly misquotes the beginning of the line, 'I wander, like a lost soul ...' (letter to George and Georgiana Keats, October 1818, in *Letters*, Vol. I, 404; cf. *Troilus and Cressida* III. ii, where Troilus actually says, 'I stalk about her door, / Like a strange soul'.
77. Keats, 'Bright Star', ll. 5–6 (2003), 247.

Heaney's line, 'mad for the kill, and that much madder'.[78] Hughes's biography is arguably exerting pressure on Heaney's translation here, the Lucanians serving as a vehicle for the critics and biographers who verbally attacked Hughes after the suicide of Sylvia Plath.

There is also an echo of the death of Orpheus, slain by the Ciconian women whose intentions were certainly murderous (G.IV.520; Meta.XI.3). In Milton's 'Lycidas', Orpheus is recalled as the archetypal poet drowned 'by the rout that made the hideous roar'. The swain of Milton's poem counters the dissonance of the mob by mourning Lycidas in richly aural verse:

> Ay me! Whilst thee the shores, and sounding seas
> Wash far away, where'er thy bones are hurled,
> Whether beyond the stormy Hebrides
> Where thou perhaps under the whelming tide
> Visit'st the bottom of the monstrous world; (*Lyc.*154–8)

The swain's elegy recalls the song that Ferdinand hears as he mourns his drowned father in *The Tempest*. The substance of his words is tragic, of course, but for Heaney, there would be a healing process at work in the intricate alliterations, the upward iambic beat and the chiming of 'hurled' and 'world'.[79] His own Palinurus elaborates on this Shakespearean music as he recalls how 'a south wind hurled me and burled me / through horizonless surge' (*Pa* 11–12; a free translation of '*tris Notus hibernas immensa per aequora noctes / uexit me uiolentus aqua*', Ae.VI.355–6). His speech concludes with a resonant line, in which his floating corpse is at once housed and unhoused by the moving waters of the sea:

> 'Nunc me fluctus habet uersantque in litore uenti.' (Ae.VI.362)

> 'Now the waves hold me, and the winds toss me on the shore.' (trans. Horsfall, p. 27)

> 'Now surf keeps me dandled and shore winds
> roll me in closer and closer.' (*Pa* 23–4)

The syntax of the Latin functions as a kind of holding device, with '*me*' coming first, and the two sentence subjects, '*fluctus*' and '*uenti*', flanking the verbs. The envelope structure is then echoed in the enclosing alliteration of '*uersant . . . uenti*'. While the sense of the line is that Palinurus' body remains unburied, the sound and syntactic

---

78. The book-length draft preserves Virgil's ambiguity, describing the locals as 'Ignoramuses who saw me as fair game' (revised but still ambiguous, in A.478).
79. Dr Johnson famously objected to 'Lycidas' that 'where there is leisure for fiction there is little grief' (*Lives of the English Poets* (1905), Vol. I, 163). Heaney's counter-argument, I think, would be that art offers the indirection by which grief can be articulated. Milton elegised the death of his good friend Diodati in Latin ('Epitaphium Damonis', *Complete Shorter Poems* (1997), 270–86). Latin was then an international language in which Milton could write fluently, but it was still, arguably, a form of emotional cover and artistic distance.

structure of the Latin perform the opposite gesture, holding the lost body in a linguistic and environmental embrace.

Heaney elaborates on the metaphorical implications of Virgil's enveloping syntax. He particularises the nouns to suggest that the body is held in the in-between space of the shoreline waters: '*fluctus*' (waves) becomes 'surf', and '*uenti*' (winds) become 'shore winds'. More strikingly, he interprets '*habet*' metaphorically, so that the body seems restored to life and indeed child-like, 'dandled' by a parental wave. And '*uersant*' (turn, toss) is rendered as 'roll me in closer and closer', a rhyming, lullaby line, with a regular, falling rhythm. Musically and metaphorically, Heaney's two lines thus reinforce the image of the body suspended and protected by the motion of the sea. In Heaney's draft of *Aeneid VI*, the lullaby sound is intensified with an additional pair of alliterative verbs: 'Now surf keeps me dandled, / The shore winds loll and roll me'.[80] This is the only occasion where the book-length translation heightens, rather than pares back, the Old English alliteration. Arguably, this is a final tribute to Hughes's Anglo-Saxon style. For 'loll' in the transitive sense, the OED offers 'let droop or dangle' (loll, v.1, 2.), and in that sense, Heaney is reinforcing the image of the helmsman's body as an infant, cradled in the arms of the sea.[81] Metaphorically, then, the line suggests that Palinurus has recovered a childhood innocence, even though the primary sense of the line denotes his ongoing wandering and exile, bodily drifting in open water, and spiritually haunting the banks of the Styx.

Having concluded his history, the shade of Palinurus then turns to Aeneas in supplication. In Heaney's extract, this passage is subtitled Part II of the episode. The ghost begs Aeneas either to take him across the river or to cover him with earth ('*tu mihi terram / inice*', Ae.VI. 365–6) so that his spirit will have the right to cross over himself. While he remains '*inhumatus*' (from *humus*, earth, and *humo*, to cover with earth), he is scarcely considered by the gods to be human at all (*humanus*, from *homo*),[82] so his plea for burial is also a plea for restoration of his humanity. In a syntactically distorted aside, Palinurus struggles with the recognition that his leader is exempt from the fate he himself must suffer,

> . . . (neque enim, credo, sine numine diuum
> flumina tanta paras Stygiamque innare paludem), (Ae.VI.368–9)

for it is not, I believe, without divine approval that you are about to swim across such great rivers and the Stygian marsh (my trans.)

prepared as you are for this vastness //
of river and Stygian marsh – (Pa 39–40)

---

80. Retained unrevised in A.479–80. Reviewing the latter, Burrow (2016) finds Virgil's language being 'flagged much too overtly as simple and childlike'. In my view, the child-centred language is deliberate here.
81. Cf. Heaney on the poetic imagination of Virgil and Miłosz: 'each poet's imagination was like an infant being rocked and cradled in a shield' (FK 412).
82. In Hebrew, *Adam* means 'person' or 'man', and is etymologically related to *adamah*, which means 'soil, earth'. Hence, Genesis 2: 7: 'And the Lord God formed man of the dust of the ground, and breathed into his nostrils the breath of life.'

Heaney's translation simplifies the syntax but he also exaggerates the expanse of the Styx, so that it seems as vast as Keats's ocean.[83] The helmsman also addresses Aeneas as the son of Anchises and the father of Ascanius: '*per genitorem oro, per spes surgentis Iuli*' (Ae.VI.364, 'by your father, I beg, by the hope of growing Iulus'). Heaney omits the less familiar name of '*Iulus*' for Ascanius but he doubles the emphasis on fatherhood: 'by your father / and your hopes as a father yourself' (29–30).

Anticipating Aeneas' attempted embrace of Anchises later in Book VI, Palinurus then reaches out to grasp his captain's hand:

> da dextram misero et tecum me tolle per undas, (Ae.VI.370)
>
> reach out your hand to a friend
> who is suffering, take me with you //
> to the other side of the waves (Pa 41–3)

In a tragic inversion of the later *ter conatus* scene, Palinurus acts the part of a ghostly son, who finds his living father untouchable. Palinurus calls Aeneas '*inuicte*' (unconquered), while Heaney's translation calls attention to the *ter conatus* motif: 'you, the unbeaten, *untouched*' (Ae.VI.365, Pa 26, my ital).[84]

In Part III of Heaney's translation, the Sibyl makes her reply to the unhappy ghost. In a carefully balanced sentence, Virgil freeze-frames the moment in which Palinurus expects Aeneas' reply and the Sibyl answers in his place: '*talia fatus erat coepit cum talia uates*' (Ae.VI.372). The pathos of Aeneas' silence is even more keenly felt in Heaney's version, where the name of the respondent is withheld to the end of the tercet:

> That was his plea to Aeneas, and this
> was the answer he got
> from the Sibyl (Pa 46–8)

Being '*inhumatus*', she informs him, he cannot cross the river, and she adds this harsh rebuke: '*desine fata deum flecti sperare precando*' (Ae.VI.376). Heaney translates, 'Banish the thought // that praying can ever affect / the edicts of gods.' (Pa 54–6)[85] This is bleak enough, but it does not quite convey the flat finality of '*desine sperare*' ('cease to hope'). 'Hope' has been a theme of Palinurus' speech, as he asks himself of the unguided ship 'what hope had she then?', and he appeals to Aeneas by 'your hopes as a father yourself'. If Palinurus' history constitutes a *katabatic* journey of its own, then this is the nadir of his descent. His body already lost, his shade has retained hope, for this much is suggested in the buoyant rhythms of his speech to Aeneas.

At this point, however, the Sibyl changes tack and offers consolation to her listener. Her assurances differ markedly from the encouraging reply she gives Aeneas at

---

83. Keats describes 'The ocean with its vastness' in his sonnet 'To My Brother George' (2003), p. 26, l. 5.
84. The book-length draft has 'you the unbowed, the unbroken' (retained in A.481).
85. Unchanged in the book-length version, apart from lineation.

Cumae, where the hero's request to enter Hades alive was equally beyond his natural rights. If a way across is found for the divinely favoured Aeneas, Palinurus has the human consolation of being remembered with honour and affection:

> 'sed cape dicta memor, duri solacia casus.
> nam tua finitimi, longe lateque per urbes
> prodigiis acti caelestibus, ossa piabunt
> et statuent tumulum et tumulo sollemnia mittent,
> aeternumque locus Palinuri nomen habebit.' (*Ae*.VI.377–81)

> 'Your plight
> is a hard one, but hear and remember
>
> my words; they should be a comfort.
> What will happen is this:
> your bones will be reverenced; the sky
>
> will reveal signs and wonders, in cities
> on every side populations will know
> to build you a tomb
>
> and solemnize it with offerings
> year after year. And the place for all time
> will bear the name Palinurus.' (*Pa* 56–66)

The Sybil assures the *pius* helmsman that he will be 'reverenced' in turn (the Latin uses the same verb, '*piabunt*') and his tomb will be 'solemnized' with all the rites due to a *humatus*, a buried human being. She implies, moreover, that the 'populations' who will revere Palinurus (the subjects of '*piabunt*', '*statuent*', '*mittent*') are the very Lucanians who caused his death. They will be driven to it ('*acti*') by divine signs and portents. The tomb ('*tumulo*' recurring twice in the Latin) will be a compensatory, human form of *terra*, covering but also prolonging the memory of the corpse lost at sea. And Palinurus will be further 'earthed', in the land ('*terra*', again) bearing his name. These promised transformations will all occur on the human plane. Indeed, the Sibyl prophetically casts his imagination forward to *urbes*, cities, already populating the Lucanian coast. And finally, the Sibyl predicts that the land will hold and preserve his name, '*locus . . . nomen habebit*', just as Palinurus has said that the sea waves hold his body, '*me fluctus habet*' (*Ae*.VI.362). So he is to be 'freed and enlarged' by the two forces that once overwhelmed him: the sea and the Lucanian people. In the larger context of Aeneas' mission to found a city and a new nation in Italy, moreover, Palinurus will serve as a bridge between cultures. He is the first Trojan to bear the brunt of the native Italians' hostility to foreign invasion, but also the first to be naturalised as an Italian and ritually honoured in communal memory.

Heaney's translation liberally expands the Sibyl's succinct reply to eleven lines. He omits the note of retributive justice and further underlines her conciliatory tone. There are no Old English-style rhymes or rhythms in her decorous speech, which is retained almost verbatim in the book-length draft. But in the extract, Heaney emphasises the Sibyl's decisiveness that this is a right and fitting outcome: signs of divine favour are *revealed*, and the people *know* to build a tomb. The verb 'to bear' means both 'to carry' and 'to endure', so in a sense the endurance of suffering is being answered by the place carrying the sufferer's name into the future. If there is a ghost of Ted Hughes in Heaney's Palinurus, the Sibyl's words assure him of an eventual reconciliation with his critics and recognition of his attachments to nature and local district. Beyond that biographical connection, Hughes's conviction of poetry's originally sacred function is borne out in the example of Palinurus, as he is henceforth integrated into the community's ritual acts of remembrance.

The episode ends with Palinurus being comforted by the Sibyl's reply. Virgil relates that the helmsman rejoices:

his dictis curae emotae pulsusque parumper
corde dolor tristi: gaudet cognomine terra. (Ae.VI.382–3)

These words lifted his heart and raised,
for a moment, his spirits. The thought
of the land in his name makes him happy. (Pa 67–9)

The Sibyl's prophecy does nothing to change Palinurus' present and actual condition of exile, and his cares are relieved only '*parumper*', for a short while. But Virgil's readers would have known the name of Cape Palinuro, a headland on the Lucanian coast of Italy, around forty miles southwest of Salerno.[86] To a Roman reader, then, her prophecy would be substantiated in the historical fact of this headland bearing the helmsman's name. Virgil's episode fittingly ends with the word '*terra*', as if the name, in absence of the body itself, were being returned to earth.[87] Heaney's translation instead ends with the phrase 'makes him happy', shifting Virgil's verb '*gaudet*' ('he rejoices') to the final foot of the line. The register is boldly colloquial, like the 'baby talk' that ends 'Route 110'. And complementing that shift to colloquial intimacy, Heaney introduces a stronger sense of uplift to Palinurus' response. Virgil's verbs for his change of mood are '*emotae*' and '*pulsus*': his cares are *driven away* from his grieving heart; in Heaney's translation, his heart and spirits are 'lifted' and 'raised'. The anapaestic rhythm of the final two lines drives home this sense of emotional uplift. Thus, while Heaney preserves the tragic arc of Palinurus' death and non-burial, his translation offers poetic redress in the sense of bringing out the *gaudeamus* latent in Virgil's *lacrimae rerum*. The helmsman rejoices for a moment in the hope of surviving in the cultural memory, forever attached to a particular place and community.

*

In his letter about the 'vale of soul-making', Keats remarks on the idea of a life spent in pursuit of happiness: 'I do not at all believe in this sort of perfectibility

---

86. See Austin (1977), 136.
87. Fairclough (1978) has a textual variant here, '*terrae*' instead of the ablative '*terra*'. See Horsfall (2013), p. 297, for a discussion of this passage.

– the nature of the world will not admit of it'.[88] His notion of soul-making is not conceived as an escape from the conditions of the actual world but rather as a way of meaningfully coping with them. Heaney expresses a similar view in his review of Nadezhda Mandelstam's memoir, *Hope Against Hope*. He agrees with the Czech playwright and former President Vaclav Havel, that hope is 'a state of mind, not a state of the world; ... not the conviction that something will turn out well, but the certainty that something makes sense, regardless of how it turns out.'[89] Virgil's Palinurus sounds the shape of his own destiny, both in the sense of narrating (sounding out) his own history and in the sense of 'making it sound' in the afterlife of human memory. Recalling Milton's Lycidas, Heaney's wandering Palinurus is a 'genius of the shore', a figure haunting the border between different cultures and languages.[90] He is the figure of the poet who speaks from Keats's 'human shore', not translatable to an absolute, eternal bliss, yet steadfastly capable of renewal from year to year, from one reader to the next.

88. Keats, *Letters*, Vol. II, 101.
89. Ibid. Heaney also points out that, in Russian, 'Nadezhda' means 'hope'.
90. Invoking Milton's swain in 'Lycidas', Heaney described his translation work as a difficult schooling in cultural reappropriation, at the end of which he could tell himself to 'Fret no more, woeful Seamus' (SS 440).

8. Cadence and Lapse in *Human Chain*

In 2009, Heaney told Robert McCrum, 'between the stroke and the 70th birthday, I suddenly realised I had boxed myself into a kind of closing cadence. I'm trying to finish a book of poems to counteract that.'[1] *Human Chain* was published a year later and turned out to be Heaney's final volume of original English poems.[2] From the opening poem to the last, Heaney counterbalances his awareness of mortality with poems exploring the regenerative powers of nature and of human memory and imagination. Virgil is Heaney's guiding classical exemplar in this volume, with 'The Riverbank Field' and 'Route 110' revised and republished to form its centrepiece.[3] The motif of the River Lethe, which features so prominently in *The Riverbank Field*, here generates a series of reflections on mortality, natality and the transformative handing-on of human culture.[4] Other familiar motifs and phrases from *Aeneid* VI come into play as well, such as the *'lapsa cadunt'* of souls crossing the River Styx, and the *'manus effugit'*, or slipping away, of underworld shades. As in *The Riverbank Field*, Heaney celebrates the freedom, spontaneity and rejuvenative powers of lyric in *Human Chain*, although these powers operate within a more pervasively elegiac context than in the earlier volume. With concentrated intensity, Heaney confronts his tragic awareness of the *lacrimae rerum*, the 'tears at the heart of things', with a comedic vision of life continually renewing itself in *altera corpora*, transformed by the waters of the mythical river of oblivion.[5]

Heaney's experience of translating *Aeneid* VI permeates the entire volume of *Human Chain*, in ways that have yet to be fully recognised.[6] The majority of

---

1. Heaney, 'A Life of Rhyme' [Interview with Robert McCrum], *The Guardian* (19 July 2009).
2. Heaney's *The Last Walk* (2013) and *Aeneid Book VI* (2016) were published posthumously.
3. HC 46–59. These versions are slightly revised from *The Riverbank Field* (2007); see Chapter 6.
4. For a philosophical exploration of natality and mortality in modern Western culture, see Robert Harrison's *Juvenescence* (2014).
5. Ae.I.462; VI.714. Heaney, BBC (2008).
6. Exceptionally, Colm Tóibín (2010) writes, 'If there is a presiding spirit haunting this book, it is Virgil's *Aeneid*', and Hugh Haughton (2014/15) observes, 'the whole book is a journey into the poet's first landscapes guided by a sense of the after-life evoked in *The Aeneid*' (197).

the poems in Heaney's last collection were composed while, or just after, writing 'Route 110', and/or while he was working on his translation of *Aeneid Book VI*.[7] In advance of their publication in *Human Chain*, several of the English poems were published in earlier versions, just as translation extracts from *Aeneid Book VI* were beginning to appear in various journals.[8] In Poem XI of 'Route 110', Heaney pictures two figures standing on the banks of a Lethean river, feeling '[n]eedy and ever needier for translation' (*HC* 58). If they are responding to the pressure of a 'closing cadence' of mortal life, they also serve to highlight the volume's preoccupation with the process of literary translation. Several poems address this subject explicitly, while *Human Chain* contains translations and adaptations of medieval Irish, French and Italian poems, alongside the Virgilian material.[9] Having completed a draft of *Aeneid VI*, Heaney moved on to finalising his collection of translations from the medieval Scots of Robert Henryson.[10] The last poem of *Human Chain* is adapted from Pascoli's 'L'Aquilone', which was to have been the lift-off to a new volume of Pascoli translations.[11] One way Heaney extricates himself from a sense of 'closing cadence', then, is by entering into the slippery, playful *labor* of translating words across different languages, cultures and historical eras.

In *Human Chain*, Heaney's imagination is especially stimulated by the play of words between English and Virgil's Latin. Apart from 'The Riverbank Field' and 'Route 110', there are allusions to Heaney's favourite underworld motifs - the golden bough, Charon's barge, the father's ghost and the River Lethe – to be found in 'Album', 'The Conway Stewart', 'Uncoupled', 'The Butts' and other poems.[12] But

For general criticism on *HC*, see especially Auge (2016), Heiny (2013), P. McDonald (2010, 2019), K. Murphy (2016), O'Brien (2016), O'Donoghue (2018), Parker (2012). For criticism on 'Route 110', see Chapter 6, note 3.

7. For dating of these two works, see Chapters 6 and 8. One of the earliest poems in *Human Chain* is 'The Baler', a draft of which is dated 10 August 2006. This predates Heaney's stroke by several weeks, which makes its 'cardiac-dull' clunk eerily prophetic (*LP* I.xviii.1; *HC* 24).
8. In 2008, 'Album' with 'Palinurus' (*Parnassus*); 'Loughanure' with 'The Fields of Light' (*Archipelago*). In 2009, 'Three Freed Speeches' (*Modern Poetry in Translation*) and 'Chanson d'Aventure', 'Miracle', 'The Butts', 'The door was open and the house was dark' and other original poems, published in various journals (see *LP* I.xvii.vi). On Ash Wednesday, February 2010, Heaney read out poems from the first section of *Human Chain* ('Had I not been awake', 'The Conway Stewart', 'The Butts', 'Chanson d'Aventure', 'The Charioteer at Delphi' and 'Miracle') at the National Gallery of Ireland.
9. Translation is the subject of 'The Riverbank Field', 'Wraiths' and 'Loughanure, IV'. On translation in *HC*, see Parker (2012).
10. Heaney, translation of Robert Henryson, *The Testament of Cresseid & Seven Fables* (2009). With thanks to Patrick Crotty.
11. Heaney's translation of Pascoli's madrigal cycle, *Myricae*, was published posthumously by The Gallery Press in 2013. The title, *The Last Walk*, was suggested by Marco Sonzogni. See Heaney, 'On Home Ground' (2012–13), Morisco (2013), Sonzogni (2014), Falconer, 'Heaney, Pascoli and the Ends of Poetry' (2019), Parker (forthcoming 2022).
12. In 'The Conway Stewart', Heaney describes his parents' parting gift of a pen with '14-carat nib' and '[t]hree gold bands', on the day he first attends boarding school (*HC* 9). Metaphorically, the gold-rich pen has magical properties akin to the golden bough because it transports him from his first world into the world of literature.

there is also a more pervasive and delicate tracery of Virgilian language animating the entire volume. In *Human Chain*, Heaney's poetic element is air, and the Latin passages that preoccupy him most are those in which an *anima*, breath or soul, is seen to fall (*cadere*), lapse or glide (*labor*) into another state of being.

1. THREE VIRGILIAN LAPSES

While there are many allusions to *Aeneid VI* in *Human Chain*, three passages in particular contribute to shaping its overall tone and mood. One of these, quoted in Heaney's BBC radio essay, likens the souls of the dead to falling leaves and migrating birds:[13]

> quam multa in siluis autumni frigore primo
> lapsa cadunt folia, aut ad terram gurgite ab alto
> quam multae glomerantur aues, ubi frigidus annus
> trans pontum fugat et terris immittit apricis. (*Ae*.VI.309–12)

> Continuous as the streaming leaves nipped off
> By first frost in the autumn woods, or flocks of birds
> Blown inland from the stormy ocean, when the year
> Turns cold and drives them to migrate
> To countries in the sun. (A.409–13)[14]

In Virgil's narrative, the shades are flocking to the River Styx, where they will beg Charon to ferry them over into Hades. This celebrated simile anticipates their passage across the river. What is more, the simile traverses an entire narrative arc in itself, moving from tragedy to consolation.[15] There is a double fall implied in Virgil's condensed phrase, '*lapsa cadunt folia*' (literally, 'the fallen leaves fall', *Ae*.VI.310).[16] Nicholas Horsfall delivers the basic sense by putting both verbs in the active tense: 'slip and fall'.[17] But Heaney responds more imaginatively to the aural contrast between '*cadunt*' and '*lapsa*', and the juxtaposition of two temporalities in the past participle and present tense Latin verbs. His translation captures the sound and sense of temporal flow and temporal rupture, condensed into

---

13. BBC (2008); see Chapter 7.
14. The text is as read on BBC (2008), with one slight variant (see Chapter 7, note 13).
15. Virgil himself is imitating Homer, *Il*.VI.146. The Virgilian simile is in turn imitated by Dante (*Inf*.III.112f.) and Milton ('Thick as autumnal leaves that strew the brooks / In Vallombrosa', *PL*.I.302–3), to whom Dryden nods, in translating Virgil's lines as 'Thick as the leaves in autumn strow the woods,' (*Ae*.6.428).
16. '*Lapsa*' comes from *labor*, meaning to 'glide, move gently along, slide or slip down', and metaphorically to 'pass away, die away, or be lost' (LS I, II), so it intensifies the downward movement of '*cadunt*', from *cadere*, meaning to 'decline, or die away' (LS I).
17. Horsfall (2013), I, p. 23.

one runover line: 'Continuous as the streaming leaves nipped off / By first frost' (A.409).[18]

The colloquial register of 'nipped off / By first frost' also conveys Heaney's affection for Virgil as a country poet.[19] By giving a georgic realism to this first line, Heaney prepares us for the consolatory lift and lightening of mood at the end of Virgil's extended simile. Twice-fallen leaves become birds escaping the cold, who eventually finding their way into southern warmth and light. This naturally regenerative lapsing will eventually extend to the human souls crossing into Hades as well. As Aeneas learns at the end of his journey, after an allotted time has elapsed ('*concretam . . . labem*'), these souls will be returned to the world in new bodies.[20]

In *Human Chain*, Heaney's parents are remembered as underworld ghosts in two poetic sequences, 'Album' and 'Uncoupled'. Previously published with the title 'Lapse of Time', the five-poem sequence 'Album' enacts a Virgilian '*lapsa cadunt*' in ways we will consider below.[21] A still closer analogy for Heaney's parental poems is Virgil's *ter conatus* scene, where Aeneas tries and fails to embrace his father's ghost:

sic memorans largo fletu simul ora rigabat.
ter conatus ibi collo dare bracchia circum;
ter frustra comprensa manus effugit imago,
par leuibus uentis uolucrique simillima somno. (Ae.VI.699–702)

          And as he spoke he wept.
Three times he tried to reach arms round that neck.
Three times the form, reached for in vain, escaped,
Slipped his hands like the wind, like a dream on wings.[22]

This draft version of Heaney's 2016 translation gives a particular emphasis to Virgil's '*manus effugit*'. Heaney renders the verb twice, with 'escaped, / Slipped his hands', a phrase that captures both the aural music and the doubleness of '*lapsa cadunt*'. Heaney has imitated the elegiac *ter conatus* scene in many previous poems, most notably in *Seeing Things*.[23] But the sensation of things slipping (from) the

---

18. Heaney's unusual rendering of '*cadunt*' as 'nipped off' was questioned by two readers of the 2008 draft but he retained it through all subsequent revisions.
19. There may also be a punning nod to Robert Frost, whose country poems Heaney greatly admired.
20. Ae.VI.746, where '*labem*' is again from *labor*, to glide, slide or slip away.
21. HC 4, 10. An early version of 'Album' was published in 2008, with its first line as a title (*Parnassus* 30:1–2, 75–7). A revised version was published in 2009, as 'Lapse of Time' (*Poetry Ireland Review* 98: 6–8).
22. December 2008 draft of A.941–4, courtesy of Sarah Ruden. In A (2016), line 944 reads: 'escaped / Like a breeze between his hands, a dream on wings.' The revision adheres more strictly to the Latin, with 'escaped' for '*effugit*', and 'breezes' for '*leuibus uentis*'. Cf. Dryden, 'Then thrice, around his Neck, his Arms he threw; / And thrice the flitting Shadow slip'd away; / Like Winds, or empty Dreams, that fly the Day.' (*The Works of Virgil, The Sixth Book*, ll. 950–2, p. 559)
23. See Chapter 2, Section IV.

hands becomes a leitmotif that runs right through *Human Chain*, from 'Album' to 'A Kite for Aibhín'. As Hugh Haughton suggests, the volume as a whole explores the slippage between first and last things, anticipated in Heaney's earlier poem, 'Mint' ('My last things will be the first things slipping from me').[24] While the image of the beloved form slipping away is intensely elegiac, the slip or lapse is also what generates the poetic response. Heaney's translation of line 702 thus evokes not only the son's grief but also the sense of a consolatory release: 'like the wind, like a dream on wings'.

In *The Haw Lantern*, Heaney had described a hailstone melting in his hand, and offered that bite of cold as a metaphor for the way poetry attempts to capture 'the melt of the real thing / smarting into its absence' (*HL* 16). As Fintan O'Toole has rightly said of this poem, 'absence *is* memory; it requires memory to reconjure the real.'[25] In the same way, the ghost's slipping out of reach is what releases and generates the new poetic form. Heaney elsewhere associates this verb 'slip' with the spontaneous generation of poetry. He was fond of quoting a line from the opening scene of Shakespeare's *Timon of Athens*, where an unnamed Poet describes 'poesy' as 'A thing slipp'd idly from me . . . a gum, which oozes / From whence 'tis nourish'd.'[26] Neil Corcoran notes that Heaney's 'lengthy, almost entranced close reading focuses on the word "slipp'd"'.[27] In *Human Chain*, as we will see, the slip or lapse of memory invariably triggers in the poet some new, imaginative flight.

The *ter conatus* motif, in which a ghost slips out of an attempted embrace, is, then, closely associated in this volume with the riverbank scene where souls drink from the River Lethe, lose their memories and cross back into the material world. This third key passage, in which Anchises explains Lethe's role in the reincarnation of souls, is part-quoted, part-translated in 'The Riverbank Field' (*HC* 46–7). I discussed Heaney's notably optimistic interpretation of the end of this passage, *Aeneid* VI.748–51, in Chapter 6.[28] The opening lines, where Anchises first identifies the River Lethe, are also important for the English poems of *Human Chain*:

> tum pater Anchises: 'animae, quibus altera fato
> corpora debentur, Lethaei ad fluminis undam
> securos latices et longa obliuia potant.' (*Ae*.VI.713–15)

>   'Spirits,' Father Anchises answered,
> 'They are spirits destined to live a second life
> In the body; they assemble here to drink
> From the brimming Lethe, and its water

---

24. Heaney, 'Mint', *SL* 6. See Haughton (2014/15).
25. O'Toole (2014). See also N. Corcoran (2014/15).
26. *Timon of Athens* I.i.21–3, the text as quoted by Heaney in 'A Flourish for the Prince of Denmark' (1973) and 'The Fire i' the Flint' (*P* 79–80). He also quotes it from memory in an interview with Paul Muldoon, at The New Yorker Festival (2008).
27. Corcoran (2020, 75), commenting on Heaney's 'A Flourish' (1973).
28. See Chapter 6, I and cf. Chapter 9, III.

Heals their anxieties and obliterates
All trace of memory. (A.959–64)[29]

Heaney's translation fills out Virgil's concise description by almost twice the original length, giving additional emphasis to 'spirits' (*'animae'*), the 'drink / From the brimming Lethe', and its effects. The spirit's relation to material existence (*'corpora'*) is explored in a number of poems about artists and their work, beginning with Heaney himself, in the volume's opening poem, as we will see in Section III below. In line 715, Virgil balances the positive and negative effects of drinking from the Lethe, with a symmetrical arrangement of *'securos latices'* ('carefree / untroubled waters') and *'longa obliuia'* ('long oblivion'). Heaney draws attention to this balance of contrasts by placing two diametrically opposing verbs, 'Heals' and 'obliterates', at the beginning and end of a single line. Virgil's *'obliuia potant'* ('they drink oblivion') is recalled in the draft title of Heaney's penultimate poem, 'Wind-Drink', eventually renamed 'In the Attic'.[30] In the English literary tradition generally, the River Lethe is often invoked as a metonymy for existential oblivion, death and the underworld. Thus, Keats's 'Ode on Melancholy' begins, 'No, no, go not to Lethe, neither twist / Wolf's-bane, tight-rooted, for its poisonous wine'; and Ezra Pound intones, 'so ordered the dark petals of iron we who have passed over Lethe'.[31] But Heaney counteracts these associations, invoking Virgil's River Lethe as the *'securos latices'*, as the waters of baptismal healing and rebirth. Poem XI of 'Route 110' depicts the 'black // Quick water' of the Lethean Moyola, where 'black' (deathly) is counteracted by 'quick', meaning both 'alive' and 'swift' (*HC* 58). These three Virgilian passages, in which the souls-as-leaves lapse across the Styx, the ghost of Anchises slips out of Aeneas' embrace and the spirits of the dead prepare to drink forgetfulness, weave their way in and through Heaney's memories of his Northern Irish past, and of family, friends and fellow artists in *Human Chain*. In this dialogue with Virgil, Heaney ponders the mysterious fleetness of time, while also discovering possibilities of regeneration and renewal.[32]

II. 'THE PHANTOM' *VERUS*

Heaney's five-poem sequence 'Album' recounts a series of memories about his late parents, and in each poem, the lapse of time between the remembered past and the present delivers a more or less explicitly Virgilian sense of Lethean loss and renewal. The form of the sequence is the same as that of 'Route 110', each poem consisting of

---

29. Cf. 'The Riverbank Field' (*HC* 46, ll. 13–16). Apart from punctuation, this 2016 translation is as drafted in 2008.
30. *HC* 83. For 'Wind-Drink', see *LP* I.xviii.1. Other titles, such as 'Attic S̶k̶y̶l̶i̶g̶h̶t̶ Tableau', are handwritten on to the typescript draft.
31. Keats (2003), 283; Pound, Canto LXXIV (1996), 469.
32. This is, of course, not only Virgil's theme; cf. Horace (1975), *'fugaces labuntur anni'* ('the years glide fleetingly by'), *Carmina* II.14, 1–2.

four unrhymed tercets. These squared-off, twelve-line sonnets are loosely linked by overlapping images and phrases, rather than by linear chronology, again reflecting the associative structure of 'Route 110'.[33] In 'Album', the image of cut oaks in Poem I is reiterated in the oak tree on Heaney's school motto in Poem II; the 'getting' of Poem II prompts the oblique allusion to his own begetting, or conception, in Poem III; the mention of 'home' of Poem III leads to a memory of leaving home in Poem IV; and the empty embraces of Poem IV are resolved in the snatched kiss of a grandson in Poem V (HC 4–8).

In the first poem of 'Album', the poet recalls a childhood memory of standing with his parents, looking out over the countryside above Magherafelt (HC 4, ll. 4–9). The memory is triggered, surprisingly, by the sound of a boiler switching on:

> Now the oil-fired heating boiler comes to life
> Abruptly, drowsily, like the timed collapse
> Of a sawn down tree, I imagine them (HC 4, ll. 1–3)

In this opening tercet, the abrupt, drowsy 'coming to life' of the boiler is paradoxically associated with the sound of a dying tree. The remembered cut and collapse of the tree in turn produces the memory of Heaney's prelapsarian childhood, 'in summer season', 'before the oaks were cut' (l. 6). In the 2009 version of this poem, line 3 ends with 'another time and lapse', which relates these sawn-down oak trees to another felled tree from Heaney's past.[34] The seventh poem of 'Clearances' associates the felling of a chestnut tree, planted in the year of Heaney's birth, with the death of his mother (HL 33). I suggested in Chapter 1 that Heaney linked this absent tree to the miraculous laurel tree heralding the birth of Virgil. In 'Album, I', the tree's absence leads once more to a compensatory discovery of a poetic resource: 'I imagine them . . .'. What swims into view next is the tableau of 'often stand[ing]' with his parents 'on airy Sundays', gazing over the countryside (l. 7). The last tercet delivers the moral of this recovered tableau:

> Too late, alas, now for the apt quotation
> About a love that's proved by steady gazing
> Not at each other but in the same direction. (HC 4, ll. 10–12).

Although the belated proof of love is not available to the three figures in the poem, it still seems available to the poet and reader, and it anticipates the grandson's more direct 'proof' of affection in Poem V (HC 8, ll. 4–5). This particular cadence of a severance and/or collapse, accompanied by a fresh burst of insight, mirrors the double movement that Heaney admires in the flow of Virgil's River Lethe.

In the second poem of 'Album', Heaney recalls his first day at St Columb's College boarding school and his loneliness watching his parents turn and walk away

---

33. As in 'Route 110', the time scale moves roughly from the poet's adolescence to the present, but Poem III flashes further back to his parents' marriage.
34. LP I.xviii.1.

(HC 5). In the opening tercet, he quotes the Latin words, derived from Matthew 6: 33, and the images of a dove and an oak tree embedded in the school's coat of arms. While these details give a strong indication of the college's Catholic affiliation, they also suggest a Virgilian analogy for this momentous turning point in the poet's life. The boy in the poem is losing his childhood but also entering the world of literature, where he is destined to discover his poetic voice. The Latin words derived from the school motto, '*Quercus*, the oak. And *Quaerite*, Seek ye' (l. 1), are also a radically distilled version of the Sibyl's advice to Aeneas as he seeks to enter the underworld.[35] With this analogy in mind, it follows that the boy will encounter the '*columba*' (dove) in the college arms (l. 3), mirroring the way Aeneas is met by '*geminae . . . columbae*' gliding down, '*per aëra lapsae*', to lead him to the golden bough (*Ae*.VI.190, 202). The adult poet, moreover, looks back on this scene with an elegiac, Orphic gaze ('*A grey eye will look back*'), just as Aeneas looks back on the loss of Troy.[36] As with Aeneas, the poet's backward look brings him to a new understanding of loss:

> Seeing them as a couple, I now see, //
> For the first time, all the more together
> For having to turn and walk away, as close
> In the leaving (or closer) as in the getting. (HC 5, ll. 9–12)

For the poet in the present, the lapse of time has sealed off the lost first world, putting it beyond recovery, but it simultaneously discovers a closeness in his parents that had been unavailable to the boy at the time.

The third poem of 'Album' pursues the secret behind Heaney's wry, parenthetical phrase 'or closer', delving into the history of his own conception (HC 6). This is the only poem in the series to be narrated in the present tense, giving it a dream-like atmosphere, which is further accentuated by fragmented imagery in the second tercet ('A skirl of gulls. A smell of cooking fish'). The scene takes place at the seaside, where the poet's parents have gone for their wedding meal. The poet imagines a strained awkwardness between them: 'Stranded silence. Tears.' (l. 5) While the parallel with Virgil's underworld ghosts is far from explicit, Aeneas is also met with stony silence from Dido, and is himself silent in the presence of Palinurus' tears.[37] The poet hints mysteriously that he had already been present at his parents' marriage feast, 'Uninvited, ineluctable.' (l. 3)[38] The couple's distressing secret is not told in the poem, and like the anniversary of their marriage, will not be observed 'in the years to come' (ll. 8–10). But in the last line, the poet hints again that he

---

35. To cut down trees for the funeral pyre of Misenus, then seek out the golden bough.
36. Paraphrasing 'A Blue Eye Will Look Back' from the medieval Irish *Colum Cille*, 'Fil súil n-glas' (G. Murphy, ed., 1956, 64). Heaney later translates the lyric in full (HC 73).
37. 'Album' was originally published with Heaney's translation extract, 'Palinurus' (see Chapter 7).
38. Line 3 of a draft of 'Album, III' reads, 'I am / With them in the flesh and imagination' (*LP* I.xviii.1).

was with them at the time, hence conceived before wedlock: 'by evening we'll be home' (l. 12).[39] In this poem, the lapse of time allows the poet to half-reveal his parents' untold secret, a serious moral lapse according to the strict Catholic *mores* of their time. Unlike the other 'Album' poems, this one was originally composed as a fourteen-line, rhyming sonnet, and there are traces of regular end-rhymes in the final twelve-line version: 'table / ineluctable'; 'cooking fish / clinking dish'; 'tears / chandeliers'.[40] The poem ends with alternating near-rhymes 'observe / drive'; 'come / home', which, together with the traces of regular end-rhyme, give the impression of a poem not quite achieving the formal cohesion for which it strives. But the final line, promising 'by evening we'll be home', might be read as a form of retrospective consolation. In a future beyond the lifetime of the couple in the poem, their shared, unspoken secret would not be such cause for grief or shame.

The last two poems of 'Album' are more explicitly modelled on Virgil's *ter conatus* scene, each replaying the hero's unsuccessful attempt to embrace his father's shade. In Poem IV, Heaney describes three separate episodes in which he and his father might have, or did, come into physical contact. While Aeneas' three tries occur in a single moment, Heaney's poem stretches the experience of loss over a time-lapse of thirty years. In the opening tercet, he assumes the reader's prior knowledge of the Virgilian context (*Ae*.VI.700–2), and situates his first *conatus* on a riverbank like Virgil's:

> Were I to have embraced him anywhere
> It would have been on the riverbank
> That summer before college, him in his prime (HC 7, ll. 1–3)

As in 'The Riverbank Field' and 'Route 110, XI', Heaney is alluding to evenings spent fishing on the Moyola river, in the summer before leaving for boarding school. Like Aeneas on the Lethean riverbank, the son fails to embrace his father: 'That should have been the first, but it didn't happen.' (l. 6) On two subsequent occasions, they do make physical contact: once when his father was drunk and needed help dressing, and another time, very near the end, when he needed help washing. But these are not properly embraces, and in the course of the poem, the father's material body reduces from a man 'in his prime' to an elderly figure with 'webby weight' in his arms (ll. 3, 12). As a physical presence, he is gradually receding from the poet's reach, like the ghost who escapes from Aeneas' outstretched arms, '*manus effugit imago*' (*Ae*.VI.701). At the same time, however, the poem counteracts the diminishing form of the father figure, by bringing each memory more vividly to life. While the first non-embrace is set in a summer dream-time, with son and father suspended between 'coming' and 'leaving' (l. 5), the next contact is specific ('at New Ferry

---

39. Again, this is far more explicit in the draft version: 'and yet I never had the nerve / To let her know I knew. Each time I shied / And spared the bridal blush I had denied.' (ll. 12–14, *LP* I.xviii.1)

40. The draft version has a regular Shakespearean rhyme pattern, ABAB CDCD CECE GG (*LP* I.xviii.1).

one night') and materially real ('do[ing] up trouser buttons'). The third embrace is poignantly recalled in precise detail, 'during his last week, ... my right arm / Taking the webby weight of his underarm.' (ll. 10–12) Each successive encounter, then, adds material detail to his memory of the attempted embrace. In this way, the ghostly image is forwarded in *altera corpora*.

Finally, in 'Album V', Heaney recalls his father receiving a quick kiss from his grandson, and the sight of this 'snatch raid', further mediated through poetry and translation, produces a parallel sense of connection between father and son. The 'closing cadence' of 'Album' thus mirrors the endings of 'Route 110', and of *Human Chain* as a whole. The sense of arriving at a destination is coupled with the surprise of a fresh departure, the latter symbolised in the youthful energy of an infant or child. Once again, Heaney assumes a familiarity with the Virgilian context:

> It took a grandson to do it properly,
> To rush him in the armchair
> With a snatch raid on his neck, //
> Proving him thus vulnerable to delight (HC 8, ll. 1–4)

A secondary meaning of 'prove' is 'test with a weapon' (*OED* 1b), and in this sense, the poet's son is playing the part of an armed Cupid in this opening tercet. There may also be a contrast intended with Aeneas' son, Ascanius, who, upon their arrival in Italy, accidently kills a sacred stag.[41] The stag's mortal wound (another '*uulnus*', echoing Dido's) provokes the first outbreak of violence between the Trojans and the native Italian tribes. In Heaney's poem, by contrast, the grandson's snatch raid is a 'proof' and 'steady dawning' of love.

The sight of this successful raid reminds the poet of Virgil's *ter conatus* scene, which he has just been translating:

> Just as a moment back a son's three tries
> At an embrace in Elysium
>
> Swam up into my very arms, and in and out
> Of the Latin stem itself, the phantom
> *Verus* that has slipped from 'very'. (ll. 8–12)

In this recollection, Virgil's text seems to take on the form of a ghost itself, and the poet does seem momentarily to arrive at a sense of closeness that has been eluding him, as it 'Swam up into my very arms'. The following phrase suggests that this shape or illusion of closeness cannot be captured but remains elusively adrift between two languages, somewhere between the English 'very' and Latin '*verus*' (truth). The 'phantom *Verus*' is not exactly the ghost of Anchises (the word '*verus*' does not

---

41. Ae.VII.483–99; Cf. Claude Lorrain's painting of the scene, 'Landscape with Ascanius Shooting the Stag of Sylvia' (1682). The military metaphor of the 'raid' is one that Heaney used to describe a swift, spontaneous mode of translation, as opposed to a 'settlement' in *Sounding Lines* (1999), 1.

appear in the Latin passage); nor is it simply a memory of the poet's own father. The image seems to have 'slipped' into view, from the coincidence of autobiographical and literary memory. The verb 'slipped' has two senses in line 12: first, that the phantom is slipping *away* out of reach again, and second, that it is slipping *into* being for the first time. Heaney's 'phantom *Verus*' thus epitomises the fleetness of poetry, both its attempt to capture ephemeral reality (Virgil's '*manus effugit*') and its effortless invention of the new (Shakespeare's 'A thing slipp'd idly from me').

Virgil's image of hands reaching to clasp an insubstantial ghost recurs in different permutations throughout the *Aeneid*, and most concentratedly in Book VI. Aeneas' journey into the underworld begins at Cumae, where the Trojans find the doors of a temple carved by Daedalus (*Ae*.VI.32f.). The fall of Icarus is missing from the bas-relief, Virgil tells us, because his father could not bring himself to depict the death of his son. In his translation, Heaney lingers over the empty hand motif:

Twice // Dedalus tried to model your fall in gold, twice
His hands, the hands of a father, failed him. (A.50–2)

In *Human Chain*, Heaney modulates continually on this Virgilian motif, often effortlessly reworking it from minor to major key. A brief instance occurs in the title poem, 'Human Chain', where bags of meal are passed 'hand to hand' by aid workers (in an earlier version, this section of the poem was subtitled 'Lent Hands'[42]). On a more personal level, Heaney pursues the '*manus effugit*' motif in two poems about the stroke he suffered in August 2006. 'Chanson d'Aventure' describes his partial paralysis, the ambulance ride to hospital accompanied by his wife, Marie, and his recovery (*HC* 14–16).[43] And 'Miracle' alludes to being lowered downstairs to the ambulance by his friends (*HC* 17). In both poems, Heaney focuses on the loss or recovery of sensation in the hands as a proof of mortal, human love.

In 'Chanson d'Aventure', Heaney remembers his paralysed hand as it 'lay flop-heavy as a bellpull' in his wife's hands (*HC* 15, l. 9). Alluding to a late sonnet by Keats, Heaney describes the strangeness of a touch without physical sensation: 'my once capable // Warm hand, hand that I could not feel you lift' (ll. 6–7).[44] But as the ambulance careers on, their locked gaze, with 'eyebeams threaded laser-fast', transcends their physical separation, like the parted lovers in Donne's 'The Ecstasy'.[45] The third part of 'Chanson d'Aventure' goes on to liken the recovering poet to the famous sculpture of the charioteer at Delphi, who 'holds his own' despite 'His left

---

42. *LP* I.xviii.1. Draft dated 11–12 November 2009.
43. *HC* 18; 'Chanson d'Aventure' was composed nearly three years after the stroke, c. 25 June 2009 (McCrum, 2009). Heaney describes being paralysed down one side at his reading in Dublin (2010).
44. Keats, 'This Living Hand' (1819), where the poet's 'living hand, now warm and capable / Of earnest grasping' is imagined returning cold from the tomb, to haunt his beloved (*Complete Poems* (2003), 384).
45. *HC* 14, l. 8. Heaney's subtitle quotes from Donne's 'The Ecstasy', which continues, 'Our eyebeams twisted, and did thread / Our eyes, upon one double string; / So to' intergraft our hands, as yet / Was all the means to make us one' (Donne (1983), 53–4).

hand lopped // From a wrist protruding like an open spout' (HC 16). The memory of the one-handed charioteer, with 'reins astream' in his remaining hand, in turn triggers a personal childhood memory of being taught to steer a horse and plough:

> myself in step //
> Between two shafts, another's hand on mine,
> Each slither of the share, each stone it hit
> Registered like a pulse in the timbered grips. (ll. 9–12)

The poet thus counteracts the evident lack of sensation in the charioteer's missing hand with the recovery of a personal memory: the touch of the ploughshare retained over a time lapse of some sixty years.[46]

The next poem, 'Miracle', transposes the Virgilian hand motif to the New Testament story of Jesus healing the man sick with palsy (HC 17).[47] Bypassing the story of Jesus' miraculous healing powers, Heaney's poem concentrates on the ordinary miracle of the friends who lower the sick man through the roof of the house where Jesus was at work. While Heaney makes no mention of his own rescue in the poem, he explains elsewhere that he was recalling being lowered downstairs by his friends when he was paralysed by his stroke.[48] What the poem imagines is the sensation in their hands as 'they stand and wait // For the burn of the paid-out ropes to cool'. Heaney repeats in the second and final lines that the burn of the rope is felt by 'those ones who had known him all along'. Once again, a sensation in the hand acts as a kind of '*uulnus*', or wounding, that proves – discovers, confirms - a love that was already there but unspoken.

By far the most insistent modulation on the '*manus effugit*' motif, however, occurs in the poems about Heaney's parents. After 'Album', Heaney conjures memories of each parent separately, in a diptych entitled 'Uncoupled', then again recalls his father in 'The Butts' and '"Lick the Pencil"' (HC 10, 12, 80). In 'Uncoupled', Heaney imagines first his mother, then his father, in a ghostly tableau which emphasises each figure's solitude and remoteness from the poet.[49] Both poems begin with a formal question, 'Who is this . . .', and the first poem in particular ('Who is this coming . . . as if in a procession') imitates Virgil's invocation of the parade of Roman heroes, '*Quis procul ille*' ('who is he, over there', Ae.VI.806), and Keats's questioning of the silent figures on the Grecian urn, 'Who are these coming to the sacrifice?'[50] All these apparitions are related to the originary *nekyia* in Homer's Odyssey XI, in which the hero's mother leads a procession of ghosts up from Hades to drink the proffered sacrificial blood and exchange words with Odysseus (Od.XI.51–138). In contrast to Anticleia, the mother figure in Heaney's poem is silent and remote; she

---

46. 'a little sensation remembered for roughly 66 years' (Heaney, introducing 'Chanson d'Aventure' at *Poetry Ireland* (National Gallery of Ireland, Dublin, 2010).
47. See Mark 2: 1–12.
48. McCrum (2009).
49. Alternatively titled 'Diptych' in a draft version, LP I.xviii.1.
50. Keats (2003), p. 282, l. 31.

bears a pan of ash in her hands, and a strong wind is blowing ash into her mouth and eyes, impeding any possible exchange of word or look. But there is a fleeting sense of physical connection with the maternal ghost when Heaney observes the strain in her hands as she bears the 'weighty' ash (l. 5) to the ash-pit, 'Hands in a tight, sore grip round the metal knob' of the pan (l. 10).[51] Like the sparking embers she bears, this phantom image quickens into life, then fleetingly recedes in the last two lines. As Colm Tóibín suggests, the two figures in 'Uncoupled' offer 'something hovering between what is lost and what has now been found'.[52]

In the second part of 'Uncoupled', Heaney conjures a memory of his father at work in a cattle pen, 'His ashplant in one hand' (HC 11, l. 3). Already associated with Virgil's golden bough in *Seeing Things*, the ashplant here seems to possess only limited powers.[53] 'Lifting and pointing' and 'Waving and calling', the fatherly ghost cannot make himself heard over the herd noise of 'lowing and roaring, lorries revving' (ll. 4, 7, 8). Heaney pictures his childhood self in the poem, perched on a gate and already feeling cut off from his father, even within the remembered scene. The boy tries to retain his father's gaze across the busy yard but the father is distracted by someone hailing him, so that 'his eyes leave mine' and the boy 'know[s] / The pain of loss before I know the term' (ll. 11–12). Unlike in the previous poem, there is little sense of a counteraction to the pain of loss in this final line.[54] But in Freudian terms, Heaney's paternal poems are works of mourning rather than melancholia in this volume, as the memory of loss is taken up in succeeding poems and worked through.[55]

Immediately following, in a poem called 'The Butts', Heaney remembers rifling through his father's empty suit pockets, looking for cigarette butts (HC 12). Working titles of this poem, 'A Restitution' and 'As Close as We Got', and an excised line, 'closeness, that's what I stole', all suggest that as well as stealing nicotine, the boy was looking for a closer sense of connection with his father.[56] At the time, his 'snatch raid' on his father's suit pockets returned only 'a kind of empty-handedness' (l. 16). But, as at the end of 'Album, IV', the poem ends with the memory of their physical closeness in his father's last days:

And we must learn to reach well in beneath
Each meagre armpit
To lift and sponge him,[57]

---

51. This ash-pan, and the father's ashplant in the following poem, are the kind of well-handled tools which, for Neruda, open the time capsule of the past (Heaney, 'Place, Pastness, Poems' (1985/6), quoting Neruda, [1939] (1974), 31).
52. Tóibín (2010).
53. See Chapter 2, Section II.
54. O'Donoghue (2018) observes that, in Heaney's poetry, memories of the father are more spectral, disruptive and destabilising than memories of the mother (17–19).
55. Freud (1958), 147–56.
56. *LP* I.xviii.1.
57. Heaney is crossing Virgil's Anchises with Yeats's figure of Death as 'a coat upon a coat-hanger' in 'The Apparitions' (Yeats (1992), 391); cf. also 'Sailing to Byzantium, II', ll. 9–11: 'An aged

This memory of filial *labor*, 'having to . . . work, . . . having . . . To keep working', is reworked into poetry as partial restitution of the father's lost material presence. And in '"Lick the Pencil"', towards the end of the volume, his father's own *labor* becomes the subject of the poem (HC 80). The family cattle farm has taken on a shimmery, Elysian quality, but the way his father worked his stick of keel on the cattle's backs is recovered in the most vivid, material detail: 'So quick he was to wet the lead, so deft / His hand-to-mouth and tongue-flirt round the stub' (ll. 2–3).[58] At the end of the poem, the father's ghost merges with, or transmutes into, Colmcille, the 'dove of the church' who, according to the saint's *Vita*, was mourned by his own horse on the day he died (HC 81). As in previous poems, the restitution offered in the closing section is a recovered sensation of touch, and a *uulnus* (the monk's habit stained by the horse's tears) that again proves an unspoken love. In such ways, Heaney's memories of his parents and his first world are deepened and amplified by *sotto voce* allusions to Virgil's *Aeneid*. As well as providing epic structure and depth, these Virgilian analogies contribute greatly to the lyric intimacy of Heaney's late poems.

III. 'THE SECOND LIFE OF ART'

Heaney's dialogue with Virgil also enriches his thinking about the artistic imagination and the afterlife of art in the collective, cultural memory. In *Human Chain*, Virgil's description of the soul's lapse across the River Lethe is invoked, as well, as a metaphor for two different aspects of artistic creation. Firstly, the way an *anima* arrives from elsewhere to enter a mortal being is deployed as a classical analogue for the modern artist's experience of an epiphany. And secondly, the process by which an individual *anima* is forgetfully forwarded beyond itself, in Anchises' explanation of the doctrine of reincarnation, is reworked into a metaphor for the transformation of an artistic work as it enters the stream of cultural life.

Heaney's thoughts about the posthumous translation of art are much inspired by Eugenio Montale's notion of 'the second life of art'. Released from the biographical life of its creator, writes Montale, the work of art begins 'its obscure pilgrimage through the conscience and memory of men, its entire flowing back into the very life from which art itself took its first nourishment'.[59] Bachelard's philosophical meditation on the poetics of air, published in an English translation in 1988, seems to have been a further inspiration for Heaney's aerial poetics in *Human Chain*.[60]

---

man is but a paltry thing, / A tattered coat upon a stick, unless / Soul clap its hands and sing' (Yeats (1992), 239).
58. The red lead pencil is also mentioned in HC 11, l. 4.
59. Montale, 'The Second Life of Art' (1982), 20. Cited by Heaney in 'On Kavanagh' (2005) and elsewhere.
60. Bachelard, *Air and Dreams: An Essay on the Imagination of Movement* (1988). Heaney alludes to this volume in *An Open Letter* (1983). Bachelard's *The Poetics of Space* (trans. 1969) is a likely influence on *Seeing Things*, and his various meditations on the poetics of earth, water, fire and air resonate closely with Heaney's poetry in (respectively) *Field Work, Seeing Things, District and Circle* and *Human Chain*.

A philosophy of art's transformative properties now informs his reading of particular Virgilian lines, such as 'animae, quibus altera fato / corpora debentur' ('They are spirits destined to live a second life / In the body'[61]). The 'courier blast' in the opening poem (HC 3) and the 'Air from another life and time and place' in the final poem (HC 85) play on several senses of the Latin noun 'anima', meaning 'a current of air, a breeze, wind' (LS I), 'a breath, inhalation' (LS II.b) and 'the life principle' or 'soul' (LS II.b.2). If the created work of art has an *anima* of its own, it seems to originate from an 'elsewhere world' (HC 43) but it is also continually 'laps[ing] ordinary' and changing into another, mortal, form (HC 3, l. 11).

The opening poem of *Human Chain*, 'Had I not been awake', begins dramatically with a sudden gust of wind rousing the poet from his bed (HC 3). The mysterious wind fills him with a vital energy, 'the whole of me a-patter / Alive and ticking like an electric fence' (ll. 4–5). This 'courier blast' (l. 10), though not explicitly identified as such, works as a metaphor for artistic inspiration, which Heaney elsewhere describes as a kind of 'visitation'. He uses this term in a 2008 essay on Wordsworth to describe the moment when a poet 'comes face to face with something or someone in the outer world recognized as vital to the poet's inner creative life', as a result of which you are 'brought beyond your uncertain individual self'.[62] In 'Had I not been awake', the poet's 'I' drops out of the second half of the poem, dramatising the sense of a translation beyond the 'uncertain individual self'. Introducing the poem at public readings, Heaney referred to it as 'Pentecostal stuff', likening the artist's epiphany to the breath of Christ entering the Apostles after the resurrection.[63] In the closing lines of the poem, Heaney alludes to the Pentecostal hymn '*Gloria Patri*', which ends, 'now and ever, and unto the ages of ages. Amen'. His own final lines seem to contrast divine revelation with artistic inspiration, which remains subject to time: 'But not ever / After. And not now.' (ll. 11–12) However, read as a continuation of the previous sentence, these phrase fragments also negate the idea of 'laps[ing] ordinary':

> A courier blast that there and then
> Lapsed ordinary. But not ever
> After. And not now. (HC 3, ll. 10–12)

So, if the blast of wind dies away a moment later, its revelatory effect seems *not* to have lapsed, either at the time of writing or 'ever after'. The artistic epiphany is life-changing, not only in spite of, but *because* of its being experienced so fleetingly.

Indeed, while he refers to the poem as 'Pentecostal', the experience Heaney describes in the poem is arguably closer to Virgil's evocation of prophetic inspiration. The Sibyl imbibes divine revelation as a drink of supernatural air: '*adflata*

---

61. Ae.VI.713–14; A.960–1.
62. '"Apt Admonishment"' (2008), 19, later rpt. as 'Visitations' (2012). Based on a lecture delivered in 2006.
63. Heaney read 'Had I not been awake' at *Poetry Ireland* (National Gallery of Ireland, Dublin, Ash Wednesday, February 2010) and *Marché de la Poésie* (Le Centre Culturel Irlandais, Paris, 3 June 2013).

est numine quando / iam propiore dei' (*Ae*.VI.50–1). Heaney's *Aeneid VI* translation emphasises this by rendering '*adflata*' as 'breath' twice over: 'she is changed by the breath of the god / Breathing through her.'[64] In 'Had I not been awake', the way the roof 'Pattered with quick leaves', combined with the poet's quickened heartbeat, 'the whole of me a-patter', recalls the leaves that famously scatter on the floor of the Sibyl's cave as Apollo approaches (*Ae*.VI.74–5).[65] And, like the poet in 'Had I not been awake', the Sibyl is electrified by the god's presence. The resemblance is even more striking in Heaney's 2008 translation draft:

> Her countenance suddenly
> Convulsed and changed colour, . . .
> Breast was a-heave, heart beating wilder and wilder'.[66]

Some reviewers, reading Heaney's description of 'the whole of me a-patter / Alive and ticking', took him to be referring to his stroke in 2006.[67] Whether or not one agrees with that interpretation, the whole poem does present the artistic 'visitation' as something unpredictable, destabilising and almost dangerous.

The third stanza, furthermore, invites comparison with one of Ted Hughes's most widely read poems, 'The Thought Fox', which characterises poetic inspiration as a fox moving stealthily through a snowy forest.[68] In the last two lines, the fox, in all its creaturely material reality, disappears into the poet's imagination: 'Till, with a sudden sharp hot stink of fox / It enters the dark hole of the head.' (ll. 21–2) Heaney's third tercet arguably alludes to this scene, though with an added Virgilian frame of reference:

> It came and went so unexpectedly
> And almost it seemed dangerously,
> Returning like an animal to the house, (*HC* 3, ll. 7–9)

Comparing the wind to 'an animal', Heaney is punning on different senses of the Latin '*anima*'. While it can simply mean 'wind' or 'breeze' (*LS* I), '*anima*' also denotes the 'animal principle of life' (*LS* II.b.2), as opposed to the '*animus*', denoting reason or the rational principle, which accords with Hughes's notion of human creativity being wild, instinctual and creaturely. I would suggest Heaney is also alluding to Virgil's Lethean river-crossing, where the '*anima*' leaves Elysium to return to another, mortal, body ('*in corpora . . . reuerti*', *Ae*.VI.751). This helps to explain

---

64. A.75–6, unchanged from December 2008 draft.
65. Cf. Dryden, 'But, oh! commit not thy prophetick Mind / To flitting Leaves, the sport of ev'ry Wind' (*The Works of Virgil, The Sixth Book*: ll. 116–17, Vol. 5, p. 530).
66. December 2008 draft, later revised to 'the more she froths at the mouth / And contorts, the more he controls her, commands her / And makes her his creature.' (A.116–18)
67. For example, Nick Laird, 'The opening poem, "Had I not been awake", replays the stroke in allegory, setting a new unfamiliar tenor of uncertainty and precariousness.' (*Telegraph*, 2 September 2010)
68. Hughes, 'The Thought Fox', in *Collected Poems* (2005), 21.

Heaney's description of the wind 'returning . . . to the house' in the simile in line 9, even though the actual breeze is passing through his bedroom very quickly ('came and went'). The artist's forgetfulness of self in the act of creation is thus drawn into the chain of metaphors comparing death and regeneration to a Lethean crossing or cadence. The poem (or any other work of art) takes on a new material form just as the artist's 'I' slips away.[69]

In several of the elegies for artists in *Human Chain*, Heaney explores the image of an artistic work being released, like a kind of supernatural '*anima*', from the corporeal 'house' of its creator to enter the common *corpus* of cultural life. In 'Death of a Painter', for example, the late painter Nancy Wynne Jones, now unfixed from her physical 'coign of vantage in the studio', has become an elusive '*anima*' that slips from one likeness to the next: 'Not a tent of blue but a peek of gold', 'not Cézanne, / More Thomas Hardy', 'not Hardy' but a butterfly in one of his novels, then 'not a butterfly' but Jonah in the whale's mouth, entering 'Like a mote through a minster door.' (HC 60) In this chain of similes, the artist's presence gets progressively smaller and more aerial while the house or *corpus* to which the *anima* returns grows more capacious and welcoming.

Similarly, in 'Loughanure', the painter Colin Middleton is depicted as an imposing physical presence at work: chain-smoking, grunting, doubled over and staring with his head hanging between his legs (HC 61, 63). And yet, while devoted to the 'mystery of the hard and fast', he is continually vanishing into streaks of paint and wreaths of his own smoke, until the poet is left wondering, 'So this is what an afterlife can come to? / A cloud-boil of grey weather on the wall' (HC 63, l. 8; 62, ll. 1–2). In Part IV of 'Loughanure', the poet suggests that, had he himself been well enough versed in Irish folklore,

> Language and longing might have made a leap
> Up through that cloud-swabbed air, the horizon lightened
> And the far 'Lake of the Yew Tree' gleamed. (HC 64, ll. 10–12)

In line 12, Heaney gives the English translation of the Anglicised name, 'Loughanure', and at the same time imagines himself (or the painter) translated to an aerial realm of the marvellous.[70] Syntactically, 'lightened' and 'gleamed', are past participles of the conditional 'might have', but they are placed so far from the conditional that they also read as active verbs, in the simple past tense. So, the tercet performs, or almost performs, the leap of faith required for the magical translation from actual being to folkloric legend to take place.[71]

---

69. Cf. Hughes, 'Across clearings, an eye, / A widening deepening greenness', 'The Thought Fox', ll. 17–18.
70. The poem relates a tale from Irish mythology, in which the hero, Caolite, follows a fawn into a faery underworld, where he is welcomed (or entrapped) by a yellow-haired girl playing a harp (HC 64).
71. In an alternative interpretation, Auge argues that Heaney presents the Celtic faery world here as an outdated illusion, no longer persuasive to his imagination (2016, 45).

In Part V, the poem then moves in the opposite direction, leaving the painter behind but seeking out the 'mystery of the hard and fast' in the landscape he has vacated. The 'unhomesick, unbelieving' poet drives home past the actual lake, which is here named in the original Irish, *Loch an Iubhair* (*HC* 65, l. 10). He tries 'to remember the Greek word signifying / A world restored completely' (ll. 7–8).[72] Though he fails to remember the word, the poem still recovers sensory fragments of the lost past in 'Hannah Mhór's turkey-chortle of Irish', 'hard iced caramels' and the names of those who had made and sold them (ll. 9–12). In this way, the poem performs a return to the material world, as if possessed by the '*anima*' of the late painter.

In a similar way, in the first poem of a sequence entitled 'Wraiths', dedicated to Ciaran Carson, Heaney develops the legend of Caolite disappearing into a magical, faery underworld (*HC* 66).[73] He pictures himself being led 'into the ground' by an unnamed, mysterious 'she' (l. 1), a homonym of the poem's title, '*Sidhe*', meaning 'fairy'. As they follow the 'gleam / And seam of sand like white gold', the two Irish figures briefly take on the appearance of Aeneas and the Sibyl, following the gleam of the golden bough (*HC* 66).[74] The second part of the poem pictures them looking out from under the hill to the light, 'holding hands, / Inhaling the excavated bank.' (ll. 8–9) Holding hands, the poet seems to have been led across into the otherworld as, in the last tercet, he imagines his own disappearance:

Zoom in over our shoulders,
A tunnelling shot that accelerates and flares.
Discover us against weird brightness. Cut. (*HC* 66, ll. 10–12)

He addresses the reader directly in filmic language, as if he were an actor–director instructing his cameraman how to shoot the scene: 'zoom in', 'a tunnelling shot', 'cut'. The last shot, freeze-framing the two figures 'against weird brightness', moves in two directions at once. The imperative 'Cut' drops the shutter down on the poet and his *sidhe*, sending him, like Caolite, into the faery otherworld. But it also finalises the filmic tableau of the two figures as they face outwards, with their backs to the weird brightness. Just as the poet's 'I' disappears, the tableau of the two illuminated figures enters the viewer's gaze as a separate *poesis*, or made thing. In Virgilian terms, this dramatises the poet becoming a wraith, slipping across the River Styx into Hades, while the art work slips across the River Lethe in the other direction, entering its second life in *altera corpora*.

In the last artist's elegy in the volume, '"The door was open and the house was dark"', Heaney commemorates David Hammond, the Belfast singer, filmmaker, broadcaster and 'lord of misrule', who died almost exactly two years after helping to bear Heaney downstairs after his stroke (*HC* 82).[75] Heaney's elegy for his friend

---

72. In Acts 3: 19–21, *apokatastasis* is the Greek word for a return of the universe to its ideal state.
73. Ciaran Carson was alive when Heaney dedicated these poems to him (he died on 6 October 2019).
74. On '*Sidhe*', see P. McDonald (2019), 177.
75. Heaney, 'David Hammond' (2008); McCrum (2009).

reportedly came to him in a dream, already fully fashioned in four tercets with a Dantean trailing last line.⁷⁶ The opening tercet has a dream-like bareness and simplicity:

> The door was open and the house was dark
> Wherefore I called his name, although I knew
> The answer this time would be silence (*HC* 82, ll. 1–3)

The 'wherefore' adds a touch of Biblical formality to an otherwise intimate tone.⁷⁷ A familiarity with 'his name' is assumed, as is the poignancy of 'silence' coming from the house that had formerly been a 'veritable court of music and poetry.'⁷⁸ The silence seems to be a negative imprint of the late singer's presence, and as the poet stands and listens, it flows out from the house of death into the material world again: 'it grew / Backwards and down and out into the street' (ll. 4–5). So, once again, as the artist's presence is withdrawn, a made thing, in this case a silence with a musical shape, enters its second life in cultural memory. The poet feels cut off from his friend, 'for the first them there and then, a stranger' (l. 8). But he is also aware of

>   a not unwelcoming
> Emptiness, as in a midnight hangar
> On an overgrown airfield (ll. 10–13).

As Andrew Auge notes, an airfield hangar is a point of departure as well as a destination.⁷⁹ The 'not unwelcoming / Emptiness' beckons Heaney to 'take flight' (ll. 11–12, 9), a gesture of release that seems to be enacted in the next two poems, which bring the volume to a close. There are also close thematic links between the elegy and these last two, valedictory, poems. In his 2008 obituary for Hammond, Heaney remembered how his friend had once climbed the mast of a fibreglass boat 'and very nearly capsized us in the middle of Lough Erne.'⁸⁰ In 'In the Attic', Heaney imagines himself as a ship's boy confidently climbing the mast of a boat that is tossed 'to and fro' but does not capsize (*HC* 83, l. 15). Both these poems end with a sense of imminent, otherworldly departure, which is mirrored by the kite's arrival, as if from the underworld, in the volume's final poem.

---

76. '"The dream is just recorded in verse that rhymes. It was an extremely strange, haunting dream. One of those dreams that marks, that you don't forget", he said.' (Heaney, qtd in Flanagan, 2010).
77. A typescript draft crosses out the Biblical 'Wherefore', replacing it with a plain 'Which is why'. He also added 'only' before 'answer'. But the final version reverts to the original, exactly as it came to him from the dream (*LP* I.xviii.1).
78. Heaney, 'David Hammond' (2008).
79. Auge (2016), 36. Contrastingly, Kevin Murphy notes that the adjective 'overgrown' recurs four times in *Human Chain*, and with each repetition has an 'increasingly and cumulatively dolorous' effect (2016, 367).
80. Heaney, 'David Hammond' (2008).

IV. 'WIND-DRINK' AND WINDFALL

As at the end of 'Route 110', the last two poems of *Human Chain* weave together images of mortality and natality, counteracting the sense of a closing cadence with the discovery of new beginnings. Memories of the poet's grandfather and reflections on his own ageing are translated into a celebration of childhood imagination and infant birth. At the same time, both poems develop the notion of art slipping from the hands of its individual creator and entering the common *corpus* of cultural memory.

In the penultimate poem, 'In the Attic', Heaney recalls a childhood exchange with his grandfather (*HC* 83–4). His boyhood self has just returned from seeing a film version of Robert Louis Stevenson's coming-of-age novel, *Treasure Island*. His grandfather asks him about a character in the novel, a villainous pirate named Israel Hands, but he misremembers the first name as 'Isaac'. 'Somehow in that little slip,' Heaney later reflected,

> I was vouchsafed a glimpse of the mysterious gulf between childhood and old age . . . What that shift from Israel to Isaac told me was that he had read *Treasure Island* decades before, and that it had stayed with him and was a part of everything that had happened to him in between and the fleetness of all that was somehow processed into his slip of memory. (*SS* 27)

The grandfather's memory lapse is a sign of old age and a premonition of the final, 'once and for all' rupture (III.8), but it also reveals a deep continuity of identity: '*Treasure Island* . . . had stayed with him and was a part of everything that had happened to him'. Heaney draws on the analogy with Stevenson's two protagonists, Jim Hawkins and Israel Hands, to reflect on the gulf between childhood and old age, in his grandfather's life and in his own, and at the same time he discovers the continuities that bind them into one human chain.

As a classic adventure novel read by both children and adults, *Treasure Island* is a particularly apt intertext for Heaney's interweaving of childhood and old age.[81] But the poem also evidences his recent preoccupation with Virgil's *ter conatus* episode, as well as the forgetful draught from the River Lethe, as suggested by the draft title, 'Wind-drink'. The typescript draft is dated 24/5 April 2008: that is, within days of Heaney's RTÉ interview on *The Riverbank Field*, within weeks of his beginning the book-length translation of *Aeneid VI*, and in the same year as his publication of the Palinurus translation.[82] In the fall of Israel Hands there is an elegiac echo of Virgil's Palinurus, the ghost whose body had been plunged in the sea and drowned, but whose name survives in the cultural memory, in part thanks to Heaney's own translation of the episode. The way his grandfather forgets the pirate's first name associates old age with Lethean oblivion. And the pirate's last name, 'Hands', punningly reprises all the other outstretched hands that try and fail to embrace phantoms elsewhere in

---

81. The novel was originally serialised in a children's magazine (1881–2), then published as *Sea Cook: A Story for Boys* (1883). On the child–adult crossover novel, see Falconer (2009).
82. See Chapter 7, Section I.

Human Chain. Even Israel's double-death ('"being both shot and drowned"', I.9) is reminiscent of Virgil's twice-fallen leaves, lapsing across the River Styx.

Heaney's poem contrasts the pirate's fall with the surefootedness of Jim Hawkins, aloft on the mast of the *Hispaniola*. In doing so, he counteracts the cadence of old age with a buoyancy he associates with childhood and the lyric imagination. The first two sections of his four-part poem focus on images of suspension and uplift, beginning with an extended simile which compares himself in his attic studio to Stevenson's young protagonist:

> Like Jim Hawkins aloft in the cross-trees
> Of *Hispaniola*, nothing underneath him
> But still green water and clean bottom sand, (HC 83, I.1–3)

In the typescript draft, Heaney introduces the 'I' as the subject of the simile in the opening line: 'These mornings I wake up out of it, / Like Jim' and so on.[83] But in the published version, the pronoun is withheld for another eleven lines, so that the reader is held in suspense for the duration of the simile, mirroring the boy's suspension on the ship's mast. Even Jim's enemy, Israel, participates in this comedic, upward cadence in the first section of the poem: surfacing in the water as Jim looks down from above, his corpse 'Appears to rise again' (I.8).

In Part II, Heaney pursues the analogy further, comparing the birch tree outside his window to the ship's mast, and himself to the boy on the rigging. '[W]ind-drunk', he has slipped backwards in time and opened himself to the marvellous, 'Rubbing his eyes to believe them' (II.6, 8). At the same time, he is clearly an adult poet in his prime, 'Shipshaped in the crow's nest of a life, . . . braced // By all that's thrumming up from keel to masthead' (II.6–7). The poet's skill requires powers of divination (to read what thrums up from below) and also mental buoyancy (to stay aloft against the buffeting wind). In the final line, his imagination surpasses the scene in the novel in the sense that, while Jim is stuck on the mast of a grounded ship, Heaney is aloft in a boat of poetry that is alive and seemingly full sail. Though firmly rooted in the garden below, the crown of his 'most / Buoyant, billowy, topgallant birch' (II.8–9) is full of lively movement, accentuated by triple alliteration on the run of stressed first syllables in line 9.

The third part of the poem, however, hosts a series of counter-images of falling and temporal decline. Unlike the grandfather in 'Album, V', who is successfully surprised into an embrace, this one returns to Heaney as an ungraspable phantom, 'Ghost-footing' in the hallway, 'His voice a-waver' (III.1, 3). The memory lapse strikes the poet as a sign of imminent mortality: 'His mistake perpetual, once and for all, / Like the single splash where Israel's body fell.' (III.8–9) The memory slip is 'perpetual', perhaps because Heaney recalled it repeatedly, but in any case, the repetition itself works as an uncanny signifier of death. The twice-killed Israel, in this section of the poem, suffers a singular, absolute and irreversible fall (which is 'perpetual', perhaps, in that it recurs every time the novel is read). In Part IV,

---

83. 'Wind-drink', *LP* I.xviii.1.

Heaney identifies with his grandfather's forgetfulness, with his unsteady step, and with the image of Israel's fall: 'As I age and blank on names, / As my uncertainty on stairs', 'As the memorable bottoms out / Into the irretrievable' (IV.1–2, 5–6). The third section, meanwhile, comes to rest on a chilling phrase, 'when Israel's body fell', which sums up the weight of mortal cadence in the poem (III.9).

In Part IV, the sense of Lethean cadence is once again reversed or counteracted, this time with a series of images balancing uplift and fall. The poet's sensation of vertigo is paradoxically caused by his mounting the attic stairs. And conversely, his lapsing memory is compared to 'the lightheadedness // Of a cabin boy's first time on the rigging', thus creating a rise out of his imminent fall. These reversals might lead us to reflect that 'Isaac', the name mistakenly recalled by Heaney's grandfather, means 'he shall laugh' in Hebrew, and in Genesis, Abraham's son Isaac is the boy saved from death.[84] In the final tercet, the poet is left anticipating a sea voyage that sounds at once like a closing cadence and the start of a fresh adventure:

> It's not that I can't imagine still
> That slight untoward rupture and world-tilt
> As a wind freshened and the anchor weighed. (*HC* 84)

The typescript draft's original phrase, 'it's not that I forget', is much reworked and eventually replaced by 'can't imagine still'.[85] The change of verb concedes the Lethean loss of memory but the poet declares he can *imagine* being a cabin-boy high on the ship's mast. And 'still' insists on a continuum of memory, at some level, because he is imagining something he knows he has imagined before. As with the phrase 'it can't not conjure' in 'The Riverbank Field', here the double negative registers the effort of counteracting the given, but the lift-off into the marvellous is still achieved. Youth and age are finely balanced in the last two verbs, 'freshened' and 'weighed'. That final verb even contains two opposing cadences within itself: 'weighed' implies a gravitational fall, but also, in the nautical sense, 'weighing anchor' refers to the anchor being lifted and the ship being released.

All the same, the nature of the release is left in the balance. The 'untoward rupture' of the ship starting to move could equally imply a final, fatal departure, as in the last line of '*Sidhe*'. In the final line, the poem undergoes a lapse of time from present to past tense, which would support such an interpretation. On the other hand, the tense shift might also signal a change of genre and chronotope, from lyric present to the historic past of narrative fiction. This would suggest that the poet has successfully re-entered the world of *Treasure Island*, and is even experiencing the novel as if reading it for the first time. With the Virgilian parallel in mind, moreover, the tense change implies another genre shift, from lyric to epic, which characteristically begins

---

84. In Genesis 17, Abraham laughs at the thought of fathering a son at a hundred years old, by his wife Sarah, aged ninety, and so calls his son 'Isaac' or 'Yshaq', meaning 'he shall laugh'. In Genesis 22, God tests Abraham's faith by commanding him to sacrifice his son, but then saves the boy at the last minute.
85. 'Wind-drink', *LP* I.xviii.

with a sea voyage. Heaney would shortly translate the opening lines of *Aeneid VI*, where the hero sets forth: 'In tears as he speaks, Aeneas loosens out sail / And gives the whole fleet its head' (A.1–2). Whatever world-tilt has taken place, the poet's 'I' has dropped away with the tense shift, suggesting that the poem has, in the process, escaped its individual author and rejoined the common sea of poetry.

'In the Attic' originally brought the collection to a close, but after the birth of his second grandchild, Heaney composed 'A Kite for Aibhín', adding it to the end of *Human Chain* to ensure a 'parity of esteem' with Anna Rose, the dedicatee of 'Route 110'.[86] As in 'Route 110, XII', where the infant arrives from across the Lethe, so this time a kite, symbolising the new grandchild, arrives borne on 'Air from another life and time and place' (HC 85, l. 1). Apart from this relatively overt allusion to the Lethean passage, 'A Kite for Aibhín' remembers and recapitulates a whole chain of associations with Virgil and earlier poems by Heaney. The poem is adapted from a literal translation of Giovanni Pascoli's 'L'Aquilone', which Heaney had recently completed and published in full.[87] This fresh adaptation transforms Pascoli's kite poem from an elegy for a young boy into a thanks-offering for a new birth. At the same time, Heaney is modulating Virgil's elegies for fallen youth into a celebration of generational, artistic and cultural renewal.

Pascoli's 'L'Aquilone' is a sixty-four-line poem written, like much of *Human Chain*, in Dantean *terza rima*. It begins with a paradisal scene of children flying kites in Urbino and then shifts to elegy in its final section: one of the kite-fliers, a beautiful young boy, has died, and lies 'like a flower in bloom that closes and reforms / Its petals into itself', in the presence of his grieving mother.[88] When Heaney was first shown a copy of 'L'Aquilone', on a visit to Urbino, he was struck by how the poem and the setting formed a triangular connection with Yeats's poem 'Upon Urbino's windy hill' and his own earlier poem 'A Kite for Michael and Christopher', addressed to his two young sons.[89] In 'A Kite for Aibhín', he adapts his earlier, full-length translation of 'L'Aquilone' to include a reference to the kite-flying episode with his own boys. The 2009 translation had rendered Pascoli's lines in this way:

So now we take our stand, halt opposite
Urbino's windy hill: each scans the blue
And picks his spot to launch his long-tailed comet. (ll. 22–4)

---

86. Heaney wrote poems for three granddaughters: Christopher Heaney's daughter, Anna Rose ('Route 110, XII'); Michael Heaney's daughter, Aibhín ('A Kite for Aibhín'); and Christopher Heaney's second daughter, Síofra ('In Time', composed 18 August 2013, two weeks before Heaney's death). See Falvey (2018).
87. 'The Kite, a literal translation of Pascoli's "L'Aquilone" by Seamus Heaney', in Mulligan, ed., *Augury: To Mary Kelleher* (2009). For Heaney's account of the poem's genesis, see 'On Home Ground' (2012–13), 21f. See also, Sonzogni (2014). Lines 30–64 of the translation were later published in Brock, ed., *The FSG Book of Twentieth Century Italian Poetry* (2012), 14–17. For 'L'Aquilone' [1907], see Pascoli (1971), 147–50.
88. Translation by Heaney (2009), ll. 55–6.
89. Yeats, 'To a Wealthy Man . . .', l. 17 (1992, 158); Heaney, 'A Kite for Michael and Christopher' (*SI* 44). Heaney discusses the Urbino encounter in 'On Home Ground', 21ff.

In 'A Kite for Aibhín', Heaney transports the scene in Urbino to his Irish home ground, turning the Italian kite-fliers into members of his own family:

> I take my stand again, halt opposite
> Anahorish Hill to scan the blue,
> Back in that field to launch our long-tailed comet. (HC 85, 7–9)

While maintaining the present tense, Heaney shifts back in time to the event described in 'A Kite for Michael and Christopher', where the poet had placed a kite-string into his children's hands and told them to get used to its 'long-tailed pull of grief.' (SI 44) Part of the kite-string's pull of grief was the memory of a family tragedy in the earlier generation, the death of Heaney's brother Christopher at four years old. At his public reading in Dublin, Heaney drew out the links in this elegiac human chain by reading, first, 'Midterm Break', a heart-breaking poem about Christopher's fatal accident, then the kite poem for his own two sons Michael and Christopher, and finally, 'A Kite for Aibhín'.[90]

In comparing the kite to 'a thin-stemmed flower', Heaney also draws on a Virgilian chain of reference that extends and amplifies the elegiac resonance of these family memories. Last to be identified among the souls waiting by the River Lethe is the shade of Marcellus, Augustus' nephew and heir. In *Aeneid VI*, Anchises foresees the early death of this talented, much-loved youth and calls for flowers to mourn him: '*manibus date lilia plenis, / purpureos spargam flores*' ('Load my arms with lilies, let me scatter / Purple flowers').[91] These lines, when read aloud to Augustus' family, are said to have caused Marcellus' mother to collapse in a faint. This eulogy for Marcellus in turn recalls the death of the young Trojan soldier Euryalus, whose death is compared to a flower bowing 'its head upon its tired stalk' in *Aeneid IX*.[92] When the poet 'takes his stand' on an Irish hillside in 'A Kite for Aibhín', he does so in remembrance of these collected griefs, and his most intimate, familial memories become interwoven with sorrows from Italy, both ancient and modern.

At the same time, the kite in this poem flies higher, with more energy and *élan*, than in any of these recollected episodes. Heaney delights in the upward climb of this creature of air, with a run of quick, lively verbs: 'And now it hovers, tugs, veers, dives askew, / Lifts itself, goes with the wind' (ll. 10–11). With the arrival of the new-born *anima*, we watch the poem itself taking shape, also symbolised in the upward cadence of the kite. As it 'Rises, and my hand is like a spindle, / Unspooling', the poet becomes its receptive diviner on the ground (ll. 13–14). Here he divines a longing for translation that recalls the figures waiting on Lethe's riverbank, in Poem XI of 'Route 110' and at the end of 'The Riverbank Field':

---

90. Heaney, at *Poetry Ireland* (Dublin, February 2010). The elegiac chain begins even earlier, with Heaney's positive memory of a rare moment in childhood when his father did this 'extraordinary thing' of flying a kite with him, but 'there was gravity in that string' ('Out of the Marvellous', 2009).
91. Ae.VI.883–4. Trans. Heaney, A.1119–200.
92. Trans. Fitzgerald (1983), 275. See Chapter 7, Section I.

> Climbing and carrying, carrying farther, higher //
> The longing in the breast and planted feet
> And gazing face and heart of the kite flier (ll. 15–17)

In the last two lines of the poem, Heaney breaks away from his Italian model and the poem veers at last into its own clear space:

> Until string breaks and – separate, elate – //
> The kite takes off, itself alone, a windfall. (ll 18–19)

The snap of the kite-string, like an umbilical cord being cut, releases the child into the world, and the poem from its chain of inter- and intra-texts. The final word, 'windfall', which has no exact equivalent in Pascoli's poem, commonly applies to fruit 'blown down by the wind', and metaphorically, to an 'unexpected profit', such as a legacy in a will (OED 1–3).[93] In Heaney's poem, the windfall describes the lucky arrival of a new grandchild and the change of direction in a long series of kite poems. Not only is the poem escaping the originary, Italian text, but it is slipping out of reach of Heaney's own elegiac kite poems. Such writing is, as Heaney puts it elsewhere, 'an escape from self-obsession . . . If the made thing happens, you have escaped'.[94] The 'fall' in 'windfall' also reminds us that this kite will presumably come to earth somewhere. So this is a breakaway and release into the mortal condition, not out of it, in Heaney's last, joyful variation on Virgilian cadence. In fact, it perfectly complements the end of 'In the Attic', since 'windfall' contains the metaphor of something light falling, while 'anchor weighed' describes something heavy being raised.

*

As elsewhere in *Human Chain*, this final poem demonstrates the uplift and release of lyric working to counterbalance the weight of remembered loss. Heaney's continuous allusions to the lapse of Virgilian *animae* and the Lethean release from memory all show how poetry, and art in general, are transformed and refreshed as they are forwarded in time.

For Heaney, Virgil's poetry is still the music of the *lacrimae rerum*, the tears of things. But the poet's underworld journey is no longer only or primarily concerned with memory and the passing on of wisdom. It is also about the capacity to be surprised; it is about babyhood, catharsis and the shedding of old griefs.

---

93. Heaney's full-length translation uses the word twice, but on both occasions he is paraphrasing a different image in the Italian: (1) 'the kite a thin-stemmed flower / Borne far away to flower again as windfall' translates '*come un fiore che fugga su lo stelo / esile, e vada a rifiorir lontano*' (ll. 29–30); (2) 'You who were lucky to have seen the fallen / Only in the windfall of a kite' translates '*felice te che al vento / non vedesti cader gli aquiloni!*' (ll. 44–5)
94. Heaney, 'Out of the Marvellous' (2009).

9. A Double Music: *Aeneid* Book VI

Heaney's translation of *Aeneid VI* was published three years after his death, so it was, in a sense, delivered to us like an *anima* from the underworld, newly borne across the River Lethe. While Heaney meditates on the afterlife of poetry in *Human Chain*, his *Aeneid Book VI* performs that posthumous flight into the common *corpus* of cultural memory. The book-length translation constitutes the final act in Heaney's ongoing dialogue with Virgil, which centres on the good of poetry both for the individual and for society as a whole. In terms of Heaney's inner debate between poetry's contrasting virtues – steadfastness or spontaneity, *pietas* or lyric release, the *Aeneid* translation swings the pendulum back towards epic *labor* and *pietas*. But, as we shall see, Heaney also foregrounds the possibilities of lyric flight in Aeneas' journey underground.

In this translation, Heaney deliberately takes on Virgil's role as the bridge or mediator between different cultures and historical eras. By modelling his three major works on Theocritus, Hesiod and Homer, respectively, Virgil had 'carried the heritage of ancient Greek poetry forward into the civilisation of Rome.'[1] Heaney is likewise forwarding the heritage of ancient Rome into the twenty-first century, in a translation that distinctively accentuates Virgil's love of *patria* rather than Roman *imperium*. Moreover, while, in *Human Chain*, Heaney draws on a compendium of Virgilian phrases and motifs to meditate on the nature of mortal cadence, here he is immersed in transposing the poetic cadence: that is, the voicing and rhythmic flow, of Virgil's lines. He bridges the temporal distance between Virgil's times and our own, in part, by mediating between two poetic rhythms and two tonal registers, creating a continuous dialogue at the very heart of his translation.[2] This chapter will explore this doubleness of rhythm and tone, a fundamental aspect of Heaney's

---

1. Heaney, *BBC* (2008).
2. For further commentary on Heaney's *Aeneid Book VI*, see Balmer (2016), Burrow (2016); Craven (2016); S. J. Harrison (2019), 244–62; Haughton (2016); Hexter (2016); Jarman (2016); Kirchwey (2016); Lysaght (2016); McNamara (2017); Motion (2016); Nelis (2017); O'Donoghue (2016); Padel (2016); and Sexton (2016).

translation that was largely overlooked by reviewers of the volume in 2016. The final section of the chapter will consider Aeneas's *katabasis* as a mythic analogue for the poet's redress to historical adversity. But we should begin with Heaney's paratextual remarks on his translation, which, though brief and fragmentary, help to clarify what is at stake for him in this last settlement with Virgil's Book of the Dead.[3]

I. INTRODUCING *BOOK VI*

In a note entitled 'Katabasis, Eschatalogical', Heaney begins what may have been intended as an Afterword to his translation:

> For the contemporary reader, it is the best of books and the worst of books. Best because of its mythopoeic visions, the twilit fetch of its language, the pathos of the many encounters it allows the living Aeneas with his familiar dead. Worst because of its imperial certitude, its celebration of Rome's manifest destiny and the catalogue of Roman heroes . . .[4]

Despite its mock-scholarly title, this brief note introduces *Aeneid* VI as a text that is already firmly embedded in popular cultural memory. It assumes a familiarity with Book VI as one of the canonical texts in the literary tradition of *katabasis*, with a cultural reach that extends far beyond its already pivotal role as the threshold crossing between the Odyssean and Iliadic halves of Virgil's *Aeneid*. Like Dickens's *A Tale of Two Cities*, echoed in the first sentence, Aeneas' journey into the underworld is an already familiar story.[5] This assumption of our familiarity with the poem is reduplicated on the cover of the Faber edition, which presents a block of six-letter names, 'Seamus', 'Heaney', '*Aeneid*' and 'Book VI', while omitting 'Virgil' as already too present to need naming.

Beyond being familiar, Book VI is the 'best' and worst' of the *Aeneid*'s twelve books because it is at once the most poetically attractive and the most entrenched in Augustan political ideology. Stephen Harrison remarks of this description that Heaney seems 'unaware of the pessimistic "Harvard" interpretation of the poem . . . and can only envisage a straightforwardly triumphalist reading'.[6] I would agree that this is how Heaney read Anchises' catalogue of heroes but he has a more complex, nuanced approach to other parts of the book, and the poem as a whole. His translation of Anchises' speech, '*parcere subiectis*' ('to spare the conquered'), is carefully restrained, and an anti-imperialist slant emerges in many other passages, as we will

---

3. 'Paratext' refers to the textual elements surrounding the main body of a work; in this case, the 'Translator's Note' (A vii–ix), *Note on the Text* (A 51) and quotation on the back cover of the 2016 Faber edition. For the concept, see Gérard Genette, *Paratexts* (1997).
4. The volume's editors, Catherine Heaney and Matthew Hollis, provide this 'tantalising fragment' of an Afterword, at the head of their 'Note on the Text' (A 51).
5. 'It was the best of times, it was the worst of times', the opening sentence of Charles Dickens's *A Tale of Two Cities* (London: Penguin, 2003).
6. S. J. Harrison (2019), 254.

see below. More importantly, as this note makes clear, Heaney suggests the *poetry* of Book VI is at odds with its *political* agenda; as he puts it in his radio essay, there is a 'latent tension' between Virgil's 'poetic personality' and his official role as spokesman for Augustus.[7] In his 'Translator's Note', Heaney admits that he finds the imperial parade the least poetic lines in the book:[8]

> the beginning and middle ... are alive with poetic and narrative energy, but not so the ending. By the time the story reaches its climax in Anchises' vision of a glorious Roman race ..., the translator is likely to have moved from inspiration to grim determination (viii–ix)

Heaney had in fact completed an entire first draft of the book by the end of 2008, although he had 'quailed' over translating Anchises' 'voice-over prophecy / history of Rome'.[9] By 2011, he had approved a proof of the final draft, up to line 1065, for an arthouse edition to be published by Bonnefant Press (A 52).[10] But the Bonnefant edition stalled, and Heaney still had not approved the final 150 lines of the manuscript; his Faber editors describe the published version as 'final' but not 'finished', much like Virgil's *Aeneid*, which was unfinished when Virgil succumbed to a fatal fever in Brundisium, in 19 BCE.[11] In Heaney's case, the delays to publication suggest that he continued to wrestle with the imperial vision that surfaces at the end of Book VI. If translating the book fulfilled some need for epic structure and myth in his writing, he seems to have been constitutionally averse to the epic as a foundational narrative for nation, state or empire. Anchises' catalogue of heroes might have been celebratory for Virgil's readers, but for Heaney it was depressing, in the way that Michael's prophecy is at the end of *Paradise Lost*:

> so shall the world go on,
> To good malignant, to bad men benign,
> Under her own weight groaning till the day
> Appear of respiration to the just (*PL*.XII.537–40)

But counterbalancing the triumphant parade of military heroes, Book VI offers the contemporary reader 'its mythopoeic visions, the twilit fetch of its language, the pathos of the many encounters it allows the living Aeneas with his familiar dead'.

---

7. See Chapter 7 for a discussion of Anchises' '*parcere subiectis*' speech and the 2008 BBC Radio 3 essay.
8. Ae.VI.756–886; in Heaney's translation, A.1022–202.
9. Letter to Sarah Ruden, 26 July 2008. See Chapter 7, Section II.
10. With illustrations by Jan Hendrix, the Bonnefant volume corresponds to the 'bijou limited edition' that Heaney initially thought would 'give me some cover', in his letter to Sarah Ruden, 9 May 2009. Helen Vendler published a number of extracts from the planned Bonnefant Press edition in her 2012 anthology of Heaney's classical poems, *Stone from Delphi*.
11. A 53. Famously, the *Aeneid* survives only because Virgil's friend Varius disobeyed his instructions to burn the work after his death. See *Vita Suetonii Vulgo Donatiana*, in Ziolkowski and Putnam, *The Virgilian Tradition*, 193.

These aspects of the book are fruits of Virgil's 'poetic personality', which for Heaney clearly work against the poem's Augustan ideology. As this brief description already suggests, Heaney's Aeneas is more the grieving son, motivated by love and loss, than the founder of Rome; and Anchises is more the lost, familiar father than the dynastic patriarch. With its 'twilit fetch', the very language of Book VI is endowed with subversive, *katabatic* agency and intention since, as a noun, 'fetch' has a primary meaning of 'bringing from a distance, or reaching after' (*OED*, n.1, 1a). In its proximity to the adjectival form, 'fetching' ('alluring, fascinating'), 'fetch' suggests a language possessing Orphic charm and power to summon the dead. Moreover, 'fetch' has another sense, only ever in popular use in Ireland, which is 'apparition, double, or wraith of a living person' (*OED*, n.2, 1). So the poetry of Book VI is ghostly in a way that will allow Heaney to speak to and for his own familiar dead, as he follows in the footsteps of Aeneas.

The back cover blurb on the Faber edition gives a further indication of what the underworld journey had come to mean for Heaney, by the time he came to translate Book VI in its entirety:

> All the great myths are consistent with what you need. You need a sense of moving on, crossing something – into the dark ... into the unknown. The great mythical stories of the afterworld are stories which stay with you and which ease you towards the end, towards a destination and a transition.

We have seen how Heaney's interest in Orpheus shifts from the poet's first trial in Hades to his greater trial in Thrace, where he meets his end but his song is taken up and transformed by other singers. In *The Riverbank Field* and *Human Chain*, Heaney takes up Virgil's description of the River Lethe as a transformative threshold space where oblivion leads to regeneration and new life. His book-length translation invites us to read Aeneas' entire journey into the dark in similar terms, as a mythic story that can 'ease you towards the end', throwing light on the mortal condition but also transforming the sense of closure into openness ('the end' becoming 'a destination and a transition'). At the level of sound, the opening line of Heaney's translation enacts this fundamental shift of perspective on mortality and loss: 'In tears as he speaks, Aeneas loosens out sail' (A.1). From the very start of the book, Aeneas is a character in mourning: he has lost his old world and not yet laid claim to the new one, *Italia*. The line starts with tight-fisted assonance (tears, speaks, Aeneas), the scrunched-up sound of grief, and then unfolds into a lovely series of open vowels: 'loosens out sail'. A destination and a transition.

The 'Translator's Note' prefacing the translation evinces this same preoccupation with *katabasis* as a journey into the dark which simultaneously opens up possibilities of regenerative renewal. Heaney begins by acknowledging his gratitude to his former Latin teacher, Father Michael McGlinchey. The present translation is 'the result of a lifelong desire to honour [his] memory', he tells us (A vii). After his father's death, he 'took special note of ... Aeneas' journey to meet the shade of his father Anchises' (ibid.). In translating Book VI, Heaney is pursuing an underworldly encounter with these two familiar shades. 'But the impulse to go ahead ... arrived', finally, with the celebration of new birth in 'Route 110', 'written to greet the birth of a first granddaughter' (ibid.). This is to suggest that Heaney's book-length translation is motivated both by *pietas* (writing 'in memory' of his teacher) and a desire for spontaneity and new life ('elated and inspired' by the infant birth, A viii). In the following paragraph, where he expounds on his 'mythic method' in 'Route 110', he draws our attention to Anchises' description of the souls awaiting rebirth, but he makes no mention of the catalogue of heroes destined for glorious military careers (A viii).

Heaney's *pietas* includes a sense of attachment and obligation to his former Latin schoolmaster, to his local district in County Derry, to the Northern Irish Catholic community, to his absent parents and literary mentors, to Virgil himself and other poetic exemplars, to the mainstream European literary tradition and its foundational myths and imaginary landscapes, and to marginalised literary voices challenging that mainstream tradition and changing the inherited mythic landscape. The list of attachments could be greatly extended, but what the 'Translator's Note' establishes is that Heaney conceives the work as a gesture of *pietas*, an expression of gratitude, obligation and attachment. The book-length translation thus develops Heaney's preoccupations in the 'Palinurus' extract, and his earlier identifications with the Tollund Man, about whom he had written, 'I had a sense of crossing a line really, that my whole being was involved in the sense of – the root sense – of religion, being bonded to something, being bound to something. I felt it a vow; I felt my whole being caught in this'.[12] Heaney identifies with the *pius* Aeneas' descent into the underworld as an act of 'surrendering one's imagination' to a greater good.[13] At the same time, however, Heaney still sees the supernatural threshold crossing as the model of a possible, antithetical gesture of lyric release from such attachments, as a 'door into the light' which affirms the seeker's integrity and inner freedom.[14] As a fragment detached from Virgil's twelve-book epic, Heaney's translation of Book VI offers the poet and his readers a chance 'to be liberated and distanced, . . . to be open, unpredictably susceptible, lyrically opportunistic.'[15]

In the last paragraph of the 'Translator's Note', Heaney paints two pictures of himself as a translator. There is firstly, the 'sixth form homunculus' who proceeds dutifully, disentangling the Latin syntax and striving for accuracy (A ix). And secondly, there is the poet,

> who has things other than literal accuracy on his mind and in his ear: rhythm and metre and lineation, the voice and its pacing, the need for a diction decorous enough for Virgil but not so antique as to sound out of tune with a more

---

12. 'An Interview with Seamus Heaney by James Randall', *Ploughshares* (1979).
13. Ibid.
14. 'I want a door into the light. And I suppose as a natural corollary or antithesis to the surrender, to surrendering one's imagination to something as embracing as myth or landscape, I really wanted to come back to be able to use the first person singular to mean me and my lifetime' (ibid.).
15. Heaney and Deane, 'Unhappy and At Home' (1977), 66.

contemporary idiom – all the fleeting, fitful anxieties that afflict the literary translator. (A ix)

Rhythm is central to Heaney's writing, as is evident in the pacing of this sentence: 'in his ear' followed by the accumulating beat of an affective parataxis ('and . . . and . . . and'). The very reach of the syntax conveys the 'literary' translator's sense of release from the constraints of the 'inner literalist'. There is a certain melancholy in his admission of 'fitful anxieties' but the playful use of alliteration gives those anxieties an Ariel lift and fleeting lightness. Like the bird-king Sweeney and Virgil's migrant hero, Heaney's condition as a poet translator is unhoused and airborne; he flits between languages, fully at home in neither.[16] Rhythmically, his translation oscillates between two poetic traditions, as we will see below.

In terms of tone and register, Heaney identifies 'the need for a diction decorous enough for Virgil', which, although seemingly straightforward enough, reveals a new emphasis in his book-length translation. Previously, what he has wanted us to hear in Virgil's poetry is the sound of the carthorse rather than the court, and the speech of 'hard-wrought, hard-bitten countrymen'.[17] Compared to his earlier translation extracts, the book-length translation has a greater elegance and formality. Here, perhaps for the first time, we hear a 'canonical serenity' in Heaney's rendering of *Aeneid VI* (BBC). But this note also alerts us to the way Heaney plays with different tonalities, bridging the distance between 'antique' and 'contemporary', and juxtaposing an outward-facing, public voice with one of intimate reverie and introspection.

II. BETWEEN TWO RHYTHMS

Introducing his translation of *Beowulf* in 1999, Heaney had suggested that rhythm and tone comprise the twin prongs of a translator's 'tuning fork':

> It is one thing to find lexical meanings for the words and to have some feel for how the metre might go, but it is quite another thing to find the tuning fork that will give you the note and pitch for the overall music of the work. Without some melody sensed or promised, it is simply impossible for a poet to establish the translator's right of way into and through a text. (*Beowulf*, xxvi)

This virtual, auditory instrument operates like a divining rod, or golden bough, providing the translator with a means of accessing the music of the originary text. So

---

16. Cf. Dryden, *The Works of Virgil*, *The Sixth Book*: 'But, oh! commit not thy prophetick Mind / To flitting Leaves, the sport of ev'ry Wind:' (ll. 116–17, Vol. 5, p. 530); 'Then thrice, around his Neck, his Arms he threw; / And thrice the flitting Shadow slip'd away; / Like Winds, or empty Dreams, that fly the Day.' (ll. 950–2, p. 559)
17. BBC (2008), where he is referring to the mixed style of the *Eclogues*, but I think he hears a 'country voice' in all of Virgil's poetry.

what is Heaney's 'tuning fork' for his new translation of *Aeneid VI*? Rhythmically, the book-length translation differs from the translation extracts, 'The Golden Bough' and 'Palinurus'. Indeed, without some familiarity with these earlier experiments, it is possible to miss the subtle complexity of the meter and rhythm in Heaney's 2016 translation. Most of the volume's reviewers assumed the translation was composed in a loose iambic pentameter. Thus, the meter was variously described as 'easy, flowing post-Shakespearean blank verse', 'loose pentameters, generally 11-syllable lines of blank verse', 'a loose five-beat line' and 'loose pentameters and hendecasyllabics – 11-syllable lines – of post-Shakespearean English blank verse.'[18] While the regular meter of English blank verse is certainly audible in Heaney's book-length translation, it is heard against the counterpoint of a persistent dactylic beat (˜˜) and/or six-beat line, reminiscent of classical epic hexameter. This double heartbeat is sustained throughout the entire book-length translation. Two reviewers, Andrew Motion and Colin Burrow, also noticed a counterpoint in Heaney's rhythm, although their judgement of the effect was less favourable than mine.[19]

That Heaney's translation does not adhere to a regular five-beat rhythm becomes evident when it is set beside his mentor Robert Fitzgerald's translation, which *is* in iambic pentameter. Here are the Trojans landing in Italy and leaping ashore, in Fitzgerald's version:

. . . Some struck seeds of fire	
Out of the veins of flint, and some explored	10. 5
The virgin woods, lairs of wild things, for fuel,	11. 5
Pointing out, too, what streams they found. Aeneas,	11. 5
In duty bound, went inland to the heights	10. 5
Where overshadowing Apollo dwells	10. 5
Ănd neárbý, ĭn ă pláce ăpárt – ă dárk	10. 5
Enormous cave – the Sibyl feared by men.[20]	10. 5

The two numbers in the right-hand column respectively denote the total number of syllables, and the probable number of stresses per line. Fitzgerald adheres closely to the ten syllables and five stresses of blank verse, even when he inverts the iambic rhythm for dramatic effect, as notated in the penultimate line above.

Heaney's version sounds quite different rhythmically. His translation begins in this way (leading up to and including the passage of Fitzgerald quoted above):

In tears as he speaks, Aeneas loosens out sail	12. 5
And gives the whole fleet its head, so now at last	11. 6

---

18. Respectively, David Sexton (*London Evening Standard*, 2016), Ruth Padel (*Financial Times*, 2016), Karl Kirchwey (*New York Times*, 2016); Bernard O'Donoghue (*The Irish Times*, 2016).
19. Andrew Motion (*The Spectator*, 2016) and Colin Burrow (*London Review of Books*, 2016), both excellent reviews deserving close consideration.
20. Fitzgerald (1983), 159.

They ride ashore on the waves at Euboean Cumae.	13. 5
There they turn round the ships to face out to sea.	11. 7
Anchors bite deep, craft are held fast, curved	9. 7
Sterns cushion on sand, prows frill the beach.	9. 6
Now a band of young hotbloods vaults quickly out	11. 7
On to the shore of Italia, some after flint	13. 6
For the seedling fire it hides in its veins,	10. 4
Some crashing through woodland thickets, the haunts	10. 5
Of wild beasts, pointing amazed at new rivers.	11. 6
But Aeneas, devoted as ever, has taken the road	15. 5
Up towards a fort, the high seat of Apollo,	12. 6
Then on to a place apart, a vast scaresome cavern,	13. 6
The Sibyl's deep-hidden retreat. There the god breathes	12. 7
Into her, overwhelmingly, knowledge and vision,	13. 4
Opening her eyes to the future. (A.1–17)[21]	

When contrasted with Fitzgerald's, it is clear at a glance that Heaney's translation is not regular or even 'loose' blank verse. In the passage above, his syllable count per line varies from nine to fifteen, and the probable number of stresses from four to seven.

Heaney's rhythm for the new project also differs from the long-line meter he had adopted for the 1989 'Golden Bough' extract. By trimming back the number of syllables and reducing the number of stresses per line, he moves further from the rhythm of Virgil's lines in Latin. But he comes closer to the effect of 'canonical serenity' (*BBC*) because the English literary tradition has already attuned our ears to an iambic stress pattern and a pentameter line length, particularly for epic and long narrative poems. By reducing the syllable count and number of accents (shifting the meter closer to blank verse), Heaney creates a sense of coming home to the English literary tradition. To take two brief examples, in the following revision a five-beat, dactylic line is reduced in syllable count: 'Hídden in the thíck of a treé is a boúgh made of góld' becomes 'Híd in the thíck of a treé is a gólden boúgh' (*ST* 3, A.187). And a six-beat line is reduced to five: 'Plúcked this gólden-flédged grówth oút of its treé' is revised to 'Plúcked this sproút of flédged góld from its treé' (*ST* 3, A.193). Over the entire passage, the syllable count is reduced, and the number of stresses varies between five and six per line:

Híd in the thíck of a treé is a gólden boúgh	12. 5
Góld to the típs of its leáves and the báse of its stém,	13. 5
[. . .] Nó one is éver allówed	
Dówn to eárth's hídden pláces unléss he has fírst	12. 6
Plúcked this sproút of flédged góld from its treé	9. 5
[. . .]	
And whén it is plúcked, a sécond one gróws évery tíme	13. 6

21. Translating *Ae*.VI.1–12.

In its pláce, gólden agaín, émanáting 11.5
That sáme sheén and shímmer . . . (A.187–98)²²

In the new version, the syntax is simpler and the visual image clarified, with the Hopkinsian double stress picking out 'flédged góld', rather than '-flédged grówth'. But the dactylic, falling rhythm is still distinctly audible (note that two of the lines above retain the six beats of classical epic). Virgil's golden bough has not been wholly transplanted to the received measure of English heroic verse. In fact, fewer than twenty of the 1,222 lines of Heaney's *Aeneid VI* fall into the rhythm of regular blank verse.²³ Of these, the only significant cluster occurs in the passage where Aeneas meets the ghost of his father, a scene that evokes a powerful desire for homecoming, as we will see below.

While the blank verse elements in Heaney's translation alert the ear to a sound of at-homeness (for English-language readers), this is not at all the same as actually being at home, comfortably embedded in the blank verse of the English literary tradition. When Aeneas comes to the darkest region of Hades, Tartarus, where the ancient enemies of Jupiter are punished, Heaney increases the proportion of dactylic feet. Indeed, the whole passage is introduced with a classical slant, as Aeneas stops short, terrified: 'Thén ăsked thĕ Síbyl: 'Whát wróng-dóĭng / Ĭs bĕíng deált wĭth hére?' (A.758–9). The pause after 'Sibyl' creates a Latin, mid-line caesura effect. In the passage that follows, Heaney dips repeatedly into a classical hexameter rhythm. Thus, he has a run of dactyls, and a six-stress line, in this description of infernal punishment: 'Véngefŭl Tĭsíphŏnĕ keéps beárĭng dówn, ă whíplăsh / Lápped ănd líthe ĭn hĕr ríght hánd' (774–5). And for the Lapiths, tormented with the sight of a feast they cannot eat, Heaney varies between dactyls and trochees, maintaining a falling rhythm: 'Góldĕn heádrĕsts / Gleám ŏn their hígh bánquĕt coúchĕs, ă súmptŭoŭs / Róyăl feást' (820–1). The classical epic meter also surfaces in moments of high pathos, as when the mutilated ghost of Deiphobus, the Trojan Prince, asks Aeneas what destiny forces him 'Dówn tŏ thĕse súnlĕss, poór ăbódes, thĭs lánd / Ŏf troúblĕs' (721–2). The 'land of troubles' containing an unmistakable echo of Northern Ireland's 'Troubles', the run of dactyls here serves to underline the sense of estrangement from peace or homeliness in this exchange, both for the Trojan princes and for Heaney's Irish readers.

To complicate this dialogue of two meters, Heaney continues to draw on the older, half-line metrical units of Anglo-Saxon poetry, used to such powerful effect in the 'Palinurus' translation.²⁴ Although Palinurus' speech is reshaped, in the book-length version, to fall into mostly blank verse or hexameter lines, Heaney preserves many of the distinctive half-line, two-stress units and alliterative pairings from the earlier translation. Here, for example, Palinurus describes his approach to the shore

---

22. Cf. Ae.VI.136–44.
23. Lines 644, 660 (concerning Greek heroism); 807 (echoing Milton); 861; 925, 927, 929, possibly 942, 943 (all related to Anchises); 988, 992 (concerning the reincarnation of souls); 1023, 1121 (concerning the glory of Rome).
24. See Chapter 7, Section III.

of Italy (my notations are added):

| Slúgging towards lánd | in my wáterlogged clóthes, |
| Gétting a gríp | on the rázor-backed rídges, | (A.475–6)

The final line of his account of drowning at sea is even more accentuated by Anglo-Saxon alliterative pairing than in the self-standing translation extract. Thus, 'shore winds / roll me in closer and closer' (Pa 23–4) becomes, in the book-length version:

| The shóre wínds | lóll me and róll me | (A.480)

This Anglo-Saxon rhythm can be heard elsewhere in the translation as well. For example, in the opening verse paragraph (lines 1–19), two nine-syllable lines fall into four half-line units, with the exception of 'curved', which links the two lines in an alliterative chain of 'c's:

| Ánchors bíte deép, | cráft are héld fást, | cúrved
Stérns cúshion on sánd, | próws fríll the beách. | (ll. 5–6)

But as with Palinurus' speech, these tautly sprung lines are embedded within a longer verse paragraph that tends either to a flowing pentameter or to a hexameter line. In the opening nineteen lines, as indeed in the translation as a whole, the dominant auditory pattern is either five or six stresses per line - approximately the same number of each.

Broadly speaking, Heaney draws in equal measure on the metrical patterns of English blank verse and classical epic hexameter. From time to time, one line will sing out in one or other of the basic metrical units of the two verse traditions, as if to make visible the structure of the whole. Thus, 'Aenéas, devóted as éver, has táken the roád': iambic. And, 'Ínto her, óverwhélmingly, knówledge and vísion': dactylic. This double rhythm is laid down from the start of the book-length project, as is evident from the 2008 draft.[25] To borrow from Heaney's introduction to *Beowulf*, it is a 'tuning fork' establishing his 'right of way into and through' Virgil's underworld book.

This sense of operating between two metrical systems, mediating between and bridging their opposing currents, distinguishes Heaney's translation from other recent translations of the *Aeneid*. Most translators have opted either for blank verse or for a long-line approximation of Latin hexameter, but only Heaney's *Book VI* mediates so consciously and systematically between the two rhythms. For example, Sarah Ruden's *Aeneid* ([2008] 2021) is composed in iambic pentameter; she matches Virgil's text line for line, which requires a springy, compressed diction to keep pace with the Latin. Conversely, Frederick Ahl (2007), with great dexterity, approximates Virgil's dactylic hexameter, using long lines of around twelve to seventeen syllables. Robert Fagles (2006) employs a free verse which sometimes

25. With thanks to Sarah Ruden; see further, Chapter 7.

dips into dactylic hexameter; of modern translators, he comes perhaps the closest to the double music of Heaney's translation.[26] In his review of Heaney's volume, Andrew Motion (2016) writes that he misses Virgil's 'ocean-roll', which Tennyson famously described as 'the stateliest measure known to man'.[27] But that steady, tolling measure is antithetical to the restless, shifting rhythm of Heaney's translation. The deliberate oscillation between two rhythms produces a version of *Aeneid VI* that hovers between centre and circumference of the Western literary tradition.

III. HE DO THE *AENEID* IN DIFFERENT VOICES

If the rhythm of Heaney's *Aeneid Book VI* is deliberately doubled, there is a similar tension in the way he voices the text, by which I mean his tone, diction, register and style.[28] Robert Frost thought that carrying over the tone of an originary work was the most difficult, if not impossible, task of a translator; thus, 'a foreign masterpiece . . . must be read in the original because while the words may be brought over, the tone cannot be.'[29] In part, Heaney bridges this impossibility by layering his *Book VI* translation with different tonalities, doing the *Aeneid* in different voices, as Eliot might say.[30] Once again, Heaney's skilful orchestration of tone was largely missed in reviews of the volume in 2016. Most reviewers described the text in terms of a single tone, although tellingly there was no critical consensus on what tone Heaney was aiming for. One reader admired the translation's 'elegant sobriety' while another criticised its exaggerated, mannered intensity (it 'stamps over the face of Virgil'). In another case, its 'Derry earthiness' was praised, while elsewhere, its over-use of contemporary colloquialisms was criticised.[31] All of these accounts catch at a particular tone, register or mood, whereas what is particularly striking about Heaney's translation is how frequently the tonal weather shifts and changes.

Just as the translation oscillates between two rhythms, so, broadly speaking, we could say that the voicing swings between two opposing scales. At one end, there is an assured, outwardly directed voice, confidently commanding a broad range of Latinate and Anglo-Saxon vocabulary. At the opposite end of the scale, there is

---

26. Brad Leithauser describes Fagles's meter as 'free verse, with the ghost of a hexameter serving as loose armature' ('Wars and a Man', 17 December 2006, *The New York Times*). On Fagles's translation, see also Willard Spiegelman, 'Unforced Marches: A Virgilian Memoir', *Parnassus* 30:1–2 (2008), 81–106.
27. Tennyson, 'To Virgil', Vol. III, p. 102. See Chapter 1.
28. This doubleness of tone might be compared to Heaney's 'airy' versus 'laden' lines, discussed by Helen Vendler (1998, 139); see also Vendler (1988, 149–65).
29. Robert Frost, 'New American Poet', *Boston Evening Transcript*, 8 May 1915, Part 3, p. 10, qtd by Robert Newdick (1937), 292.
30. T. S. Eliot's working title for *The Waste Land* was 'He Do the Police in Different Voices', quoting Charles Dickens's *Our Mutual Friend* (see Bedient, 1986).
31. Respectively, Nelis (2017), Burrow (2016), Balmer (2016), Hexter (2016). Lysaght (2016) and Craven (*The Sydney Herald*, 2016) also comment on the translation's unadorned, plain style.

a more intimate, inwardly directed voice, often plain-spoken and inflected with Hibernian idioms. At the former end, there is indeed a new, 'elegant sobriety' in Heaney's translation of Book VI, which is unmistakable when set beside his earlier translation of 'The Golden Bough'.[32] Thus, in the later version, the Sibyl speaks, not 'from the back of her shrine' (GB.1), but from 'her innermost shrine' (A.140). Her 'scaresome equivocal words' (GB.2) are planed down to 'menacing riddles'(A.141). In place of her vividly 'mad mouthings' (GB.6), for '*rabida ora*' (Ae. VI.102), she now succumbs to sacerdotal 'raving', which carries over the sound of the Latin word (A.145). And Aeneas replies with more dignified restraint:

> 'No ordeal, O Priestess,
> That you can imagine would ever surprise me
> For I have already foreseen and foresuffered them all.' (GB.7–9)

> 'No ordeal, O Sibyl, no new
> Test can dismay me, for I have foreseen
> And foresuffered all.' (A.146–8)[33]

In the later version, the quotation of Eliot's Tiresias is more terse and impactful, and Aeneas' 'surprise' is dignified into 'dismay'.[34] Aeneas uses more formal phrasing, as in 'vouchsafe me one look'. And the Sibyl answers him with like formality: 'Only a few have prevailed'. There are thirty or more such upward shifts of register and tone in the 130 lines of the golden bough episode alone. What was an exchange between private equals, or between master and disciple, is raised to the level of resonant, public discourse. With the more compact phrasing, Aeneas' speech becomes more memorable not just to an individual listener, but potentially to a collective audience.

There is also a heightened formality to Heaney's description of the golden bough itself, possibly the most reworked lines in all of his poetic corpus. In the 1989 'Golden Bough' extract, Aeneas enters a 'huge belt of forest', which becomes a 'high stretch' in 2016 (GB.101; A.251). In the earlier version, Aeneas begs Venus' doves to show him where 'that blessed bough casts its shades on the rich forest floor' (GB.112). The homely 'blessed bough' is exchanged for a more elevated register, and at the same time, a more exact translation. In the book-length version, Aeneas implores them to reveal 'the grove where that opulent bough / Overshadows the rich forest floor.' (A.263–4) Virgil's '*dives . . . ramus*' is opulent, being solid gold, and 'Overshadows' introduces a dactylic foot in the line ('-shádŏws thĕ'). The new phrasing has a more obvious musicality, with the short 'o' of 'opulent' lengthening out to long 'o's in the next line.

By mixing registers in his description of the golden bough, Heaney transforms the familiar Virgilian talisman into a symbol of his own linguistically hybrid inherit-

---

32. A.140–282, corresponding to lines 1–129 of GB (1989).
33. Trans. Ae.VI.103–5.
34. Also ST 1; quoting Eliot, 'And I Tiresias have foresuffered all' (2015), Vol. I, p. 64.

ance. Heaney's 1989 version had focused on the bough's double nature as an organic growth and a made thing:

> gemina super arbore . . .
> discolor unde auri per ramos aura refulsit. (Ae.VI.203–4)
> a tree that grew like two trees
> For a glow came from it, and a gold aura tarnished its branches. (GB.120–1)

In the book-length version, the bough's double nature triggers a double-voiced translation, in which demotic Anglo-Saxon words are grafted together with elevated, Latinate vocabulary:

> a tree that was two trees
> In one, green-leafed yet refulgent with gold. (A.273–4)

This juxtaposition of registers, 'green-leafed' alongside 'refulgent', makes the golden bough seem at once homely and exotic.[35] The two registers are inextricably woven together by the complex alliteration threading through both lines: *t*, *r* in line 273, then *n*, *g*, *r*, *l*, *f*, *t*, *d* in line 274. This display of technical artistry, along with the command of different linguistic registers, seems designedly performed for a public audience.

In the book-length translation, Heaney also situates Aeneas's underworld journey in the distant, classical world, with proper names retaining their Latin and Greek forms.[36] This deliberate classicism could not be more different to the familiar commingling of Mossbawn and Elysium, in his 'Route 110' sequence. In the 2016 volume, '*Italia*' has a particular emotive resonance as it evokes the home ground of Virgil, as well as Aeneas' adoptive country (for example, A.8, 90, 969, 1091).[37] Certain phrases retain a classical otherness, such as Dedalus 'Rowing with wings', which captures the oddity of Virgil's mixed metaphor for his flight, '*remigium alarum*' (A.24; Ae.VI.19). The spelling of 'Dedalus' (instead of Daedalus) is an homage to Joyce's *Ulysses*, as Catherine Ware discusses in detail.[38] As well as alluding to Eliot's Tiresias, Heaney also uses the Yeatsian phrase 'the last inheritor' to describe Marcellus in the 2008 draft, but he trims this down to 'my inheritor' in the published

---

35. For the tonal shift, recall Shakespeare's 'this my hand will rather / The multitudinous seas incarnadine, / Making the green one red.' (*Macbeth* II.ii.54–60)
36. Heaney does, however, choose more familiar names where Virgil chooses esoteric ones; thus, 'Ulysses' (A.714) instead of 'Aeolides' (Ae.VI.529), and 'Tuscan' (A.939) for 'Tyrrhenian' sea (Ae.VI.697).
37. Heaney gives 'Italia' in each case for Ae.VI.6 ('*Hesperium*'), 61, 718, 807 ('*Ausonia*'). In his adolescent copy of Mackail's translation of the *Aeneid*, there is a vertical line marking this passage in Book XII: 'Ausonia shall keep her native speech and usage, and as her name is, it shall be.' (Mackail, 296) Edith Hall concludes from this and other youthful marginalia in the Mackail edition that Heaney 'had begun to sense parallels between Trojan/Roman imperialism and the British conquest of Ireland before he even arrived at university' (2019, 238).
38. Ware (2018) has a fine analysis of the 'Dedalus' *ekphrasis* (A.20–52).

version.³⁹ By combining these modern allusions with a more overt classicism in the 2016 translation, Heaney enters into the epic *labor* of sustaining and expanding the common storehouse of cultural memory, bridging Virgil's Roman epic and our own times.

Heaney's use of Biblical language, in accordance with Virgil's own borrowings from the Orphic and mystery cults, adds to this outward-facing, public and 'epic' dimension of his book-length translation. He draws freely from his Catholic word hoard to accentuate the mysterious, visionary and sacred elements of Virgil's underworld. In preparation for the burial of Misenus, Aeneas moves round his company, 'sprinkling / Clean water for purification, asperging men lightly' (A.304–5). 'Asperging', the technical term for purification at Mass, is what the dewy trefoil does to the ground, at the end of Heaney's 'Bann Valley Eclogue' (*EL* 12). Here, too, the 'pure in spirit' cannot cross 'the god-cursed threshold' of Tartarus, where the stern judge Rhadamanthus 'exact[s] / Confession' from 'unatoned' souls, like a Catholic priest.⁴⁰ And the '*laeta arua*' (literally, 'happy meadows', *Ae*.VI.744) are the 'blessèd fields' of Elysium, where Aeneas finds his father dwelling in paradisal peace (A.1007).

To the formality of these Latinate and Biblical phrases Heaney sometimes adds the chiselled masonry of Anglo-Saxon kenning, such as 'horn-cruel bull' for the Minotaur (A.35). There is an Anglo-Saxon rasp and growl to Heaney's underworld monsters, like Cerberus,

> Growling from three gullets, his brute bulk couched
> In the cave, facing down all comers. (A.559–60)

And each underworld river has its own distinctive, haunting sound. A dark, silent forest is encircled by 'a ring of dark waters, the river Cocytus, furls / And flows round it' (A.181–2). In contrast to this quiet desolation, the fortress of Tartarus is noisily 'encircled / By a hurtling torrent, a surge and rush of flame, / Rock-rumbling, thunder-flowing Phlegethon' (744–6). From beyond the fiery river, Aeneas hears 'the flinge and scringe and drag / Of iron chains.' (755–6) Andrew Motion finds such dense, consonantal collisions 'more appropriate to *Beowulf* (where it fitted and worked brilliantly) than the *Aeneid*.'⁴¹ But they are inappropriate only if one associates the *Aeneid* with a heightened, elegant register throughout. Virgil himself uses jagged, consonant sequences: for example, in Anchises' final instructions to Aeneas, '*et quo quemque modo fugiatque feratque laborem*' (*Ae*.VI.892). Heaney mirrors Virgil's *f*-alliteration in this version: 'How he should face or flee each undertaking' (A.1211). Moreover, Heaney's adoption of Anglo-Saxon diction and meter has its

---

39. Cf. Yeats's description of Lady Gregory (who also lost a son) in 'Coole and Ballylee, 1931', l. 30 (1992, 294). Heaney comments on 'last inheritor' as 'an echo [of] Yeats, that was, or maybe, come to think of it, of *Beowulf*, which has a famous "last veteran" passage' (letter to Ruden, 9 May 2009).
40. A.763–4 (trans. *Ae*.VI.563); A.770–3 (trans. *Ae*.VI.567–8).
41. Motion, 'Gifts from Beyond the Grave' (2016).

correspondence in Virgil's mixed style, which likewise dips into archaisms drawn from Ennius and other Roman predecessors.

Heaney sometimes 'ups the verbal voltage', as Colin Burrow argues, but I would not agree that he 'always' does so.[42] In describing Tartarus, the region of Hades where gods and heroes are racked with torture, Heaney does ramp up the volume and dissonance. Thus, Tityos lies prone as

> a huge, horrendous
> Vulture puddles forever with hooked beak
> In his liver and entrails teeming with raw pain (A.811–13)

But Heaney can just as suddenly turn down the *fortissimo*, as happens in this direct invocation of the gods of the underworld:

> Gods who rule over souls! Shades who subsist
> In the silence! Chaos and Phlegethon, O you hushed
> Nocturnal expanses, let assent be forthcoming (A.351–3)

The *forte* comes from the accent falling on the first syllable of a rhythmic foot: Gods! Shades! Chaos! Phlegethon! With the last invocation, though, the accent falls differently, producing a diminuendo and a held breath at the end of the line, before we arrive at 'Nocturnal expanses'.

Heaney's virtuosic aural effects, Anglo-Saxon archaisms and heightened linguistic registers all contribute to the constellation of tonalities I would loosely group together as constituting the translation's outward-facing, public forms of address. In contrast to these, the translation sometimes dips into an intimate voice, one that seems addressed to a familiar reader, whether a Derry countryman, a close literary exemplar or the elusive authorial voice (part poet, part translator) itself. The linguistic register here is spare, demotic and locally accented, so that Heaney seems to ventriloquise through Virgil, conveying his own attachments to his childhood *patria* and the weathered, familiar features of its inhabitants. If the former constellation demonstrates the epic *labor* of Heaney's translation, the latter conveys its lyric intimacy.

'In relation to my own job,' Heaney writes of the translation, in July 2008, 'I keep thinking of Patrick Kavanagh saying he wanted to play a true note on a slack string.'[43] Kavanagh's exact phrase was 'a true note on a dead slack string', by which he meant 'complete casualness'.[44] Perhaps Heaney drops the colloquial 'dead' for the sake of rhythm, or perhaps it was too close to the mark for thinking about Virgil's Land of the Dead. But the colloquial, Irish-inflected voice is an unmistakeable undercurrent in his translation, from 2008 to 2016. It is the voice missing from Ian McKellen's

---

42. Burrow (2016).
43. Heaney, letter to Ruden (26 July 2008), where he adds, 'and Brodsky, who once said to me, "intensity isn't everything", although neither he nor I believed it.'
44. 'Anyhow, I did arrive at complete casualness, at being able to play a true note on a dead slack string.' (Kavanagh, *Self-Portrait* (1962))

otherwise wonderful reading of the poem for BBC Radio, shortly after its publication.[45] The casual, 'slack string' note sounds in Heaney's Hiberno-English phrasing, such as: Dedalus 'away and afloat' (A.22), the Sibyl's breast 'aheave' (73), the cave with 'stone jaws agape' (314), the woods 'atremble' (340), and the upper reaches of Hades pictured as 'a nowhere of deserted dwellings' (358). The Sibyl sounds Hibernian when she instructs Aeneas to bury Misenus: 'Carry this man to a right / Resting place, lay him into his tomb' (208–9). And the translator shows his country familiarity with livestock when he describes ghost horses being 'loosed out' by their riders (884). Virgil's Trojan Prince Deiphobus is an angry, unappeased ghost and Heaney preserves the note of bitter resentment in his translation. But the ghost also becomes a veteran with an Irish past when, as mentioned above, he describes Virgil's underworld as 'this land / Of troubles' (A.721–2). Further on and further in, the avuncular poet, Musaeus, tells Aeneas, 'None of us has one definite home place' (909), but Heaney describes the woods, riverbanks and meadowland of Elysium in terms that conjure his remembered childhood landscape, 'the green welcome' of those 'happy vistas' in and around Mossbawn (867).

Rather than 'up the voltage' of the translation, these Irish inflections dampen it down, giving the underworld the appearance of ordinary, unmythical turf. Readers familiar with Heaney's earlier adaptations of Virgil, in 'Route 110' and the pastoral eclogues of *Electric Light*, will also experience a sense of *déjà-vu* when finding Derry meadows and streams in Virgil's Elysium. But even a first-time reader will find this region of the underworld familiar because, from the start, Heaney presents us with characters and gestures we are assumed to know already. In the opening lines, Aeneas is described as 'devoted *as ever*', implying that we have already witnessed his *pietas* many times before (A.12, my ital.). And later, when we first glimpse '*pater Anchises*' in Elysium, he is 'fatherly' as if we already knew to regard him as a modern figure remembered from childhood, rather than a distant Roman patriarch (*Ae.* VI.679, A.917). Aeneas' attempt to embrace him - 'Three times he tried to reach arms round that neck' - implies familiarity because of the demonstrative 'that', which Heaney slips into Virgil's '*collo dare bracchia circum*' (A.942, *Ae.*VI.700). Aeneas recognises the beloved shape of his father's body and the translator assumes we share that filial intimacy.

At the same time, however, 'that' body, along with everything else dear and familiar in the underworld, is given a layer of remoteness, so that the experience of reading the translation itself feels like a *ter conatus* embrace of a cherished absence. The late Kavanagh's 'slack string' voice is casual but also dream-like, conjuring the *heimlich* in the *unheimlich*, and vice versa.[46] For example, this line describes Aeneas' first glimpse of his father:

At pater Anchises penitus conualle uirenti (*Ae.*VI.679)

---

45. *Book of the Week: Seamus Heaney's Aeneid Book VI*, broadcast 7–13 March 2016, <https://www.bbc.co.uk/programmes/b073grjb>. Reviewed by Reynolds (2016).
46. Sigmund Freud, 'The Uncanny' [*Das Unheimliche*, 1919], trans. Alix Strachey (1925), in *The Standard Edition of the Complete Psychological Works of Sigmund Freud*, Vol. 4, 368–407.

> Elsewhere Anchises,
> Fatherly and intent, was off in a deep green valley (A.916–17)

Heaney translates 'at' (literally, 'but') as 'elsewhere . . . off', which greatly increases the distance separating father and son. While accurately rendering '*penitus conualle uirenti*', Heaney's phrase, 'a deep green valley', is also familiar from ballad songs. And it echoes the 'dearest freshness . . . deep down things' that Heaney admired from Hopkins's 'God's Grandeur'.[47]

The emotional core of Heaney's translation, and the passage where his lyric voicing is most prominent, is the riverbank scene where Aeneas first sees his father's ghost. Anchises is busy 'surveying and reviewing' the souls of future children and grandchildren, 'taking note / Of his whole posterity' (A.918, 920–1), somewhat resembling a cattle-dealer surveying his stock, in Heaney's translation. And then the father catches sight of his son:

> isque ubi tendentem aduersum per gramina uidit
> Aenean, alacris palmas utrasque tetendit,
> effusaeque genis lacrimae et uox excidit ore: (*Ae*.VI.684–6)

> But seeing Aeneas come wading through the grass
> Towards him, he reached his two hands out
> In eager joy, his eyes filled up with tears
> And he gave a cry (A.923–6)

The voicing here is intimate and emotional, and the sense of nostalgia, or longing for home, is heightened by the shift into a predominantly iambic rhythm. Line 925, with its 'joy' and 'tears', is one of the translation's rare instances of regular blank verse; the meter recurs in lines 927 and 929, where Anchises addresses his son. Virgil has Aeneas approach him '*aduersum*' ('from the other direction'), which Heaney renders as 'comes wading towards'. This added detail diminishes the hero in size and shifts the perspective to Anchises', so that we watch Aeneas approach like a child through tall meadow grasses. The altered perspective recalls the moment in 'Man and Boy' where Heaney identifies his childhood self with his father's:

> My father is a barefoot boy with news,
> Running at eye-level with weeds and stooks
> On the afternoon of his own father's death. (*ST* 15)[48]

In both passages, the figure in the grass occupies two temporalities, a present moment of joy and an impending experience of loss. The spectral presence of Heaney, *fils et père*, is not easily missed in this touching encounter between Aeneas

---

47. Hopkins (1990), 139. Cf. also Richard Llewellyn's *How Green Was My Valley* (1939).
48. In section V of 'Album', too, Heaney pictures his father being rushed with an embrace by his own small son (*HC* 8).

and the ghostly Anchises.

There follows the well-known *ter conatus* motif, in which Aeneas tries three times to embrace his father. As noted in earlier chapters, Virgil's description of the empty embrace is densely memorious, recalling scenes from Homer and his own earlier writing. Aeneas' gesture is itself iterative, which Virgil underlines with three opening monosyllables, *ter*, *ter* and *par*:

> ter conatus ibi collo dare bracchia circum;
> ter frustra comprensa manus effugit imago,
> par levibus ventis volucrique simillima somno. (Ae.VI.700–2)

In Heaney's new translation of this passage, the son's failed embrace echoes all these scenes, as well as scenes of failed intimacy between father and son, in his own English poems. In the first two lines below the meter is iambic pentameter, with an initial double stress, and a midline double/trochaic stress, but in the third line this familiar rhythm breaks down.[49] The voicing is again extremely simple, almost entirely monosyllabic. Aeneas has arrived at the *telos* of his underworld quest, and it should be a scene of homecoming but it is not:

> Three times he tried to reach arms round that neck.
> Three times the form, reached for in vain, escaped
> Like a breeze between his hands, a dream on wings. (A.942–4)

The concentration of intimacy and distance is captured in the juxtaposition of 'that neck' with 'the form', so that the loved, familiar body becomes, in the very next line, a shape without name or substance. There is even a suggestion of welcome release for the ghost, which 'escapes' and, in the last line, seems to take flight unsorrowfully.[50] Immediately after this elegiac *ter conatus*, Virgil lifts the mood and brings Aeneas within sight of the riverbank of River Lethe. In Heaney's translation, this scene evokes the most powerful sense of homecoming in Book VI, as we will see below. The intimate lyric voicing of the father–son encounter, and the subsequent description of the Elysian fields, stand in marked contrast to Heaney's extrovert and virtuosic voicing elsewhere in the translation.

---

49. The first two lines are, I think, the only instance of consecutive iambic pentameters in the whole volume.
50. Cf. Fairclough (1978): 'even as light wings, and most like a winged dream.' (p. 555); and Fitzgerald: 'Weightless and wind and fugitive as dream' (p. 184). Both these translations come to earth on the word 'dream'. But Heaney has a triple assonance, in 'breeze', 'between' and 'dream', from which the last word, 'wings', breaks free.

IV. *KATABASIS* AS POETIC REDRESS

We have seen in Heaney's previous translations and reworkings of Virgil that Aeneas' mythic descent into the underworld and return is associated with the introspective journey into the otherworld of art, in search of redress (comprehension, perspective, resistance) to real-world suffering, whether from violent political conflict or personal loss. In the 2016 volume, although the shape of the *katabatic* journey, its threshold-crossings, encounters with the dead, trajectory and *telos*, are all laid down by Virgil, nevertheless Heaney's translation continues this *labor* of seeking redress to historical adversity through the medium of poetry.[51] These longstanding preoccupations of Heaney's are evident not only in the orchestration of the tone and rhythm of the translation, but also in the weight he gives to particular, threshold moments, the careful phrasing of certain familiar motifs, and the elaboration of Virgil's vision of a country at peace. The good of poetry that emerges from this dialogue with Virgil is ultimately its capacity to offer inner resilience, hope, and the memory or vision of a more just and peaceful society.

In terms of its overall characterisation of Aeneas, Heaney's translation shows great sympathy for the hero in his role as a Trojan refugee longing for home, as an obedient servant of the gods and as the bearer of the household *penates*. Heaney has the Sibyl address Aeneas as 'blood relation / Of gods', a respectful title he emphasises on several occasions (A.1723).[52] He translates Aeneas' epithet '*pius*' as 'devoted' and 'devout', and the hero's '*pietas*' as 'goodness' and 'sense of right'; these values are always positively connoted, but not with any particular emphasis on Aeneas being a good *Roman*.[53] Indeed, 'Rome' and 'Roman' are nominatives that never carry the same emotional weight as '*Italia*' does in his translation.

By contrast with his sympathy for the *pius émigré*, Heaney shows a marked reserve towards Aeneas as a coloniser of Italy. In the 'Freed Speech' published in 2009, which is carried over unmodified in 2016, the Sibyl suggests that Aeneas will play the part of a Homeric Greek aggressor in the upcoming invasion of Italian lands. The cause of the new, internecine conflict will be Aeneas himself:

causa mali tanti coniunx iterum hospita Teucris
externique iterum thalami. (*Ae*.VI.93–4)

           And again the cause of such pain
And disaster for the Trojans will be as before: a bride
Culled in a host country, an outlander groom. (A.133–5)

Virgil describes Aeneas' future wife, Lavinia, in ambiguous terms as a '*hospita coniunx*'. Fairclough translates this as 'foreign bride', meaning foreign to the Trojans,

---

51. On the 'poetic quest for repose', see Heaney's review of Kavanagh, 'Strangeness and Beauty' (2005).
52. For example, BBC (2008).
53. See A.240, 540, 543, 927 and 1192 (of Marcellus). At 308, he omits Virgil's '*pius*' altogether (*Ae*.VI.232).

but *hospita*, from *hospes*, can also mean 'host', 'friend' or 'stranger' (*LS* I, II), so the phrase could equally mean 'bridal *host* to the Trojans', a reminder of the hospitality extended to the Trojans by Lavinia's father, King Latinus.[54] Heaney brings out this latter sense of '*hospita*' by linking 'bride' with 'host country'. Adding the verb 'culled', moreover, imputes the Trojans with a charge of violence against their hosts. Lavinia becomes one of a series of young victims culled for sacrifice, along with Euryalus, Marcellus and Pallus. The free translation of '*externi thalami*' (literally, a 'foreign marriage') as 'an outlander groom' emphasises Aeneas' alien otherness to the Italian tribes, and his similarity to Paris, whose theft of Helen sparked the outbreak of war between Trojans and Greeks. And if the wars in Italy constitute a traumatic repetition of the Trojan War, Heaney clears the hospitable Lavinia of any guilt by association with Helen, the 'foreign bride' who helped to betray her adoptive city of Troy.

Heaney's Aeneas is not only a Trojan prince but also an everyman figure like Dante's pilgrim, '*nel mezzo del cammin di nostra vita*', whose journey through the dark wood is also ours.[55] He is also, at times, a figure for the wayfaring poet, seeking redress to 'the actual condition of the times', the 'brutality of war, the reality of cruelty and bloodshed.'[56] Thus, in the 2016 translation, Aeneas's discovery of the golden bough is even more strongly associated with poetic inspiration than in earlier translation extracts. When instructing Aeneas how to pluck the golden bough, the Sibyl predicts that the bough will yield easily to to the right hero's touch:

ergo alte uestiga oculis et rite repertum
carpe manu; namque ipse uolens facilisque sequetur,
si te fata uocant; (*Ae*.VI.145–7)

    Therefore look up
And search deep and as soon as you find it
Take hold of it boldly and duly. If fate has called you
The bough will come away in your hand. (A.198–201)

But when Aeneas comes to break off the bough, it does not yield '*ipse uolens facilisque*'; it resists his grasp ('*cunctantem*', *Ae*.IV.211). In 1989, Heaney had translated the Sibyl's phrase as 'by its own will and easily' (*GB*.57), underlining the mismatch between divine prophecy and heroic deed in Virgil's poem. In this new, pared-down version, the Sibyl's problematic phrase is all but omitted. Instead, Heaney introduces the haptic motif 'will come away in your hand', incorporating '*manu*' ('in hand') from the previous phrase, which offers this scene as a moment of redress to the tragic *ter conatus*, where the beloved ghost of his father slips from Aeneas' hands ('*ter frustra comprensa manus effugit imago*', *Ae*.VI.701).[57] When Aeneas does come to tear off

---

54. See Horsfall (2013), p. 128, l. 94.
55. 'Midway on the journey of our life' (Dante, *Inf*.I.1).
56. Heaney, *SS* 389, *BBC*. Cf. 'the brutality of the historical onslaught' (*GT* 107).
57. Dedalus' hands failing to carve the image of Icarus (A.52); Palinurus reaching for Aeneas' hand (A.493–4); the souls by the Styx, 'stretching out / Arms that hankered towards the farther

the bough, he does so 'greedily' and with force (A.281). While the violent action is still jarring, it no longer directly contradicts what the Sibyl had predicted. As a figure of the wayfaring poet, Aeneas is harnessing epic will and *pietas* to lyric instinct.

The outlines of Heaney's poetic *katabasis* are also visible in the episode where Aeneas steps into Charon's boat to cross the River Styx. For Virgil's '*accipit*' (Charon 'received' the hero into the boat), Heaney writes that the god 'Hands mighty Aeneas down' (Ae.VI.414; A.552), which continues the notion of the poet's redress to the tragic *ter conatus* motif. When Aeneas then crosses the River Styx and reaches the farther shore, this scene can be read symbolically as the poet's successful threshold-crossing out of historical reality into the realm of memory and imagination. Virgil describes the crossing thus: '*tandem trans fluuium incolumis uatemque uirumque*', a long, alliterative line that stretches the duration of the crossing and underlines the difficulty of Aeneas' undertaking (Ae.VI.415). Heaney dismisses this emphasis almost entirely ('in the end it is a safe crossing'), and instead deploys the heavy alliteration for the hero's landfall in Hades:

> He lands
> Soldier and soothsayer on slithery mud, knee-deep
> In grey-green sedge. (A.566–8)

The muddy, 'slithery' landfall of the hero captures the moment of poetic rebirth and regeneration as he enters the supernatural realm.

Aeneas' journey through the underworld begins in shadowy darkness and ends in warmth and sunlight, a trajectory that corresponds precisely to Heaney's notion of poetic redress. Thus, he takes great care over the translation of two passages that mark the beginning and end of that Orphic 'haulage' from darkness to light.[58] The first describes Aeneas setting forth into the realms of Dis (Hades), and the latter describes his arrival in the valley of Elysium. Virgil's description of the hero's setting forth is justly famous, with its rich alliterations, word order inversions and mysterious beginning with the imperfect verb '*ibant*' ('they were going'):

> Ibant obscuri sola sub nocte per umbram
> perque domos Ditis uacuas et inania regna:
> quale per incertam lunam sub luce maligna
> est iter in siluis, ubi caelum condidit umbra
> Iuppiter, et rebus nox abstulit atra colorem. (Ae.VI.268–72)

> On they went then in darkness, through the lonely
> Shadowing night, a nowhere of deserted dwellings,

---

shore.' (A.414–15); Deiphobus, 'mutilated in every part, his face / In shreds – his face and his two hands –' (A.665–6); Anchises 'reach[ing] his two hands out / In eager joy' to Aeneas, and addressing his descendants: 'be you the first / In clemency: rid your hands of those weapons.' (A.1131–2). See also Chapter 8.

58. 'the Orphic effort to haul life back up the slope against all the odds' (*RP* 158); see Chapter 3, Section II.

> Dim phantasmal reaches where Pluto is king –
> Like following a forest path by the hovering light
> Of a moon that clouds and unclouds at Jupiter's whim,
> While the colours of the world pall in the gloom. (A.357–62)

Heaney responds very expressively to Virgil's evocation of underworld melancholy.[59] His translation emphasises the psychological dimensions of Aeneas' quest, while also giving a specifically Irish dimension to this universal realm of shadows. The infernal stretch of time implied in Virgil's '*ibant*' is conveyed here through word order inversion: 'On they went then', where 'then' carries the sense of causation as well as temporality ('therefore', as well as 'at that time'). The line-end pause after 'lonely' encourages us to attach the adjective to the wayfaring Aeneas, as well as the 'Shadowing night' it modifies. Heaney's idiomatic phrase, 'a nowhere of deserted dwellings', conjures the material reality of a Northern Irish town, post-military conflict. At the same time, both 'a nowhere' and 'deserted dwellings' are phrases that posit, and cancel out, a sense of place. 'Phantasmal *reaches*' recall the 'phantasmal comrades' of Joyce's *Portrait*, while draining away the presence of even companionable ghosts at the start of Aeneas' lonely journey.[60] Heaney begins the simile with uncertain syntax, so that it is at first unclear who is 'following a forest path'. By the time we realise this must refer to Aeneas and the Sibyl, we have experienced their sense of disorientation on the dim-lit path. Virgil's '*atra*' is a blackness associated with funerals, for which Heaney's 'pall in the gloom' is a perfectly apt translation. In Virgil's lines 271–2, '*Iuppiter*' and '*nox*' are the subjects of the phrase, and they impose darkness on the sky and world. In Heaney's corresponding lines 361–2, the subjects are the moon and 'the colours of the world'. Both are overshadowed by 'Jupiter's whim', but since they are active agents, they retain the capacity to restore the world to its full radiance. In other words, Heaney redistributes the balance of power between darkness and light, giving an equal weight to each in the line: 'moon' against 'Jupiter's whim', and 'colours' against 'gloom'. The possibility of the moon *un*clouding, and overthrowing Jupiter's whim, exists only in the simile, since Aeneas at the start of his journey is in Pluto's realm (his translation of the less familiar name, '*Dis*'), where the darkness and negation appear absolute.

At the end of his journey, however, Aeneas arrives at a region of the underworld that is unexpectedly bathed in light. He has just found, and attempted to embrace, his father's ghost. The pathos of the empty embrace is then checked and redirected by a powerfully understated adverb, '*interea*' ('meanwhile'). Virgil thus introduces his vision of a familiar *patria*, entirely at peace:

> Interea uidet Aeneas in ualle reducta
> seclusum nemus et uirgulta sonantia siluae,

---

59. For excellent close analyses of this passage in Heaney's translation, see Nelis (2017) and S. J. Harrison (2019).
60. Joyce, *A Portrait of the Artist as a Young Man* (1992), 89. S. J. Harrison notes this allusion as well (2019, 258).

Lethaeumque domos placidas qui praenatat amnem.
hunc circum innumerae gentes populique uolabant:
ac ueluti in pratis ubi apes aestate serena
floribus insidunt uariis et candida circum
lilia funduntur, strepit omnis murmure campus. (Ae.VI.703–9)

In Heaney's translation, the Elysian valley rapidly transforms from a remote place to one that looks and sounds like home, full of dappled light and a gentle, insect hum:

Meanwhile, at the far end of a valley, Aeneas saw
A remote grove, bushy rustling thickets,
And the river Lethe somnolently flowing,
Lapping those peaceful haunts along its banks.
Here a hovering multitude, innumerable
Nations and gathered clans, kept the fields
Humming with life, like bees in meadows
On a clear summer day alighting on pied flowers
And wafting in mazy swarms around white lilies. (A.945–53)

Virgil's '*reducta*' means literally 'receding', which Heaney translates as 'at the far end of a valley'. This introduces a sense of spatial distance, which is then dramatically telescoped, so as to bring us close enough to see and hear the insects swarming. Heaney's use of the demonstrative pronoun, '*those*' fields, again heightens the sense of familiarity with this country scene. Readers familiar with 'The Riverbank Field' will recall Heaney's earlier association of the Lethe with his own River Moyola, swarming with evening moths and midges, 'not bees in sunlight' (*HC* 46). The rich aural effects (alliteration, assonance, onomatopoeia of bee sounds), the slow participial verbs, and the echo of Hopkins and Keats in 'pied flowers' and 'mazy swarms' of bees all contribute to the sense that Heaney's translation is here deliberately restoring the lost 'colours of the world'.[61] 'Those peaceful haunts' are the exact inverse of 'a nowhere' of 'phantasmal reaches', since a 'haunt' is both a place one frequents fondly (*OED*, *n*., 3) and the repeated action of a ghost presenting itself (*OED*, *v*., 5b). That Heaney identified particularly strongly with these lines is suggested by the fact that he translated and published them as a self-standing extract, entitled 'The Fields of Light'.[62] In contrast to his translation of the Palinurus episode, which was much revised for the book-length version, Heaney retained this description of the riverbank scene unchanged from 2008. So when we get to this passage of the 2016

---

61. Cf. G. M. Hopkins, 'Pied Beauty' ('Glory be to God for dappled things'), in *Poetical Works* (1990), 144, l. 1; and John Keats, 'To Autumn' ('they think warm days will never cease, / For summer has o'er-brimm'd their clammy cells.' (2003, 360, l. 11). There is a copy of Keats's ode, written out in Heaney's longhand, in McCabe Heaney Collection, II.xi, dated 23 October 1990.
62. 'The Fields of Light' [trans. Ae.VI: 638–78], published with 'Loughanure', in *Archipelago* II (Spring 2008), 9–14.

translation, we have a strong sense of Aeneas arriving home, where home evokes the memory not only of Virgil's Mantuan countryside, but also of Heaney's homeplace in Mossbawn.

In Heaney's translation, moreover, the underworld sun sets the bees 'humming with life' (A.951). That incongruous word, 'life' (not in the Latin), underlines the translator's notion of Elysium as a vision of the regenerated, actual, material world. More than recalling Heaney's homeplace, this scene depicts an entire society at peace, with its 'multitude' of 'innumerable, / Nations and gathered clans' (A.949–50). This is a glimpse of a *patria* not yet divided by civil war, and the irenic image precedes and counterbalances the description of imperial wars to follow, wars in which these very spirits will play their part. If Kavanagh hears Homer's ghost whispering to him to make 'the *Iliad* from such / A local row', Heaney hears in Virgil's underworld the *urlar* of a longing for peace.[63]

In the next section of the riverbank scene, Heaney steers a middle course between these alternative futures, the one irenic, the other dominated by warfare. When Aeneas first catches sight of the unborn souls milling at the water's edge, Virgil tells us he is shocked and frightened: '*horrescit uisu subito causasque requirit / inscius Aeneas*' ('Aeneas shuddered at the sudden sight, and blankly sought an explanation', *Ae*.VI.710–11, my trans.). In Heaney's translation, the hero is more surprised than stupefied: 'Aeneas startled at this unexpected sight / And in his bewilderment asked what was happening' (A.954–5). What follows is Anchises' explanation of the Orphic–Pythagorean doctrine of metempsychosis, which Heaney interprets as a joyful symbol of natural and cultural regeneration, in *The Riverbank Field* and *Human Chain*.[64] But here, the celebratory aspect is more muted, in line with Virgil's more ambivalent tone in this passage. For Virgil's elevated, Lucretian register and diction, Heaney finds an equivalence in the sonorous opening of Dylan Thomas's *Under Milk Wood*: 'To begin at the beginning: a nurturing inner spirit / Works to sustain sky, earth, the fields of ocean' (A.977–8).[65] But when Anchises comes to the description of the souls' purgatorial suffering, Heaney drops the elevated register. Virgil's ambiguous phrase, '*quisque suos patimur manis*', Heaney renders coolly as 'Each of us suffers / The death we're due' (*Ae*.VI.743; A.1004–5). There is little sense of a Keatsian intelligence being schooled into a soul through suffering, as Heaney's dramatises in his earlier translation of the Palinurus episode.[66]

Heaney also maintains Virgil's ambivalent tone when he comes to translating Anchises' description of the souls' approach to the River Lethe, the passage that most directly informs the regenerative poetics of *Human Chain*. In Virgil's lines, the god who inflicts oblivion on the souls sounds stern and punishing:

---

63. Patrick Kavanagh, 'Epic' (1960). Qtd in *P* 139. An *urlar*, from Gaelic, is the 'ground-theme' of a melody, on which variations are played (*OED*).
64. See Chapters 6 and 8.
65. *Ae*.VI.724f. S. J. Harrison also argues for the analogy between Lucretius and Thomas (2019, 255).
66. See Chapter 7.

'has omnis, ubi mille rotam uoluere per annos,
Lethaeum ad fluuium deus euocat agmine magno,
scilicet immemores supera ut conuexa reuisant
rursus, et incipiant in corpora uelle reuerti.' (Ae.VI.748–51)

In 'The Riverbank Field', Heaney rendered '*immemores*' as 'memories . . . are shed', and for '*rotam uoluere*' he offered 'rolled time's wheel'.[67] Here, his translation mirrors the cooler mood of the Latin:

'The rest, when they have trod
Time's mill for a thousand years, the god commands
Wave upon wave into the Lethe river, so at that stage
Their memory is effaced and they go once more
To dwell beneath sky's dome and start again
To long for the old life of flesh and blood.' (A.1010–15)[68]

Now more harshly, memories are 'effaced' when the souls 'have trod / Time's mill'. The image of the mill, suggested by the proximity of '*mille*' ('a thousand') in line 748, may allude to the tread mills operated by Roman slaves.[69] In this new translation, Heaney is also echoing Hopkins's joyless line, 'Generations have trod, have trod, have trod'.[70] And again, there is a likely reference to his own phrase, 'the treadmill of assault // turned waterwheel', in 'Mycenae Lookout' (*SL* 37). These allusions suggest that the turn of time's wheel, far from effecting a regenerative renewal, may simply lead to an eternal repetition of war and suffering.[71] From this perspective, the souls' desire for 'the old life of flesh and blood' might indicate their readiness to return to military conflict. Heaney's new translation does not cancel out his earlier, optimistic, reading of this passage, but he opens up the possibility of a tragic interpretation and leaves the reader to decide between them.

While the description of the metempsychosis of souls is more ambivalent than previously, Heaney counterbalances the patriotic spectacle of the Roman parade by enclosing it within a deliberately anti-heroic, georgic–pastoral frame (lines 1016–18 and 1203–5). Anchises pauses between his explanation of Pythagorian doctrine and his prophetic account of 'The future glory of the Trojan race' (A.1023). Before he resumes his speech, Anchises leads Aeneas downhill into the crowd of waiting souls:

Dixerat Anchises natumque unaque Sibyllam
conuentus trahit in medios turbamque sonantem, (Ae.VI.752–3)

---

67. HC 46–7; still more positively, in the earlier version, 'done their turn' (*RF* 2007).
68. Heaney's text here follows the line order of the OCT edition and Fairclough's Loeb edition (1978), but not Goold's revised Loeb (1999).
69. This is Stephen Harrison's intriguing suggestion (2019, 260).
70. G. M. Hopkins, 'God's Grandeur', l. 5 (1990, 139).
71. Cf. Ezra Pound's despairing final line of Canto CXIII: 'but the mind as Ixion, unstill, ever turning' (Pound, Canto CXIII (1996), 810; for Pound, see Whittier-Ferguson (2010), 230).

In Nicholas Horsfall's prose translation, this passage reads:

> Then Anchises finished speaking and took his son and the Sibyl with him, into the midst of the crowded, ringing assembly. (2013, p. 53)

Horsfall suppresses the bee-like sound of the swarming souls, Virgil's '*turbam sonantem*' picking up on their '*sonantia . . . ubi apes*' in the description above (704, 707). Arguing that armed souls would make a much more robust sound than insects humming, Horsfall opts for 'a ringing crowd'.[72] Heaney, by contrast, insists on their descent into a bee-loud glade:

> Anchises concluded and led his son
> Accompanied by the Sibyl into the crowd,
> Into the thick and buzzing throb of it, (A.1016–18)

Heaney exaggerates the souls' likeness to bees, translating '*sonantem*' as 'the thick and buzzing throb'. And he emphasises that Anchises and Aeneas enter the very heart of the swarm: 'into the crowd / Into the thick . . . of it'. The 'throb' of the swarm, moreover, suggests the pulse of a heartbeat, reminding us that these souls are on the verge of bursting into corporeal life. The bee simile further recalls the hive of dying bees that revives when Aristaeus placates the shade of Orpheus, at the end of *Georgics IV* (ll. 557–8). And for Heaney, as we saw in *The Riverbank Field*, this Virgilian hive is associated with Yeats's honey-bees, who are invoked to rebuild Ireland in a time of civil war.[73] Heaney's subtle emphasis on the bee-like throb of the crowd offers a moment of lyric release, a glimpse of an alternative, pastoral future for the waiting souls, instead of the conflict and bloodshed that awaits them.

In Heaney's translation, the parade of Roman heroes concludes with a similar lyric swerve away from the prophecy of future wars. Anchises concludes his roll call of heroes with a lament for Augustus' nephew, Marcellus, destined to die young. Famously, he calls for lilies to mourn his death ('*manibus date lilia plenis*', *Ae*.VI.883), flowers that might be gathered from the peaceful, Lethean riverbank (l. 709). But then, as quickly as before, Virgil lightens the mood, and shows the father and son enjoying a leisurely tour of Elysium together:

> sic tota passim regione uagantur
> aëris in campis latis atque omnia lustrant. (*Ae*.VI.886–7)

> And so
> Far and wide in those fields, through regions of air,
> They go wandering at will, surveying all. (A.12003–5)

---

72. Horsfall (2013), Vol. II, p. 508. Other translators favour 'murmuring': for example, Fairclough (1978 edition), 'murmuring'; Fitzgerald, 'Into the middle of the murmuring throng'; and Fagles, 'into the midst of the vast murmuring throng'.
73. See Chapter 6, and Yeats, 'Meditations' (1992, 250). The 'bee-loud glade' is from Yeats's 'Lake Isle of Innisfree'.

Heaney's phrase, 'regions of air', comes from combining Virgil's '*tota regione*' ('whole region') with '*aëris in campis latis*' ('spreading plains of air'). Placed at the end of the imperial parade, the phrase conjures a sense of spacious release and freedom. Like the freshening wind in 'In the Attic' and the 'Air from another life and time and place' in 'A Kite for Aibhín', these 'regions of air' offer space for reflection, and the opportunity 'to be liberated and distanced' from what is to come.[74] Heaney renders '*uagantur*' as 'wandering at will', which underlines Aeneas' unexpected freedom of movement through the gathering crowd of souls.[75] It is almost as if he has become a weightless soul himself and is able to hover, bee-like, over the fields. If 'Ariel's spirit music' can generate a 'transitory' and 'momentary sensation of resolution, a healing moment', these two lines perform a comparable healing action, perhaps in response to the imperial future Aeneas has just seen.[76] At the very least, they return the reader to the Elysian fields, where the souls have not yet been reborn as heroes and Aeneas has not yet waged war on the Latin tribes.

At the end of Virgil's *Aeneid VI*, Aeneas leaves Hades via the Gates of Sleep, rejoins his comrades and immediately sets sail for Gaeta, about 35 miles from Cumae.[77] Heaney's translation captures the accelerated pace and famous ambiguity of Virgil's ending, but his own preoccupations with the poet's *katabasis* also emerge clearly in this final verse paragraph. Instead of a definitive return to the actual, material world, his translation hints at a further threshold-crossing into the marvellous. In this way, Heaney transforms the destination into a transition, and the entire book comes to figure for the unceasing *labor* and play of poetry itself.

Virgil tells us there are two gates, one of horn and one of ivory. For reasons unspecified, Anchises opens the ivory gate for his son and the Sibyl:

> Sunt geminae Somni portae, quarum altera fertur
> cornea, qua ueris facilis datur exitus umbris,
> altera candenti perfecta nitens elephanto,
> sed falsa ad caelum mittunt insomnia Manes.
> his ibi tum natum Anchises unaque Sibyllam
> prosequitur dictis portaque emittit eburna, (*Ae*.VI.893–9)

> There are two gates of Sleep, one of which, they say,
> Is made of horn and offers easy passage
> To true visions; the other has a luminous, dense
> Ivory sheen, but through it, to the sky above,
> The spirits of the dead send up false dreams.
> Anchises, still guiding and discoursing,

---

74. HC 84, 85; 'Unhappy and At Home' (1977), 66.
75. Cf. Milton, *PL*.XII.646–9: 'The world was all before them, where to choose / Their place of rest, and providence their guide: / They hand in hand with wand'ring steps and slow, / Through Eden took their solitary way.'
76. Heaney, 'The Whole Thing' (2002), 10, drawing on W. H. Auden's contrast between Prospero's realism and Ariel's imagination, *The Dyer's Hand* (1987: 239–50).
77. Horsfall (2013), Vol. 2, p. 622.

Escorts his son and the Sibyl on their way
And lets them both out by the ivory gates. (A.1212–19)

Virgil's narrative leaves us wondering why Aeneas leaves Hades via the ivory gate, used for issuing '*falsa insomnia*' (false dreams), rather than the horn gate for '*ueris umbris*' (true shades). Is this meant to indicate that the underworld journey has been a dream, not a prophecy?[78] Or, in a 'pessimistic' reading of the poem, is Virgil encouraging his readers to be sceptical about the '*famae uenientis*', the future glory of Rome (*Ae*.VI.889)? Or is it simply that Aeneas has to avoid the horn gate because he is a living man, not an '*umbra*'? The asymmetrical function of the two gates is also problematic: why does one send forth '*umbris*' (shades, spirits) while the other releases '*insomnia*' (dreams, apparitions)?[79] Heaney's translation does not help us immediately decide between these interpretations.[80] 'True visions' sound preferable, yet the 'easy passage' suggests they might be too simplistic. 'False dreams' are undeniably negative and yet they are 'luminous', a word very positively connoted in his vocabulary.[81]

A closer comparison with the Latin, however, reveals an added dimension to the ivory gate in Heaney's translation. Virgil describes the gate of false dreams as '*candenti perfecta nitens elephanto*', which translates literally as 'glistening with the sheen of polished ivory'. Heaney renders this as 'a luminous, dense / Ivory sheen'. By turning 'ivory' into an adjective and 'sheen' into a noun, he shifts the emphasis to the gleaming light of the gate, rather than its material substance. The 'sheen' recalls the light of the golden bough, which, when plucked, immediately recovers its supernatural powers: 'golden again, emanating / That same sheen and shimmer.' (A.197–8) In this connection, the 'dense' light of the ivory recalls the dark grove in which the golden bough was concealed. And 'luminous', derived from *lumen* (light), reminds us of the *limen* (threshold) of Persephone, where Aeneas plants the bough in the underworld, as well as the *numen* (divine will) which guides his entire journey from the moment he catches sight of Venus' doves. These echoes suggest that, in passing through the ivory gate, Aeneas is not simply returning to the fate that awaits him and the 'wars that will first have to be waged' before Rome attains its 'future

---

78. David West (1987) argues that the ivory gate, along with the golden bough, are images Virgil borrowed indirectly from Plato, and the exit via '*falsa insomnia*' indicates to readers that they should interpret Anchises' account of metempsychosis as a narrative device, not as religious truth.
79. For a review of recent classical scholarship on the Gates of Sleep, see Horsfall (2013), pp. 612–21.
80. Cf. Dryden, who privileges the 'transparent' truth of the horn gate over the polish (opacity, ornate style) of the ivory: 'Two Gates the silent House of Sleep adorn; / Of polish'd Iv'ry this, that of transparent Horn: / True Visions through transparent Horn arise, / Through polish'd Iv'ry pass deluding Lyes.' (*The Sixth Book*, ll. 1235–8, p. 568) The adjective 'transparent' is Dryden's addition.
81. For example, in an essay Heaney much admired, Ted Hughes describes how primary 'memories, images, sounds, feelings, thoughts' become 'luminous at the core of [the poet's] mind'. For Heaney's quotation of this essay, see, for example, '"Apt Admonishment"' (2008), 23.

glory' (A.1208–9). In Heaney's self-standing translation of Book VI, this future path is no longer an inevitability for the hero, and for the wayfaring poet the ivory gate may be a new way into the 'luminous core of the mind'.[82]

The final lines of Heaney's translation reinforce this sense of a return to the beginning, which is already implicit in the way Virgil brings the underworld book to a close. The Sibyl famously warns Aeneas that, although it is *'facilis descensus Auerno'*, easy to go down to Hades, it is hard and rare to return.[83] But in the event, the hero's *anabasis* is swift and unimpeded. He returns to his comrades, takes his fleet across the Bay of Naples to Gaeta, and casts anchor in the harbour. The last line of Virgil's narrative recalls the opening of the book, with ships anchored (*'ancora'*) and prows (*'puppes'*) once again facing out to sea:

>   tum dente tenaci
> ancora fundabat nauis et litora curuae
> praetexunt puppes. (*Ae*.VI.3–5)
>
> ancora de prora iacitur; stant litore puppes. (*Ae*.6.901)[84]

In Heaney's translation, this verbal echo is amplified into a formal repetition:

> Anchors bite deep, craft are held fast, curved
> Sterns cushion on sand, prows frill the beach. (A.6–7)
>
> Anchors are cast from the prow; sterns cushion on sand. (A.1222)

While the last phrase repeats part of line 7 verbatim, Heaney's choice of verb, 'cast', also retains the sound of 'craft' and 'fast' in line 6 of his translation. The effect of this ampler repetition is two-fold. In one sense, it makes Heaney's ending sound even more classically epic than Virgil's.[85] By having the epic narrative circle back on itself in a formal ring composition, Heaney gives the impression of stepping away from the book as, with a hard-won, 'veteran detachment', he hands it back to the collective, cultural memory.[86]

In another sense, though, his final line is full of personal, lyric resonance for readers of Heaney's poetry. In 'Crediting Poetry', he had defended the 'adequacy of lyric' as 'both the ship and the anchor. It is at once a buoyancy and a holding,

---

82. See Hughes, in note 81 above.
83. *Ae*.VI.126–9; A.174–7.
84. 'then with firm-holding teeth, the anchors began to secure the ships and the curved hulls fringed the shore'; 'Anchors were cast from the bows; the ships stand along the shore' (trans. Horsfall, pp. 3, 61).
85. Repetition of stock phrases is a common feature of classical epic, originally an aid to oral performance. Dryden also formalises the repetition: 'Their Heads are turn'd to Sea, their Sterns to Shoar' (l. 1247, p. 568), echoing this opening passage: 'They turn their Heads to Sea; their Sterns to Land;' (l. 4, p. 527).
86. Heaney and Deane, 'Strangeness and Beauty' (2005), reviewing the new *Collected Poems* of Patrick Kavanagh.

allowing for the simultaneous gratification of whatever is centrifugal and whatever is centripetal in mind and body' (OG 466). For Heaney's readers, the image of Aeneas' fleet frilling the beach at Gaeta will recall the 'shiftiness and heft' of the Inishbofin ferry, the miniature golden ship from the Broighter Hoard, the miraculous air ship in 'What the annals say', and the 'untoward rupture and world-tilt' of Stevenson's ship at the end of *Human Chain*.[87] In each of these poems, a 'boat of imagination' is allowed to carry forward 'poetry's impulse to outstrip the given' (SS 327). So, when Heaney turns our attention again to the start of the book, we have the impression that Aeneas' fleet, though anchored on the shore, is about to set forth again.

*

In his lecture 'The Whole Thing: On the Good of Poetry', Heaney had declared that the 'virtue of poetry' resides in its being 'a whole thing, a hale thing, a thing formally and feelingly sound, right within itself'.[88] His lecture title recalls an earlier poem in which he praised the artist for venturing alone to the island and returning with 'the whole thing', the 'given note' (*DD* 36). And yet, Heaney's translation of Book VI is the more powerful and resonant for not being 'whole', in the sense of perfected and complete. Like Virgil's golden bough, its powers of renewal are released when it is broken off from the stem. As a self-standing, lyric fragment, Heaney's *Book VI* reverberates in a condition 'of unceasing sound'; like Mandelstam's cicada, 'having once seized hold of the air, it will not let it go.'[89] In this way, Heaney's translation of *Aeneid Book VI* successfully harnesses the twin drives of his poetry and poetics, both the impulse towards lyric spontaneity and self-sufficiency, and the epic sense of obligation to a community and to the common, cultural memory. In dialogue with Virgil, his poetry speaks to us powerfully both as individual readers, and as inheritors of our oldest and most enduring myths about the underworld and the afterlife.

87. Heaney, *ST* 16, 27, 62; *HC* 84.
88. Heaney, 'The Whole Thing' (2001), 8.
89. Heaney, quoting Mandelstam (comparing a quotation extract to a cicada), in 'The Freedom Writer: Poetry is the Plough that Turns up Time' (*The Guardian*, 1991). Cf. Keats, 'On the Grasshopper and Cricket' (2003, 54).

Coda: 'Mossbawn via Mantua'

'The poetry is not that which is lost in translation but that which survives it.' So Heaney writes in an essay originally delivered in Vienna, at a conference devoted to the 'cross-currents' linking Ireland to the rest of Europe.[1] The 'moment of consciousness' caught in a poem 'speaks beyond itself and its origins'; it can reach us across languages, historical eras and geographical distances (ibid.). Such poetry offers us new perspectives, or 'planes of regard', from which to view the familiar home ground in a new way.[2] The title of Heaney's essay, 'Mossbawn via Mantua', indicates that one of the ways he finds his way home is through his engagement with Virgil's poetry, Mantua being Virgil's birthplace.[3] While the title suggests that Virgil's poetry has a particular and unique importance for Heaney, the Roman poet occupies quite a modest place in the essay itself. Heaney takes the occasion in Vienna to identify five 'zones of operation', or areas of engagement with European literature, which have given him fresh perspectives on the Irish home ground. After an introductory reference to 'Route 110' and *Aeneid VI*, Virgil's poetry is cited near the end of the essay in connection with the fifth zone, that of 'more or less direct translation'. But if we examine his argument in more detail, we find that Heaney's dialogue with Virgil extends into all five of these types or territories of European engagement. As this study has shown, when Heaney responds to Virgil's poetry, he is also engaging with other writers such as Hesiod, Theocritus, Homer, Sophocles, Horace, Ovid, Dante, Shakespeare, Wordsworth, Keats, Mandelstam, Eliot, Yeats, Synge, Kavanagh, Miłosz and Hughes. So Virgil's poetry is 'translatable' both in its own right and as a transmitter of other European texts; it 'carries over' Virgil's

1. Heaney, 'Mossbawn via Mantua' (2012), 26 [based on the keynote lecture, 'Mossbawn via Mantua: A Reading with Commentary', delivered at the Seventh Conference of the European Federation of Associations and Centres of Irish Studies (*EFACIS*), *Ireland in/and Europe: Cross-Currents and Exchanges*, 3–6 September 2009].
2. 'Mossbawn via Mantua' (2012), 19.
3. The title alludes to Joyce's Dedalus in *A Portrait*: 'the shortest way to Tara is via Holyhead'. See Chapter 4, note 39, and Cillian O'Hogan, 'Irish Versions of Virgil's *Eclogues and Georgics*' (2018), 402.

particular 'moment of consciousness' in Roman times, and it mediates and builds bridges with other writers and their times. As a literary exemplar, Virgil triangulates and amplifies Heaney's 'planes of regard' on Ireland 'in/and' the European literary tradition.

In 'Mossbawn via Mantua', Heaney identifies five 'zones' of 'European operations': that is, five areas in which his own writing has engaged with Continental European literature, ancient, medieval and modern (20). The first zone he names the 'classical', all we have inherited from the Greek, Roman and Judaic past (20). The second zone is the 'barbarian', the 'antithetical European inheritance' of Northern, Viking and Germanic tribes, 'all that babble beyond the pale', with whom Heaney closely identifies (20). The third zone he calls the 'Hyperborean', the group of 'twentieth century poets of Russia and Eastern Europe', who, in their witness of the century's most brutal wars, comprise Heaney's 'republic of conscience' (21). His fourth zone consists of one poet alone, Dante Alighieri. And the fifth is 'more or less direct translation', in relation to which Heaney mentions his translations of texts by Virgil, Horace, Aeschylus, Sophocles, *Beowulf* and, again, Dante (21). Time and again, however, we will find that Heaney's dialogue with Virgil is implicated in all these areas of literary engagement.

Heaney's first 'zone of operations' consists of what he terms 'the classical': that is, all the 'mythological, cultural and intellectual baggage which European civilisation holds in common' (20). This shared cultural inheritance, he argues, 'provides the first co-ordinates of the Western mind, its common vocabulary, a system of longitude and latitude whereby the individual can locate himself or herself in culture and consciousness' (ibid.). Heaney's grammar school education had provided access to this classical inheritance (23). Later, he comes to regard Virgil as the poet who 'carried the heritage of ancient Greek poetry forward into the civilization of Rome and . . . the Europe that was to come' (*BBC*). So Virgil's poetry helps to forward an entire world of ancient Greek and Roman thought and literature. The classical figure in Heaney's writing who most completely embodies the poet's labour of forwarding the 'mythological, cultural and intellectual baggage [of] European civilisation' is Virgil's hero Aeneas, who bears the sacred *penates* out of burning Troy.

Moreover, as Heaney reminds his readers, all this inheritance of 'the classical' had come to Ireland in the fifth century, with Patrick and his Christian missionaries (20). Unlike Milton in *Paradise Lost*, for example, Heaney is not troubled in this essay by a sense of the incompatibility of classical and Christian literature. His first 'zone' of European 'intellectual baggage' capaciously accommodates both, in what he terms the 'Christian humanist inheritance, . . . a religious order amplified and inflected by the discoveries of the Renaissance' (ibid.). His classical education at St Columb's 'happened to be Roman as in Roman Catholic' (23). Heaney's first 'zone of operations', the classical, is, in his own experience, fully compatible with his fourth zone, the one 'invigilated' by Dante, 'whom Yeats called "the chief imagination of Christendom"' (21). In the *Commedia*, the pilgrim is guided through the first two realms of the afterlife by Dante's guide and literary exemplar, Virgil. Heaney, in turn, takes Dante as his guide through the purgatorial journey of *Station Island* (1984). When he turns to Virgil's *Aeneid VI* as a model for his descent into the past, in *The Riverbank Field* and *Human Chain*, he brings the shaping influence of Dante's *terza rima* forward into these Virgilian poems. Heaney's own relation to his beloved 'hedge-schoolmaster' is more familiar and more homely than either Eliot or Dante's relation to Virgil, but for him, Virgil and Dante still inhabit compatible worlds. Both writers take him over the threshold into imagination's realm of the marvellous, where poetry seeks redress to the 'Heaviness of being . . . / Sluggish in the doldrum of what happens.' (*ST* 50)

Heaney's second 'zone of operations' *is* antithetical to 'the classical', consisting of the 'barbarian element in European culture', all that originates from territories 'north of the Alps and north of Hadrian's Wall, all that is symbolised by the runic Germanic letter or the Irish ogham stone rather than the lines of Roman script.' (20) The 'barbarian element' in Heaney's poetry is given fullest expression in his 1975 volume, *North*, but all his writing is inflected in one way or another by this 'antithetical' European tradition. His dialogue with Virgil is shot through with an awareness of, and identification with, 'all that babble beyond the pale' (20). This 'antithetical' cultural inheritance is precisely what gives poetic energy and tension to his translations of Virgil, as we saw in Heaney's 'The Golden Bough', 'Palinurus' and other poems. In the *Aeneid*, Heaney hears the voice of one who 'celebrates, very deliberately, the origins and triumph of Roman power', but he also hears the undersong of Virgil's 'sympathy and intimacy with the world of nature . . . his closeness to the life of the land, . . . his raw inwardness, with the *lacrimae rerum*, the brutality of war, the reality of cruelty and bloodshed.' (*BBC*) In Virgil's poetry, Heaney detects signs of conflict between these two antithetical elements of European culture, and this tension in turn fuels his own inner self-questionings: 'how should a poet properly live and write? What is his relationship to be to his own voice, his own place, his literary heritage and his contemporary world?' (*FK*, x)

These self-questionings are also raised in Heaney's third 'zone of operations', where we find the modern Russian and Eastern European poets Osip Mandelstam and Czesław Miłosz, and the Polish poet Zbigniew Herbert, whom Heaney calls 'dual citizens of the republic of letters and the republic of conscience' (21). In their ice-calm witness of the twentieth century's world war atrocities, these writers produce poems '"like a slingstone / Whirled for the desperate"' (quoting Mandelstam, 21). One aspect of their armoury is a searing use of classical form, imagery and myth. Indeed, he gives this group of poets a classical name, the 'Hyperboreans', after the cultured people living in the mountains north of ancient Greece.[4] More specifically, Mandelstam's reading of Dante directly influences the way Heaney reads Virgil's poetry in the mid-1980s, as we saw in Chapter 1. A few years later, Heaney describes the 'curve of Miłosz's whole destiny' as Virgilian (*FK* 411). And he compares the '*integritas, consonantia* and *claritas*' of Virgil's *Eclogues* to that of Miłosz's pastoral poem, 'The World', composed during the occupation of Warsaw in 1943.[5] As Heaney remarks elsewhere, in the *Eclogues* Virgil deploys this 'almost vindictive

---

4. An early typescript of Heaney's poem 'To the Shade of Zbigniew Herbert' (*EL* 67) is entitled 'A Hyperborean' (*LP* I.v.3).
5. '*Eclogues in Extremis*' (2003), 7. See Chapter 4.

artistry' against the 'power of Rome and the brutal might of the legions'.⁶ So in this 'republic of conscience', Heaney sees Virgil sitting at the same table as his most admired Russian and Eastern European poets. In this connection, we should recall that Virgil's Orpheus meets his death in the 'Hyperborean glacial peaks' of Thrace (G.IV.517). The modern 'Hyperboreans' are comparable to Orpheus in the sense that their poetry attempts 'to haul life back up the slope against all the odds'; and some of them, like Orpheus, suffer brutally violent deaths at the hands of their enemies (*RP* 158).

Virgil is named in Heaney's fifth 'zone of operations': that is, the zone of direct translation from Latin, ancient Greek and other European literatures. Although, elsewhere, Heaney is guarded and oblique about the political context of his translations, here he stresses that each was composed in response to a particular contemporary crisis (22). Thus, his translation work is closely related to his engagement with Eastern European and Russian poets, his 'republic of conscience'. 'With Dante, as with my Hyperboreans', he writes, it was 'a matter of example, of being shown how to deal with conditions on the home ground, of trans-lation in a wider, looser, more general sense as "carry over"' (21–2). In his translation of Dante's *Inferno* 33, 'Ugolino', for example, Heaney responds to the dirty protest in Maze Prison, which led on to the IRA hunger strikes in 1981; and in his adaptation of Horace's *Odes* I, 34, Heaney reflects on the 9/11 destruction of the Twin Towers and 'approaching terror via Holyhead' (22). In Chapter 5 of this study, I explored the close structural and thematic connections between this adaptation of Horace and the Virgilian *katabasis* in 'District and Circle'. In his essay, Heaney cites another Virgilian poem, his translation of Virgil's ninth *Eclogue*. Amongst the examples of translation cited here, *Eclogues IX* stands out as the poem which best articulates Heaney's own preoccupation with the poet's role in times of historical crisis and conflict. 'The Ninth Eclogue is fundamentally concerned with the frail but vitally necessary work of poetry in a time of violence', Heaney writes; 'I did that job as a poet's *apologia pro vita mea* over the previous thirty years.' (22)

Heaney's mid- to late-career dialogue with Virgil likewise extends over a span of roughly thirty years, from the mid-1980s to 2013. As we observed in preceding chapters, this dialogue brings Heaney continually back to his home ground, in part because Virgil is a poetic resource remembered from his childhood and adolescence in rural County Derry. In terms of his engagement with Virgil's poetry, T. S. Eliot's prediction in 'Little Gidding' proves largely true: 'the end of all our exploring / will be to arrive where we started / And know the place for the first time.'⁷ Towards the end of his intense and richly productive dialogue with Virgil, Heaney's central focus shifts from the importance of poetry's *labor* in the 'republic of conscience' to its pleasurable implication in the natural cycles of rebirth and regeneration. From 2006 onwards, Heaney takes up Virgil's image of Aeneas and his father watching souls gather on the banks of the River Lethe, as a symbol of cultural renewal and the second life of art. The poetic recovery of this riverbank encounter, from Virgil's

---

6. Heaney, *SS* 389; 'Eclogues *in Extremis*' (2003), 3.
7. Eliot, 'Little Gidding', IV.27–9 (2015), Vol. I, p. 209.

poem and his own adolescent memories of Mossbawn, produce a powerful sense of uplift and release in the closing pages of The Riverbank Field, Human Chain and Heaney's translation of Aeneid Book VI. We can even hear the distinctively light step of this lyric Virgil in one of Heaney's last poems, 'In Time', written for his granddaughter Síofra. Heaney delights in the child's 'toddler wobbles' on the bare floor: 'Energy, balance, outbreak / At play for their own sake'.[8] The three nouns in that opening line encapsulate what Heaney prizes as the spontaneous, generative impulse of lyric poetry. As one of a trio of poems devoted to Heaney's granddaughters, this poem's dancing toddler recalls the new-born infant in 'Route 110, XII', and the lively kite that 'hovers, tugs, veers, dives askew, / Lifts itself' in 'A Kite for Aibhín'. On a secondary level, all these poems enact a Lethean return of language to its infancy, as suggested in the adults' 'baby talk' at the end of 'Route 110'. When Heaney recalls the beautiful riverbank scene at the end of Aeneid VI, then, he is not only finding a way back to his own home ground; he is also recovering the home ground of poetry itself, with its origins in 'infant babbling' (FK 176).

At every stage of this unfolding dialogue, Heaney's relations to Virgil can be regarded as an essentially enabling friendship. He admires and identifies with the Roman poet, who retains a strong attachment to his rural origins in the Mantuan countryside. He shares Virgil's melancholy awareness of the *lacrimae rerum*, the 'tears at the heart of things'. He is drawn to Virgil's Aeneas as the model for a poet on a marvellous quest for recovery of his lost first world. In Heaney's writing, Virgil's talismanic golden bough comes to symbolise poetry's doubleness in harnessing instinct and technical skill, its 'impulse to outstrip the given', and its power to renew and regenerate human culture (SS 327). Aeneas' crossing of the Styx in Charon's boat, along with other Virgilian motifs, provides a visual image for Heaney to weigh up his competing attachments and obligations to his artistic life, to his Irish community and to society as a whole. And Aeneas' helmsman, Palinurus, is an intelligence schooled into a soul through suffering and loss; as such, he offers Heaney a poetic image of human endurance and artistic staying power. For Heaney, Virgil's *Eclogues* epitomise the staying power of pastoral in their brilliant confluence of heightened, literary cadence and hard-bitten, country realism. And Virgil's poetry, in general, offers Heaney the means of transforming the sense of an ending into a fresh departure in his own late poems. Heaney's dialogue with Virgil spans some 2,000 years of European literature and culture, yet its lasting impression is that of a warm and intimate friendship between one *poeta natus et doctus* and another. One of the outstanding goods of Heaney's poetry is to make us feel included in that intimate and wide-ranging conversation.

---

8. Heaney, 'In Time', *The New Yorker* (23 December 2013), written 18 August 2013.

Appendix: 'Palinurus': *Aeneid* Book VI, lines 349–83

I

'Bound to hold course and hold fast
to the wheel, I refused to let go
when gale-force dislodged it - and went down

when the helm went down.
                    But by tempest
and tide I swear my fear for myself

was less than my fear for the ship: what hope
had she then, her tiller torn off
and her steersman gone overboard, at the mercy

of mountainous seas? For three nights
a south wind hurled me and burled me
through horizonless surge,

then the fourth day at dawn
there was Italy, barely glimpsed
as I rose on a wave.

Little by little I was making headway,
slugging and struggling to land
in my waterlogged clothes, getting a grip

on razor-backed ridges,
when savage locals came at me
mad for the kill, and that much the madder

at the thought of me as rich pickings.
Now surf keeps me dandled and shore winds
roll me in closer and closer.'

II

'You, therefore,
You the unbeaten, untouched,
I implore

by the cheerful light of the sky
and its winds, by your father
and your hopes as a father yourself,

get me out of this place, put an end
to my woes. Either
scatter the handful of earth

on my corpse, which you easily can
once you make your way back
above, to the anchorage, or else –

and this I ask in the knowledge
that gods take cognizance of you,
prepared as you are for this vastness

of river and Stygian marsh –
reach out your hand to a friend
who is suffering, take me with you

to the other side of the waves
so that in death at the least
I will find a calm haven.'

III

That was his plea to Aeneas, and this
was the answer he got
from the Sibyl:

'What madness is this, Palinurus?
You who aren't even buried, what makes you think
you can look on the flow of the Styx

or the Furies' grim river? Your time
has not come, you don't have the right.
Banish the thought

that praying can ever affect
the edicts of gods. Your plight
is a hard one, but hear and remember

my words; they should be a comfort.
What will happen is this:
your bones will be reverenced; the sky

will reveal signs and wonders, in cities
on every side populations will know
to build you a tomb

and solemnize it with offerings
year after year. And the place for all time
will bear the name Palinurus.'

These words lifted his heart and raised,
for a moment, his spirits. The thought
of the land in his name makes him happy.

Translated by Seamus Heaney
Parnassus: Poetry in Review (2008) 30:1–2, 78

Bibliography

I. VIRGIL (P. VERGILIUS MARO)

Editions and commentaries

Aeneid 6: Text and Commentary, (ed.) Nicholas Horsfall, 2 vols (Berlin: De Gruyter, 2013).
Aeneidos Liber Sextus, (com.) R. G. Austin (Oxford: Clarendon, 1977).
Aeneis Buch VI, (ed.) Eduard Norden (Leipzig: B. G. Teubner, 1903).
Eclogues, Georgics, Aeneid 1–6, (trans.) H. R. Fairclough (Cambridge, MA: Loeb, 1978).
Eclogues, Georgics, Aeneid 1–6, (trans.) H. R. Fairclough, revised by G. P. Goold (Cambridge, MA: Loeb, 1999).
P. Vergili Maronis Opera, (ed.) R. A. B. Mynors (Oxford: Clarendon, [1969] 1980).
Vergil, Aeneid Book VI, (eds) H. E. Gould and J. E. Whiteley (London: Macmillan, 1946, rpt. 1960).
Virgil, Aeneid I–VI, (ed.) R. D. Williams (London: Macmillan, 1972).
Virgil: Georgics Books III–IV, (ed.) R. F. Thomas (Cambridge: Cambridge University Press, [1988] 2001), Vol. 2.

Translations (in order of publication)

The Sixth Book of Virgil's Aeneid *Translated and Commented on by Sir John Harington* [1604], (ed.) Simon Cauchi (Oxford: Clarendon, 1991).
The Aeneid of Virgil, (trans.) J. W. Mackail (London: Macmillan, [1885] 1920).
Virgil: The Eclogues, The Georgics, (trans.) C. Day Lewis [1940], (intro.) R. O. A. M. Lyne (Oxford: Oxford University Press, 1983).
Virgil: The Aeneid, (trans.) C. Day Lewis [1952], (intro.) Jasper Griffin (Oxford: Oxford University Press, 2009).
Virgil: The Aeneid, (trans.) Robert Fitzgerald (New York: Random House, 1983).
The Eclogues of Virgil, (trans.) David Ferry (New York: Farrar, Straus and Giroux, 1999).
The Georgics of Virgil, (trans.) David Ferry (New York: Farrar, Straus and Giroux, 2006).
Virgil: The Aeneid, (trans.) Robert Fagles (London: Penguin, 2006).
The Aeneid, (trans.) Frederick Ahl (Oxford: Oxford University Press, 2007).
Aeneid Book VI, (trans.) Seamus Heaney (London: Faber, 2016).
The Aeneid: Virgil, (trans.) David Ferry (Chicago: University of Chicago Press, 2017).
The Aeneid, (trans.) Sarah Ruden (New Haven: Yale University Press, 2008; revised 2021).

II. SEAMUS HEANEY

Unless otherwise indicated, all websites were last accessed 19 May 2021.

Archives

Seamus Heaney Literary Papers, 1963–2010, The National Library, Dublin.
  <http://catalogue.nli.ie/Collection/vtls000358500>
McCabe Heaney Collection, 1977–2010, The National Library, Dublin.
  <http://catalogue.nli.ie/Collection/vtls000552515>
Seamus Heaney Papers, 1939–2013, Emory University, Stuart A. Rose Manuscript, Archives and Rare Book Library, Atlanta, Georgia.
  <https://findingaids.library.emory.edu/documents/heaney960>
The British Library Sound and Moving Image Catalogue.
  <https://www.bl.uk/subjects/sound>
Henry C. Pearson Collection of Seamus Heaney, Rare Book Collection, University of North Carolina at Chapel Hill.
Woodberry Poetry Room, Harvard University
  <https://library.harvard.edu/libraries/poetryroom#collections>

Publications, interviews, broadcasts (arranged by date of first publication)

Eleven Poems (Belfast: Festival Publications, Queen's University, 1965).
Death of a Naturalist (London: Faber, [1966] 2006).
Door into the Dark (London: Faber, [1969] 1972).
A Lough Neagh Sequence (Didsbury: Phoenix Pamphlets Poets Press, 1969).
Boy Driving His Father to Confession (Farnham: Sceptre Press, 1970).
Night Drive (Crediton: Richard Gilbertson, 1970).
Servant Boy (Detroit: Red Hanrahan Press, 1971).
Wintering Out (London: Faber, 1972).
'A Flourish for the Prince of Denmark', in Graham Fawcett (ed.), *Poems for Shakespeare 2* (London: The Globe Playhouse Trust, 1973), Part II.
After Summer, (illus.) Timothy Engelland (Old Deerfield, MA, and Dublin: Deerfield Press and Gallery Press, 1975).
Bog Poems (London: Rainbow Press, 1975).
The Fire i' the Flint: Reflections on the Poetry of Gerard Manley Hopkins (London: Oxford University Press, 1975).
North (London: Faber, [1975] 2000).
Stations (Belfast: Ulsterman, 1975).
in their element: a selection of poems by Seamus Heaney & Derek Mahon (Belfast: Arts Council of Northern Ireland, 1977).
'Unhappy and At Home' [Interview with Seamus Deane and Seamus Heaney], *The Crane Bag* 1:1 (Spring 1977), 61–7.
The Makings of a Music: Reflections on the Poetry of Wordsworth and Yeats (Liverpool: University of Liverpool, 1978), 1–18.
Robert Lowell: A Memorial Address and Elegy (London: Faber and John Roberts Press, 1978).
Field Work (London: Faber, 1979).
Gravities (Newcastle: Charlotte Press, 1979).
Hedge School: Sonnets from Glanmore, (illus.) Claire Van Vliet (Newark, VT: Janus Press for Charles Seluzicki Fine Books in Salem Oregon, 1979).
'An Interview with Seamus Heaney by James Randall', *Ploughshares* 18 (Fall 1979).

Ugolino [trans. of Dante, *Inferno* Cantos 32–3] (Monkstown, Co. Dublin: Andrew Carpenter, 1979). Rpt. *Antaeus* (Spring 1979), 20–31; *Lower Stumpf Lake Review* (Spring 1979), 6–7.
Preoccupations: Selected Prose 1968–1978 (London: Faber, 1980).
Selected Poems: 1965–1975 (London: Faber, 1980).
The Names of the Hare, sculptures by Barry Flanagan [Yorkshire Sculpture Park exhibition] (Barnsley: Derek Hattersley & Son, [1981] 1992).
Sweeney Praises the Trees, (illus.) Henry Pearson (New York: Kelly Winterton Press, 1981).
Poems and a Memoir (New York: Limited Editions Club, 1982).
The Rattle Bag, (eds) Heaney and Ted Hughes (London: Faber, 1982).
'Among Schoolchildren: A John Malone Memorial Lecture' (Queen's University, Belfast: John Malone Memorial Committee, 1983).
A Hazel Stick for Catherine Ann (Private publication: Peter Fallon, 1983).
An Open Letter (Derry: Field Day, 1983).
Sweeney Astray: A Version from the Irish (London: Faber, [1983] 2001).
Hailstones (Oldcastle, Co. Meath: The Gallery Press, 1984).
Place and Displacement: Recent Poetry of Northern Ireland (Grasmere: Trustees of Dove Cottage). Rpt. *The Agni Review* 22 ([1984] 1985), 158–77.
Station Island (London: Faber, 1984).
'Envies and Identifications: Dante and the Modern Poet', *Irish University Review* 15 (1985), 5–19. Rpt. Heaney, *Finders Keepers* (2002), 168–79; and *The Poets' Dante*, (eds) Peter S. Hawkins and Rachel Jacoff (New York: Farrar, Straus and Giroux, 2002), 239–58.
'Robert Fitzgerald: Memorial Address' [Audiofile], Emory University, Stuart A. Rose Manuscript Archives and Rare Book Library, Atlanta, Georgia (1985).
'Place, Pastness, Poems: A Triptych', *Salmagundi* 68/9 (Fall–Winter 1985/6), 30–48.
The Haw Lantern (London: Faber, 1987).
'The Placeless Heaven: Another Look at Kavanagh', *Massachusetts Review* 28:3 (Autumn 1987), 371–80. [Based on lecture delivered in 1985.]
'Anglo-Irish Occasions', *London Review of Books* 10:9 (5 May 1988), <https://www.lrb.co.uk/the-paper/v10/n09/seamus-heaney-anglo-irish-occasions>.
'The Dark Wood' [trans. of Dante, *Inferno*, Canto I], in Robert Welch (ed.), *Literature and the Art of Creation* (New Jersey: Barnes & Noble, 1988), 247–51.
The Government of the Tongue (London: Faber, 1988).
'The Crossing' [trans. of Dante, *Inferno*, Canto III, ll. 82–129], *Agenda* 27:1 (Spring 1989), 5–31.
'Crossings', *The New Yorker* (17 April 1989), 35.
'The Golden Bough' [trans. of *Aeneid* VI: 98–211], *Translation: The Journal of Literary Translation* XXII (Fall 1989), 197–201.
'Interview with Sue Lawley' [Audiofile], *Desert Island Discs*, BBC Radio 4 (19 November 1989), <https://www.bbc.co.uk/programmes/p009mdcy>.
The Place of Writing (Atlanta, GA: Scholars Press, 1989).
'Varieties of Irishness', *Irish Pages* 9:1 (1989), 9–20.
The Cure at Troy: A Version of Sophocles' Philoctetes (London: Faber, 1990).
New Selected Poems, 1966–1987 (London: Faber, 1990).
The Tree Clock (Belfast: Linen Hall Library, 1990).
'Above the Brim', *Salmagundi* 88/9 (1990–1), 275–94. Rpt. Joseph Brodsky, Heaney and Derek Walcott, *Homage to Robert Frost* (London: Faber, 1997), 61–92.
'The Freedom Writer', *The Guardian* (7 June 1991), 27.
'The Lost People' [trans. of Dante, *Inferno*, 1–3], in Noel Connor (ed.), *Confounded Language* (Hexham: Bloodaxe, 1991), 13–14.
'Man and Boy' and 'The Golden Bough', *Poetry Review* (Spring 1991), 72–4.
Seeing Things (London: Faber, 1991).
'A soul on the washing line' [Interview], *The Economist* (June 1991). Rpt. 5 September 2013.

'The Underground', *Folger Shakespeare Library* (7 April 1991).
The Golden Bough, screenprints by Jan Hendrix (Mexico City: Los Tropicos, and Bannholt, Netherlands: In de Bonnefant, May 1992).
'An Invocation', *London Review of Books* (6 August 1992).
'Introduction', Homer, *The Odyssey*, (trans.) Robert Fitzgerald (London: Everyman Library, 1992).
Keeping Going (Concord, NH: Bow and Arrow Press, 1993).
The Midnight Verdict (Oldcastle, Co. Meath: The Gallery Press, 1993).
'Orpheus and Eurydice' and 'The Death of Orpheus', in Michael Hofmann and James Lasdun (eds), *After Ovid: New Metamorphoses* (London: Faber, 1994), 222–9.
'Between North and South: Poetic Detours' [Interview with Richard Kearney, 1992], in Richard Kearney (ed.), *States of Mind* (1995), 101–8.
Crediting Poetry: The Nobel Lecture (London: Faber, 1995). Rpt. in *Opened Ground* (1998), 445–67. <http://www.nobelprize.org/nobel_prizes/literature/laureates/1995/heaney-lecture.html>.
The Redress of Poetry: Oxford Lectures (London: Faber, 1995).
'The Connection' [Audiofile], Henry C. Pearson Collection of Seamus Heaney, Rare Book Collection, University of North Carolina at Chapel Hill. [Interview with Christopher Lydon, 16 May 1996].
The Spirit Level (London: Faber, 1996).
'The Art of Poetry No. 75' [Interview with Henri Cole], *The Paris Review* 144 (Fall 1997), <https://www.theparisreview.org/interviews/1217/the-art-of-poetry-no-75-seamus-heaney> (last accessed 23 May 2021).
'Further Language', *Studies in the Literary Imagination* 30:2 (Fall 1997), 7–16. [Based on an address delivered in Belfast, 26 June 1995.]
Opened Ground: Poems, 1966–1996 (London: Faber, 1998).
'The Stick', in Richard English and Joseph Morrison Skelley (eds), *Ideas Matter: Essays in Honour of Conor Cruise O'Brien* (Lanham, MD: University Press of America, [1998] 2000), 51–3.
'Bann Valley Eclogue', *Times Literary Supplement* (8 October 1999), 32. Rpt. *Sunday Business Post* (26 December 1999), 1.
Beowulf: A New Translation (London: Faber, [1999] 2000).
'The Child That's Due' [extract of 'Bann Valley Eclogue'], Bank of Ireland Group Treasury, December 1999.
The Light of the Leaves, screenprints by Jan Hendrix (Mexico City: Los Tropicos, and Bannholt, Netherlands: In de Bonnefant, 1999). [Includes ten poems by Heaney: 'On a New Work in the English Tongue', 'A Norman Simile', '"Would they had stayed"', 'The Stick', 'W. H. Auden', 'Audenesque', 'Our Lady of Guadeloupe', 'The Little Canticles of Asturias', 'Willow, Ophelia, Moyola' and 'Hyperborean'.]
Sounding Lines: The Art of Translating Poetry [Interview with Robert Hass] (University of California at Berkeley, Townsend Center for the Humanities, Occasional Papers, 1999), <http://townsendcenter.berkeley.edu/sites/default/files/publications/OP20_Sounding_Lines.pdf>.
'Glanmore Eclogue', in Nicholas Grene (ed.), *Interpreting Synge: Essays from the Synge Summer School* (Dublin: Lilliput Press, 2000), 17–19.
'In Small Townlands: For Colin Middleton', in Carlo Eastwood (ed.), *Colin Middleton: A Millennium Appreciation* (Belfast: Eastwood Gallery, 2000), 13.
W. B. Yeats, *Poems* selected by Seamus Heaney (London: Faber, 2000).
Electric Light (London: Faber, 2001).
'Lux Perpetua', *The Guardian* (16 June 2001).
'Time and Again: Poetry and the Millennium', *The European English Messenger* 10:2 (2001), 19–23.

'On Elegies, Eclogues, Translations, Transfusions' [Interview with Rui Cavalho Homem], *The European English Messenger* 10:2 (2001), 24–30.

'Horace and the Thunder' [trans. of Horace, *Odes I*, 34], *The Irish Times* (17 November 2001), Weekend 10; *Times Literary Supplement* (18 January 2002), 40; *Translation Ireland* (Spring 2002), 8–11.

'Secular and Millennial Miłosz', in Heaney, *Finders Keepers: Selected Prose, 1971–2001* (2002), pp. 410–16. Originally published in Danish translation, in *Weekend Avisen* (Denmark, 1999).

'Towers, Trees, Terrors, a Rêverie in Urbino', in *In forma di parole: Seamus Heaney poeta dotto, a cura di Gabriella Morisco* 23:2 (2007), 145–56. [Based on a lecture delivered in Urbino, 23 November 2001.]

'The Whole Thing: On the Good of Poetry', *The Recorder: Journal of the American Irish Historical Society* (2002), 5–20. [Based on Heaney's Annual Distinguished Lecture, Royal College of Surgeons in Ireland, delivered 5 November 2001.]

Finders Keepers: Selected Prose 1971–2001 (London: Faber, [2002] 2003).

Heaney and Jan Hendrix, *Yagul: Three Books with Seamus Heaney* (*Diario de fatigas*) (Mexico: Turner/Fundación Cultural Artención/Universidad Autónoma Metropolitana, 2002).

'Ramifications: A Note on Jan Hendrix', in Heaney and Jan Hendrix, *Yagul: Three Books with Seamus Heaney* (*Diario de fatigas*) (Mexico: Turner/Fundación Cultural Artención/Universidad Autónoma Metropolitana, 2002), 229–31.

'Reality and Justice: On Translating Horace', *Irish Pages* I:2 (2002/3), 50–3.

'Sixth Sense, Seventh Heaven', *Dublin Review* 8 (Autumn 2002), 115–26.

'Staying Power' [Lecture, 22 October 2002, Audiofile], Woodberry Poetry Room, Harvard University.

'Eclogues *in Extremis*: On the Staying Power of Pastoral', *Proceedings of the Royal Irish Academy: Archaeology, Culture, History, Literature*, Vol. 103C:1 (2003), 1–12.

'"Glory be to the World"' [Review of Fallon (trans.), *The Georgics of Virgil*], *The Irish Times* (23 October 2004).

Anything Can Happen: A Poem and Essay by Seamus Heaney with Translations in Support of Art for Amnesty (Dublin: Townhouse, 2004).

The Burial at Thebes: A Version of Sophocles' Antigone (London: Faber, 2004).

A Shiver (Thame: Clutag Press, 2005).

'Strangeness and Beauty: Seamus Heaney Salutes a New Collection of Patrick Kavanagh's Poetry', *The Guardian* (1 January 2005).

'To the Poets of St Andrews', in Robert Crawford (ed.), *The Book of St Andrews: An Anthology* (Edinburgh: Polygon, [2005] 2007).

District and Circle (London: Faber, [2006] 2011).

'One Poet in Search of a Title', *The Times* (25 March 2006), 7.

'Afterword: Petals on a Bough', in Irene De Angelis and Joseph Woods (eds), *Our Shared Japan: An Anthology of Contemporary Irish Poetry* (Dublin: Dedalus, 2007), 211–18. Rpt. as 'The Pathos of Things', *The Guardian* (24 November 2007). [Based on a talk delivered in Dublin, 15 November 2000.]

'Our Mystery' and 'Fragment: "Nairn in darkness and in light"', *Archipelago* 1 (Summer 2007), 1, 62.

The Riverbank Field (Oldcastle, Co. Meath: The Gallery Press, 2007).

'The Staying Power of Poetry' [Interview with Simone Kearney], *Irish Literary Supplement* (Boston College Imprint), 27:1 (1 September 2007), 14, <https://newspapers.bc.edu>

'"Apt Admonishment": Wordsworth as Example', *The Hudson Review* 61:1 (Spring 2008), 19–33. [Based on a lecture delivered at the Morgan Library and Museum, 8 June 2006.]

'Articulations: Poetry, Philosophy and the Shaping of Culture', *Publication of Lecture upon Receipt of Royal Irish Academy Cunningham Medal* (Dublin: Royal Irish Academy, 2008).

'David Hammond' [obit.], *The Guardian* (28 August 2008), <https://www.theguardian.com/world/2008/aug/28/ireland.folk>

'The Fields of Light' [trans. of *Aeneid* VI: 638–78] and 'Loughanure', *Archipelago* II (Spring 2008), 9–14.

'Greek and Latin Voices: (Virgil): Episode 2', *The Essay*, BBC Radio 3 (transmission 15 July 2008). British Library Sound Archive BBC Catalogue WT 07035/7. Extract, <https://www.bbc.co.uk/sounds/play/p019bpl5>.

'Interview with Mark Lawson', *Front Row*, BBC Radio 4 (transmission 14 November 2008), <https://www.bbc.co.uk/programmes/b00f9gq4>.

'Palinurus' [trans. of *Aeneid* VI: 349–83] and 'Now the oil-fired burner comes to life', *Parnassus* 30:1–2 (2008), 75–80.

'Poetry Taught Me to Trust Derry as well as Derrida' [Interview with Denis O'Driscoll], *The Arts Show*, RTÉ Radio 1 (24 November 2008), <https://www.rte.ie/archives/exhibitions/1982-seamus-heaney/1991-21st-century-heaney/607215-stepping-stones/>.

'The Riverbank Field' [Interview with Gerald Dawe], *The Poetry Programme*, RTÉ (transmission 4 October 2008).

Stepping Stones: Interviews with Seamus Heaney, (ed., interviewer) Dennis O'Driscoll (London: Faber, [2008] 2009).

'Interview with Mark Lawson' [Heaney's seventieth birthday], *Front Row*, BBC Radio 4 (13 April 2009), <https://www.bbc.co.uk/programmes/b00jm364>.

'"The Kite" by Giovanni Pascoli', in Fergus Mulligan (ed.), *Augury: To Mary Kelleher* (Dublin: Dublin Royal Society, 2009).

Robert Henryson: The Testament of Cresseid & Seven Fables (London: Faber, 2009).

'Seamus Heaney: A Life of Rhyme' [Interview with Robert McCrum], *The Guardian* (19 July 2009), <https://www.theguardian.com/books/2009/jul/19/seamus-heaney-interview>.

'Seamus Heaney: Out of the Marvellous', (dir.) Charlie McCarthy (RTÉ, April 2009; retransmission BBC Radio 4, 22 January 2014), <https://www.youtube.com/watch?v=YJekPyV2rJM> (last accessed 15 December 2020).

Spelling It Out, (illus.) Basil Blackshaw (Oldcastle, Co. Meath: The Gallery Press, 2009).

'Three Freed Speeches from Aeneid VI' [trans. *Aeneid* VI: 42–76; 77–97; 847–54], in David and Helen Constantine (eds), *Modern Poetry in Translation*, 3:12 (2009), 58–61.

'Title Deeds: Translating a Classic', in S. J. Harrison (ed.), *Living Classics: Greece and Rome in Contemporary Poetry in English* (Oxford: Oxford University Press, 2009).

'Writer and Righter' (Dublin: Irish Human Rights Commission. Publication of the Fourth IHR Annual Human Rights Lecture, [9 December 2009] 2010).

Human Chain (London: Faber, [2010] 2012).

'Poetry Prom Interview' [with Michael Laskey], *Poetry Trust Archive*, 2010, <https://www.poetryfoundation.org/podcasts/75876/seamus-heaney>.

'From "The Kite" by G. Pascoli' [ll. 30–64], in Geoffrey Brock (ed.), *The FSG Book of Twentieth Century Italian Poetry* (New York: Farrar, Straus and Giroux, 2012), 14–17.

'Mossbawn via Mantua', in Werner Huber, Sandra Mayer and Julia Novak (eds), *Ireland in/and Europe: Cross-Currents and Exchanges. Irish Studies in Europe* 4 (Trier: Wissenschaftlicher Verlag Trier, 2012), 19–28. [Based on a lecture delivered in Vienna, 3–6 September 2009.]

The Stone from Delphi: Poems with Classical References, selected with intro. by Helen Vendler (San Francisco: The Arion Press, 2012).

'Visitations', in Lindsay Clarke (ed.), *The Gist: a Celebration of the Imagination* (Arvon and The Write Factor, 2012), 61–72. A reprint of 'Apt Admonishment' (2008).

'On Home Ground', *Rivista Pascoliana* 24–5 (2012–13), 19–26. [Based on a lecture delivered at the University of Bologna, 2012, on the 200th anniversary of the death of Giovanni Pascoli.]

The Last Walk. From the Italian, by Giovanni Pascoli, illus. Martin Gale (Oldcastle, Co. Meath: The Gallery Press, 2013).

'On the Gift of a Fountain Pen', *Beall Poetry Festival Brochure* (4 March 2013).
'"The Owl" translated from the Italian of Giovanni Pascoli', *Translation* 4/10 (Dublin: Graphic Studio Dublin, 2013).
'Suffering and Decision', in T. Gifford, N. Roberts and M. Wormald (eds), *Ted Hughes: From Cambridge to Collected* (Basingstoke: Palgrave Macmillan, 2013). [Based on the Ted Hughes Memorial Lecture, delivered at Dartington Hall, Devon, 2007.]
'Banks of a Canal', *Anthology of National Gallery of Ireland* (Dublin, 2014). Rpt. *The Guardian* (3 October 2014).
'Four Poems', *Irish Pages* 8:2 (2014), 9–11.
New Selected Poems 1988–2013, (ed.) Marco Sonzogni (London: Faber, 2014).
Aeneid Book VI (London: Faber, 2016).
Aeneid Book VI, screenprints by Jan Hendrix (Bannholt, Netherlands: Bonnefant Press, 2016).
Seamus Heaney's *Aeneid Book VI*, read by Ian McKellen, broadcast in 5 episodes, *Book of the Week*, BBC Radio 4 (7–13 March 2016), <https://www.bbc.co.uk/programmes/b072jomn> (last accessed 24 May 2021).
Given Notes: The Complete Translations of Seamus Heaney, (ed.) Marco Sonzogni (London: Faber, forthcoming).

III. GENERAL BIBLIOGRAPHY

Ahmed, Samira [Review], *Front Row*, BBC Radio 4 (8 March 2016), <https://www.bbc.co.uk/radio/play/b072hlnt>.
Allen, Michael (ed.), *Seamus Heaney* (Basingstoke: Macmillan, 1997).
Alpers, Paul, *The Singer of the* Eclogues: *A Study of Virgilian Pastoral* (Berkeley: University of California Press, 1979).
—, *What is Pastoral?*, 2nd edn (Chicago: Chicago University Press, 1997).
Aristotle, *Poetics*, (ed., trans.) S. Halliwell (London: Harvard University Press, 1995).
Armitage, Simon, *Sandettie Light Vessel Automatic* (London: Faber, 2019).
Auden, W.H., *The Dyer's Hand* [1962], (London: Faber, 1987).
—, '"The Sea and the Mirror": A Commentary on Shakespeare's *The Tempest*', in Auden, *Collected Longer Poems* (New York: Random House, 1965).
Auge, Andrew J., 'Surviving Death in Heaney's *Human Chain*', in E. O'Brien (ed.), *'The Soul Exceeds Its Circumstances'* (Notre Dame, IN: Notre Dame University Press, 2016), 29–48.
Auerbach, Erich, *Mimesis: The Representation of Reality in Western Literature*, (trans.) W. Trask (New York: Doubleday Anchor Books, 1957).
Averill, James H., *Wordsworth and the Poetry of Human Suffering* (Ithaca, NY: Cornell University Press, 1980).
Bachelard, Gaston, *La Terre et les rêveries de la volonté* (Paris: Librairie José Corti, 1947).
—, *The Poetics of Space* (*La Poétique de l'espace* [1958]), (trans.) Maria Jolas (Boston: Beacon Books, 1969).
—, *Air and Dreams: An Essay on the Imagination of Movement* (*L'Air et les songes, essai sur l'imagination du mouvement* [1943]), (trans.) E. R. and C. F. Farrell (Dallas: The Dallas Institute Publications, [1988] 2011).
—, *Water and Dreams: An Essay on the Imagination of Matter*, (trans.) E. R. and C. F. Farrell (Dallas: The Dallas Institute Publications, [1994] 2011).
Bakhtin, Mikhail, —, *The Dialogic Imagination: Four Essays*, (ed.) Michael Holquist, (trans.) Caryl Emerson and Michael Holquist (Austin: University of Texas Press, 1981).
—, *Art and Answerability: Early Philosophical Essays*, (eds) M. Holquist and V. Liapunov, (trans.) V. Liapunov (Austin: University of Texas Press, 1986).

Balmer, Josephine, 'Seamus Heaney's Translation of Aeneid Book VI: A Fitting End to a Life's Work' [Review], *New Statesman* (6 April 2016).
Banville, John, 'Living Ghosts', *The New York Review* (11 November 2010), 20–1.
Barrell, John and John Bull (eds), *The Penguin Book of Pastoral Verse* (London: Penguin, [1975] 1982).
Barrett, William and Theodore Besterman, *The Divining-Rod: An Experimental and Psychological Investigation* (London: Methuen, 1926).
Basto, Ronald, 'Horace's "proempticon" to Vergil: A Reexamination', *Vergilius* 28 (1982), 30–43.
Bate, Jonathan, *The Song of the Earth* (Cambridge, MA: Harvard University Press, 2000).
Beckett, Samuel, *The Unnameable*, (ed.) Steven Connor (London: Faber, [1953] 2010).
Bedient, Calvin, *He Do the Police in Different Voices: The Waste Land and Its Protagonist* (Chicago: University of Chicago Press, 1986).
—, '*District and Circle* by Seamus Heaney; *Cracks in the Universe* by Charles Tomlinson', *Chicago Review* 51:3 (Spring 2007), 160–5.
Bennett, Alice, 'Afterlife', *Oxford Research Encyclopedias: Literature* (June 2019), <https://oxfordre.com/view/10.1093/acrefore/9780190201098.001.0001/acrefore-9780190201098-e-1046>.
Bevis, Matthew, 'Unknowing Lyric', *Poetry Magazine* (2017), 575–89, <https://www.poetryfoundation.org/poetrymagazine/articles/92372/unknowing-lyric>.
Bilbro, Jeffrey, 'Sounding the Darkness and Discovering the Marvellous: Hearing "A Lough Neagh Sequence" with Seamus Heaney's Auditory Imagination', *Irish Studies Review* 19:3 (2011), 321–40.
Bloom, Harold, *The Anxiety of Influence: A Theory of Poetry* (New York: Oxford University Press, 1973).
— (ed.), *Seamus Heaney* (New York: Chelsea House, 1986).
Bloomer, W. Martin, 'Marble Latin', in Bloomer (ed.), *The Contest of Language: Before and Beyond Nationalism* (Notre Dame, IN: University of Notre Dame Press, 2005), 207–26.
Bonnefoy, Yves, *The Arrière-pays*, (trans.) Stephen Romer (Calcutta: Seagull Books, [1972] 2012).
Borges, Jorge Luis, 'The Maker', in Borges, *Collected Fictions*, (trans.) Andrew Hurley (London: Penguin, 1998), 192–3.
Brandes, Rand, and Michael J. Durkan, *Seamus Heaney: A Bibliography 1959–2003* (London: Faber, 2008).
Bremmer, Jan, *The Rise and Fall of the Afterlife* (Abingdon: Routledge, 2002).
—, 'The Golden Bough: Orphic, Eleusinian, and Hellenic–Jewish Sources of Virgil's Underworld in *Aeneid VI*', *Kernos* 22 (2009), pp. 183–208, <https://journals.openedition.org/kernos/1785> (last accessed 23 May 2021).
—, *Initiation into the Mysteries of the Ancient World* (Berlin: de Gruyter, 2014).
Braund, Susanna and Zara Martirosova Torlone (eds), *Virgil and His Translators* (Oxford: Oxford University Press, 2018).
Buell, Lawrence, *The Environmental Imagination: Thoreau, Nature Writing, and the Formation of American Culture* (Cambridge, MA: Harvard University Press, 1995).
Burris, Sydney, *The Poetry of Resistance: Seamus Heaney and the Pastoral Tradition* (Athens: Ohio University Press, 1991).
Burrow, Colin, 'You've listened long enough' [Review], *London Review of Books* 38:8 (21 April 2016), <http://www.lrb.co.uk/v38/n08/colin-burrow/youve-listened-long-enough> (last accessed 15 December 2020).
Buxton, Rachel, *Robert Frost and Northern Irish Poetry* (Oxford: Oxford University Press, 2004).
Byron, Catherine, *Out of Step: Pursuing Seamus Heaney to Purgatory* (Bristol: Loxwood Stoneleigh, 1992).

Calvino, Italo, *Why Read the Classics?*, (trans.) M. McLoughlin (London: Penguin, 2009).
Cardinale, Philip, *Verse Translations of Virgil's Aeneid in Britain, 1787–1824* (University of Oxford, Humanities Division, D.Phil. thesis, 2005).
Carruth, Allison, 'On Bog Lands and Digital Markets: Seamus Heaney's Recent Poetry', *Pacific Coast Philology* 46:2 (2011), 232–44.
Cavanagh, Michael, *Professing Poetry: Seamus Heaney's Poetics* (Washington, DC: Catholic University of America Press, 2009).
Cavarero, Adriana, *Relating Narratives: Storytelling and Selfhood*, (trans.) Paul Kottman (London: Routledge, 2000).
Chapman, George, *Chapman's Homer: The Iliad*, (ed.) Allardyce Nicoll (Princeton: Princeton University Press, [1598] 1998).
Clark, Raymond, *Catabasis: Vergil and the Wisdom Tradition* (Amsterdam: B. R. Gruner, 1979).
Clarke, Charles and Mary, *Recollections of Writers* (London: Gilbert and Rivington, 1878).
Clausen, Wendell, 'Theocritus and Virgil', in E. J. Kenney and W. V. Clausen (eds), *Cambridge History of Classical Literature*, Vol. 2 (Cambridge: Cambridge University Press, 1982), 301–19.
—, *A Commentary on Virgil: Eclogues* (Oxford: Clarendon Press, 1994).
Cohen, Jeffrey Jerome, *Elemental Criticism: Thinking with Earth, Air, Water and Fire* (Minneapolis: University of Minnesota Press, 2015).
Connor, Noel (ed.), *Confounded Language: New Poems by Nine Irish Writers* (Hexham: Bloodaxe, 1991).
Constable, John, 'What Happened after *Field Work*?', *Poetry Wales* 34:3 (1999), 48–56.
Corcoran, Brendan, 'Seamus Heaney's Cold Heaven: "The Ecological Lament"', *Irish Pages* 10/1 (2011), 127–45.
Corcoran, Neil, *A Student's Guide to Seamus Heaney* (London: Faber, 1986).
—, 'Seamus Heaney and the Art of the Exemplary', *Yearbook of English Studies* 17 (1987), 117–27.
— (ed.), *The Chosen Ground: Essays on the Contemporary Poetry of Northern Ireland* (Dufour: Seren Books, 1992).
—, *The Poetry of Seamus Heaney: A Critical Study* (London: Faber, 1998).
—, 'The Melt of the Real Thing', *Irish Review* 49/50 (2014/15), 5–18.
—, 'Heaney's Shakespeare', *Essays in Criticism* 70:1 (January 2020), 64–86.
Coughlan, Patricia, '"Bog Queens": The Representation of Women in the Poetry of John Montague and Seamus Heaney', in Michael Allen (ed.), *Seamus Heaney* (London: Macmillan, 1997), 185–205.
—, '"The Whole Strange Growth": Heaney, Orpheus and Women', *The Irish Review* 35 (Summer 2007), 25–45.
Craven, Peter, 'The Aeneid Review: Heaney's Translation of Virgil in a Heroic Mode', *The Sydney Morning Herald* (18 June 2016).
Crowder, Ashby Bland and Jason David Hall (eds), *Seamus Heaney: Poet, Critic, Translator* (Basingstoke: Palgrave Macmillan, 2007).
Culler, Jonathan, *Theory of the Lyric* (Cambridge, MA: Harvard University Press, 2015).
Cullingford, Elizabeth, '"Thinking of Her & as & Ireland": Yeats, Pearse and Heaney', *Textual Practice* (1 January 1990), 1–21.
Curtis, Tony (ed.), *The Art of Seamus Heaney*, 4th edn (Bridgend: Seren, 2001).
Danchev, Alex, *Cézanne: A Life* (London: Profile Books, 2012).
—, *The Letters of Paul Cézanne* (London: Thames and Hudson, 2013).
Dante (Dante Alighieri), *The Divine Comedy* [1320], bilingual edition, (trans.) Charles Singleton (Princeton: Princeton University Press, 1989).
D'Avanzo, Mario L., 'Keats' and Virgil's Underworlds: Source and Meaning in Book II of *Endymion*', *Keats–Shelley Journal* 16 (Winter 1967), 61–72.
Davidson, Peter, *The Last of the Light: About Twilight* (London: Reaktion Books, 2015).
Dawe, Gerald, 'Shifting Ground', *Fortnight* 285 (1990), 23–4.

De Man, Paul, *Blindness and Insight* (Abingdon: Routledge, 1983).
Deane, Seamus, *Celtic Revivals: Essays in Modern Irish Literature, 1880–1980* (London: Faber, 1985).
—, 'Powers of Earth and Visions of Air', *Times Literary Supplement* (16 March 1990), 275–6. Rpt. in Catherine Malloy and Phyllis Carey (eds), *Seamus Heaney: The Shaping Spirit* (London: University of Delaware Press, 1996), 27–33.
—, 'The Production of Cultural Space in Irish Writing', *Boundary 2* 21:3 (Autumn 1994), 117–44.
—, *Strange Country: Modernity and Nationhood in Irish Writing Since 1790* (Oxford: Oxford University Press, 1999).
Dennison, John, *Heaney and the Adequacy of Poetry* (Oxford: Oxford University Press, 2015).
Dick, Bernard F., '*The Waste Land* and the *descensus ad inferos*', *Canadian Review of Comparative Literature* 2:1 (Winter 1975), 35–46.
Dickens, Charles, *A Tale of Two Cities* (London: Penguin, 2003).
Dolan, Terence Patrick (compiler, ed.), *A Dictionary of Hiberno-English* (Dublin: Gill and Macmillan, 1999).
Donne, John, *John Donne: The Complete English Poems*, (ed.) A. J. Smith (Harmondsworth: Penguin, 1983).
Douglas, Gavin, *Gavin Douglas's Translation of the Aeneid* [1513], (ed.) Gordon Kendal (London: MHRA, 2011), 2 vols.
Dryden, John, *The Works of Dryden: The Works of Virgil in English* [1697], (eds) W. Frost and V. A. Dearing (Berkeley: University of California Press, 1987), Vol. 5.
Dyson, Julia, *King of the Wood: The Sacrificial Victor in Virgil's Aeneid* (Norman: University of Oklahoma Press, 2001).
The Economist [Anon. review], 'Music from the Underworld: Seamus Heaney's "Aeneid"', *The Economist* 419:8985 (16 April 2016), 72–3.
Eliot, T. S., *Selected Prose*, (ed.) John Hayward (Harmondsworth: Penguin, 1953).
—, *On Poetry and Poets* (London: Faber, [1957] 1969).
—, *Selected Prose of T. S. Eliot*, (ed.) Frank Kermode (London: Faber, 1975).
—, 'Tradition and the Practice of Poetry' [1936], *The Southern Review* 21:4 (October 1985), 873–88.
—, *The Poems of T. S. Eliot*, (eds) Christopher Ricks and Jim McCue (London: Faber, 2015), 2 vols.
Empson, William, *Some Versions of Pastoral* (New York: New Directions, 1974).
Faggen, Robert (ed.), *Cambridge Companion to Robert Frost* (Cambridge: Cambridge University Press, 2001).
Falconer, Rachel, *Orpheus Dis(re)membered: Milton and the Myth of the Poet Hero* (London: Bloomsbury, 1996).
—, 'Bakhtin and the Epic Chronotope', in Carol Adlam, Rachel Falconer, Vitalii Makhlin and Alastair Renfrew (eds), *Bakhtin in Russia and the West* (Sheffield: Sheffield Academic Press, 1997), 254–72.
—, *Hell in Contemporary Literature: Western Descent Narratives Since 1945* (Edinburgh: Edinburgh University Press, [2005] 2007).
—, *The Crossover Novel: Contemporary Children's Fiction and Its Adult Readership* (Routledge: London, 2009).
—, 'Genres and Modes: Epic', in Michael Hattaway (ed.), *A Companion to English Renaissance Literature and Culture*, 2nd edn (Oxford: Blackwell, 2010).
—, 'Hell in Our Time: 9/11 and its Aftermath', in M. Toscano and I. Moreira (eds), *Hell and Its Afterlife: Historical and Contemporary Perspectives* (Farnham: Ashgate, 2010), 217–36.
—, 'Is There Freedom Afterwards? A Dialogue between *Paradise Lost* and DeLillo's *Falling Man*', in Laura Knoppers (ed.), *Milton Studies* 53 (2012), 235–55.

—, 'Facing the Other Through Metaphor: Primo Levi's *The Periodic Table*', *British Journal of Literature and Science* 8:2 (2015), 53–71.
—, 'The Music of Heaney's *Aeneid VI*', *Comparative Literature* 69:4 (December 2017), 430–48.
—, 'Heaney and Virgil's Underworld Journey', in S. J. Harrison et al. (eds), *Seamus Heaney and the Classics: Bann Valley Muses* (Oxford: Oxford University Press, 2019, 180–204.
—, 'Heaney, Pascoli and the Ends of Poetry', in Thomas Harrison (ed.), *The Ends of Poetry: California Italian Studies* 8 (2019), <https://escholarship.org/uc/item/9cf9h0qc>.
—, 'Wordsworth's Soundings in the *Aeneid*', *Romanticism* 26:1 (2020), 23–37.
Falconer, Rachel and Madeleine Scherer (eds), *A Quest for Remembrance: The Underworld in Classical and Modern Literature* (London: Routledge, 2020).
Falvey, Deirdre, 'Seamus Heaney, Our Dad the Poet, by Catherine, Chris and Mick Heaney', *The Irish Times* (30 June 2018), <https://www.irishtimes.com/culture/books/seamus-heaney-our-dad-the-poet-by-catherine-chris-and-mick-heaney-1.3546885>.
Farrell, Joseph and Michael Putnam, *A Companion to Vergil's* Aeneid *and Its Tradition* (Oxford: Wiley-Blackwell, 2010).
Felstiner, John, *Can Poetry Save the Earth?* (New Haven, CT: Yale University Press, 2009).
Finn, Christine, *Past Poetic: Archaeology and the Poetry of W. B. Yeats and Seamus Heaney* (London: Duckworth, 2004).
Fitzgerald, Robert, 'Dryden's *Aeneid*', *Arion* 2:3 (Autumn 1963), 17–31.
— (trans.), Homer, *The Odyssey* (London: Everyman Library, 1992), <http://www.randomhouse.com/knopf/classics/intro/odyssey_homer.pdf>.
— (trans.), *Oedipus at Colonus*, in Mark Griffith, Glenn Most, David Greene and Richmond Lattimore (eds), *Sophocles I: Antigone, Oedipus the King, Oedipus at Colonus* (Chicago: University of Chicago Press, 2013).
Flanagan, Eimear, 'Seamus Heaney: "I live in panic over the next poem"', *BBC News* (23 September 2010), <https://www.bbc.com/news/uk-northern-ireland-11400255>.
Fowler, Rowena, '"Purple Shining Lilies": Imagining the *Aeneid* in Contemporary Poetry', in S. J. Harrison et al. (eds), *Living Classics: Greece and Rome in Contemporary Poetry in English* (Oxford: Oxford University Press, 2009), 238–54.
—, 'Heaney and Hesiod', in S. J. Harrison et al. (eds), *Seamus Heaney and the Classics: Bann Valley Muses* (Oxford: Oxford University Press, 2019), 38–49.
Frazer, Sir James George, *The Golden Bough*, Abridged edn (London: Macmillan, 1922).
—, *The New Golden Bough*, (ed.) Theodor Gaster (New York: Criterion Books, 1959).
Freer, Nicholas and Bobby Xinyue, *Reflections and New Perspectives on Virgil's* Georgics (London: Bloomsbury, 2019).
Freud, Sigmund, 'A Project for a Scientific Psychology' [1894], in James Strachey (gen. ed.), *The Standard Edition of the Complete Psychological Works of Sigmund Freud* (London: Hogarth Press, 1950), Vol. 1, 283–388.
—, 'Remembering, Repeating, and Working Through' [1914], in James Strachey (gen. ed.), *The Standard Edition of the Complete Psychological Works of Sigmund Freud* (1958), Vol. 12, 147–56.
—, 'Mourning and Melancholia' [1917], in James Strachey (gen. ed.), *The Standard Edition of the Complete Psychological Works of Sigmund Freud* (1958), Vol. 14, 239–60.
—, *The Standard Edition of the Complete Psychological Works of Sigmund Freud*, gen. ed. James Strachey, in collaboration with Anna Freud (London: Hogarth Press and the Institute of Psycho-Analysis, 1955–1974), Vols 1–24.
Friel, Brian, *Translations* (London: Faber, 1981).
Frost, Robert, *The Collected Poems of Robert Frost* (New York: Halycon House, 1939).
Frye, Northrop, *The Secular Scripture: A Study of Romance* (Cambridge, MA: Harvard University Press, 1976).

Garrard, Greg, *Ecocriticism*, 2nd edn (Abingdon: Routledge, 2011).
Garrard, Greg and Susanna Lidström, '"Images adequate to our predicament": Ecology, Environment and Ecopoetics', *Environmental Humanities* 5 (2014), 35–53.
Garratt, Robert F. (ed.), *Critical Essays on Seamus Heaney* (New York: G. K. Hall, 1995).
Genette, Gérard, *Paratexts: Thresholds of Interpretation* (Cambridge: Cambridge University Press, 1997); originally *Seuils* (Paris: Éditions du Seuil, 1987).
Gifford, Terry, *Pastoral*, 2nd edn (Abingdon: Routledge, 2019).
—, N. Roberts and M. Wormald (eds), *Ted Hughes: From Cambridge to Collected* (Basingstoke: Palgrave Macmillan, 2013).
Gilgamesh, The Epic of, (intro.) N. K. Sandars (London: Penguin, 1972).
Gilsenan Nordin, Irene, *Crediting Marvels in Seamus Heaney's Seeing Things* (Uppsala: Acta Universitatis Upsaliensis, 1999).
Girard, René, *Violence and the Sacred*, (trans.) Patrick Gregory (Baltimore: Johns Hopkins University Press, 1977).
Glob, P. V., *The Bog People: Iron-Age Man Preserved* (London: Faber, 1969).
Goodman, Kevis, *Georgic Modernity and British Romanticism: Poetry and the Mediation of History* (Cambridge: Cambridge University Press, 2006).
Gowing, Alan, *Empire and Memory: The Representations of the Roman Republic in Imperial Culture* (Cambridge: Cambridge University Press, 2005).
Greenblatt, Stephen (ed.), *The Norton Anthology of English Literature: The Sixteenth Century, the Early Seventeenth Century*, 8th edn (New York: Norton, 2006).
Grillo, Luca, 'Leaving Troy and Creusa', *The Classical Journal* 106:1 (October–November 2010), 43–68.
Guthrie, W. K. C., *A History of Greek Philosophy* (London: Cambridge University Press, 1962), Vol. I.
Haffenden, John (ed.), *Viewpoints: Poets in Conversation with John Haffenden* (London: Faber, 1981).
Hall, Edith, 'Paving and Pencilling: Heaney's Inscriptions in J. W. Mackail's Translation of the *Aeneid*', in S. J. Harrison et al. (eds), *Seamus Heaney and the Classics: Bann Valley Muses* (Oxford: Oxford University Press, 2019), 223–43.
Hall, Jason David, *Seamus Heaney's Rhythmic Contract* (Basingstoke: Palgrave Macmillan, 2009).
Hanson, Kristin and Paul Kiparsky, 'A Parametric Theory of Poetic Meter', *Language* 72:2 (1996): 287–325.
Hardie, Philip, *The Epic Successors of Virgil: A Study in the Dynamics of a Tradition* (Cambridge: Cambridge University Press, 1993).
—, 'Virgil and Tragedy', in Charles Martindale (ed.), *The Cambridge Companion to Virgil* (Cambridge: Cambridge University Press, 1997), 312–26.
—, *The Last Trojan Hero: A Cultural History of the Aeneid* (London: I. B. Tauris, 2014).
Hardie, Philip and Helen Moore, *Classical Literary Careers and Their Reception* (Cambridge: Cambridge University Press, 2010).
Hardwick, Lorna, 'Classical Texts in Post-Colonial Literatures: Redress and New Beginnings in the Work of Derek Walcott and Seamus Heaney', *International Journal of the Classical Tradition* 9 (2002), 236–56.
— and Christopher Stray (eds), *A Companion to Classical Receptions* (Oxford: Blackwell, 2008).
Harrison, Robert Pogue, *Forests: The Shadow of Civilization* (Chicago: University of Chicago Press, 1992).
—, *The Dominion of the Dead* (Chicago: University of Chicago Press, 2003).
—, *Juvenescence: A Cultural History of Our Age* (Chicago: Chicago University Press, 2014).
Harrison, S. J., 'Virgilian Contexts', in L. Hardwick and C. Stray (eds), *A Companion to Classical Receptions* (Oxford: Blackwell, 2008), 113–26.

— (ed.), *Living Classics: Greece and Rome in Contemporary Poetry in English* (Oxford: Oxford University Press, 2009).
—, 'Heaney as Translator: Horace and Virgil', in S. J. Harrison et al. (eds), *Seamus Heaney and the Classics: Bann Valley Muses* (Oxford: Oxford University Press, 2019), 244–62.
—, Fiona Macintosh, Claire Kenward and Helen Eastman (eds), *Seamus Heaney and the Classics: Bann Valley Muses* (Oxford: Oxford University Press, 2019).
Hart, Henry, *Seamus Heaney: Poet of Contrary Progressions* (Syracuse: Syracuse University Press, 1992).
—, 'What is Heaney Seeing in *Seeing Things?*', *Colby Quarterly* 30:1 (March 1994), 33–42.
—, 'Seamus Heaney and Ted Hughes: A Complex Friendship', *The Sewanee Review* 120:1 (Winter 2012), 76–90.
—, 'Seamus Heaney's Gifts', in E. O'Brien (ed.), *'The Soul Exceeds Its Circumstances': Later Poetry of Seamus Heaney* (Notre Dame, IN: Notre Dame University Press, 2016), 219–38.
Haughton, Hugh, 'Seamus Heaney: First and Last Things', *Irish Review* 49–50 (2014/15), 194–207.
—, '"Heaneid" Breathes Fresh Life into Virgil's Book of the Dead' [Review], *The Irish Times* (20 March 2016).
Hawkins, Peter S. and Rachel Jacoff (eds), *The Poets' Dante: Twentieth-Century Responses* (New York: Farrar, Straus and Giroux, 2002).
Heiny, Stephen, 'Virgil in Seamus Heaney's *Human Chain*: "Images and symbols adequate to our predicament"', *Renascence* 65:4 (Summer 2013), 304–18.
—, '"Puny in My Predicaments": Seamus Heaney's Readings of Virgil's Ninth Eclogue', *Vergilius* 64 (2018), 53–70.
Henryson, Robert, *The Testament of Cresseid & Seven Fables*, (trans.) Seamus Heaney (London: Faber, 2009).
Hexter, Ralph J., 'Aeneid VI, by Seamus Heaney' [Review], *Vergilius* 62 (2016), 158–62.
Hickey, Ian, 'The Haunted Bog and the Poetry of Seamus Heaney', *Nordic Irish Studies* 17:2 (2018), 35-54.
—, 'Virgilian Hauntings in the Later Poetry of Seamus Heaney', *Estudios Irlandeses* 13:13 (1 March 2018), 27–40.
—, 'Elegising the Past and Future: Seamus Heaney's "Route 110" Sequence', *Irish University Review* 49:2 (November 2019), 340–55.
Hofmann, Michael and James Lasdun (eds), *After Ovid: New Metamorphoses* (London: Faber, 1994).
Homem, Rui Carvalho, *Poetry and Translation in Northern Ireland: Dislocations in Contemporary Writing* (Basingstoke: Palgrave, 2009).
Hopkins, David and Charles Martindale (gen. eds), *The Oxford History of Classical Reception in English Literature* (Oxford: Oxford University Press, 2012–), 5 vols.
Hopkins, Gerard Manley, *The Poetical Works of Gerard Manley Hopkins*, (ed.) N. M. Mackenzie (Oxford: Clarendon Press, 1990).
Horace [Q. Horati Flacci], *Opera*, (ed.) E. C. Wickham (Oxford: Oxford University Press, 1975).
—, *Horace: Odes and Epodes*, (trans.) C. E. Bennett (Cambridge, MA: Harvard University Press, 1999).
Hornblower, Simon and Antony Spawforth (eds), *Oxford Classical Dictionary*, 3rd edn (Oxford: Oxford University Press, 2003).
Hughes, Ted, *Tales from Ovid* (London: Faber, 1997).
—, *Collected Poems* (London: Faber, 2005).
Impens, Florence, '"Help me please my hedge-school master": Virgilian Presences in the Work of Seamus Heaney', *Irish University Review* 47:2 (2017), 251–65.
—, *Classical Presences in Irish Poetry after 1960* (Basingstoke: Palgrave Macmillan, 2018).

Jarman, Mark, 'You Are Not Finished: Seamus Heaney's Translation of the *Aeneid* Book VI', *Hudson Review* 69:3 (Autumn 2016), 506–12.
Jenkins, Nicholas, 'Walking on Air: Travel and Release in Seamus Heaney', *Times Literary Supplement* (5 July 1996), 10–12.
Johnson, Dr Samuel, *Lives of the English Poets* [1779–81], (ed.) G. B. Hill (Oxford: Clarendon Press, 1905).
Jones, Chris, *Strange Likeness: The Use of Old English in Twentieth-Century Poetry* (Oxford: Oxford University Press, 2006).
Joyce, James, *A Portrait of the Artist as a Young Man*, (ed.) Seamus Deane (London: Penguin, 1992).
—, *Ulysses: The Corrected Text*, (pref.) Richard Ellmann (London: Penguin, 1986).
Kallendorf, Craig, *The Other Virgil: Pessimistic Readings of the* Aeneid *in Early Modern Culture* (Oxford: Oxford University Press, 2007).
Kassovitz, Mathieu (dir.), *La Haine* ['Hate'] (France: Canal+, 1995).
Kavanagh, Patrick, *Self-Portrait* (RTÉ, 30 October 1962; Dublin: Dolmen Press, 1964).
Kay, Magdalena, *In Gratitude for All the Gifts: Seamus Heaney and Eastern Europe* (Toronto: Toronto University Press, 2018).
Kearney, Richard (ed.), *The Irish Mind: Exploring Intellectual Traditions* (Dublin: Wolfhound 1984).
—, 'Seamus Heaney: Between North And South: Poetic Detours', in R. Kearney (ed.), *States of Mind: Dialogues with Contemporary Thinkers* (Manchester: Manchester University Press, 1995), 101–8.
—, 'Dialogue with Borges and Heaney: Fictional Worlds', in R. Kearney, *Navigations: Collected Irish Essays, 1976–2006* (Dublin: Lilliput, 2006).
—, *Reimagining the Sacred* (New York: Columbia University Press, 2016).
Keats, John, *The Letters of John Keats*, (ed.) H. E. Rollins (Cambridge, MA: Harvard University Press, 1958), 2 vols.
—, *Complete Poems*, (ed.) Jack Stillinger (Cambridge, MA: Belknap Press of Harvard University, 2003).
Kelleher, Margaret and Philip O'Leary (eds), *The Cambridge History of Irish Literature* (Cambridge: Cambridge University Press, 2006), 2 vols.
Kermode, Frank, 'The Man who Returned to Earth', *The Sunday Times* (6 September 1998).
Kerrigan, John, 'Ulster Ovids', in Neil Corcoran (ed.), *The Chosen Ground* (Dufour: Seren Books, 1992), 237–69.
—, 'Earth Writing: Seamus Heaney and Ciaran Carson', *Essays in Criticism* 48:2 (April 1998), 144–68.
Kirchwey, Karl, '*Aeneid* Book VI, by Seamus Heaney' [Review], *New York Times* (10 June 2016).
Koethe, John, *Poetry at One Remove* (Michigan: University of Michigan Press, 2000).
Lacan, Jacques, *Écrits: A Selection* (London: Routledge, 1997).
Latour, Bruno, *Politics of Nature: How to Bring the Sciences into Democracy*, (trans.) Catherine Porter (Cambridge, MA: Harvard University Press, 2004), 25–31.
Lavan, Rosie, *Seamus Heaney and Society* (Oxford: Oxford University Press, 2020).
Levi, Peter, *Virgil: A Life* (London: I. B. Tauris, [1997] 2012).
Levi, Primo, *The Periodic Table*, (trans.) R. Rosenthal (New York: Schocken Books, 1984).
—, *The Drowned and the Saved*, (trans.) Raymond Rosenthal (London: Abacus, 1989).
—, *If This Is a Man* and *The Truce*, (trans.) Stuart Woolf (London: Abacus, 1995).
—, *Opere*, (ed.) Marco Belpoliti (Turin: Einaudi, 1997), 2 vols.
—, *The Search for Roots*, (trans.) Peter Forbes (London: Allen Lane, Penguin, 2001).
Liu, Allen, *Wordsworth: The Sense of History* (Stanford: Stanford University Press, 1989).
Longley, Edna, '"Inner Emigré" or "Artful Voyeur"? Seamus Heaney's *North*', in Longley, *Poetry in the Wars* (Newcastle upon Tyne: Bloodaxe, 1986), 140–69.

—, *Poetry & Posterity* (Newcastle upon Tyne: Bloodaxe, 2000).
—, 'Too Much Confectionary?', *Metre* 11 (Winter 2001/2), 14–18.
Longley, Michael, *The Weather in Japan* (London: Jonathan Cape, 2000).
Lyne, R. O. A. M., *Further Voices in Vergil's Aeneid* (Oxford: Clarendon Press, 2004).
Lyons, Tony, '"Inciting the lawless and profligate adventure" - the Hedge Schools of Ireland', *18th–19th Century Social Perspectives* 24:6 (November to December 2016), <https://www.historyireland.com/volume-24/inciting-lawless-profligate-adventure-hedge-schools-ireland/>.
Lysaght, Seán, 'Aeneid Book VI' [Review], *New Hibernia Review* 20:3 (Autumn 2016), 141–4.
MacCana, Proinsias, 'Early Irish Ideology and the Concept of Unity', in Richard Kearney (ed.), *The Irish Mind: Exploring Intellectual Traditions* (Dublin: Wolfhound 1984), 56–78.
McConnell, Gail, *Northern Irish Poetry and Theology* (London: Palgrave Macmillan, 2014).
MacDonald, Joyce Green, *Women and Race in Early Modern Texts* (Cambridge: Cambridge University Press, 2010).
McDonald, Henry, 'Heaney Tells of his Stroke Ordeal', *The Observer* (19 July 2009).
McDonald, Marianne, 'Seamus Heaney: An Irish Poet Mines the Classics', in S. J. Harrison et al. (eds), *Seamus Heaney and the Classics: Bann Valley Muses* (Oxford: Oxford University Press, 2019), 121–46.
McDonald, Peter, *Mistaken Identities: Poetry and Northern Ireland* (Oxford: Oxford University Press, 1997).
—, 'Last and First', *The Times Literary Supplement* (15 October 2010), 10.
—, '"Weird Brightness" and the Riverbank: Heaney, Virgil and the Need for Translation', in S. J. Harrison et al. (eds), *Seamus Heaney and the Classics: Bann Valley Muses* (Oxford: Oxford University Press, 2019), 160–79.
MacGórain, Fiachra, 'Vergil's Sophoclean Thebans', *Vergilius* 64 (2018), 131–56.
Mackenzie, Tom, '*Georgica* and *Orphica*: The *Georgics* in the Context of Orphic Poetry and Religion', in Nicholas Freer and Bobby Xinyue (eds), *Reflections and new Perspectives on Virgil's Georgics* (London: Bloomsbury, 2019).
McKibben, Bill, *The End of Nature* (New York: Random House, 1989; repr. New York: Random House Trade Paperbacks, 2006).
McNamara, Charles, 'Report from the Afterlife' [Review], *Commonwealth* (6 January 2017), 32–4.
MacNeice, Louis, *The Collected Poems of Louis MacNeice*, ed. E. R. Dodds (London: Faber, 1966).
Maritain, Jacques, *Creative Intuition in Art and Poetry* (Princeton, NJ: Princeton University Press, 1977).
Marlowe, Christopher, *The Complete Works of Christopher Marlowe*, 2nd edn, (ed.) Fredson Bowers (Cambridge: Cambridge University Press, 1981).
Martindale, Charles (ed.), *The Cambridge Companion to Virgil* (Cambridge: Cambridge University Press, [1997] 2008).
Martiny, Erik, 'Modern Versions of Nostos and Katabasis: A Survey of Homeric Hypertexts in Recent Anglophone Poetry', *Anglia* 127:3 (2009), 469–79.
Marvell, Andrew, *The Poems and Letters of Andrew Marvell*, 3rd edn, (ed.) H. M. Margoliouth (Oxford: Oxford University Press, 1971), Vol I.
Mathews, Steven, *Irish Poetry: Politics, History, Negotiation* (Basingstoke: Palgrave Macmillan, 1997).
—, 'Bucketful by Glistering Bucketful', *Poetry Review* 97:1 (2007), 91–3.
Michels, Agnes, 'The Golden Bough of Plato', *American Journal of Philology* (1945), 59–63.
Miller, Karl, *Seamus Heaney in Conversation with Karl Miller* (London: Between the Lines, 2000).
—, *Tretower to Clyro: Essays* (London: Quercus, 2011).
Miłosz, Czesław, *The Collected Poems: 1931–1987* (New York: The Ecco Press, 1988).
—, *Provinces: Poems 1987–91*, (trans.) Miłosz and Robert Hass (Manchester: Carcanet Press, 1993).

—, *The Separate Notebooks*, (trans.) Renata Gorczynski, Robert Pinsky and Robert Hass (New York: The Ecco Press, 2001).
—, *Second Space: New Poems*, (trans.) Miłosz and Robert Hass (New York: The Ecco Press, 2004).
—, *Selected and Last Poems*, (trans.) Robert Hass, (intro.) Seamus Heaney (New York: The Ecco Press, 2011).
Milton, John, *The Complete Prose Works of John Milton*, (ed.) Don M. Wolfe (New Haven, CT: Yale University Press, 1953).
—, *Complete Shorter Poems*, (ed.) John Carey (London: Longman, 2nd edn, 1997).
—, *Paradise Lost* [1667], (ed.) Alastair Fowler (London: Longman, 2nd edn, 1998).
—, *The John Milton Reading Room*, (gen. ed.) Thomas H. Luxon (Dartmouth: Dartmouth College, 1997–2018), <https://www.dartmouth.edu/~milton/reading_room/contents/text.shtml>.
Mitchell, Andrew J., *The Fourfold: Reading the Late Heidegger* (Evanston, IL: Northwestern University Press, 2015).
Moi, Ruben, '"The cure by poetry that cannot be coerced": Text, Canon and Context in Seamus Heaney's Electric Light', in A. B. Crowder and J. D. Hall (eds), *Seamus Heaney: Poet, Critic, Translator* (Basingstoke: Palgrave Macmillan, 2007), 172–88.
Montale, Eugenio, *The Second Life of Art: Selected Essays*, (trans.) Jonathan Galassi (New York: The Ecco Press, 1982), 20–4. Rpt. from *The New York Review of Books* (16 April 1981).
Morgan, Llewelyn, *Patterns of Redemption in Virgil's Georgics* (Cambridge: Cambridge University Press, 1999).
Morisco, Gabrielle, 'Two Poets and a Kite: Seamus Heaney and Giovanni Pascoli', *Lingua* 12:1 (2013), 35–45, <http://www.ledonline.it/linguae/allegati/linguae1301Morisco.pdf>.
Morrison, Blake, *Seamus Heaney* (London: Methuen, 1982).
—, 'Encounters with Familiar Ghosts', *Times Literary Supplement* (19 October 1984), 1191–2.
Motion, Andrew, 'Digging Deep' [Review], *The Guardian* (1 April 2006).
—, 'Gifts from Beyond the Grave – From Virgil and Seamus Heaney' [Review], *The Spectator* (March 2016), <http://www.guardian.co.uk/books/2006/apr/01/poetry.seamusheaney1>.
Muldoon, Paul, *Moy Sand and Gravel* (London: Faber, 2002).
—, *One Thousand Things Worth Knowing* (New York: Farrar, Straus and Giroux, 2016).
Mulligan, Fergus (ed.), *Augury: To Mary Kelleher* (Dublin: Dublin Royal Society, 2009).
Murphy, Gerard (ed.), *Early Irish Lyrics, Eighth to Twelfth Century* (Oxford: Clarendon Press, 1956).
Murphy, Kevin, 'Heaney Translating Heaney: Coupling and Uncoupling the Human Chain', *Texas Studies in Literature and Language* 58:3 (Fall 2016), 352–68.
Murphy, Patrick D., 'The Four Elements and the Recovery of Referentiality: Ecocriticism as a Pivotal Localist Theory', *Studies in the Humanities* 29:1 (2002), 70–82.
Nancy, Jean-Luc, *Listening*, (trans.) Charlotte Mandell (New York: Fordham University Press, [2002] 2007).
Neiman, Susan, *Evil in Modern Thought* (Princeton, NJ: Princeton University Press, 2002).
Nelis, Damien, '*Aeneid*: Book VI, Translated by Seamus Heaney' [Review], *Translation and Literature* 26:2 (June 2017), 226–31.
Neruda, Pablo, 'Towards an Impure Poetry' [1939], in Ben Belitt (ed. and trans.), *Five Decades: Poems 1925–1970* (New York: Grove Press, 1974).
Newdick, Robert S., 'Robert Frost and the Sound of Sense', *American Literature* 9:3 (1937), 289–300.
Ní Anluain, Clíodhna and Declan Kiberd (eds), *Reading the Future: Twelve Writers from Ireland in Conversation with Mike Murphy* (Dublin: The Lilliput Press, 2000).
Ní Ríordáin, Clíona, '"Puddling at the Source": Seamus Heaney and the Classical Text', *Études Anglaises* 56:2 (April to June 2003), 173–84.
Nisbet, R. G. M., 'The Style of Virgil's *Eclogues*', in K. Volk (ed.), *Oxford Readings in Classical Studies: Vergil's Eclogues* (Oxford: Oxford University Press, 2008), 48–63.

Obert, Julia C., *Postcolonial Overtures: The Politics of Sound in Contemporary Irish Poetry* (Syracuse, NY: Syracuse University Press, 2015).
O'Brien, Eugene, 'Seamus Heaney and the Ethics of Translation', *Canadian Journal of Irish Studies* 27:2/28:1 (2001–2), 20–37.
—, *Seamus Heaney and the Place of Writing* (Florida: University Press of Florida, 2002).
—, *Seamus Heaney: Creating Irelands of the Mind* (Dublin: Liffey Press, 2002).
—, 'The Anxiety of Influence: Heaney and Yeats and the Place of Writing', *The Nordic Journal of Irish Studies* 4 (2004), 30–50.
—, *Seamus Heaney as Aesthetic Thinker: A Study of the Prose* (Syracuse, NY: Syracuse University Press, 2012).
— (ed.), *'The Soul Exceeds Its Circumstances': Later Poetry of Seamus Heaney* (Notre Dame, IN: Notre Dame University Press, 2016).
O'Donoghue, Bernard, *Seamus Heaney and the Language of Poetry* (London: Harvester Wheatsheaf, 1994).
—, 'Seamus Heaney and the Classics', *Omnibus* 36 (September 1996), 21–3, <https://archive.org/details/omnibus36>.
—, 'Heaney's *ars poetica*: The Government of the Tongue', in Tony Curtis (ed.), *The Art of Seamus Heaney* (Bridgend: Seren, 2001).
— (ed.), *The Cambridge Companion to Seamus Heaney* (Cambridge: Cambridge University Press, 2009).
—, 'Heaney's Classics and the Bucolic', in O'Donoghue (ed.), *The Cambridge Companion to Seamus Heaney* (Cambridge: Cambridge University Press, 2009), 106–21.
—, 'The Boat' (trans. *Piers Plowman*, passus 8), *The Irish Times* (15 February 2014), <https://www.irishtimes.com/culture/books/the-boat-1.1687755>.
—, '*Aeneid* Book VI, Seamus Heaney's Miraculous Return from Literary Afterlife' [Review], *The Irish Times* (27 February 2016).
—, '"Chosen Ancestors": *Aeneid* 6 and Seamus Heaney's Pieties' (London: UCL Dept of Greek and Latin, 2018).
—, 'Heaney, Yeats, and the Language of Pastoral', in S. J. Harrison et al. (eds), *Seamus Heaney and the Classics: Bann Valley Muses* (Oxford: Oxford University Press, 2019), 147–59.
O'Driscoll, Dennis, *Stepping Stones: Interviews with Seamus Heaney* (London: Faber, 2008).
O'Hogan, Cillian, 'Irish Versions of Virgil's *Eclogues and Georgics*', in Susanna Braund and Zara Martirosova Torlone (eds), *Virgil and His Translators* (Oxford: Oxford University Press, 2018), 399–411.
O'Toole, Fintan, panel contributor, 'A Conversation about Seamus Heaney - Feeling into Words' (Emory University, 22 February 2014), <https://www.youtube.com/watch?v=67MxifaG8UA>.
Ovid [P. Ovidius Naso], *The.XV.Bookes of P.Ouidius Naso, entytuled Metamorphosis, translated oute of Latin into English meter, by Arthur Golding Gentleman*, (trans.) Arthur Golding (London: Willyam Seres, 1567).
—, *Ovid's Metamorphosis Englished, Mythologiz'd and Represented in Figures*, (trans.) George Sandys (Oxford: John Lichfield, 1632), <http://ovid.lib.virginia.edu/sandys/11.htm>.
—, *Ovid's Metamorphoses in Fifteen Books Translated by the Most Eminent Hands*, (ed.) Samuel Garth (London: Shakespear's-Head, 1717).
—, *Metamorphoses Books 9–15*, (trans.) Frank J. Miller, (rev.) G. P. Goold (Cambridge, MA: Loeb, 1984).
—, *Metamorphoses IX-XII*, (ed.) D. E. Hill (Warminster: Aris & Phillips, 1999).
—, *Metamorphoses*, (ed.) R. J. Tarrant (Oxford: Clarendon Press, 2004).
Owen, Wilfred, *The Collected Poems of Wilfred Owen*, (ed.) C. Day Lewis (London: Chatto and Windus, 1977).
Padel, Ruth, 'Beyond the Golden Bough with Seamus Heaney' [Review], *Financial Times* (24 March 2016).

Padilla, Juan Ráez, 'Seamus Heaney's *Elemental* Ecopoetics: Earth, Water, Air and Fire', *Journal of Ecocriticism* 1:2 (July 2009), 21–30.
Parker, Michael, *Seamus Heaney: The Making of the Poet* (Basingstoke: Macmillan, 1993).
—, 'Fallout from the Thunder: Poetry and Politics in Seamus Heaney's *District and Circle*', *Irish Studies Review* 16:4 (2008), 369–84.
—, '"His Nibs": Self-Reflexivity and the Significance of Translation in Seamus Heaney's *Human Chain*', *Irish University Review* 42:2 (Autumn–Winter 2012), 327f.
—, '"Back in the heartland": Seamus Heaney's "Route 110" sequence in *Human Chain*', *Irish Studies Review* 21:4 (2013), 374–86.
—, '"Past master": Czesław Miłosz and his Impact on the Poetry of Seamus Heaney', *Textual Practice* 27:5 (2013), 825–50.
—, 'Czesław Miłosz's "World"', *The Seminary Co-op* (posted 25 April 2017), <https://www.semcoop.com/blog/post/czes%C5%82aw-mi%C5%82osz%27s-world>.
—, *Seamus Heaney: Legacies, Afterlives* (London: Palgrave, forthcoming 2022).
Pascoli, Giovanni, 'L'Ultima Passeggiata' [1886–94], in *Myricae: Tutte le poesie di Giovanni Pascoli*, Vol. 1. (Milan: Arnoldo Mondadori, 1935), 56–64.
—, *Poemetti*, (ed.) Edoardo Sanguineti (Turin: Einaudi, 1971).
Pellicer, Juan Christian, 'Pastoral and Georgic', in David Hopkins and Charles Martindale (gen. eds), *The Oxford History of Classical Reception in English Literature* (Oxford: Oxford University Press, 2012–), Vol. 3 (1660–1790), 287–321.
Perloff, Marjorie, 'Eliot's Auditory Imagination: A Rehearsal for Concrete Poetry', *Raritan* 38:3 (Winter 2019), 69–91.
Phillips, Adam, *On Flirtation* (London: Faber, 1994).
Pike, David, *Passage Through Hell: Modernist Descents, Medieval Underworlds* (London: Cornell University Press, 1997).
Plato, *Lysis, Symposium, Gorgias*, (ed., trans.) W. R. M. Lamb (London: Harvard University Press, 1991).
—, *Republic*, (eds, trans.) Chris Emlyn-Jones and William Preddy (London: Harvard University Press, 2013), Vols 5–6.
Potts, Donna, *Contemporary Irish Poetry and the Pastoral Tradition* (London: University of Missouri Press, 2011).
Pound, Ezra, *Three Cantos 3, Poetry* 10:5 (1917), 250–1.
—, *The Selected Letters of Ezra Pound, 1907–1941*, (ed.) D. D. Paige (New York: New Directions, 1971).
—, *The Cantos of Ezra Pound* (New York: New Directions, 1996).
Putnam, Michael, *Virgil's Pastoral Art: Studies in the Eclogues* (Princeton, NJ: Princeton University Press, 1970).
—, *Virgil's Poem of the Earth* (Princeton, NJ: Princeton University Press, 1979).
—, 'Vergil and Seamus Heaney', *Vergilius* 56 (2010), 3–16.
—, 'Virgil and Heaney: "Route 110"', *Arion* 19:3 (2012), 79–108.
Quint, David, *Virgil's Double Cross: Design and Meaning in the Aeneid* (Princeton, NJ: Princeton University Press, 2018).
Radnóti, Miklós, *Camp Notebook*, (trans.) Francis Jones, (intro.) George Szirtes (Todmorton: Arc, 2000).
Ramazani, Jahan, *Poetry of Mourning: The Modern Elegy from Hardy to Heaney* (Chicago: University of Chicago Press, 1994).
—, 'Seamus Heaney's Globe', *Irish Review* 49–50 (2014/15), 38–53.
Randall, James, 'An Interview with Seamus Heaney by James Randall', *Ploughshares* 18 (Fall 1979).
Reeves, Gareth, *T. S. Eliot: A Virgilian Poet* (London: Macmillan and St Martin's Press, 1989).
Ricks, Christopher, 'Literary Sources, Literary Allusions', in Susan J. Wolfson (ed.), *The Cambridge Companion to Keats* (Cambridge: Cambridge University Press, 2001), 152–69.

—, *Allusion to the Poets* (Oxford: Oxford University Press, 2002).
Ricoeur, Paul, *Memory, History, Forgetting* (Chicago: Chicago University Press, 2004).
Riley, Kathleen, '"The Forewarned Journey Back": *Katabasis* as *Nostos* in the Poetry of Seamus Heaney', in S. J. Harrison et al. (eds), *Seamus Heaney and the Classics: Bann Valley Muses* (Oxford: Oxford University Press, 2019), 205–22.
Robbins, Jim, 'The Dilbit Hits the Fan', *Places* (October 2015), <https://placesjournal.org/>.
Roe, Nicholas, *John Keats* (New Haven, CT: Yale University Press, 2013).
Rollins, Hyder Edward (ed.), *The Keats Circle: Letters and Papers 1816–1878 and More Letters and Poems 1814–1879*, 2nd edn, 2 vols (Cambridge, MA: Harvard University Press, 1965).
Rushdie, Salman, *The Satanic Verses* (London: Penguin, 1988).
Russell, Richard Rankin, *Poetry and Peace: Michael Longley, Seamus Heaney, and Northern Ireland* (Notre Dame, IN: University of Notre Dame Press, 2010).
—, *Seamus Heaney: An Introduction* (Edinburgh: Edinburgh University Press, 2016).
Said, Edward, *On Late Style* (New York: Random House, 2006).
Scherer, Madeleine and Rachel Falconer (eds), *A Quest for Remembrance: The Underworld in Classical and Modern Literature* (London: Routledge, 2020).
Schirmer, Gregory A., *Out of What Began: A History of Irish Poetry in English* (Ithaca, NY: Cornell University Press, 1998).
Schneider, Michael, 'Linguistic Sparks' [Review of *District and Circle*], *Pittsburgh Post-Gazette* (8 October 2006), 64.
Scranton, Roy, *Learning to Die in the Anthropocene: Reflections on the End of a Civilization* (San Francisco: City Lights Books, 2015).
Segal, Charles, '"Tamen Cantabitis, Arcades": Exile and Arcadia in "*Eclogues* One and Nine"', *Arion* 4:2 (1965), 237–66.
—, *Orpheus: The Myth of the Poet* (London: Johns Hopkins University Press, 1989).
Sexton, David, '*Aeneid Book VI* translated by Seamus Heaney' [Review], *London Evening Standard* (10 March 2016).
Shakespeare, William, *A Midsummer Night's Dream*, (ed.) R. A. Foakes (Cambridge: Cambridge University Press, 2003).
—, *Timon of Athens*, (eds) Anthony B. Dawson and Gretchen E. Minton (London: Bloomsbury, 2008).
—, *The Tempest*, (ed.) David Lindley (Cambridge: Cambridge University Press, 2013).
—, *The Merchant of Venice*, (ed.) John Drakakis (London: Bloomsbury, 2019).
Sheats, Paul, *The Making of Wordsworth's Poetry* (Cambridge, MA: Harvard University Press, 1973).
Sheehan, Thomas, *Making Sense of Heidegger: A Paradigm Shift* (Evanston, IL: Northwestern University Press, 2015).
Sonzogni, Marco, 'A Jobber in His Shadow', 'Heaney and Pascoli' and 'Note on Heaney and Pascoli', in R. Brandes (ed.), *Remembering Heaney: Special Issue of Irish Studies South* 1:1 (2014), 30–6.
— (ed.), *Translation, Transnationalism and World Literature: Essays in Translation Studies, 2011–2014* (Novi Ligure: Edizioni Joker, 2015).
—, '"Out of the Marvellous" as I Have Known It: Translating Heaney's Poetry', in Jean Boase-Beier (ed.), *The Palgrave Handbook of Literary Translation* (Basingstoke: Palgrave Macmillan, 2018), 337–405.
— (ed.), *Given Notes: The Complete Translations of Seamus Heaney* (London: Faber, forthcoming).
Sonzogni, Marco and Marcella Zanetti (eds), *Raids and Settlements: Heaney as Literary Translator* (Amsterdam: John Benjamins, 2018).
Soper, Kate, *What is Nature? Culture, Politics and the Non-Human* (Oxford: Blackwell, 1998).
Sophocles, *Antigone, The Women of Trachis, Philoctetes, Oedipus at Colonus*, (ed.) Hugh Lloyd-

Jones (London: Harvard University Press, 1994).
Spiegelman, Willard, 'Unforced Marches: A Virgilian Memoir', *Parnassus* 30:1–2 (2008), 81–106. Rpt. in Spiegelman, *Imaginative Transcripts* (Oxford: Oxford University Press, 2009), 3–24.
Spufford, Francis, *The Child That Books Built* (London: Faber, 2003).
Stafford, Fiona, 'Local Attachments', *Archipelago* 2 (Spring 2008), 103–15.
Steiner, George, *In Bluebeard's Castle: Some Notes Towards the Re-definition of Culture* (London: Faber, 1971).
Strabo, *The Geography of Strabo*, (trans.) H. L. Jones (Cambridge, MA: Harvard University Press, 1969), 8 vols.
Synge, J. M., *Collected Works*, (ed.) Ann Saddlemyer (London: Oxford University Press, 1968).
Takács, László, 'The Eclogues of Miklós Radnóti: A Twentieth-Century Vergil', *Acta Antiqua Academiae Scientiarum Hungaricae* 53:2–3 (2013), 311–22.
Tarrant, R. J., 'Poetry and Power: Virgil's Poetry in Contemporary Context', in Charles Martindale (ed.), *The Cambridge Companion to Virgil* (Cambridge: Cambridge University Press, [1997] 2008).
Tennyson, Alfred Lord, *The Poems of Tennyson*, 2nd edn, (ed.) Christopher Ricks (Harlow: Longman, 1987).
Thomas, R. F., *Virgil and the Augustan Reception* (Cambridge: Cambridge University Press, 2001).
—, 'Domesticating Aesthetic Effects: Virgilian Case Studies', in Susanna Braund and Zara Martirosova Torlone (eds), *Virgil and His Translators* (Oxford: Oxford University Press, 2018), 239–59.
Thorne, Kip S., *Black Holes and Time Warps: Einstein's Outrageous Legacy* (London: Papermac, 1995).
Thurston, Michael, *The Underworld in Twentieth-Century Poetry: From Pound and Eliot to Heaney and Walcott* (Basingstoke: Palgrave Macmillan, 2009).
Tobin, Daniel, *Passage to the Center: Imagination and the Sacred in the Poetry of Seamus Heaney* (Lexington: University Press of Kentucky, 1998).
Tóibín, Colm, '*Human Chain* by Seamus Heaney' [Review], *The Guardian* (21 August 2010), <https://www.theguardian.com/books/2010/aug/21/seamus-heaney-human-chain-review>.
Tola, Eleonora, 'Memories of Rome's Underworld', in Madeleine Scherer and Rachel Falconer (eds), *A Quest for Remembrance: The Underworld in Classical and Modern Literature* (London: Routledge, 2020), 87–107).
Tolkien, J. R. R., 'On Fairy Stories', *Tree and Leaf* (London: Allen and Unwin, 1964).
Travaglia, Teresa, '*Latet aureus ramus*: Presenze di Virgilio nell'opera di Seamus Heaney'. University of Trieste, Dept of Humanist Studies, MA thesis, 2017.
Tuma, Kathryn, 'Cézanne and Lucretius at the Red Rock', *Representations* 78:1 (Spring 2002), 56–85.
Twiddy, Iain, *Pastoral Elegy in Contemporary British and Irish Poetry* (London: Bloomsbury, 2012).
Tyler, Meg, *A Singing Contest: Conventions of Sound in the Poetry of Seamus Heaney* (New York: Routledge, 2005).
—, '"The Whole of Me A-Patter": Image, Feeling, and Finding Form in Heaney's Late Work', in O'Brien (ed.), *'The Soul Exceeds Its Circumstances': Later Poetry of Seamus Heaney* (Notre Dame, IN: Notre Dame University Press, 2016), 129–48.
Vance, Norman, *Irish Literature: A Social History* (Oxford: Blackwell, 1990).
Vendler, Helen, *The Music of What Happens: Poems, Poets, Critics* (Cambridge, MA: Harvard University Press, 1988).
—, *Seamus Heaney* (Cambridge, MA: Harvard University Press, 1998).
— (ed.), *The Stone from Delphi* (San Francisco: The Arion Press, 2012).
Volk, Katharina, *Oxford Readings in Classical Studies: Vergil's Eclogues* (Oxford: Oxford University Press, 2008).
—, *Oxford Readings in Classical Studies: Vergil's Georgics* (Oxford: Oxford University Press, 2008).

Ware, Catherine, 'The Ashplant and the Golden Bough: Heaney in Vergil's Labyrinth', *Classical Receptions Journal* 10:3 (July 2018), 229–48.

Washiguka, Naho, '"How With This Rage Shall Beauty Hold a Plea?": Seamus Heaney's *Electric Light*', *Journal of Irish Studies* 26 (2011), 106–16.

Weber, Clifford, 'The Allegory of the Golden Bough', *Vergilius* 41 (1995), 3–34.

Welch, Robert (ed.), *Literature and the Art of Creation* (New Jersey: Barnes & Noble, 1988).

West, David, 'The Bough and the Gate', *Jackson Knight Memorial Lecture*, 24 October 1986 (Exeter: Exeter University Publications, 1987).

Wheatley, David, 'Orpheus Risen from the London Underground', *Contemporary Poetry Review* (29 October 2006), n.p.

—, '"Atrocities against his Sacred Poet": The Orpheus Myth and the Poetry of the Northern Irish Troubles', in Alex Houen and Jan-Melissa Schramm (eds), *Sacrifice and Modern War Literature: From Waterloo to the War on Terror* (Oxford: Oxford University Press, 2018), 222–36.

Whittier-Ferguson, John, 'Ezra Pound, T. S. Eliot and the Modern Epic', in Catherine Bates (ed.), *The Cambridge Companion to the Epic* (Cambridge: Cambridge University Press, 2010), 211–33.

Wieseltier, Leon, 'Czesław Miłosz, 1911–2004', *New York Times Book Review* (12 September 2004), <http://www.nytimes.com/2004/09/12/books/Review/12WIESELTIER.html> (last accessed 15 December 2020).

Williams, Gordon, 'Review: Robert's Fitzgerald's *Aeneid*', *The Sewanee Review* 92:4 (Fall 1984), 630–9.

Wolfson, Susan J. (ed.), *The Cambridge Companion to Keats* (Cambridge: Cambridge University Press, 2001).

Wordsworth, William, *The Fourteen-Book Prelude*, (ed.) W. J. B. Owen (Ithaca, NY: Cornell University Press, 1985).

—, *Lyrical Ballads and Other Poems, 1797–1800*, (eds) J. Butler and K. Green (Ithaca, NY: Cornell University Press, 1992).

—, *Poems Selected by Seamus Heaney* (Faber: London, [1998] 2001).

—, *Translations of Chaucer and Virgil*, (ed.) Bruce E. Graver (Ithaca, NY: Cornell University Press, 1998).

—, *Last Poems 1821–1850*, (eds) Jared Curtis, Apryl Lea Denny-Ferris and Jillian Heydt Stevenson (Ithaca, NY: Cornell University Press, 1999).

Yeats, W. B., *The Poems*, (ed.) Daniel Albright (London: Dent, 1992).

Ziolkowski, Jan and Michael Putnam, *The Virgilian Tradition: The First Fifteen Hundred Years* (New Haven, CT: Yale University Press, 2008).

Zirzotti, Emanuela, '"Pius Seamus": Heaney's Appropriation of Aeneas's Descent to the Underworld', in Ben Pestell, Pietra Palazzolo and Leon Burnett (eds), *Translating Myth* (Abingdon: Routledge, 2016), 195–204.

Index

'A Kite for Michael and Christopher', 226, 227
Acheron, 28–9, 41
Adam, 81
Aeneas
   attempted rescue of Creusa, 60
   contrasted with Orpheus, 30, 68–9
   contrasted with Palinurus, 187–8
   on a country road, 120, 121–2, 124
   encounter with Dido, 142–4, 145, 166–7
   encounter with the Sibyl, 2, 28–30, 40, 41
   and the fall of Troy, 60, 62–3, 66, 81, 145
   as the grieving son, 232, 245–6
   Heaney's characterisation of, 247–9
   Heaney's identification with, 59
   pius/pietas, 1, 14, 120, 233
   quest for his father, 14, 28–30
   as a questing artist (Ae.I.1), 26, 29, 30, 32–3, 37, 248
   see also *katabasis*; *ter conatus*
'Aeneas meeting Dido at Carthage' (Cézanne), 60, 65
Aeneid
   arma uirumque cano (Ae.I.1), 19
   blank verse translations, 24–5
   ending, 168
   fall of Troy (Ae.II), 60, 62–3, 66, 81, 145
   in Heaney's first world, 59, 60, 61–3; see also Virgil
   Heaney's study of, 2
   Mackail's prose translation, 2
   Nisus and Euryalus (Ae.IX), 180–1
   nota maior imago (Ae.II.773), 60
   other translations of, 183–4
   parallels with *Metamorphoses* X and XI, 68–9
   urbs antiqua fuit (Ae.I.12), 144, 179
   verse forms for translations, 24–7
   see also Virgil, biography: *lacrimae rerum*
Aeneid VI
   Aeneas' encounter with Dido, 142–4, 145, 166–7
   Anchises' catalogue of heroes, 230–1
   animae, quibus altera fato (Ae.VI.713), 158, 171, 172, 208–9, 218, 228
   Augustan ideology, 230–1
   bella, horrida bella (Ae.VI.86), 28, 185
   Charon's barge, 19, 40–1, 54–9, 69, 81, 142, 249
   Cumaean Sibyl, 2
   death of Palinurus, 165
   Deiphobus, 6, 167, 168
   in 'District and Circle', 140–2
   'domestic' treatment of, 151
   facilis descensus Auerno (Ae.VI.126), 30, 179, 257
   father's shade (ghost), 153; see also *ter conatus*
   flocking of souls of the dead, 152, 153, 163, 181; see also *lapsa cadunt folia*
   ibant obscuri sola sub nocte (Ae.VI.268), 249
   lapsa cadunt folia (Ae.VI.310), 163, 181, 204, 206, 207

lost memories of tormented souls, 153–4, 155–6, 158–9
manus effugit imago (Ae.VI.701), 59, 204, 207, 212, 214, 215, 246, 248
Modern School Classics edition, 15, 31, 161, 162
noctes atque dies patet atri ianua Ditis (Ae.VI.701), 30, 62, 198
parcere subiectis (Ae.VI.853), 186, 230
Roman imperial parade (catalogue of heroes), 173, 215, 231, 253–5
Roman power, 182, 186–7
in 'Route 110', 152
twilit fetch of its language, 177, 230, 231–2
Venus' doves, 33, 164, 240, 256
see also golden bough (motif); *ter conatus*
Aeneid Book VI (Heaney's translation)
allusions to in *Human Chain*, 159, 178, 204–5, 206
decision to translate, 48, 178, 183, 184
doubleness of rhythm and tone, 229–30, 233–9
'Katabasis, Eschatological', 230–4
meter, 24–6, 191, 235–42, 245–6
posthumous publication, 229
rhythm, 229, 233, 234–8
secularised language, 4
tonal registers, 229, 239–46
Translator's Note, 178, 183, 231, 232–4
Virgil as Heaney's inner interlocutor, 5
Aeschylus, 6
aisling (genre), 71, 72
'Album'
backward gaze, 211
Heaney's parents remembered, 207, 210–11, 216
the lapse of memory, 208
'Lapse of Time', 207, 209, 211–12, 225
manus effugit, 212–15; see also *Aeneid* VI
paired with 'Palinurus', 178, 187, 209
sonnet form, 210, 212
ter conatus motif in, 212–14
Alexander, Michael, 190
Alpers, Paul, 91, 93, 95, 104, 115
anabasis, 146, 257
Anchises
catalogue of heroes, 230–1, 233
as the lost father, 232, 245–6

Marcellus' death foretold, 173, 227
parcere subiectis speech, 230
Roman history, 14, 135, 167–8, 185, 187
souls awaiting rebirth, 153–4, 158–9, 185, 186, 208–9, 233, 253–4
see also *ter conatus*
Aristaeus the beekeeper, 73, 84, 86, 115, 120, 148, 254; see also bees
art
Aeneas as a questing artist, 26, 29, 30, 32–3, 37, 248
poet's artistic imagination, 54, 57, 58, 218–20
transformative power of, 217–18, 228
Ascanius, 63, 200, 213
'The Ash Plant', 50–2
Atlas, 135
Auden, W. H., 76, 141
Auge, Andrew, 222
Avernus, Lake, 17–18, 26, 30, 33–4, 162, 179

Bachelard, Gaston, 23, 217
Bakhtin, Mikhail, 49–50, 92, 93
'Banks of a Canal', 52
'Bann Valley Eclogue'
birth of child, 96, 97, 106–7, 173
dactylic rhythm, 99
'hedge-schoolmaster' Virgil, 99–100, 102
Lucina, 101–2
Northern Irish Roman Catholicism, 98–9
parallels with *Eclogues IV*, 94, 96–106
peace agreements, 96–7, 103–6
postlapsarian knowledge, 104, 109
relational exchange with 'Virgil', 92, 97, 98–101, 102–3
semi-autobiographical 'Poet', 96, 98–100, 101–4, 105–6
solar eclipse in, 104, 105
Barth, John, 76
bees
in Elysium, 86, 252
in *Georgics IV*, 85
and lyric song, 85–6
in Mandelstam, 174–5
in 'The Riverbank Field', 174–5, 254
'Sic tua Cyrneas' (Ecl.IX.30), 110–11
in Yeats's work, 175
see also Aristaeus

Belfast
  Good Friday Agreement, 97, 107
  sectarian conflict, 167
  Smithfield Market, 15, 160, 161, 162–3
Belfast Group, 2
bella, horrida bella (Ae.VI.86), 28, 185
Beowulf, 27, 182–3, 190, 193, 234, 238
Bishop, Elizabeth
  'The Fish', 171
  'At the Fishhouses', 171
  'The Monument', 77
  'One Art', 77
  in *The Redress of Poetry*, 69, 76–7, 171
  transmutation of suffering, 76–7
  'In the Village', 77
Boland, Eavan, 5, 74
Bonnefoy, Yves, 47, 49
Braund, Susanna, 5
broagh (noun), 155, 156, 157
Broch, Hermann, 68
Brueghel, 8
Buile Suibhne (*Sweeney Astray*), 38–9, 100
The Burial at Thebes, 6, 127
Burrow, Colin, 151, 243

Caillebotte, 52
Carson, Ciaran, 221
Carthage, 144
Catholicism
  in Dante, 18
  funerals, 165
  of Heaney's childhood, 2, 8
  Heaney's loss of faith, 45–6
  in Heaney's poetry, 4, 7
  lux perpetua, 117
Cavanagh, Michael, 19
Cavarero, Adriana, 98, 102
Cézanne, Paul, 60, 65
Charon's barge
  in Dante's *Inferno*, 40, 41–2, 43, 44, 54
  in 'District and Circle', 140, 142
  in Eliot's 'Little Gidding', 19
  in Heaney's later writing, 13
  Heaney's translation of, 249
  motif in *Seeing Things*, 40, 41–2, 44, 50, 54–9, 72
  in 'Route 110', 163
  in *Squarings*, 43–4
  see also *Aeneid VI*

Christianity, 98, 101, 126–7
chronotope
  of the country road, 93, 120, 124, 225
  of the threshold, 49–50
classical literature
  ancient Greek literature, 6–7
  Heaney's engagement with, 2
  Heaney's translations of, 4–5, 6–7
  Latin literature, 6–7, 9
Clausen, Wendell, 93
'Clearances', 20, 32
Cole, Henri, 69, 72, 76
Constantine, David and Helen, 184–5
Corcoran, Neil, 95, 208
Creusa, 60, 65, 69, 81
'Crossings', 42–4; see also *Seeing Things*
Cúirt an Mheán-Oíche (*The Midnight Court*), 71
Cumaean Sibyl *see* Sibyl of Cumae
The Cure at Troy, 6

Daedalus/Dedalus, 214, 241
Dante
  biography, 193
  Commedia, 18, 161, 260
  Eliot's treatment of, 18–19
  form creation, 152, 161, 174, 175
  Heaney's translations of, 19, 22, 26
  Inferno III, 40, 41
  influence on Heaney, 1, 4, 5
  Mandelstam's treatment of, 18, 19
  nel mezzo del cammin, 248
  Purgatorio, 54
  in *Seeing Things*, 40, 41
  selva oscura, 18, 43, 44
  'Ugolino', 26, 121, 182, 262
  Virgil and, 18–19
  see also *Inferno*
Dawe, Gerald, 155–6, 157, 160, 161, 167, 179
Day Lewis, C., 26, 27, 29, 37, 101
Deane, Seamus, 8 n.32, 17
death
  black, open door metaphor, 30, 61–2
  commemoration of victims of violence in 'Route 110', 166–9
  elegies in *Electric Light*, 116
  elegies in *Human Chain*, 220–2
  of Euryalus, 180–1

funerals in Irish Catholicism, 165
  of Heaney's brother, 128–9
  lux perpetua of Mass, 117
  of Margaret Heaney, 20, 32, 45, 210
  of Miklós Radnóti, 119
  of Orpheus, 67, 68, 74–5, 81–9, 198
  Orpheus' song and the loss of Eurydice, 78–82, 86–7
  Orphic song's power over, 9–10, 67, 74, 76, 78–82, 84, 89
  of Patrick Heaney, 13, 14, 23, 45, 46
  and poetry's redress, 64, 70, 74–7, 141, 202, 248–9
Death of a Naturalist
  'Digging', 2
  'Personal Helicon', 2–3
Deiphobus, 6, 166, 167, 168, 237, 244
Dennison, John, 4
Derry, County
  Heaney's rural first world, 8, 46, 103, 129, 141, 150, 233
  parallels with *Aeneid VI*, 152, 157, 239, 244
  in 'Route 110', 160, 161, 164
  sectarian conflict, 127–8, 139, 169
Dido, 60, 142–4, 145, 166–7
'District and Circle'
  Aeneas' encounter with Dido, 142–4, 145
  Aeneid Book VI in, 140–2
  Charon's barge in, 140, 142
  father's shade (ghost) in, 136, 139–40, 141–2, 144, 145
  golden bough in, 140, 141
  Heaney's response to 7/7 London bombings, 125, 137, 140, 144
  katabasis, 10, 136, 145, 146
  lacrimae rerum in, 144
  Livy's sense of *urbs* in, 141
  Petrarchan sonnet form, 129, 136–7
  poet-as-relict, 145–6
  rural/urban dynamic, 144–5
  sonnet form, 125, 129, 136–7, 138, 139, 140, 141–2
  threshold crossings, 139–41
  title, 145
  Tollund Man in, 136–7, 140–1, 156
District and Circle
  allusions to Virgil, 5, 135–6
  'Anahorish 1944', 129

'The Blackbird of Glanmore', 128–9, 165
  environmental pollution, 147
  fragility of the mortal earth, 125–6, 147
  katabatic narrative arc, 124, 125, 126, 129, 131, 136, 146, 148–9
  Livy's sense of *urbs* in, 125–6, 141
  'poet' as witness, 128
  response to 9/11 and terrorism in, 125–6, 129–30, 132, 134–5
  'A Shiver', 129, 130
  title, 129
  'The Tollund Man in Springtime', 125, 131, 137, 146–8
  translations of Horace's *Odes I*, 131–3
divination
  as a 'feminine' poetic function, 16–18
  poetic divination, 16–17, 19, 32–3, 37
divining rods, 15–16
'The Diviner', 16
Door into the Dark, 2
Dryden, John, 24, 27, 32, 35

eclogues
  Eastern European tradition, 119–20
  as resistance to historical conditions, 95
  see also 'Bann Valley Eclogue'; *Eclogues IX*; *Electric Light*; 'Glanmore Eclogue'
Eclogues (Virgil)
  covenant with truth, 92, 93
  Heaney's treatment of, 1–2, 8, 94–5
  integritas of, 94
  land confiscations, 92
  Miłosz compared to, 119–20
  mix of artistry and realism, 92–4
  pietas of, 92, 94, 95
  praise for Augustus, 92, 93
  structure, 93–4
Eclogues I, 108, 114
'*Eclogues in Extremis*', 6, 108, 118–21
Eclogues IV
  in '*Bann Valley Eclogue*', 94, 96–106
  as a bridge between cultures, 111
  end-stopped rhythm, 97
  idea of historical progression, 100–1
  Lucina, 101–2
  pacatum orbem (*Ecl.IV.17*), 96, 104, 105, 172
  peace agreements, 96, 101

Eclogues IV (cont.)
    prophesying of a Golden Age, 96, 97–8, 100, 103–4
    prophetic mode, 100–1, 117
Eclogues IX
    herdsmen's dialogic exchange, 107–13
    Hibernian/Latin language, 109–11
    mixed prosody, 109
    political change in Rome, 107–8
    postlapsarian knowledge, 109
    Virgil: *Eclogues IX* (Heaney's translation), 6, 94, 96–7, 107
Electric Light
    'Electric Light', 117–18
    'Known World', 104–5
    'Sonnets from Hellas', 116
    'Sonnets to Hellas', 6, 107
    'At Toomebridge', 117
    translation of *Eclogue IX*, 94, 96–7, 107
    Virgil as Heaney's inner interlocutor, 5
    see also 'Bann Valley Eclogue'; *Eclogues* (Virgil); *Eclogues IX*; 'Glanmore Eclogue'
'Elegy', 56–7
elegy
    in *Electric Light*, 116
    in *Human Chain*, 220–2
Eliot, T. S.
    auditory imagination, 17
    as 'epic' poet, 18
    on Joyce, 151
    'Little Gidding', 1 n.2, 19, 48, 73, 190 n.46, 262
    and Mandelstam, 18–19
    portrayal of Virgil, 123
    'Preludes', 122
    Tiresias, 29, 240, 241
    treatment of Dante, 18–19
    view of history as futile and violent, 70, 151
    Virgil and Christianity, 98
    The Waste Land, 18, 29, 117
Elysium
    Anchises' ghost in, 42, 59, 142, 153, 154, 171, 213
    as Heaney's homeplace, 157, 244, 252
    Heaney's translation of, 157, 184, 251–2
    peace of, 250–1
Ennius, 69, 243

The Epic of Gilgamesh, 8–9, 126
epic poetry
    in blank verse, 24
    in Heaney's writing, 14, 177
    iambic pentameter, 24
    lyric poet's shaping of, 23, 37
    'In Memoriam', 25
    and myth, 17–18
    pietas, 14
    poetic *labor*, 47, 74, 205, 217, 242, 247, 262
    T. S. Eliot, 18
    virtues of, 177
    W. B. Yeats, 17, 18
    see also memory; *pietas*
essays
    'Anglo-Irish Occasions', 47–8, 55
    'Crediting Poetry', 3, 175, 257–8
    'Envies and Identifications', 6, 14, 18, 48, 49
    'Feeling into Words', *Preoccupations*, 16–17
    'The Government of the Tongue', 50
    'Mossbawn via Mantua', 259–62
    'Place, Pastness, Poems', 48
    'The Place of Writing', 45
    'The Placeless Heaven: Another Look at Kavanagh', 14
    'The Sense of Place', 17
    'Suffering and Decision', 6, 194
    'Towers, Trees, Terrors, a Rêverie in Urbino', 6, 121–2, 125, 133, 144–5
    'Varieties of Irishness', 47, 48
    'The Whole Thing: On the Good of Poetry', 258
    see also 'Greek and Latin Voices'; *The Redress of Poetry*
Eurydice
    'Orpheus and Eurydice' (Heaney), 78–81
    'Orpheus and Eurydice' (Miłosz), 86
    Orpheus' descent, 67, 69
    Orpheus' song and the loss of, 77–82, 86–7
    Platonic union with Orpheus, 86–7
    parallel with *ter conatus* in Ae.II, 60, 69
    in 'The Underground', 70
Eve, 35, 81–2
exemplars, literary *see* poetics

INDEX 293

facilis descensus Auerno (Ae.VI.126), 30, 179, 257
Fairclough, H. Rushton, 100, 101, 105, 106, 111, 112–13, 156, 157, 158, 247
fairytales, 63, 64, 65
Fallon, Peter, 6, 8 n.30, 93 n.13, 271
fathers
  death of Dylan Thomas's father, 75
  as Hermes, 65–6
  of John Keats, 195–6
  pietas towards, 14, 23, 32, 54, 92, 246
  see also Heaney, Patrick
father's shade (ghost)
  Aeneid Book VI, 153, 245–6
  of Anchises, 14, 15, 22, 42, 142, 144, 186, 200, 213–14, 245–6
  in 'District and Circle', 136, 139–40, 141–2, 144, 145
  motif in Heaney's writing, 3, 13, 15
  motif in *Seeing Things*, 42, 50, 59–66
feminist critique
  of Heaney's *The Midnight Verdict*, 72–3
  of Merriman's *The Midnight Court*, 71
Ferry, David, 94
Field Day Theatre Company, 6, 72
Field Work, 2
'The Fields of Light', 178, 184, 251
Fitzgerald, Robert, 19, 21, 22–3, 24, 48, 180, 235
Frazer, Sir James, 17–18
Freud, Sigmund, 61–2
Friel, Brian, 144
'From the Frontier of Writing', 44–5
Frost, Robert, 118–19

Gale, Martin, 152
The Gallery Press, 150, 152
Garth, Samuel, 88
Gates of Sleep, 45, 71, 171, 255–6
gender
  double-gendered authority of the golden bough, 14–17
  femininity of divination, 16–18
  masculine/feminine poetic functions, 14
Georgics IV
  Aristaeus the beekeeper, 73, 84, 86, 115, 120, 148
  Hesiod's *Works and Days* and, 6
  influence on Heaney, 1, 2, 6
  as a model for *The Midnight Verdict*, 73–4
  Orpheus' *katabasis*, 58, 67
  and pastoral, 118
  Virgil as author, 8
ghosts (shades)
  child's, 61–3
  confluence of bodies and shades, 171–2
  of Creusa, 60
  of Deiphobus, 167
  of Dido, 60, 142–6, 166, 211
  Eliot's compound ghost, 19
  in Homer's *Odyssey XI*, 15
  manus effugit (Ae.VI.701), 204, 207 *see also Aeneid* VI
  of Margaret Heaney, 207
  of Palinurus, 165, 187–8, 199–200
  underworld games, 169
  see also father's shade (ghost); *ter conatus*
Glanmore Cottage, 23, 37, 47, 57, 113, 114, 151, 183
'Glanmore Eclogue'
  country road chronotope, 115
  land resettlement schemes, 114
  pastoral song, 115–16
  rural community, 113, 114–15
  semi-autobiographical 'Poet' in, 94, 113–16
  Synge as Meliboeus, 113, 115
'Glory be to the world', 6
golden bough (episode, motif)
  advice on the golden bough, 30–2, 33, 40, 41
  Aeneas encounter with the Sibyl, 28–30, 40, 41
  in 'The Ash Plant', 51–2
  boundary/threshold function, 13–14
  dangers of Aeneas' quest, 30
  discovery of the bough, 22, 33–5, 37–8, 41, 248–9
  in 'District and Circle', 140, 141
  as a divining rod, 15–16
  feminine/masculine authority, 14–17
  in *The Haw Lantern*, 14–15
  language of, 26–7
  latet arbore opaca (Ae.VI.136), 31
  Misenus in, 13, 21–2, 32–3, 165–6
  in *Seeing Things*, 1, 13, 14, 40, 41, 42, 45, 50–3, 59

golden bough (episode, motif) (*cont.*)
  tree-clock and the golden bough, 52
  see also Sibyl of Cumae
'The Golden Bough' (Heaney's translation),
    3, 13–39, 40, 59
  Aeneas as a questing artist, 26
  feminine/masculine authority, 14–17
  language of, 26–7
  meter, 24–6, 235–6
  poetic divination, 15–16, 32–3, 37
  rejection of iambic pentameter, 24–5
  rhythm, 25–7, 30–2
  as self-standing narrative, 21
  shifts of register, 240–1
  the Sibyl of Cumae, 27–30
The Golden Bough (Frazer), 17–18
Golding, Arthur, 88
Good Friday Agreement, 91, 96–7, 105
'Greek and Latin Voices' (BBC radio essay)
  identification with Virgil, 179–80
  poetry and collective memory, 179–80, 182

Hades
  boat crossing into, 55–6
  exit from *see also* Gates of Sleep; Lethe, River
  Orpheus in, 73–4, 75, 76, 80, 84, 87, 108, 232
  Tartarus, 28, 237, 242, 243
  see also Elysium; golden bough; *katabasis*
Hammond, David, 221–2
Hardie, Philip, 5
Hardy, Thomas, 48, 49
Harington, Sir John, 24
Harrison, Stephen, 135, 230
Harvard University, 19, 21, 23, 150
'The Harvest Bow', 170–1, 172
Hass, Robert, 22, 23, 37, 182
The Haw Lantern
  'Alphabets', 7
  golden bough episode, 13–14
  the lapse of memory, 208
  Latin language, 7
Heaney, Anna Rose, 151, 172–3, 226, 233
Heaney, Christopher (brother), 128–9, 165, 227
Heaney, Christopher (son), 151, 226
Heaney, grandfather, 223

Heaney, grandmother, 117
Heaney, Margaret (neé McCann, mother)
  in 'Album', 212–13
  in 'Clearances', 20, 32, 210
  death, 20, 32, 45, 210
  and the fallen chestnut tree, 20
  maternal association with the golden bough, 13, 14, 20–1, 22
  memories of, 187, 207, 209–11, 215–16
  in 'Uncoupled', 215–16
Heaney, Patrick (father)
  in 'Album', 211–12
  in 'The Butts', 215, 216–17
  cattle-dealer's stick, 50–2
  death, 13, 14, 23, 45, 46
  diminished figure of, 212–13
  fishing with Seamus, 170–2, 212
  ghost of in 'District and Circle', 136, 139–40, 141–2, 145
  Heaney's memory of, 61, 63, 65, 187, 207, 209–11, 212–13, 215, 216–17
  in *Human Chain*, 215
  in '"Lick the Pencil"', 215, 217
  'Man and Boy', 61, 62, 65, 245
  in 'Running Water', 42–3
  'Seeing Things, III', 63–5
  shade (ghost) of, 3, 13, 15, 50, 207, 212–13
  see also ter conatus
Heaney, Seamus
  chestnut tree and birth, 20–1, 32, 210
  childhood in Co. Derry, 8, 46, 103, 129, 141, 150, 233
  education, 1, 8
  engagement with European literature, 259–60
  50th birthday, 40, 41, 53
  identification with Virgil, 1, 7–8, 122–3, 150, 179
  loss of faith, 45–6
  McGuire's portrait, 56
  memorial address for Robert Fitzgerald, 22–3
  Mossbawn farm, 7, 20, 22, 61–2, 129, 141, 147, 151, 157, 161, 217, 252
  Nobel Prize for Literature, 3, 95, 96, 114, 150
  Northern Irish identity, 137, 138, 141, 144

pseudonym *Incertus*, 108
70th birthday, 183
stroke, 150–1, 214–15
see also Catholicism
Heaney, Sheena, 102
Hebrus, River, 67, 82, 84, 85
hedge schools, 99–100
Hendrix, Jan, 23–4, 30
Henryson, Robert, 205
Hermes, 65
Hesiod
  Golden Age, 96, 97
  Works and Days, 6, 100
Homem, Rui, 107, 108
Homer, 15, 126, 215
Hopkins, Gerard Manley, 48–9, 171
Horace, 2, 7, 10, 57, 129, 131, 145, 148; *see also Odes I*, 34
Horsfall, Nicholas, 206
Hughes, Ted
  Anglo-Saxon verse forms, 192, 193
  association with Palinurus, 194–5, 197, 198
  'Crow's Song of Himself', 134–5
  pietas, 193, 194
  Ted Hughes Memorial Lecture, 192–3, 195
  'The Thought Fox', 219
  transformation through suffering, 192, 193–5
  see also essays; 'Suffering and Decision'
Human Chain
  '"The door was open and the house was dark"', 221–2
  '"Lick the Pencil"', 215, 217
  and *Aeneid VI*, 159, 178, 204–5, 206
  anima motif, 219–20
  artistic creation, 217–20
  'In the Attic', 223–6
  'The Butts', 215, 216–17
  'Chanson d'Aventure', 214–15
  childhood and old age, 223, 224–5
  elegies for artists, 220–2
  element of air, 206, 217, 218, 219–20
  'Had I not been awake', 218–19
  hand motif, 207–8, 214–15, 223–4
  'A Kite for Aibhín', 181, 208, 226–8
  lacrimae rerum in, 204
  lapsa cadunt folia, 206–7
  the lapse of memory, 208, 223, 224–5
  Lethean loss and renewal, 204, 208–10, 252–3
  'Loughanure', 178, 184, 220–1
  manus effugit leitmotif, 207–8
  medieval Irish poems, 205
  memories of Heaney's parents, 215–17
  'Miracle', 215
  mortality theme, 204
  souls as falling leaves, 181–2, 206–7
  terza rima form, 4, 226
  'Uncoupled', 215–16
  underworld motifs, 205
  Virgil in, 1, 4, 5, 204
  'Wraiths', 221
  see also 'Album'; *The Riverbank Field*; 'Route 110'

imagination
  Ariel and Prospero, 76, 78, 89, 91 *see also* Auden, W. H.
  auditory imagination, 17, 20, 22
  Catholic imagination, 4, 46–7
  in *Eclogues IV*, 98
  poet's artistic imagination, 54, 57, 58, 218–20
  role of memory, 50
  transformative power of, 40, 45, 49
Inferno
  Charon's barge, 40, 41–2, 43, 44, 54
  crossing of the Styx, 40, 43–4
  fireflies, 43
  selva oscura, 18, 43, 44
  threshold crossings, 41–2, 43–4
interviews
  'On Elegies, Eclogues, Translations Transfusions', 6
  with Henri Cole, 69, 72, 76
  with Richard Kearney, 69, 70, 119
  with Robert Hass, 22, 23, 37
  with Robert McCrum, 204
  with Rui Homem, 107, 108
  with Seamus Deane, 17
  see also RTÉ Poetry Programme (interview with Gerald Dawe)
Italian
  of Dante, 152, 174, 175
  translation in *Human Chain*, 205, 226–8

Johnston, Arthur, 154–5
Jones, Nancy Wynne, 220
journey to the underworld, see *katabasis*
Joyce, James, *Ulysses*, 151, 152, 160, 165, 241
Julius Caesar, 92, 112

katabasis
  of Aeneas, 15, 50, 58, 60
  defined, 15
  in 'District and Circle', 10, 136, 145, 146
  familiarity of, 230
  fusion of lyric and epic, 49
  Lawrence's *katabatic* flower, 53, 164
  as a mythic structure, 8–9
  narrative arc in *District and Circle*, 124, 125, 126, 129, 131, 136, 145, 146, 148–9
  of Orpheus, 58, 67, 68–9
  as poetic redress, 249–58
  regenerative renewal and, 232–3
  as a response to violence, 126–8
  in 'The Riverbank Field', 156
  in 'Route 110', 160, 161–5, 167, 169, 172
  threshold crossings, 139, 230, 232, 233
  via Lethe, 156
  Virgilian model, 41
Kavanagh, Patrick
  Canal Bank sonnets, 52
  Catholicism, 46
  fusion of lyric and epic, 14, 17, 19–20, 49
  Heaney's identification with, 20–1
  'In Memory of My Mother', 20
  in 'The Placeless Heaven', 19–20
  'true note on a slack string', 243
Kearney, Richard, 69, 70, 119
Keats, John
  Endymion, 195–6
  idea of soul-making, 202–3
  negative capability, 17
  'Ode on Melancholy', 209
  'On the Sea', 196
  transformation through suffering, 192, 195–7
Kipling, Rudyard, 112

labor (glide), 206
lacrimae rerum (*Ae*.I.462),
  in the *Aeneid*, 8, 68, 123, 144, 153, 179, 181, 192, 228, 261, 263
  in 'Bann Valley Eclogue', 105, 106
  in 'District and Circle', 144
  in *Electric Light*, 116, 117
  in *Human Chain*, 204
  in 'Strange Meeting' (Owen), 127
  Virgilian sense of tragic mortality, 1, 8, 68–70, 105–6, 116–7, 123, 127, 136, 144, 153, 192, 202, 204, 228, 263
language
  Anglo-Saxon, 28, 141, 190, 239, 241, 242–3
  Biblical, 242
  formal/vernacular, 27, 29
  in Heaney's *Aeneid Book VI*, 239–42
  Hibernian/Latin, 27–8, 109–11
  Hiberno-English, 27, 29, 103, 244
  Irish colloquial, 243–5
  secularisation of, 4
  see also Latin
lapsa cadunt folia (*Ae*.VI.310), 204, 206
Larkin, Philip, 75
Latin
  and Anglo-Saxon, 27–8
  and Dante's *Commedia*, 18
  Heaney's familiarity with, 2, 7
  Hibernian/Latin, 27–8, 109–11
  in Irish culture, 47
  as the language of Mass, 2, 46
  urbs (noun), 125
  see also McGlinchey, Michael (Heaney's Latin teacher)
Lavan, Rosie, 48
Lavinia, 186, 247–8
Lawrence, D. H., 53, 164
lectures
  address to the Royal Academy, 92, 118–21
  address to the Royal College of Surgeons, 124, 126
  at Emory University, 45
  at Oxford University, 69
  Robert Fitzgerald memorial address, 22–3
  Ted Hughes Memorial Lecture, 192–3, 195
  at the University of Urbino, 121–2, 125, 133, 144–5
  see also essays

Lethe, River
  in *Human Chain*, 204, 209–10, 224–5, 232
  memory loss, 153–4, 155–6, 158–9, 208, 209
  in 'The Riverbank Field', 153–4, 156–7, 159–60, 170, 204, 208, 251
  Roman army's crossing, 154–5
  in 'Route 110', 153, 170, 171, 172–3, 205, 209
  as the '*securos latices*' (Ae.VI. 715), 209
Lewis, C. Day, 115
Liffey, River, 152
Livy, 125, 141
Loeb translation of Virgil, *see* Fairclough, H. Rushton
Longley, Michael, 5, 118, 119
Lowell, Robert, 57
lyric poetry
  fusion of lyric and epic in Kavanagh, 14, 17, 19–20, 49
  generation of poetic form, 151
  hum of bees and lyric song, 85–6
  lightness of, 52, 57, 65, 66
  local-associative, 19, 20
  lyric impulse in Heaney, 37–8, 52, 177
  Orpheus' lyre, 69, 75, 78, 79, 84–5
  poet's shaping of, 23, 37
  in relation to epic, 23, 27
  rhythmic cadence, 151, 161
  of 'Route 110', 160–1
  associated with Virgil, 14, 151–2, 160–1
  virtues of, 177
  see also Human Chain

MacCana, Proinsias, 47
McCrum, Robert, 204
McGlinchey, Michael, 158, 180, 183, 184, 232, 233
McGuire, Edward, 56
Mackail, J. W., 2
MacNeice, Louis, 69, 99, 119
Mahon, Derek, 5
Mandelstam, Nadezhda, 203
Mandelstam, Osip
  bees, 175
  on Dante, 18, 19, 152, 161, 174
  Heaney's dialogue with, 5
  as a lyric poet, 14, 17

Mantua farm (Virgil's family), 1, 8, 92, 95, 97–8, 102, 110, 114, 122, 165, 252
manus effugit (Ae.VI.701)
  in 'Album', 212–15
  in *Human Chain*, 214–15
  as slipping away, 204, 207
  see also Aeneid VI; ter conatus
Marcellus, 173, 227, 241, 248, 254
Marlowe, Christopher, 76, 77, 143
Matthews, Stephen, 144
memory
  descent into the underworld of, 2–3, 19, 38, 39
  of fathers, 65
  of Heaney's grandmother, 117–18
  of Heaney's parents, 207, 209–11 215–16
  lapse of, 208, 223–5
  Lethean loss of, 153–4, 155–6, 158–9, 208, 209
  poetry's transmission of cultural memory, 178, 179–80, 182, 202, 223
  repetition compulsion, 62
  in 'The Riverbank Field', 156–9
  in 'Route 110', 156, 160–1, 165–9
  threshold crossings into, 46–7
  tribal and literary memory, 48–9, 65
Merriman, Brian, 71, 79, 82
Metamorphoses
  After Ovid (translation), 70–1
  arboreal metamorphosis, 87–9
  Charon's barge motif, 69
  Heaney's translations of, 67–8, 70–1, 76, 77–8, 80–1, 82–4, 89
  parallels with *Aeneid*, 68–9
  ter conatus motif, 69
  see also The Midnight Verdict; Orpheus
Metamorphoses (Garth), 88
Metamorphosis (Golding), 88
metempsychosis, Pythagorean, 158, 252, 253
meter
  Aeneid Book VI translation, 26
  Anglo-Saxon, 192, 193
  ballad, 115–16
  dactylic hexameter, 14, 26, 27, 30, 31–2, 71, 72, 99, 109, 235, 237, 238–9
  iambic pentameter, 14, 24–5, 235, 238, 246, 10910
  iambic tetrameter, 25

meter (*cont.*)
    long-line meter, 236
    mixed meters, 109, 234–8
Middleton, Colin, 184, 220–1
The Midnight Court (Merriman), 71, 72, 73, 79, 82
The Midnight Verdict (Heaney)
    Augustan heroic couplets, 71–2
    critical reception, 72
    Orpheus as poet on trial, 73
    'Orpheus in Ireland', 71, 72, 73
    Orpheus myth, 70–4
    as tragi-comedy, 73–4
    Virgil as Heaney's inner interlocutor, 5
Miller, Karl, 46
Miłosz, Czesław
    contrasted with Virgil, 68, 119–20
    as a lyric poet, 14
    'Orpheus and Eurydice', 86
    and pastoral, 119
    role of poetry, 130
    'Secular and Millennial Miłosz', 6
    'The World', 120
Milton, John
    treatment of Orpheus, 33, 82–3
    engagement with Virgil, 7
    'Lycidas', 82–3, 198, 203
Misenus, 13, 21–2, 32–3, 165–6
Montale, Eugenio, 217
Mossbawn farm (Heaney family), 7, 20, 22, 61–2, 129, 141, 147, 151, 157, 161, 217, 252
'Mossbawn via Mantua', 6, 259–63
Moyola, River, 62, 118, 122, 147, 152, 153, 157, 161, 162, 170
'Mycenae Lookout', 6

nekyia, 3, 15, 215
Neruda, Pablo, 48
Ní Dhomhnaill, Nuala, 38
9/11 terrorist attacks
    aftermath of fear, 118, 121, 124
    Bush administration's response, 127–8, 134–5
    Heaney's turn to Horace, 125, 128, 131, 133
    religious language and, 126, 127
    staying power of pastoral post-9/11, 124

in 'Towers, Trees, Terrors, a Rêverie in Urbino', 121, 125, 133, 144–5
Nobel Prize for Literature, 3, 95, 96, 114, 150
North, 3, 4
Northern Ireland
    British media coverage, 48
    checkpoint crossings, 42, 43–5, 50, 103
    sectarian conflict, 10, 41, 66, 96, 107, 118, 127–8, 153, 161, 166, 168, 172, 179
    see also Belfast; Derry, County

O'Brien, Conor Cruise, 38
O'Brien, Flann (Myles na Gopaleen), 113–14
Octavian Augustus, 92, 96
Odes I, 34 (Horace)
    in *District and Circle*, 131–3
    Heaney's post-9/11 re-reading, 125, 128, 131, 133
    Heaney's translation of, 7, 129, 131–3
    Horace and Virgil's friendship, 57
    rapax/ Fortuna (*Odes I*, 34.14–5), 134–5
O'Donoghue, Bernard, 4–5, 25, 65
Odyssey XI, 15, 126, 215
O'Hogan, Cillian, 109
Orpheus
    contrasted with Aeneas, 30, 68–9
    death of, 67, 68, 74–5, 81–9, 198
    Duino Elegies (Rilke), 70, 74
    importance to Heaney, 69
    katabasis of, 58, 67, 68–9
    loss of Eurydice, 77–82, 86–7
    lyre, 69, 75, 78, 79, 84–5
    in *The Midnight Verdict*, 70–4
    Orphic song, 9–10, 33, 67, 74, 76, 78–82, 84, 86–7, 89
    in *The Redress of Poetry*, 68, 70, 74–5
    Segal's reading, 68, 73–4, 76, 79, 80, 86
    song of the severed head, 82, 84–6
    and the trial of the poet, 73–4
    in 'The Underground', 70
'Orpheus and Eurydice' (Miłosz), 86
Ovid
    Augustan heroic couplets, 71
    dactylic hexameter, 72
    dialogue with Virgil, 67–9, 73–4, 77–8, 79, 82

Heaney's translation of, 67–8, 70–1
Metamorphoses X and XI, 7, 67
see also *Metamorphoses*
Owen, Wilfred, 'Strange Meeting', 126–7
Oxford University, 23, 69

Pact of Brundisium, 92, 96, 100
Palinurus
   in cultural memory, 200–2, 223
   encounter with the Sibyl, 200–2
   ghost of, 165, 187–8, 199–200
   in 'Route 110', 187
   shipwreck and drowning, 197–9, 223
   and Ted Hughes, 194–5, 197, 198
'Palinurus' (Heaney's translation)
   Anglo-Saxon verse forms, 190–1, 198–9, 237–8
   paired with 'Album', 178, 187
   pietas of Palinurus, 189
   poetry and suffering, 192
   ter conatus motif in, 200
   terza rima, 178, 191
   three-part structure, 188–9, 192
Paradise Lost (Milton), 7, 33, 35, 82–3, 87, 143, 161, 231, 260
Parnell, Charles, 38
Pascoli, Giovanni, 'L'Aquilone', 181, 205, 226–8
pastoral
   Aeneas' wanderings, 120, 121–2, 124
   chronotope, 93, 120, 124, 225
   composer/audience dynamic, 114
   country road, 92, 115, 120, 121
   figure of the shepherd, 93, 129
   form in Heaney's poetry, 91
   Heaney's theory of pastoral, 118
   as a knowing genre, 104
   links with georgic, 118
   modern pastoral, 119
   pastoral song, 97, 109–13, 115–16
   post-9/11, 124
   rural poetic tradition and, 92–3
   staying power of, 91, 95, 118–19, 121, 122, 263
   the subject of, 115
   see also eclogues
patria, 8, 11, 229, 243, 250–1, 252
Persephone, 15, 21, 30, 32, 37, 38, 42, 79, 256

pietas
   of Aeneas, 1, 14, 120, 233
   in 'District and Circle', 139–40
   of the *Eclogues*, 92, 94, 95
   of Heaney's *Aeneid* translation, 233
   for Michael McGlinchey, 184, 233
   of Palinurus, 189
   Ted Hughes and, 193, 194
   of translation, 184
   of Virgil, 92, 95, 194
   see also Aeneas
'The Placeless Heaven', 19–20
Plath, Sylvia, 194, 198
Plato, 70, 86–7, 89
poetics
   Ariel–Prospero dichotomy, 76, 78, 89, 91
   crediting marvels, 1, 4, 45, 46, 53
   doldrums of what happens, 4, 40, 45, 55, 261
   exemplars, literary, 10, 18, 20, 42, 47, 49, 50, 95, 98, 120, 122–3, 153, 204, 233, 260
   heard/herd pun, 58, 83
   'hedge-schoolmaster' Virgil, 7, 10, 52, 99–100, 102–3, 107, 109, 120, 123, 150, 158, 178, 261
   immanentist, 74, 75
   masculine/feminine poetic functions, 14
   music of what happens, 52
   poetic divination, 16–17, 19, 32
   redress of poetry, 1, 70, 76
   reverie/dream-work, 8–9
   transcendent, 74–5
poetry
   Ariel–Prospero dichotomy, 76, 78, 89, 91
   boat-as-poetry imagery, 54–9
   during times of poetic crisis, 14
   redress of poetry, 1, 70, 76
   social and individual role of, 1, 6, 9
   task of, 47, 130, 151
   transformative power of, 74–7, 192, 195–7
   transmission of cultural memory, 178, 179–80, 182, 202, 223
   see also epic poetry; lyric poetry
Poetry Review, 61
Polydorus, 89
Pope, Alexander, 24

Pound, Ezra, 36, 49, 209
Preoccupations, 116
'Punishment', 72
Putnam, Michael, 112, 113, 168

Queen's University, Belfast, 2, 45

Radnóti, Miklós, 119, 120
The Redress of Poetry
   allusions to Orpheus, 68, 70, 74–5
   'Counting to a Hundred: On Elizabeth Bishop', 76–7
   defence of poetry, 70
   'Dylan the Durable?: On Dylan Thomas', 74
   'Extending the Alphabet: On Christopher Marlowe's…', 76
   'Introduction', 69–70
   'Joy or Night: Last Things in the Poetry of W. B. Yeats and Philip Larkin', 8 n.33, 70 n.15, 75
   'Orpheus in Ireland: On Brian Merriman's…', 71, 73
   poetry's transmutation of suffering, 74–7
   'The Redress of Poetry', 70
   revised from the Oxford lectures, 69
Rilke, Rainer Maria, 79
   Duino Elegies, 70, 74
   'Sonnets to Orpheus', 70, 74
The Riverbank Field
   confluence of bodies and shades, 172
   Gale's river painting, 152–3
   local, lyric Virgil, 150–1
   see also 'Route 110';
'The Riverbank Field'
   in *Human Chain*, 204
   Lethean crossings, 153–4, 156–7, 159–60, 204, 208, 251
   memory in, 156–8
   as a threshold to 'Route 110', 156, 160
   translation of *Aeneid VI*, 157, 158–9
   Virgil's bees, 174–5, 254
Roe, Nicholas, 196
Rome
   identification with London, 144
   resettlement schemes, 8, 92, 93, 97–8, 107, 114, 122
   Roman *imperium*, 8, 125, 180, 186–7, 229
Romulus and Remus, 101, 103

'Route 110'
   Charon's barge, 163
   crossing of the Styx, 163, 164, 181
   dactylic rhythm, 162
   Dido and Aeneas, 143, 166–7
   Elysian fields of, 169–70
   first copy of *Aeneid VI*, 15, 161, 162
   fishing with Patrick Heaney, 170–2, 212
   free flowing form, 152, 161
   ghost of Ted Hughes and, 192
   in *Human Chain*, 204
   katabatic journey, 160, 161–5, 167, 169, 172
   Lethean crossings, 153, 170, 171, 172–3, 205, 209
   light leitmotif, 173–4
   lyric temporality, 160–1
   memory in, 156, 160–1, 165–9
   memory of sectarian conflict, 166–9
   mythic method, 151–2, 153, 157, 233
   Palinurus in, 187
   parallels with *Aeneid VI*, 152, 156
   'The Riverbank Field' as a threshold to, 156, 160
   Smithfield Market, 160, 161, 162–3
   'spots of time' (Wordsworth), 161
   tercet form, 152
Royal College of Surgeons in Ireland, 124, 126
RTÉ *Poetry Programme* interview with Gerald Dawe
   County Derry, 157, 160
   Heaney's identification with Virgil, 179
   riverbank setting of 'The Riverbank Field', 155–6
   'Route 110', 160, 161, 167, 179
   translation work as *pius*, 184
Ruden, Sarah, 183, 238
rural poetry, 92–3

Saddlemyer, Ann, 128–9
scelus (noun), 87, 100, 101, 102, 108–9
Seeing Things
   Anchises' ghost, 42
   'The Biretta', 54
   boat-as-poetry, 54–9
   Charon's barge motif, 40, 41–2, 44, 50, 54–9, 72

chronotopic images of the threshold, 49–50
'The Crossing' (translation of *Inferno* III), 40, 41, 45
death's door, 61–2
poetic detachment, 55–6
father's shade (ghost) motif, 42, 50, 59–66
'Fosterling', 4, 45, 46, 52–3
golden bough motif, 40, 42, 50–3, 59
'The Golden Bough' (translation), 1, 13, 14, 41, 45, 52
dialogue with Virgil and Dante, 4, 41–2
loss of the first world in, 59–60, 61–3
'Man and Boy', 61, 62, 65, 245
'Seeing Things', 54–5
'Seeing Things, III', 61, 63–5
'Skylight', 40
ter conatus motif in, 61, 63–5
threshold crossings, 41–3, 45, 49–50, 139
water element, 54, 117
see also *Squarings*
Segal, Charles, 68, 73–4, 76, 79, 80, 86
7/7 London Underground bombing, 125, 137
Shakespeare, William
Dido, 143–4
in *District and Circle*, 129
King Lear, 196
Sonnet 65, 130
The Tempest, 78, 80, 190, 196, 198
Timon of Athens, 208
use of the vernacular, 19
Sibyl of Cumae
advice on the golden bough, 30–2, 33, 40, 41, 248–9
Aeneas' encounter with, 2, 28–30, 40, 41
bella, horrida bella, 28, 185
divine revelation, 218–19
Heaney's grandmother as, 117
in Heaney's translation, 27–30, 240
double gendered authority, 14–15
Palinurus' encounter with, 200–2
prophecy of the Golden Age, 96, 97–8, 100, 103–4
as shopkeeper in 'Route 110, I', 162
in Turner's painting, 17–18
'Song', 52
song
in *Eclogues IV*, 111–13

hum of bees and lyric song, 85–6
Orpheus' song and the loss of Eurydice, 78–82, 86–7
Orphic song, 9–10, 33, 67, 74, 76, 78–82, 84, 89
pastoral song, 97, 109–13, 115–16
sonnet form
in 'Album', 210, 212
Canal Bank sonnets (Kavanagh), 52
in 'District and Circle', 125, 129, 136–7, 138, 139, 140, 141–2
of Keats, 196, 197214
Petrarchan sonnet, 129, 136–7, 152
Sonnet 65 (Shakespeare), 130
sonnets, 130
'Sonnets from Hellas', 6, 107, 116
in 'The Tollund Man in Springtime', 146, 148
twelve-line sonnets, 210, 212
Sophocles, 6, 7, 62, 127
Sounding Lines, 6, 19, 23, 37–8, 182, 192, 213 n.41
Spiegelman, Willard, 183
Squarings
'The annals say', 57–8
Charon's barge in, 43–4
'Crossings', 55
questions of faith, 46
'Running Water', 42–3
tercet form, 152
terza rima form, 49
threshold crossings, 42–4, 50
St Brigid's hoops, 42
'St Kevin and the Blackbird', 160
Station Island, 2, 4
'staying power'
of pastoral, 91, 95, 118–19, 121, 122, 263
the Tollund Man's, 147–8
Stepping Stones
'A Basket of Chestnuts', 56
on the classics, 6
on crediting marvels, 52
figure of the Tollund Man, 147
poetry as redress, 64–5, 76
reception of *The Midnight Verdict*, 72
'A Royal Prospect', 56
'Seeing Things, I', 56
tree-clock and the golden bough, 52, 164
Stevenson, R. L., 223–5

'The Stick', 38
Strabo, 154
Styx, River
　in *Aeneid* VI, 136, 142, 145, 163, 164, 165, 181, 200, 206, 249, 263
　in Dante's *Inferno*, 40, 43–4
　in Horace, 133
　lapsa cadunt folia, 204, 206
　Palinurus on the banks of, 187, 188, 199
　Smithfield Market as, 162
　souls crossing, 163, 164, 181, 196, 206, 209
　in Heaney's work, 3, 9, 106, 178
Suchard, Ronald, 45
'Suffering and Decision', 6, 194
Sweeney, Jack, 23
Sweeney, King, 38–9, 65, 79, 100, 141, 160
Synge, John Millington, 113, 114, 115

Tartarus, 28, 237, 242, 243
Tennyson, Alfred, 25
ter conatus (Ae.VI.700)
　Aeneas' attempted embrace of his father, 59–60, 61, 63, 65, 81, 187, 207, 212–13, 246
　in 'Album', 212–14
　empty hands motif, 207–8, 214, 223–4
　Heaney's memory of his father, 61, 63, 65, 187, 207, 212–13
　Heaney's memory of his mother, 187, 207
　in *Metamorphoses*, 69
　of Orpheus for Eurydice, 69, 81
　in 'Palinurus', 200
terrorism, 10, 91, 121–2, 125–9, 131, 133–5, 137–8, 144–6, 262
Theocritus, 6, 92–3, 108, 111
Thomas, Dylan
　'Do Not Go Gentle into That Good Night', 75
　not confronting death, 74–5, 77
'Three Freed Speeches'
　political slant, 184–5
　publication, 178, 184
　Roman *imperium*, 186–7
　threat of warfare, 184–7
threshold crossings
　in 'A Basket of Chestnuts', 56
　checkpoint crossings in Iraq, 128
　chronotope of, 49–50

　in Dante's *Inferno*, 41–2, 43–4
　'District and Circle', 139–41
　of 'Fosterling' in *Stepping Stones*, 52–3
　'From the Frontier of Writing', 44–5
　Hermes, the god of, 65
　of the *katabatic* journey, 139, 230, 232, 233
　loss of faith and, 45–6
　into memory, 46–7
　in Northern Ireland, 42, 43–5, 50, 103, 139
　in *Seeing Things*, 41–3, 45, 49–50, 139
　in *Squarings*, 42–4, 50
'To the Poets of St Andrews', 154–5, 173
Tollund Man
　in 'District and Circle', 136–7, 140–1, 156
　'The Tollund Man in Springtime', 125, 131, 137, 146–8
Torlone, Zara Martirosova, 5
translation
　of *Aeneid*, 183–4
　as being forwarded, 172
　of the classics, 4–5, 6, 9
　commingling, 3, 143, 152, 157, 171–2, 173, 174–5
　of Dante, 19, 22, 26
　doubleness of rhythm and tone, 234–9
　of the golden bough episode, 3, 13, 22–4, 27–30, 38, 40, 59, 240–1
　Greek translations, 6–7
　in Heaney's later writing, 178
　Heaney's Ovid translation, 67–8, 77–8
　of the *katabatic* journey, 249–58
　parallel original composition and, 178
　pietas of, 184
　as *Raids and Settlements*, 37–8, 178, 182–3, 213
　as speech given freedom, 184–5
　transfusion and, 10, 94, 111
　use of Augustan heroic couplets, 71–2
　of 'To a Wine Jar' (Horace), 2
Translation, 13, 23, 24
Treasure Island (Stevenson), 223–5
trees
　in 'Album', 210
　arboreal metamorphosis in Ovid, 87–9
　ashplants, 51–2, 65, 216
　chestnut tree, 20–1, 32, 210

laurel tree, 9, 21, 210
  for Misenus' funeral pyre, 22, 32, 165–6
  oak of St Columb's College, 211
  Polydorus, 89
the Troubles
  civilian victims, 167–8
  ghosts of, 3
  lack of overt reference to in 'The Golden Bough' translation, 26
  in 'Route 110', 156, 166–8
  in *Aeneid Book VI*, 236, 244
truth
  Ariel–Prospero dichotomy, 76, 78, 89, 91
  covenant with the truth, 91, 92
  of the *Eclogues*, 92, 93
Turner, J. M. W., 17–18
Turnus, 168, 187

Ulysses (Joyce), 151, 152, 160, 165, 241
'The Underground', 70
underworld *see* Hades; *katabasis*
Urbino, Italy, 121, 133, 144–5, 226
Urbs antiqua fuit (Ae.I.12), 179

Vendler, Helen, 4, 6
Venus, 15, 33, 42, 164, 166, 240, 256
verse forms
  Anglo-Saxon, 111–12, 190–1, 192, 193, 198–9, 237–8, 242–3
  Augustan heroic couplets, 71–2
  couplets, heroic, 24, 27, 35, 71–2, 77, 88–9
  ottava rima, 24
  blank verse, 24
  tercets, unrhymed, 43, 152, 156–9, 162, 169, 172, 173, 189–90, 191, 200, 210–11, 212, 220, 221–2, 225
  terza rima, 4, 49, 152, 161, 178, 191, 226, 261
  for translations of *Aeneid*, 24
  villanelle, 77
violence of history
  World War I, 126–7
  World War II, 119–20
  see also terrorism
Virgil
  assassination of Julius Caesar, 92, 96, 122

  Augustan Virgil, 34, 180, 182, 232
  Battle of Actium, 68, 92, 123
  biography, 1, 3 n.8, 8, 98, 102–3, 122, 193
  as bridge between cultures, 229–30, 259–60, 262
  and Catholic faith, 45–6, 102, 146
  and the Christian era, 98
  civil war experience, 68, 92, 103–4
  Czesław Miłosz contrasted with, 68
  epitaph in Naples, 182
  friendship with Horace, 57
  Heaney's dialogue with, 1, 5–6, 7, 47–8, 95, 262–3
  in Heaney's first world, 7, 46–7, 49, 59, 60, 61–3, 66–7, 217, 263
  Heaney's homely image of, 120, 121, 122
  Heaney's identification with, 1, 7–8, 122–3, 150, 179
  Heaney's tragic view of, 68
  as 'hedge-schoolmaster', 99, 120, 122
  influence on Heaney's early poetry, 1–3
  land confiscations, 8, 110, 122
  laurel tree and the birth of, 9, 21, 210
  Mantua farm, 1, 8, 92, 95, 97–8, 102, 110, 114, 122, 165, 252
  serenity of Virgil, 180, 182, 232
  as *summus artifex decori* (for Milton), 7
  see also Eclogues (Virgil)

What is Pastoral? (Alpers), 91, 93, 95
Wheatley, David, 72
Wilde, Oscar, 76, 77
Wintering Out, 2, 3, 4, 136
women
  aisling (genre), 71, 72
  arboreal metamorphosis in Ovid, 87–9
  divine female power, 42
  St Brigid's hoops, 42
  see also Sibyl of Cumae
Wordsworth, William
  'The Prelude', 161
  translation of *Aeneid I–III*, 24
  'wise passiveness', 17

Yeats, William Butler
  'The Circus Animals', 162
  in 'Crediting Poetry', 175

Yeats, William Butler (*cont.*)
  'Cuchulain Comforted', 65, 152
  in 'Joy or Night', 69–70, 75–6
  'Meditations in Time of Civil War', 175–6
  mythological poetry, 17, 18
  poetry's role to transmute the suffering of, 75
  tower of Urbino, 121, 133
  'Upon Urbino's windy hill', 226